Multilateralism and Security Institutions in an Era of Globalization

Featuring an outstanding international line-up of contributors, this edited volume offers a timely examination of two of the most crucial and controversial issues in international relations, namely the evolution of particular concepts of multilateralism and whether international security institutions are the objects of state choice and/or consequential.

The book combines a variety of theoretical perspectives with detailed empirical examples. The subjects covered include:

- the development and contemporary application of the concept of multilateralism
- American foreign and security policy in the post 9/11 era (unilateralism vs. multilateralism)
- humanitarian intervention and liberal peace
- case studies of a variety of security institutions including the EU, UN and NATO
- a broad selection of geographical examples from North America, Europe and Asia.

This book is a significant contribution to the contemporary debate on multilateralism and the effects of multilateral security institutions and will be of great interest to scholars of international relations and security studies.

Dimitris Bourantonis is an Associate Professor of International Relations at Athens University of Economics and Business. His previous books include *The History and Politics of UN Security Council Reform* (Routledge, 2006) and *The UN's Role in Nuclear Disarmament Negotiations* (Dartmouth, 1993).

Kostas Ifantis is an Associate Professor of International Relations at the University of Athens, Greece. His books include *Turkish-Greek Relations: The Security Dilemma in the Aegean* (Routledge, 2004) and *International Security Today* (SAM, 2006).

Panayotis Tsakonas is an Assistant Professor of International Relations and Security Studies at the University of the Aegean, Rhodes. His books include *A Breakthrough in Greek–Turkish Relations? Understanding Greece's "Socialization Strategy"* (Palgrave-Macmillan, 2007).

Multilateralism and Security Institutions in an Era of Globalization

Edited by
Dimitris Bourantonis, Kostas Ifantis and
Panayotis Tsakonas

LONDON AND NEW YORK

First published 2008
by Routledge
2 Park Square, Milton Park, Abingdon, Oxon OX14 4RN

Simultaneously published in the USA and Canada
by Routledge
270 Madison Ave, New York, NY 10016

Routledge is an imprint of the Taylor & Francis Group, an informa business

© 2008 Selection and editorial matter, Dimitris Bourantonis, Kostas Ifantis and Panayotis Tsakonas; individual chapters, the contributors

Typeset in Times New Roman by
RefineCatch Limited, Bungay, Suffolk
Printed and bound in Great Britain by
MPG Books Limited, Bodmin, Cornwall

All rights reserved. No part of this book may be reprinted or reproduced or utilized in any form or by any electronic, mechanical, or other means, now known or hereafter invented, including photocopying and recording, or in any information storage or retrieval system, without permission in writing from the publishers.

British Library Cataloguing in Publication Data
A catalogue record for this book is available from the British Library

Library of Congress Cataloging in Publication Data
A catalog record for this book has been requested

ISBN10: 0–415–44945–6 (hbk)
ISBN10: 0–415–44946–4 (pbk)
ISBN10: 0–203–93350–8 (ebk)

ISBN13: 978–0–415–44945–8 (hbk)
ISBN13: 978–0–415–44946–5 (pbk)
ISBN13: 978–0–203–93350–3 (ebk)

Contents

List of figures vii
List of tables viii
Notes on contributors ix
Acknowledgments xi
List of abbreviations xiii

Introduction 1
DIMITRIS BOURANTONIS, KOSTAS IFANTIS AND
PANAYOTIS TSAKONAS

PART I
Multilateralism and security: concepts, issues and strategies 19

1 **State power and international institutions: America and the logic of economic and security multilateralism** 21
   G. JOHN IKENBERRY

2 **Unipolar empire and principled multilateralism as strategies for international change** 43
   JACK SNYDER AND LESLIE VINJAMURI

3 **US military commitments: multilateralism and treaties** 60
   LISA L. MARTIN

4 **The crisis of the transatlantic security community** 78
   THOMAS RISSE

5 **State attributes and system properties: security multilateralism in central Asia, southeast Asia, the Atlantic and Europe** 101
   JAMES SPERLING

6 Is multilateralism bad for humanitarianism? 136
MICHAEL BARNETT

7 Horizontal and vertical multilateralism and the liberal peace 163
OLIVER RICHMOND

PART II
Assessing multilateral security institutions 181

8 Transatlantic relations, multilateralism and the transformation of NATO 183
FRANK SCHIMMELFENNIG

9 Persuasion and norm promotion: international institutions in the western Balkans 202
GEOFFREY EDWARDS AND MLADEN TOŠIĆ

10 From "perverse" to "promising" institutionalism? NATO, EU and the Greek-Turkish conflict 223
PANAYOTIS TSAKONAS

11 Evaluating multilateral interventions in civil wars: a comparison of UN and non-UN peace operations 252
NICHOLAS SAMBANIS AND JONAH SCHULHOFER-WOHL

12 Why no UN Security Council reform? Lessons for and from institutionalist theory 288
ERIK VOETEN

13 The reform and efficiency of the UN Security Council: a veto players analysis 306
ARIS ALEXOPOULOS AND DIMITRIS BOURANTONIS

References 324
Index 359

Figures

3.1	Number of references in the *New York Times* to multilateral and bilateral agreements	69
3.2	Fraction of all agreements that are multilateral, by year	74
3.3	Total multilateral agreements, by year	75
4.1	The European-American value space	86
4.2	Foreign policy coalitions in the USA and Europe	95
7.1	Multilateralism and gradations of liberal peace	176
7.2	Unilateralism, multilateralism and liberal peacebuilding	177
12.1	Annual number of Chapter VII resolutions, 1946–2004	291
12.2	Bargaining with heterogeneous preferences: the effects of outside options	299
13.1	Three- and five-member unanimity cores in two dimensions, where five members can reach a decision more easily than a three-member decision body that is more distant	308
13.2	A fifteen-member decision body in a two-dimensional policy space	311
13.3	The core of the UNSC	312
13.4	The UNSC's preference mapping	314
13.5	The UNSC's preference mapping in 25 years: a hypothetical scenario	320
13.6	A fifteen-member decision body in a two-dimensional policy space, with majority core 10/15 (compared with a majority core 9/15)	321

Tables

1.1	Incentives and opportunities behind the institutional bargain	27
3.1	Incidence of treaties: bilateral versus multilateral agreements	69
3.2	Treaties versus executive agreements: logit analysis	70
3.3	Multilateral agreements and the president's party	73
3.4	Multilateral agreements and the president's party: logit analysis	73
3.5	Descriptive statistics and data sources	77
4.1	US image in Germany and France (June 2003)	87
4.2	Structure of foreign policy attitudes in the US and Europe	88
5.1	State attributes	105
5.2	System properties	107
5.3	Constituent elements of security multilateralism	109
5.4	Characteristics of the varieties of security governance	111
5.5	State attributes found in central Asia, southeast Asia, the Atlantic and Europe	115
5.6	Regional system properties of central Asia, southeast Asia, the Atlantic and Europe	121
5.7	The varieties of security multilateralism	126
6.1	Humanitarianism: classical and solidarist	144
8.1	Multilateralism in post-Cold War NATO co-operation	192
8.2	Community and multilateralism in post-Cold War NATO co-operation	199
11.1	Matching problem type and strategy type	260
11.2	The effect of UN and non-UN peace operations on participatory peace	263
11.3	The effect of UN and non-UN peace operations on participatory peace, without the undivided sovereignty criterion	265
11.4	The effect of UN and non-UN peace operations on components of participatory peace	268
11.5	The effect of UN and non-UN peace operations on sovereign peace	269
11.6	Non-UN operations involving the participation of advanced militaries and peacebuilding	271
11.7	Non-UN operations involving the participation of advanced militaries and war recurrence (survival model of peace duration)	272

Contributors

Aris Alexopoulos is Lecturer in Politics in the Department of Political Science at the University of Crete, Greece.

Michael Barnett is Harold Stassen Chair of International Affairs at the Humphrey School of Public Affairs and Professor of Political Science at the University of Minnesota, USA.

Dimitris Bourantonis is Associate Professor of International Relations in the Department of International and European Economic Studies, Athens University of Economics and Business, Greece.

Geoffrey Edwards is Reader in European Studies in the Centre of International Studies at the University of Cambridge and a Fellow of Pembroke College, Cambridge, UK.

Kostas Ifantis is Associate Professor of International Relations in the Department of Political Science and Public Administration, University of Athens, Greece.

G. John Ikenberry is the Albert G. Milbank Professor of Politics and International Affairs at Princeton University in the Department of Politics and the Woodrow Wilson School of Public and International Affairs, USA.

Lisa L. Martin is Clarence Dillon Professor of International Affairs in the Department of Government at Harvard University, USA.

Oliver Richmond is Professor of International Relations at the School of International Relations, University of St Andrews, UK.

Thomas Risse is Professor of International Politics in the Department of Political and Social Sciences at the Free University of Berlin, Germany.

Nicholas Sambanis is Associate Professor of Political Science in the Department of Political Science at Yale University, USA.

Frank Schimmelfennig is Professor of European Politics at the Centre for Comparative and International Studies, ETH Zurich, Switzerland.

Jack Snyder is the Robert and Renée Belfer Professor of International Relations in the Department of Political Science and Institute of War and Peace Studies at Columbia University, USA.

James Sperling is Professor of Political Science in the Department of Political Science at the University of Akron, USA.

Mladen Tošić is a PhD candidate in the Centre of International Studies and a member of Gonville and Caius College, Cambridge, UK.

Panayotis Tsakonas is Assistant Professor of International Relations in the Department of Mediterranean Studies, University of the Aegean, Greece.

Leslie Vinjamuri is a Lecturer at the School of Oriental and African Studies (SOAS), University of London.

Eric Voeten is Peter F. Krogh Assistant Professor of Global Justice and Geopolitics in the Edmund A. Walsh School of Foreign Service and Government Department at Georgetown University, USA.

Jonah Schulhofer-Wohl is a PhD candidate in the Department of Political Science at Yale University, USA.

Acknowledgments

The origins of this volume are to be found in an international conference that took place in Delphi, Greece in June 1995. The conference brought together IR scholars who presented their research findings on the evolution of multilateralism and its relationship to particular issues and strategies, as well as on the important, if not critical, question of how and under what conditions international security institutions matter. The discussion that ensued was invaluable and provided an opportunity for the contributors to this book to improvise their papers. The editors of this volume, who were the convenors of the meeting in Delphi, wish to thank all the participants at the conference including Jeffrey Checkel and John Duffield who, for reasons beyond their will, did not contribute papers to this volume but actively participated in the Delphi conference.

In the period since the Delphi conference the papers have been redrafted. Contributors have been patient during this process and our thanks go to them. Additionally we would like to thank the Department of International and European Economic Studies at the Athens University of Economics and Business for organizing the conference on which this volume is based. The work of preparing the manuscript for publication was ably assisted by Dr Spyros Blavoukos and the staff of the Hellenic Center for European Studies. Finally the editors wish to express their appreciation to Craig Fowlie of Routledge for providing encouragement and his role in overseeing the technical details of publishing.

Abbreviations

ABM	Anti-ballistic Missile
AFOR	Albanian Force
APEC	Asian Pacific Economic Forum
ARF	ASEAN Regional Forum
ASC	ASEAN Security Community
ASEAN	Association of Southeast Asian Nations
BiH	Bosnia and Herzegovina
CEECs	Central and Eastern European Countries
CFSP	Common Foreign and Security Policy
CJTF	Combined Joint Task Force
DRC	Democratic Republic of the Congo
ECB	European Central Bank
ECJ	European Court of Justice
ECOSOC	Economic and Social Council
EDC	European Defence Community
ESDI	European Security and Defence Identity
EU	European Union
GATT	General Agreement on Tariffs and Trade
GDP	Gross Domestic Product
HR	High Representative
ICC	International Criminal Court
ICJ	International Court of Justice
ICRC	International Committee of the Red Cross
ICTY	International Criminal Tribunal for Yugoslavia
IFIs	International Financial Institutions
IFOR	Implementation Force
IMF	International Monetary Fund
INTERFET	International Force for East Timor
IOs	International Organizations
ISAF	International Stabilization and Assistance Force
JHA	Justice and Home Affairs
KFOR	Kosovo Force

MONUC	UN Organization Mission in the Democratic Republic of the Congo
MSF	Medécins Sans Frontières
NAC	North Atlantic Council
NAFTA	North America Free Trade Agreement
NATO	North Atlantic Treaty Organization
NGOs	Non-Governmental Organizations
OEEC	Organization for European Economic Co-operation
OHR	Office of the High Representative
OSCE	Organization for Security and Co-operation in Europe
PCO	Peacekeeping Operation
PfP	Partnership for Peace
PIC	Peace Implementation Council
PRC	Police Restructuring Commission
ROs	Regional Organizations
RS	Republika Srpska
SAA	Stabilization and Association Agreement
SALT	Strategic Arms Limitation Treaty
SAP	Stabilization and Association Process
SC	Security Council
SCO	Shanghai Co-operation Organization
SFOR	Stabilization Force
SQ	Status Quo
START	Strategic Arms Reduction Talks
TAC	Treaty of Amity and Co-operation
TLEs	Treaty Limited Equipments
TRNC	Turkish Republic of Northern Cyprus
UN	United Nations
UNAMA	United Nations Assistance Mission in Afghanistan
UNAMSIL	United Nations Mission in Sierra Leone
UNDP	United Nations Development Program
UNGA	United Nations General Assembly
UNHCR	United Nations High Commissioner for Refugees
UNOC	United Nations Operation in the Congo
UNSC	United Nations Security Council
UNTAET	United Nations Transitional Administration in East Timor
WMD	Weapons of Mass Destruction
WTO	World Trade Organization

Introduction

*Dimitris Bourantonis, Kostas Ifantis
and Panayotis Tsakonas*

The perception of the Cold War nuclear era in the West was of a clear and present threat from the Soviet Union that had to be matched by the United States and its allies. The Cold War superimposed on the international security agenda a political and conceptual framework that simplified most issues, while magnifying some and obscuring others. During this period, almost every Western government defined national security in excessively narrow, military terms. That meant there was an enduring acceptance of the need for a balance of terror, with mutually assured destruction ensuring a stable international system. The end of the Cold War has allowed for burgeoning of the security agenda to include a different set of threats and dangers, not really new but previously kept outside the Cold War context. These new threats are again global in scope, persistent in nature, and potent in their implications (Lynn-Jones and Miller 1995: 3).

A NEW SECURITY AGENDA

Among the new factors that transcend boundaries and threaten to erode national cohesion, the most perilous are the "new risks": drug trafficking, transnational organized crime and nuclear smuggling, refugee movements, uncontrolled and illegal immigration, environmental risks, and international terrorism. As already noted, these are not new sources of potential conflict. They all existed to some extent during the Cold War, but were largely subsumed by the threat of military conflict between NATO and the Warsaw Pact. A new/old issue is the proliferation of Weapons of Mass Destruction (WMD) and Nuclear, Biological, Chemical, and Radiological (NBCR) agents. The issue of proliferation is profoundly old, but the dimension of threat is new. Indeed, trans-sovereign problems – problems that move beyond sovereignty and traditional state responses – have started to fill the post-Cold War agenda and make a mockery of state borders and unilateral state responses. The rise of trans-sovereign problems has been made possible by changes since the end of the Cold War: the opening of societies, economies, and technologies (Cusimano 2000: 4).

The spread of religious fundamentalism, the "criminalization" of state institutions and economic transactions, the increase in cross-border narcotics trafficking, and the potential proliferation of WMD represent an interrelated network of transnational challenges to states and societies in regions like the Caspian, Caucasus, Central Asia, North Africa, and (to a lesser extent) Southeast Europe, and they can serve as a potential catalyst for future conflicts. Moreover, trans-sovereign issues present a very difficult dilemma for policy makers: the very same policies that work to bring about open, democratic, pluralist societies and open markets also make trans-sovereign threats possible. It is obvious that these problems can be difficult for states to address, because effective action requires greater international co-ordination.

The same can be true for environmental problems, which are profoundly trans-sovereign in nature: they do not respect state borders and they defy unilateral state action. Recent times have witnessed an explosion of attention to and concern about environmental challenges, which have become much more salient in public discourse, more prominent in media coverage, more visible and important in political deliberations. Indeed, the environment has become a significant factor in international politics. Although not all environmental problems are relevant to international security, many of them can be a source of political conflict and can contribute to violence within and between states. In any case, much depends on the capacity of states to adapt and respond to the social and economic effects of environmental degradation – for example, reduced agricultural production, declining economic performance, the displacement of populations, the disruption or even destruction of communal relations, and the collapse of legitimate authority.

The developing world is particularly vulnerable to the social consequences of eco-problems, because those states have fewer or no technical, financial, and institutional resources to devote to containing or coping with the consequences. In such cases, conflicts are easily born of scarcity, deprivation, or ethnic, racial, or cultural strife exacerbated by scarcity and deprivation (Homer-Dixon 1995). It is beyond doubt that environmental degradation leads to refugee flows and violent conflicts, thus undermining state institutions and authority, as occurred in Chiapas in Mexico, and in Rwanda. The flow of refugees can cause further environmental damage, which in turn adds more pressure on state authority and economic capacity, thus providing fertile ground for drug trafficking and organized criminal activity. Trans-sovereign problems tend to be mutually reinforcing.

Refugee movements, along with uncontrolled or illegal immigration, represent yet another non-traditional threat to international security and stability. Refugees place economic and social burdens on government services, burdens that have become substantial. In some cases they have overwhelmed and drained the already fragile institutions and infrastructure of host states, resulting in violent conflicts and military interventions. Former Yugoslavia is a case in point. There are 30 to 40 million people displaced across state boundaries or within states, and this figure is expected to rise.

As a result, numerous countries in Europe are beginning to re-examine their immigration policies and enforce more stringent standards, thus moving towards neo-conservative, undemocratic practices. This could have a destabilizing effect on the less economically advanced nations in Europe and could threaten inter-state relations. It also could lead to domestic unrest if more is not done soon to regulate the flow of refugees and expedite safe repatriation of those not accepted for long-term residence. Such policies will almost inevitably result in much suffering and not a little "militant migration" as marginalized migrants are radicalized. In the interim, Europe is experiencing an increase in crime rates and hatred crimes, any of which could lead to instability and thence to conflict and insecurity.

At the same time, international terrorism has become more than ever a source of grave concern. This was true even before 11 September 2001, but "9/11" finally answered the question of what the dominant security problem in the post-Cold War world is: "mega-terrorism", a non-state form of terrorism in which a readiness to take life knows no limits (Muller 2003: 7). Constraints on the use of violence are not effective. There are no bounds to the number of fatalities a group like al-Qaeda wishes to cause. The new breed of terrorist seems to want only to kill, create havoc and cause destruction on a massive scale; in most cases they are not seeking to negotiate to achieve certain objectives; they are very well organized, trained, funded, and supported; and their worldwide networks include an excellent intelligence and communications structure that gives them enough information about their targets to be able to direct their operatives, often over the internet, from thousands of miles away. The challenge has been enormous, especially for the United States.

A NEW SECURITY DISCOURSE?

Post-Cold War global processes have been changing the nature of threat and forcing some adaptation of basic strategic principles, and the patterns of allegiance associated with them. Each of these dimensions – threat, strategy, and affiliation – is understood most readily "in terms of a sharp conceptual distinction: the difference between a deliberate opponent and a natural process, between strategies of prevention and strategies of reaction, and between cooperative and confrontational alignments" (Steinbruner 2000: 195). Security challenges become more complex when one turns to those issues that may not directly challenge the viability of the state, in traditional terms, but may nevertheless undermine its sovereignty, compromise its ability to control the penetrability of its borders, and exacerbate relations – either between groups within the polity or between states in the regional or global system. Moreover, the 9/11 terrorist attacks by militant Muslims, the subsequent counter-terrorist campaigns in Afghanistan and Pakistan, and the war against Saddam's regime in Iraq have further changed the post-Cold War security discourse.

Throughout the 1990s, the security debate remained rather tentative, unfocused and vague. The formulations of threat now in use – ranging from major regional contingencies, via lesser nationalist or fundamentalist war-prone regimes and groups, to the eventual emergence of peer competitors – refer to the deliberately aggressive actions of calculating enemies, who are assumed to have conscious identity even if they are not mentioned explicitly. Armed conflicts like the ones in Kosovo and Afghanistan have clearly demonstrated the difficulty of anticipating and meeting the new problems that have arisen from the debris of the old order.

The scope of political change and the complexities of international security are making the new challenges much harder to understand. All the above represent a new class of security problem, in which dispersed processes pose dangers of potentially large magnitude and incalculable probability. In reaction to those problems, policies seem to be shifting from contingency reaction to anticipatory prevention, pre-emptive action and coalitional crisis management. In that context, contemporary security discourse seems to be aimed at taking account of security's geographical and functional scope, its degree of institutionalization, its strength and fragility, and its ideological and normative elements. Also, more often than in the past, there are new and sometimes unexpected linkages between political, security and economic concerns, which have challenged the capacity of the state to recognize and respond to new dangers and needs for action. They have also challenged international institutions – the adequacy of existing bodies for action, and the potential for multilateral co-ordination.

A CHANCE FOR MULTILATERALISM AND MULTILATERAL SECURITY INSTITUTIONS?

The 9/11 terrorist attacks truly changed the world security system. The scale of these attacks, the destruction they caused, the relative ease with which they were organized and executed against the most powerful country in the world, made it very clear to everybody that no country was immune. The attacks that followed in Madrid and London showed that no country could afford to be complacent about terrorism any more. Like drug traffickers, nuclear smugglers, and international crime cartels, terrorist groups take advantage of the infrastructure that open societies, open economies, and open technologies afford. Such groups are more easily able to move people, money, and goods across international borders thanks to democratization, economic liberalization, and technological advances. They rely on international telecommunications to publicize their acts and political demands. Even if propaganda is nothing new, tools like CNN and the Internet dramatically extend the scope of a terrorist's reach. Terrorists also take advantage of weaker or developing states to serve as operational bases for training and carrying out attacks against Western targets. As the 11 September attacks indicated, counter-state and counter-society abilities have already become more available to radical and fundamentalist groups. Overall these trends suggest that seemingly invulnerable states, however powerful and wealthy they may be, have innate weaknesses.

All these trends, probably as much as the proliferation of weapons of mass destruction (nuclear, chemical, and biological) and their means of delivery as well as human-rights abuses, pose profound challenges to efforts to build a new global order. They contribute to terrorist groups' capability for violence and other forms of coercion. Contrary to other global challenges (the communications revolution, water shortages, access to energy resources, financial flows), they call directly into question the very authority of the state, and are therefore potentially, if not openly, subversive. However, this multifaceted conception of security entails a multifaceted approach to security. That does not mean analysis cannot be state-centered. Rather, it means that, while a state-centered analysis is capable of illuminating most facets of discord and conflict in the 1990s (for example, proxy wars and irredentism), it should acquire a multidimensional optic, beyond accounts of military power distribution.

This multifaceted/multidimensional security concept means that there is no rigid link between a comprehensive concept for understanding a new situation and the quality of the response. On the contrary, a broad concept – where military force and defense policy continue to occupy a central place – allows a flexible, tailored policy in which force is a major element, but only one of the means that could be employed. In the final analysis, security is a politically defined concept. It is open to debate whether the widening of security might be a good or a bad political choice, but security is not intrinsically a self-contained concept, nor can it be related to military affairs only. If political priorities change, the nature and the means of security will inevitably follow and adapt to the different areas of political action.

In an age of protean threats, transnational in nature, trans-sovereign in quality, and coupled with insidious weapons of enormous destructive capability, the only way forward seems to be through co-operation, preparedness, vigilance, and creative diplomacy. The tools to make a safer world already exist: political fora, international law, economic levers, intelligence assets, and (where necessary) military power. What remains to be harnessed is a collective will to succeed, a will grounded in the UN Universal Declaration of Human Rights and the International Law.

Moreover, the deepening of global interdependence has bred multiple transnational problems that no country can resolve on its own, from humanitarian catastrophes to financial instability, from environmental degradation to terrorism and weapons of mass destruction. By implication, and given the spread of liberal principles and the rise of a new global agenda, multilateralism would seem to offer the USA the obvious way to advance its national interests, pursue common objectives, and exercise leadership. Yet, the United

States has been deeply ambivalent about multilateral engagement (Patrick 2002: 2).

In fact, instead of viewing multilateralism as a tool for expanding – rather than limiting – US options, the G. W. Bush Jr. administration clearly indicated from the outset its intention to pursue unilateral strategies. Based on a state-centric world view in the most traditional sense – formed by a concern with traditional conceptions of security, such as great powers, rogue states, and proliferation of WMD – and equipped with unmatched military capacity and the world's largest national economy, Washington has found multilateral cooperation constraining. This is not surprising, because multilateralism implies a relationship based on rules rather than power, with states agreeing that behavior on a certain issue should be governed by shared principles, rules and norms, regardless of individual interests and circumstances (Caporaso 1993: 53–4). US policy makers have also been sensitive to potential pathologies of multilateral institutions, such as "free-riding" and "buck-passing", while viewing the institutions as constraints that could slow decisions, dilute objectives, and even entangle the United States in foreign adventures on behalf of global agendas.

By implication, multilateralism was seen as carrying certain costs for a dominant power like the United States and did not appear to be a very attractive grand strategy or/and foreign-policy option. Instead, the combination of unprecedented military might and the most vibrant single national economy drove the political and military strategy of "engagement and enlargement" that has become the lynchpin of US foreign and national security policy. Indeed, the 1991 Gulf war, the 1995 and 1999 Balkan campaigns, and most of all the 2001 Afghanistan intervention and the spring 2003 war against Iraq have been impressive US exhibitions of its capacity to go to war. They have demonstrated that military power is not obsolete.

Indeed, the most profound effect of 9/11 has been the reordering of America's international engagement, coupled with reinforcement of the administration's strident unilateralism. America's attempt to make its own international rules is the most vivid example of unilateralism. Washington pushes a military agenda that aims self-confidently to master the "contested zones" because it believes that primacy depends only on vast, omni-capable military power. It also believes that the USA need not tolerate plausible threats to its safety from outside American territory. These threats are to be eliminated. Insofar as pre-emptive war is perceived negatively abroad, this strategy requires a unilateral, global, offensive military capability. The effort to achieve such a capability will further alienate America's traditional allies, it will definitely produce balancing tendencies, it will drive the costs of sustaining US military pre-eminence to unacceptable levels, and it will thus create great difficulties in sustaining, improving, and expanding the global network of US military bases (Posen 2003: 45). Most importantly, with its pre-emptive strategies and tendency to treat different global challenges as being all in the same category, the Bush doctrine is seen as damaging the fabric of international law and the world multilateral *acquis*.

In that context, the Iraq war has been a crisis for the United States, because UN members saw a prospect of unchecked American power being tested. For many around the world the Iraq war is viewed as a step towards seizing global energy control, or hegemonic world economic and trade domination, or to assure Israel's ambitions. They have seen the United States as being unable to provide a rationale for its Iraq policy that can convince the majority of the democracies, its natural supporters. They have seen it intemperately denounce those who criticize it. In short, they have seen Washington demand submission and take steps to obtain it by force. To the rest of the world, this is not very reassuring, to put it mildly. Unchecked American global power seems to be rapidly losing its appeal. Indeed, rather than proving the unilateralists' point, Iraq illustrates the continuing need for co-operation and a return to multilateralism as a rich source of legitimacy and order.

MULTILATERALISM AND SECURITY INSTITUTIONS IN AN ERA OF GLOBALIZATION

In Ruggie's influential account of multilateralism, it is defined as "an institutional form that coordinates relations among three or more states on the basis of generalized principles of conduct" (Ruggie 1993b: 8). Moreover, multilateralism is closely related to legitimacy, and it has three aspects. First, multilateralism entails a commitment to common ways of working, including agreed rules and norms: creating common rules and norms, solving problems through rules and co-operation, and enforcing the rules. Secondly, it means a commitment to working with, and through the procedures of, international institutions. Thirdly, multilateralism also has to include co-ordination, rather than duplication or rivalry.

But multilateralism is, first and foremost, about envisioning and implementing a system of international legitimacy and empowerment. It is about defining the rules of the game in international life, with the aim of socialization, co-ordination of relations and co-operation among states, on the basis of generalized principles or codes of conduct. In the various applications of multilateralism, these codes of conduct express the values that significant actors consider to be indispensable elements of the quest for a workable and justice-oriented international system (Coicaud 2001).

All three aspects of multilateralism and its development as an institution highlight the critical link to multilateral security institutions. Their role has been central to the study of world politics since the end of the Second World War. Yet there is some disagreement on what exactly international security institutions should be about. The end of the Cold War has further blurred the limits of the contested concept of security and made the task of defining international security institutions even more problematic. In order to place some reasonable limits in the debate, we employ herein a definition that treats international security institutions as relatively formal and consciously constructed "sets of rules meant to govern international behavior" (Simmons and Martin 2002: 194), especially those that are negotiated and endorsed by states (Duffield 2006).[1]

It is worth noting that there is as yet no distinct body of theory on the effects of multilateral security institutions. By implication, as has been aptly demonstrated by a prominent student of international institutions,

> one should turn to the more general theoretical literature on the significance of international institutions, identifying where possible the distinct ways in which international security institutions might (or might not) make a difference. Especially international security is an issue-area, which can provide a particularly valuable arena for adjudicating among the competing claims of different theories insofar as it is the area where theorists of all stripes have expected international institutions to be least consequential.
> (Duffield 2006: 639)

This volume brings together world-renowned scholars from various theoretical perspectives to present their research findings on the evolution of multilateralism and its relationship to particular issues and strategies. The book also attempts to explore a rather timely question in international relations theory, namely how multilateral security institutions matter and under what conditions. Accordingly, its range of topics is rather broad: contributions examine the ambivalent US position on multilateralism in the post-9/11 era, empirical assessments (qualitative and quantitative) of whether international security institutions are objects of state choice and/or are consequential (with case studies of certain functions of the UN, NATO and EU), and multilateralism at the periphery (in certain sub-systems and/or bilateral conflicts).

The volume is divided into two parts. In the first part – entitled Multilateralism and Security: Concepts, Issues and Strategies – the contributions discuss the evolution of particular concepts of the term "multilateralism," such as "opportunistic," "effective," "humanized" and "principled" multilateralism, and their relationship to the most important issues and strategies of current world affairs. In the second part – entitled Assessing Multilateral Security Institutions – the analysis turns into a more detailed empirical assessment of the difference that particular multilateral arrangements and institutions (such as the UN, EU and NATO) can make in the security domain.

Part I of the book

More specifically, the contributions in the first part provide a wide assessment of the contemporary discourse on multilateralism, not just as an institution, but in the context of novel developments in global security.

In his contribution, John Ikenberry discusses US ambivalence about multilateral institutions and variations in the USA's institutional relations with Europe and the rest of the world. The central question in regard to US economic and security ties, one that American policy makers have confronted over the decades since 1945, Ikenberry argues, is how much the policy "lock-in" of other states – ensured by institutionalizating various commitments and obligations – is worth, and how much reduction in US policy autonomy and constraint of its power is politically sustainable? Ikenberry claims that institutions are best seen as tools of political control. Their basic value to states is that they alter the levels of state autonomy and political certainty. Seen in this way, the leading state's ability to credibly restrain and commit its power is, ironically, a type of power. The leading state wants to lock other states into specific institutional commitments. It could use its power to coerce them, but this would be costly and lose any chance of building a legitimate order. If the leading state can bind itself and institutionalize the exercise of its power – at least to some credible extent – offering to do so becomes a bargaining chip that may obtain the institutional co-operation of other states. But it is only a bargaining chip when power disparities make limits and restraints desirable to other states and when the leading state can in fact establish such limits and constraints. It is variations in these enabling circumstances, Ikenberry argues, that explain why the USA sometimes seeks to build multilateral institutions, binding itself to other states, and in other cases does not.

Jack Snyder and Leslie Vinjamuri critically examine the two dominant strategies for promoting a more democratic and just international order. They argue that the unilateralist and multilateralist policy agendas are both problematic because both are based on flawed theories of social change. For Snyder and Vinjamuri, both strategies suffer from a wilful voluntarism, which inevitably runs up against hard political and social facts. The liberal activists overstate the efficacy of normative persuasion; the unilateralist strategy as expressed by the Bush administration overestimates the efficacy of military force. Both underestimate the need to ground international change firmly in a set of facilitative preconditions: an economic basis to support a liberal political order, a strong political coalition that supports political reform, and the creation of administrative and judicial institutions that support the rule of law. In particular, both approaches underestimate the need to develop a strategy for creating these preconditions in the right sequence, taking into account the realities of particular political and social contexts. In their contribution, Snyder and Vinjamuri examine what happens when weak theories of social change run into the hard realities of social facts, and offer some thoughts on change that have a better sociological grounding.

At a micro-level, Lisa Martin examines why and how the USA chooses to commit itself to multilateral and bilateral agreements on security issues. Her chapter takes further the previous arguments that the choice of an international agreement's form is a strategic one, taking into account both domestic and international considerations. This choice is of interest, Martin argues, because it tells us something about the president's freedom of maneuver in security affairs and the factors that constrain his choices. By introducing international strategic considerations, Martin argues that the major expectation derived from the purely domestic perspective cannot be sustained in equilibrium. The president does face domestic constraints, but he must also address the concerns that other governments have about the president not living up to the terms of an agreement.

Thomas Risse focuses on the transatlantic relationship and the crisis that plagued it after the Iraq war. For Risse, the current crisis stems from domestic developments on both sides of the Atlantic, which have led to different perceptions of security threats, including transnational terrorism, and – more importantly – to different prescriptions on how to handle them. For Risse, a major source of concern is that unilateral and even imperial tendencies in contemporary US foreign policy, and particularly its official discourse, have violated constitutive norms on which the transatlantic security community has been built over the years, namely multilateralism and close consultation with allies. Although unilateralism is currently receding into the background of US foreign policy, the danger, Risse warns, remains that "instrumental multilateralism" is still the preferred course in Washington. In this sense then, the current disagreements between Europe and the United States go beyond ordinary policy conflicts: they touch issues of common values and the core of the security community.

In the face of this crisis, Risse argues forcefully that a new transatlantic bargain is needed, a bargain that dismisses calls for European balancing or bandwagoning responses against US unilateralism. Instead, Risse argues for a new transatlantic dialogue to be started in the EU, with its unique capacities and experience in the economic and political aspects of international security. An EU that puts "teeth" into its concept of a "civilian power" and gets its foreign-policy act together is the pre-condition – Risse argues – for a new transatlantic bargain.

James Sperling's contribution offers an understanding of how the interaction of state attributes and system properties produces specific forms of security multilateralism. By capturing the precise interaction of system- and unit-level variables – and the forms of security multilateralism arising from that interaction – Sperling assesses whether the varieties of security multilateralism in the contemporary international system can be explained by changes in the nature of the state. Sperling also examines the extent to which there are identifiable patterns of internal and external variables that produce a narrow range of outcomes in multilateral security, and criteria that effectively differentiate between varieties of security multilateralism. The substantive purpose of Sperling's contribution is to identify and explain the type of security multilateralism represented by the Shanghai Cooperation Organization (SCO), ASEAN, NATO, and the EU. The key hypothesis emerging from Sperling's survey is that the post-Westphalian state provides the permissive context for the creation of an international civil society, just as the Westphalian state precludes it.

Michael Barnett examines how the emergence of a humanized multilateralism and a politicized humanitarianism can compromise the provision of relief and the protection of civilians in zones of conflict. He explores the factors that contributed simultaneously to the humanization of multilateralism and the politicization of humanitarianism. Barnett, in order to explore these issues, focuses on NATO's "humanitarian war" in Kosovo. He argues that, though the willingness of states to use force in the defense of civilian populations can be interpreted as a victory for principled action, this principled action also represents a potential threat to humanitarianism, especially since many agencies felt rather comfortable associating so closely with a combatant and suspending their sacrosanct principles of impartiality, independence, and neutrality. Barnett concludes by reflecting on how different versions of institutionalism help us understand the different kinds of control mechanisms exerted by the environment over humanitarian organizations, the need for an interpretive perspective to understand why humanitarian organizations might view this principled development – a humanized multilateralism – as a threat to their principles, and humanitarianism's relationship to world order.

Last, but by no means least in this first part of the volume, Oliver Richmond's contribution takes as its starting point the debate about the qualities and dynamics of the liberal peace in the context of multilateral relations between IOs, states, NGOs and other non-state actors. By focusing on the multilateral activities of non-state actors, Richmond goes beyond the traditional, horizontal, state-to-state multilateral architecture. According to the author, there is a "new," vertical multilateralism, which is defined by any relationship between an official and a private/unofficial actor. Vertical multilateralism allows a replication of the norms that arise in the context of horizontal multilateralism within conflict societies. Richmond argues that new and often informal forms of multilateralism have had an important impact on liberal peacebuilding. Moreover, horizontal and vertical forms of multilateralism are vital if the peacebuilding process is to receive wide support and, with the transmittal of norms of governance, have a plausible chance of leading to a sustainable peace. Whether or not these new forms operate an as extension of the old multilateralism or are representative of a radical departure from it, remains to be seen, but it is now mainly through vertical multilateralism – Richmond argues – that norm transmittal and diffusion occurs within conflict zones.

Part II of the book

In the second part of this volume, an attempt is made to empirically assess the difference that particular international security institutions, such as the

UN, EU and NATO, can make in the security domain. Moreover, contributions from various theoretical perspectives do not explore simply whether institutions matter but, more importantly, how they matter and under what conditions. By implication, then, the theoretical gap addressed by relevant accounts of the effects of international institutions is also limited: "research should increasingly turn to the question of how institutions matter in shaping the behaviour of important actors in world politics . . . and emphasize theoretically-informed analysis based on observable implications of alternative theories of institutions" (Martin and Simmons 2001: 437).

Obviously, contributions in this part of the volume are not based on approaches covering the entire theoretical spectrum of the existing literature on the effects of international institutions. Indeed, highly sceptical – if not negative – realist and neo-realist views about the influence international institutions can exert over state behavior are self-excluded from any attempt to test institutional effects. By implication, analysis is mainly based on rational (mainly neo-liberal institutionalist or neo-institutionalist) and social constructivist accounts – and/or on a synthesis of these two approaches – of the effects of particular international security institutions. Both approaches assume, though for different reasons and through different channels, that international institutions can affect and alter states' interests as well as their identities.

For neo-institutionalists, international institutions can make the difference and affect states' strategies through a plethora of channels, including – among others – their ability to serve as focal points that help states solve co-ordination problems, to function as well-defined standards of behavior that reinforce the incentives to co-operate, to reduce uncertainty about each other's capabilities, behavior, and interests, and to reduce transaction costs, thus facilitating co-operation and making it easier for states to resolve disputes over distributional conflicts (Keohane 1984; Martin 1992; Duffield 1994; Hasenclever, Mayer and Rittberger 1997).

From a social constructivist perspective, international institutions can have more profound effects and can succeed in changing states' preferences and even their identities. This happens mainly through the dispersion of norms, beliefs and standards of appropriate behavior (Finnemore 1993) and the subsequent internalization of the institutions' rules and norms into states' domestic legislation and practice (Muller 1993; Finnemore and Sikkink 1998; Risse and Sikkink 1999). Teaching, learning and/or the use of international institutions as discourse fora that facilitate argumentative goals are the most common mechanisms through which ideational change might take place (Finnemore 1993; Checkel 1997 and 2001b; Risse 2000).

Most recently, rational and constructivist efforts have generated some promising propositions to better specify the mechanisms of institutional effects, as well as the conditions under which international institutions are expected to lead to the internalization of new roles or interests from their member states (*International Organization* special issue, Fall 2005). However,

Introduction 13

a series of interesting and important issues seem to remain under-researched and thus unanswered.

More specifically, attention in the institutional literature has turned to the causal significance of institutions, which, as a result of the fact that only a few studies take the problem of institutional endogeneity seriously, has remained inadequately demonstrated (Botcheva and Martin 2001: 3). Apart from constructing well-delineated causal mechanisms, however, a rationalist inquiry has so far given rise to a series of related research directions and issues, such as how institutions might resolve bargaining and distributional conflicts (Hasenclever et al.,1997), how to bring domestic politics more systematically into the study of international institutions (Cortell and Davis 1996), and how to explain variation in institutional effects.

It is worth noting that only a few empirical studies specify the conditions under which institutions should have the predicted effects (Botcheva and Martin 2001: 3). By implication, the existence of unanticipated effects poses a challenge to a rationalist approach and calls for a more synthetic approach, namely one that might integrate the premises and insights of other schools of thought. From a sociological point of view, this would mean that future research should address how non-state actors can not only be empowered by institutions, but how they can also use the latter as leverage to promote their agenda. This point brings to the fore another important area for future research: international institutions as dependent variables. Indeed, as pinpointed by Duffield, "literature has not paid particular attention to international security institutions and the ways in which they may differ both among themselves and from international institutions in other issue areas" (Duffield 2006: 649). Last, but not least, recent research also draws particular attention to research enterprises that would allow for a departure from the currently dominant single-issue, single-organization and single-country format to more theory-guided comparative research across time, across states and/or across international institutions (Simmons and Martin 2002: 205).

The contributions in the second part of the volume treat particular international institutions as both independent and dependent variables, and are constructed methodologically as tests of different influencing variables. By doing so, all contributions address some of the aforementioned issues that remain under-researched while their findings provide theoretically significant insights. It should be noted, however, that these contributions should not be viewed as integral parts of a concrete analytical framework in which one may situate these insights. Rather, each contribution should be viewed as an independent source of theoretical refinement of particular under-researched issues on the effects of international security institutions on states' behavior, which could, in turn, be fruitfully integrated in any future attempt to refine, elaborate, and confirm the state of the art on the sources and, most importantly, on the effects of international institutionalization. One should also highlight the policy relevance each contribution carries with it. Indeed, given that institutions evaluate their domestic impact, learn from the unintended or counterproductive effects of their policies and change them accordingly, studying the effects of a series of multilateral security institutions can also provide those particular institutions with insights on the limits and/or on the unintended effects of their actions and thus contribute to their ability to refine the strategies they choose to follow.

Serving the purpose of helping interested readers think more systematically about how international institutions matter, Frank Schimmelfennig raises the question of how multilateralism has developed in NATO since the end of the Cold War. In assessing NATO's post-Cold War multilateralist quality, the author analyzes both the formal institutional development of NATO and co-operative behavior within the alliance. Schimmelfennig argues that, due to the change in the nature of the threat and NATO's co-operation problems, multilateral institutions within the post-Cold War, "new NATO" have been expanded but at the same time weakened as a result of flexibilization and decentralization.

However, the more flexible and less multilateralist structure of the "new NATO" does not lead *per se*, the author argues, to less multilateralist behavior among its members. Rather, behavior varies with the kind of security threats or challenges at issue. Multilateral co-operation has been strongest when core values and norms of the liberal transatlantic community were at stake – either as a result of their massive violation (as in the "ethnic cleansing" in the Balkans) or their strong reaffirmation (as in the candidates for NATO membership). It was weakest in the Iraq case, which was neither located in the core community region nor related initially to the protection of liberal community values. In between are the Afghanistan and Darfur cases. Thus, in the absence of a common and clearly identifiable threat to their security, the member states of NATO are mainly held together – and bound to act together – by their common liberal democratic identity and the shared liberal values and norms of the transatlantic community of all member states. Whenever this identity was at stake, member states eventually felt compelled to co-operate even in the absence of a threat to their own security.

The contribution of Geoffrey Edwards and Mladen Tošić and that of Panayotis Tsakonas attempt to analyze the effects of "international socialization" in a systematic, theory-informed and comparative way.[2] Edwards and Tošić explore the role that international institutions can play in promoting norms and bringing about changes in the domestic systems of states. The instruments and policies by which organizations have sought to achieve compliance with such norms and bring about a process of socialization have been explored particularly fruitfully in relation to the EU, and especially in terms of its policies towards its near-neighbors to the south or east. However, in the part of Europe where the involvement of international institutions and organizations has been most intense, the western Balkans, these models – outlining conditions under which policies have been effective – have not accounted for compliance/socialization of the local governments.

Starting with the two most prominent models in the literature on persuasion and international norm promotion – the thick persuasion/social learning model and the external incentives model – the authors re-examine the conditions under which compliance by target governments comes about. More specifically they show that, though the conditions identified in the existing models hold for the cases in the western Balkans, they are not sufficient. Looking closely at the role of particular international organisations in Bosnia and Herzegovina – the Office of the High Representative and the EU – the authors identify four further conditions that affect compliance/socialization: the impact of war, the level of co-ordination among international institutions, the levels of economic activity, and the impact of coercion.

Although rational and constructivist efforts have generated some promising propositions to better specify the mechanisms of institutional effects and the conditions in which international institutions are expected to lead to the internalization of new roles or interests by member states, Tsakonas argues that much less has been done on the role of institutions as facilitators of co-operation and conflict management and/or transformation. Bridging "rational-institutionalist" and "constructivist" accounts, the author explores the impact the two most successful and prominent international institutions, namely NATO and the EU, have had on the management and/or transformation of the long-standing Greek–Turkish territorial dispute.

The author specifies the reasons that NATO's role has always been – and is doomed to remain – poor and parochial, whereas the EU appears able to change the interests and/or identity scripts of the conflict parties. To this end, certain core arguments are being developed about when and under what conditions NATO and the EU may have a positive impact on the conflict parties' strategies toward co-operation and conflict transformation. Through a comparative assessment of the empirical record of NATO and EU roles in the transformation of the Greek–Turkish dispute, the author identifies two conditions that accounts most for NATO's pervasive and the EU's promising role in the Greek–Turkish conflict: the strength of the norms each institution exerts *vis-à-vis* the conflict parties, and the "type of socialization" or depth of internalization the two institutions' mechanisms have produced. The author also draws attention to the need for international security institutions that fulfill the aforementioned conditions to be careful enough to promote the right mix of conditionalities and incentives to the disputants in order to positively contribute to the transformation and/or resolution of an inter-state dispute.

In a pioneer study on the UN peacebuilding enterprise, by employing new quantitative methods to measure peacebuilding success defined by self-sustaining peace (two or more years after the peacekeepers have left), Nicholas Sambanis and Jonah Schulhofer-Wohl find that the UN has been much more successful in peacekeeping than other organizations. Building on a particular "ecological model of peacebuilding" Sambanis and Schulhofer-Wohl test the hypothesis of the effectiveness of non-UN operations empirically and find that non-UN operations have no significant effect on peacebuilding success, unlike UN operations, which have a rather positive effect. The authors postulate several possible explanations why non-UN operations seem to have no significant effect on peacebuilding success and they explore the differences between the outcomes of UN and non-UN peace operations as a way to analyze the determinants of the composition of a peace operation.

In their chapter, Sambanis and Schulhofer-Wohl make a valuable contribution to our understanding that certain peace operations are more successful than others. However, a better approach, as the authors admit, would be to isolate at a high level of detail those aspects of peace operations that are important for success and to ensure that, whatever the originating organization or state, a peace operation possessed these characteristics. Thus, a new challenge for analysts of peacekeeping and policy makers is still to grasp the political process by which peace operations are created and placed in the field. Pursuing this line of research further promises to generate policy recommendations on how to design any type of peace operation for the maximum positive impact on peacebuilding.

In the contribution by Erik Voeten and that by Aris Alexopoulos and Dimitris Bourantonis, analysis turns to treating international security institutions as dependent variables. More specifically, Erik Voeten's chapter tries to shed light on the timely issue of reform in the world's leading multilateral organization, the UN Security Council. Voeten evaluates various plausible explanations for the UNSC's institutional persistence despite its increased activity and shows why traditional explanations for the persistence of suboptimal institutional configurations provide insufficient explanations and do not contribute much to our understanding of this question.

The author argues that, in order to understand the UNSC's institutional persistence, we need a fuller appreciation of how the UNSC fits into its strategic environment. After introducing the issues that arise in delegating decisions on uses of force to an international institution, Voeten provides some simple illustrations of how outside power affects bargaining in an institution such as the UNSC. His empirical findings suggest that the most promising account focuses on the institutional characteristics of the bargaining process that underlies the reform process. In addition, Voeten's chapter evaluates various other aspects of the bargaining process and draws conclusions about the UNSC and institutionalist theories of change and continuity in the international system. His analysis points – inter alia – to the limits of the impact that institutional reform and design have when decisions need to be self-enforcing and non-institutionalized power asymmetries matter. In addition, the benefits of clever constitutional engineering will most likely be relatively small, both for the production of public goods (peace) as well as for the private interests of individual states.

On a more positive note, on the ability of the UNSC to successfully reform, Alexopoulos and Bourantonis apply the work of George Tsebelis – a theory produced to explain the function of domestic political institutions – in order to examine the element of enlargement of the UN decision body and its correlation with its decision efficiency. The authors analyse the current structures of the UNSC and discuss the decision capacity of the UN system under alternative reform scenarios on the membership and institutional arrangements of the future UNSC.

The authors convincingly argue that it is misleading to connect, as many used to do, enlargement with less decision capacity in the UNSC. Hence, a UNSC larger than the current one, with more permanent members equipped with institutional veto power, could arrive at a decision with less difficulty than the current, more restricted UNSC. The important element for the decision capacity of the UNSC is therefore not its size but the location of the ideal preference points of its members and the decision rule according to which these members vote for the proposed draft resolutions.

Notes

1 As all the contributions in Part II deal with (mostly the effects of) particular multilateral security institutions, such as the UN, EU and NATO, this volume adheres to the definition of international institutions given by Robert Keohane, who includes international organizations in his definition of international institutions (Keohane 1989: 3–4).
2 For the need of future research undertakings to follow these directions, see Schimmelfennig (2002: 22).

Part I
Multilateralism and security
Concepts, issues and strategies

1 State power and international institutions
America and the logic of economic and security multilateralism

G. John Ikenberry

Introduction

The United States has been one of the great champions of multilateral, rule-based international order, but it has also frequently sought to resist and exempt itself from entangling institutional obligations. Across the twentieth century – and in particular at the major postwar turning points of 1919, 1945 and 1989 – the United States pursued ambitious strategies that entailed the use of an array of multilateral institutions to remake international order. No other great power has advanced such far-reaching and elaborate ideas about how institutions might be employed to organize and manage the relations between states. But despite this enthusiasm for creating institutions and a rule-based international order, the United States has been reluctant to tie itself too tightly to these multilateral institutions and rules (Ikenberry 2003).

After World War I, the United States put the League of Nations at the center of its designs for world order: collective institutions were to play an unprecedented role in organizing security and providing mechanisms for dispute resolution and the enforcement of agreements. After World War II, the United States pushed onto the world a remarkable array of new institutions – multilateral, bilateral, regional, global, security, economic, and political. After the Cold War, the United States again pursued an institutional agenda – the expansion of NATO and the launching of the North America Free Trade Agreement (NAFTA), the Asian Pacific Economic Co-operation (APEC), and the World Trade Organization (WTO). But at each turn, the United States also resisted the loss of sovereign authority or the reduction of its policy autonomy. The League of Nations in 1919, the International Trade Organization in 1947, and the recent cases of the International Criminal Court (ICC), the Kyoto Protocol, and the Nuclear Test Ban Treaty are all monuments to America's reluctance to bind itself to international institutions. Indeed, the George W. Bush administration has made resistance to binding international agreements a hallmark of its foreign policy.

The puzzle is to explain the logic and variation in the extent to which the United States has agreed to establish binding institutional ties – particularly multilateral ties – with other states. Why did the United States at the zenith of its hegemonic power after World War II and again after the Cold War seek the establishment or expansion of multilateral institutions and agree to insert itself within them? Why did it agree to bind itself to Europe in a 1949 security pact, deepen that commitment in the years that followed, and seek the expansion of NATO in the 1990s, even after the Soviet threat that prompted security co-operation disappeared? Why did the United States seek to establish order after World War II in western Europe through multilateral commitments and pursue a series of bilateral security agreements in Asia?

The most basic hypothesis is that the United States organizes and operates within international institutions when it can dominate them and resists doing so when it cannot. But a slightly more complex set of calculations seem to be involved. This chapter argues that American ambivalence about multilateral institutions – along with variations in its institutional relations with Europe and the rest of the world – reflects a basic dilemma that lies at the heart of international institutional agreements. The attraction of institutional agreements for the leading states is that they potentially lock other states into stable and predictable policy orientations, thereby reducing its need to use coercion. But the price that the leading state must pay for this institutionalized co-operation is a reduction in its own policy autonomy and its unfettered ability to exercise power. The central question that American policy makers have confronted over the decades after 1945 in regard to its economic and security ties is: how much policy "lock-in" of other states – ensured by the institutionalization of various commitments and obligations – is worth how much reduction in American policy autonomy and restraint on its power?

The result is a potential institutional bargain – a bargain that lies at the heart of America's multilateral ties to other Western democracies and the wider array of postwar multilateral institutions championed by the United States. It is a bargain that is most fully available when the old order has been destroyed and a newly powerful state must engage weaker states over the organization of the new order. In the institutional bargain, the leading state wants to reduce compliance costs and weaker states want to reduce their costs of security protection – or the costs they would incur trying to protect their interests against the actions of a dominating lead state. This is what makes the institutional deal attractive: the leading state agrees to restrain its own potential for domination or abandonment in exchange for the long-term institutionalized co-operation of subordinate states. Both sides are better off with an institutionalized relationship than in an order based on the constant threat of the indiscriminate and arbitrary exercise of power. The leading state does not need to expend its power capabilities to coerce other states, and the other states do not need to expend resources seeking to protect themselves from such coercion. It is the mutually improving nature of this exchange that makes the institutional deal work.

The central theoretical claim is that institutions are best seen as tools of political control. Their basic value to states is that they alter the levels of state autonomy and political certainty. Seen in this way, the ability of the leading state to credibly restrain and commit its power is, ironically, a type of power (Schelling 1960: 22–8). It wants to lock other states into specific types of institutional commitments. It could use its power to coerce them, but to do so is costly and it loses any chance of building a legitimate order. If the leading state can bind itself and institutionalize the exercise of its power – at least to some credible extent – offering to do so becomes a bargaining chip it can play as a way to obtain the institutional co-operation of other states. But it is only a bargaining chip when the power disparities make limits and restraints desirable to other states and when the leading state can in fact establish such limits and constraints. It is the variations in these various enabling circumstances that explain why the United States sometimes seeks to build multilateral institutions and bind itself to other states and why in other cases it does not.

State power and institutions

Why would a leading state surrounded by a world of weaker states want to establish multilateral institutions? The answer is that institutional agreements can lock other states into a relatively congenial and stable order. The institutions help create a more favorable and certain political environment in which the leading state pursues its interests. This is possible because institutions can operate as mechanisms of political control. When a state agrees to tie itself to the commitments and obligations of an inter-state institution, it is agreeing to reduce its policy autonomy. A leading state that has created an institutionalized order that works to its long-term benefit is better off than a leading state operating in a free-floating order requiring the constant and costly exercise of power to get its way.

Institutions can serve two purposes. First, as neo-liberal institutionalists argue, institutions can help solve collective action problems – reducing the commitment problems and transaction costs that stand in the way of efficient and mutually beneficial political exchange (Keohane 1984). But institutions are also instruments of political control. As Terry Moe argues, "political institutions are also weapons of coercion and redistribution. They are the structural means by which political winners pursue their own interests, often at the expense of political losers" (Moe 1990: 213). A winning political party in Congress will try to write the committee voting rules to favor its interests. Similarly, in international relations, a powerful state will want to make its advantages as systematic and durable as possible by trying to rope weaker states into favorable institutional arrangements.[1]

The attraction of institutional agreements for the leading state is two-fold. First, if the leading state can get other states to tie themselves to a multilateral institution that directly or indirectly serves its long-term interests, it will not need to spend its resources to constantly coerce other states. It is the most powerful state, so it is likely that it would win many or most of the endless distributive battles in a non-institutionalized relationship with subordinate states, but locking these lesser states into institutional agreements reduces these costs of enforcement (Ikenberry and Kupchan 1990; Martin 1993).[2] Second, if the institutional agreement has some degree of stickiness – that is, if it has some independent ordering capacity – the institution may continue to provide favorable outcomes for the leading state even after its power capacities have declined in relative terms. Institutions can both conserve and prolong the power advantages of the leading state.

In general, when deciding whether to sign a multilateral agreement, a state faces a trade-off. In agreeing to abide by the rules and norms of the agreement, the state must accept a reduction in its policy autonomy. That is, it must agree to some constraints on its freedom of action – or independence of policymaking – in a particular area. But in exchange it expects to get other states to do the same. The multilateral bargain will be attractive to a state if it concludes that the benefits that flow to it through the co-ordination of policies achieved through rule-based constraints on policy choice are greater than the costs of lost policy autonomy. In an ideal world, a state might want to operate in an international environment in which all other states are heavily rule-bound, while leaving itself entirely unencumbered by rules and institutional restraints. But because all states are inclined in this way, the question becomes one of how much autonomy each must offer in order to get rule-based behavior out of the others.

A state's willingness to agree to a multilateral bargain will hinge on several factors that shape the ultimate cost–benefit calculation. One is whether the policy constraints imposed on other states (states B, C, D) by the multilateral agreement really matter to the first state (state A). If the "unconstrained" behavior of other states is judged to have no undesirable impact on state A, then state A will be unwilling to give up any policy autonomy of its own. It also matters if the participating states are actually able to credibly restrict their policy autonomy. If state A is unconvinced that states B, C, and D can actually be constrained by multilateral rules and norms, it will not be willing to sacrifice its own policy autonomy (Fearon 1997). Likewise, state A will need to convince the other states that it too will be constrained. These factors are all continuous rather than dichotomous variables – so judgments must be made by states about the degree of credibility and relative value of constrained policies.

But why would weaker states agree to be roped in? After all, they might calculate that it is better to not lock themselves into an institutional agreement now (T1) and wait until some later time (T2 or T3) when the power asymmetries do not favor the leading state as much. Weaker states have two potential incentives to buy into the leading state's institutional agreement. First, if the institutional agreement also put limits and restraints on the behavior of the leading state, this would be welcome. In a non-institutionalized relationship, these lesser states are subject to the unrestrained and unpredictable domination of the leading state. If they believed that credible limits could be placed on the arbitrary and indiscriminate actions of the leading state, this might be enough of an attraction to justify an institutional agreement at T1. Second, when the leading state does in fact circumscribe its behavior, it is giving up some opportunities to use its power to gain immediate returns on its power – it settles for fewer gains at T1 by operating within institutional rules and obligations than it could otherwise achieve with its brute power. It does this with an eye toward longer-term gains that are specified above. But weaker states may have reason to gain more sooner rather than later. The discount rates for future gains are potentially different for the leading and lesser states, and this makes an institutional bargain potentially more mutually desirable.

So the leading state is faced with a choice: how much institutional limitation on its own policy autonomy and exercise power is worth how much policy lock-in of weaker states? Institutionalization tends to be a two-way street. A newly powerful state can try to embed other states in a set of multilateral institutions, but it will likely need to give up some of its own discretionary power to get the desired outcome. Terry Moe (1990: 227–8) notes this in regard to a ruling party's control of government institutions:

> They can fashion structures to insulate their favorable agencies and programs from the future exercise of public authority. In doing so, of course, they will not only be reducing their enemies' opportunities for future control; they will be reducing their own opportunities as well. But this is often a reasonable price to pay, given the alternative. And because they get to go first, they are really not giving up control – they are choosing to exercise a greater measure of it ex ante, through insulated structures that, once locked in, predispose the agency to do the right things. What they are moving away from – because it is dangerous – is the kind of ongoing hierarchical control that is exercised through the discretionary decisions of public authority over time.

Several hypotheses follow immediately from this model of state power and institutions. First, a leading state should try to lock other states into institutionalized policy orientations, while trying to minimize its own limitations on policy autonomy and discretionary power. This is the story that Michael Crozier tells about politics within large-scale organizations. Each individual within a complex organizational hierarchy is continually engaged in a dual struggle: to tie his colleagues to precise rule-based behavior – thereby creating a more stable and certain environment in which to operate – while also trying to retain as much autonomy and discretion as possible for himself (Crozier 1964). Similarly, leading states will try to lock other states in as much as possible while also trying to remain as unencumbered as possible by institutional rules and obligations. Second, the leading state will make use of its ability – to the extent the ability exists – to limit its capacity to exercise power in indiscriminate and arbitrary ways as a "currency" to buy the institutional co-operation of other states.

The availability of the institutional bargain will depend on several circumstances that can also be specified as hypotheses. First, the amount of "currency" available to the leading state to buy institutional co-operation of weaker states is determined by two factors: the ability of the leading state to potentially dominate or injure the interests of weaker states and its ability to credibly restrain itself from doing so. Although all states might offer to restrain and commit themselves in exchange for concessions by other states, the willingness and ability of powerful states to do so will be of particular interest to other states. Chad may offer to lock itself into an institutional agreement that lowers its policy autonomy and make its future policy orientation more predictable, but few states will care much about this offer to bind itself and they are not likely to offer much in return to get it. But if a powerful state with the capacity for serious domination and disruption offers to restrain itself – this will get the attention of other states and they are likely to be willing to offer something to get it. But it is not just the domination and disruption potential of the leading state that generates "currency" to buy the institutional co-operation of other states. It is also the capacity to actually make good on restraint and commitment. If a powerful state cannot credibly limit its power, its currency will amount to very little.

Two other factors will also determine if the leading state – if it has the "currency" with which to buy institutional co-operation – will in fact want to do so. One is the degree to which the leading state is in fact interested in locking in the policy behavior of other states. This is a question about the extent to which the actions of other states actually impinge on the interests of the leading state. The security policy orientation of Europe states would tend to qualify as important, but other policy orientations of European states – and the wide range of policy orientations of other states around the world – are not significant enough to justify efforts by the leading state to lock in stable and favorable policy behavior, particularly if the price of doing so entails a reduction of policy autonomy. The other factor is simply the ability of weaker states to be locked in. The United States may want to lock in the policy behavior of other states – particularly the security policy behavior – but not have enough confidence that these institutionalized commitments and obligations can be effectively locked in.

Taken together, these considerations allow us to see how a leading state and weaker states might make trade offs about binding themselves together through multilateral institutions. The four factors are summarized in Table 1.1. The more that the leading state is capable of dominating and abandoning weaker states, the more that weaker states will care about restraints on the leading state's exercise of power – and the more they are likely to make some concessions to get leading state restraint and commitment. Similarly, the more that a potentially dominating state can in fact credibly restrain and commit itself, the more that weaker states will be interested in pursuing an institutional bargain. When both these conditions hold – when the leading state can dominate and abandon, and when it can restrain and commit itself – that state will be particularly willing and able to pursue an institutional bargain. From the perspective of the leading state, the less important that the

Table 1.1 Incentives and opportunities behind the institutional bargain

Variable	Implications
Domination/abandonment potential of the leading state	Weaker states more willing to make concessions to gain restraint Leading state has enhanced institutional bargaining advantage
Restraint/commitment potential of the leading state	Weaker states more willing to make concessions Leading state has enhanced institutional bargaining advantage
Lock-in importance to leading state	Leading state has greater incentive to offer restraint and commitment
Lock-in potential of weaker states	Leading state has greater incentive to offer restraint and commitment

policy behavior is of weaker states (that is, the less consequential it is to the leading state), the less the leading state will offer restraints on its own policy autonomy to achieve policy lock-in. Likewise, the less certain that the leading state is that policy lock-in of weaker states can in fact be accomplished, the less the leading state will offer restraints on its own policy autonomy.

American institution building

This model is useful in making sense of the broad sweep of American institution building over the twentieth century. The major patterns of American policy toward multilateral institutions can be sketched. It is not only that the United States has tended to support the creation of multilateral institutions when it can dominate them. This is the most straightforward hypothesis, and there is a great deal of evidence to support it. But there is also a slightly more complicated calculation in American institutional thinking. The United States has tended to weigh the costs of reducing its policy autonomy in relation to the gains that it would realize by locking other states into enduring policy positions.

Postwar institution building

The United States has been most active in seeking institutional agreements after major wars – as it did in 1919, 1945, and 1989. The reason why is made clear in the foregoing model. There are several distinctive features of postwar moments that lend themselves to new institutional initiatives. First, the old institutional order has been cleared away by the war and therefore, in contrast to more "normal" moments in international relations, basic issues of order are on the table. It is difficult simply to fall back on the status quo. Second, wars tend to create new winners and losers – and ratify a new and often heightened asymmetrical distribution of power. As a result, the new leading state will be faced with a decision how to use its new power assets. It has, in effect, received a windfall of power. Should it simply use these new power assets to win in the endless distributive struggles after the war or use them to invest in an order that serves its long-term goals? The leading state does have incentives at these junctures to act in a relatively far-sighted way. Institutional agreements are potentially a form of investment in the future – but only if they are capable of playing a shaping and constraining role even in the face of shifts in the distribution of power.

Third, because the leading state is newly powerful, secondary states will be particularly eager to gain assurances about the actions of the leading state. They will be interested in agreements that reduce the ability of the leading state to dominate or abandon them. The more powerful and potentially disruptive the new leading state is, the more other states will worry about this problem and the more they will be willing to concede in order to get credible restraints and commitments. Fourth, the war itself also tends to disrupt the domestic institutions of the new leading state and the new secondary states. Often the leading state is actually in a position to occupy and help rebuild the secondary states. As a result, the postwar moment may be particularly congenial for the establishment of institutional agreements that lock weaker states into a long-term policy orientation. Put differently, the lock-in capacity is particularly high after major wars.

Finally, if the leading state does want to create an order that is legitimate, it will be attracted to institutional agreements that not only lock weaker states into a desirable order but also render the postwar order legitimate – that is, mutually acceptable or desirable. To the extent that the institutional agreements restrain and commit the power of the leading state, this may be an attractive option. The institutional agreement lowers its costs of enforcement. After wars, newly powerful states are confronted with these sorts of dilemmas and trade-offs.

Variations in postwar institutional outcomes

The United States pursued a much more elaborate and wide-ranging institutional agenda after 1945 than it did after 1919. The proposal for a League of Nations was an ambitious and demanding institution that sought to establish a global system of collective security. But the hard work of building these institutions was not in the institutional concessions and obligations that the United States and the other countries agreed to, but in the democratic revolution that Wilson saw as insuring the success of the League of Nations (Knock 1992). In contrast, the scope and depth of the post-1945 proposals and the ambition with which the United States sought to remake Europe and Asia entailed a more fully institutionalized postwar order than Wilson could imagine. Why did the United States pursue a much more far-reaching institutional agenda after 1945?

The model presented earlier is helpful in untangling this postwar variation. The United States was in a much more asymmetrical power relationship with Europe after 1945 than it was in 1919. This had a major impact on the ability and willingness of the leading and weaker states to seek an institutional bargain. More so than in 1919, the United States was a full-fledged hegemonic power after 1945, and because of this the Europeans attached a premium to harnessing and restraining this newly powerful state. Europe was much more willing to accept an institutional agreements in return for a more restrained and committed America. Likewise, the United States had tremendous "currency" with which to buy the institutional agreement of other states, particularly the Europeans.

Other factors also facilitated the unprecedented post-1945 institutionalism. The United States ended World War II with a much more sophisticated critique of what had caused the world war and what would be necessary to insure a peaceful and stable postwar order. In 1919, the Wilson administration did have a strong view about how Europe needed to transform itself. It made stark contrasts between its new thinking and the militarism and balance-of-power thinking of the Old World. The leaders in France and Britain also felt threatened by Wilson's crusade to remake the world. But the American position after World War II entailed a much more comprehensive critique of European and world politics. Europe needed to integrate itself more fully. Wider social and economic reform would be needed to sustain liberal democratic regimes, and these reforms would need to be embedded in regional and global multilateral institutions. Just as importantly, the domestic systems in Japan and Germany would need much more thorough-going reform – made possible by the unprecedented opportunity of the American and allied occupation (Smith, T. 1994: ch. 6). Compared to 1919, in 1945 the United States saw more lock-in importance and more lock-in opportunity in Europe. As a result, it was willing to give more to get it. Likewise, the Europeans were more willing after 1945 to give more concessions in order to get institutionalized American restraints and commitments.

This analysis suggests that three of the four variables that bear on the incentives and opportunities for an institutional bargain were more evident in 1945 than in 1919. What about the fourth variable: the ability of the leading state to make credible restraints and commitments? It is difficult to argue that the institutional character of the United States was radically different after 1945 in a way that facilitated the establishment of credible restraints and commitments. But there was a difference. The sheer density of post-1945 institutional initiatives provided more "strings" with which to tie the United States down and tie it to Europe. American restraint and commitment to Europe in 1919 was based on the fragile tie of a single treaty. In 1945 it was based on dozens of inter-governmental agreements, most importantly NATO.

Variations in American policy toward Europe and Asia

American institution building after 1945 took different forms in Europe and Asia. The United States pursued a multilateral strategy in Europe – with NATO as the anchor – while in Asia it pursued a series of bilateral security agreements with Japan, Korea, and several southeast Asian states. This contrast provides an important puzzle that can sharpen the logic of American multilateralism.

The first observation is that the United States actually did float the idea of a multilateral security institution in Asia – in the early 1940s and during 1950–1 – that was to be a counterpart to NATO. The second observation is that some of the elements that allowed security multilateralism to be embraced in Europe did not exist in Asia – quite apart from American interests or intentions. Europe did have a group of roughly equal sized and situated states that were capable of being bound together in a multilateral security institution tied to the United States, while Japan was alone and isolated in east Asia. The third observation is that the countries in east Asia that might have been party to a multilateral security pact – South Korea, South Vietnam, and Taiwan – were all countries that were interested in reunification. The NATO pact in Europe seemingly made permanent the division of Germany. This was a development that these Asian states sought to avoid.

The model presented earlier adds to these explanations. The basic difference between Asia and Europe is that the United States was more dominant in Asia but also wanted less out of Asia. This meant that as a practical matter it was less necessary for the United States to give up policy autonomy in exchange for institutional co-operation in Asia. In Europe, the United States had an elaborate agenda for uniting the European states, creating an institutional bulwark against communism, and supporting centrist democratic regimes. It had ambitious lock-in goals. These goals could not simply be realized through the brute exercise of power. To get what it wanted it had to bargain with the Europeans and this meant agreeing to restrain its exercise of power.[3] In Asia, the United States did not have goals that were sufficient important enough to purchase with an agreement to restrain its power. Bilateralism was the desired strategy because multilateralism would have required more restraints on policy autonomy. Put differently, the United States had much more unchallenged hegemonic power in Asia than in western Europe, and therefore it had fewer incentives to secure its dominant position with international institutions. Peter Katzenstein (1997) argues that

> [i]t was neither in the interest of the United States to create institutions that would have constrained independent decision making in Washington nor in the interest of subordinate states to enter institutions in which they would have minimal control while foregoing opportunities for free-riding and dependence reduction. Extreme hegemony thus led to a system of

bilateral relations between states rather than a multilateral system that emerged in the North Atlantic area around the North Atlantic Treaty Organization (NATO) and the European Community.

This view is also consistent with the more recent developments. As American hegemony has declined in relative terms within east Asia and as the United States has developed more specific lock-in goals for the states within the region, its interest in multilateral institutional building has increased somewhat (Crone 1993). American support for APEC – while not an institution that requires much, if any, real policy restraint by the United States – is emblematic of this new multilateralism in Asia.

Institutionalism on the cheap

The United States has consistently attempted to get as much institutionalized order building after major wars as possible on the cheap – that is, with minimal cost to it in real restraints on its policy autonomy or political sovereignty. This is the basic logic that the model illuminates: the leading state will try to lock in other states and create as stable and favorable a political environment as possible with the least possible cost in policy encumbrances.

This logic is seen in the American impulse after 1919 and 1945. At both moments, the United States did not initially foresee specific or legally demanding American commitments to the rest of the world. Instead, the United States sought to encourage general tendencies in the international system that would work independently to foster a stable and favorable international order. In 1919, Wilson understood that the major leverage that the United States had over the policies of other states was not an offer of American commitments and restraints. The leverage was the worldwide democratic revolution. It was Wilson's optimism about the trajectory of history and the groundswell of world public opinion that was to launch the League of Nations and transform world politics. The democratic structure of the world, rather than the legal character of binding ties, was to be the source of America's stable and favorable world order.

The American president's view of international law and inter-government agreements was firmly rooted in nineteenth-century understandings. The inter-governmental institutions themselves were not the mechanisms that bound states to each other. It was the democratic disposition to co-operate that was the critical source of institutional co-operation. As a result, Wilson did not think the United States was giving up much policy autonomy to get a desired institutionalized order. The League of Nations treaty had an escape clause that made the American commitment to a postwar collective security system consistent with the United States constitution and the wishes of the American Senate. Wilson ultimately did not object to his antagonists in the Senate – and their proposed "reservations" – because he thought their proposals would break the American commitment to Europe. His rejection of their reservations was more symbolic: that the Senate would send the world the wrong message. This in turn was consistent with his view of the unfolding postwar political situation. The United States needed to encourage the world democratic revolution because that – not specific agreements to reduce American policy autonomy – was the motor of world order building.

After 1945, the United States again began its thinking about postwar order with a view of an "automatic" world order that would require little direct American involvement – or specific commitments or restraints on its power (Ikenberry 1989). Throughout the war, Secretary of State Cordell Hull and the American State Department anticipated a postwar order built around free trade. This was before the postwar social and economic debilitations and potential for political collapse in Europe were fully apparent to American officials and before the Cold War rudely shifted official thinking. But the free trade idea was perfect. The United States would get a stable and favorable postwar order without either directly managing the system or placing restraints on its policy autonomy. An open world economy, once the major states moved in this direction, would be self-generating. It would lock other states into a liberal internationalist policy orientation and the United States would not need to offer concessions or reduce its policy discretion.

What was different after 1945 is that the situation changed quickly. The United States realized almost immediately that more direct and specific institutional commitments would be needed to stabilize and orientate Europe. In effect, American lock-in goals expanded. They expanded as a result of numerous developments discussed below. Also, for the Europeans the costs of not securing postwar agreements that restrained and committed the United States would be much greater after World War II than after the earlier war. These considerations drove the institutional bargain forward. But even as this rolling process of institutional bargaining proceeded, the United States sought to squeeze out as much policy lock-in from Europe with as few restraints on its policy discretion as possible.

The institutional bargain with Europe

The postwar order in Europe and across the Atlantic was built around multilateral institutions that created an elaborate system of restraint, commitments and reassurances. The United States and Europe each attempted to lock the other party into specific postwar institutional commitments. They accomplished this in part by agreeing in turn to operate within those institutions as well, even if sometimes reluctantly (Ikenberry 2001: ch. 6).

This institutional bargain between the United States and Europe after World War II was a rolling process. The United States saw its goals for Europe expand. It progressively came to realize that the stabilizing and reorientation of Europe would require active intervention and engineering, including the creation of a variety of new multilateral institutions that would bind the United States to Europe. It increasingly valued this European stabilization and reorientation as tensions with the Soviet Union increased. In both these ways, American lock-in goals expanded throughout the 1940s. At the same time, the Europeans drove a hard bargain. They actively sought American institutional involvement in postwar Europe and their institutional agreement with the United States was tightly contingent on specific American commitments and restraints. The order that emerged – the European order, the Atlantic order, and the wider postwar world order – was the result of a complex set of rolling institutional agreements that tightly linked the reorganization of Europe to an expanding American multilateral commitment. Along the way, the United States only grudgingly gave up increments of policy autonomy and restraints on its exercise of power but it did so with the explicit understanding that in doing so it would be buying the institutional lock-in of Europe.

The most elaborate and consequential institutional bargain was the security alliance. Although established to respond to a growing Soviet threat, the Atlantic pact was also designed to play a wider role in stabilizing relations and reassuring partners within the alliance. The NATO alliance provided a mechanism for the rehabilitation and reintegration of western Germany, an instrument of what has been called "dual containment." But it also locked in America's reluctant security commitment to Europe and tied the European states together, reinforcing their movement toward regional integration. In this way, the NATO alliance operated along with other postwar institutions as a multifaceted instrument of "quadruple containment."

The most consistent British and French objective during and after the war was to bind the United States to Europe. The evolution in American policy, from the goal of a European "third force" to acceptance of an ongoing security commitment within NATO, was a story of American reluctance and European persistence. The European search for an American security tie was not simply a response to the rise of the Soviet threat. As early as 1943, Winston Churchill proposed a "Supreme World Council" (composed of the United States, Britain, Russia, and perhaps China) and regional councils for Europe, the western hemisphere, and the Pacific. In an attempt to institutionalize an American link to Europe, Churchill suggested that the United States would be represented in the European Regional Council, in addition to its role in its own hemisphere. Reflecting American ambivalence about a postwar commitment to Europe, one historian notes, "Roosevelt feared Churchill's council as a device for tying the United States down in Europe" (Harper 1996: 96).

During and after the war, Britain and France sought to bind the United States to Europe in order to make American power more predictable, accessible, and useable. The NATO alliance was particularly useful an as institution that made the exercise of American power more certain and less arbitrary. Despite the vast differences in the size and military power of the various alliance partners, NATO enshrined the principles of equality of status, non-discrimination, and multilateralism (Weber 1993). The United States was the clear leader of NATO. But the mutual understandings and institutional mechanisms of the alliance would reduce the implications of these asymmetries of power in its actual operation.

The security alliance also served to reduce European fears of resurgent and unbridled German military power. The strategy of tying Germany to western Europe was consistently championed by George Kennan:

> In the long run there can be only three possibilities for the future of western and central Europe. One is German domination. Another is Russian domination. The third is a federated Europe, into which the parts of Germany are absorbed but in which the influence of the other countries is sufficient to hold Germany in her place. If there is no real European federation and if Germany is restored as a strong and independent country, we must expect another attempt at German domination.[4]

Two years later, Kennan was again arguing that "without federation there is no adequate framework within which adequately to handle the German problem."[5]

If NATO bound both West Germany and the United States to Europe, it also reinforced British and French commitment to an open and united Europe. The United States not only was intent on the rehabilitation and reintegration of Germany, but it also wanted to reorientate Europe itself. In an echo of Wilson's critique of the "old politics" of Europe after World War I, American officials after 1945 emphasized the need for reform of nationalist and imperialist tendencies. It was generally thought that the best way to do so was to encourage integration. Regional integration would not only make Germany safe for Europe, it would also make Europe safe for the world. The Marshall Plan reflected this American thinking, as did Truman administration support for the Brussels Pact, the European Defence Community (EDC), and the Schuman Plan. In the negotiations over the NATO treaty in 1948, American officials made clear to the Europeans that a security commitment hinged on European movement toward integration. One State Department official remarked that the United States would not "rebuild a fire-trap."[6] The American goal was, as Dean Acheson put it in reference to the EDC, "to reverse incipient divisive nationalist trends on the continent."[7] American congressional support for the Marshall Plan was also premised, at least in part, on not just transferring American dollars to Europe but also on encouraging integrative political institutions and habits.

When Marshall Plan aid was provided to Europe, beginning in 1948, the American government insisted that the Europeans themselves organize to jointly allocate the funds. This gave rise to the Organization for European Economic Co-operation (OEEC), which was the institutional forerunner of the European Community. This body eventually became responsible for European-wide supervision of economic reconstruction, and it began to involve the Europeans in discussion of joint economic management. As one

American official recalls, the OEEC "instituted one of the major innovations of postwar international co-operation, the systematic country review, in which the responsible national authorities are cross-examined by a group of their peers together with a high-quality international staff. In those reviews, questions are raised which in prewar days would have been considered a gross and unacceptable foreign interference in domestic affairs."[8] The United States encouraged European integration as a bulwark against intra-European conflict even as it somewhat more reluctantly agreed to institutionalize its own security commitment to Europe.

The various elements of the institutional bargain among the Atlantic countries fit together. The Marshall Plan and NATO were part of a larger institutional package. As Lloyd Gardner argues: "Each formed part of a whole. Together they were designed to "mold the military character" of the Atlantic nations, prevent the balkanization of European defense systems, create an internal market large enough to sustain capitalism in Western Europe, and lock in Germany on the Western side of the Iron Curtain" (Gardner 1984: 81). NATO was a security alliance, but it was also embraced as a device to lock in political and economic relations within the Atlantic area.

Taken together, American power after the war left the European more worried about abandonment than domination and they actively sought American institutionalized commitments to Europe. Multiple layers of multilateral economic, political, and security institutions bound these countries together, reinforcing the credibility of their mutual commitments. The dramatic asymmetries of postwar power were rendered more acceptable as a result. As the post-1945 period unfolded, American lock-in goals for Europe expanded. Stabilizing the European economies, solving the German problem, and reorientating British and French security policies required much more "engineering" than American officials at first expected. To get these institutional concessions by Europe also entailed reluctant American willingness to make an institutionalized security commitment and reduce its policy autonomy.

Post-Cold War multilateralism

The United States emerged from the end of the Cold War in a newly advantaged position, and during the 1990s the world increasingly moved toward unipolarity. In these circumstances, and across security and economic areas, the United States sought to build and expand regional and global institutions. NATO expansion and the creation of NAFTA, APEC, and the WTO were elements of this agenda. This pattern of policy is consistent with the logic of post-1945 institution building and it is captured in the model of the institutional bargain. The United States employed institutions as a mechanism to lock in other states to desired policy orientations and it was willing to exchange some limits on its own autonomy to do so. Other states also seized upon these institutions as ways to retrain and commit the United States.

In the immediate aftermath of the Cold War, the Bush administration pushed forward a variety of regional institutional initiatives. In relations with Europe, State Department officials articulated a set of institutional steps: the evolution of NATO to include associate relations with countries to the east, the creation of more formal institutional relations with the European Community, and an expanded role for the Conference on Security Co-operation in Europe (CSCE) (Baker 1995: 172–3). In the western hemisphere, the Bush administration pushed for NAFTA and closer economic ties with South America. In east Asia, APEC was a way to create more institutional links to the region, demonstrating American commitment to the region and insuring that Asian regionalism moved in a trans-Pacific direction. The idea was to pursue innovative regional strategies that resulted in new institutional frameworks for post-Cold War relations.

These institutional initiatives, Baker later observed, were the key elements of the Bush administration's post-Cold War order-building strategy, and he likened its efforts to American strategy after 1945: "Men like Truman and Acheson were above all, though we sometimes forget it, *institution builders*. They created NATO and the other security organizations that eventually won the Cold War. They fostered the economic institutions . . . that brought unparalleled prosperity . . . At a time of similar opportunity and risk, I believed we should take a leaf from their book" (Baker 1995: 605–6; emphasis in original). The idea was to "plant institutional seeds" – to create regional institutional frameworks that would extend and enhance America's influence in these areas and encourage democracy and open markets.[9]

An institution-building agenda was also articulated by the Clinton administration in its strategy of "enlargement." The idea was to use multilateral institutions as mechanisms to stabilize and integrate the new and emerging market democracies into the Western democratic world. In an early statement of the enlargement doctrine, National Security Advisor Anthony Lake argued that the strategy was to "strengthen the community of market democracies" and "foster and consolidate new democracies and market economies where possible." The United States would help "democracy and market economies take root" which would in turn expand and strengthen the wider Western democratic order.[10] The target of this strategy was primarily those parts of the world that were beginning the process of transition to market democracy: countries of central and eastern Europe and the Asia-Pacific region. Promising domestic reforms in these countries would be encouraged – and locked in if possible – through new trade pacts and security partnerships.

NATO expansion embodied this institutional logic. At the July 1997 NATO summit, Poland, Hungary, and the Czech Republic were formally invited to join the alliance. These invitations followed a decision made at the January 1994 NATO summit in Brussels to enlarge the alliance to include new members from eastern and central Europe. Led by the United States, the alliance embarked on the most far reaching and controversial reworking of institutional architecture in the post-Cold War era.

The Clinton administration offered several basic rationales for NATO expansion, but it consistently emphasized its importance in consolidating democratic and market gains in eastern and central Europe and building an expanded Western democratic community. NATO enlargement would provide an institutional framework to stabilize and encourage democracy and market reform in these reforming countries. NATO would help lock in the domestic transitions under way in eastern and central Europe. The prospect of membership would itself be an "incentive" for these countries to pursue domestic reforms in advance of actually joining the alliance. Once they were admitted to NATO, the process of alliance integration was further assumed to lock in institutional reforms. Membership entailed a wide array of organizational adaptations, such as standardization of military procedures, steps toward interoperability with NATO forces, and joint planning and training. By enmeshing themselves within the wider alliance institutions, the ability of the new NATO members to revert to old ways was reduced, and ongoing participation in alliance operations tended to reinforce the governmental changes that were made on the way toward membership. As one NATO official remarked: "We're enmeshing them in the NATO culture, both politically and militarily so they begin to think like us and – over time – act like us" (quoted in Towell 1998: 275). NATO membership rewarded steps toward democratic and market reform, pushed it forward and locked it in.

NAFTA and APEC initiatives also embodied this logic, though the commitments and lock-in mechanisms were less demanding. The Bush administration supported bringing Mexico into the United States–Canada free trade area for political reasons as well as for the anticipated economic gains. Mexico was undergoing a democratic revolution and American officials wanted to lock in these watershed reforms. Mexican officials also championed the trade accord, for the same reason: it would lock in their successors to policy commitments and economic relations that would thwart political backsliding. APEC had at least a trace of this same reasoning. A multilateral economic dialogue was possible within east Asia because of the long-term shift in the developmental orientation of the emerging economies of the region. Japan and Australia were the initiators of the APEC process, but the United States quickly lent its support. At least part of the appeal of APEC within the region was that it was a counterweight to American unilateral trade tendencies: the multilateral process would help restrain the worst impulses of American trade policy – symbolized in the "Super-301 Authority," the trade authority that Congress gives the executive, under which the United States can act unilaterally to punish countries for restrictive or subsidized trade. In return, the United States was able to encourage an open east Asian economic regionalism and reinforce the market reforms that were unfolding across Asia and the western hemisphere. The actual ability of APEC to lock in policy orientations in the region was limited, but the restraints on American policy autonomy were also more symbolic than real.

This pattern of institution building can be seen as a continuation of the logic that underlay the Western postwar settlement. Institutional agreements were pursued in order to reinforce domestic governmental and economic changes which, in turn, tended to fix into place desired policy orientations. As a leading State Department official describes the institutional strategy: "Our intention was to create institutions, habits, and inclinations that would bias policy in these countries in our direction."[11] The United States was able to insure political and economic access to these countries and regions, and gain some confidence that these countries would remain committed to political and market openness. In exchange, these countries gained some measure of assurance that American policy would be steady and predictable. The United States would remain engaged and do so through institutions that would leave it open to market and political access by these countries.

The Bush administration appears to have made a break with this American strategy of using institutions to order the international system. The current administration appears much less willing to make binding institutional commitments. Quite the contrary, across a range of policy areas – arms control, environment, security alliances, and the UN – the Bush administration has sought to reduce American exposure to global multilateral entanglements in a remarkable sequence of rejections of pending international agreements and treaties, including the Kyoto Protocol on Climate Change, the Rome Statute of the ICC, the Germ Weapons Convention, and the Programme of Action on Illicit Trade in Small and Light Arms. It also unilaterally withdrew from the 1970s ABM treaty, which many experts regard as the cornerstone of modern arms control agreements. Perhaps most dramatically, spurred by its war on terrorism and war in Iraq, the Bush administration has advanced new and provocative ideas about the American unilateral and pre-emptive use of force.[12] The question is: why?

The most straightforward answer is that the Bush administration brought into office a different set of ideas about making institutional commitment trade-offs. Indeed, President Bush himself and many of his advisors do have a distinctly skeptical view of the merits of compromising American policy autonomy and political sovereignty. Neo-conservative thinkers who have influenced Bush policy bring with them a deep resistance to liberal institutional ideas. Some observers see today's unilateralism as practiced by the Bush administration as something much more sweeping – not an occasional ad hoc policy decision but a new strategic orientation. Capturing this view, one pundit calls it the "new unilateralism":

> After eight years during which foreign policy success was largely measured by the number of treaties the president could sign and the number of summits he could attend, we now have an administration willing to assert American freedom of action and the primacy of American national interests. Rather than contain power within a vast web of constraining international agreements, the new unilateralism seeks to strengthen American power and unashamedly deploy it on behalf of self-defined global ends.[13]

Indeed, Richard Holbrooke, former US ambassador to the UN has charged that the Bush administration threatens to make "a radical break with fifty-five years of a bipartisan tradition that sought international agreements and regimes of benefit to us."[14]

This is surely part of the explanation. But the international context in which the United States is making decisions about institutional commitments has also changed. In particular, the rise of unipolarity and the shifting character of international threats have altered the "values" that go into institutional bargaining calculations by the United States and its postwar partners. The rise of unipolarity gives the United States a near-monopoly on global military power. Increased power advantages give the United States more freedom of action. It is easier for Washington to say no to other countries or to go it alone. Growing power – military, economic, technological – also gives the United States more opportunities to control outcomes around the world. But unipolarity also creates problems of governance. Without bipolar or multipolar competition, it is not clear what can discipline or render predictable American power. Other countries worry more than in the past about domination, exploitation, and abandonment. They may not be able to organize a counter-balancing alliance, but they can resist and undermine American policies. At the very least, they would like to see the unipolar state tied down through institutional constraints in the manner at the heart of the postwar institutional bargain.

So unipolarity alters the terms of the institutional bargain. The United States does not need other countries as much under conditions of unipolarity, so – everything else being equal – it is less willing to reduce its policy autonomy. It would in fact like to use its rising power position to reduce its binding institutional obligations. Other countries, on the other hand, have growing worry about American power, and so they in fact would like to see more restrictions in American policy autonomy.

The second shift in the international environment that alters the institutional bargain is the shift in security threats. Under the bipolar Cold War, the United States and its institutional partners were all threatened by the same external threat – Soviet communism. Indeed, front-line states in Europe and Asia actually, in some ways, felt the threat more immediately and intensely than the United States. But the upshot of the security situation was that the United States had security to offer and other countries wanted the American provision of security. The end of the Cold War changed this situation. The rise of terrorist threats compounds this shift. Now it is the United States that feels threatened – but it does so in a way that other states do not experience. There is a growing divide in the experience of "insecurity." The United States feels insecurity but other states are only secondarily able to be of assistance in addressing America's security problem. Other states do not feel the same threats – and they are less dependent on the United States for the provision of security. These multiple shifts have the same effect – they reduce incentives on both sides for an institutional bargain on security (Ikenberry 2005).

In other areas, the rise of unipolarity or new security threats should not directly impact on the institutional bargain. This is most obviously true in terms of the world economy. American support for multilateralism is indeed likely to be sustained – even in the face of resistance and ideological challenges to multilateralism in the Bush administration – in part because of a simple logic: as global economic interdependence grows, the need for multilateral co-ordination of policies also grows. The more economically interconnected that states become, the more dependent they are for the realization of their objectives on the actions of other states. Rising economic interdependence is one of the great hallmarks of the contemporary international system. If this remains true in the years ahead, it is easy to predict that the demands for multilateralism – even and perhaps especially by the United States – will increase and not decrease.

Conclusion

Several general conclusions can be offered. First, there is a general institutional logic that combines the instincts of both realist and liberal theory. Institutional bargains are driven by concerns about policy autonomy, legitimacy, the exercise of power, and political certainty. The struggle is to promote as predictable and favorable international environment in which to operate. States are self-interested actors who jealously guard their policy autonomy and sovereign authority, but who also are willing to bargain if the price is right. Ironically, it is precisely the asymmetry of power that creates the potential mutually beneficial exchange. The leading state has an incentive to take advantage of its newly dominant position to lock in a favorable set of international relationships – institutionalizing its pre-eminence. The subordinate states are willing to lock themselves in – at least up to some point – if it means that the leading state will be more manageable as a dominant power.

Second, this model assumes that institutions can play a role in muting asymmetries in power – thereby allowing the leading state to calculate its interests over a longer time frame, with institutions serving as a mechanism to invest in future gains, and allowing the weaker states to be confident that there can be credible restraints on the arbitrary and indiscriminate exercise of power. If institutions are unable to play this role, than the calculations and trade-offs that are highlighted in the model are not likely to be of much consequence. But American officials themselves have acted in a way that suggests that at least they think institutions can in fact play such a shaping and restraining role.

Third, the actual costs and benefits behind the trade-off between policy autonomy and policy lock-in are difficult to specify in advance. The postwar crisis in Europe and the multiple engineering tasks that the United States saw as absolutely critical were real enough and they justified the restraints and commitments that the United States offered to get these institutionalized arrangements in Europe. But some of the other lock-in goals – such as economic reforms, human rights standards, and war crimes laws – are not easy to evaluate as goals worthy of X or Y amount of reduced policy autonomy. Because of this the institutional model is perhaps better at identifying a dilemma that states face and less effective at specifying in advance how the trade-offs will be made.

Notes

This chapter is adapted from G.J. Ikenberry (2003) "State Power and the Institutional Bargain: America's Ambivalent Economic and Security Multilateralism," in R. Foot, S. Neil MacFarlane and M. Mastanduno (eds) *US Hegemony and International Organizations: The United States and Multilateral Institutions*, New York: Oxford University Press, pp. 49–70.

1 Institutions are potentially sticky for at least three reasons. First, they can create difficult and demanding legal or political procedures for altering or discontinuing the institutional agreement. Second, the institution can itself over time become an actor, gaining some independence from states and actively promoting institutional compliance and continuity. Third, growing vested interests – groups with stakes in the success and continuation of the institution – along with other positive feedback effects produce "increasing returns" to institutions that raise the costs of ending or replacing the institutions. This view of institutions can be contrasted with two other perspectives. One is a more narrowly drawn rationalist account that sees institutions as contracts – agreements that remain in force only so long as the specific interests that gain from the agreement remain in place. It is the interests and not the institution that are sticky. The other view is a constructivist view that sees institutions and the institutionalization of inter-state relations as built upon shared ideas and identities.
2 To the extent that the locking in of institutional commitments and obligations is mutual – that is, the leading state also locks itself in, at least to some extent – this makes the asymmetrical relationship more acceptable and legitimate to the weaker and secondary states. This, in turn, reduces the enforcement costs.
3 On the ways in which NATO multilateralism restrained the American exercise of power, see Weber (1993).
4 See "Report of the Policy Planning Staff," 24 February 1948, *Foreign Relations of the United States*, 1948, I, Part 2 (Washington, DC: US Government Printing Office), p. 515.
5 See "Minutes of the Seventh Meeting of the Policy Planning Staff," 24 January 1950, *Foreign Relations of the United States*, 1950, III (Washington, DC: US Government Printing Office), p. 620.
6 See "Minutes of the Fourth Meeting of the Washington Exploratory Talks on Security," 8 July 1948, *Foreign Relations of the United States*, 1948, III (Washington, DC: US Government Printing Office), pp. 163–9.
7 See "The Secretary of State to the Embassy in France," 19 October 1949, *Foreign Relations of the United States*, 1949, IV (Washington, DC: US Government Printing Office), p. 471.
8 L. Gordon in Ellwood (1989: 48–9).
9 Interview of Robert B. Zoellick (US State Dept), 28 May 1999.
10 See A. Lake, "From Containment to Enlargement," *Vital Speeches of the Day*, 60 (15 October 1993).
11 Interview, Robert B. Zoellick, 28 May 1999.

12 For an overview of this shift in American policy toward institutions under the Bush administration, see Daalder and Lindsey (2003).
13 See C. Krauthammer, "The New Unilateralism," *Washington Post*, 8 June 2001, p. A29.
14 Quoted in T.S. Purdum, "Embattled, Scrutinized, Powell Soldiers On," *New York Times*, 25 July 2002, p. 1.

2 Unipolar empire and principled multilateralism as strategies for international change

Jack Snyder and Leslie Vinjamuri

Enthusiasts for international change have put forward two strikingly different strategies for promoting a more democratic and just international order, one unilateralist and the other multilateralist. Both are problematic because both are based on flawed theories of social change.

During the 1990s, the loudest lobbyists for change were principled transnational activist groups in league with like-minded officials in international organizations, idealistic international lawyers, and liberal internationalists in some powerful democratic governments. Using the multilateralist tools of transnational civil society networks and international organizations, with intermittent help from liberal states, they promoted a universalistic agenda of human rights, democratization, civil society promotion, peacekeeping, peace-building and juridical accountability. The legacy of their handiwork has included the liberation of Kosovo from Serbian tyranny, the trial of Slobodan Milosevic, the extradition of Augusto Pinochet, the creation of the International Criminal Court (ICC), and the democratic enlargement of the EU, but it also includes the passivity of the UN peacekeepers during the Srebrenica massacre and the Rwanda genocide, as well as internationally mandated voting that triggered mass violence in Burundi in 1993 and in East Timor in 1999.

After September 2001, the initiative for promoting international change shifted to the Bush administration, and the neo-conservative ideologists who articulated its principles. Like the principled multilateralists' agenda, this strategy too stressed the goal of promoting democracy and bringing evil-doers to justice as means to end threats to global peace and security, but its means were distinctively unilateralist, military, and non-legalistic. The mixed legacy of its handwork has been the invasions of Afghanistan and Iraq, disputes over the application of international legal principles to perpetrators of atrocities and prisoners, and the election in Middle Eastern states of candidates favoring terrorism (Hamas in the Palestinian territories), nuclear proliferation (President Ahmadinejad in Iran), sectarianism, and warlordism. In the wake of a May 2005 surge of terror attacks by Sunni insurgents in Iraq, the American president belatedly added the too-mild disclaimer that "no nation in history has made the transition from tyranny to a free society without setbacks and false starts."[1]

These strategies suffer from a willful voluntarism that is inevitably running up against hard political and social facts. The liberal activists overstated the efficacy of normative persuasion; the Bush strategy overestimated the efficacy of military force. Both underestimated the need to ground international change firmly in a set of facilitative preconditions: an economic basis to support a liberal political order, a strong political coalition that supports political reform, and the creation of administrative and judicial institutions that support the rule of law. In particular, they underestimated the need to develop a strategy for creating these preconditions in the right sequence, taking into account the realities of particular political and social contexts.

In this chapter, we want to look at concepts for promoting change in two areas: democracy promotion and international justice. Our goal will be to study what happens when weak theories of social change run into the hard realities of social facts, and then to offer some thoughts on change that have a better sociological grounding.

Theories of change in a time of change

The pace of change is accelerating in international politics, yet social science remains a notoriously poor guide to understanding and shaping it. The waning of sharp military rivalries among the great powers, America's unprecedented position of material dominance, its struggle against hydra-headed terrorist networks, and the rise of global advocacy politics together suggest that the basic shape of the international order is changing. Old conceptions of international order and the role of violence in it have been overtaken by events. However, new visions of international order that are prominent in the academy and in the world of affairs often misunderstand the relationship between material and normative change. People who act on these mistaken assumptions may unintentionally hinder the achievement of their goals of peace and democracy.

According to the realist school of international relations, which dominated American academic thought for half a century, politics among states is ordered only in the thin sense that their struggle for security in international anarchy recurrently produces balance-of-power behaviors, such as the formation of military alliances against strong, threatening states. Realists portray this order as timeless, changing only in its details since Thucydides, depending on the number of great powers and the ebb and flow of their relative strength (Waltz 1979; Mearsheimer 2001).

In today's unipolar circumstances, where American power cannot be balanced in the traditional sense, many prominent international relations scholars still adopt a state-centered power-politics framework as a starting point, though not necessarily the endpoint, of their analyses. Even Robert Jervis, whose main contributions have focused on the ways that leaders misperceive the strategic problems they face, argues that "the forceful and unilateral exercise of U.S. power is not simply the by-product of September 11, the Bush administration, or some shadowy neoconservative cabal – it is the logical outcome of the current unrivaled U.S. position in the international system" which permits the US to indulge its nightmarish fears and its Wilsonian hopes (Jervis 2003: 84, 86).

Realists' assumptions about international power politics have come under challenge from diverse quarters in academic and policy circles. Social constructivists and principled activists, for example, argue that the familiar game of international power politics is not based on some inexorable, timeless logic, but was constructed at a particular moment in time out of the discourse of state sovereignty and *raison d'état*. Anarchy, they say, was what states made of it. Consequently, the norms that constitute international relations can be remade through campaigns of principled persuasion spearheaded by transnational activist networks. If more benign ideas and identities are effectively spread throughout the globe by cultural change and normative persuasion, then "ought" can be transformed into "is": support for warlike dictators can be undermined, perpetrators of war crimes and atrocities can be held accountable, benign multicultural identities can be fostered, and international and civil wars will wane (Finnemore and Sikkink 1998: 916; Risse and Sikkink 1999; Wendt 1999: 141, 377–8; Ruggie 1998: 199).[2]

Not only human rights activists, legalists, and social constructivists see international order as a norm-guided project for social change. The highest officials of the Bush administration argue that power politics must serve the agenda of democratic idealism. President Bush, in his preface to the September 2002 National Security Strategy Memorandum that laid out the doctrine of preventive attack that subsequently justified the Iraq war, stated: "the United States enjoys a position of unparalleled military strength," which creates "a moment of opportunity to extend the benefits of freedom across the globe. We will actively work to bring the hope of democracy, development, free markets, and free trade to every corner of the world" (US President's Office 2002: 1–2). The text of the strategy document itself pulls the concept of the "balance of power" inside-out and conflates it with ideological expansionism: "Through our willingness to use force in our own defense and in the defense of others, the United States demonstrates its resolve to maintain a balance of power that favors freedom" (US President's Office 2002: 29). In explaining the new strategy, National Security Advisor Condoleezza Rice mused about the theoretical debates of her erstwhile days as a Stanford international relations professor, remarking that power-political realism and idealism should not be seen as alternatives.[3] Paul Wolfowitz and the neoconservative proponents likewise saw the Iraq war as the opening round of a campaign to overturn prevailing political patterns in the Arab world and generate momentum towards democracy there (Herrmann 2004: 191–225).

Many activists, legalists, and constructivists share this urge to use coercive power to bring about change in the international order. Secretary of State Madeleine Albright justified the Kosovo war as, above all, a human rights necessity. Samantha Power's prize-winning book on America's repeated failures to prevent genocide helped galvanize a generation of idealistic activists to argue in favor of humanitarian military interventions (Power 2002). Constructivist international relations scholar John Ruggie worked in support of the war effort as an advisor to the UN Secretary General, Kofi Annan. In constructivist accounts of international change, the main aim of transnational activists' normative persuasion campaigns is often to convince powerful states to use their leverage to coerce rights abusers (Keck and Sikkink 1998; Risse and Sikkink 1999).[4]

Each of these schools of thought gets part of the story right – and part of it dangerously wrong. The traditionalist realists, most of whom spoke out against the 2003 attack on Iraq, are right in insisting that any world view and any policy derived from it must start with a realistic appreciation of the positional interests of entrenched powers, especially states. However, they are wrong insofar as they underrate the role of normative convictions in constituting social orders and in promoting change in them. Liberal activists and constructivists have made that point well, but their theory of normative change is too voluntarist and lacks an understanding of the preconditions needed to sustain change. The Bush administration war hawks were right that American power was crucial to the fate of normative change in international relations, but their strategies were likely to be counterproductive in bringing about the goals they claimed to seek.

What then might be a better-grounded approach to understanding the potential for change in the international order and the role in it of political violence?

First, in the period before a hoped-for change, the norms needed to bring about the change should be understood as aspirations, as standards outlining what might be achieved after a great deal of hard work and subtle politicking (Beitz 1979). They should not be understood legalistically, as if they were unconditional rights in need of immediate and universal enforcement regardless of the political consequences.

Second, the potential for normative change should be assessed in light of the material, political, and institutional preconditions for it. Any normative aspiration – democracy, human rights, justice – is only as good as the soil that is available to nurture it. Typically, this requires the existence of favorable (or at least permissive) material conditions, a powerful coalition of global and local actors with an interest in bringing it about, and the construction of institutions with the administrative capacity to give real effect to the norms. Normative persuasion may help to shore up these preconditions and consolidate them once they are in place, but it cannot create them out of whole cloth.

Third, sequence matters in effecting normative change. Generally, the creation of a powerful reform coalition internationally and locally must be the first step. It does no good and may even do harm to try to implement aspirational norms if they are supported only by weak institutions and fragile coalitions. In the short run, aspirational norms may have to be put on hold in order to pursue the pragmatic political maneuvers that are needed to neutralize potential spoilers and strengthen coalitions for reform (Stedman 1997).

Fourth, the promotion of normative change is a strategic interaction. Would-be norms exist in a crowded field. They must contend with prevailing traditional norms, with other new candidate norms, and with powerful, self-interested actors that seek to evade being bound by any norms other than ones that are temporarily convenient. New norms may be threatening to powerful actors, who will respond with their own normative countercampaigns and perhaps even with violence. Norms entrepreneurs should make sure that they can win normative battles – or at least contain the damage from the possible backlash – before they start the fight.

To show how this general argument might apply to concrete items on the agenda of international normative change, I will briefly examine the issues of democracy promotion and justice for perpetrators of atrocities.

Democracy promotion

One of the few points that the Bush administration and the principled activists agreed upon is that the assertive promotion of democracy is a good idea.[5] In particular, both argued that democracy and free speech are pillars of peace; therefore, to promote peace, you promote democracy. Of course, this is in principle. In fact, the Bush administration was rightly worried about the consequences for interethnic relations of holding early elections in Iraq. The occupation authorities shut down newspapers that spread falsehoods that inflamed Iraqis to resist the occupation. This is the kind of problem that the US is likely to face wherever it tries to install democracy in countries that lack a strong reform coalition and useable institutions for the rule of law.

It is true that no two mature democracies have ever fought a war against each other. The basic workings of this democratic peace rely on supports in the material, institutional, and cultural domains. The absence of war between mature democracies depends on the material motivation of the average member of society to avoid needless death and impoverishment (goals widely if not universally shared across cultures), political institutions that predictably empower the median voter, and a set of cultural symbols sanctifying civil rights, free speech, and electoral legitimacy in ways that underpin those institutions, facilitate peaceful bargaining, and establish a non-threatening, "in-group" identity among democratic states. The democratic peace works best when these material, institutional, and cultural elements are all in place (Russett 1993; Owen 1997).

Moreover, democracy itself has material preconditions. Adam Przeworski finds that transitions to democracy are almost always successfully consolidated in countries with average annual income above $6,000 per capita in 1985 constant dollars, whereas democratic transitions almost always suffer reversals below $1,000, with a very few exceptions, such as India (Przeworski et al. 2000: ch. 2). These economic levels may to some degree be proxies for closely related factors such as literacy and the development of a middle class. Between those levels, consolidation seems to depend on a number of institutional preconditions, such as the strength of the rule of law and the development of civil society organizations (Linz and Stepan 1996: 7–15). The fact that these material and institutional preconditions often arise along with symbols and ideas supportive of democracy does not mean that democratic culture can somehow be a substitute for those conditions. Not surprisingly, Western arguments in favor of free speech, fair elections, and human rights have borne little fruit in countries that lack these preconditions (Carothers 1999). There is no cultural shortcut to a global democratic peace.

Proponents of democratic transformation are often too direct and non-strategic in their approach to achieving their objectives. For example, Thomas Carothers notes that the typical "strategy" of democracy assistance efforts is to generate a checklist of the attributes of mature democracies, and then mount parallel programs to try to install each of them in the targeted country right away. This approach is flawed because it pays insufficient attention to interaction effects between these efforts, issues of sequencing and preconditions, strategic responses from resistant actors, and other negative feedback effects.

Demanding a democratic transition and accountability to international human rights norms can be risky in settings that lack even the rudiments of the rule of law or the material resources needed to sustain an independent civil society and media. In such settings, transformative projects may unleash a populist form of mass politics at an inopportune, premature moment, when elites threatened by such changes can exploit social turmoil by playing the ethnic card. Untimely voting demanded by the international community in such places as Burundi in 1993 and East Timor in 1999 has led directly to hundreds of thousands of deaths and refugees (Lund et al. 1998). Arguably, it has also led to the deepening of ethnic and social cleavages and to the tainting of democratic remedies.

The risk of such backlashes may be increasing. The "third wave" of democratization consolidated democratic regimes mainly in the richer countries of eastern Europe, Latin America, southern Africa, and east Asia (Diamond 1996). A fourth wave would have to take on harder cases: countries that are poorer, more ethnically divided, and starting from a weaker base of governmental institutions and citizen skills.

In an era in which troubled, incomplete democratic transitions may engulf such geopolitically salient locations as the Middle East, this dynamic could be one of the fundamental determinants of the course of world politics. Although democratization in the Islamic world might contribute to peace in the very long run, Islamic public opinion in the short run is, in most places, hostile to the United States. Although much of the belligerence of the Islamic public is fueled by resentment of the US-backed authoritarian regimes under which many of them live, simply renouncing these authoritarians and pressing for a quick democratic opening is unlikely to lead to peaceful democratic consolidations. All of the risk factors are there: the media and civil society groups are inflammatory, as old elites and rising oppositions try to outbid each other for the mantle of Islamic or nationalist militancy.[6] The rule of law is weak, and existing corrupt bureaucracies cannot serve a democratic administration properly. The boundaries of states are mismatched with those of nations, making any push for national self-determination fraught with peril. Per capita incomes, literacy rates, and citizen skills in most Muslim Middle Eastern states are below the levels normally needed to sustain democracy (United Nations 2004; Przeworski et al. 2000: 101; Council on Foreign Relations 2005: 61–2; Donno and Russett 2004). Electoral results in Egypt, Iraq, Iran, and the Palestinian territories in 2005 bear out the prediction that inadequately prepared democratic transitions risk political polarization.

This does not necessarily mean that all steps toward democracy in the Islamic world would lead to disaster. Etel Solingen argues, for example, that reforms leading toward "democratization from above," combined with economic liberalization, have been consistent with support for peaceful policies in such Arab states as Jordan, Tunisia, Morocco, and Qatar. "The more consolidated democratizing regimes become," she notes, "the less likely they are to experiment with populism and war" (Solingen 1998: 213). Consistent with my argument, these modest success cases indicate that the most promising sequence for democratization in such settings begins with reforms of the state and the economy, together with limited forms of democratic participation, rather than a headlong jump into popular elections before the strengthening of the institutions – such as efficient and even-handed public administration, the rule of law, professional journalism, and political parties – that are needed to make a democratic system work.

In facing this challenge, culturally creative activists and thinkers may play an important role in changing behavior in the international system, but they must do so within a context that is structured by the system's material and institutional possibilities. This is true for both unilateralist and multilateralist strategies of change.

Justice for perpetrators of atrocities

Advocacy groups such as Human Rights Watch and Amnesty International have made a historic contribution to the cause of international human rights by publicizing the need to prevent mass atrocities such as war crimes, genocide, and widespread political killings and torture.[7] However, a strategy that many such groups favor for achieving this goal – the prosecution of perpetrators of atrocities by multilateral institutions according to universal standards – risks causing more atrocities than it would prevent, because it pays insufficient attention to political consequences.[8] Recent international criminal tribunals have failed to deter subsequent abuses in the former Yugoslavia and central Africa. Because tribunals, including the ICC, have often failed to gain the active co-operation of powerful actors in the United States and in countries where abuses occur, it is questionable whether this will succeed as a long-run strategy for international change unless it is implemented in a more pragmatic way.

Amnesties, in contrast, have been highly effective in curbing abuses when implemented in a credible way, even in such hard cases as El Salvador and Mozambique. Truth commissions, another strategy favored by some advocacy groups, have been effective mainly when linked to amnesties, as in South Africa. Simply ignoring the question of punishing perpetrators – in effect, a de facto amnesty – has also succeeded in ending atrocities when combined with astute political strategies to advance political reforms, as in Namibia.

The shortcomings of the strategies preferred by most advocacy groups stem from their flawed understanding of the role of norms and law in establishing a just and stable political order. Like some scholars who write about the transformative impact of such groups, these advocates believe that rules of appropriate behavior constitute political order and consequently that the first step in establishing a peaceful political order is to lobby for the universal adoption of just rules (Finnemore and Sikkink 1998: 898; Roth 2001). This reverses the sequence that is necessary for the strengthening of norms and laws that will help prevent atrocities.

Justice does not lead; it follows. A norm-governed political order must be based on a political bargain among contending groups and on the creation of robust administrative institutions that can predictably enforce the law. Preventing atrocities and enhancing respect for law will frequently depend on striking politically expedient bargains that create effective political coalitions to contain the power of potential perpetrators of abuses (or so-called spoilers). Amnesty – or simply ignoring past abuses – may be a necessary tool in this bargaining. Once such deals are struck, institutions based on the rule of law become more feasible.[9] Attempting to implement universal standards of criminal justice in the absence of these political and institutional preconditions risks weakening norms of justice by revealing their ineffectiveness and hindering necessary political bargaining. Although the ultimate goal is to prevent atrocities by effectively institutionalizing appropriate standards of criminal justice, the initial steps toward that goal must usually travel down the path of political expediency.

The social psychologist Tory Higgins posits three different logics whereby a person may decide on the rightness of a choice of action: whether it follows right principles, whether it leads to the right outcome, and whether it feels right given the person's current emotional state (Higgins 2000; Camacho, Higgins, and Luger 2003). These correspond to the logics of appropriateness, consequences, and emotions, which between them reflect the prevailing range of views on justice for perpetrators of atrocities.

These logics are ideal types. The strategies adopted by real political actors inevitably include a mix of these elements, as do those advocated by scholars. For example, human rights "norms entrepreneurs" argue not only that following their prescriptions is morally right; they also claim that these principles are grounded in a correct empirical theory of the causes of behavior and will therefore lead to desirable outcomes (Finnemore and Sikkink 1998: 896–9). Thus, even arguments based on the logic of appropriateness usually also make claims about consequences (Schulz 2001).[10] Conversely, proponents of the logic of consequences might argue that bargains based on the expediency of power and interest are often a necessary precondition for creating coalitions and institutions that will strengthen norms in the long run. For example, in September 2002, the UN administrator for Afghanistan, Lakhdar Brahimi, resisted calls from out-going Human Rights Commissioner Mary Robinson to investigate war crimes by key figures in the UN-backed government of Hamid Karzai on the grounds that such investigations would undercut progress toward peace and stability (Burns 2002). In short, all three logics are concerned with reducing the chance of future atrocities, and consequently it is justifiable to compare the validity of their empirical claims (Finnemore and Sikkink 1998: 910–14).

The logic of appropriateness

Martha Finnemore and Kathryn Sikkink, leading social-scientific scholars studying human rights, adopt a social constructivist definition of a norm as "a standard of appropriate behavior for actors with a given identity" (Finnemore and Sikkink 1998: 889). Norms, for them, imply a moral obligation that distinguishes them from other kinds of rules. In this constructivist view, norms do more than regulate behavior: they mold the identities of actors, define social roles, shape actors' understanding of their interests, confer power on authoritative interpreters of norms, and infuse institutions with guiding principles (Finnemore and Sikkink 1998: 913; Wendt 1999). In this sense, norms – and discourse about what norms ought to be – help to constitute social reality. Powerful states and social networks matter, too, but principled ideas and arguments often animate their actions. In that sense, world society is what its norms make of it.

According to this perspective, norms entrepreneurs attempt to persuade others to accept and adhere to new norms; targets of persuasion respond with arguments and strategies of their own (Finnemore and Sikkink 1998: 914). Persuasion may work through any of several channels, including logical arguments about consistency with other norms and beliefs that the target already adheres to, arguments from legal precedent, and emotional appeals (Finnemore and Sikkink 1998: 912–13). Once persuasion has succeeded in establishing a norm within a social group, norm entrepreneurs seek to promote conformity with the norm by "naming and shaming" violators, to use the terminology of constructivist theorists and human rights activists (Keck and Sikkink 1998: 16–25).

Finnemore and Sikkink conceive of the process of normative change as a three-stage "cascade." First, norms entrepreneurs use their organizational platforms to call attention to issues by naming, interpreting, and dramatizing them. Second, once these entrepreneurs achieve widespread success in their campaign of persuasion, a tipping process pushes the norm toward universal acceptance as international organizations, states, and transnational networks jump on the bandwagon. This occurs in part because of these actors' concern to safeguard their reputation and legitimacy, and in part because processes of socialization, institutionalization, and demonstration effects convince people that the rising norm is a proper one. In the third stage, the logic of appropriateness is so deeply imbued in law, bureaucratic rules, and professional standards that people and states conform unquestioningly out of conviction and habit (Finnemore and Sikkink 1998: 904–5).

Constructivist social scientists have only recently begun to apply the logic of appropriateness to the study of judicial accountability for war crimes or genocide (Lutz and Sikkink, 2000: 644; Kim and Sikkink, 2007). Nonetheless, NGOs and legalists advocating war crimes tribunals implicitly hold to the constructivist theory. These activists assume that efforts to change the prevailing pattern of social behavior should begin with forceful advocacy for generalized rules embodied in principled institutions, such as courts.

Proponents of war crimes prosecutions have long been prone to exaggerate the centrality of rule following in ordering world politics. Judith Shklar's 1964 book discussing the Nuremberg and Japanese war crimes trials charged some of their proponents with excessive, apolitical legalism, which she defined as "the ethical attitude that holds that moral conduct is to be a matter of rule following, and moral relationships to consist of duties and rights determined by rules" (Shklar 1964: 1). Contemporary activists argue that handing down indictments and holding trials strengthen legal norms even when perpetrators are hard to arrest and convict. Many of them favor generalizing norms through such measures as universal jurisdiction for prosecuting war crimes and crimes against humanity (Roth 2001). They also encourage setting up judicial institutions that will embody the norm of accountability, such as the ICC, even when its short-term effect is to reduce the chance that a powerful, skeptical actor such as the United States will co-operate with the implementation of the norm.[11]

In the realm of international criminal justice, the logic of appropriateness generates several predictions. None of them has been supported by evidence from recent tribunals.

First, as norms of criminal accountability for war crimes and other violations of international humanitarian and human rights law begin to cascade, the notion of individual responsibility should gain international momentum. Local actors, not just proponents in the advanced liberal democracies, should increasingly blame atrocities on individuals (e.g., specific Serbian leaders), not collectivities (e.g., the Serbian ethnic group as a whole). In fact, the Hague Tribunal's indictments and trials have sometimes been polarizing in Serbia and Croatia, and local trials overseen by international authorities in Kosovo have spurred resentment and violence. The political parties of two war criminals on trial at The Hague, Slobodan Milosevic and Vojeslav Seselj, made a strong showing in the December 2003 Serbian parliamentary elections, unseating the incumbent liberal government by running against the tribunal's interference with Serbian sovereign rights. In contrast, trials in Latin America, which for the most part have not pitted ethnic communities against each other, have more effectively focused guilt on individuals.

Second, if the vast majority of individuals worldwide accept the basic principles of the laws of war and prohibitions against genocide and torture, then prevailing practices should tip in favor of a universal system of international criminal justice. In this view, changes in behavior follow the adoption of new beliefs about appropriate standards of behavior. In fact, that the prevailing pattern of political power and institutions shapes behavior in ways that are difficult to change simply through normative persuasion. For example, an extensive survey commissioned by the International Committee of the Red Cross (ICRC) shows that large majorities of people in powerful democracies and in conflict-ridden developing countries agree that it is wrong to target civilians for attack or to engage in indiscriminate military practices that result in widespread civilian slaughter (Greenberg Research 1999). However, the vast majority of those polled were not participating as fighters in the conflicts. Respondents who said they were participants in the conflict or who identified with one side expressed significant reservations about the laws of war. The report finds that "the more conflicts engage and mobilize the population," as in Israel and Palestine, "and the more committed the public is to a side and its goals, the greater the hatred of the enemy and the greater the willingness to breach whatever limits there exist in war" (Greenberg Research 1999: 32). Moreover, "weak defenders feel they can suspend the limits in war in order to do what is necessary to save or protect their communities" (Greenberg Research 1999: 33). Despite the convergence on abstract principles, these data imply that one person's terrorist is often another's freedom fighter.

Third, as the norm is embodied in institutions like the war crimes tribunals for Yugoslavia and Rwanda, and the ICC, it should begin to have some deterrent effect (Kritz 1999). In fact, the indictments and trials initiated by the Yugoslav and Rwanda tribunals failed to deter the Srebrenica massacre, the ethnic cleansing of Kosovo, or atrocities involving Hutu and Tutsi in eastern Congo, let alone subsequent atrocities in other parts of the globe, such as East Timor, that failed to be impressed by the example of The Hague's justice.

Human rights abusers – such as repressive states, extremist factions, and warlords – stand outside any normative consensus, whether global or local. They need to be deterred through the predictable application of coercive force. The problem is, however, that they are often too powerful to deal with simply as criminals. Indeed, they can sometimes be indispensable allies in efforts to bring war criminals to justice. For example, the 2001–2 US war against the terrorist-harboring Taliban would have been infeasible without the self-interested participation of the Afghan Northern Alliance, whose own leadership was earlier responsible for horrendous crimes in the Afghan civil war in the 1990s. Strategies that deal with rights abusers on a political rather than criminal basis may be indispensable for the advancement of the international justice project itself, let alone other practical objectives, including national self-defense.

In such circumstances, legalists need to exercise prosecutorial discretion: A crime is a crime, but not all crimes must be prosecuted (Roth 2001: 153). Such choices, however, risk putting judges and lawyers in charge of decisions that political leaders are better suited to make. For example, the investigations of the International Criminal Tribunal for Yugoslavia (ICTY) have complicated a peace settlement between the Macedonian government and ethnic Albanian former guerrillas accused of committing atrocities.[12] The settlement granted these rebels an amnesty except for crimes indictable by the international tribunal. The ICTY's decision to investigate rebel atrocities led the guerrillas to destroy evidence of mass graves, creating a pretext for hard-line Slavic Macedonian nationalists to renew fighting in late November 2001 and to occupy Albanian-held terrain.[13]

In sum, the logic of appropriateness and the theory of norms cascades capture the mind-set and strategies of advocates of international criminal accountability. However, this social constructivist theory of normative change fundamentally misunderstands how norms gain social force. As a result, legalist tactics for strengthening human rights norms can backfire when institutional and social preconditions for the rule of law are lacking. In an institutional desert, legalism is likely to be either counterproductive or simply irrelevant.

The logic of consequences

Drawing on the work of James March and Johan Olsen, Finnemore and Sikkink distinguish between the logic of appropriateness and the logic of consequences (March and Olsen 1989: ch. 2). Whereas Finnemore and Sikkink place the former at the center of their analysis, our approach emphasizes the latter. The logic of consequences assumes that actors try to achieve their objectives using the full panoply of material, institutional, and persuasive resources at their disposal. Norms may facilitate or co-ordinate actors' strategies, but actors will follow rules and promote new norms only insofar as they are likely to be effective in achieving substantive ends, such as a reduction in the incidence of atrocities.

If norms are to shape behavior and outcomes, they must gain the support of a dominant political coalition in the social milieu in which they are to be applied. The coalition must establish and sustain the institutions that will monitor and sanction compliance with the norms. Strategies that underrate the logic of consequences – and thus hinder the creation of effective coalitions and institutions – undermine normative change.

This perspective has important implications for rethinking strategies of international criminal justice. Sporadic efforts by international actors to punish violations in turbulent societies are unlikely to prevent further abuses. Deterrence requires neutralizing potential spoilers, strengthening a coalition that supports norms of justice in the society, and improving the domestic administrative and legal institutions that are needed to implement justice predictably over the long run. Meeting these requirements must take precedence over the objective of retroactive punishment when those goals are in conflict. Where human rights violators are too weak to derail the strengthening of the rule of law, they can be put on trial. But where they have the ability to lash out in renewed violations to try to reinforce their power, the international community faces a hard choice: either commit the resources to contain the backlash, or else offer the potential spoilers a deal that will leave them weak but secure. Efforts to prosecute individuals for crimes must also be sensitive to the impact of these efforts on relations between dominant groups in a future governing coalition. Where trials threaten to create or perpetuate intra-coalition antagonisms in a new government, they should be avoided.

According to the logic of consequences, decisions about prosecution should be weighed in light of their effects on the strengthening of impartial, law-abiding state institutions. In the immediate aftermath of a state's transition to democracy, such institutions may already be capable of bringing rights abusers to trial, as for example, in Greece following the collapse of the junta in 1974. However, in transitional countries that are rich in potential spoilers and poor in institutions, such as contemporary Indonesia, the government may need to gain spoilers' acquiescence to institutional reforms, especially the professionalization of police and military bureaucracies and the development of an impartial legal system. In these cases, decisions to try members of the former regime should be weighed against the possibly adverse effects on the strengthening of institutions. Trials may be advantageous if they can be conducted efficiently, strengthen public understanding of the rule of law, add to the institutional capacities of domestic courts, help to discredit rights abusers, help to defuse tensions between powerful groups in society, and produce no backlash from spoilers. Where these conditions are absent, punishment for the abuses of the former regime may be a dangerous misstep and should be a low priority.

The main positive effect of truth commissions has probably been to give political cover to amnesties in transitional countries with strong reform coalitions. In South Africa, for example, the truth commission recommended amnesties for the vast majority of the perpetrators who testified. In El Salvador, the truth commission helped to discredit the appalling practices of the former regime, but its release triggered a blanket amnesty for both government and rebel perpetrators (Hayner 2001: 101–5).

The international criminal justice regime should permit the use of amnesties when spoilers are strong and when the new regime can use an amnesty to decisively remove them from power. Deciding what approach to adopt in a particular case requires political judgment. Consequently, decisions to prosecute should be taken by political authorities, such as the UN Security Council or the governments of affected states, not by judges who remain unaccountable to both domestic electorates and international politicians.

Nonetheless, purely pragmatic approaches are inadequate if they do not address the long-term goal of institutionalizing the rule of law in conflict-prone societies. Opportunistic "deals with the devil" are at best a first step toward removing spoilers from positions of power so that institutional transformation can move forward. Institution building must begin with the strengthening of general state capacity and then move on to regularize the rule of law more deeply. Both amnesties and trials require effective state institutions and political coalitions to enforce them. Without those conditions, neither approach is likely to succeed. In cases where legal accountability is not barred by the danger of backlash from spoilers, trials should be carried out through local justice institutions in ways that strengthen their capacity, credibility, and legitimacy. When international jurists must get involved, mixed international-domestic tribunals, such as the one in Sierra Leone, are preferable to strictly international bodies like the ICC.

In short, the logic of consequences generates the following empirical predictions: When a country's political institutions are weak, forces of reform there have not won a decisive victory, and potential spoilers are strong, attempts to put perpetrators of atrocities on trial are likely to increase the risk of violent conflict and further abuses, and therefore hinder the institutionalization of the rule of law.

The logic of emotions

A third approach to dealing with past atrocities and preventing their recurrence reflects the logic of emotions. Scholars and advocates suggest that eliminating the conditions that breed atrocities depends on achieving an emotional catharsis in the community of victims and an acceptance of blame by the perpetrators. Without an effort to establish a consensus on the truth about past abuses, national reconciliation will be impossible, as resentful groups will continue to use violence to voice their emotions. For these reasons, proponents of truth commissions stress the importance of encouraging perpetrators to admit responsibility for their crimes, sometimes in exchange for amnesty (Rotberg and Thompson 2000).

Some proponents of the logic of emotions speak in the language of psychotherapy (Pupavac 2001). Others ground their arguments in evolutionary biology, claiming that the emotional aspects of reconciliation are central to social cohesion. For example, an important study by William Long and Peter Brecke contends that successful civil war settlements tend to go through a trajectory that starts with truth telling and limited justice, culminates in an emotionally salient call for a new relationship between former enemies, and sometimes accomplishes a redefinition of social identities (Long and Brecke 2003: 31). One problem with their research design, however, is the difficulty of knowing whether the emotional theater of reconciliation is causally central to establishing peace or whether it is mainly window-dressing that makes political bargaining and amnesties more palatable to the public.

Approaches based on the logic of emotions locate the solution to human rights abuses at the popular level. Reconciliation, in this view, resolves conflict because it reduces tensions between peoples, not between elites. However, elites, not masses, have instigated many recent ethnic conflicts with high levels of civilian atrocities. Solutions that mitigate tensions at the mass level need to be combined with strategies that effectively neutralize elite spoilers and manipulators (Kaufman 2001).

No one contends that emotion should be entirely removed from an analysis of the politics of punishing atrocities. Emotion plays some role in both the logic of appropriateness and the logic of consequences. Finnemore and Sikkink, for example, discuss the importance of emotional appeals in proselytizing for new norms. Likewise, in the logic of consequences, the goals of political action are valued in part for emotional reasons (Elster 1999). Many people worldwide, including those that have experienced atrocities first hand, feel that judicial punishment is intrinsically satisfying, even apart from any effect that trials may have in deterring future abuses (Liberman 2006). Nonetheless, few would want to base a global strategy of justice simply on the emotional satisfactions of retribution. The logic of emotions is useful to the extent that it can be integrated into a broader approach that has as its principal aim the prevention of future abuses.

Conclusion: the potential for transforming international politics

The long-run trend of history at the most general level has favored processes of popular liberation. More societies with a greater share of the world's people have come to live under regimes that observe the principles of democracy, human rights, and the impartial rule of law. The underlying reasons for this are best captured by modernization theory: economic development and related improvements in mass education tend to distribute social power more widely, go hand-in-hand with the strengthening of the rule of law, give rise to ideas of universal rights and popular sovereignty, and create a strong constituency that insists on governmental accountability to the people. Exactly what causes what in this syndrome of mutually supportive phenomena remains a matter of debate, but this seems to be the general trend – if not necessarily the end – of history.

Nonetheless, the path of modernization and liberation is hardly smooth or universally traveled. Some societies still have not taken the path: their GDP per capita and literacy are low, and they are typically autocracies or anarchies. Others have started down the path, but have taken a detour. Some developed economically without dispersing social power, or their development created key powerful constituencies that resisted accountability to the people. In many, the development of their institutions of accountability lagged behind the demand for mass political participation (Huntington 1968). In fact, most of the world's countries took such detours, sometimes long ones.

All these detours, with the possibly important exception of China, have turned out to be dead ends. States that sustained development did so by getting back on the path predicted by modernization theory. This might be because the theory is right, or it might be because the United States and Great Britain have been powerful enough to set up rules that forced states onto that path if they were to succeed.

Understanding the prospects for liberation, the obstacles that stand in its path, and the strategies that will advance it depends in part on understanding these background tendencies – both the general processes of modernization and the specific circumstances that affect the path that it is likely to take in any given setting. However, these conditions are not only varied, but also probabilistic and complexly interactive in their effects. A country as poor as India, a late developer at the periphery of the world economy, has become a stable democracy, whereas wealthy, worldly Singapore retains its own brand of authoritarianism. Moreover, the factors that can take a country on a detour depend not only on the society's circumstances, but also the choices that key actors – including liberation movements – make in those circumstances. Indeed, choices made at one moment help to create circumstances at the next.

Among the important causes of detours from the path of liberation are flaws in the strategy of liberation projects themselves – tactical errors that galvanize resistance to the project or deformations in the movement that lead it to subvert its own goals. Those who seek to transform the culture of contemporary anarchy need to work within an existing material and institutional setting that may enable, derail, or pervert efforts to promote change. Efforts to force the pace of change risk unintended consequences that could wind up hindering change and increasing its costs.

Normative aspirations can be fulfilled only in the presence of permissive material conditions, a powerful coalition of global and local actors with an interest in bringing it about, and the construction of institutions with the administrative capacity to give real effect to the norms. Moreover, sequence matters in effecting normative change. Generally, the creation of a powerful reform coalition internationally and locally must be the first step. This holds true equally for unilateral and multilateral efforts to promote international change.

Notes

1 R.W. Stevenson, "Bush Says Patience Is Needed As Nations Build a Democracy," *New York Times*, 19 May 2005, p. A12, reporting his speech to the International Republican Institute of 18 May.
2 These scholars adhere to the constructivist approach to the study of international

politics, but not all constructivists are so clearly wedded to this transformative political agenda. For more qualified views, see Katzenstein (1996: 536–7), and Owen (1997: 232–5).
3 "Dr. Condoleezza Rice Discusses President's National Security Strategy," Waldorf Astoria Hotel, New York, 1 October 2002.
4 Bukovansky (2002) explores changing bases of legitimacy as a power resource.
5 This section draws on Snyder (2002).
6 Berman (2003: 265) draws parallels to belligerent civil society in the flawed democracy of Weimar Germany and stresses the "Huntingtonian gap" between high demand for political participation and ineffective state institutions.
7 For elaboration on the arguments in this section, see Snyder and Vinjamuri (2003/4). On the advocacy community, see Clark (2001). On international human rights law, which applies to all people at all times, and international humanitarian law, which concerns the actions of combatants during military conflict, see Best (1994).
8 On proposals for international tribunals, see Kritz (1996) and Minow (1998), as well as the numerous publications by Human Rights Watch, Amnesty International, and the Coalition for International Justice. See also the sources cited in the balanced critical commentary in Bass (2000: 284–310).
9 On institutionalization of the rule of law as a precondition for successful human rights promotion, see Putnam (2002) and Ignatieff (2001: 25, 40).
10 Schulz is the executive director of Amnesty International USA. On a philosophical plane, see Nagel (1988: 60).
11 For historical background, see Weschler (2000) and Scheffer (2000).
12 "Macedonia Bolsters Albanian Rights: After Constitutional Change, Amnesty Is Declared for Former Rebels," *International Herald Tribune*, 17–18 November 2001.
13 G. Ash, "Macedonia Is Seeking Control of Land Harboring Ex-Rebels," *New York Times*, 26 November 2001, p. A11.

3 US military commitments
Multilateralism and treaties

Lisa L. Martin

The United States reaches dozens of agreements with other countries on security issues each year, both multilateral and bilateral. These agreements typically commit the United States to take particular actions, such as limiting the development of certain types of arms, or to provide military assistance to other states and organizations. As such, the credibility of the United States is of intense interest to its bargaining partners. Will the United States actually live up to its commitments? How can other states improve their information about US credibility?

Building on other work on credibility and the form of international agreements, in this chapter I focus on the form of military agreements. I make a number of arguments. First, I argue that the form that an agreement takes is a strategic decision of the president. While this may not sound like a controversial statement, it does go against the grain of much legal literature on international agreements, which sees their form as primarily a matter of precedent and normative concerns. Second, I argue that the form of an agreement sends signals to other countries about US reliability, and that the president takes this signaling process into account when deciding on an agreement's form. Again, this may sound obvious, but this claim goes against the substantial body of work on US agreements in the American politics literature, which considers only domestic incentives facing the president. A signaling model gives rise to a number of hypotheses about the conditions under which a president will bear the costs of undergoing the formal (Article II) treaty procedure. These hypotheses are tested on, and borne out by, a dataset made up of all US security agreements reached between 1980 and 1999.

The first section of this chapter spells out the theoretical framework. It summarizes previous research on agreement form, and the legal and domestic arguments. It then specifies my alternative signaling model, taking into account international strategic motivations. The second section of the chapter then tests predictions about the form that security agreements take, finding support for the signaling model but not the purely domestic or legal perspectives. The third section turns to contrasting multilateral and bilateral agreements, asking about the conditions under which we see the United States reaching more multilateral or bilateral agreements.

Theoretical framework

This chapter builds on previous work arguing that the choice of an international agreement's form is a strategic one, which takes into account both domestic and international considerations. This choice is of interest because it tells us something about the president's freedom of maneuver in security affairs and the factors that constrain his choices. Most literature on US international agreements has looked only at the domestic considerations that go into the choice of form. I introduce international strategic considerations and argue that the major expectation derived from the purely domestic perspective cannot be sustained in equilibrium. The president does face domestic constraints, but he must also address the concerns that other governments have about the president not living up to the terms of an agreement. A president attempting to advance his policy agenda needs to consider the interaction of both sets of constraints.

The choice between executive agreements and treaties lies with the president, and induces strategic behavior on his part (Moe and Howell 1999a: 164). As specified in the Constitution, treaties must receive the approval of two-thirds of voting senators to go into effect. Executive agreements are not mentioned in the Constitution, and can be approved through a number of different mechanisms, from a legislative vote to sole executive approval (Millett 1990).[1] Congress has at times attempted to set binding guidelines for the choice of agreement form, but without success, so this choice remains a strategic decision by the executive branch (Setear 2002: 12).

A substantial legal literature has emerged asking whether, in fact, the president is unconstrained in his choice. While some have argued, on legal or normative grounds, that the president should limit reliance on executive agreements so that Congress is not bypassed (Tribe 1995), in practice the "doctrine of full interchangeability" has prevailed (Ackerman and Golove 1995; Yoo 2001: 759).[2] This doctrine means that all international agreements have the same standing in domestic courts, regardless of the ratification procedure. New thinking by legal scholars has called into question the long-standing view of their colleagues about the normativity of agreement form, arguing instead for a strategic perspective that sees agreements as primarily sources of information (Goldsmith and Posner 2005: 90). My argument is consistent with this new turn in legal studies.

The political-science literature on executive agreements sees them as a mechanism by which the president can evade legislative constraints, and thus as a way for the president to enhance his dominance over the legislature in foreign affairs. Since executive agreements create binding commitments to other countries (they have the same legal standing as treaties), but do not involve the Senate in its constitutionally-prescribed formal "advise and consent" role, they could be a potent source of executive power. By the 1990s, the president was signing hundreds of these agreements each year, while the number of treaties signed each year is just a couple of dozen (Congressional Research

Service 1993). Nathan and Oliver (1994: 99) summarize the consensus view of American politics scholars about the use of executive agreements: "Presidents ... have developed and employed the executive agreement to circumvent Senate involvement in international agreements almost altogether."

Legal scholars have long been concerned about the constitutionality and legitimacy of unilateral presidential action, and have seen devices such as executive orders as powerful mechanisms for the president to evade Congress. For example, Fleishman and Aufses (1976: 38) conclude that "executive orders allow the President, not only to evade hardened congressional opposition, but also to preempt potential or growing opposition." More recently, political scientists have echoed the same theme and elaborated the political logic behind these concerns. Moe and Howell (1999b) argue that the president has substantial powers of unilateral action because the Constitution is an incomplete contract, that the president has incentives to exploit this incompleteness to enhance the powers of the office, and that Congress and the courts can do little to resist. Statistical analysis by Deering and Maltzman (1999) largely supports this claim, although they also find that a cohesive Congress can sometimes threaten to overturn executive orders and so constrain the president.

William Howell (2003), in an extended and systematic study of executive orders, finds that Congress is in fact quite diffident when it comes to overturning or opposing the use of executive orders. He concludes that such devices allow the president to exercise power unilaterally, without the need to persuade other branches of government to support his efforts. However, his work really cannot be read to directly support the idea that executive orders allow the evasion of congressional opposition. For example, he finds that the president relies more heavily on executive orders during periods of unified than divided government; we would expect the opposite pattern if executive orders were merely evasive devices. Mayer (1999: 460) also finds more use of executive orders under unified government.

The hypothesis that executive agreements allow the president to evade congressional opposition has been labeled the "evasion hypothesis" (Martin 2000). It has at least one implication that can be tested quantitatively: that when the president expects the most congressional opposition to an agreement, he should be the most likely to choose an executive agreement rather than a treaty. Thus, we should expect to see a higher percentage of international agreements taking the form of executive agreements when Congress (or at least the Senate) is in different partisan hands than the presidency, or when the president receives low levels of support in general from Congress.

There are many reasons to question the logic of the evasion hypothesis, as simple and compelling as it may appear initially. One difficulty is that most executive agreements do in fact require some legislative action, such as appropriating funds, and thus are not likely to allow the president complete freedom of maneuver. Few agreements, even formal treaties, are self-executing. They thus require implementing legislation of some sort. Even agreements that do not require explicit implementing legislation can be overturned by congressional action, as legal doctrine provides that the most recent action takes precedence in the courts. Therefore, executive agreements do not allow the president the unfettered freedom to make commitments that many assume. Attempting to evade congressional opposition can backfire, as Congress has many methods it can use to void or refuse to implement executive agreements.

Perhaps even more telling, the evasion hypothesis completely neglects the process of negotiation with other countries. Assume that the hypothesis was correct, and that the president used executive agreements to evade legislative opposition. Other states would then see these agreements as a sign of lack of domestic support, and would therefore become more reluctant to sign on to them. Signing a security agreement that the president then reneges on can be highly costly for other states, as they may have changed their force structure or taken other steps that enhance their vulnerability in anticipation of US compliance with the agreement. Thus governments should follow domestic debates about agreements closely, and take them as signals about the likelihood that the president will actually live up to the terms of the agreement. While an agreement's form likely has a number of consequences, one of the most important may be its impact on the beliefs of other parties to it. That is, agreements are signaling devices. The idea that unilateral presidential actions can send signals to other political actors has been mentioned in the American politics literature (e.g. Mayer and Price 2002), but this insight has not been developed.

The proposition that treaties can serve as signals rests on two crucial assumptions. The first is that there is some uncertainty about whether the president will live up to the terms of the agreement. Empirically, this seems a reasonable assumption. The United States does sometimes renege on its international commitments. Such reneging rarely takes the form of legal abrogation of a treaty. More often, the president simply does not fully implement the terms of the agreement, or chooses to "reinterpret" the agreement in such a manner that the United States does not behave as the other parties anticipated it would.

There is little doubt that the United States is sometimes unreliable on security commitments. A well-known example of unreliability involves the ABM Treaty with Russia. This treaty constrained the United States and Russia to build no more than two ABM installations, one to protect the capital city and one elsewhere. Beginning under Ronald Reagan, and continuing through recent administrations, these limitations conflicted with the desire to pursue defensive systems that would shoot down incoming missiles, whether from Russia or small attacks from rogue states. Rather than simply stating that the United States was withdrawing from or abrogating the ABM treaty, administrations have engaged in contorted attempts to "reinterpret" it to allow large-scale development of these anti-missile systems. While debate has ensued regarding the legalities of reinterpretation, there is no doubt that development of ABM systems is a substantial deviation from the behavior expected under the terms of the ABM treaty. Thus, other states can reasonably ask when reaching an agreement with the United States whether the president will, in practice, live up to the terms of the agreement.

Why renege on international agreements? Typically, the reason lies in domestic politics. While some domestic groups benefit from the terms of agreements, others see these commitments as costly and would prefer to renege. This dynamic is clear, for example, in arms-control agreements. If actors who believe that these commitments are too costly and constraining are in positions of decision-making authority, there is an increased chance of reneging. Thus, the chance that the president will live up to the terms of an agreement is a direct function of the levels of domestic support for and opposition to the agreement. A president that has a high probability of being reliable is one who enjoys high domestic support for the agreement and a low level of opposition.

Considering the level of domestic opposition to an agreement leads us to the second crucial assumption of a signaling model: that the signals sent are costly, and the costs vary for different sorts of actors. Here, we are interpreting treaties as a signal of the reliability of the president. They can only serve as such a signal if, first, treaties are more costly to conclude than executive agreements and, second, there is a cost differential so that reliable types bear lower costs for treaties than do unreliable types. Both aspects of this assumption are highly plausible (see also Goldsmith and Posner 2005: 93). Consider first whether it is more costly for a president to gain approval of a treaty than an executive agreement. If the agreement is a sole executive agreement, the comparison is obvious: treaties require the support of two-thirds of the Senate, which involves bargaining, arm-twisting, concessions, and sometimes delays. None of this is necessary for a sole executive agreement.

More serious questions may arise when comparing treaties to executive agreements that involve some degree of *ex ante* legislative participation. Is it always the case that treaties will be more costly? While there may be exceptions, I would argue that the assumption that treaties are more costly for the president is reasonable. Consider what would be the most costly form of a congressional-executive agreement, one that required majority support from both the House and Senate.[3] Would the president have to pay a higher cost to get this agreement approved than a treaty? No, unless the distribution of preferences in the House diverged substantially from that in the Senate. If the distribution of preferences were similar, then the median voter in the House would be similar to that in the Senate. Satisfying this median voter would be less difficult than satisfying the swing voter when two-thirds of the Senate was required, since this swing voter would be more extreme. There might be occasions when preference outliers in the House were able to hold an agreement hostage and demand high side-payments or concessions from the president. However, these occasions should be rare, and the assumption that the president bears higher costs to gain approval for treaties than for nearly any executive agreement is plausible.

Anecdotal evidence suggests that the image developed here of treaties as signaling devices is one held by governments. If other states believe that treaties signal that the president intends to live up to the terms of an agreement, they should under some conditions demand that an agreement take the form of a treaty rather than an executive agreement. In fact, such demands are easy to find. Negotiations between the United States and Russia on Nuclear Arms Reduction found Russian President Putin working hard to persuade US President Bush to sign a "full-blown" treaty to provide "certainty."[4] Bush had preferred a "gentlemen's agreement" that would avoid high negotiation costs.[5]

The SALT II negotiations in 1977–9 showed a similar dynamic, as the Soviet foreign minister objected that an executive agreement would not require the approval of two-thirds of the Senate and so would have an "inferior" status.[6] At times, US allies demand that long-standing executive agreements be transformed into formal treaties, explicitly stating that such changes would signal US long-term commitment. This has been the case, for example, in security agreements with Pakistan[7] and aid agreements with Turkey. The Turkish case is especially interesting, as it was complaints that Washington had not lived up to the terms of previous executive agreements that led to calls for a treaty.[8]

In previous work (Martin 2005), I have developed a formal signaling model of agreement form. The game considers the interaction between the president, who determines the form any potential agreement will take in the United States, and its negotiating partner.[9] The first move is by Nature, which determines whether the United States is reliable or not. A reliable United States is one that will live up to the terms of the agreement as expected, while an unreliable United States will renege on the agreement. The president knows whether the United States is reliable or not, but the negotiating partner has only an estimate of reliability. The president then decides whether to offer his negotiating partner a treaty or an executive agreement. If he offers a treaty, he bears an immediate cost, for the reasons discussed above. This cost is higher for unreliable than reliable types. If the United States is unreliable, that means there is significant domestic opposition to the agreement, which will prevent it from being fully implemented. For the president to offer a treaty in such circumstances means higher political costs than for a reliable president, one facing little domestic opposition to the agreement.

After observing the US offer, the negotiating partner decides whether or not to sign the agreement. If no agreement is signed, all get a payoff of zero, minus the costs of a treaty for the United States, if one was offered. If an agreement is signed, the United States receives a positive payoff, as does the negotiating partner if the United States is reliable. However, if the negotiating partner signs an agreement with an unreliable United States, it receives a payoff of less than zero.

Under some conditions, the negotiating partner can use its observation of the form of the agreement offered to update its beliefs about the US type. This leads to a separating equilibrium, in which reliable and unreliable types are clearly distinguished from one another, and the negotiating partner will sign treaties only with reliable types under these circumstances. This separating equilibrium occurs when the cost of offering a treaty for the United States is in an intermediate range, where a reliable United States is willing to bear the cost but an unreliable one is not. Separating equilibria are efficient, in the sense that no mutually-beneficial agreements are forgone.

Under other conditions, both unreliable and reliable types will behave in the same manner, and the negotiating partner will not be able to update its beliefs about the US type. In this case, the partner has to rely on its prior beliefs about US reliability when deciding whether to sign the agreement. If it believes that the United States is likely reliable, it will sign; otherwise, it will not. Such pooling equilibria occur when the potential benefits of an agreement for the United States are quite low, so that no types are willing to bear the costs of a treaty. They also occur when the potential benefits are very high and the negotiating partner has a prior belief that the United States is likely reliable. Under these conditions, an unreliable United States has incentives to bluff by bearing the costs of a treaty. If benefits of the agreement to the United States are high, but the negotiating partner believes that the United States is likely unreliable, a complex semi-separating equilibrium emerges in which an unreliable United States and its negotiating partner both pursue a randomized strategy, offering treaties and signing agreements with some probability between zero and one.

Both pooling and semi-separating equilibria give rise to some inefficiency, as some agreements that could potentially benefit both sides are not signed. This occurs because a reliable United States cannot fully distinguish itself from an unreliable type. In addition, both types of equilibria create the possibility that an agreement will be reached that the United States then reneges on. This occurs because an unreliable type is sometimes able to bluff its way into an agreement.

This simple model gives rise to a rich set of hypotheses, based on parameters such as the cost the negotiating partner bears if the United States reneges, and the costs to the two types of offering a treaty. The two parameters that I focus on here as promising explanatory variables are the potential benefits of an agreement for the United States and the negotiating partner's prior beliefs that the United States is reliable. The hypotheses I focus on are those that specify the relative frequency of executive agreements and treaties relative to all completed agreements. That is, I take into account the potential for selection bias that has plagued other studies of agreement form, which have neglected the fact that some potential agreements are never reached. In the next empirical section, I concentrate on two hypotheses, H1 and H2:

H1. The chance that a completed agreement takes the form of a treaty increases as the benefits of the agreement for the United States grow.
H2. The chance that a completed agreement takes the form of a treaty decreases as the reliability of the United States grows.

This prediction is in direct contrast to the predictions of a purely domestic perspective. Previous studies have argued that it is precisely the inability of the president to generate approval from the Senate that gives rise to the use of executive agreements. However, taking signaling considerations into account, we see that such a move would be interpreted as a sign of unreliability.

Understanding the signals that treaties send to other states leads to new insights about the form that particular agreements take. In particular, we should expect the president to be most willing to bear the costs of the treaty process when the potential benefits of an agreement are particularly high. In addition we should not see a president who is facing substantial domestic opposition attempt to evade it by using an executive agreement; such a maneuver would only confirm his unreliability in the eyes of negotiating partners. The next section turns to explore these insights with evidence on US security agreements reached between 1980 and 1999.

Treaties versus executive agreements

To examine these propositions, and see whether the evidence tends to support the signaling model or the evasion hypothesis, I turn to a dataset of US international agreements signed between 1980 and 1999 (with a few in 2000). These data were obtained from Oceana, a firm that collects this information for the use of lawyers. This is the most comprehensive list of US agreements available, containing many agreements that do not show up on official State Department lists or in the UN database.

The full database contains information on all issue areas, and has nearly 5,000 observations. The subset of the data I look at here was coded by Oceana as being about "defense" or "arms limitation." This subset includes 798 agreements. Oceana indicates whether the agreement is multilateral; for bilateral agreements, it indicates what country the agreement is with, and its title. It also shows a treaty number for those agreements that are formal treaties. I have supplemented this information with data on domestic politics in the United States, particularly the party of the president and whether he faces divided government – a Congress in the hands of the other party. These data came from Stanley and Niemi (2001).

A first important observation is that the incidence of formal treaties in this subset of the data is very low. For the full dataset, over 4 per cent of the agreements are treaties. This itself may seem a low number. But considering the large number of agreements reached each year, the time necessary to shepherd a treaty through the Article II process, and the relatively inconsequential nature of many of these agreements, the high frequency of executive agreements should not be surprising. In the subset of agreements dealing with security issues, only 1.25 per cent of them – 10 out of 798 – were treaties. This in itself is an interesting observation. Conventional wisdom among legal scholars is that security agreements, especially arms control agreements, tend to take the form of treaties. Instead, we find just the opposite, that these agreements are even more often executive agreements than those in other issue areas.

The 1980s and 1990s were an active period for US negotiations and agreements on security issues. In the 1990s, especially, the end of the Cold War created a large number of opportunities and demands for the United States to reach new security accommodations with other states – including new states. For example, a large number of the agreements in this dataset aim to resolve security concerns with former Soviet states, specifying their relationship to the United States and their control of stocks of arms. The transformation of NATO during this period also led to many agreements, including with potential new members. In addition, in the earlier years of the dataset, some landmark arms-control agreements were reached with the Soviet Union. The dataset is filled out with the day-to-day stuff of interaction in the security realm, amending earlier agreements, specifying military assistance and arms sales, setting the conditions for US military bases overseas, and so on.

The hypotheses derived from the signaling model focused on two major explanatory variables related to the form of an agreement: the potential benefits to the United States and its reliability. In previous work, I have argued that, on balance, multilateral agreements will be more valuable to the United States than bilateral agreements. This is not to deny that some bilateral agreements – including some in this subset of data – are immensely valuable. However, on average, multilateral agreements, because they are with a number of states, offer greater potential advantages than bilateral agreements.

As a check on whether the multilateral proxy is a plausible measure of agreements' benefits, in previous work I randomly chose 25 multilateral and 75 bilateral agreements. For each, I undertook a search of the *New York Times* for the three months surrounding the signing of the agreement, identifying the number of references to the agreement. Within this subset, the multilateral agreements on average had 4.9 references in the *Times*, while the bilateral agreements had only 0.49 references on average. This figure suggests that the multilateral agreements were, indeed, much more substantial and consequential than the bilateral agreements. However, the figure on multilateral agreements was heavily influenced by one outlier (the START treaty) that received 84 references. Excluding this outlier, the mean number of references to multilateral agreements drops to 1.6. However, this is still triple the number of references to the average bilateral agreement, suggesting a significant difference and supporting the plausibility of this indicator. Figure 3.1 shows a histogram of the number of references to bilateral and multilateral agreements, excluding the multilateral outlier.

So, if multilateral agreements are more consequential than bilateral ones, on average, we should expect them more often to take the form of treaties. Previous work has shown that this insight holds strongly in the larger dataset. Does it hold for security agreements, in particular? A skeptic might argue that multilateral security agreements tend not to be particularly important, that in

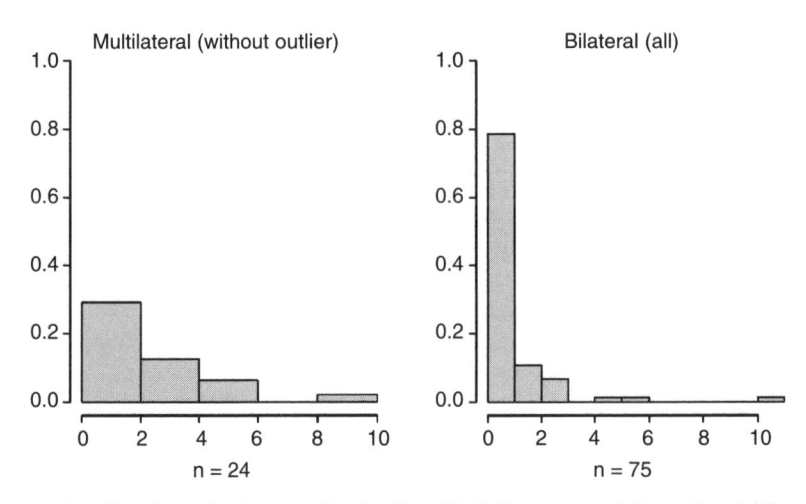

Figure 3.1 Number of references in the *New York Times* to multilateral and bilateral agreements.

Table 3.1 Incidence of treaties: bilateral versus multilateral agreements

	Bilateral		Multilateral		Total	
Executive agreement	724	99.45%	64	91.43%	788	98.75%
Treaty	4	0.55%	6	8.57%	10	1.25%
Total	728		70		798	

Chi-square 33.21, $p<0.01$

this issue area the real work is done in bilateral negotiations. If so, the results from the more general analysis would not carry over to the security realm.

Table 3.1 shows how bilateral and multilateral agreements are sorted into executive agreements and treaties. Just 0.55 per cent of bilateral agreements – 4 out of 728 – take the form of treaties. In contrast, 8.57 per cent of multilateral agreements, 6 out of 70, are treaties. This relationship is highly statistically significant, as indicated by the chi-square statistic. Thus, the general insight that multilateral agreements offer more potential benefits, and thus are more likely to take the form of treaties, holds for security agreements. The intuition behind this finding, according to the signaling model, is that the president will more often be willing to bear the costs of a treaty as a way to indicate US reliability when the potential benefits of the agreement are high.

The evasion hypothesis predicts that a president facing high domestic opposition should more often turn to executive agreements as a way to evade this opposition. In contrast, the signaling model argues that such a maneuver would send a signal of unreliability to negotiating partners. If anything, higher domestic opposition should force the president more often to use treaties as an attempt to signal reliability. Previous work has used divided government as an indicator of domestic opposition and prior beliefs about reliability.[10] While early work suggested that divided government was in fact associated with greater use of executive agreements, Martin (2000, 2005) has shown that in properly specified models, the relationship disappears or even reverses, as the signaling model predicts.

Table 3.2 presents a logit analysis that allows us to test the effect of divided government on the probability that an agreement will be a treaty, controlling for whether the agreement is multilateral. Here, I also control for whether the president is in an election year or in his first year in office. Some have suggested that presidents might more often turn to executive agreements during election years as a way to establish their own foreign policy agenda. It is also possible that a new president, who has not yet developed a working relationship with Congress, may be forced to rely more heavily on executive agreements. I also control for the party of the president, allowing for the possibility that ideological commitments might push presidents of one party to favor executive agreements that appear to enhance their autonomy from Congress.

As in the simple bivariate correlation, we find a strong positive relationship between multilateral agreements and treaties. We also find a positive relationship between a Republican president and the use of treaties, although this relationship is not quite statistically significant. This is interesting, because in the larger dataset a significant *negative* relationship appeared between Republican presidents and the use of treaties. This suggested that Republicans favored unilateral presidential action more than Democrats, probably consistent with conventional wisdom. However, this relationship does not hold for security agreements, and even appears to reverse. The circumstances that led to this pattern, at least for these decades, may be worth further speculation.

Neither of the year dummies has any effect. This suggests that a purely domestic logic of the president's relationship with Congress does not have a consistent effect on the form of agreements, lending support to a signaling

Table 3.2 Treaties versus executive agreements: logit analysis

Dependent variable = treaty	Coefficient	Estimated standard error	z
Multilateral	3.034*	0.6917	4.39
Republican president	0.8623	0.6909	1.25
Divided government	−0.4219	0.7042	−0.60
Election year	−0.5621	0.8440	−0.67
First year	−0.3457	0.8667	−0.40
Constant	−5.269*	0.8098	−6.43

Number of observations: 798
Pseudo R-squared: 0.181
* $p<0.01$

model. Importantly, divided government also has no significant effect on the probability that an agreement is a treaty, undermining the purely domestic logic of the evasion hypothesis. A finding that divided government had a significant positive relationship to the probability that an agreement took the form of a treaty would be strong support for the signaling model. Unfortunately, this finding does not materialize. However, we can conclude that there is no support for the evasion hypothesis, just as work on agreements in other issue areas has concluded. When it comes to security agreements, the president is not able to evade congressional opposition by turning to executive agreements, as this would send a signal of unreliability.

I have interpreted the positive relationship between multilateral agreements and treaties as supporting the idea that such agreements, on average, have greater value to the United States than bilateral agreements. However, particularly in the security realm, one could certainly argue that some bilateral agreements would be of tremendous value. Thus, a closer look at multilateral and bilateral treaties seems in order here. First, the multilateral treaties in this dataset are indeed consequential agreements; they are not just multilateral agreements that took the form of treaties because of legal precedence or convenience. Most involve NATO, for example planning for accession of new members. A multilateral landmine protocol is included, as is a multilateral agreement on terrorism. Thus, the assumption that many multilateral agreements are important substantive arrangements finds support in these data.

Looking at the bilateral treaties, a very interesting finding emerges. All four of these treaties are with the same country: the Soviet Union. Three of these are extensions of earlier treaties on nuclear weapons, and one regards the elimination of intermediate and short-range missiles. These are agreements of tremendous importance to the United States, and thus it is entirely consistent with the signaling model that they have taken the form of treaties. Thus, while multilateral agreements may be a decent proxy for the value of an agreement, even the cases that do not fit this rule – the bilateral treaties – support the underlying logic of the argument.

It is also interesting to note that none of the bilateral agreements in this dataset that are with US allies or with other democracies takes the form of a treaty. This may argue against some more normative arguments, for example those that predict that democracies would be more "legalistic" in their approach to security agreements. There is no evidence here that democracies will demand the formality of a treaty any more often than non-democracies. It may be interesting, in future work, to explore the impact of levels of military spending or other domestic characteristics of US negotiating partners to determine whether they have an impact on the form of agreements. Unfortunately, given the lack of variation in this dataset – all the bilateral treaties are with the same country – we cannot address these questions. Research aimed at looking at the impact of other domestic characteristics would have to extend the time frame to include more observations.

Overall, this analysis of agreement form provides moderately strong support for a signaling model, while providing no support for a purely domestic or legalistic model. To the extent that the reliability of the United States can be captured by examining divided government or other aspects of presidential relations with Congress, we do not find that lack of reliability can be overcome by turning to executive agreements. We do not find that the legalistic treaty form is preferred by democracies. Instead, the only consistent pattern we observe is that more valuable agreements more often take the form of treaties, exactly as the signaling model predicts. The next section provides a brief analysis contrasting bilateral and multilateral agreements with one another.

Multilateral versus bilateral agreements

In the context of multilateralism and security generally, it would be interesting to see whether there are any regular patterns in the degree to which US presidents are willing or able to complete multilateral agreements. The dataset analyzed here allows us to offer some preliminary insights on this question. Of course, any conclusions reached here must be treated as only initial insights. The data cover only twenty years, and there is no guarantee that each president had opportunities to complete about the same percentage of multilateral agreements each year. Nevertheless, this period covers extremely important changes in the US security environment, and offers variation in the party of the president and whether he faced divided government. Thus, it does allow us to undertake some analyses that could be of wider interest.

One intriguing question is whether partisan ideology influences the degree to which presidents complete multilateral versus bilateral agreements. Based on recent practice, with the George W. Bush administration showing an aversion to multilateral commitments, we might expect that Republican presidents would be more reluctant to conclude multilateral agreements. Thus, we would expect a lower ratio of multilateral to bilateral agreements under Republican presidents. However, a number of other factors would influence this ratio as well, and it is not obvious that partisan ideology has been consistent on the value of multilateralism. For example, in the early Cold War years, presidents of both parties concluded important multilateral security agreements.

Table 3.3 presents an initial simple analysis of the relationship between the party of the president and the relative frequency of bilateral and multilateral agreements. We do find the pattern we would expect if Republicans have typically been more skeptical of the value of multilateralism. Under Democratic presidents, about 10.8 per cent of agreements completed were multilateral during this period, while under Republicans only 6.6 per cent were multilateral. Using the chi-square statistic, we can see that this difference is statistically significant at the standard .05 level. Thus, we have suggestive evidence that Republican ideology does support the negotiation of bilateral rather than multilateral agreements.

Of course, we cannot draw too many conclusions from this crude analysis.

Table 3.3 Multilateral agreements and the president's party

	Democratic president		Republican president		Total	
Bilateral agreements	372	89.21%	356	93.44%	728	91.23%
Multilateral agreements	45	10.79%	25	6.56%	70	8.77%
Total	417		381		798	

Chi-square 4.451, $p<0.05$

Table 3.4 Multilateral agreements and the president's party: logit analysis

Dependent variable = multilateral agreement	Coefficient	Estimated standard error	z
Republican president	−0.6733*	0.2643	−2.55
Divided government	1.056*	0.2916	3.62
Constant	−2.749*	0.2592	−10.61

Number of observations: 798
Pseudo R-squared: 0.0409
* $p<0.01$

It does not control for any other factors that might influence a president's incentives or ability to conclude multilateral agreements. Although there are a large number of such potential factors, one that we can easily control here is the existence of divided government. Perhaps a president facing a Congress controlled by the other party would find it more difficult to gain support for complex multilateral agreements that could commit the United States in ways that would prove inconvenient in the future. Thus, we might expect that a president facing divided government would conclude fewer multilateral agreements. On the other hand, the analysis in the previous section of this paper suggested that divided government was not, in fact, a block to concluding agreements. While divided government might raise questions in negotiating partners' minds about the reliability of the United States, a president willing to make a costly signal of intent to live up to the terms of an agreement can overcome this liability.

In order to control for divided government and to assess its effects, Table 3.4 shows the results of a logit analysis using multilateral agreement as the dependent variable. That is, this table asks about the odds that any particular agreement will be multilateral rather than bilateral. The two explanatory variables are the president's party and divided government. As in Table 3.3, we find a significant negative relationship between Republican presidents and multilateral agreements. Thus, this finding does not simply arise because Republicans faced divided government more often than Democrats. Perhaps just as interesting, we find a strongly significant *positive* relationship between divided government and multilateral agreements. This suggests that divided government is not an impediment to negotiating multilateral agreements. However, the positive coefficient on this variable is somewhat surprising and deserves further exploration. Why might we see more multilateralism in periods of divided government? Does Congress simply have a preference for multilateral over bilateral agreements?

One further step we can take with these data is to examine the records of individual presidents. Perhaps the fact that Republican presidents concluded fewer multilateral agreements is not due to partisan ideology, but is more idiosyncratic to specific presidents, or the result of the particular era in which they were governing. The data here cover only four different presidents: Carter (1980); Reagan (1981–8); Bush 1 (1989–92); and Clinton (1993–9). Figure 3.2 presents a bar chart breaking down the data on multilateral and bilateral agreements by year.

We can see from this figure some clear differences across presidencies. The one year that we have for Carter, 1980, shows that about 13 per cent of all agreements were multilateral. During the first Reagan administration, this fraction plummeted, with no multilateral agreements in 1983 or 1984. However, in the second Reagan administration, the percentage of agreements that are multilateral returns about the same level as observed in 1980. In the first year of the Bush 1 administration we see no multilateral agreements, but the numbers return to about their usual levels for the next three years.

The first year of the Clinton administration, 1993, also shows a very low

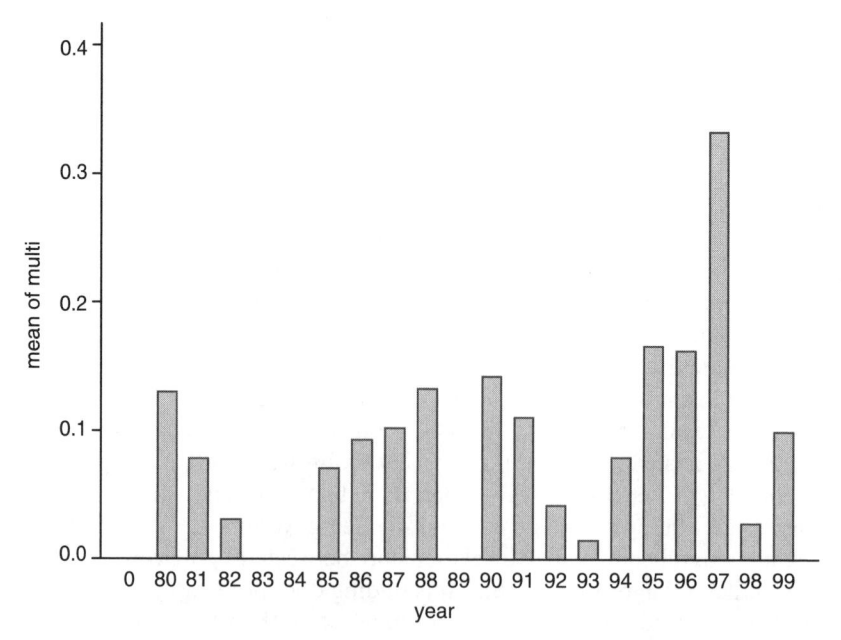

Figure 3.2 Fraction of all agreements that are multilateral, by year.

percentage of agreements as multilateral. However, this fraction grows dramatically over the next few years, reaching a maximum of over 30 per cent in 1997. Thus, the finding that Democratic presidents negotiate a higher percentage of their agreements as multilateral seems primarily to be a Clinton effect; while Reagan seemed particularly averse to multilateral agreements, at least during his first term. We would need to have data that covered a longer time span in order to see if the patterns found here could be generalized beyond this small set of presidents.

Figure 3.3 shows the total number of multilateral agreements negotiated per year, rather than the percentage, to allow us to see if any different patterns emerge. Overall, we see the same picture, exaggerated in some respects. The first Reagan administration shows almost no multilateral agreements being negotiated, but this number grows substantially toward the end of the second Reagan administration. The high point for negotiating multilateral agreements is in 1995–7, when the number negotiated per year averages about ten, well over the number for any other years. Given these data, it is not possible to sort out the precise reasons for this flurry of activity. It could be attributed to a fondness of Clinton for multilateralism in the security realm. Alternatively, it could be part of the post-Cold War aftermath, when opportunities to negotiate multilateral agreements proliferated.

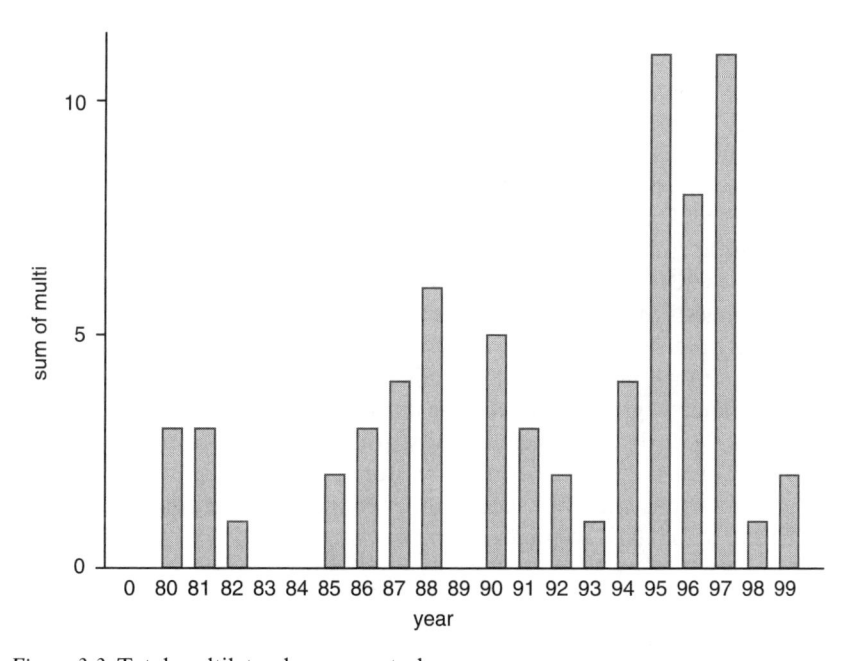

Figure 3.3 Total multilateral agreements, by year.

Conclusion

When the United States concludes security agreements with other countries, does the form of the agreement send a signal about the reliability of the United States? This question engages the extensive literature on the domestic politics of US agreements, but extends it significantly by considering how the form of the agreement provides information to other countries about the likelihood that the United States will actually live up to its terms. Work on this question from a purely American politics perspective has argued that the president is able to use executive agreements to evade the congressional constraints that a formal treaty would entail. Work by legal scholars has focused more on precedent and practice, paying little attention to the strategic issues involved in choosing the form of an agreement.

I have argued that the form of the agreement does, in fact, send signals to other countries. This means that presidents cannot simply evade congressional opposition by using executive agreements rather than treaties, as this would send a signal of unreliability. A signaling model of treaties predicts that agreements on consequential issues should more often take the form of a treaty, but that indicators of unreliability, such as divided government, should not reduce the chance that an agreement is a treaty. Analysis of data on nearly 800 US security agreements during the 1980s and 1990s supports the insights of the signaling model, while not providing evidence in support of the evasion perspective or a purely legalistic argument. Multilateral agreements, which on average are more valuable for the United States than bilateral agreements, more often take the form of treaties. Divided government does not have a significant negative relationship with the frequency of treaties. The only bilateral agreements that took the form of treaties were important agreements with the Soviet Union, again providing support for the signaling model.

In addition, these data allowed an initial exploration of the reliance of different presidents on bilateral versus multilateral agreements. Conventional wisdom suggests that Republicans are more skeptical of multilateralism than Democrats, and that hypothesis is borne out in this dataset. We also see the somewhat surprising result that periods of divided government give rise to more multilateral agreements, a finding that deserves further research. Overall, this study of security agreements suggests that they, like agreements in other issue areas, are the subject of intense strategizing by presidents, who are aware of the signals that they send to other countries, while also being swayed by partisan ideological commitments.

Notes

My thanks go to Olivia Lau for her excellent research assistance and to participants in the conference on multilateralism in the security realm in Delphi, Greece, in June 2005.

1 The legal literature draws distinctions among sole executive agreements, congressional-executive agreements, and executive agreements that are subsequent

to previous congressional approval. While this more fine-grained distinction may prove important, at this stage I examine only the broad difference between treaties and all forms of executive agreements. This is motivated by data availability (no data are readily accessible differentiating among types of executive agreements) and by the presumption, justified below, that treaties impose higher domestic costs on the president than other forms of agreements.
2 Spiro (2001) disagrees with Ackerman and Golove's conclusion (1995), arguing that sole executive agreements are constitutionally unacceptable under some conditions. However, this reasoning has found no support in the courts.
3 I would note that very few executive agreements require this high level of legislative participation.
4 *San Francisco Chronicle*, 14 May 2002; *New York Times*, 12 April 2002.
5 *Deutsche Presse-Agentur*, 13 May 2002.
6 *Washington Post*, 11 May 1979.
7 *Washington Post*, 18 January 1980; *The Economist*, 26 January 1980.
8 *New York Times*, 21 March 1986.
9 It is important to note that the agreement need not take the same form in all states party to it. It is not at all unusual for the same agreement to have to undergo very different ratification procedures in different countries. So the United States may choose to treat some agreement as a formal treaty while others treat it as a purely executive agreement, or vice versa. The model focuses only on the form the agreement takes in the United States.
10 Other indicators of reliability might be variables such as presidential victories on votes in Congress, or LPPC scores – the legislative potential for policy change. All such measures perform in the same way as divided government.

Appendix to Chapter 3

Table 3.5 Descriptive statistics and data sources

Variable	Mean	Std. Dev.	Minimum	Maximum	Source
Treaty	.0125	.1113	0	1	Oceana
Multilateral	.0877	.2831	0	1	Oceana
Republican president	.4774	.4998	0	1	Stanley and Niemi 2001
Divided government	.5614	.4965	0	1	Stanley and Niemi 2001

4 The crisis of the transatlantic security community

Thomas Risse

> Not long ago, a generation of young Germans who were liberated from the Nazi regime by American soldiers developed admiration of the political ideals of a nation that soon became the driving force in founding the United Nations and in carrying out the Nuremberg and Tokyo tribunals. As a consequence, classical international law was revolutionized by limiting the sovereignty of nation-states ... Should this same nation now brush aside the civilizing achievement of legally domesticating the state of nature among belligerent nations?
>
> (Habermas 2002)

> Europe's rejection of power politics, its devaluing of military force as a tool of international relations, have depended on the presence of American military forces on European soil. Europe's new Kantian order could flourish only under the umbrella of American power exercised according to the rules of the old Hobbesian order. American power made it possible for Europeans to believe that power was no longer important.
>
> (Kagan 2002)

Introduction

There is little doubt that the transatlantic relationship is in crisis despite the patching-up work being done on either side of the Atlantic after the Iraq war. Therefore, it is time to re-evaluate US–European relations and to take stock of their current evolution. Such an effort has to take into account, however, that the history of the transatlantic relationship is a history of crises. Compare the crowds marching against George W. Bush, his rhetoric of the "axis of evil," and the Iraq war with the demonstrations against Ronald Reagan, the talk of "empire of the evil" and the euro-missiles!

If the current conflicts are supposed to be different from the past, we need convincing analytical arguments pointing to structural changes in world politics rather than editorial adhocery. Three such changes come to mind: the end of the Cold War; unprecedented American preponderance; and 11 September 2001, and the rise of transnational terrorism.

I argue in the following that none of these changes (alone or in combination) offers sufficient evidence to conclude that structural changes in the international system are about to spell the end of the transatlantic community as we have known it over the past fifty years. The transatlantic security community used to rest on three things: collective identity based on common values, (economic) interdependence grounded in common material interests, and common institutions based on norms regulating the relationship. The current conflicts stem from domestic developments on both sides of the Atlantic leading to different perceptions of contemporary security threats including transnational terrorism and, more importantly, different prescriptions on how to handle them. Such differences have existed before and they have been dealt with through the institutions of the transatlantic community including European use of domestic access opportunities into the US political system. Recent evidence suggests that European and US leaders are currently busy (re-)developing their working relationships to deal with the most urgent international problems such as Iran's compliance with the Nuclear Non-Proliferation Treaty. This is the good news.

The bad news is that unilateral and even imperial tendencies in contemporary US foreign policy and particularly its official discourse have violated constitutive norms on which the transatlantic security community has been built over the years, namely multilateralism and close consultation with the allies. The more US foreign policy in general acts unilaterally and the more it renounces international agreements and institutions that the US itself has helped to build, the more it touches upon fundamental principles of world order and the rule of (international) law in dealing with international conflicts. The National Security Strategy (US President's Office 2002) is indeed partly at odds with some principles of world order which have been part of the Western consensus in the post-World War II era. Even though unilateralism is currently receding into the background of US foreign policy, the danger remains that "instrumental multilateralism" remains the preferred course in Washington. In this sense then, the current disagreements between Europe and the US go beyond ordinary policy conflicts and touch issues of common values and the core of the security community. Moreover, the transatlantic tensions and, most importantly, the thoroughly negative image of the Bush administration in the rest of the world including Europe, are beginning to eat away at the "sense of community" or collective identity as a cornerstone of the transatlantic security community. To put it differently, the most severe and global legitimacy crisis of US foreign policy in recent decades affects the transatlantic relationship directly. The pictures of Abu Grahib and Guantanamo Bay are not only destroying what is left of a positive image of the United States in the Islamic world, but they also challenge the Western community of values.

In short, the transatlantic community faces a severe crisis. It is no longer possible to paper over the differences in joint communiqués and nice photo opportunities. Rather, we need a new transatlantic bargain (Moravcsik

2003). Fortunately, the EU has been quick to get its foreign policy act together after the disastrous internal rows over Iraq. For the first time, the EU has articulated its own Security Strategy adopted by the European Council in December 2003 (European Council 2003). It substantially differs from George W. Bush's National Security Strategy in that it embraces what has been called "effective multilateralism," that is, a foreign policy vision of a "civilian power with teeth." Moreover, the European foreign policy strategy is already being expressed in practice – from European efforts in conflict prevention and peacekeeping to European support for the International Criminal Court (ICC) and multilateral efforts at dealing with global environmental challenges. Last not least and slowly but surely, Europe is putting the "teeth" into its concept of a "civilian power." In sum, an EU that gets its foreign policy act together is the pre-condition for a new transatlantic bargain.

Yet, a European (counter-)vision of world order is not meant to wreck the transatlantic security community. The rhetoric of building a counterweight to American hyperpower emanating from politicians and intellectuals in parts of "old Europe" is bound to fail, since it will split Europe further apart in foreign policy. Rather, efforts at a common European foreign policy and a European "grand strategy" should revive a serious transatlantic dialogue and (re-)create the transnational alliances across the Atlantic among like-minded groups that seem to have been silenced after 9/11.

I proceed in three steps. First, I take stock of and discuss the fundamentals of the transatlantic security community, including some alternative accounts. Second, I analyze domestic developments in the US and Europe in order to account partially for the current crisis. I conclude with some suggestions for the necessary transatlantic dialogue concerning world order questions.

A crisis of the transatlantic security community?

It is wrong to argue that policy disagreements between Europeans and North Americans dominate the transatlantic agenda. There is still quite some variation across policy areas in the extent to which the US and European governments disagree with each other. In transatlantic economic affairs, for example, things are fundamentally intact. The two main powers in the world economy – the US and the EU – still co-operate in managing international economic relations through multilateral institutions, particularly the World Trade Organization. Even in security issues, it would be hard to argue that disagreements prevail. As to the top priority on the current international security agenda – the fight against transnational terrorism – both sides have established a rather smooth co-operative relationship concerning transnational law enforcement and intelligence sharing. Military and political security co-operation in the Balkans, in Afghanistan, and elsewhere has not been affected by the crisis in the transatlantic relationship. Thus, not all is bad in the transatlantic relationship.

Yet, policy disagreements between the US and Europe extend over a wide range of issues these days. During the Cold War, such conflicts were rather normal, but they were mostly confined to specific questions. Today, things seem to be different. "Regime change" by force, "preventive war," and other policies of the Bush administration are not considered legitimate means of international politics in Europe. And this includes the United Kingdom and those European countries that have participated in the "coalition of the willing" in the Iraq war. Moreover, European and US foreign policies are at odds with each other on almost all issues of global governance (except for international economic affairs). This relates to, among others, nuclear and conventional arms control, international human rights (the fight over the ICC only constitutes the tip of the iceberg here), and the international environment (for details see Krell 2003: 22–5). The underlying problematique of these policy disagreements concerns rather fundamental world order questions, such as the role of multilateral institutions including the UN in global governance, understandings of international law, and the like. It has to be noted here that many of these policy conflicts predate both 11 September 2001, and the Bush administration. The ICC and the European–American rift on the climate change regime were with us already during the Clinton administration.

Three claims about the contemporary crisis in US–European relations

The end of the Cold War

Mearsheimer and Waltz were already arguing more than ten years ago that the end of the Cold War and the resulting end of the bipolar international system would lead to a decline of the Western alliance (Mearsheimer 1990; Waltz 1993). The argument was straightforward and came out of the structural realist theory of international relations: alliances are partnerships of convenience and joint interest to balance the power of an adversary. Once the power of the adversary has collapsed, the forces decrease that bind an alliance together. NATO and the transatlantic relationship are no exceptions. More than ten years after the end of the Cold War, it is still unclear whether the argument is right or wrong. Worse, the neo-realist claim is too indeterminate to tell us what would count as evidence confirming or falsifying it. As a result, neo-realists tend to adhocery when it comes to analyzing the transatlantic relationship. In 1990, for instance, Mearsheimer predicted not only the collapse of NATO, but also of the EU, and he expected Germany to go nuclear. Even if one concedes that NATO is in a deep crisis, the EU is not in decline and Germany still has no intention to acquire nuclear weapons.

US power (and European weakness)

A second argument holds that the end of the Cold War has led to an unprecedented supremacy of US power in the international system (e.g. Wohlforth 1999; Brooks and Wohlforth 2002; Huntington 1999). The US does no longer require allies to pursue its goals and can go it alone. At the same time, Europe is militarily weak and its military expenditures have declined sharply since the end of the Cold War. Kagan argued in this context that the US lives in a Hobbesian "dog-eat-dog" world and sees itself as the world policeman, while Europeans have made themselves comfortable in a Kantian world of peace and multilateralism (Kagan 2003).

There are various problems and inherent contradictions with these claims. First, it is more than questionable whether concepts such as "unipolarity" or "multipolarity" are still adequate to describe a partially globalized world in which states are all but one among many sites of power. Second, it is certainly true that we live in a unipolar world when it comes to military power. Concerning economic power, though, the argument only holds true if the EU is treated as twenty-seven individual states rather than an economic power with a single market and a single currency. Concerning various categories of "soft power" (knowledge, ideas etc.; Nye 1990, 2002), it is rather unclear whether the US is in a league of its own, since "soft power" seems to be rather diffuse and more widely spread in the contemporary world system. Moreover, since legitimacy arguably constitutes a significant ingredient of "soft power," US power might actually be in rapid decline in this regard.

Second, as to superpower behavior in a unipolar world, we need to distinguish clearly between (benign) hegemony and imperialism. Hegemonic power rests on the willingness of the superpower to sustain an international order, on its preparedness to commit itself to the rules of that order and on the smaller states' acceptance of the order as legitimate. The latter is a function of the former as a result of which small states gain "voice opportunities" to influence the hegemon's behavior, as Ikenberry has convincingly argued (Ikenberry 2000, 2001). Imperial power also rests on the willingness of the superpower to sustain world order, but the main difference from hegemony is that the superpower only plays by the rules when it suits its interests. In other words, imperial power is above the rules of the order (Ikenberry 2002; see also Krell 2003).

Unipolarity as a structural condition of the international system does not tell us whether we live in a hegemonic or an imperial order. The behavioral consequences of a unipolar world for US foreign policy are unclear. Yet, for allies and for the sustainability of the transatlantic alliance it makes all the difference in the world whether they are faced with a hegemonic or an imperial power. US hegemony and leadership have been readily accepted by the European allies throughout the post-World War II period. US imperialism, however, would indeed lead to the end of the transatlantic partnership and would have to be maintained by the use of US power against its allies in the long run. The crucial point is that we need to look inside the US itself in order to explain whether it behaves like a benign hegemon or like a malign imperialist. In other words, domestic politics and domestic structures become central to accounting for US foreign policy, even if we accept realist assumptions about the (unipolar) structure of the international system.

11 September 2001 and the rise of transnational terrorism

There is a final claim that 9/11 and the reactions to it constitute a watershed in the transatlantic relationship. If this means that differences in domestic responses to transnational terrorist threats result in transatlantic conflicts over the means to handle the threat, there is certainly some truth to it (see Katzenstein 2002). The securitization of many aspects of US foreign policy and the re-emergence of the "national security state" in the US cannot be understood without reference to the rise in the intensity of threat perceptions in the US following the attacks on the World Trade Center.

If this means, however, that the transatlantic community as such is endangered because of 9/11, the argument makes no sense. On the contrary, the transatlantic alliance faces a new threat which endangers the survival of highly industrialized democracies precisely because transnational terrorist networks exploit the vulnerabilities of open and liberal societies (Schneckener 2002; Arquilla and Ronfeldt 2001; Deibert and Stein 2002). Increased transatlantic co-operation in intelligence and law enforcement is necessary, which should strengthen alliance cohesion rather than weakening it.

In sum, neither the end of the Cold War nor US unipolarity as such, nor the new threats of terrorist networks, constitute changes in world politics that spell the end of the transatlantic community. These processes have in common that they are indeterminate with regard to their consequences for the US–European relationship. Let me now examine the fundamentals of the transatlantic relationship to determine whether it is still intact.

The transatlantic alliance: still a liberal security community?

Debates about US foreign policy, unipolarity, and the transatlantic relationship mostly overlook the obvious fact that the Western world consists of liberal and capitalist democracies.[1] Enduring liberal democracies rarely fight each other and, therefore, the security dilemma is almost absent in interactions among them. The literature about the "democratic peace" is enormous and the proposition does not require further elaboration (see, e.g., Russett 1993; Russett and Oneal 2001; Owen 1997; for reviews see Chan 1997 and Elman 1999). Recent quantitative studies suggest that economic interdependence measured in trade dependence of GDP and joint membership in international organizations (IOs) also add to peaceful relations among states (Russett and Oneal 2001). Interdependence effects and IO membership are apparently not as robust as the consequences of joint democracy, but they add to the absence of war among states.

Joint democracy, economic interdependence, and highly institutionalized international relations – these are indicators for what Karl W. Deutsch was already calling a "pluralistic security community" in 1957, defined as "a group of people which has become "integrated". By *integration* we mean the attainment, within a territory, of a "sense of community" and of institutions and practices strong enough and widespread enough to assure, for a "long" time, dependable expectations of "peaceful change" among its population" (Deutsch et al. 1957: 5–6, 9). A security community constitutes a particular social structure of international relations which then generates peaceful relations among the members (see also Adler and Barnett 1998b).

Inside a stable security community, behavior will not be regarded as threatening which might be perceived as highly dangerous and worth a response if it came from states outside the community. The US, e.g., has never been concerned about British and French nuclear weapons of mass destruction even though "objectively" they could inflict heavy damage on the US mainland. Europeans and Japanese might strongly disagree with US attempts to change the ABM Treaty, with the failures to ratify the Comprehensive Test Ban Treaty, to sign the international treaty banning landmines, or to join the regime against climate change, and the decision to go to war against Iraq. They might feel annoyed by American unilateralism. But none of this is seen as a military security threat to the other democratic powers in the contemporary international system giving rise to balancing behavior or to building counter-alliances.

But what explains the expectations of peaceful change among members of a security community? Three factors – "three Is" – mutually reinforce each other and serve to account for the democratic peace in the contemporary security community of major powers (see also Adler and Barnett 1998a):

1   a common sense of belonging together in terms of a collective *identity*;
2   strong (economic) *interdependence* among societies, creating substantial social interests in each other's well-being;
3   robust *institutions* to manage the relationship, creating social order and enduring norms among the members of the community (see Haftendorn et al. 1999).

The "three Is" can also be used as indicators for the current state of the transatlantic security community.

Collective identity

Among the three factors, collective identity is probably the most difficult to measure without getting into tautological reasoning (members of security communities do not fight each other; therefore, they must identify with each other, which explains their peacefulness). To measure the strength of collective identities, we should distinguish them along two dimensions: the salience of the "self/other" or "in-group/out-group" distinction, on the one hand, and the price people are prepared to pay for their sense of loyalty to the group, on the other. As to the in-group/out-group distinction, democratic security communities usually score rather high in this regard. Liberal democracies hold what Giesen and Eisenstadt called a "sacred" identity construction (Eisenstadt and Giesen 1995). We are the "shining city on the hill" (to quote from the American collective mythology; similar self-descriptions can easily be found in French discourses), but others can convert and become part of us, that is, also become liberal democracies. Liberal security communities engage in rather strong boundary constructions along the "self/other" divide, which is a function of a country's internal order. Once states democratize, they are eligible as members of the security community. The sharp self/other distinction explains, for instance, the missionary impulse in American foreign policy. It also explains why non-democracies are often constructed as "empires of the evil" and why autocratic leaders are often demonized (cf. the comparisons of both Saddam Hussein and Slobodan Milosevic with Adolf Hitler, as well as the description of Osama bin Laden as "personified evil").

Moreover, there are sufficient examples to sustain the argument that the often-proclaimed "value community" of the Western alliance does not simply represent sheer rhetoric. After all, the US prepared itself to sacrifice New York for Berlin during the Cold War. The hot debates about the credibility of extended deterrence during the Cold War document that this was not regarded as an empty threat. And in the post-Cold War era, the Western security community did fight for its principles several times, from the Gulf war to the war in Kosovo. While there are material-interest-based explanations for the Gulf war, the Kosovo war and the transformation of most of ex-Yugoslavia into a Western protectorate can hardly be explained on material grounds. Rather, the liberal identity of the community and its commitment to humanitarian principles accounts to a large extent why Western powers agreed to spend substantial economic, military, and human resources in the Balkans.

But do US Americans and Europeans hold a sufficiently large share of common values? Evidence from the *World Value Surveys* demonstrates overall similarities as well as some differences (Figure 4.1; see also the chapter by Fuchs and Klingemann in Anderson et al. 2008). Overall, North Americans and Europeans still occupy the same value space, that is, the north-eastern corner of both "secular-rational" and "self-expression" values. When it comes to support for democracy, human rights, and market economy, the core values of the transatlantic security community, we can discern very few differences between Europe and the US At least, the variation in support for these and other "self-expression values" is greater inside Europe than between Europeans and North Americans. And there is little evidence that this picture has changed over the past few years. There is a widening gap across the Atlantic, though, which concerns the "traditional vs secular-rational values" continuum. There is only one EU member state, Ireland,

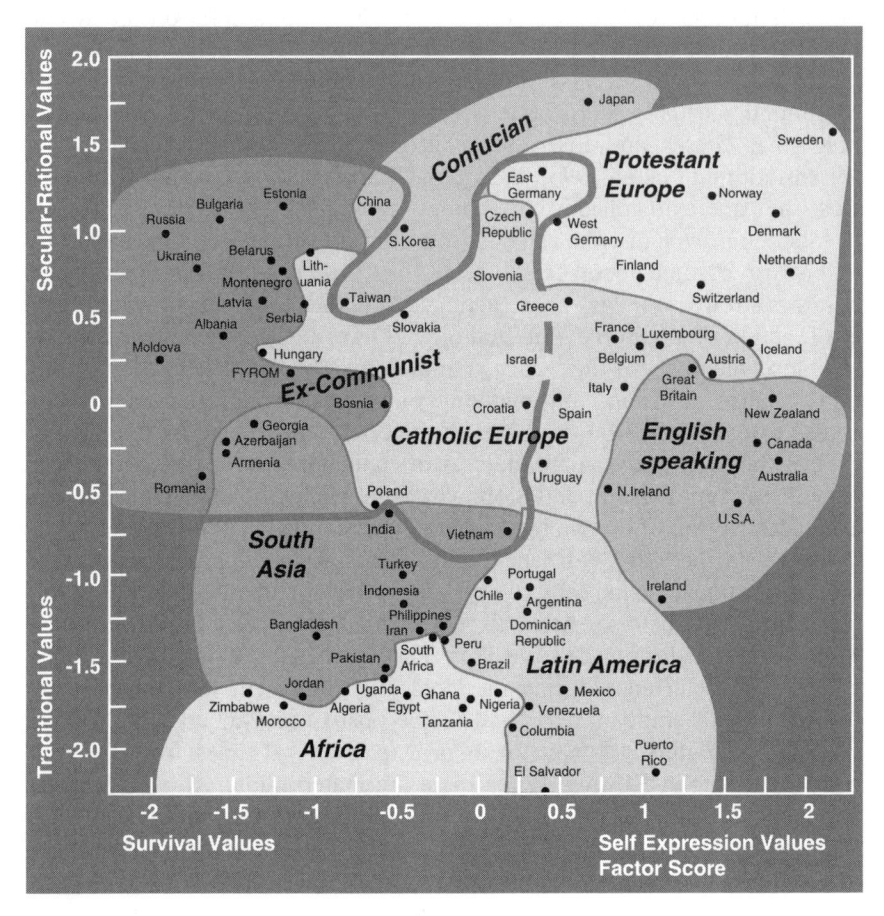

Figure 4.1 The European–American value space.

whose citizens are more supportive of both traditional-religious and so-called "family" values than US Americans (predominantly Catholic Poland equals the US on this scale). Northern and western Europeans in general are far more secular than North Americans (including Canada).[2]

However, this juxtaposition of a "religious America" versus a "secular Europe" overlooks the fact that the US is itself a deeply divided country when it comes to moral values. The eastern and western parts of the US look pretty much like "secular Europe" in this regard, where religion is considered one's private affair that should not interfere with politics. It is no coincidence that "secular America" pretty much coincides with those states that voted for John Kerry in the most recent Presidential elections. Among the demographic markers that impacted upon a person's vote for the president, religious engagement and race were the two top factors in 2004 (Pew Research Center 2005: 29). Two thirds of those who regularly attend church voted for President

Bush in 2004 (ibid.: 27; see also Braml 2004). The consequences of this religious divide for the transatlantic relationship are far from clear – apart from a fact that the religious right in the US strongly supports a foreign policy that tends to antagonize even the most pro-American Europeans (but also the other half of America).[3]

Let me now move toward issues that are more closely related to political relations in the transatlantic community than general value orientations. To begin with, is anti-Americanism on the rise in Europe? We need to distinguish mass public and elite opinion here. Concerning the former, the main measurement problem is not to confuse support for each other's foreign policies with collective identification. All public opinion polls agree that many Europeans – including British, Italian, Spanish, and central eastern European citizens – disagree sharply with the Bush administration's foreign policy.[4]

Whether rejection of particular US foreign policies translates into "anti-Americanism" is hard to tell overall. The Iraq crisis and war has certainly led to a steep decline in European sympathy for the US (for the following, see the Pew Global Attitudes Project 2003: 19–22). Whereas 75 per cent of the British, 61 per cent of the Germans, and 63 per cent of the French held favorable views of the US in summer 2002, these numbers declined to 48 per cent (British), 25 per cent (German), and 31 per cent (French) in March 2003. Yet, the pre-Iraq war image of the US in Europe was more negative than the post-war image. In March 2004, once again 58 per cent of the British, 38 per cent of the Germans, and 37 per cent of the French held favorable views of the US (Pew Research Center 2005: 106). Yet, while people might dislike the US, they still hold "Americans" in very high esteem – 73 per cent of the British, 68 per cent of the Germans, 53 per cent of the French (Pew Research Center 2005: 114). This further indicates that attitudes toward US (foreign) policies tend to color people's views of the US in general: 65 per cent of the French, 56 per cent of the Germans, and even 48 per cent of the British agreed that the re-election of George W. Bush made them feel worse toward the American people (BBC World Service 2005). In sum, negative feelings toward America stem from the Bush administration's policies rather than from some underlying resentments toward the US in general (see Table 4.1).

Table 4.1 US image in Germany and France (June 2003)

	Favorable views of Americans		What's the problem with the US?	
	in 2002	in 2003	Mostly Bush	America in general
Germany	70%	67%	74%	21%
France	71%	58%	74%	22%

Source: The Pew Global Attitudes Project (2003: 21–2)

Moreover, opinion poll data confirm a remarkable degree of transatlantic consensus with regard to foreign policy, threat perceptions, and support for a multilateral world order. Threat perceptions in Europe and the US are still remarkably similar, even though support for the "US-led war on terrorism" declined in France and Germany (Pew Global Attitudes Project 2003: 28). Europeans and Americans also agree that religious and ethnic hatred constitutes one of the greatest dangers in the world, while US citizens seem to be somewhat more concerned about the spread of nuclear weapons than their European counterparts. Finally and perhaps most significantly in light of the current transatlantic disputes, it is significant to note that support for multilateral institutions remains equally high in western Europe as in the United States. In 2005, 66 per cent of Republican voters and 79 per cent of Democratic voters agreed that the US should work more closely with other countries to fight terrorism. Similar bipartisan majorities agreed that strengthening the UN should be an important goal of US foreign policy (Kull 2005: 5, 7). International organizations in general are still held in very high esteem on either side of the Atlantic (Pew Global Attitudes Project 2002: 97). These data have remained stable for a long period of time (Krell 2003: 7; Worldviews 2002; Holsti 1996, 2001).

A deeper look at the structure of foreign policy attitudes on either side of the Atlantic reveals some important differences between US citizens and Europeans, though (for the following, see Asmus et al. 2003). Asmus, Everts, and Isernia have suggested grouping public opinion depending on the answers to two questions: (a) whether people view economic power as more or less important than military power, and (b) how people assess the use of military force (Table 4.2).

Table 4.2 reveals, first, that there are very few "isolationists" on either side of the Atlantic. It is particularly significant that isolationism has significantly declined in the US over recent years, which might be a post-9/11 phenomenon. Second, it is far too simplistic to state that US citizens are predominantly Martians, while Europeans tend to originate from Venus, as Kagan tried to argue. Instead, while there are many more hawks in the US than in Europe, the overwhelming majority of US citizens hold what Asmus et al. call a

Table 4.2 Structure of foreign policy attitudes in the US and Europe

	Economic power		*Military power*	
	US	Europe	US	Europe
War necessary	"Pragmatists" 65%	43%	"Hawks" 22%	7%
War unnecessary	"Doves" 10%	42%	"Isolationists" 3%	8%

Source: Asmus, Everts, and Isernia (2003: 3, 5)

"pragmatic" foreign policy outlook. And Europeans are almost equally split between "doves", on the one hand, and "pragmatists", on the other. One can conclude from these differences that it is much more difficult in Europe than in the US to build political coalitions in support of using military force – and indeed, it was this issue that drove Europe and the US apart during the Iraq war. At the same time, however, there is enough public support on either side of the Atlantic for pragmatic foreign policies to allow for transatlantic bridge-building.

In sum, there is no doubt that the collective identity of the transatlantic security community has taken a beating in recent years. Concerning European mass public opinion, the Bush Administration's foreign policy in general and the Iraq war in particular have led to a steep decline in the image of America and the US. The pictures of US troops engaged in torture have not helped to improve the US image. At the same time, however, it is hard to construct a widening value gap given the deep divisions about moral and religious values in the US itself. Last not least, foreign policy attitudes remain largely in sync across the Atlantic. Thus, the picture that emerges is too complex to come to any firm conclusion. It seems to show a transatlantic community in motion.

Transnational interdependence

Concerning the second factor contributing to a security community, transnational (economic) interdependence, the transatlantic community is alive and kicking. Combined indicators for trade, foreign investment, and capital flows show that the transatlantic region is highly integrated economically and is only surpassed by the EU's single market itself. In 1999, 45.2 per cent of all US foreign investment went to Europe, while 60.5 per cent of all European foreign investment went to the US European investments in Texas alone are higher than all Japanese investments in the US combined. A German firm – Siemens – is among the largest employers in the US. Moreover, intra-firm trade constitutes a large portion of transatlantic trade. EU subsidiaries of US companies import more than one third of all US exports to the EU, while US subsidiaries of EU companies import more than two fifths of all EU exports to the US. Six million jobs on each side of the Atlantic depend on transatlantic economic relations (data according to Krell 2003: 10–17).

The transatlantic market is highly integrated and remains so despite the ups and downs in the political relationship. The US and the EU not only constitute each other's most important economic partners, but are also the two leading world economic powers. The current international economic order is largely guaranteed and stabilized by the transatlantic economic relationship. What is less clear, though, is the degree to which high economic interdependence serves to smooth increasing political conflicts. The spill-over effects from one area to the other are not clear, in either direction. To what extent can transatlantic economic interdependence substitute for a lack in transatlantic identity when it comes to maintaining and nurturing the political relationship? Historical lessons, particularly the decades preceding World War I, appear to suggest that economic interdependence does not suffice to stabilize a deteriorating political relationship, as generations of neorealists have always been quick to point out (e.g. Waltz 1979; see also chapters by van Scherpenberg and McNamara in Anderson et al. 2008).

Multilateral institutions

The third factor reinforcing a security community pertains to multilateral institutions managing the relationship. Again and in parallel to the density of transnational interdependence, Europe and the transatlantic region constitute the most tightly coupled institutionalized settings within the larger Western community. This region of the world also hosts the two strongest political, economic, and security institutions in terms of robustness of norms, rules, and decision-making procedures, the EU and NATO. The multilateral institutions of the transatlantic community serve to manage the inevitable conflicts inside a security community (Risse-Kappen 1995; see also Haftendorn et al. 1999). Strong procedural norms of mutual consultation and policy co-ordination insure that the members of the community have regular input and influence on each other's policy-making processes. These procedural norms and regulations are among the major tools mitigating power asymmetries among community members.

Of course, these "voice opportunities" (Ikenberry 2001) suffer, the more US foreign policy pursues a unilateralist course or falls victim to "imperial ambitions" (Ikenberry 2002). Unilateralism violates norms of multilateralism, which are constitutive for the transatlantic community. If unilateral tendencies, which have always been a temptation in American foreign policy, become the prevailing practice, the transatlantic security community's constitutive norms are endangered. The discourse emanating from Washington over the past few years concerning "coalitions of the willing" – now enshrined in the foreign policy doctrine of the United States (US President's Office 2002) – stands in sharp contrast to the idea of multilateralism on which the transatlantic alliance has been based over the past fifty years. NATO was so successful in the past as an instrument of alliance management, precisely because it served as a clearing house for potential policy disputes before firm decisions were taken on either side of the Atlantic. The more consultations in the alliance framework are reduced to merely informing each other about decisions already taken, the more NATO becomes irrelevant for the future of the transatlantic relationship.

This is why the North Atlantic alliance has taken such a toll in the past years, even before 9/11 and certainly before the Iraq crisis. Neither the US nor Europeans have made good use of NATO in recent years as the primary institution to manage their security relationship. After 9/11, Article 5 of the North Atlantic Treaty was invoked for the first time in the history of the alliance – without any further consequences. During the Iraq crisis and war, the NATO Council apparently never discussed the transatlantic dispute in detail (see Pond 2004). Both sides violated norms of consultation that are fundamental for the transatlantic security relationship. If we are in a fundamental crisis of the transatlantic relationship, it primarily concerns the norms governing it, which have been enshrined in its institutions. As long as the US continues to build its foreign policy on "coalitions of the willing," this constitutes unilateralism in disguise and is fundamentally at odds with the norms of the transatlantic security community. No wonder then, that we have seen rather hectic attempts on both sides to repair the security relationship after the Iraq crisis. More recently, the US has indeed resumed regular consultations with its allies. Whether this constitutes a break from unilateral temptations remains to be seen. It also remains to be seen whether NATO is able to resume its role as the most important institution to manage the transatlantic security relationship (see below).

In sum, if we use the "three Is" – identity, interdependence, and institutions – as indicators for the state of the transatlantic security community, we get a rather precise picture of its current situation. While transatlantic economic interdependence remains strong, the collective identification with each other has taken quite a beating since 2002/3. US post-9/11 foreign policy has resulted in a strong spill-over from anti-Bushism to anti-Americanism in Europe, including Great Britain. At the same time, either fundamental value and foreign policy orientations on either side of the Atlantic remain rather comparable or else the value differences point to more fundamental cleavages dividing American society. Moreover, in the wider world community, European and North American societies have more in common than any other societies in the world. Current challenges to the community concern its institutions and the constitutive norms on which they are based. NATO has taken quite a beating, and whether it is beyond repair remains to be seen.

In short, the Atlantic has indeed become wider in recent years, but we still lack an explanation. To understand the sources of conflicts, we need to open up the black box of the states on both sides of the Atlantic and look at domestic politics.

Domestic sources of the transatlantic disputes

The domestic side of US foreign policy

To some extent, one is reminded of the transatlantic tensions during the first Reagan administration in the early 1980s (see Kubbig 1988; Risse-Kappen 1988; Talbott 1984). While George W. Bush is widely perceived as a unilateralist president in Europe, Ronald Reagan was seen as abandoning nuclear arms control in a similar fashion.

These similarities run deeper than perceptions in public opinion. Most importantly, US foreign policy has been controlled in recent years by a domestic coalition whose world views differ substantially from dominant European foreign policy outlooks. Three competing groups dominate the Bush administration's foreign policy and they hold strikingly similar world views as compared to the prevailing and equally competing domestic coalitions during Reagan's first term (on the latter, see in particular Talbott 1984, 1988; Kubbig 1988). During the early 1980s, a conservative group hating détente and arms control as well as despising the "wimpish" European allies was largely in control of the Pentagon. Now and then, this group consisted of devoted militant internationalists preferring American unilateralism over entangling alliances. During the early 1980s, unilateralist conservatives were convinced that arms control had to be abandoned in favor of arms racing in order to ruin the Soviet economy and, thus, to win the Cold War. Twenty years later, this group believes in the "unipolar moment" as a unique opportunity for the US to (re-)create international order following an American design. Their "imperial ambition" (Ikenberry 2002) is prepared to accept temporary alliances, but their fundamental beliefs reject stable partnerships such as the transatlantic community as too entangling to suit US interests. In other words, this group rejects the principles upon which the security community between the US and Europa has been built. It is anti-European to the degree that it considers the transatlantic alliance as largely superfluous and constraining US foreign policy.

However, we need to distinguish between two versions of conservative thinking in foreign policy (for a broader analysis of these various strands, see Mead 2001; Hassner 2002; Nau 2002). They are both unilateral and aggressive internationalists and prepared to use American power offensively when they see US interests at stake. But they differ in how they view the world and which values they want to promote. One group – among them Vice President Cheney and Secretary of Defense Rumsfeld – see the world in Hobbesian terms as a "dog-eat-dog" world. They are aggressive realists who believe in the US role as world policeman to keep order in an anarchic international system (on offensive realism, see Mearsheimer 2001).

But there is also another group of neoconservative hawks, who are prepared to use American power to promote liberal values and to construct a world order based on liberal democracies, universal human rights, and American-style capitalism. Paul Wolfowitz, Undersecretary of Defense of the first Bush administration used to be the most prominent representative of this group, which Hassner has aptly called "Wilsonians in boots," analogous to Napoleon's "revolution in boots" (Hassner 2002: 43; on the historical origins of Wilsonianism in American foreign policy, see Mead 2001). In their view, the purpose of American power in the world is to promote democracy and capitalism. US power is to be used aggressively and unilaterally toward a liberal world order. This is why they supported regime change in Iraq. The particular strength of the neo-conservative group during the first Bush administration results from the fact that they were able to forge a domestic coalition with the religious right, which constitutes the backbone of the Republican party (see also Braml 2004).

Yet, the unilateralists of the early Reagan as well as the current Bush administrations have been balanced domestically and bureaucratically by a more moderate and traditional conservative group. Officials such as Richard Burt and Paul Nitze during the early 1980s, Bush senior's foreign policy team of the late 1980s, as well as George W. Bush's two Secretaries of State, Colin Powell and Condoleezza Rice, see the world in more moderate realist terms. While they certainly share liberal values, they are not Wilsonians in the sense of supporting a multilateral liberal world order. But they resent the "imperial ambition" of the unilateralists and are convinced that the US cannot go it alone – even in a unipolar system. At the same time, this group is rather sceptical of the nation-building implications which the neo-conservatives' liberal visions imply. Today as well as twenty years ago, this group has remained committed to the transatlantic security community. With a little help of their European friends, the traditional conservatives succeeded in gradually moving Ronald Reagan toward the resumption of nuclear arms control – and in moving George W. Bush to repair relations with the allies, particularly in Europe, after the Iraq adventure.

From the beginning of the Bush administration, a tug-of-war between the neo-conservatives and the traditional conservatives – between the "Pentagon party" supported by the Vice President and the "State Department party" – characterized the foreign policy decision-making process in Washington. It became the task for President Bush's then National Security Advisor and now Secretary of State, Condoleezza Rice, to find a balance between these competing views. Rice's academic credentials, prior to her work for the Bush administration, seem to suggest that her world views come closer to the traditional conservative camp.

Then came 11 September 2001, and the attack against the US homeland by transnational terrorism: 9/11 – and the understandable shock and sense of vulnerability it generated among Americans – had profound consequences for the domestic balance of power in US foreign policy (for details, see Woodward 2002, 2004). It created a policy window of opportunity for neo-conservative policy entrepreneurs. As a result, the domestic balance of power in the US changed in favor of the neo-conservative group whose liberal unilateralist vision ("Wilsonianism in boots") was increasingly shared by the president.

The presidential National Security Strategy of September 2002 as well as the focus on Iraq constituted expressions of the new domestic balance of power in Washington. Nevertheless, both examples also show that neo-conservative unilateralists of the offensive realist and the liberal variety both had to make concessions to the traditional conservatives and their allies in Congress and in Europe. As to the much-criticized National Security Strategy document, for example, it expresses a liberal vision of world politics: "Finally, the United States will use this moment of opportunity to extend the benefits of freedom across the globe. We will actively work to bring the hope of democracy, development, free markets, and free trade to every corner of the world" (US Presidents Office 2002: V). Incorporating the foreign policy views of the neo-conservatives, the document commits the US to:

- pre-emptive, if not preventive warfare against terrorism and "rogue states" possessing weapons of mass destruction;
- unilateralism "when our interests and unique responsibilities require" (US President's Office 2002: 31);
- military superiority "to dissuade potential adversaries from pursuing a military build-up in hopes of surpassing, or equaling, the power of the United States" (ibid.: 30).

None of these statements as such is new. However, it is the combination of a liberal vision with unilateral action "if necessary" (but who decides?) that represents a shift from previous foreign policy strategies of the US. The document also contains quite a few paragraphs expressing the standard repertoire of the traditional conservatives, such as the commitment to NATO, the EU, and other allies. It also commits the US to active engagement in regional crises and to a substantial increase in foreign aid. Finally and significantly, the US remains supportive of a multilateral and liberal international economic order. This latter point is often overlooked in Europe, but it is of utmost importance for the future of world order. In sum, the much criticized National Security Strategy document represents a policy compromise between neo-conservative unilateralists and traditional conservatives in the Bush administration.

Since the Iraq war, the domestic balance of power inside the second Bush administration has shifted yet again. The unilateralist neo-conservative group which has led the US into its worst foreign and security policy disaster in decades, seems to have lost ground at the expense of the more traditional conservative group who realize that the US needs stable allies. As a result, the Bush administration is gradually moving back toward the political center in the US and toward the mainstream "pragmatism" of the US public (see above). This, of course, makes life easier for Europeans who have to deal with the US. At the same time, however, the liberal vision of promoting democracy and capitalism as primary goals of US foreign policy seems to remain a centerpiece of the president's rhetoric, if not practice. In all of this, one should not overlook the fact that the dominant foreign policy elite coalitions in Europe differ substantially from their American counterparts – and this includes the Democrats. Last not least, the damage done by the neo-conservative group to the international legitimacy of US foreign policy has lasting consequences.

In sum, if we want to understand the shifting positions of US foreign policy, it's domestic politics, stupid! Unipolarity and the structure of the international system do not tell us much about the oscillation between unilateralism and instrumental multilateralism in the current Bush administration.

Crisis of the transatlantic security community 95

Unipolarity only enters the picture insofar as unilateralism is an option for US foreign policy to begin with. While systemic pressures push almost all other states in the international system toward more co-operative and multilateral behavior, the US enjoys the luxury of having real choices, at least in the short run. Systemic pressures and foreign policy crises, such as the one the administration experiences at the moment, work themselves out through the domestic policy process. While the various domestic factions in US foreign policy have been rather stable over time, it is their relative strength and their balance of domestic power that goes along way to explain American foreign policy. The same holds true for Europe, at least to some extent.

The domestic side of European foreign policy

While the coalition in charge of US foreign policy during the first Bush administration was composed of neo-conservatives (liberal as well as realist unilateralists) and traditional conservatives (realists with a preference for traditional alliances), the dominant coalitions running the EU's foreign policy as well as the foreign policies of the most important member states look rather different (see Figure 4.2). The diagram depicts the foreign policy elite coalitions on both sides of the Atlantic in a two-dimensional space. A third

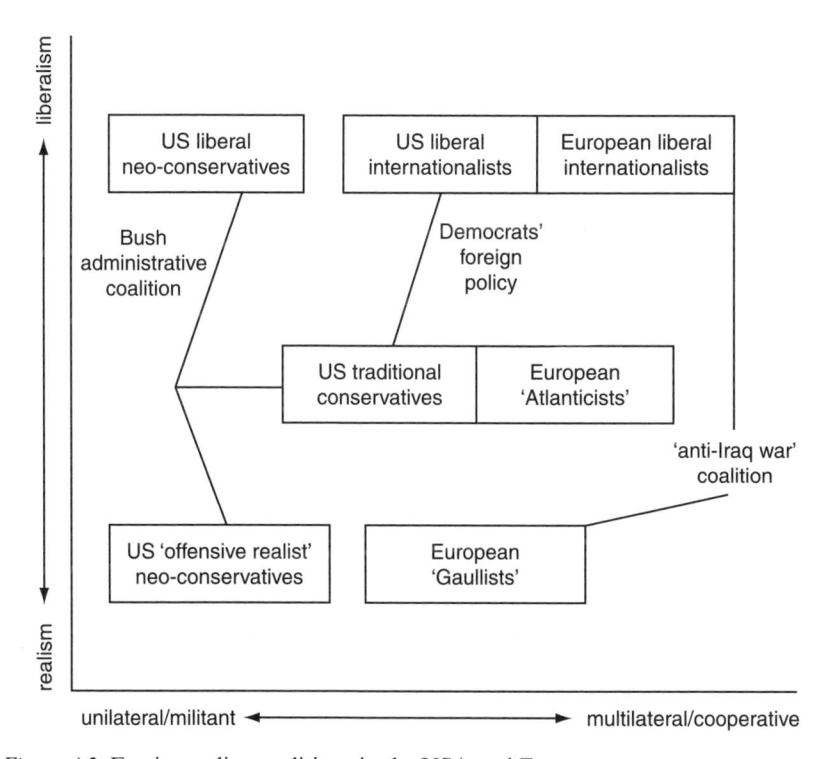

Figure 4.2 Foreign policy coalitions in the USA and Europe.

dimension that is often used to describe foreign policy attitudes – isolationism versus internationalism – is omitted here, since the dominant foreign policy elites in the US and in Europe share a commitment to internationalism. Rather, the various groups differ from each other in two dimensions:

1 A "realist–liberal" continuum (the y-axis), which depicts whether people view the world in realist terms and thus security interests dominate their vision of foreign policy, or whether they are primarily committed to the promotion of a liberal vision, that is, the spread of human rights, democracy, and market economy;
2 A "unilateral/militant – multilateral/cooperative" continuum (the x-axis), delineating whether foreign policy-makers favor unilateralism and the use of force to promote foreign policy goals or whether they support a co-operative foreign policy working with and through multilateral institutions.

The three factions dominating the Bush administration's foreign policy are situated on the left-hand side of Figure 4.2. I have also included the dominant foreign policy coalition in the Democratic Party which is composed of "traditional conservatives" on the one hand and "liberal internationalists" on the other. The graph also depicts three European foreign policy groups according to their views. The first group in the upper right corner of the figure could be called "liberal internationalists." It is often overlooked that the European center-left shares with American "liberal" neo-conservatives a commitment to the promotion of democracy and human rights as their foreign policy priorities. The same is true for the EU's foreign policy strategy (see also Börzel and Risse 2004). In sharp contrast to the US right, however, this group is equally firmly committed to a co-operative foreign policy and to work with and through multilateral institutions. This group – which, for example, was in charge of German foreign policy in the Schröder/Fischer coalition – pursues the foreign policy of a "civilian power" (Maull 1990; Harnisch and Maull 2001) and thus shares a Kantian vision of world order in the sense of the "perpetual peace" – that is, building a pacific federation of democratic states and strengthening the rule of law in international affairs (Kant 1795/1983). European Kantians are not pacifists; they support the use of military force if necessary (cf. Chancellor Schröder's stance on Kosovo and Afghanistan). Yet, military power has to be embedded in political and diplomatic efforts. Unilateralism is anathema for the European center-left.

There is a second group among the European foreign policy elites which holds a more realist view of the world than either the American neo-conservatives or the European center-left. Since this group thinks primarily in realist, balance-of-power terms, it is very much concerned about the growth of US power and promotes a European foreign policy of balancing and building a counter-weight to US primacy. One could call this group the "European Gaullists" (see e.g. Bahr 2003; Schöllgen 2003), given that French presidents from de Gaulle to Chirac shared that world view. Their mantra is to build a multipolar world in contrast to a unipolar one dominated by US hyperpower. Interestingly and strangely enough, the Franco-German anti-Iraq war coalition brought together the European center-left and the European "Gaullists" who joined forces for different reasons. Both were concerned about American unilateralism. But the center-left primarily opposed the use force for liberal purposes ("regime change"), while the "Gaullists" opposed the war because of concern about US "hyperpower."

The third group among European foreign policy elites can be located in a similar position as the American traditional conservatives. This group holds rather moderate world views on either the liberal–realist axis or the militant–co-operative axis. Above all, however, this group is strongly committed to preserving the transatlantic partnership, almost no matter what. This group of "European Atlanticists," which formed the core of the European "coalition of the willing" during the Iraq war, is strongly motivated to avoid policy disagreements with Washington that could weaken the transatlantic community. British Prime Minister Tony Blair (and his successor Gordon Brown) as well as German Chancellor Angela Merkel belong to this group. Thus, Germany's current grand coalition government is composed of European Atlanticists as well as European liberal internationalists, thus bringing the country closer to the US.

Two main conclusions follow from this attempt at locating the various foreign policy groupings on either side of the Atlantic in a two-dimensional political space:

1 The core of the transatlantic disagreements does not concern value commitments such as the goals of promoting democracy or human rights. When it comes to the question whether foreign policy should primarily promote liberal values rather than serving strategic or economic interests (the realist view), European elites are as much divided among themselves as Americans. Despite all the different positions over Iraq, however, Europeans are overwhelmingly in favor of multilateralism and co-operative foreign policies, while a strong group in Bush's foreign policy coalition is composed of unilateralists. Thus, the main dividing line between the US and Europe concerns the commitment to multilateral norms, which have been constitutive to the transatlantic security community. This is fairly obvious if one compares the national security strategy of President Bush (US President's Office 2002) with the strategy document adopted by the European Council (European Council 2003). For all the talk about "preventive engagement," the EU security strategy remains firmly committed to international law and to multilateralism.

2 It is also obvious that the two opposing camps in Europe that emerged during the Iraq crisis ("new vs old" Europe) constitute anything but stable foreign policy coalitions. To put it more bluntly: Neither European Gaullism nor European Atlanticism of the old kind can form the basis of

a common European foreign policy consensus. I come back to that point in the conclusions.

To sum up: The crisis in the transatlantic relationship has to be understood on the basis of differing world views of dominant foreign policy coalitions on either side of the Atlantic. Domestic forces – rather than structural changes in the international system – have made the Atlantic a wider ocean. This does not imply that the crisis is less serious. First, one of the core groups that dominated US foreign policy of the first Bush administration does not believe in the values and norms of the security community. This is a new development compared to previous US governments. While unilateralists formed part of the foreign policy coalition during Ronald Reagan's first term, they have never been as powerful as during the first Bush administration. Second, the unilateralist group might have been weakened inside the second Bush administration as a result of the Iraq disaster. Yet, the damage to the transatlantic relationship, and particular to the social underpinnings of the security community, has been done. Of course, European "Gaullists" and their rhetoric – which was primarily motivated by domestic election concerns in the case of Chancellor Schröder – have also done their fair share of damage to the transatlantic community. But this does not make things much better.

Conclusions: how to repair the transatlantic security community

The argument of this paper can be summarized as follows. As to the fundamentals of the transatlantic security community, a mixed picture emerges. One of the three Is – interdependence – appears to be still intact completely. Sense of community and collective identity have taken a beating, while the institutional basis (NATO) and the norms governing the community are in serious crisis. These conflicts stem from domestic developments on both sides of the Atlantic leading to different perceptions of contemporary security threats and, more importantly, different prescriptions on how to handle them. Diverging elite coalitions have been in charge of foreign policies on either side of the Atlantic. An uneasy coalition of unilateralist conservatives and more traditional conservatives have been in charge of President Bush's foreign policy. The EU's foreign policy as well as the foreign policies of the member states are dominated by varying coalitions of European "Gaullists," liberal internationalists, and "Atlanticists." The split between "new Europe" and "old Europe" during the Iraq war was mainly one between "Gaullists" and "Atlanticists," with liberal internationalists trying to balance between the two.

What policy consequences follow from this assessment, particularly for European responses to America's "imperial ambitions?" I see three major conclusions. First, neither balancing nor bandwagoning can be a valid basis for a European response to American imperial ambitions. Building Europe as a "counterweight" to US power is neither feasible in practical terms nor can a European consensus be built around it, which would have to include the

United Kingdom as well as the new EU member states of central eastern Europe. Bandwagoning is not an option, either, since it would betray core principles of European foreign policy when dealing with US unilateralist tendencies. Thus, there is a European paradox: On the one hand, Europe and the EU need to speak out with one voice in order to be listened to in Washington. On the other hand, a European common foreign policy will fail and split Europe further apart if it is constructed as a counter-hegemonic project.

Second, however, there is a way out. I would argue against Kupchan (2003) that the social structure of the transatlantic relationship and its institutional basis in particular can be (and indeed should be) repaired. The traditional European reaction to US unilateralist impulses remains valid even today. In the past, Europeans have usually responded to transatlantic conflicts by increased binding, through strengthening the transatlantic institutional ties, rather than counter-balancing. They have used the open US domestic system for their purposes by successfully forming transnational and transgovernmental coalitions across the Atlantic in order to increase their leverage on American foreign policy (for evidence, see Risse-Kappen 1995). There is no compelling reason why this strategy, which worked well during the Reagan administration with a similar domestic configuration of forces, cannot be successfully employed today. Now and then, the natural allies of Europeans inside the administration and in Congress are the moderate conservatives who care about the transatlantic community. Moreover, as strange as it sounds, the Iraq disaster provides a "window of opportunity" for European liberal internationalists to enter a strategic dialogue with neo-conservatives, particularly in the Washington-based think tanks. There seems to be a growing awareness and recognition that democracy promotion by force might not work the way neo-conservatives had envisioned it. There is also a growing sense that US foreign policy needs some international legitimacy in order to be effective. Last not least, European foreign policy can exploit the fact that American public opinion continues to hold views much closer to European outlooks than to those of the neo-conservatives inside and outside the administration.

The third conclusion concerns the necessity of a new transatlantic bargain. While transatlantic collective identities can only be re-constructed through active policies to a very limited degree, the institutional setup of the transatlantic community is in serious need of repair. As I have argued above, concepts such as "coalitions of the willing" or "the mission defines the coalition" are inherently inconsistent with the institutional norms of a security community. Europeans need a firm and explicit commitment from Washington to an enduring alliance rather than to ad hoc coalitions. And the US needs to understand that the Europeans are the ones to primarily deliver the international legitimacy required to make US foreign policy effective. Such a new transatlantic bargain also entails a re-affirmation of the rule that consultations with allies and partners have to precede policy decisions. There can always be an "agreement to disagree" and Europeans must not always follow

US decisions, and vice versa. But we need some serious talk about ground rules governing the transatlantic relationship if disasters such as Iraq are to be prevented.

What is less clear is the institutional framework in which a new transatlantic bargain can be forged. On the one hand, NATO continues to be the most densely institutionalized transatlantic organization, including its military integration. It also has more than fifty years of experience in managing the transatlantic relationship. On the other hand, NATO has thoroughly failed in this latter regard over the past five years. With its emphasis on military and defense affairs, it is ill-suited to tackle the political dimensions of the contemporary security agenda, such as transnational terrorism, failing states, and state-building. In this regard, a new transatlantic dialogue must bring in the EU with its unique capacities and experiences as regards the economic and political aspects of international security. While US–EU summitry might not be the right institutional framework for a renewed transatlantic security dialogue, it is clear that a new transatlantic bargain must include the European Union as the emerging polity of Europe.

In sum, the transatlantic security community is in need of repair. "Friendly divorce" as suggested by Kupchan (2003) does not resolve any of the world's problems, while transatlantic co-operation might at least make a significant contribution to it. Re-invigorating the security community, however, requires sustained efforts on both sides of the Atlantic. It remains to be seen whether Europeans and Americans are up to the task.

Notes

This is an updated and revised version of a paper presented at the American Institute for Contemporary German Studies, Washington DC, 24 January, 2003, published as AICGS Seminar Papers, and at the 2004 Annual Convention of the American Political Science Association. Various versions have been published as Risse (2003, 2006). I owe a lot to discussions in the research seminar of the Center for Transnational Relations, Foreign and Security Policy at the Freie Universität Berlin. Last not least, this chapter benefited from discussions in a transatlantic study group which Jeffrey Anderson, G. John Ikenberry, and I have chaired over the past few years. See Anderson, Ikenberry, and Risse 2008. I thank my students as well as Tanja Börzel and Ingo Peters for their critical comments.

1 This part of the chapter summarizes Risse (2002).
2 For a detailed analysis of religious orientations in Europe showing clear differences between the old EU, on the one hand, and the accession countries, on the other, see Gerhards and Hölscher (2005).
3 According to the Pew surveys, the war in Iraq figures as by far the most divisive issue in the 2004 US elections (Pew Research Center 2005: 12).
4 See e.g. Pew Global Attitudes Project (2002); Pew Research Center for the People & the Press (2002). In a poll 77 per cent of the Germans, 75 per cent of the French, and still 64 per cent of the British agreed that the re-election of George W. Bush was negative for peace and security in the world (BBC World Service 2005).

5 State attributes and system properties

Security multilateralism in central Asia, southeast Asia, the Atlantic and Europe

James Sperling

Why does security multilateralism, particularly its institutionalization, become a regular feature of interstate interaction in some geopolitical regions of the world and episodic or absent in others? An answer to this question may be found in the confluence of state attributes and system properties, which combine to produce a narrow range of viable security governance outcomes. The dominant system-level theories of international relations generally treat state attributes as given and homogeneous. This homogeneity assumption no longer comports with the contemporary international system, because at least two categories of states – the Westphalian and post-Westphalian – constitute the system. System properties fall along a continuum describing, at one end, a primitive state of nature reacting unvaryingly to changes in relative power and, at the other, an international civil society governed by a dense and comprehensive network of norms codified as binding law.

Capturing the precise interaction of system- and unit-level variables – and the forms of security multilateralism that arise from it – raises three questions: Can the varieties of security multilateralism in the contemporary international system be explained by changes in the nature of the state? Are there identifiable patterns of internal and external variables that produce a narrow range of security multilateralism outcomes? What criteria effectively differentiate between the varieties of security multilateralism? The conceptual nomenclature defining the varieties of security multilateralism has become flabby: different forms are conflated or have acquired different and contradictory meanings; their essential and distinguishing characteristics have been glossed over. The substantive purpose of this chapter is to identify and explain the type of security multilateralism represented by the Shanghai Co-operation Organization (SCO), ASEAN, NATO, and the EU. In the conclusion, a final and critical question is addressed: Why do states participate in seemingly suboptimal forms of security multilateralism even though superior forms exist?

The post-Westphalian hypothesis

There has been a sustained debate about the importance of domestic constitutional orders as the determinant of international order. Phillip Bobbitt (2002) linked the historical evolution of the European state system to changes in domestic constitutional form. The democratic peace hypothesis, which ignited one of the most heated post-Cold War debates, holds that democratic constitutional orders present the best guarantee of peace and stability (Owen 1994; Lipson 2003). Stochastic analyses generally support the hypothesis, but the data supporting the hypothesis are largely drawn from the European and Anglophone worlds (Oneal and Russett 1997: 3; Ward and Gleditsch 1998).[1] This particular use of the European state system as the primary benchmark for testing theories of international politics has become hazardous, particularly when the hypothesis is supported by a circumscribed empirical base and precludes from consideration the more fundamental change that is taking place – the rise of the post-Westphalian state. The post-Westphalian state better explains the emergence of a security community than does reliance upon a single form of constitutional order, liberal democracy. Conversely, the persistence of the Westphalian state elsewhere better explains the continuing force of anarchy and the continued reliance on "primitive" forms of security governance, regardless of constitutional form.

The post-Westphalian hypothesis challenges the assumption that states are homogeneous actors. Rather states fall along a continuum bounded by the Westphalian and post-Westphalian forms: each form seeks alternative forms of security and practices alternative forms of statecraft – instrumentally and substantively. Post-Westphalian states are more vulnerable to the influence of non-state actors – malevolent, benevolent, or benign – in international politics. Non-state actors fill or exploit the gaps left by the (in)voluntary loss or evaporation of sovereignty attending the transformation of the state, while others are purposeful repositories for sovereignty ceded, lent, pooled or forfeited. The changing nature of the security agenda, particularly its functional expansion and the changing agency of threat, necessitates a shift from coercive to persuasive security strategies (Kirchner and Sperling 2007).

Westphalian sovereignty forms a significant barrier to security co-operation – even in the transatlantic area. John Herz (1957) identified territoriality as the key characteristic of the Westphalian state and characterized it as the "hard shell" protecting states and societies from the external environment. Territoriality is increasingly irrelevant, particularly in Europe. States no longer enjoy the "wall of defensibility" that leaves them relatively immune to external penetration. The changed salience and meaning of territoriality has not only expanded the number and type of security threat, but shifted attention from the "hard" to the "soft" manifestations of power. Westphalian states are preoccupied with protecting autonomy and independence, retaining a gatekeeping role, and avoiding external interference in domestic constitutional arrangements. Post-Westphalian states, while not indifferent to territorial integrity, have largely abandoned their gate-keeper role owing to the interdependency of openness, welfare maximization, and democratic political principles. Autonomy and independence have been devalued as sovereign imperatives; sovereign prerogatives have been subordinated to the demands of the welfare state and the preferences of individual agents.

The success of the European project in the post-war period reinforced Europe's material, ideational, and cultural interconnectedness (March and Olsen 1998: 944–7). Geography, technological innovations, the convergence around the norms of political and economic openness, and a rising dynamic density have progressively stripped away the prerogatives of sovereignty and eliminated the autonomy once afforded powerful states by exclusive territorial jurisdiction. The ease with which domestic disturbances are transmitted across national boundaries, and the difficulty of deflecting those disturbances, underline the strength and vulnerability of the post-Westphalian state: the ever expanding spectrum of interaction provides greater levels of collective welfare than would otherwise be possible, yet the very transmission belts facilitating those welfare gains serve as diffusion mechanisms hindering the state's ability to inoculate itself against exogenous shocks or malevolent actors. Those actors, in turn, are largely immune to sovereign jurisdiction as well as strategies of dissuasion, defense, and deterrence. Consequently, broad and collective milieu goals have been substituted for particularistic, national security goals, conventionally conceived. Perforated sovereignty has rendered post-Westphalian states incapable of meeting their national security requirements alone.

Stephen Krasner (1999) has challenged the post-Westphalian hypothesis, referring famously to sovereignty as organized hypocrisy. While his deconstruction of sovereignty into its constituent components is welcomed, his rebuke of the hypothesis is contingent on the validity of three claims: "the principles of territoriality and autonomy" had never been sacrosanct in practice (Krasner 1995–6: 123); states have never been able "to regulate perfectly transborder flows"; and the EU (and presumably the states constituting it) is dismissed as a "neutral mutation" without apparent consequence for the international system (Krasner 2001: 234, 244). These claims cannot withstand superficial scrutiny: first, the violation of the principles of territoriality and autonomy is distinct from the voluntary acceptance of mutual governance and loss of autonomy attending it; second, the question is not whether states have been able to control transborder flows, but the nature and volume of those flows as well as the barriers to controlling them effectively; and finally, dismissing the EU as a "neutral mutant" represents at a minimum the suppression of the inconvenient.

Two "kinds" of states populate the contemporary international system, an assumption that may pose a barrier to a unified system-level of theory (Powell 1991: 1305). The existence of two distinct categories of state with different *kinds* of preference structures and vulnerabilities lacks theoretical elegance, but many states do approximate the post-Westphalian ideal-type. Introducing the post-Westphalian state better comports with the empirical world. It better explains the emergence and consolidation of a security community in Europe as well as the Westphalian embrace of less effective forms of security multilateralism elsewhere.

A model of security multilateralism

Security multilateralism is either nominal or qualitative. Nominal multilateralism exists where states merely co-ordinate national policies, while qualitative multilateralism also requires that appropriate conduct be defined "without regard to the particularistic interests of the parties or the strategic exigencies that may exist" (Ruggie 1992: 565, 571). Both forms require that security be indivisible and its provision nonexcludable, that the participants have a reasonable expectation of diffuse reciprocity, and that states "sacrifice significant levels of flexibility in decision-making" (Martin, L.L. 1992: 786). These four criteria are too restrictive (e.g., security interests need only be overlapping) and are not met in equal measure across the broad spectrum of multilateral arrangements. While some claim that most forms of security multilateralism constitute gradations of collective security (Kupchan and Kupchan 1995), these forms may nonetheless be differentiated with respect to the security referent, the regulator of conflict, the normative framework, and the interaction context. The model developed below links specific constellations of state attributes and system characteristics to a range of security multilateralism outcomes.[2]

State attributes

Four state attributes – identity, interests, sovereign control, and use of force – demarcate the range of viable security arrangements in which any given state will participate. These attributes do not manifest themselves in fixed relationships or individually exert an unvarying explanatory power, although the range of values assessed for any one attribute is likely to set the boundary conditions for the others (see Table 5.1).

Identity has emerged as the central causal variable for those seeking to explain the emergence and persistence of the European and transatlantic security communities and by inference the persistence of more primitive forms of multilateralism elsewhere in the world (Wendt 1994; Jepperson, Wendt, and Katzenstein 1996; Finnemore and Sikkink 1998; Checkel 1998). Such analysts emphasize the role of identity in interest formation and claim that collective identities create shared interests, normatively disciplined patterns of behavior, and ultimately the stable expectation of non-violent conflict resolution (Adler and Barnett 1998b). State identities range from the mutual recognition that states, as states, have the sovereign right of self-preservation to a fused identity where interstate differentiation is literally nonexistent. Moreover, identities may be positive or negative: the former indicates an

Table 5.1 State attributes

	Westphalian state	Post-Westphalian state
Identity	National and egotist	Denationalized and other-regarding
Force	Instrument of first resort; use is a function of a utilitarian, rather than normative, calculus	Renunciation as policy instrument; non-use a function of normative rather than utilitarian calculus
Sovereign Control	State functions as effective gate-keeper between internal and external flows; disinclination to surrender sovereignty to individual agents domestically or to international institutions	There is a *de facto* erasure of sovereign boundaries and governments are unable to act as effective gate-keepers between internal and external flows; there exists a sanctioned loss of sovereign control to individual economic agents and a willingness to transfer sovereignty to international institutions
Interest Calculus	Interests are calculated on a narrow, self-regarding set of criteria orientated towards the goals of territorial integrity and power maximization	Interests are constituted by a broad, other-regarding set of criteria orientated towards the milieu goals of economic and political stability

underlying source of affinity that reinforces co-operation along a broad spectrum of policy issues; the latter indicates that rivalry is set aside in the presence of a common, but epiphenomenal threat.

The calculation of interest is best formulated as a question: do states calculate their security interests with respect to a narrow, self-regarding frame of reference or to a broad, collective, other-regarding frame of reference? Alliance theorists consider interests to be material, enduring, and particularistic (Osgood 1953; Wolfers 1962; Walt 1987); yet, where states do share a broadly collective identity or act in accordance with a set of intrinsically valued norms, the material interest is intermediated by the ideational (Risse-Kappen 1996). The focus of security co-operation, much like the concept of security itself, has been unduly restricted to considerations of defense and deterrence. The expanded security agenda and the rise of non-state actors as antagonists have made the calculation of interest less parochial for all states, but the subordination of the national interest to the cosmopolitan is not everywhere evident. Where national interests remain solely self-regarding, so too do the more primitive forms of security multilateralism.

Sovereign control identifies a government's *de facto* capability and desire to control transborder flows of people, ideas, and commerce. The loss of sovereign control may be evaluated positively or negatively. In open societies and economies, the loss of sovereign control is positive insofar as it provides the channels whereby domestic welfare is maximized and the rationale for the external co-operation necessary to sustain it (Hanrieder 1978). This patterned behavior establishes the necessary preconditions for advanced forms of security co-operation. In closed societies or failing states, the retention of sovereign control or efforts to reclaim it erect a considerable barrier to more advanced forms of security multilateralism: a failing state can only offer implausible assurances of compliance, while the opacity of closed societies makes potential security partners uncertain whether the costs of entering into an arrangement are likely to exceed the benefits of doing so.

A reliance on force is central to realist understandings of foreign policy (Waltz 1978; Mearsheimer 2001). The use of force does not depend solely upon the external context of action or level of threat, but also upon the societal consensus on when force should be used and in what measure. Historical cases exist where a domestic consensus against the use of force has trumped the sovereign imperative of national survival,[3] while other states appear to be predisposed to rely reflexively upon it.[4] Moreover, even where force is recognized as a legitimate instrument of statecraft, its imputed utility or the normative aversion to its use varies across states. Independent of the external context, the domestic consensus delimits the forms of security arrangement in which a state will participate.

System properties

If an international (sub)system is minimally independent of its parts, then system properties play an important role in establishing the possible range of viable security governance outcomes for any group of states. Four system properties constrain or enable the likely forms of security multilateralism: the role of power in ordering relations between states, the attachment to the sovereignty principle, the breadth and depth of shared norms, and the legitimacy of war (see Table 5.2).

Power as a system determinant has the longest pedigree in the study of international relations (Meinecke 1929; Carr 1938; Dehio 1948; Gilpin 1981; Mearsheimer 2001). Power is both subjective (is a peer friend or foe?) and material (where do states fall along the hierarchy of power?). The intersection of the subjective understanding of power and its material distribution affects the pattern of interaction between members of the group and those outside it, as well as the calculation of interest with respect to the source of threat and how it should be met.

The strength of the sovereignty principle indicates the (un)willingness of states to abnegate sovereign prerogatives where national interests collide with group interests, to cede sovereignty to international or supranational institutions, or to accept that group norms constrain states, particularly when those norms collide with particularistic national interests. Where the sovereignty principle is undiluted, states are unlikely to enter into any form of security multilateralism beyond contingent and temporary alliances; where the sovereignty principle is relaxed, an enabling condition for advanced forms of institutionalized security multilateralism arises.

Table 5.2 System properties

	Westphalian system	Post-Westphalian system
Power	Numeraire of interaction; defined in terms of military and economic capabilities; decisive arbiter of conflicts	Unimportant in negotiations between individual members of the system; interactions based on prearranged rules independent of power distribution and adheres to democratic governance
Sovereign recognition	Sovereignty principle uncontested	Sovereignty principle abrogated
Normative framework	Shallow, narrow and contingent	Broad, deep and binding
War	Legitimate form of conflict resolution; states prepare for war as the final arbiter of conflict; constraint on recourse to war is determined by a state's utility calculation	Illegitimate form of conflict resolution; expectation that states will enter into rule-governed negotiations to resolve conflicts; rejection of force is normative rather than instrumental

Normative frameworks do shape state interests, particularly in late- or post-Westphalian states. Although the material structure of power is observer-independent, power and its elements lack exclusively intrinsic (observer-independent) properties (Searle 1999: 37–8). States operate in normative and historical contexts that generate proscriptive and prescriptive norms. These norms may be comprehensive or rudimentary. In primitive forms of security multilateralism, where the normative framework is rudimentary, norms – if they exist at all – are at best likely to be shallow and narrow with a contingent validity for the participants; where the normative framework is deep and broad, norms are more likely to be substantively valued and intrinsically valid.

War is the one constant in interstate relations. The utility of war was only seriously questioned after the industrial slaughter of the Great War, but even then it did not prevent the European powers from going to war twenty years later or virtually any other state going to war after 1945. War remains an available and relied upon instrument of statecraft, owing largely to the self-help imperative of an anarchical state system. Yet, the probability of war between specific dyads or sets of states ranges from zero to a near certainty. Where the probability of war is low – whether it reflects a normative aversion or the utilitarian calculation that war doesn't pay – the greater is the likelihood that an advanced (and institutionalized) form of security multilateralism will emerge. Where those conditions are lacking, security multilateralism will be contingent and institutionally primitive or nonexistent.

Security multilateralism

Any form of security multilateralism has four components: the referent; the regulator; the normative framework; and the interaction context. The security referent identifies the target of the security arrangement. The system regulator identifies the range of mechanisms relied upon to resolve conflicts. The normative component assesses the function norms play in the calculation of states' interests and behavior. The interaction context, the final component, identifies the level of intramural amity and enmity as well as the intensity of the security dilemma. Each component is the product of specific dyads of state attributes and system properties.

The security referent may be directed inwardly towards the contracting states (as in a collective security system) or outwardly towards an "other" (as in an alliance) or the regional milieu (as in a co-operative security). The referent emerges from the interaction of identity and power: as identity moves from the egotist to other-regarding, the more likely are states to enter into security arrangements focusing on the within-group dynamic; as the role of power wanes in the security system, the transformation of identity will accelerate and reinforce the within-group orientation. Where the role of power dominates interstate relations, even among states sharing a common identity, security arrangements will be outwardly directed towards an "other" or the regional milieu.

The purpose of security multilateralism is the regulation of conflict. Regulatory mechanisms range from the rule of war to the rule of law. The regulator is the product of the system-wide legitimacy of war and the propensity of states to rely upon force. As the utility or legitimacy of war or force declines, states will seek alternative mechanisms for conflict regulation. The opportunities and rationale for constructing institutionalized conflict mechanisms are retarded where national identities and the sovereignty principle are undisturbed; when identities coalesce or merge, then sovereign recognition becomes less important, providing the space for constructing effective institutional mechanisms for conflict resolution.

The mere existence of international norms does not reveal whether those norms are intrinsic or extrinsic to state calculations or how binding those norms are likely to be. Those two aspects of a normative framework are determined by the relevance of system-level norms to the national security calculus, in conjunction with the strength of the sovereignty principle and the use of force. If sovereignty is jealously guarded, particularly with regard to the associated principles of non-interference and autonomy, then states retain the presumptive right to determine domestic behavioral norms and interests, while a reliance upon force as an instrument of statecraft limits the cases where states will act in accordance with the "logic of appropriateness" associated with norm derived behaviors (Hyde-Price 2000; Bulmer, Jeffery and Paterson 2000). Where system-level norms govern within-group interactions, the sovereignty principle is necessarily discounted and a reliance on force for the regulation of within-group conflicts is delegitimized. When those conditions are met, system-level norms become intrinsic to the calculation of interest, and produce outcomes at a variance with material interests or the structure of power. When they are not met, narrow national interests will win out over system norms when they collide.

The interaction context refers to the level of amity and enmity in the system and the intensity of the security dilemma. Where states have lost sovereign control and discounted sovereign prerogatives, the states will have developed a positive affect for one another owing to the positive externalities associated with openness. Amity is reinforced when the loss of sovereignty initiates the pooling or ceding of sovereign prerogatives to international or regional institutions. The security dilemma will be most acute where war remains a viable option, normatively and instrumentally, and states retain an "egotist" national interest. Where states share a common set of interests (or identity) and war becomes normatively proscribed, the security dilemma will dissipate and create an enabling condition for the advanced forms of security multilateralism; where those conditions do not hold, the security dilemma is exacerbated.

Alternative forms of security multilateralism

A primitive state of nature and an international civil society provide the end points of a continuum along which seven general forms of security multi-lateralism fall: co-operative security, alliances, concerts, collective defense, collective security, and two types of security community – the civilianized and fused. Two categories of security governance, the state of nature and an international civil society, are easily disposed of since neither exists nor is likely to exist.[5] The state of nature and international civil society nonetheless serve as useful benchmarks against which the different forms of security

Table 5.3 Constituent elements of security multilateralism

	Identifies	*Range of values*
Security referent	Target of security concern	Inwardly or outwardly directed (adversarial "other" or regional milieu)
Regulator	Mechanism for conflict resolution	Warfare to binding arbitration within well-defined institutional frameworks
Function of norms	Role of norms in defining national or group interests	Instrumental and extrinsic (marginal impact on state behavior or interest formation) to substantive and intrinsic to the definition of interest (constitutes state interests and governs behavior)
Interaction context	Intensity of the security dilemma; the level of amity and enmity	Enmity and intense security dilemma to amity and the absence of a security dilemma

multilateralism may be measured. In a state of nature, the security referent is any and all other states, war regulates conflict, norms are absent, and states face unremitting enmity and an acute security dilemma. In an international civil society, the security referent is inwardly directed towards the requirements of social stability and economic welfare, conflict is regulated by binding law, compulsory adjudication and centralized enforcement, norms are institutionalized as a comprehensive legal code, and the interaction context is one of social solidarity where the security dilemma is bereft of its conceptual purchase (see Table 5.4).

A co-operative security arrangement presents the most rudimentary form of security multilateralism. This form is relatively novel: co-operative security arrangements usually lack specific obligations to undertake or lend military aid in the event of aggression, primarily reference within group or milieu security threats, and do not entail a significant loss of independent decision-making. States enter into co-operative security arrangements owing to structural interdependencies with security implications. This kind of multilateralism targets threats that originate within the group rather than threats emanating from outside it (Adler and Barnett 1998: 50, 56). Norms are limited in scope and revolve around the protection of sovereign prerogatives. Security co-operation remains contingent on the persistence of interdependencies, but it does have a salutary effect on the interaction context: enmity and distrust are necessarily suppressed. Moreover, the security dilemma undergoes a contingent inversion: the enhancement of one state's security enhances the security of the others.

A system of impermanent alliances or the balancing of power emerges where, as Palmerston noted, states have permanent interests, rather than permanent allies or adversaries. Alliances, as either formal or informal institutions, contingently bind together two or more sovereign states to balance, deter, or defeat a common enemy. Alliances rely on deterrence or defense for regulating disequilibria in the international system. In an alliance system, norms possess an instrumental role and lack a substantive or intrinsic value. The interaction context of an alliance system is outward enmity and a classic security dilemma, but the underlying strategic reason for forming an alliance determines whether there is inward amity (as in NATO) or muted enmity (the Allied powers during the Second World War).

The lines demarcating concerts, collective defense, and collective security arrangements have become unnecessarily blurred (cf: Kupchan and Kupchan 1995; Acharya 1999). Six characteristics define a concert: a set of fixed rules and behavioral norms that only discipline within-group balancing; the sovereignty principle is unmolested, particularly formal equality and non-interference; an (in)formal dispute resolution mechanism exists for brokering intramural conflicts; the contracting states contingently renounce war with one another; the states engage in multilateral consultations on issues of mutual interest; and there is a collective commitment to protect the essential members of the system (Morgan 1993: 335; Mearsheimer 1994–5: 35–6; Soutou 2000: 329–33). The security referent of a concert is inwardly directed,

Table 5.4 Characteristics of the varieties of security governance

	Security referent	Regulator	Function of norms	Context of interaction
State of nature	Other states in system	War	None	Unrelenting enmity; intense security dilemma
Co-operative security	Generally within group	Negotiation with rudimentary institutional framework; recourse to war remains an option	Neither deep nor binding; provides a limited basis for co-operation	Security dilemma abated; distrust persists; enmity suppressed
Impermanent alliances	Great power "other"	War and balancing of power	Limited to rules of war	Neither a permanent state of amity nor enmity towards any state; classic security dilemma
Concert	Great powers	Multilateral consultation, managed balance of power; war proscribed but viable	Norms support limited co-operation; defend the status quo and existing domestic regimes; and support the qualified renunciation of war	Conditional amity; mitigated security dilemma
Collective defense	Identifiable enemy outside the group	Balancing, deterrence, defense, or war	Alliance norms are substantive and intrinsic to interests along a narrow range of issues	Amity within group; enmity without; security dilemma intact
Collective security	Within group	Collective, compulsory adjudication of conflicts; collective enforcement when group norms violated	Norms replace sovereign prerogatives in issues of war and peace. Renunciation of war is intrinsically and substantively valued	Amity; security dilemma resolved

(*Continued overleaf*)

Table 5.4 Continued

	Security referent	Regulator	Function of norms	Context of interaction
Civilianized security community	Within group	International law, institutionalized conflict resolution mechanisms	Norms replace sovereign prerogatives across a wide range of issues; constitute state interests; are substantively and intrinsically valued	Deep amity derived from a positive or collective identity; a common set of norms have been internalized; security dilemma atrophied
Fused security community	Within group	International law, institutional conflict resolution mechanisms	Same as in civilianized security community	Deep amity derived from a single identity and total absence of differentiation between within-group members; security dilemma not a relevant conceptual category
Civilian international system	Within group	Civil contract law in effect; compulsory adjudication; voluntary compliance or effective enforcement	Sovereignty principle no longer defines interactions within the group; normative framework substantive and intrinsic	Amity derived from an inviolable social contract among the group members

conflict resolution is (in)formally institutionalized although the option of war remains, a limited number of substantive norms creates a sense of community and regulates how states interact, and the interaction context is one of contingent amity and a muted security dilemma.

Since a collective defense arrangement only emerges when one group of states identifies another state or group of states as a common threat, the security referent is outwardly directed. Within-group conflicts are mediated by institutionalized procedures of dispute management and decision-making, while deterrence and defense mediate conflicts with the adversary. A binding normative framework is required to offset the required abnegation of sovereignty: military forces are likely to be aggregated at some level, defense acquisition and expenditures become a matter of common concern, and strategy is likely to serve the collective rather than the particularistic interests of its members. Yet, each state retains the right to decide whether an act of aggression has occurred and whether it constitutes a threat. Moreover, when an act of aggression does occur, the member states have the option, rather than the obligation, to intervene on behalf of their ally (Wolfers 1962: 182–3; Kelsen 1948: 793–4). A collective defense arrangement emerges in the context of internal amity and external enmity; the security dilemma gives the arrangement its *raison d'être*.

Collective security differs fundamentally from collective defense. In a collective security arrangement, the security referent is inwardly directed at a contracting state that initiates an act of aggression. Any party to a collective security arrangement is contractually and normatively obligated to assist any other contracting state that is the victim of aggression and to punish the aggressor. A collective security arrangement makes provision for the compulsory adjudication of within-group conflicts. Finally, in a collective security system, the use of force – except in cases warranting immediate self-help measures – must be wielded and legitimized by a quasi-sovereign entity (Kelsen: 1948: 784–90; Wolfers 1962: 182–6). States, in effect, are required to abnegate a core element of sovereignty; viz, the right to decide the where, when, and why of war. This form of security multilateralism only exists where there is a strong prohibitionary norm against war and an interaction context characterized by amity and a moribund security dilemma.

A civilianized security community is the most advanced form of security multilateralism that has yet emerged in the international system.[6] A civilianized security community exists where states have replaced "the military enforcement of rules (politics based on power) with the internalization of socially accepted norms (politics based on legitimacy)" (Harnisch and Maull 2001: 4). Five conditions must be met: there are normative constraints on the use of force and an unwillingness to rely on it for resolving conflicts; international law serves as the basis for conflict resolution; formal institutional mechanisms must exist to adjudicate within-group conflict; decision-making is participatory; and sovereignty plays an instrumental rather than substantive role in the calculation of interest (Harnisch and Maull 2001; Eberwein

1995: 350–2). The security referent is predominantly within the group, conflict is regulated by rule of law, the normative framework is binding and codified, and an abiding amity complements the absence of a security dilemma.

A fused security community differs from a civilianized security community in one critical respect – the nature of the identity shared between the members. "Fused" replaces "civilianized" as a modifier where states retain *de jure* sovereignty and a nominal notion of nationality, but not where there is a within-group "other" or the persistence of negative identities. A "fused" security community would have two primary characteristics: first, a member state would not differentiate between a threat to the group and a threat to itself; second, members would have a single set of security interests derived from an identical set of norms, values and interests.

Four systems of security multilateralism: SCO, ASEAN, NATO and the EU

What kind of security multilateralism best describes the SCO, ASEAN, NATO and the EU? The answer to that question entails a two-step process: the state attributes and system properties underpinning each system must first be identified and then the pattern of interaction between these variables, which define the elements of a security system, traced. Once those steps are completed, the SCO, ASEAN, NATO and EU can be classified as specific forms of security multilateralism consistent with the criteria summarized in Table 5.4.

State attributes: central Asia, southeast Asia, and Euro-Atlantic

The member states of the SCO and ASEAN share the attributes of Westphalian states, while the member states of NATO and the EU approximate the attributes of late- or post-Westphalian states. The SCO member states – China, the Russian Federation, Kazakhstan, Kyrgyzstan, Tajikistan, and Uzbekistan – deviate least from the Westphalian ideal-type. Of those states, only China and Russia exercise something other than nominal sovereign control over borders and territory. The majority of the ASEAN states – Brunei, Cambodia, Indonesia, Laos, Malaysia, Myanmar, the Philippines, Singapore, Thailand, and Vietnam – exercise *de facto* control over national territory. NATO states, with the exceptions of Turkey and the new eastern European members, can be described as late- or post-Westphalian. The EU, prior to its eastern enlargement, consisted almost entirely of post-Westphalian states; arguably, conformity with the *acquis communautaire* will accelerate the evolution of the new members towards the post-Westphalian form (see Table 5.5).

Table 5.5 State attributes found in central Asia, southeast Asia, the Atlantic and Europe

	Identity	Interests	Sovereign control	Force
Central Asia	National	National with some overlap	No juridical loss, although some territory sovereign-free	Yes, particularly within actors' own territory
Southeast Asia	National, modified by the notion of an "ASEAN Way"	National with overlapping interests	Largely retained in all areas	Yes, but effort to avoid intramural conflicts
Atlantic	National, but underpinned by a weak notion of community	Common, over-lapping and broad	Largely retained in security affairs, but largely lost in areas related to the economy	Not within area, but out of area
Europe	Community	Joint and very broad	Largely lost	No; reliance upon persuasion and compromise

Central Asia

The SCO states retain a national identity without the underlay of either a regional or civilizational identity. The Chinese and Russian identities are national, based on distinct cultures, civilizations, languages and histories; at the best of times they only share an opposition to an "other" in the form of the United States or Japan. The other four SCO states, ruled by autocratic governments deriving their legitimacy from clan loyalties, are all former republics of the Soviet Union and have weak national identities (Trofimov 2003: 46). Unlike NATO or the EU, there is no mythologized common culture or civilization that serves as an ideational epoxy providing a rationale for co-operation. Instead, the SCO states explicitly recognize that they represent "different civilizations and different cultural traditions" (Shanghai Co-operation Organization 2001a; Perlo-Freeman and Ståhlenheim 2003: 16). This cultural barrier to the formation of regional identity is reinforced by anemic interaction densities: only 2.4 per cent of their total exports, for example, are intramural (IMF 2004, author's own calculations).

The SCO emerged from the "Shanghai Process", the purpose of which was to settle pre-existing Sino-Soviet border conflicts that involved Tajikistan, Kazakhstan, and Kyrgyzstan after the dissolution of the Soviet Union in 1992. The Sino-Soviet border had been heavily militarized; confidence-building measures taken in 1990, 1996 and 1997 led to the renunciation of Chinese claims against Russia (and its successor states) and produced agreements on the mutual reduction of armed forces (Fravel 2005: 55ff). Compared to the not-so-distant past, force has become less an issue between states: the Sino-Russian Treaty of Friendship and Co-operation in July 2001, for example, renounced "the use or threat of the use of force" in their mutual relations. Force does remain an issue within states, particularly the combating of Muslim Uighur and other ethnic separatists. Defense expenditures as a percentage of GDP are low, but the increases between 1995 and 2004 have been staggering.[7] Military co-operation has been limited: the first joint SCO exercise, which did not include every member, occurred on Chinese and Kazakh territory in August 2003, Russian troops are stationed along the Tajik-Afghan border, and the four Central Asian republics are members of the Russian-led Collective Security Treaty Rapid Reaction Force (Carlson 2003). This co-operation is leavened by distrust: Uzbekistan, for example, built new military bases along its border with Russia and has conducted 22 military exercises with the United States.

All six SCO members have long, porous, and ineffectively policed borders. Domestic order is threatened by civil conflict between competing, non-integrated ethnic groups with antagonistic confessions. Governments do not exercise control over ill-defined and "soft frontiers" (Bailes 2003: 2). Despite the inability to exert full sovereign control over borders and territory, these states have not chosen to pool their sovereign prerogatives in formal multilateral institutions – the SCO has only a small secretariat in Beijing and a recently established regional anti-terrorism center in Tashkent.

State attributes and system properties 117

Interests remain nationally rather than collectively defined. National calculations of interest shape Sino-Russian bilateral co-operation as well as their support for the SCO. Both Russia and China desire the withdrawal of American troops stationed in central Asia, a region that is arguably a natural sphere of influence for either. The SCO states share an overlapping interest in preserving their own territorial integrity and regime stability, both of which are threatened by militant Islam and ethnic rivalries. The Islamic Movement of Uzbekistan, for example, is active in Kyrgyzstan and Tajikistan, and supports Uighur separatists in China's Xinjiang province (Yom 2002; Dongfeng 2004). The 2001 SCO Charter and the 2004 Tashkent Declaration commit each member to "assign priority to regional security" and seek the "joint definitions of interests . . . on the basis of respect of their individuality and sovereign rights," respectively. Those interests are defined as threats to internal security posed by the "three forces" of terrorism, separatism, and extremism. Yet, as the Astana Summit declaration made clear, the member states retained the right to determine when and how those forces represent a *national* security threat (Guang 2005).

Southeast Asia

Identity formation within ASEAN was initially "negative" insofar as it rested upon a shared "anti-communism" without a reinforcing "positive" identity derived from a common culture or constitutional form (Acharya 1991: 175; Gallant and Stubbs 1997: 216). These states are culturally, religiously and ethnically heterogeneous, their economies fall along the entire development spectrum, their relations are marked by telling asymmetries of power and influence, and they have social compacts that strike different balances between social stability and individual liberty.[8] Regional heterogeneity is perhaps best captured by religious confessions anchored in different civilizations – European Roman Catholicism in the Philippines, Arabic Islam in Indonesia, and indigenous Buddhism in Indochina. Diverse European imperialisms in the region – the British in Malaysia and Burma, the French in Indochina, the Dutch in the East Indies, the Americans in the Philippines – left behind different legacies: weak or nonexistent political infrastructures, poorly drawn borders that created ethnic and linguistic conflicts where none had previously existed, and economies servicing imperial rather than local requirements. Collective identity formation is also impeded by historical animosities preceding the age of European imperialism and gross disparities in economic wealth – GDP per capita ranges from a low of $104 in Myanmar to a high of $20,515 in Singapore. The modestly interdependent ASEAN economies – only 23 per cent of total exports are intramural (ASEAN 2003b: 74, table V.12) – and their mutual vulnerability to financial panics provides some foundation for collective identity formation, positive and negative.[9] The ASEAN community is imagined in Benedict Anderson's (1991) sense that governing elites purposively created a sense of community based on appeals to the "ASEAN way". It is also imagined in the narrower sense that it doesn't exist because the raw materials for community are absent (Hemmer and Katzenstein 2002: 599).

The ASEAN states exercise greater control over their territory and borders than do the SCO states, but nonetheless face a transborder security complex arising from borders made porous by geography and regional economic interdependencies (Dosch 2003: 490). ASEAN governments can and do control the flow of individuals, goods and even ideas across national borders, unencumbered as they are by the legal inhibitions on individual liberty found in Western democracies.

Even though the ASEAN states have encouraged economic interdependence as a strategy of growth and regional autonomy, they cling to relatively narrow definitions of self-interest even at the expense of protecting regional autonomy (Khoo 2004; Narine 1998). Some point to the Bali II Concord declaration on comprehensive security as evidence that a common culture and identity are emerging in the region (Dosch 2003: 485). The intervention in East Timor belies that claim. Each ASEAN state participating in the peacekeeping mission did so for narrow national purposes, rather than for the community interest. Some participated out of the fear that a successful revolt in East Timor would stoke their own separatist movements and others wanted to rein in Thailand's eagerness to stake a leadership claim within ASEAN. The ASEAN states did share an immediate interest in thwarting the Australian effort to lead the expedition and claim a regional leadership role, an interest not inconsistent with the longer-term concern with protecting against Chinese or American encroachments on regional autonomy (Nabers 2003: 127).

One hallmark of the "ASEAN way" is the rejection of force (Khoo 2004; Ba 2005). That normative injunction, however, has not banished force from the diplomatic toolbox. Disputes have been militarized, including but not limited to the 1999 Philippines–Malaysia dispute over reefs in the South China Sea and the 2001 border clashes between Thailand and Myanmar. While the militarized incidents in the region have been few in number and can be plausibly be described as "minor military incidents" (Haacke 2003), it also remains the case that ASEAN defense expenditures have risen from $11.7 bn in 1994 to $28.8 bn in 2002, an increase of 246 per cent. Even though regional specialists insist that those expenditures do not constitute an arms race (Simon 1996: 338; Narine 1998: 203), it would not be unreasonable to infer that military power remains a highly valued commodity.

Euro-Atlantic

Over the course of the post-war period, positive identity formation between the states of North America and Europe, as well as within Europe itself, was facilitated by democratic governments and a shared civilization, both of which were reinforced by the legitimizing rhetoric of NATO and the EU. The common identity shared within the Atlantic was initially "negative" insofar as the glue holding NATO together was the common Soviet military threat and the fear that national communist political parties would enjoy success at the polls in Western Europe. Europe's common identity was also initially negative; it consisted not only of the external threat posed by the Soviet Union and internal threat posed by national communist parties, but also a fear of a renascent Germany. While the Europeans and Americans have shared a commitment to liberal democracy, elites manufactured a common European and American identity, where arguably only a contingent one exists: the United States has a "culture" while the Europeans have a "civilization"; Americans are ostentatiously religious, while Europeans are generally secular; Americans favor a Darwinian market economy alien to European social democracy; the American identity remains pristinely national, whereas the EU states possess in different measure a muddied identity that is both national and European. These differences have consequences: they partially account for the mutual suspicion and acrimony that creep periodically into European–American relations, particularly on security issues.[10]

The most conspicuous characteristic these states share is the loss of sovereign control. Economic and political interdependence were postwar American and European foreign policy objectives. The European states have ceded control over most aspects of economic management to the EU, individual economic agents, and most recently the European Central Bank (ECB). The real and financial sectors of the EU economies are fully integrated, a process begun in earnest with the Single European Act (1986). The euro has replaced national currencies in the EU (with a few exceptions) and the ECB rather than national central banks sets monetary policy. The integration of the North American and European economies is likewise broad and deep. Trade in manufactured goods is free from high tariffs, capital markets are integrated, the euro and dollar are the world's two major transaction and investment currencies, and prior to 11 September 2001 personal travel faced few administrative hindrances. Philosophical design and technological default reinforce these interdependencies: the privileging of the individual vis-à-vis the state and the ubiquity of cyberspace and other forms of electronic communication constrain further the state's inability to monitor or control individual actions.

The interest calculus reveals the largest divergence within the Euro-Atlantic region. The European states have opted to create or at least strive for a common foreign and security policy, a European security and defense policy, and an entire range of common policies along their periphery and beyond. The United States retains an almost exclusively national calculus for arriving at its definition of interest, a tendency evident during the Clinton administration and a hallmark of the Bush administration (Carter and Perry 1999; Carter 1999–2000; US President's Office 2002, 2006). The current administration's rhetoric and definition of interest have slipped into the solipsism that a threat only exists if it threatens America. Europeans, however, have largely denationalized the definition of interest within specific spheres of activity, particularly the promotion of democracy and market economies in their "neighborhood". Traditional security concerns remain national at some fundamental level, but even here the EU's solidarity principle represents an important step towards replacing discrete national interests with a single European interest (European Union Council 2004).

The transatlantic area is free from the intramural use of force. European defense expenditures have declined markedly since the end of the Cold War.[11] Only the United Kingdom and France actively seek a power projection capability; the other EU states are content to rely on "civilian" instruments of statecraft, which in their view are not only normatively preferable, but are also the more effective means for ameliorating the security threats Europe faces. American defense expenditures (in constant dollars) declined over much of the 1990s, but rose from $290.48 bn in 1999 to $417.36 bn prior to the invasion of Iraq. As important, American expenditures on the non-military requirements of security have not been negligible, notably the billions spent on the co-operative threat-reduction program. It remains true that the security challenges facing Europe generally resist military solution, while the global challenges facing the United States are not always militarized out of choice, but sometimes of necessity.

System characteristics: central Asia, southeast Asia, and Euro-Atlantic

Muted great power competition and interaction overshadows the central and southeast Asian subsystems. This singular characteristic constitutes a high barrier to more advanced and institutionalized forms of security multilateralism. As compared to central Asia, southeast Asia presents a more favorable climate for advanced forms of security multilateralism given the moderate level of economic integration, a common desire to protect regional autonomy, and the American security umbrella providing the necessary reassurance for broadened multilateral commitments. The Euro-Atlantic region is free from intraregional great power competition, although outside the transatlantic area competition between Europe and the United States occasionally flares into open conflict. Those disputes, however, have not yet torn the underlying fabric that supports the advanced forms of security multilateralism found in the transatlantic area (see Table 5.6).

Central Asia

Power relationships dominate the dynamic of the central Asian subsystem: China and Russia both seek regional dominance and both are wary of American troops stationed in Uzbekistan, Kyrgyzstan, and Tajikistan; the Indian and Pakistani acquisition of nuclear weapons has not only made more acute the regional security dilemma facing China and Russia, but threatens

Table 5.6 Regional system properties of central Asia, southeast Asia, the Atlantic and Europe

	Power	Sovereign recognition	Normative framework	War
Central Asia	Coin of realm	Retained; central principle of interaction; no *de jure* abnegation	Narrow range of norms that lack binding character	Yes
Southeast Asia	Continues to play a role	Retained; central principle of interaction	Broad range of proscriptive and prescriptive norms that is highly developed in economic affairs and underdeveloped in security affairs	Possible
Atlantic	Residual role	Compromised and shared within NATO integrated military structure	Very deep in defense, but on a narrow range of issues and dependent upon voluntary compliance	No
EU	No role	Pooled; compromised	Very deep, broad, binding; adjudication of conflicts with expectation of voluntary compliance	No

the nuclear-free status of the central Asian republics; and the United States, China and Japan seek control over or assured access to central Asian energy resources (Yom 2002; Guang 2005: 506; Dongfeng 2004: 13; Choo 2003).

The protection of sovereign prerogatives, the organizing principle of the SCO, is codified in the Declaration on Creating the Shanghai Co-operation Organization [hereafter the Declaration] (SCO 2001a: para 5), the Charter of the Shanghai Co-operation Organization [hereafter the Charter] (SCO 2001b: Article 1 and 2), and the Tashkent Declaration (SCO 2004). The SCO mutually guarantees the member states' independence, sovereign equality, non-interference in domestic affairs, and recognition of each state's territorial integrity. The preoccupation with preserving *de jure* sovereignty reflects the insecurities of nominally sovereign states (Dawisha and Parrott 1997; Jonson 1998), China's unwillingness to accept any constraints on its freedom of action (Dongfeng 2004: 5), and a mutual desire to avoid outside meddling in internal affairs (SCO 2001b: Article 1). Even where China and Russia have a direct interest in the withdrawal of American troops based in the region, the SCO Astana Declaration in 2005 left the terms and timetable of those withdrawals to bilateral negotiations (Guang 2005: 503).

The normative framework governing intra-SCO interactions is rudimentary, but consistent with the unwillingness of the SCO states to surrender sovereignty to an institution or one another. The Shanghai Communiqué (SCO 2001c) and the Declaration (SCO 2001a: para 5) put forward the basic ground rules for behavior: the non-use of force; the renunciation of unilateral military superiority in "contiguous" areas; non-alignment and rejection of military alliances; and the peaceful resolution of disputes. These behavioral norms do not deviate significantly from the principles underpinning the law of nations in eighteenth-century Europe.

War as a means of conflict resolution remains a normatively and instrumentally sanctioned option. There is an explicit preference to resolve conflicts peacefully, but China has not yet demonstrated any greater willingness to forgo military force possibly leading to war than has the United States when its interests are threatened. Civil wars and separatist movements are endemic to the region (Eriksson and Wallensteen 2004: 132 ff). Although the 4,600-mile Sino-Russian border has been demilitarized, a financially stretched Uzbekistan nonetheless devoted scarce resources to constructing a military base along its common border with Russia. Finally, the SCO Charter lacks a mutual defense or collective security clause; it only provides an obligation to resolve disputes peacefully which in the not-so-distant past were militarized.

Southeast Asia

Considerations of power bind ASEAN states together and lend ASEAN an important part of its *raison d'être*. The region lies at an intersection of the three great Pacific powers – the United States, China, Japan – with divergent interests and objectives in the region (Narine 1998: 211; Acharya 1999: 84). ASEAN increasingly functions as a mechanism for assuring regional autonomy and forestalling great power competition between an already established United States and a presumably aspiring hegemonic China (Dosch 2003: 488). Yet, ASEAN elites recognize that regional autonomy remains dependent upon the United States providing the region with the "oxygen of security" (Segal 1996: 135; cf. Dibb 1995; Leifer 1996; Acharya and Tan 2006). Power relationships also shaped ASEAN: elites purposely designed ASEAN so that it would mitigate the power asymmetry between Indonesia and the others, thereby diminishing the prospects of either an unrestricted arms race or Indonesian dominance.

Sovereign recognition is ASEAN's "main feature" and "highest principle" (Emmerson 2005: 176). The 2003 Bali II Declaration restated ASEAN's two cardinal principles: non-interference in domestic affairs and sovereign equality (ASEAN 2003a). Sovereign equality is manifest in the formal commitment to reach decisions on the basis of consensus. Non-interference places criticism of domestic political arrangements out of bounds and precludes a positive obligation to intervene, even in the case of gross violations of human rights. Thailand, in response to domestic developments in Myanmar, proposed a modification of the non-intervention principle to allow "enhanced interaction" or "flexible engagement". This proposal would have created a principled basis for the intramural monitoring of domestic political developments, but the proposal violated the sovereignty principle, did not gain traction, and was subsequently withdrawn.

The normative framework governing intra-ASEAN relations is shallow, but relatively broad in scope. A set of treaties, conventions and declarations spell out a set of internally consistent regulatory norms, including the 1995 Treaty on the Southeast Asian Nuclear Weapons Free Zone (the Bangkok Treaty), the 1976 Treaty of Amity and Co-operation in Southeast Asia (TAC), and the 2003 Declaration of ASEAN Concord II (Bali Concord II). The TAC, which has served as the touchstone for subsequent ASEAN agreements, codified the renunciation of the threat or use of force, the peaceful settlement of disputes, and non-interference in bilateral disputes between ASEAN members (Emmerson 2005: 176; Haacke 2003: 59). Other governing norms include decision-making by consensus, the rejection of military pacts and European-style multilateral security institutions, and regional nuclear non-proliferation (Ba 2005: 257; Khoo 2004: 40).[12] These normative injunctions are the constituent elements of the so-called "ASEAN way," defined somewhat ambitiously as a "process of identity building which relies upon conventional modern principles of interstate relations as well as traditional and culture-specific modes of socialization and decision-making" (Acharya 2001: 28). The 2003 ASEAN Security Community (ASC) declaration, hailed as a signal departure for ASEAN, failed to expand mutual obligations or deepen the normative framework governing regional security co-operation. The ASC simply expresses the signatories' intention to protect the region's status as a nuclear-free zone and to deepen co-operation in the fight against terrorism. Moreover, the ASC declaration explicitly declared that it was *not* the basis for a military alliance, a defense pact or a joint foreign policy (ASEAN 2003a). Sovereign prerogatives were left unmolested.

A key feature of ASEAN security co-operation is the proscription of war as an instrument of statecraft. Although the last major regional conflict ended in 1998 with the Sino-Vietnamese war, war remains a practical option although normatively proscribed in treaty. That war should remain viable should not come as a surprise, but the absence of war and the low number of militarized conflicts in the region probably should. The absence of war within ASEAN, however, does not exclude the possibility of it erupting in the future; there is little empirical evidence supporting the proposition that the aversion to war is normative rather than instrumental.

Euro-Atlantic

Despite the economic and military power wielded by individual EU states, power asymmetries do not determine outcomes in EU policy debates. While little of significance has happened in the EU without a prior Franco-German agreement, the converse has not been not true: their bargain does not inexorably become Europe's. Institutional arrangements have also muted power asymmetries: the smaller EU states wield influence disproportional to their size owing to the assessment of voting weights; qualified majority voting precludes a unit veto; and the double majority rule has aligned population size with voting strength, which does not always favor the most economically or militarily powerful. In the transatlantic area, the United States acts in accordance with the prerogatives that its power confers upon it. NATO's integrated military command has placed a mild constraint on the American exercise of power, but a significant one on the European. Moreover, there has been – and there is – little that the NATO allies can do if the United States acts unilaterally. Thus, within the transatlantic context two contrary dynamics exist: a growing reliance upon democratic decision-making in the EU tenuously linked to power traditionally measured; and intra-alliance relations still mediated by the sometimes raw exercise of American power.

The three pillars of the EU – the European Communities, the Common Foreign and Security Policy (CFSP), Justice and Home Affairs (JHA) – have progressively encroached on sovereign prerogatives. The two institutional manifestations best illustrating this development are the European Court of Justice (ECJ) and the ECB. The ECJ adjudicates conflicts within the EU, and member states treat those decisions, in principle, as binding.[13] The ECB manages euro-zone monetary policy, regulates aspects of the European financial system, and monitors member-state budgetary policies. The ECB and ECJ are politically unaccountable and possess sovereign prerogatives historically reserved to states. Unlike its European allies, the United States has resisted the sacrifice of significant sovereign prerogatives to international institutions, particularly in the formulation and execution of security policy. The United States is the signatory to any number of international treaties and agreements – and the author of many – but successive administrations have ignored the provisions of international agreements when they have come into conflict with material national interests. Moreover, successive American administrations have acted as if NATO's integrated command functioned primarily to keep America's European allies on a short leash.

Norms in the European political space have become institutionalized as hard law (Abbott et al. 2000: 405; Alter 2000: 492). As the scope and domain of EU law have expanded, the member states are increasingly "pushed toward outcomes other than those predicted by power and the pursuit of national interest" (Ann-Marie Slaughter, quoted in Beyers 1999: 17). Alec Stone Sweet and Thomas Brunell (1998: 65) detect a "vertically integrated legal regime" that is transforming the EU into "a multi-tiered system of governance founded on higher law constitutionalism" (cf. Caldeira and Gibson 1995: 358; Mattli and Slaughter 1995). The institutionalization of norms as hard law is ongoing in Pillar I, although the norms and principles governing EU security policy under the aegis of Pillars II and III are not yet binding (Kirchner and Sperling 2007). In JHA, the EU has made progress in crafting a common strategy towards transborder crime and terrorism. It has, for example, established common minimum maximum penalties for specific categories of crime

State attributes and system properties 125

and a common definition of terrorism, agreed on a common list of terrorist groups, created common standards governing the collection of evidence, and instituted a common European arrest warrant. It would be very difficult to argue that international norms have recently constrained American behavior or defined its interests with regard to security matters – the questionable legality of the Iraq war and the clear violation of the Geneva Convention provisions on the treatment of prisoners of war are only two of the most egregious examples. Norms play very different roles on either side of the Atlantic. Arguably, norms constitute European interests across a broad spectrum of policy issues; norms, albeit central to American rhetoric, are valued instrumentally and remain peripheral to the definition of American interests.

The role of war in the Euro-Atlantic region may be summarily dismissed. Unlike other regions of the world, war plays no role in resolving intramural disputes. Ole Wæver (1998: 104) has correctly characterized the EU as a "non-war community"; there is no conceivable set of circumstances that could serve as a *casus belli* between Europe and the United States.

Forms of security multilateralism: SCO, ASEAN, NATO, and EU

There is considerable debate over the precise form of security multilateralism found in the SCO, ASEAN, NATO and EU. The SCO has been categorized as an alliance balancing the United States in central Asia (Kay 2003; Allison 2004) and as a collective security arrangement (Gleason and Shaihutdinov 2005). ASEAN has been defined as a "thin" (Emmerson 2005) and "thick" security community (Acharya 1991, 1999, 2004; Wanandi 2005), a defense community (Simon 1998), a concert (Kang 2003; Shambaugh 2004/05), and as a co-operative security arrangement (Acharya and Tan 2006). NATO has been categorized as a security community (Risse-Kappen 1996), as a collective defense organization (Osgood 1953), and as a collective security arrangement (Kupchan and Kupchan 1995). The EU has been classified as a security community (Wæver 1998), but many are skeptical that it even plays an important security role (Gordon 1998; Smith, M. 1996). Yet, it is highly unlikely that the SCO, ASEAN, NATO and the EU suffer from the institutional equivalent of a multiple personality disorder; each represents a single, specific form of security multilateralism (see Table 5.7 on page 126).

SCO

The SCO, and the "Shanghai Process" that preceded it, originally arose out of Sino-Soviet efforts to resolve outstanding border disputes and to demilitarize their common border. Shared concerns over the transborder threats posed by terrorism, separatism, and organized crime have slowly eclipsed in importance the demilitarization process and implementation of confidence-building measures (Gill 2004: 213–16). These shared security interests have not produced collective or positive identities and Sino-Russian strategic interests define the regional dynamic. Thus, the SCO security referent is outwardly

Table 5.7 The varieties of security multilateralism

	Security referent	Regulator	Function of norms	Context	Type of multilateralism
Central Asia	Internal and regional	Balance of power	Instrumental and extrinsic to interests; serve to bolster internal repression and territorial integrity	Enmity; intense security dilemma	Co-operative security
Southeast Asia	Internal and regional	Consensus and force	Norms defining "ASEAN way" have substantive value, but are not intrinsic to interest calculation	Muted enmity; security dilemma managed	Concert towards co-operative security
Atlantic	External and global	Force outside group	Norms are substantively and intrinsically valued over a narrow range of security issues; there has been a weakening of those norms after 11 September	Strained amity, security dilemma weak	Collective defense towards concert
EU	Internal and neighborhood	Law and institutions	Norms are substantively and intrinsically valued across a broad range of issues spanning the entire spectrum of internal and external governance policies	Amity; security dilemma not a relevant category of analysis	Civilianized security community

directed to the regional milieu (managing the "three threats") and inwardly directed at the management of within-group conflicts.

Intramural conflict is regulated by traditional statecraft, particularly the reliance upon informal mechanisms for policy co-ordination. War and force remain viable instruments. Although the renunciation of force is a central norm of the "Shanghai process", it remains contingent and instrumental rather than intrinsic and substantive. China has embarked upon an ambitious military modernization program, Russia only exercises influence in the region owing to its military preponderance, and the other SCO states extended the United States basing rights, arguably defense expenditure and deterrence by proxy. The persistence of the sovereignty principle and a particularistic definition of interest together provide a formidable barrier to the deeper institutionalization of the SCO process and a greater reliance upon multilateral mechanisms for resolving conflict.[14]

The function that norms play in defining national interests is contingent on whether system-level norms are substantive or instrumental and intrinsic or extrinsic to national values. The strength of the normative framework is contingent upon the overlapping of norms and interests. The strength of the sovereignty principle and continuing importance of relative power in intra-regional relations retard the emergence of a robust normative framework constituting a part of the national security calculus. SCO framework documents enumerate a consistent set of norms, but those norms only legitimize repressive political regimes, leave unmolested sovereign prerogatives, and reinforce the primacy of national interests. No SCO state is obligated to carry out an SCO policy if it conflicts with the national interest; there is no expectation of sovereign abnegation to further a collective goal (SCO 2001b: Article 7; SCO 2001a: para. 10). Thus, SCO norms are weakly regulative rather than constitutive, contingent rather than binding. As such they have had little impact on either identity formation or the definition of interest.

The strength of the sovereignty principle, in conjunction with the sovereign control the member states exercise and seek to exercise over their territory and citizenry, sustain an interaction context of enmity and bilateral security dilemmas. The Chinese and Russian governments retain a high degree of sovereign control over closed political systems, exploit political cultures privileging the state over society, and highly discount civil and political liberties. Despite "soft borders" repressive governments in the four remaining SCO states act as gate-keepers over those aspects of society most likely to touch upon national security. The sovereignty principle reinforces the "national" in the national interest and the preoccupation with territorial and political integrity. Correspondingly, the development of a positive or collective identity, which would build trust and mitigate the bilateral security dilemmas, is blocked by a constellation of factors, particularly the militarized intramural conflicts of the not-too-distant past, the unabated great power competition between China and Russia for regional dominance, and the absence of a civilizational or threat-based foundation for constructing either a "we" independent of the external environment or a common "other" against which the members are jointly opposed.

The SCO does not meet the criteria of an outwardly directed impermanent alliance. It would be difficult to demonstrate that the organization's origin, continuing rationale, and cohesion (such as it is) can be attributed to a common interest in "balancing" the United States or the "bandwagoning" calculations of the smaller central Asian states. The basing of American troops in three of the SCO states also suggests that an alternative classification is in order. The SCO fails to meet any of the criteria for the more demanding forms of security multilateralism that require even a partial abnegation of sovereignty. Instead, the attributes of the central Asian states and the characteristics of the regional subsystem have produced a weak form of co-operative security: these states jointly seek an overlapping set of milieu goals that serve narrowly defined national interests. The multilateralism that does take place is severely constrained by the external dynamic of anarchy and the internal dynamic of repression.

ASEAN

The ASEAN states have rejected as undesirable both collective security and collective defense arrangements. The structure of power continues to play an important, but not dominant, role in defining relations within ASEAN and southeast Asia more broadly. ASEAN states seek regional autonomy, a goal that can only be achieved in opposition to the presumed hegemonic ambitions of China and insulated from the Sino-American competition for Asia-Pacific dominance. The American security guarantees, which pose a significant barrier to Chinese suzerainty or hegemony, permit ASEAN states to discount intramural considerations of power. The external threats posed to ASEAN – initially communism and now China – have created a common identity between the member states, but that identity remains largely negative. Nonetheless, that negative identity serves as a foundation for the joint definition of interests and policy co-ordination in a circumscribed set of policy areas, including security. The ASEAN security referent is both internal (within group co-operation on jointly defined security threats) and external (maintaining regional autonomy and mitigating great power conflicts).

The regulator is decentralized and weakly institutionalized by design. Decentralization represents the confluence of the ASEAN states' willingness and preparedness to use force and the episodic eruption of militarized conflict within and between them. As the defense budgets of the ASEAN states attest, the military option remains in place despite the prohibitionary norms against force found in the TAC and Bali II Concord. The continuing relevance of power and force is moderated by the relatively high levels of economic interaction among the more powerful ASEAN states – Thailand, Singapore, Indonesia, and the Philippines – and a common interest in expanding commercial and financial ties with China, Japan and the United

States. While the structure of trade could contribute steadily to the creation of a positive identity, if not a sense of "we-ness," it will remain counterbalanced by the continuing resilience of southeast Asian nationalisms, lingering historical enmities, and domestic political systems ranging from the democratic to the despotic. These factors work against surrendering significant sovereign prerogatives to a regional institution for the purposes of regulating intramural conflict or securing regional milieu goals.

A series of treaties enumerate the norms governing intra-ASEAN relations. Those norms, which proscribe and prescribe intramural behavior, have taken on a substantive value for the members, but are not yet intrinsic to the calculation of national interests (Emmerson 2005). Successful appeals to the "ASEAN way" have managed intramural disputes and shaped the broader dynamic of the Asia-Pacific. At a minimum, the ASEAN norms have created the basis for positive identity formation. The sovereignty principle inhibits progress towards a more fully formed collective identity or the transition of norms from the instrumental to the substantive, from the extrinsic to the intrinsic. As a consequence, the more demanding forms of security multilateralism are unavailable, albeit the ASEAN states have explicitly rejected Western-style multilateral frameworks as alien to the region (ASEAN 2004). The southeast Asian interaction context combines muted enmity between dyads of states (such as Thailand and Myanmar; Singapore and Malaysia; Vietnam and Laos) with fully unresolved within-group security dilemmas overlain by a collective security dilemma vis-à-vis China. The region suffers from a set of unpropitious circumstances for co-operation – border and territorial disputes persist, sovereign prerogatives remain inviolable, and distrust remains high. The persistence of narrowly defined national interests and the role of power in shaping the regional context hinder the development of a more fully formed positive identity and preclude the emergence of a collective one. The ASEAN states' economic success and acknowledged interdependencies, both economic and strategic, offset these negative factors and contribute to the muted enmity and the absence of an acute within-group security dilemma.

What kind of security multilateralism does ASEAN represent? ASEAN shares some of the characteristics found in co-operative security arrangements, but closely approximates a concert. As a concert, ASEAN has been enabled to facilitate weakly institutionalized balances of power within ASEAN + 3 (China, Japan and South Korea) or the ASEAN Regional Forum (ARF), the pan-Pacific security institution. ASEAN + 3 directs its energies towards containing a Sino-Japanese competition in Asia; ARF pursues the balancing of the major Pacific powers (China, Japan, and the United States). Both auxiliary institutions seek general milieu goals of political and strategic stability in the Asia-Pacific that serve the long-term ASEAN interest in regional autonomy. It is overly broad and misleading to claim that the Asia-Pacific exists "somewhere between a balance of power and a community-based security order" (Ikenberry and Tsuchiyama 2002), particularly since "somewhere" includes virtually every conceivable form of security multilateralism.

Security multilateralism in the Asia-Pacific is relatively weak, but ASEAN represents a regional concert striving to manage intramural conflicts, protect regime integrity, and create a favorable regional milieu.

NATO

The classification of NATO as a collective defense arrangement ought to be relatively uncomplicated and uncontested, particularly given the provisions of the North Atlantic Treaty's Article 5. Alas, this is not the case. NATO's precise character is muddied by those seeking to press NATO into the pigeon hole of a "security community" based on the confluence of democratic government, a shared civilization, and the expectation that conflicts will be resolved non-violently. A second barrier to the simple classification of NATO is the fundamental geopolitical change occasioned by the end of the Cold War; viz, NATO was transformed virtually overnight from a compulsory alliance that derived its cohesive power from a common Soviet threat to a voluntary alliance with no specific adversary or obvious purpose. Thus the evolution of the Atlantic area initiated the transformation of the NATO security referent from a specific, adversarial "other" into a non-specific set of milieu goals. That change has eroded the negative identity that the Soviet threat gave the alliance. In the absence of an equally cohesive alternative "other", power has been reintroduced into NATO's internal dynamic, particularly with respect to the defining of common milieu goals and the appropriate geographic reach for NATO. Paradoxically, the absence of the Soviet Union has placed into question the causal relationship between democracy, collective identity, and interest formation. NATO remains outwardly orientated, but the target of the alliance is uncertain and internal cohesion has weakened.

The regulator of conflict within the alliance is highly institutionalized within the North Atlantic Council and more importantly within the integrated command structure. Deterring war and relying upon force to address "common" security problems was the core function of NATO, but in the changed environment that consensus has weakened. During the Cold War, Western Europeans and Americans alike relied upon military force to deter a Soviet attack and actively prepared for war within the North Atlantic area; conflicts of interest over how those goals would be best met were resolved within the NATO unified command or between the member governments within the institutionalized forum provided by the North Atlantic Council. The sovereignty principle was asymmetrically compromised within that framework; the Europeans by and large yielded to American preferences out of necessity rather than conviction, particularly on the use of nuclear weapons and deterrence strategy. While some argue that the Alliance shared a common identity, which would imply an undifferentiated understanding of threat and response, there was in fact a highly differentiated concept of interest outside the general interest of deterring the Soviet Union. Simply put, the Europeans hoped that if deterrence failed the subsequent nuclear exchange would take place over their heads, while the United States was determined that a nuclear exchange would first occur on European soil. That conflict was resolved largely in the American favor owing to its preponderance of power; after the Cold War similar fissures within the alliance over strategy are not so easily contained, as the division over Iraq proved.

The norms embodied in the North Atlantic Treaty are intrinsic and substantive to the calculation of interest on both sides of the Atlantic over a narrow range of issues. Norms have been endowed with these characteristics despite the relative strength of the sovereignty principle within the treaty itself (sovereign equality) and the American tendency to identify its interests according to a national rather than collective referent (Carter and Perry 1999; US President's Office 2002, 2006). The absence of force as an instrument for resolving intramural disputes, albeit somewhat offset by the American willingness to exploit the asymmetry of power between itself and its European allies, created an environment that allowed the transformation of instrumental norms created in the early 1950s into substantive norms intrinsic to national calculations of interest. Even the existential threat posed to the United States on 11 September 2001 and the plausible insularity of the European allies from a similar attack did not deter them from invoking Article 5 for the first time in the Alliance's history and participating in the pacification and occupation of post-Taliban Afghanistan. This chain of events demonstrates that the collective defense obligation in the North Atlantic Treaty is indeed an intrinsic norm.[15]

Amity interrupted by occasional fits of pique defines the NATO interaction context. There is no security dilemma within the alliance; controversy does exist, however, on what constitutes a threat, the sources of those threats, the best means of addressing those threats, and the geographic reach of the Alliance. These kinds of controversies existed during the Cold War, but multiplied after 1992. Russia and Ukraine are unlikely to emerge as a geostrategic "other" reintroducing a renewed source of negative identity to hold the alliance together. But the Russian failure to evolve into a robust democracy could reintroduce at a minimum regional enmity.

The durability of NATO as a collective defense organization may be attributed to the postwar confluence of common interests, common values, and a manufactured common identity, even though positive and negative identities coexisted (Hampton and Sperling 2002: 281–302). NATO falls short of meeting fully the requirements of a security community or a collective security organization. While it may have appeared to have been more than a collective defense arrangement during the postwar period, developments within NATO since 2001 in particular have revealed schisms that are deep and probably enduring. The NATO states are democracies and there is no conceivable circumstance under which they would resort to war with one another. But the selective participation of NATO allies in different peacekeeping missions and, most tellingly, the invasion of Iraq also suggest that NATO may be developing a dual personality: an inwardly directed collective defense organization without a specific or likely enemy and an outwardly directed concert pursuing a disputed set of milieu goals.

EU

The EU has been both a foreign policy objective of its member states as well as a foreign policy actor. As in the case of NATO, the EU referent is both inwardly and outwardly directed, although there is no adversarial "other". The inward orientation of the EU focuses on the non-traditional aspects of security that arise from the post-Westphalian character of the member states; the outward orientation is directed towards a broad and consistent set of regional milieu goals along its eastern and southern peripheries. The EU members share a collective identity reinforced by supranational institutions that have muted asymmetries of power. Power does not play a significant role in EU relations with its neighboring states. A benign external environment in combination with the absence of differentiation between member state interests across a broad spectrum of security issues explains the character of the EU security referent.

The EU states have pooled or ceded considerable sovereignty to supranational institutions (the Commission, ECJ, and ECB) and have constructed a collective identity over the course of the postwar period. While a European identity has not superseded the national identities of its members, there nonetheless exists a denationalized understanding of threats common to Europe and the expectation that those threats will be met jointly. War between the EU states has become unthinkable; no other state or group of states constitutes a military threat. The willingness to rely on force remains, but the resort to force is limited by treaty to the Petersberg Tasks of peace-keeping, humanitarian intervention, rescue tasks, crisis-management and conflict prevention. These permissive internal factors in combination with a settled external environment have enabled the EU to institutionalize conflict resolution to a degree only exceeded within states: intramural conflicts are resolved within the Council of Ministers and European Council, the European Commission drafts policies meeting common needs, and the ECJ adjudicates conflicts and the plaintiffs expect voluntary compliance with the court's decisions.

The norms governing the EU states are substantive and intrinsic to the calculation of interest. National interests are themselves subject to the solidarity principle, which has established the expectation that national security policies will serve not only the particularistic interests of the member state, but the collective interests of the Union (EU 2004). The erosion of the sovereignty principle, the absence of force in mediating intramural conflicts, and a broad and deep normative framework progressively institutionalized as hard law create a context where EU norms constitute the definition of interest.

Amity and the absence of a security dilemma characterize the EU interaction context. The within-group dynamic has created and sustained amity: the states have progressively sacrificed ever greater levels of sovereignty to supranational institutions, while the purposeful loss of sovereign control has required that transfer of sovereignty. While the rationale for the European project may have been initially instrumental (Milward 1992), it could only persist and broaden if accompanied by intramural trust and amity. This same dynamic altered the calculus of interest from the particular to the collective, a process unhindered by the prospect of war (a function of the American security guarantee and occupation of Germany in the early postwar years). By the time that the EU acquired a security writ in the late 1980s, the fear of a renascent Germany and the corresponding security dilemma perceived by its neighbors (the original motivation for the Brussels Treaty Organization) had evaporated.

The EU is positioned to adopt the defining characteristic of a collective security system: Article V of the Western European Union treaty provides for the positive obligation to intervene on behalf of a signatory state in the event of aggression.[16] The EU does represent a civilianized security community. This conclusion should not come as a surprise since the concept was developed to account for the EU as a system of governance. Classifying the EU is not as important as understanding why the EU developed into a security community, since the answer to that question has policy implications for those wishing to reproduce the number of security communities across the globe. What distinguishes the EU from the other regions is the post-Westphalian character of the member states and the systemic dynamic of post-Westphalianism that pushes states towards security co-operation (Falk 2002).

Conclusion

Security multilateralism is about effective governance of the international system, particularly the supply of order and the regulation of conflict. The primary task set in this chapter was to understand how the interaction of state attributes and system properties produced specific forms of security multilateralism and to establish the limits of security governance in disparate parts of the world. Secondary objectives included crafting a set of criteria that differentiate between the different forms of security multilateralism and classifying the SCO, ASEAN, NATO and the EU as systems of security multilateralism.

The assessments of the four regional systems of security multilateralism are relatively conservative. Contrary to much of the existing literature, the SCO, ASEAN, and NATO can not be described as a form of collective security or security community if those concepts are to retain any explanatory or descriptive power. Neither the SCO nor ASEAN represents a very ambitious form of security multilateralism. NATO's qualified classification as a collective defense arrangement – despite the provisions of the North Atlantic Treaty – and its devolution towards an amiable concert reflects a change in systemic conditions conjoined to the asynchronous evolution of the United States and its European allies towards a post-Westphalian identity. The EU states are post-Westphalian states *and* operate in a permissive systemic milieu. These findings provide, at a minimum, preliminary support for the post-Westphalian hypothesis: the post-Westphalian state is a necessary condition for the most advanced forms of security governance, but an insufficient one. The system continues to function as a significant barrier between the possible and desirable forms of security multilateralism.

Notes

Thanks are owed to Aris Alexopoulos, Dimitris Bourantonis, Kostas Ifantis, Oliver Richmond, Keery Walker and Michael Westmoreland for comments made on a much earlier draft of this paper. The usual disclaimer applies.

1 The inclusion of nineteenth- and early twentieth-century European and North American democracies in these data sets should be troubling. Any form of disenfranchisement would disqualify a state from qualifying as democratic today. Yet a majority of Britons was disenfranchised until the early twentieth century; in the United States, a significant portion of the population were held as slaves, women were disenfranchised until the early twentieth century, and Americans of African descent were systematically excluded from the political process well into middle of the twentieth century. Edward Mansfield and Jack Snyder (1995, 2002) also demonstrate that states in the early stages of democratization are as likely to be war-prone as not. Kal Holsti (1995) rejects the emphasis on democratic constitutional orders and suggests that the absence of domestic legitimacy, regardless of constitutional form, is the better indicator of bellicosity.
2 As John Gerard Ruggie (1992: 592) notes, the assessment of multilateral arrangements is "not entirely independent of the attributes of states making the calculations." This model shifts the emphasis of the analysis: multilateral arrangements are not entirely independent of systemic conditions.
3 Denmark was unwilling to wage war against Germany at the outset of World War II, while the vastly outnumbered and outgunned Finns, for example, chose instead to wage war against Russia and subsequently Germany.
4 The postwar American experiences in Indochina and more recently in Mesopotamia are cases in point.
5 The state of nature would require a complete breakdown of the contemporary international system, while an international civil society would eradicate the "stateness" of states.
6 The civilianized security community is similar to a pluralistic security community (Deutsch et al. 1957) as well as a loosely coupled security community (Adler and Barnett 1998), although the latter is so broadly defined that it accommodates concerts and collective defense arrangements.
7 Between 1995 and 2004, expenditures increased 352 per cent for Tajikistan, 241 per cent for Kyrgyzstan, 163 per cent for China, 123 per cent for Kazakhstan and 54 per cent for Russia (IISS 2004: author's own calculations).
8 The ASEAN states range from reasonably well-functioning democracies (such as the Philippines) to some of the least democratic in the world (Myanmar and Vietnam) (WorldAudit.org).
9 The impact of the Asian financial crisis on identity formation is contested. Nabers (2003: 121) claims that the financial crisis created the notion that ASEAN was a community of fate; Acharya and Tan (2006: 52) detect instead a loss of cohesion reinforced by an expanded membership and intramural territorial disputes.
10 On the schism that developed between "old" Europe and the United States over Iraq, see Merkl (2005).

11 EU member-state defense expenditures increased by 12.8 per cent between 1995 and 2004, while the comparable US figure is 32 per cent. German defense expenditures remained essentially flat, while Italy, Britain, and France experienced increases of 38 per cent, 28 per cent and 12 per cent respectively (Scons, Stålenheim, Omitoogun, Perdomo 2005: table 8A.3, 356–61). British and French defense expenditures have been devoted to enhancing force projection capabilities out of area in addition to the costs attending peacekeeping in southeastern Europe and Africa as well as war-fighting in Afghanistan and Iraq.
12 The provisions of the TAC inform the secondary institutional elaborations of ASEAN, particularly ASEAN + 3 and even the ARF (Khoo 2004: 40).
13 The supremacy of EU law to national law is increasingly cited as evidence of a common identity and the subsequent reshaping of national interest calculations. See Stone Sweet and Brunell (1998), Caldeira and Gibson (1995), and Alter (2000). For a skeptical view, see Huelshoff, Sperling and Hess (2005).
14 The SCO can only intervene in a conflict between its members if two conditions are met: the two states concerned initiate the request for SCO intermediation and the other foreign ministers agree to honor the request (SCO 2001b: Article 7).
15 Article 5 does not provide a binding obligation to come to the defense of a NATO member under attack; a card of condolence would satisfy the letter of the Treaty.
16 Not all EU member states were signatories to the WEU, and Article 5 remains outside the EU legal framework.

6 Is multilateralism bad for humanitarianism?

Michael Barnett

Developments since the end of the Cold War have encouraged multilateral security organizations and humanitarian organizations to orientate their activities in the same direction. Although the formal structures of multilateral security organizations have not appreciably altered, their purpose has. During the Cold War most multilateral security organizations operated with a statist concept of security, restricted their activities to the defense of states, and viewed security in strictly military terms. Yet over the past fifteen years many of these same organizations have introduced a humanitarian dimension into their strategic doctrines and stated purpose. Reflective of the member states that define their activities, many regional and international organizations increasingly view as legitimate the idea of humanitarian intervention, believe that human rights are an important part of security, and occasionally fancy themselves as humanitarian actors. As they have warmed to the idea and importance of humanitarian action, many major powers and regional organizations not only see humanitarian action as an important supplement to their goals, they also imagine that states and humanitarian organizations are crime-fighting partners. As former Secretary of State Colin Powell told a gathering of NGOs in 1991, "just as surely as our diplomats and military, American NGOs are out there [in Afghanistan] serving and sacrificing on the frontlines of freedom. NGOs are such a force multiplier for us, such an important part of our combat team."[1]

The meaning and practice of humanitarian action also have expanded over the last fifteen years. Humanitarian agencies have traditionally defined themselves in opposition to "politics" (Nyers 1999: 21).[2] Certainly they recognized that humanitarianism was the offspring of politics, that their activities have political consequences, and that they are inextricably part of the political world. Yet the widely accepted definition of humanitarianism – the impartial, independent, and neutral provision of relief to those who are in avoidable danger of harm – emerged in opposition to a particular meaning of politics and helped to depoliticize relief-orientated activities.[3]

The foundational purpose of humanitarian action, the provision of assistance to those at immediate risk, removed it from politics. Many activities might alleviate suffering and improve life circumstances, including human rights and development; but these are political because they aspire to restructure underlying social relations. Humanitarianism provides relief: it offers to save individuals, but not to eliminate the underlying causes that placed them at risk.

Humanitarian's original principles also were a reaction to politics and designed to obstruct this "moral pollutant." The principle of humanity commands attention to all humankind and inspires a cosmopolitanism. The principle of impartiality demands that assistance be based on need and not discriminate on the basis of nationality, race, religious belief, gender, political opinions, or other considerations (Pictet 1979). The principles of neutrality and independence also help to inoculate humanitarianism from politics. Relief agencies are best able to perform their life-saving activities if, and only if, they are untouched by state interests and partisan agendas.[4] Neutrality involves refraining from taking part in hostilities or from any action that either benefits or disadvantages the parties to the conflict. Neutrality is both an end and a means to an end, because it helps relief agencies gain access to populations at risk. Independence demands that assistance should not be connected to any of the parties directly involved in the conflict or who have a stake in the outcome. Accordingly, many agencies have either refused or limited their reliance on government funding if the donors have a stake in the outcome. The principles of humanity, impartiality, neutrality, and independence have served to depoliticize humanitarian action and create a "humanitarian space" – a space insulated from politics.

Yet over the last decade humanitarian action has expanded significantly beyond its "apolitical" confines and now shares space with "politics" as it works to promote development, human rights, democracy, and peacebuilding. Push and pull factors were responsible for this expansion, and while some agencies resisted the flow, others went with it. For many agencies this transgression into politics produced considerable anxiety because of the fear that the fraternization of politics and humanitarianism would corrupt this sacred idea and undermine the ability to provide relief. Not only might they lose their impartiality as they became attached to broader political projects, but they also would sacrifice their independence as they associated with states.[5] For other agencies, especially those championing human rights and development, this was a welcome expansion because it deepened their solidarity with the weak and vulnerable, extended the assistance activities that might be provided to them, and enabled them to work toward the elimination of the root causes of conflict. Although there remain important divisions in the humanitarian community, "fundamentalists" have lost ground to the "new" humanitarians who accept a politicized humanitarianism (Weiss 1999; Minear 2002; Chandler 2002; Stoddard 2002).

This chapter examines how the emergence of a humanized multilateralism and a politicized humanitarianism can compromise the provision of relief and protection of civilians. The first section explores the various factors that contributed simultaneously to the humanization of multilateralism and the politicization of humanitarianism. To better understand how these changes shaped the meaning and practices of humanitarian action, the second section looks at external control and examines three branches of organizational theory. The first two, principal–agent analysis and sociological institutionalism, highlight how the different dimensions of the environment can lead to greater control over humanitarian organizations. Principal–agent analysis highlights how states that are increasingly prone to see humanitarian action as an important feature of their foreign policy might now be encouraged to introduce new control mechanisms on agencies, mechanisms that might threaten agencies' independence, impartiality, and neutrality. Sociological institutionalism focuses on how the desire by organizations for external legitimacy – legitimacy that can bring resources and status – can encourage agencies to expand their activities and associate with states.

The legitimation of international human rights norms was a powerful magnet for relief agencies. Yet organizations were not only forced into new areas, they also were drawn because of internal dispositions. Although organizational interests played a part, also present was an organizational culture that compelled staff to try to resolve the tensions they confronted between their aspirational mandates to help the suffering and the demanding situations on the ground. Relief can be a temporary salve in the face of ongoing threats against civilians and the concern that relief does not address the root causes that make populations vulnerable. To try to reduce suffering, humanitarian organizations reached into new areas and toward states.

The third section of this chapter explores these issues in the case of NATO's "humanitarian war" in Kosovo. Although the willingness of states to use force in the defense of civilian populations can be interpreted as a victory for principled action, in this case principled action also represented a potential threat to humanitarianism. Indeed, the humanitarian sector sponsored over two dozen evaluations of Kosovo, something of a record for the time and indicative of the desire to assess not only their technical prowess (or lack thereof) but also the larger political implications of this event.[6] At issue was why so many agencies felt so comfortable associating so closely with a combatant and suspending their sacrosanct principles of impartiality, independence, and neutrality, whether that association had harmed their ability to provide relief and protection, and what this event meant for the future of humanitarian action. I conclude by reflecting on how different versions of institutionalism help us understand the different kinds of control mechanisms exerted by the environment over humanitarian organizations, the need for an interpretive perspective to understand why humanitarian organizations might view this principled development – a humanized multilateralism – as a threat to their principles, and humanitarianism's relationship to world order.

Humanizing multilateralism and politicizing humanitarianism

A defining feature of the post-Cold War period was the foregrounding of the "civilian" as an object of concern.[7] The meaning of security underwent a perceptible change, expanding from an emphasis on state security to include elements of human security. Reflective of this change, many states, regional organizations, and international organizations redefined the military's activities to include peacekeeping, civilian policing, political stabilization, and even nation-building, and to consider the legitimacy of humanitarian intervention. Although many security organizations resisted this expansion on the grounds that it was outside – and would dilute – their core mandate, the secular trend was toward a humanized multilateralism. The factors that led to a humanized multilateralism also had a second-order effect on humanitarian action. Certainly humanitarian organizations did not have to be convinced of the importance of organizing their activities around the principle of humanity, but they did require a more permissive environment that would allow them to expand into new areas that would enable them to protect populations at risk. Once states and their regional organizations became more open to the idea of humanitarian action, humanitarian organizations quickly discovered that the constraints on their activities decreased and the opportunity structure increased. Although many humanitarian organizations worried that this engagement with politics might injure humanitarian action, the secular trend was toward a politicized humanitarianism.

Humanized multilateralism

A widely accepted definition of multilateralism is that it "coordinates behavior among three or more states on the basis of generalized principles of conduct" (Ruggie 1993b: 14). This definition points us to the formal organizational structure and its organizing principles. However, I am less concerned with the formal structure than I am with the purpose. Many of the multilateral security institutions that were established during the Cold War years were organized around interstate security. Yet with the end of the Cold War there was an important shift in the purpose of many multilateral arrangements as they broadened their definition of what counts as a threat to international peace and security and incorporated the civilian as an object of concern.

Various factors produced the general trend toward the inclusion of humanitarian emergencies and human rights into the meaning and practice of international security. Geopolitical shifts associated with the end of the Cold War and the demise of the Soviet Union increased the demand for humanitarian action in several ways (de Waal 1997: 133–4). There appeared to be more humanitarian crises than ever before.[8] Although there is considerable debate regarding whether, in fact, there were more crises or whether Great Powers were now willing to recognize populations at risk because their policies were no longer the immediate cause, the emergencies now were on the international agenda (Slim 2004b: 155–6).

As states paid more attention to them, they linked these populations at risk to an expanding discourse of security. One reason for their visibility was because they now were viewed as a security issue. During the Cold War, the UNSC defined threats to peace and security as disputes between states that might (or had) become militarized, conflicts involving the Great Powers, and general threats to global stability (White 1993: 34–8; Howard 1993: 69–70). After the Cold War, and in reaction to the growing perception that domestic conflict and civil wars were leaving hundreds of thousands of populations at risk, creating mass flight, and destabilizing entire regions, the UNSC authorized interventions on the grounds that they challenged regional and international security. Operation Provide Comfort, the international intervention to help the Kurdish refugees, reflected not simply a concern with the nontraditional security threats but a recognition also that they could destabilize the more traditional kind. As an unfortunate and tragic consequence of the Gulf War, the Iraqi Kurdish population was fleeing Saddam Hussein's military to the Turkish border, but Turkish authorities, in violation of international refugee law, refused to give them temporary refuge. In response, the UNSC established safe havens for the Kurdish refugees and justified this act in the name of international peace and security. Subsequent events reinforced the broadening of international security to include humanitarian dimensions. Somalia barely qualified as an international threat to peace and security but shocked the conscience of the international community. Responding to both the post-Cold War humanitarian emergencies and the growing prominence of the UNSC in this domain, the General Assembly passed a watershed resolution that coronated the UN as the new co-ordinating body for governing the response to humanitarian action.[9]

Relatedly, states warmed to the idea of humanitarian action as they began to see it as an important instrument of their strategic and foreign policy goals. Immediate evidence of their support was their growing financial generosity (see below). Even more impressive was their growing willingness to support operations whose stated function was to protect civilians at risk, and even to consider the legitimacy of humanitarian intervention. Although it remains a matter of fierce legal and political debate whether and when human rights should be a factor in determining the legitimacy of intervention, as an empirical matter the international community became increasingly willing to avail themselves of international bodies to intervene in internal conflicts when there are threats to human rights.[10]

States also discovered that humanitarian action was functional for avoiding more costly interventions. For instance, the major powers authorized UNHCR to deliver humanitarian relief in Bosnia in part because they wanted to relieve the growing pressure for military intervention. Sometimes states will label their activities humanitarian because they want to do something; sometimes it is because they do not. Regardless of whether or not states had the right motives, they were including humanitarianism and human rights in the international peace and security discourse.¹¹

The expansion of the meaning and object of security imprinted the post-Cold War reform of various security institutions. As already suggested, the UN was one of the first international organizations to reform its understanding of security. Reflective and causative of the changes that occurred at the Security Council, the Secretariat pushed for reform. UN Secretary-General Boutros Boutros-Ghali's *The Agenda for Peace* was an ambitious, forward-looking document that represented a meditation on the changing nature of security and called for member states to recognize the salience of non-traditional security threats and to consider different forms of violence that directly harm the individual. The UN was doing more than talking; it was also acting. Between 1989 and 1994 the UNSC authorized 26 operations across the globe, doubling in five years the number of operations authorized by the council in the previous forty, and expanding the number of soldiers seven-fold. While some of these post-1989 operations resembled the "classical" prototype, most now were situated in much more unstable environments, where a ceasefire was barely in place, if at all, where government institutions were frayed and in need of repair, where there were rag-tag armies that were not parties to the agreement, and where the UN was charged with multidimensional and complex tasks that were designed to repair deeply-divided societies, divided in part because of their legacy of violence against civilians.

A humanized multilateralism also was evident in the reform of regional security institutions, including NATO. With the demise of the Cold War and the Soviet Union, NATO's very *raison d'être* appeared to vanish. Moreover, its conceptual and operational definition of security seemed inappropriate given the rise of non-traditional security threats and the growing emphasis on the need to contain and prevent domestic instability. In response to charges that it was built for bygone times and inappropriate for the new security challenges, NATO underwent a major debate regarding how to reorganize itself for the new security environment. One important result was its 1999 Strategic Concept, which emphasized: a broad concept of security that recognized the presence of non-traditional security threats and how domestic instability can produce regional instability; and a willingness to confront humanitarian emergencies within its geographical zone and near abroad for principled and strategic reasons.¹² In reference to this proposed "deepening" of NATO, US Deputy Secretary of State Strobe Talbott said that if NATO is to remain relevant it must take into account the "more diversified threats ... Disputes over ethnicity, religion or territory, can, as we've already seen trigger armed conflict, which in turn can generate cross-border political instability, refugee flows and humanitarian crises that endanger European security" (Simma 1999: 14). In general, post-Cold War developments, including new ideas about security and the idea of protecting the civilian, left its mark on various security organizations and created a humanized multilateralism.

Politicized humanitarianism

Four global processes helped to propel the expansion and politicization of the purpose of humanitarianism.[13] One was the already discussed changes in meaning and practice of international security, which obviously increased the centrality and importance of humanitarian action. A related development was the emergence of the category of "complex humanitarian emergencies." A complex humanitarian emergency is a "conflict-related humanitarian disaster involving a high degree of breakdown and social dislocation and, reflecting this condition, requiring a system-wide aid response from the international community" (Duffield, M. 2001: 12).[14] These emergencies are characterized by a combustible mixture of state failure, refugee flight, militias, warrior refugees, and populations at risk from violence, disease, and hunger, and they seem to be proliferating across the world. These emergencies have had several effects. They created a demand for new sorts of interventions and conflict management tools. Relief agencies were attempting to distribute food, water, and medicine in war zones, frequently being forced to bargain with militias, warlords, and hoodlums for access to populations in need. In situations of extreme violence and lawlessness the relief agencies frequently lobbied foreign governments and the UN to consider authorizing a protection force that could double as bodyguard and relief distributor. These emergencies also attracted a range of NGOs to become more involved in the same space (Kelly 1998: 174–5). Relief agencies that were delivering emergency assistance, human rights organizations aspiring to protect human rights and create a rule of law, and development organizations keen to sponsor sustainable growth began to interact and to take responsibility for the same populations. The growing interaction between different fields in turn encouraged them to articulate a relief–rights–development linkage within a humanitarian discourse that became tied to the construction of modern, legitimate, democratic states (Duffield, M. 2001). As various international actors began to think about the causes of and solutions to these humanitarian emergencies, they situated their arguments under a humanitarian rubric that became tied to a wider range of practices and goals.

A second factor was a change in the normative and legal environment, which created new opportunities for humanitarian action that coaxed humanitarianism into the political world. There was a shift from negative to positive sovereignty (Jackson 1990). Whereas once state sovereignty was sacrosanct, now it was conditional on states honoring a "responsibility to protect" their societies (International Commission on Intervention and State Sovereignty 2001) Whereas once their legitimacy appeared to have nearly divine origins, now it was dependent on them possessing certain characteristics, such as the rule of law, markets, and democratic principles. These developments created a normative space for external intervention and encouraged a growing range of actors to expand their assistance activities; in some cases they were intended to provide immediate relief during conflict situations, in others to eliminate the root causes of conflict and create legitimate states. Regardless of the pretext, the new normative environment greased the tracks for more wide-ranging interventions (Macrae 1999: 6–7).

There also was the related rise of an international human rights discourse. Although I will soon discuss how the logics of relief and rights differ, for the moment I want to highlight elements of overlap: they place front and center the human citizen and humanity; they contain the language of empowerment as they attempt to help the victims, the weak, and the powerless; and they favor a human-centered approach that rejects power (Chandler 2002: ch. 1). The fast-growing human rights agenda pulled humanitarianism from the margins toward the center of the international policy agenda, and many relief agencies, increasingly adopting the language of rights, were glad to ride its coat-tails (Chandler 2002: 21). Bosnia mixed humanitarian action and human rights in complicated but inextricable ways, as there was a general desire for humanitarian action to provide relief, but also the fear that such relief was unintentionally prolonging the suffering because it allowed Western states an exit. Then Rwanda caused "the great majority of humanitarian agencies [to] welcome the international community's recent introduction of the use of force more explicitly as a key part of international policy to protect human rights" (Slim 2002c: 2). Human rights ideas shaped the thinking of many humanitarian organizations, and many human rights organizations began to champion coercive humanitarianism as the best way to protect civilian populations and enforce human rights norms.

A fourth development was a growing cosmopolitanism. Cosmopolitanism concerns the central idea that each person is of equal moral worth and a subject of moral concern, and that in the "justification of choices one's choices one must take the prospects of everyone affected equally into account" (Beitz 1994: 124).[15] Cosmopolitanism underpins humanitarianism. The very principle of impartiality presumes that all those at risk, regardless of their identity, deserve equal attention and consideration. The desire to help those who are suffering regardless of place means that borders do not define the limits of obligations. This commitment to cosmopolitanism and the very desire to reduce suffering, however, creates a tension within humanitarianism (Calhoun 2004). One branch restricts it to the provision of assistance to victims of conflict; this is the version that emerged in the mid-nineteenth century and is most closely associated with the International Committee of the Red Cross. Another branch extends assistance to all those at risk and imagines eliminating the conditions that are hypothesized to render populations vulnerable. As one aid worker wrote, "in terms of the destruction of human life, what difference is there between the wartime bombing of a civilian population and the distribution of ineffective medicines during a pandemic that is killing millions of people?" (Bradol 2004: 9). If individuals are at risk because of authoritarian and repressive policies, then humanitarian organizations must be prepared to fight for human rights and democratic reforms. If individuals are at risk because of poverty and deprivation, then humanitarian organizations must be prepared to promote development. If regional and domestic conflicts are the source of violence against individuals, then humanitarian organizations must try their hand at conflict resolution and attempt to eliminate the underlying causes of conflict.

These developments expanded the meaning and practice of humanitarianism. Table 6.1 captures the significance of this shift and the principled claims that account for the divisions between different branches of humanitarianism. There is widespread agreement that humanitarian action has drift from a "classical" to a "solidarist" position, best represented by the displacement of traditional relief-based agenda with a rights-based agenda. However, this trend has been produced not only by human rights organizations but also by development organizations, which frequently come from a solidarity tradition and are concerned with long-term structural change.

This trend in humanitarianism has generated serious rifts within the sector, particularly pronounced in the clash between relief and rights organizations. Specifically, the logics of relief and rights differ in critical respects. The relief community will nearly always privilege survival over freedom, while the rights community is willing, at times, to use relief as an instrument of rights. Rights-orientated agencies are willing to make relief conditional on the observance of human rights and thus weaken the very notion of universality, a move many relief agencies view as nearly incomprehensible.[16] Relief agencies hold that neutrality and impartiality are essential for giving them access to populations, while many others in the sector believe that neutrality is a false guide in situations such as crimes against humanity, and that state involvement is a necessary solution.[17] In short, in many situations of conflict and threats to civilians, relief organizations will think long and hard before loosening their hold on long-standing principles, while solidarists and rights-based organizations will do so with ease.

Table 6.1 Humanitarianism: classical and solidarist

	Classicists	*Minimalists*	*Maximalists*	*Solidarists*
Engagement with political authorities	Eschew political confrontations			Advocate controversial public policy
Neutrality	Avoid taking sides			Selectively take sides
Impartiality	Deliver aid using proportionality and non-discrimination			Skew balance of resource allocation
Consent	Pursue as *sine qua non*			Over-ride sovereignty as necessary

Source: Weiss (1999: 4)

In general, the 1990s witnessed the emergence of a humanized multilateralism and a politicized humanitarianism. The meaning of security expanded, altering the purpose and practices of various multilateral security organizations. The meaning of humanitarianism expanded, altering the purpose and practices of any humanitarian organizations. These changes were not without controversy for either multilateral security organizations or humanitarian organizations. Many security organizations resisted this expansion into humanitarian issues on the grounds that it would potentially dilute their core competencies. So, too, did many humanitarian organizations resist this expansion into politics on the grounds that it would reduce their autonomy and potentially corrupt their soul. Although politics might not be the black widow portrayed by some critics, the growing connections between humanitarian organizations and their environment did leave their mark.

The external control of humanitarianism

The politicization and expansion of humanitarianism was made possible by environmental opportunities, but these developments also meant that environmental attributes gained control over humanitarianism. Environmental control had two dimensions. Prominent actors were now in a greater position to control what humanitarian actors *do*, features captured by principal–agent models. Now that states were taking a greater interest in humanitarian action, they had a desire to ensure that humanitarian organizations acted as their agents. The environment not only controlled what humanitarian actors do, but also what they *are*, features captured by sociological institutionalism. An environment in which states were taking a greater interest in humanitarian affairs, in which human rights were increasingly an important legitimation principle, slowly but consequently shaped the commitments of humanitarian organizations. Yet humanitarian organizations moved in this direction not only because of external forces, but also because of their attempt to better protect populations at risk. This daunting challenge is made nearly impossible in situations of conflict. In their desire to better accomplish their mandate and try and remove the root causes that leave populations vulnerable, humanitarian organizations will feel drawn to expand if they represent potential solutions to the tension between their broad aspirational mandates and their narrow capacities.

Principal–agent models

Principal–agent approaches examine why principals delegate various tasks to agents, the conditions under which such delegation is likely to happen, and the control mechanisms that principals might develop to minimize agency loss.[18] Importantly, principal–agent models recognize that all agents have some autonomy. Indeed, this can be by design. If one reason why principals such as states establish agents such as international organizations is to benefit from their expertise, then it makes good sense to give them the discretion to adapt their policies in response to new information, challenges, and circumstances. The problem, though, is that agents can use their discretion either to venture into areas that are unrelated to their mandate (shirk) or to undermine agent interests (slack). If the agent bumps up against or crosses the line, then the expectation is that the principal will sanction the agent or rewrite the contract.

Principal–agent approaches capture why states have imposed more control mechanisms on humanitarian organizations since the early 1990s. Prior to the 1990s states funded NGOs with almost no questions asked. They were a minor part of the budget, governments viewed them as more flexible and more efficient relative to international organizations, and they had a near monopoly on providing front-line relief. Beginning in the 1990s, however, states began introducing various control mechanisms. Humanitarian organizations were now consuming more of the foreign aid budget and states wanted to ensure that they were getting their money's worth. States increasingly saw humanitarian organizations as carrying out their foreign policy objectives. Moreover, the trust between donors and humanitarian organizations began to erode (Minear and Smillie 2004: ch. 9). Humanitarian organizations were now in the spotlight, and their foibles and failures began to attract as much publicity as their heroics. For these and other reasons, states wanted to assert more control over humanitarian organizations.

Four control mechanisms deserve attention because they had a significant impact on the discretion available to humanitarian organizations. First, and perhaps most important, was the bilateralization of aid and the earmarking of funds. Multilateral aid is technically defined as aid that is given to multilateral organizations and is not earmarked; these organizations, therefore, have complete discretion over how the money is spent. Bilateral aid can mean the state dictates either to the multilateral organization how the money is spent or gives the money to a non-multilateral organization such as an NGO. Earmarking is when the donor dictates where and how the assistance will be used, frequently identifying regions, countries, operations, or even projects; this is especially useful if governments have geopolitical interests or pet projects. Since the 1980s there has been a dramatic shift away from multilateral aid and toward bilateral aid and earmarking. In 1988 states directed roughly 45 per cent of humanitarian assistance to UN agencies in the form of multilateral assistance. After 1994, however, the average dropped to 25 per cent, and even lower in 1999 because of Kosovo (Randel and German 2002: 21).

States, moreover, are increasingly earmarking their aid, a trend partly driven by growing concerns over the performance of UN agencies and multilateral organizations. An important consequence of earmarking is that state interests, rather than the humanitarian principle of relief based on need, drive funding decisions. For instance, of the top 50 recipients of bilateral assistance between 1996 and 1999, the states of the former Yugoslavia, Israel/Palestine, and Iraq received 50 per cent of the available assistance (Randel and German 2002: 27). In 2002 nearly half of all funds given by donor governments to the UN's 25 appeals for assistance went to Afghanistan (Minear and Smilie 2004: 145). If funding decisions were based solely on need, then places like Sudan, Congo, northern Uganda, and Angola would leapfrog toward the top of the list rather than remain neglected at the bottom. In general, while there was more aid than ever before, it is controlled by fewer donors who are more inclined to impose conditions and direct aid toward their priorities. It is now a several-tiered system, with the least fortunate getting the least attention.[19]

States also began applying "new public management" principles to the humanitarian sector. These principles originated with the neo-liberal orthodoxy of the 1980s. One of neoliberalism's goals was to reduce the state's role in the delivery of public services and, instead, rely on commercial and voluntary organizations that were viewed as more efficient. Because government agencies justified the shift from the public to the private and voluntary sectors on the grounds that the latter were more efficient, they introduced monitoring mechanisms to reduce the possibility of either slack or shirking (Macrae et al. 2002: 18–21). Humanitarian organizations largely escaped this public management ideology before the 1990s. Because humanitarian assistance was a minor part of the foreign aid budget, states did not view humanitarianism as central to their foreign policy goals, and states trusted that humanitarian agencies were efficient and effective, so there was little reason to absorb the monitoring costs. However, once humanitarian funding increased, humanitarianism became more central to security goals, and states began to question the effectiveness of humanitarian organizations, they were willing to spend money on monitoring (de Waal 1997: 78–9).

A third development was the growing interest by states in seeing for themselves what was occurring in the field. Toward that end, they began sending representatives directly into the field to provide first-hand accounts of assistance activities, and began developing the capacity for independent needs assessments and strategic analyses. An immediate consequence was that humanitarian organizations no longer benefited from having privileged and highly authoritative information. Said otherwise, whereas once humanitarian organizations possessed private information and were the experts because of their first-hand knowledge and practical experience, the growing presence of state officials meant that humanitarian organizations lost that monopoly position, their informational advantages, and their discretion.

Fourth, as states and regional organizations became more involved in war zones and delivering relief to populations in need, they became more interested in co-ordinating the actions of humanitarian organizations. Co-ordination can appear to be a technical exercise whose sole function is to improve the division of labor, increase specialization, and heighten efficiencies. Yet this co-ordination, like all governance activities, is a highly political exercise that is defined by power (Minear 2002: ch. 2). The power behind co-ordination has not been lost on humanitarian organizations, especially when the donors are either parties to the conflict or have a vested interest in the outcome (Macrae et al. 2002: ch. 3).

The growing interest and involvement by states in humanitarian action had the consequence of giving them greater control over the behavior of humanitarian organizations. Some of these control mechanisms operated through subtle and indirect means. After all, when states earmark they are not always intentionally attempting to redirect the behavior, that is, the exercise of power in its most visible and fundamental form, but rather acting in ways that give incentives for aid agencies to shift their activities. States are not always subtle, though, and sometimes they can use control mechanisms to compel agencies to change their behavior or suffer the consequences. Western states have flexed their political and financial muscle to compel humanitarian organizations to act in ways that are consistent with state interests. In Afghanistan and Iraq, the United States unveiled these threats and communicated to NGOs that they expected humanitarian organizations to perform in ways that would help the United States with its hearts and minds campaigns and sell the war back home. One NGO official captured the US's message in the following terms: "play the tune or they'll take you out of the band" (quoted in Minear and Smilie 2004: 143).

These control mechanisms were doing more than simply reducing the autonomy available to humanitarian organizations – they also were potentially undermining the existing principles of humanitarian action. Certainly any organization, humanitarian or otherwise, will object to a reduction in its autonomy and discretion, but also at stake were their principles. This possibility is underscored by the very nature of principal–agent contract. States see themselves as principals that are providing a temporary transfer of authority to their agents, humanitarian organizations. Yet humanitarian organizations do not see themselves as agents of states or operating with delegated authority; instead they see themselves as agents of humanity and operating with moral authority. The very association with states and its presumption of delegated authority, then, potentially undermined the moral authority cherished by most humanitarian organization. Moreover, humanitarian organizations fear that any sort of association with states might compromise their independence, impartiality, and neutrality. Indeed, if states are funding humanitarian organizations in order to further their foreign policy goals, then humanitarian organizations are not unjustifiably paranoid. The very move by states to try and monitor and regulate humanitarian organizations almost, by definition, compromises these principles.

Sociological institutionalism

Organizations are embedded in an environment that can control, constrain, and constitute their practices. Two, related, features of the external environment are critical. One concerns the broad normative environment. Sociological institutionalism emphasizes the "socially constructed normative worlds in which organizations exist and how the social rules, standards of appropriateness, and models of legitimacy will constitute the organization" (Orru et al. 1991: 361).[20] The environment in which an organization is embedded is defined by a culture that contains acceptable models, standards of action, goals, and logics of appropriateness. Organizations are constituted by, and will be compelled to adopt, this culture for a variety of reasons. In the domestic context there are regulatory agencies, laws, professions, and broad public opinion that will shape organizations and their activities (H. Alford 2000: 49; DiMaggio and Powell 1991). In the international context this includes regulatory structures associated with international law and organizations, states demands, transnational actors and epistemic communities, and international public opinion.[21]

The second is their resource dependence.[22] Organizations depend on others for the resources they require to do their work. The willingness of others to fund their activities is contingent, in part, on their perceived legitimacy and whether they are viewed as acting according to the community's values. If they are out of sync with their environment, then they are likely to have their legitimacy questioned, which, in turn, will threaten their resource base. As Scott and Meyer summarize, this normative environment contains the "rules and requirements to which individual organizations must conform if they are to receive support and legitimacy from the environment" (1993: 140). Because organizations are rewarded for conforming to rules and legitimation principles, and punished if they do not, they will tend to model themselves after their environment.

The international normative environment and resource competition encouraged humanitarian organizations to expand in new directions. The growth of the international human rights discourse and the desire to "save failed states" created incentives for existing organizations to legitimate their activities along these lines. They were frequently rewarded by states for doing so.[23] For instance, by becoming the lead humanitarian agency and by framing its activities as instrumental for the pursuit of international peace and security, UNHCR was in a position not only to expand its responsibilities but also to demonstrate its relevance to the very states who paid the bills (Loescher 2001). Development agencies that were suffering something of an ideological crisis by the end of the 1980s found themselves relegitimated and rejuvenated by the possibility of claiming that development was now part of humanitarian action (Duffield, M. 2001). Although there was more money than ever before for humanitarian action, there also were more organizations competing for these funds. This produced something of a "NGO scramble," as various agencies not only competed with each other for these funds but frequently moved into new activities, outside their central areas of competence, in order to go where the money was (Cooley and Ron 2002).

Organizational culture

Principal–agent analysis and sociological institutionalism highlight the external drivers of control over humanitarian organizations, but there also can be internal dynamics that lead humanitarian organizations to introduce changes in their rules and activities that also can leave them more vulnerable to external control. The organizational culture can be understood as "the solutions that are produced by groups of people to meet specific problems they face in common. These solutions become institutionalized, remembered and passed on as the rules, rituals, and values of the group" (Vaughan 1996: 64).[24]

Although there are various features of this culture that might encourage expansion into new areas, I want to highlight one in particular: how to work out various tensions that existed between their moral commitments and their organizational mandates in new circumstances.[25] Organizations may feel the need to expand in order to resolve the contradiction between their broad aspirational goals and the more narrowly circumscribed rules that limit organizational action (Barnett and Finnemore 2004: ch. 6). Humanitarian organizations are empowered by moral or aspirational claims that can be much broader than their specific mandates or capacities. After all, while they act in the name of humanity and attempt to reduce suffering, their mandates may not necessarily extend to cover all that are at risk. Over time, the former can exert pressure on the latter: limited organizational structures make it impossible to fulfill broad mandates, creating reasons for organizational expansion into new areas. If the goal is to relieve suffering, then it is difficult to feel gratified by providing temporary relief; instead, they will desire to eliminate the very conditions that produce a demand for their services.[26]

Many humanitarian agencies more fully embraced a human rights agenda and the need to work alongside states as they confronted violent situations where they were unable to provide relief or protection. In Somalia various aid organizations, most (in)famously Care International, intensively lobbied for military intervention to protect the relief lines and aid workers. Rwanda made clear that there were no humanitarian solutions to humanitarian problems, and various aid agencies lobbied (unsuccessfully) for outside military intervention, first to halt the genocide and then to evict the *genocidaires* from the camps. Playing out alongside Rwanda was the continuing tragedy of Bosnia, where many relief agencies became convinced that humanitarian action was nothing more than a "fig leaf" for anemic Western states who were unwilling to apply the proper political and military muscle to stop the killing. Under such circumstances, they increasingly feared that their primary contribution was to help assist ethnic cleansing and make it easier for Western states and the UN to avoid military action. One lesson of Bosnia and Rwanda was that there was no substitute for military action during humanitarian emergencies, and that humanitarian agencies could and should work with states under certain conditions. Although aid agencies hotly debated the implications of the militarization of relief and working alongside states, there was a general willingness to suspend such concerns in the face of gross violations of human rights.

In general, while both principal–agent and sociological institutionalist approaches focus on the relationship between the environment and the organization, they highlight different mechanisms of control that have different kinds of effects. Principal–agent analyses highlight how states politicize humanitarianism to the extent that they establish more control mechanisms that directly alter what organizations can *do*. Sociological institutionalism recognizes this possibility but also adds how the environment might change not only what humanitarian organizations do, but also what they *are*. Major states, principal donors, and others that control resources can potentially use this leverage to control the behavior and activities of humanitarian organizations. Yet humanitarian organizations might also act in ways that are consistent with the external environment not only because of direct external pressure but also because of changes in legitimation principles and resource dependence. Not all change is externally-driven, though, for humanitarian organizations also contained cultural rules that encouraged them to expand outward as a solution to pressing problems on the ground. There were many roads to a politicized humanitarianism.

Kosovo

The events that led to NATO's intervention in Kosovo can be briefly told. Kosovo had been an autonomous province of the Yugoslavian Republic until 1990, when Yugoslav President Slobodan Milosevic formally abolished its autonomy.[27] From here on out Belgrade steadily took control of Kosovo's political, economic, and cultural affairs, and the Albanian population, which formed the vast majority of Kosovo's population, began to see their lives diminished. In response, Ibrahim Rugova, a well-known Albanian writer, advised passive resistance and established the Democratic League of Kosovo; soon thereafter, in September 1991 an underground plebiscite overwhelmingly voted for independence.

The situation in Kosovo remained fairly stable during the Yugoslavian wars, but once they ended it deteriorated. In response to continuing repression by the Federal Republic of Yugoslavia (FRY), the Kosovo Liberation Army (KLA), a previously unknown organization, carried out a series of attacks in April 1996. International involvement increased beginning in late 1997 and in response to a deteriorating and violent situation. In March 1998 the UNSC adopted Resolution 1160, which called on the KLA and Belgrade to negotiate a political settlement, imposed an arms embargo on both parties, and warned of the "consideration of additional measures" in the absence of progress toward a peaceful solution.[28] In response to further violence, including numerous civilian deaths and the displacement of hundreds of thousands of individuals, in April the Contact Group for the Former Yugoslavia (minus Russia) agreed to impose new sanctions on Belgrade. In

June, UN Secretary-General Kofi Annan informed NATO that there might be need for a Security Council authorization for future military action in Kosovo. In September the Security Council adopted Resolution 1199, declaring that Kosovo was a "threat to peace and security in the region."[29] Although Russia permitted this resolution, it served notice that it would oppose any authorization of military force by the Security Council.

Because of the Russian impediment, the Western states shifted their attention to NATO. Citing "humanitarian intervention" as the legal justification for any possible use of force, on 9 October 1998 NATO Secretary-General Javier Solana warned of future military action if Belgrade did not comply with international demands.[30] Apparently because of this warning, on 25 October Belgrade agreed to a ceasefire that would be monitored by NATO from the air and by unarmed OSCE peace monitors on the ground.[31] The humanitarian and security situation improved, but only temporarily; in the absence of a political agreement, the KLA and the Serbian authorities continued to maneuver for war. A particularly grisly incident in January 1999, in which 45 civilians were killed by Serbian troops in the city of Racak, led NATO to threaten air strikes. Indeed, at this point NATO became more fully committed to coercive diplomacy to force Belgrade to accept various principles regarding Kosovo's future status, including the restoration of its autonomy and international protection by NATO (Simma 1999: 8). Against the backdrop of the threat of force if there was no negotiated settlement, beginning on 6 February 1999 the combatants and outside parties held a series of talks at Rambouillet, France. The talks collapsed on 19 March.

Following through on its threat, NATO launched air strikes on 24 March, its first active military encounter in its 50-year history. A statement by US President Bill Clinton captured the reasons for this unprecedented action: to prevent a humanitarian emergency, preserve European stability, and maintain NATO's credibility.[32] Given the Bosnian precedent and Serbian violations of the basic human rights of Kosovar Albanians, Western officials had good reason to fear the worst either in the immediate or the medium-term future. As Michael Riesman observed: "The facts were alarming. As always, information was imperfect, but enough was available to indicate that bad things were happening, things chillingly reminiscent of some earlier as well as, lamentably, more recent events in this century; and it was reasonable to assume (and, to some, irresponsibly naive not to assume) that, given the people involved, worse things were in store" (Riesman 1999: 860). And, after having been criticized for their anemic and half-hearted response to Bosnia and Rwanda, their shadow cast a sense of shame (Roberts 1999). Consequently, NATO proclaimed Kosovo to be a "humanitarian war" that would protect the Kosovar Albanians.[33] There also were security considerations. The Bosnian conflict always threatened to expand beyond the Yugoslavian borders, and while the violence was quarantined the political and security effects were not. Kosovo's implosion might invite intervention by Greece, Italy, Turkey, and other European countries. Finally, NATO was concerned about

Is multilateralism bad for humanitarianism? 153

its own future. As NATO was debating its response to Kosovo, many were using the occasion of NATO's upcoming fiftieth anniversary to debate NATO's relevance and future. Coming on the heels of reactions to the wars of the former Yugoslavia that had led directly to the Strategic Concept, Kosovo potentially gave NATO an opportunity to answer its critics and demonstrate its continued relevance.

NATO's bombing, however, seemed to trigger the very humanitarian emergency it was designed to prevent. Milosevic responded to NATO's air campaign by unleashing the dogs of ethnic cleansing, causing hundreds of thousands of Kosovar Albanians to flee. Within two weeks, a half-million Kosovars had crossed into Albania and gathered at the Macedonian border, producing the largest refugee flight in Europe since World War II. This spectacle – mass displacement caused by a humanitarian war – was quickly becoming a major public relations disaster for an organization that had initially seen this humanitarian war as a public relations savior. Although few charged NATO with being directly responsible for this turn of events, it was heavily criticized for its failure to anticipate Milosevic's move. But NATO was not the only organization overwhelmed by the flood of refugees. So, too, were UNHCR, the lead humanitarian agency, and most relief agencies. In any event, it was NATO that was accused of creating the situation and it was NATO that was expected to do something about it. Given all of this, NATO decided that relief was too important to be left to the relief agencies (Suhrke et al. 2000; Orbinski 1999: 2). It began holding immediate discussions with UNHCR.

On 3 April UNHCR High Commissioner Sadako Ogata requested NATO's assistance. This was an unprecedented and highly controversial decision because never before had UNHCR approached a combatant for direct assistance.[34] Many at UNHCR objected on the grounds that whatever temporary benefit UNHCR might receive from NATO's assistance would be outweighed by the cost to its independence and ability to work in the field.[35] Ogata overruled these objections on the grounds that UNHCR needed NATO to help overcome Macedonia's unwillingness to permit entry of refugees (the government feared destabilizing the ethnic balance) and logistical problems in Albania (Morris, N. 1999; Ogata 2005: 144–8). NATO stepped in and acted as a "surge protector" (Minear et al. 2000: 76).

NATO made a critical contribution at the outset of the refugee crisis, but then transformed what was supposed to be a temporary and supporting role into a permanent and commandeering role throughout the war and long after its assistance ceased to be needed.[36] The agreement between NATO and UNHCR, as one evaluator observed, was a "Trojan Horse that allowed NATO to effectively take over the humanitarian operation from the inside" (Porter 2000: 5).[37] NATO became a "full-service" relief agency, helping to build camps, distribute relief, ensure security, co-ordinate the actions of relief agencies – and set the agenda (Rieff 2002: 204). Its decision to outstay its welcome and extend its activities into unauthorized areas had relatively little to do with the needs of the refugees and everything to do with NATO's need to maintain support for the air campaign (Porter 2000: 5). By continuing to play a co-ordinating role, NATO was able to cast its actions as humanitarian and thus continue to legitimate the war. For instance, the leaders of AFOR, NATO's Albanian force that was dedicated to relief, commanded that "all activities undertaken by AFOR should contribute to the enhancement of NATO's public image and the undermining of critics of the NATO air campaign."[38]

Although most agencies resented the reduction in autonomy, the surprise was that there was little outrage or outright rebellion. After all, the same agencies that had strenuously guarded their humanitarian space – their independence, impartiality, and neutrality – in places like the Congo and Sudan were now working alongside, getting assistance, from, and being directed by a combatant – and doing so with relative ease (Vaux 2001: 16–67; Roggo 2000; Porter 2000; Apthorpe 2001: 25). MSF was one of the few organizations that refused to participate on the grounds that doing so violated basic principles of humanitarian action and placed refugees at risk (Roggo 2000). In general, while some NGOs attempted to distinguish themselves from governments, "most were happy to go along with these arrangements" (Porter 2000: 5).[39]

What explains this development? Certainly some relief workers and organizations believed that they had little choice. MSF's financial independence might allow it to walk away, but many agencies did not believe they had the luxury because of their dependence on Western governments for funding. To overtly criticize NATO's heavy-handed presence in the humanitarian operation or to refuse to work in camps run by their own governments would have run against their short- and long-term interests (Porter 2000: 5). However, it was not only that protest was futile or highly discouraged. Many agencies were happy to go along because they were being rewarded handsomely by Western states that were showering funds on the relief effort. And, Kosovo was not some forgotten emergency in the middle of Africa; instead, it was a heavily-covered crisis in Europe. Therefore, it provided a spotlight for many agencies to demonstrate to the world and their donors what they could do. In general, their material interests tilted toward compliance and away from resistance.

Yet their willingness to ally themselves with NATO owed to more than the correspondence between their material interests and NATO's political interests. It also owed to their perception that they were on the same side. Human rights organizations and relief agencies that had integrated a rights discourse into their operations were more open to the idea of coercive humanitarianism. And, like NATO, many aid agencies read Kosovo with Bosnia-colored glasses.[40] In the months leading up to the war, many agencies had continuously reminded Western powers of what their impotence had wrought in Bosnia and how the end game required the threat and use of military force, and then directed the West to apply these lessons learned to Kosovo. Interaction, the association of American NGOs, wrote to the US National Security Council as early as June 1998 to encourage a military intervention to protect Kosovar Albanians (Minear et al. 2000: 63). As the violence continued with no political settlement in sight, more agencies made more urgent appeals for a more forceful response. Accordingly, once the diplomatic talks collapsed and the bombing began, they saw themselves as allied with NATO and part of a humanitarian operation designed to protect civilians.[41]

NATO's commandeering of the relief effort, the alliance between aid agencies and NATO, and the general politicization of humanitarianism had various consequences for the provision of relief and protection of civilians. To begin, it contributed to a bilateralization of the relief effort. Once NATO took charge of the relief effort, it quickly delegated different zones to different governments and their militaries. This had several implications. Now that NATO was a humanitarian actor, it had less need for multilateral humanitarian organization such as UNHCR, even though that was still formally the lead agency. NATO and other troop-contributing countries funded directly their "national" camps and their national NGOs to work in their camps (Morris, N. 1999: 19; Porter 1999: 22; Houghton and Robertson, 2001; Minear et al. 2000: 34–45). Although NATO justified this move on the grounds that it enhanced the efficiency of the relief effort, it also was consistent with their desire to control the relief effort and get credit (Roggo 2000: 3; Porter 1999: 19, 21). As one aid worker reflected, "NGOs from particular countries were often selected to work in particular camps where "their" army was in control – not necessarily because that NGO was the most competent." And, while NGOs were flush with funds, UNHCR was enduring a well-publicized shortfall (Porter 1999: 21).

More problematic, the bilateralization of relief by NATO did not necessarily benefit the refugees. Notwithstanding NATO's boast that it was more efficient that NGOs, its lack of experience showed as it made various mistakes, including choosing sites that had been previously rejected by NGOs because of their unsuitability (Porter 1999: 21). Bilateralism also led to varying standards, inequalities across camps, the failure of specific militaries to meet the basic needs of the populations, and the attempt by beneficiaries to play one national authority off against another in order to get the best aid package (Ogata 2005: 149–50).[42]

Now that humanitarian agencies and NATO were on the same side, many agencies felt the need to self-censor their views regarding its conduct of the war. They had lobbied NATO to use force, if needed, and thus implicitly or explicitly viewed the start of hostilities as an unfortunate but necessary development. Consequently, once the war began they did not feel as if they could protest when NATO's wartime conduct potentially increased civilian casualties or violated international humanitarian law (Wiles 2001: 12).[43] NATO's decision to avoid ground troops and to fight the war from the air made it easier for Milosevic to execute ethnic cleansing; that is, how NATO fought this war in the name of protection actually led to a protection crisis.

Although Oxfam and other such organizations were aware that the onset of war would hinder civilian protection, Oxfam muted its concerns in order not to distract from the case for force. Accordingly, when the consequences unfolded, it felt itself poorly positioned to criticize NATO for delivering exactly what it wanted (Vaux 2001: 20, 22). Aid agencies also were remarkably quiet when NATO was rumored to be using cluster bombs; Human Rights Watch was one of the few rights-based agencies to vocally object to this purported development. Although some agencies protested NATO's bombing of Belgrade and targeting of non-military facilities, again, the decibel level was noticeably low. Oxfam, for one, did not vocalize its concerns because it wanted to avoid confronting Western governments at a critical moment during the war (Vaux 2001: 23).

This politicized humanitarianism also shattered the sacrosanct principle of impartiality (Porter 2000: 4). The readiness of aid agencies to so quickly suspend their principles raised troubling issues regarding how primordial this principle truly is. Indeed, it revealed the extent to which these principles rested on a functionalist and interest-based logic. Relief agencies developed and defended these principles because they facilitated their access to populations at risk, gave them a measure of security and operational freedom, enhanced their legitimacy and funding, and enabled them to work virtually anywhere in the world (Leader 2000: 2). Yet in Kosovo impartiality served no immediate purpose because these goals were already assured. Indeed, in Kosovo the traditional incentives for impartiality reversed course. "There were neither security concerns nor difficulties negotiating access to the refugee populations with parties to the conflict. There were no donors insisting on strategies to minimize the incorporation of aid into the dynamics of the conflict. On the contrary, working in the camps actually required agencies to set aside impartiality. That they were prepared to do so with such dispatch creates the strong suspicion that the value of humanitarian principles for many agencies is a means more than an end" (Stockton 1998).

The willingness to forgo impartiality, however, was not without costs. From Serbia's perspective, NATO's humanitarian and military activities were one and the same (Curtis 2001: 10). Indeed, because NATO had militarized the camps, they became a legitimate target in Serbia's eyes. And, because relief agencies were allied with NATO, they also could be treated as a combatant (Krahenbuhl 2000: 4). There also was relatively little attention to the humanitarian situation in Serbia. Serbia had been hosting a very large refugee community, many of whom had fled the Croatian province of Krajina in the last act of ethnic cleansing of the Bosnian war. It then experienced civilian casualties as a result of the NATO bombing. In response to these perceived humanitarian needs, in May a UN Inter-Agency Needs Assessment Mission called for more assistance to Serbia, but none came. Although impartiality-guided aid agencies should have shown up on both sides of the border and attempted to treat all those in need according to the same allocation principles, "political considerations seem to have given rise both to humanitarian excesses on one side of the conflict, and an equally dramatic shortfall on the other" (Porter 2000: 6).[44]

Parenthetically, impartiality also means that relief is given based on need and not based on political, geographic, religious, ethnic, or other considerations. Using these criteria, the response toward Kosovo was hardly impartial. Western states and organizations demonstrated a nearly unprecedented generosity. The camps, by refugee standards, were lavish and subsequently became part of humanitarian mythology. Hot showers, video rooms, good lighting, state-of-the-art medical facilities. Such generosity, though, only highlighted the West's lack of concern for other areas in greater need. In Kosovo there was $207 for every person in need, in Sierra Leone $16 and in Congo $8. The European Community Humanitarian Office spent more money on Kosovo than the rest of world combined (Wiles 2001: 13). The US Army's expenditures at Camp Hope, Albania, which housed only 3,000 people for two months, equaled the UN's entire outlay for Angola. Although such inequities might have been tolerated had they been applied efficiently and where necessary to cover the basic needs of the refugees, there was gross duplication of services and inefficiencies.[45]

Kosovo represented a stark moment when a humanized multilateralism met a politicized humanitarianism. For a mixture of motives, NATO launched a humanitarian war, a military intervention that was designed to protect human rights. When that humanitarian war contributed to a humanitarian emergency, it quickly took control of the relief effort in order to maintain public support for the war. Most aid agencies accepted this development as the price of doing business with an organization that was acting in a way that was consistent with their principles and their interests. They were now firmly committed to human rights and willing to accept that in some cases it would be necessary to work with states. Yet the willingness to do so was not without costs to their long-standing principles and their ability to work effectively for populations in need. As many evaluations concluded, the problems confronted by aid agencies in Kosovo were only partly technical. They were profoundly political.

Conclusions

Those in the humanitarian sector continue to debate Kosovo and other episodes in humanized multilateralism because these events force them to reexamine what are the meanings and practices of humanitarianism. This debate raises three issues that deserve greater attention: how the humanitarian actors have been changed by the world they are attempting to change; the need to supplement organizational theory with interpretive analysis in order to understand the creation, fixing, and contestation of norms; and the relationship between humanitarian and world order.

Humanitarianism has been shaped and reshaped by the world in which it is embedded. So far, what little attention international relations scholars have given to principled actors has focused on how they have changed the nature of world politics (Risse et al. 1999; Keck and Sikkink 1998; Finnemore and Sikkink 1998). Yet we need to reverse the causal arrow and also examine how the world has changed these principled actors. Consider modern humanitarianism's very origins. By the mid-nineteenth century changes in military technology were making war more brutal, there was no tradition of medical relief, and the emerging profession of war reporting was transmitting gruesome pictures and accounts of soldiers left to languish and die on the battlefield. Publics were beginning to rebel at these sights and to express pacifist sentiments. In response, state and military elites coopted Henry Dunant's platform, removed its more radical proposals, accepted new rules governing how to tend to wounded soldiers on the battlefield, and thus demonstrated to their publics their commitment to humanize war. The International Committee of the Red Cross developed its principles in part to differentiate it from the world of politics and thus to help it gain access to populations in need. But, while its principal contribution was to rescue soldiers on the battlefield, it also helped to legitimate modern war. Although humanitarianism has continued to develop over the decades, such developments have been profoundly influenced, defined, and limited by global forces. I employed principal-agent and sociological institutionalist analysis to better understand how these environmental forces have shaped what humanitarian organizations do and what they are. To that extent, they do provide some of the theoretical tools necessary for conceptualizing why and how different elements of the international environment contain different control mechanisms that have had different kinds of effects on these actors.

Yet organizational and institutionalist theory devoid of interpretive analysis might very well overlook exactly how and why these features of the international environment might prove so controversial to humanitarian organizations. These should be humanitarianism's golden years. It has never been better funded, better supported, or more acclaimed. Such impressions are reinforced by international relations theory. For neo-liberal institutionalists, humanitarianism's causal importance is evident because states are using humanitarian norms to guide their behavior, and are now co-ordinating their humanitarian activities in and through an impressive number of international and regional institutions (Keohane and Martin 1995). The very development of a humanized multilateralism might very well be cause of celebration, not despair, for humanitarian organizations. As I have already suggested, constructivists, for their part, are so focused on how principled actors can change the world that they have neglected that they are not of like mind regarding what are those principles.

Yet what the theorists label as normative convergence or consensus might be labeled by the participants as a "crisis." In order to understand this contestation over norms, the debate over what is humanitarian and what are its practices, requires recapturing how the participants themselves give meaning to their actions and debate with others over what public meanings should be ascribed to their actions and events. Kosovo proved so controversial in part because it challenged humanitarian organizations to re-examine and re-imagine what are their constitutive norms – that is, what *is* humanitarian action. In general, as international relations scholars continue to investigate the role of NGOs and principled actors in world politics, they need to situate those organizations within the broader environment, consider how that environment has shaped the very principles that define principle action, and how such principles are not simply derivative of international forces but rather are a result of debate and contestation among actors who are attempting to adapt their interests and principles to new circumstances.

Kosovo raised troubling concerns regarding whether these adaptations have erased what made humanitarianism distinctive and have altered humanitarianism's role in global politics. The humanization of multilateralism and the politicization of humanitarianism destabilized the differentiation principles that once distinguished humanitarianism from other kinds of actors. Once upon a time these roles were clearly differentiated. Humanitarian organizations provided impartial relief to victims of conflict and military organizations were the ones that made necessary this impartial relief. Yet humanitarian organizations now engage in broader projects that are clearly political and turn to military organizations to defend human rights and to help deliver relief.[46] If so, then, states and their militaries also can be humanitarian actors. Many within the humanitarian sector categorically dismiss this possibility on the grounds that it is absurd that states, which are political, and militaries, which use force, could be bona fide humanitarian actors. Yet as Hugo Slim evocatively observes, humanitarianism is not owned by humanitarian agencies, a position that would be "as disastrous as making humor the sole preserve of clowns" (Slim 2002a: 4). As humanitarian agencies watch states, militaries, and commercial firms deliver relief, and as humanitarian agencies increasingly concern themselves with grander political projects and their organizational interests, there emerge more questions regarding what, if anything, makes humanitarian organizations a distinctive social kind. Although there are good reasons to conclude that humanitarian organizations are still distinct because of their motives, principles, and social purpose, the very nature of this debate only highlights how much has changed.

The willingness of humanitarian agencies to engage with politics, working with states and for grander political projects, also suggests a change in humanitarianism's function in the global order. Humanitarianism is now more firmly part of politics. Certainly it always was part of politics to the extent that its actions had political effects and relief workers saw themselves as standing with the weak and against the mighty. Yet humanitarian agencies once saw themselves as standing outside politics to the extent that their ambition was to save lives at immediate risk and to keep states at bay – for the principal reason that it might entangle them with political agendas and thus compromise their goal of relief. No longer satisfied with saving individuals today so they can be at risk again tomorrow, humanitarianism now aspires to transform the structural conditions that make vulnerable populations. Toward that end, aid agencies desire to spread development, democracy, and human rights, and to join up with a peacebuilding agenda that aspires to create stable, effective, and legitimate states. Humanitarianism is increasingly an ism that has ambitions to transform the world. In this way, aid agencies are carriers of liberal values as they help spin into existence a global liberal order.[47] Humanitarian organizations may or may not be part of a neo-liberal agenda, and they may or may not resemble the missionaries of the nineteenth century, but by their own admission they are now part of a global order that they once used to resist.

Notes

1 C. Powell, "Remarks to the National Foreign Policy Conference for Leaders of Nongovernmental Organizations", Washington, DC, 26 October 2001.
2 In this way, humanitarianism has a logocentric quality, which Jacques Derrida observes is in play whenever "one privileged term (logos) provides the orientation for interpreting the meaning of the subordinate term." For discussion of this discursive and binary relationship, see Nyers (1999: 21); Cutts (1998: 3); Minear (2002: 76).
3 This definition draws from Stockton (2004: 15).
4 The ICRC's principles are largely the "industry standard," though there are debates about the prioritization of these principles, their operational meaning, and even their relevance. For discussions, see Forsythe (2005); Terry (2002); Weiss (1999); M. Duffield (2001); Minear (2002).
5 For various statements, see Rieff (2002); Minear (2002); Donini (2004); M. Duffield (2001); Slim (2004a).
6 A fairly exhaustive list of these evaluations can be found at Humanitarian Policy Network, "Evaluative studies of the international response to the Kosovo crisis", online at http://www.odihpn.org/report.asp?ID=1040.
7 For this claim, see Slim (2004). This is related to UN Secretary-General Kofi Annan's (2000) call for a "people-centered" approach to security.
8 For an interesting discussion concerning the epistemology of "humanitarian crisis," see Stockton (2004).
9 See UN General Assembly Resolution 1991.
10 For the debate on humanitarian intervention, see Cassese (1999); Lang (2003); International Commission on Intervention and State Sovereignty (2001); Holzgrefe and Keohane (2004); Wheeler (2000); Slim (2002c).
11 See Franck (1999: 858) for a brief comment to this effect.
12 For the Strategic Concept, see http://www.nato.int/docu/pr/1999/p99-065e.htm online.
13 For this claim, see Slim (2004).
14 Also see Weiss (1999: 20).
15 Also see Linklater (1998: ch. 2).
16 For a succinct statement regarding the competing logics of relief and rights, see Bouchet-Saulnier (2000). Also see Macrae and Leader (2000); Chandler (2002); Minear (2002: ch. 3).
17 For discussions of differing attitudes toward military intervention, see Minear (2002: 101–4, 115).
18 For various statements, see McCubbins and Sullivan (1987) and Bendor, Glazer, and Hammond (2001). For applications to international relations, see Thatcher

19 Also see Macrae et al. (2002).
20 Also see Scott (1987); Scott (1995); Scott and Meyer (1993); DiMaggio and Powell (1991).
21 On organizational legitimacy, see Suchman (1995); also see Dobbin (1994: 126); Scott (1987); Meyer and Rowan (1977).
22 The heart of the resource dependence approach is that "organizations survive to the extent that they are effective. Their effectiveness derives from the management of demands, particularly demands of interest groups upon which the organizations depend for resources and support.... There are a variety of ways of managing demands, including the obvious one of giving in to them" (Pfeffer and Salancik 2003: 2).
23 See Barnett (2005) for a discussion of variation in response among humanitarian organizations.
24 For discussions of organizational and bureaucratic culture, see J. Martin (1992) and Alvesson (1993).
25 On the scramble, see Cooley and Ron (2002).
26 Another factor potentially influencing this expansion is psychological, deriving from the personal strain of relief work. Relief workers migrate from one nightmare to another, comforted only by the fact that, at best, they provide temporary relief. This sort of existence takes a very high emotional toll. Relief workers live in a twilight of hopelessness, believing that their just acts cannot begin to change the circumstances that give cause for their services. Wanting to believe that they are helping to build a better world, they begin to treat human rights, conflict resolution, and nation-building as extensions of humanitarianism (Rieff 2002).
27 The background is informed by Clark (2002); Daalder and O'Hanlan (2001); Malcom (1999); Mertus (1999); and Judah (2002).
28 UNSC Resolution 1160, 31 March 1998.
29 UNSC Resolution 1199, 23 September 1998.
30 Annan apparently approved of this tactic. See Letter from Secretary-General Solana to permanent representatives of North Atlantic Council, 9 October 1998. Cited from Simma (1999: 7).
31 The UNSC essentially backed these agreements with its Resolution 1203 of 24 October 1998.
32 Statement by President Bill Clinton Confirming NATO Air Strikes on Serb Military Targets, Federal News Service, 24 March 1999. See also Press Statement of Javier Solana, Secretary-General of NATO, NATO Press release 040, 24 March 1999.
33 Many NATO members cited the humanitarian circumstances for providing legal and moral justification for military action absent a UN Security Council authorization. See Simma (1999: 11–13) for some of these statements. In addition to Prime Minister Tony Blair's (1999) proclaimed "Doctrine of the International Community", Czech President Vaclav Havel (1999: 4, 6), also offered a defense of NATO's action in the name of humanitarian intervention: "It is fighting out of concern for the fate of others. It is fighting because no decent person can stand by and watch the systematic, state-directed murder of other people. It cannot tolerate such a thing. It cannot fail to provide assistance if it is within its power to do so."
34 UNHCR was unable to register refugees, the first step toward protecting their rights, or to play the proper role of determining the priorities surrounding assistance and protection.
35 The general observation is that the military can play three distinct roles in relief operations: providing security so that relief workers can operate; providing logistical capacity in order to move workers and supplies; and direct delivery of relief.

In Kosovo, NATO performed all three roles. Subsequent analyses focus on whether there is a "division of labor" and who might best play what role at which stage. See Minear (2002: ch. 6) for a general discussion and Minear et al. (2000) for the case of Kosovo.
36 On NATO's initial contribution, see Krahenbuhl (2000: 4); P. Morris (1999: 19).
37 Ogata (2005: 149) negatively reflects on the experience as she writes: "NATO had decided to engage in humanitarian assistance even before the NATO-UNHCR agreement of April 3 and had gone beyond the defined areas of cooperation".
38 Quoted from Minear et al. (2000: 64). They also note that NATO's working definition of CIMIC [civilian military co-ordination] as it applies to Kosovo and elsewhere, is "A military operation, the primary intention and effect of which is to support a civilian authority, population, international or non-governmental organization, the effect of which to assist in the pursuit of a military objective."
39 Also see Vaux (2001: 27–8).
40 The claim that agencies somehow lost their impartiality in this instance overlooks the simple fact that it has always been difficult for aid agencies and staff "to maintain a neutral and impartial stance in conflicts in which one party may have strong claims (including legal ones) to international sympathy and support" (Roberts 1999: 37). Any compassion NGOs felt for Kosovar Albanians invariably led to anger at those responsible.
41 While international lawyers and commentators focused on whether the NATO action was legal because it did not receive Security Council approval, aid agencies exhibited little concern with such legal niceties, preferring to judge the legitimacy of the action not on whether it followed the proper legal procedures but whether its ends were consistent with human rights goals. For the debate among international legal scholars, see the forum in the *American Society of International Law* (1999).
42 Also see Scott-Flynn (1999: x); N. Morris (1999: 17); Minear et al. (2000: 25).
43 One independent evaluation of twelve British aid agencies observed that "given the scale and profile of the Kosovo crisis, those DEC agencies with an advocacy remit appeared to carry out only limited public advocacy during the Kosovo crisis."
44 Also see MacFarlane (2000: 19); Overseas Development Institute (2000: 78); and Vaux (2001).
45 For discussions, see Vaux (2001: 30–1).
46 As Peter Fuchs of the ICRC observed: "The respective roles of politicians, generals, and humanitarian actors are not clear anymore." Quoted from Chandler (2002: 48).
47 For a general argument regarding how NGOs are constituted by a global rationalization processes, and are carriers of rational-legal values, see Boli and Thomas (1999).

7 Horizontal and vertical multilateralism and the liberal peace

Oliver Richmond

Introduction

This chapter takes as its starting point the debate about the qualities and dynamics of the liberal peace in the context of multilateral relations between IOs, states, NGOs and other non-state actors. The "problem of peace" in most regions of the world has been dealt with by strategies of both elite-level multilateralism and the promotion of vibrant civil societies, in the context of democratization, human rights, the rule of law, and development. These dimensions of the contemporary project to construct the liberal peace encompass the activities of a broad range of state, official, agency, IO, regional organizations (RO), and NGO actors, which take as their starting point an assumed conceptualization of the "liberal peace", present in most academic and policy documentation.

Multilateralism has traditionally been viewed as a way through which realist and liberal/idealist interpretations of the propensity of international relations (IR) towards anarchy can be brought under control. Traditional notions of multilateralism, prevalent in realist and liberal thinking depict an international system in which states are persuaded to adhere to a liberal form of peace by a set of international guardians. These take the shape of institutions, ROs and IOs, organized to defend and enforce a set of liberal norms in IR. These frameworks inform, guide and monitor state behavior. The focus is inevitably on state behavior, and so such thinking favors the state, officialdom, and the elites associated with the control of power and resources, those who make social, economic, developmental, legal, and political policy, and those who decide policy norms in these areas. This essentially encapsulates the multilateralism inherent in state–donor liberal peacebuilding today, and especially in the state reconstruction and transitional administrations in many conflict zones around the world at present.

It has also been increasingly recognized since about the late 1980s that non-state actors play a vital role in such activities, and this has raised the question of state–non-state actor co-ordination in terms of donor activities and project management, and more generally in terms of the complexity of the liberal peace project. State networks and officialdom no longer have absolute control over resources, whether for peace or violence. The state's Weberian control of violence or of peace has been moderated by a "global civil society", "human security" discourse, the requirement for post-conflict justice in some form, and the need for the marginalized populations of many conflict zones to be heard in any peace process. The new multilateralism reflects these new linkages between states, IOs, IFIs, ROs, agencies, and NGOs, as well as the requirement to build capacity in civil societies emerging from conflict. This reflects an "orthodox" version of the liberal peace, and is an important development. However, the inherent bias of multilateralism towards state-centricity means that even an orthodox form of the liberal peace masks what is a "virtual peace" in many conflict zones.

"Old", elite, and formal forms of multilateralism – in the context of international and regional organization, and governance – may increasingly be eclipsed by the multilateral activities of non-state actors, which have also emerged as a qualifying factor of the dominance of states, IOs, and their "rational-legal" authority (Barnett and Finnemore 1999: 699). Multilateral actors, as Barnett and Finnemore have shown, do indeed have their own agency and pathologies despite them being creatures controlled by powerful states, but so too do many other non-state actors involved in peacebuilding (Barnett and Finnemore 1999: 705). Thus differing levels of horizontal and vertical multilateralism, formal and informal, are key to understanding the efficacy and sustainability of the liberal peace model, and to its construction in post-conflict zones around the world. "Winning the peace" cannot occur without sophisticated forms of multilateralism (Ruggie 1992: 587) effectively directed and supported by "willful communities" (Ruggie 1994: 565). However, it is important to develop our understanding of multilateralism as more than merely a formal and horizontal architecture of IR (Caporaso 1992: 601), but also representative of a vertical architecture, which implicitly means that the constructivist, critical theory, and postmodernist agendas of justice, identity, inter-subjectivity, hegemony, universalism and cosmopolitanism provide points of departure for understanding the liberal peace, its construction, and its sustainability. Horizontal forms of multilateralism are defined here as relationships between official actors, states, and diplomats, and relationships between a broad range of unofficial and private actors. The "new", vertical multilateralism is defined by any relationship between an official and private/ unofficial actor. Vertical multilateralism allows a replication of the norms that arise in the context of horizontal multilateralism within conflict societies, but in tandem with at least some level of local debate and custodianship of peacebuilding.

While the liberal peace is assumed to be unproblematic in its internal structure, and in its acceptance in post-conflict zones, its methodological application may be far from smooth (Paris 2004: 18–20). Indeed its main components – democratization, the rule of law, human rights, free and globalized markets, and neo-liberal development – are increasingly being critiqued from several different perspectives. These critiques have focused upon the incompatibility of certain stages of democratization and economic reform, the ownership of development projects and thick and thin versions of the neo-liberal agenda, the possible incompatibility of post-conflict justice with the stabilization of society, the problem of crime and corruption in economic and political reform, and the establishment of the rule of law. These terrains are relatively well explored (Snyder 2000: 43; Annan 2002: 136; Chopra and Hohe 2004: 292; Rieff 2002: 10; Paris 2002: 638). In this context it is crucial to understand the way in which multilateralism affects and even facilitates the multiple interventions designed to construct the liberal peace as a self-sustaining end to war and conflict. These approaches have led to a "peacebuilding consensus" (Richmond 2004b: 85)[1] that reaches far beyond simply reconstructing the shell of the state, though with limited success. This consensus of course implies an inherent multilateralism, driven by a willful community's (the so-called international community) view of peace and what must be done to make it sustainable.

Consequently, this chapter argues that new and often informal forms of multilateralism have had an important impact on liberal peacebuilding. Horizontal and vertical forms of multilateralism are vital if the peacebuilding process is to receive wide support, for the transmittal of norms of governance, and to have a plausible chance of leading to a sustainable peace. Whether or not these new forms operate an as extension of the old multilateralism, or are representative of a radical departure from it, remains to be seen, but it is now mainly through vertical multilateralism that norm transmittal and diffusion now occurs within conflict zones – even if this does mean the export and import of dominant norms and pathologies associated with liberal state donors, the UN, EU, OSCE, World Bank, IMF, and other international organizations and agencies (Barnett and Finnemore 1999: 705). In what follows, this chapter examines the components of the liberal peace and related levels of multilateralism, and also what vertical forms of multilateralism offer in the quest to bequeath a sustainable peace to post-conflict polities by the liberal peacebuilding community.

Peace and multilateralism

The "problem of peace" has always lain in the capacity of unilateral actions to disrupt the international system, and in the international system's lack of any system of control and guardianship based upon consensus. The development of the liberal peace is exactly in order to respond to these flaws. At its heart lies a hierarchical international system, but one where international consent based upon multilateralism is the modus operandi of consensus building in order to establish a set of mutually agreed norms.

Despite this laudable impetus, the problem of peace has been caused not just by the contestation of power by sovereign actors operating unilaterally (Carter, W. H. 1936: xi), but also by the absence of broad debate on the conceptualization of peace to include so-called human security issues and actors, and the consequence of assuming it is a negative epistemology that can never fully be achieved. Liberal approaches to peace have generally assumed that the "liberal peace" is acceptable to all because it is both universal and built through multilateralism (Mandelbaum 2002: 6; Duffield 2001: 11). Such a consensus has been built multilaterally where it exists, though it is strongly predisposed towards state and official actors. Ruggie has pointed out that there is a dark side to multilateralism, which lies in its possible imperialist tendencies, which effectively deny the sovereignty of subject states (Ruggie 1992: 571). An extension of this is that non-state subjects may also be denied individual sovereignty. However, as the liberal peace assumes that all actors are agents and subjects within an international community, contemporary multilateral practises should also reflect this. Clearly this requires the concept of multilateralism to encompass a broader range of actors if this tension is to be resolved.

Before going any further, the contours of the liberal peace framework need to be sketched. It contains four main strands of thought influenced by the key antecedents of, and debates in, international theory. To examine these in detail would be a task for several other chapters (Richmond 2005: ch. 1 and 2), but they include the victor's peace, the institutional peace, the constitutional peace, and the civil peace. The victor's peace has evolved from the age-old realist argument that a peace that rests on a military victory, and upon the hegemony or domination of that victor, is more likely to survive. In its extreme forms this can be seen as a Carthaginian peace, and as the only way of containing both Hobbesian anarchy and the profligacy of human nature. The institutional peace rests upon idealist, liberal-internationalist, and liberal-institutionalist attempts to anchor states within a normative and legal context in which states multilaterally agree how to behave and how to enforce or determine their behavior, which also informs the thinking of the English School. It can be traced from the Treaty of Westphalia, through to the founding of the UN and beyond. The constitutional peace rests upon the liberal Kantian argument that peace rests upon democracy, trade, and a set of cosmopolitan values that stem from the notion that individuals are ends in themselves, rather than means to an end (Doyle 1983). This became a common refrain spanning the many European Peace projects of the medieval period and after,[2] through to Versailles in 1919, and on into the post-Cold War period. All of these three strands have been influential across the scope of the first and second "Great Debates" of IR, and depend to differing degrees on horizontal multilateralism between official actors, states, and institutions.

The final strand identifiable is that of the civil peace. This is something of an anomaly in thinking about peace because it requires individual agency, rather than state, multilateral, or international agency. The civil peace is derived from the phenomena of direct action, of citizen advocacy and mobilization, in the attainment or defense of basic human rights and values, spanning the ending of the slave trade to the inclusion of civil society in IR today

(Halliday 2001: 35). It is derived from liberal thinking on individualism and rights, and has been taken up by more recent constructivist, critical and post-structural thinking on the problem of hegemony and domination, self–other relations, identity, particularism and pluralism, as well as the need for human security and justice beyond the states system. The civil peace depends to a large degree on the connection of actors and issues within the official multilateral context in order to allow for advocacy, norm building, and the establishment of transnational networks (Keck and Sikkink 1998: xi); this is where informal multilateral dynamics have developed, which may be described as vertical multilateralism.

All four strands of thinking about peace effectively nominate omniscient third parties who are then placed in a position to transfer external notions of peace into conflict societies and environments. The liberal peace depends upon intervention, and a balance of consent, conditionality, and coercion (Ceadal 1987: 4–5). Most significantly, it depends upon co-operation and co-ordination among international actors engaged in its construction. Without this, the liberal peace project could not succeed, and as Mitrany pointed out, forms follows function (Mitrany 1975: xi): the requirement of multilateralism inherent in the liberal peace has led to the development of new forms of co-ordination and co-operation among an ever-growing group of actors. New forms of multilateralism have emerged as a consequence, notably vertical forms of multilateralism.

These notions have lengthy antecedents and the victor's peace has remained a key aspect of the liberal peace, even possibly including the emancipatory discourses, which still seem to depend on others being able to know, and install peace for those caught up in conflict. But, the victor's peace has increasingly become diluted and disguised by the long line of increasingly multilateral peace projects in the post-Enlightenment period, which were mainly European in origin and Euro-centric in nature, the emergence of a private discourse on peace with the growth of NGOs and civil society actors, and then in the twentieth century the formalization of a liberal-institutionalist discourse on peace. This later discourse, again underpinned by the victor's peace, formed the basis for the hybrid form that was to become the liberal peace, in which multiple actors at multiple levels of analysis in rigid conditional relationships with each other began its universal construction according to a mixture of conservative, liberal, regulative, and distributive tendencies (Clark, I. 2001: 216–41). This construction requires a specific ontology of peace, a methodology, mechanisms and tools deployed by epistemic communities that have the necessary expertise, by coalitions of organizations, states, institutions, involved in a conditional relationship between them and locations where the liberal peace is being constructed. It is in these communities that multilateralism, horizontal and vertical, has flourished.

Multilateralism and peacebuilding

The liberal peace is now multilaterally constituted by a number of international agencies, the UN, international financial institutions, and NGOs, as well as regional organizations like the EU and the OSCE. While in some cases as in Iraq multilateralism has been of a lower level, generally in all post-conflict peacebuilding zones the peacebuilding consensus is representative of a high level of international co-operation. This multilateral peacebuilding consensus constructs the liberal peace through the reform of governance in post-conflict zones. As outlined above, it is characterized by two key dimensions of multilateralism: horizontal linkages between official actors or between unofficial actors; and vertical linkages between official and unofficial actors. This latter is vital in confirming the sovereignty of subjects of multilateralism, rather than it merely being a disguised hegemony stemming from powerful international actors. Thus, contrary to traditional approaches to multilateralism, it is not just constituted by a broad range of states and their representatives, but also by a broad range of NGOs, agencies, and other private actors, which have now become indispensable as part of the peacebuilding consensus and the attempt to respond to human security concerns in the construction of the liberal peace.

These forms of multilateral peacebuilding aim at reforming governance in conflict zones. They entail a communicative strategy on which depends its viability and legitimacy with its recipients, both at a social and a state level. It cannot be achieved without significant resources. The allocation of those resources, the power to do so, and their control, is often the new site of power in post-conflict societies, despite or because of the emancipatory claims of the liberal peace. Both of these forms of multilateralism are necessary, and one cannot exist without the other because the liberal peace is created through the methodologies associated with a peacebuilding consensus, where like-minded liberal states co-exist in a Western-orientated international society and states are characterized by democracy, human rights, free markets, development, a vibrant civil society, and multilateralism (Richmond 2005: 85). This represents a consensus of states, donors, IOs, ROs, and NGOs as to the objectives entailed in the different components of the liberal peace.

The depth of this consensus varies according to the depth of multilateral consensus it implies. In some cases a broad level of multilateralism leads to a weak consensus that masks a dissensus, whereas in others a strong consensus emerges. The temptation is often to replace a weak consensus with unilateralism, if the liberal peace agenda is to be maintained, as seems to have occurred in both Afghanistan and Iraq since 2001. The first level of this consensus relates to security environments and humanitarian intervention. In the case of NATO intervention in Kosovo and Bosnia there was only a weak consensus. Australian involvement through INTERFET in East Timor was more broadly supported, as was British intervention in Sierra Leone, albeit being unilaterally conducted. A secondary level, but just as significant, relates to peacebuilding. In all of the above cases, amongst NGOs and agencies, and the UN family, there was a broad consensus on the breadth of requirements for democratization, the rule of law, human rights and post-conflict justice and development. There have been concerns on the part of such actors that this secondary consensus might effectively justify unilateral military actions especially on the part of the US or NATO, but generally speaking peacebuilding actors have not let this prevent them from working in these environments. Vertical multilateralism has developed between these actors and states providing military security and the necessary discursive resources required for them to operate in a relatively co-ordinated fashion, while "doing no harm", establishing the liberal peace at the civil, constitutional, institutional, and military levels, and of course conforming with the interests of dominant donor states and their agencies.

Yet, there is also a dark side to this process. Within the liberal peacebuilding framework there is disagreement on the methodologies to be applied for its creation, and also which aspect of the liberal peace should be prioritized. Yet, being part of this framework of liberal peace provides certain rights. Knowing peace empowers an horizontal and vertical epistemic community, legitimately able to transfer the liberal peace into conflict zones. This represents a continuum from war to absence of war or to peace, marked by ever increasing democratization, human rights, and development, all supported by a multilateral band of co-ordinated external actors. Not only is the peacebuilding consensus heavily contested in this manner but it has also been argued that institutional and local capacity is actually being destroyed by intervention in conflict environments (Fukuyama 2004: 53). This implies that the more external actors engage in peacebuilding, however multilateral, the more they may actually induce dependency. What is worse, the more efficiently the multilateral peacebuilding community operates, the more local capacity is destroyed and the more dependency is induced. There is strong evidence to show that this is the case: from Cambodia to the Balkans and East Timor, internationals remain in control of some aspects of domestic politics, they bankroll the state, provide expertise in every area, control foreign policy, and exercise censure when local actors misbehave. This of course raises the question of whether this is a purposive strategy on the part of the peacebuilding community, in which imperial multilateralism allows them to become trustees of conflict zones that are unable to govern themselves peacefully according to the dominant norms of the liberal international community.

Peace as multilateral governance

Clearly, the development of the liberal peace in conflict zones depends up an pre-existing blueprint for the liberal peace, and (as argued above) a vertical and horizontal multilateral consensus on this blueprint. As I have outlined in earlier work (Richmond 2005: 69), this multilateral peacebuilding consensus leads to a notion of peace-as-governance, which is heavily dependent on these forms of multilateralism. However, even within these forms of multilateralism it is clear that the role of the liberal states in building replicas of themselves dominates the project. This is partly because those working from the top down to construct the liberal peace tend to focus more on the state and its institutions. While this is often resisted by those working on bottom-up versions of peacebuilding, their conditional relationship with recipients, donors, IOs and IFIs, means that many non-state actors have developed the capacity for the most intimate forms of intervention in states and in civil society in order to develop a civil peace and to contribute the broader liberal peace project. This important capacity is of course of great benefit to the predominantly state-centric liberal peace project, in which such actors are deployed as norm entrepreneurs promoting the validity of its components (Keck and Sikkink 1998: xi). This entails a reform of governance directed by an alliance of actors, which become custodians of the liberal peace. Their control of this process rests upon a combination of inducement, consent, and co-operation, occasionally verging upon the coercive, or even the outright use of force. There is essentially a conditional relationship between different states and other actors involved in projecting the liberal peace, the agents they use to construct the peace, and the recipients of the liberal peace. There is little questioning of the validity of the liberal peace, or the way in which its various components fit together.[3] Thus, it is assumed that democratization, development, and economic reform, are complementary, along with human rights reform, and legal processes. There is also little questioning of the motivation of the projectors and agents of the liberal peace, other than among its recipients, who, whether official or non-official actors, tend to be suspicious of outsiders' objectives. Most of the critical focus therefore tends to be on the methods used to construct the liberal peace most effectively, efficiently, and as quickly as possible.

Peace-as-governance is the most common form of peace applied through a horizontal and multilateral peacebuilding consensus in conflict zones, in which a reordering occurs in the distribution of power, prestige, rules and rights. It focuses on the institutions of state as the basis for the construction of the liberal peace, followed by the governance of society. This represents both the top-down and bottom-up peacebuilding approaches. In terms of bottom-up peacebuilding, different actors contribute to the liberal peace model by installing forms of peace-as-governance associated with the regulation, control, and protection of individuals and civil society. The balance of power, hegemony, institutionalism and constitutionalism, and civil society converge in this version of peace in an era of governmentality, which is super-territorial, and multi-layered (Foucault 1991: 103). It incorporates official and private actors from the local to the global, institutionalized in the alphabet soup of agencies, organizations, and institutions. But, in its top-down guise it is also a form of the victor's peace, relying on dominant states, in the context of the states system. They give rise to "normalizing" activities involving the methodological transfer of knowledge from peaceable communities into conflict zones.

The next section argues that there are different levels of vertical and horizontal multilateralism inherent in the different gradations of the liberal peace.

Multilateralism and gradations of the liberal peace

There are four main gradations of the liberal peace, associated with differing levels and types of multilateralism. These are illustrated in Figure 7.1 (see page 176). The conservative model of the liberal peace is mainly associated with top-down approaches to peacebuilding and development incorporating horizontal multilateralism at the highest level of analysis. It tends towards the coercive and often seen as an alien expression of hegemony and domination, sometimes through the use of force, or through conditionality and dependency creation. This was the case in the Bosnia, Kosovo, Sierra Leone, Afghanistan and Iraq interventions. However, high levels of multilateralism appear to develop slowly in the context of the conservative version of the liberal peace, which is generally dependent on a major US role. What is interesting is that this also often seems to reflect the post-conflict situation in the longer term. Conservative approaches by implication seem not to make the transition to multilateralism easily because many peacebuilding actors display some resistance to their resulting association with unilateralism, which may slow down the engagement of the peacebuilding community. The peace that is created by conservative approaches is therefore marked by a strong reliance on a single actor, and little progress towards sustainability – as has been the case in Iraq recently. Of course, recent evidence suggests that there is a slow progression from horizontal to vertical multilateralism. As appears to have happened in the context of Afghanistan, humanitarian actors, while resistant to any association with the unilateralism of US military action in the first instance, tend to become drawn into the post-conflict environment eventually because of their aversion to allowing humanitarian problems to go untreated, and because of the funding that donors make available in such contexts.

In Afghanistan, the main focus of the peacebuilding community was on advisory functions, reconstruction, and reconciliation, through the work of UNAMA and UNDP. Gradually, and despite initial reluctance to work with the US military forces and in the environment they had been instrumental in creating, the UN mission took over co-ordination of the many agencies engaged in humanitarian support. UNAMA is the main provider of such capacity in the country. The UN operation has, however, been based not on international administration, but on promoting local Afghan capacity – though this has clearly been overshadowed by the sheer weight and capacity of the internationals present. This has become known in the context of state building debates as the "light footprint" approach,[4] which even though this is a conservative peacebuilding operation has necessitated both horizontal and vertical multilateralism involving grassroots actors.[5] The UN documentation on this assistance has been very careful to defer to the lead role of the local transitional administration, but even so the mandate of UNAMA includes national reconciliation, the tasks entrusted to the UN in the Bonn Agreement, human rights, the rule of law, gender issues, and the management of all UN humanitarian, relief, recovery, and reconstruction activities.[6] Given the fragmented nature of politics in Afghanistan, perhaps the most that can be achieved in the medium term is to collude with regional fiefdoms in order to construct what Ignatieff describes as a "rough and ready peace" rather than a fully fledged liberal peace, as has been the focus of efforts in Bosnia, Kosovo, and East Timor (Ignatieff 2003: 92). This is also what may transpire in the context of the attempt to construct the liberal peace in Iraq after the intervention of 2003. It is important to note the problems the UN has faced in maintaining the credibility of the "light footprint" model. There has been a lack of authority over donors, NGOs, and IFIs on the part of the UN system meaning that the co-ordination process and system between all of these actors in the case of Afghanistan has been dysfunctional (Stockton 2002: 2). This is partly because the "light footprint" approach has confused strategic ends (for example, maintaining the consent of local actors for the reform process) with the operational processes in what has been described as "aid-induced pacification" (Stockton 2002: 5).

The conservative gradation of the liberal peace equates to a hegemonic and often unilateral, state-led peace, which diplomats are fond of describing as the "art of the possible." Such charges are often leveled at the World Bank or the UN, but more often at recent US unilateral state-building efforts. This represents a fear of moving peacebuilding into a terrain where coercion and even force may used to apply it, and where it becomes an expression of external interest rather than external concern and responsibility. Where peacebuilding becomes heavily militarized, as has been seen in Somalia, the Balkans, Afghanistan, and Iraq, this represents a hyper-conservative model, mainly unilateral and heavily informed by the victor's peace in preliminary stages of intervention. In this context, the conservative liberal peacebuilding project is dogged by problems often associated with colonialism or trusteeship, and in particular with the phenomena of often violent spoiling tactics aimed at the custodians of the intervention.

Until the US interventions in Iraq and Afghanistan, the most common form of the liberal peacebuilding project was the orthodox model, which rests upon both vertical and horizontal forms of multilateralism. In this framework, intervening actors are wary and sensitive about local ownership and culture, but still also determined to transfer their methodologies, objectives, and norms into the new governance framework. Such operations are characterized by a high level of horizontal multilateralism between states, and vertical multilateralism between donors, IOs, ROs, IFIs and NGOs. This framework is dominated by consensual negotiation. This equates to a balanced and multilateral, and still state-centric peace. This is generally projected by international organizations and institutions as well as international NGOs. It represents a bottom-up approach, peacebuilding peace via grassroots and civil-society-orientated activities, as well as a top-down approach, through which peacebuilding is led by states, donors, officials, IOs, and IFIs. It focuses upon and contests needs-based and rights-based activities. However, top-down peacebuilding activity tends to dominate, particularly through the conditional models and practices of donors, organizations, and institutions, as do the interests of major states and donors. This model is exemplified by the UN family's practices of peacebuilding and governance reform, which started at the end of the Cold War and culminated in UN sovereignty for a time over East Timor. Despite its vertical multilateralism the orthodox model assumes technical superiority over recipient subjects.

East Timor provides an important example of the orthodox framework. UNTAET was deployed in October 1999 to administer East Timor during its transition to independence, during which time it was a non-self-governing territory.[7] The assumptions lying behind this mission were a natural extension of the role of the UN in Cambodia and the Balkans, and the UN became a sovereign in its own right during its attempt to construct a sustainable polity. The UN mission was mandated to establish an effective administration, support capacity building for self-government, assist in the development of civil and social services, co-ordinate and deliver humanitarian, rehabilitation and development assistance, and establish the required conditions for sustainable development. It was explicitly mandated to ". . . take all measures. . . ." The Kosovo operation provided a reference point for this mission based upon the pillars of governance and administration, humanitarian issues and rehabilitation, and peacekeeping (Suhrke 2001: 7). At least in its early stages, East Timor was effectively governed in its entirety by a coalition of UN, agency, IFI, NGO, and donor actors representing both vertical and horizontal forms of multilateralism. The governance pillar is representative of this coalescence of the different actors and roles engaged in UN peace operations as perhaps the most sophisticated process of constructing peace today.

However, even an orthodox framework such as this has not been without problems. The agencies and IFIs stood accused of doing too little, generally too late, being wasteful, excessively bureaucratic, and erecting barriers to local participation through the latter. A common complaint has been that locals cannot contribute to the state-building exercise meaningfully because of a lack of capacity and that internationals tend to ignore what local capacity there is.[8] What is more, there were also complaints that the UN has shown little leadership in terms of co-ordination of the various agencies. There has also been a failure to support indigenous peacebuilding processes, particularly because there has been little effort to initiate peacebuilding to deal with social justice and welfare issues.[9] The operation in East Timor still focused upon top-down peacebuilding at the expense of bottom-up peacebuilding, social justice, and welfare, meaning that focus was on horizontal rather than vertical multilateralism.

Though the orthodox peace in East Timor had become associated with governance of a mainly external nature, the operation found most of its local legitimacy in the sense that it was merely transitional rather than a fully competent government.[10] Not only was it a precursor of independence, which was legitimate in the eyes of the local population, but it shaped the coming peace as a liberal peace, as it was explicitly tasked to do by the international community. As a somewhat jaundiced Jarat Chopra has pointed out, the UN mission risked establishing another form of authoritarianism unless it was itself held to be accountable to the local population (Chopra 2000: 27). Indeed, Chopra charts an abrasive relationship between the World Bank and the UN over who controlled sovereignty, in which UNTAET resisted Timorese participation to "safeguard the UN's influence" (Chopra 2000: 30–1).[11] The East Timorese president, Xanana Gusmao, was evidently extremely aware of the questions relating to the nature of the peace that are apparent in this case. In one of the most explicit documents in existence from the policy world on the nature of peace he argued that the experience of East Timor indicated that peace was a basic human right and this involved not just international and civil violence, but socio-economic deprivation, a lack of development, and an engagement with the experience of recipient communities on the part of internationals.[12]

A third gradation is provided by a more critical form of the liberal peace, the emancipatory model, which is concerned with a much closer relationship of custodianship and consent with local ownership, and tends to be very critical of the coerciveness, conditionality and dependency that the conservative and orthodox models operate on the basis of. Though all liberal peace approaches aspire to be emancipatory, this is mainly found within the bottom-up approach, and tends to veer towards needs-based activity and a stronger concern for social justice. Again this approach is highly multilateral, especially in a vertical sense, and is much more influenced by transnational advocacy networks (Halliday 2001: 253) and "norm entrepreneurs" made up of an epistemic peacebuilding community rather than networks of state and official actors. Indeed, many actors operating at this level are cautious of becoming involved with international actors, even through a vertical form of multilateralism, because they are very aware of the risk of losing control of their own agendas and being susceptible to donor dependency. This critical approach to the liberal peace still envisages its universalism, but accentuates its discursive and negotiated requirements. These different actors, mainly local and international NGOs in association with major agencies and some state donors, and associated types of the liberal peace, tend to become more or less prominent in different phases of the conflict and the peacebuilding process. This peace equates to the civil peace, and generally is not state-led, but shaped by private actors and social movements. The civil peace and its emancipatory claims are indicative of a vertical form of multilateralism in which officialdom is less highly valued than function, perhaps returning to the insight of Mitrany that "form follows function" (Mitrany 1975: xi)[13] rather than defining function.

These main aspects of the liberal peace are expressed to different degrees in any one peacebuilding intervention. Which of these gradations takes precedent in any one peacebuilding operation often depends upon horizontal multilateral negotiations between key actors to establish its key priorities, which are then passed down to the many partners invovled in the liberal peacebuilding project. These are normally associated with dominant state interests, donor interests, and the capacity of peacebuilding actors. Local actors' responses may also have some impact, as has been seen in the case of the "Timorisation" campaign in East Timor (Smith, M. G. 2003: 63), or in Kosovo (Rupnik 2005). Yet, even where a high degree of horizontal multilateralism can be observed, as in cases such as Kosovo or East Timor, effective vertical multilateralism does not necessarily follow.

This means that multilateral operations actually suffer from some major disadvantages in the area of co-ordination. However, multilateral approaches appear more likely to lead to outcomes acceptable to the many rather than just to their main progenitor. Both Kosovo and East Timor became broadly multilateral after military interventions took place. In both cases the peacebuilding consensus has been sustained in an framework approximating the orthodox version of the liberal peace, even if there is doubt about how deeply engrained it has become. Similarly across the Balkans, relatively sustainable polities have been established if only on the continuation of international mandates for engagement. Yet in the case of Afghanistan and Iraq where levels of multilateralism have been low and the focus has been on a conservative version of the liberal peace, the picture is much bleaker.

What is also clear from this is that conservative, orthodox, and emancipatory versions of the liberal peace may actually contradict and undermine each other, leading to disruption in the broader peacebuilding process. Clearly, the less unilateral interventions mentioned above are still inherently liberal, but the sustainable dynamics associated with an orthodox or emancipatory version of the liberal peace seem to be held perhaps permanently in abeyance because of the security situation which has arise both before, during, and since the military intervention. There question here is whether unilateral military intervention – even if it is to produce the liberal peace – produces unintended consequences which make progression more difficult. In cases where military intervention has been multilaterally approved such as East Timor and Kosovo in 1999, Bosnia in 1994–5, and Sierra Leone in 2003, the peacebuilding process seems to progress much more quickly. This raises some important policy implications in terms of the different versions of the liberal peace and the impact of differing levels of multilateralism on the sustainability of the peace being created. It is assumed that the project of the liberal peace moves from the conservative coercive models, to the more consensual orthodox model, or even to the emancipatory model, and that this represents an increase in the numbers and types of international actors engaged in a peacebuilding project, and an increase in the networks between international and local actors. Figure 7.1 illustrates these dynamics in the context of horizontal and vertical forms of multilateralism.

Gradations of liberal peace

	Hyper-Conservative	Conservative	Orthodox	Emancipatory
Multilateralism	Negligible Horizontal	Limited Horizontal	High Horizontal/Vertical	High Horizontal/Vertical
Actors	State officials and regular/irregular military forces	State officials and regular/irregular military forces; IO, RO, IFI, which control agencies and NGOs	State officials and regular/irregular military forces; IO, RO, IFI, which control agencies and NGOs	State officials and regular/irregular military forces; IO, RO, IFI, which control agencies and NGOs
Method	Use of force	Force and diplomacy, military intervention leading to ceasefire, mediation or negotiation	Top-down peacebuilding; some bottom-up peacebuilding	Top-down and bottom-up peacebuilding
Nature of peace	Victor's peace defined solely by military superiority	Victor's peace, constitutional peace settlement/international peace treaty (but not an institutional peace); quasi-military measures such as peacekeeping deployed for long periods.	Constitutional and institutional peace; some aspects of civil peace; elements of victor's peace	Civil peace; focus on social movements, social actors, and issues, social justice as a pathway to peace; wary of external forms of domination being imported through external intervention
Sustainability of peace	Negligible	Fair	High	Complete?
Exit of internationals	Unlikely	Possible in long term?	Likely in medium to long term	Definite in medium term

Figure 7.1 Multilateralism and gradations of liberal peace.

Figure 7.2 illustrates that unilateral forms of intervention that do not have broad consent amongst internationals are unlikely to lead to sustainable outcomes. In the cases of Iraq and Afghanistan, a sustainable and orthodox version of the liberal peace looks very unlikely in the short to medium term. But, in other cases where there has been broad consent for the use of force,

Horizontal and vertical multilateralism 177

Hyper-Conservative	Conservative	Orthodox	Emancipatory
Unilateral			Multilateral

| Iraq/ Afghanistan (Bosnia 1995, Kosovo 1999, Somalia 1993) | Somalia/Bosnia/Kosovo/ Rwanda/Sierra Leone/ Congo/Haiti | East Timor/Cambodia El Salvador/Angola/Mozambique/ Namibia/Nicaragua/Guatemala | Objective of UN, ROs, IFIs, agencies, NGOs |

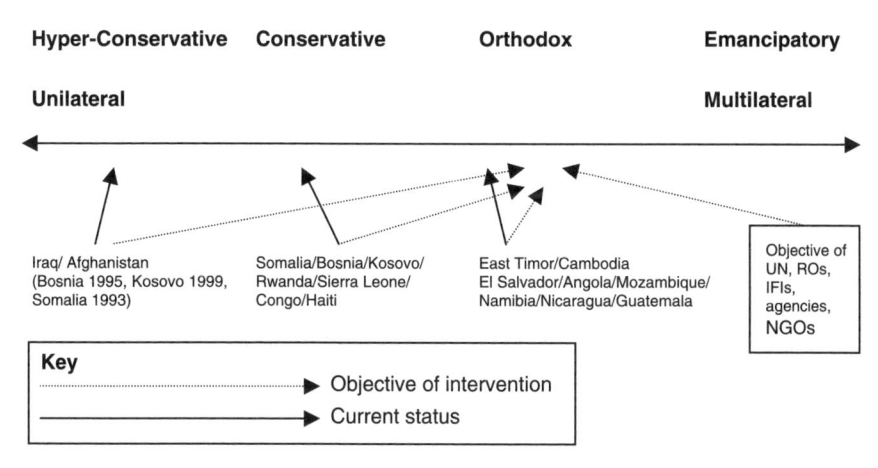

Key
·········▶ Objective of intervention
─────▶ Current status

Figure 7.2 Unilateralism, multilateralism and liberal peacebuilding.
Source: adapted from Richmond (2005)

such as in Sierra Leone, Bosnia and Kosovo, and East Timor, it seems that there has been movement along this typology to a more sustainable peace. However, even in Iraq and Afghanistan, there is now a sizeable peace constituency that seems intent on making sure that the liberal peace and its components survive. What this indicates is that what is key to the sustainability of the liberal peace is ideally multilateral international involvement that rapidly develops a vertical component, and a broad local constituency that also accepts this project. Without this in place, any progression would be unlikely or, at best, tortuous (as in Somalia).

Another aspect of this liberal peace model throws some doubt on even this minimalist prognosis. In Cambodia, depicted above as being at an orthodox stage of the liberal peace after 13 years of international peacebuilding involvement, progress has been excruciatingly slow in building a self-sustainable situation. It not just that unilateralism results in *slow* progress as the cases of Afghanistan and Iraq suggested, or *some* progress as the additional cases of the Balkans and Sierra Leone suggest, but that all of these attempts to build the liberal peace result in excruciatingly slow progress. The evidence suggests that the situation improves when more actors are involved and more consent is available – though co-ordination, conditionality, dependency, and the acquisition of the necessary resources then become problems – but also that unilateralism does not necessarily mean that progress cannot be made. What Figures 7.1 and 7.2 show most importantly, however, is that all unilateral interventions, if they are aimed at building the liberal peace, eventually become multilateral. This is because the liberal peace is such a complex project that one actor simply cannot succeed alone.

Conclusion

Multilateralism remains crucial to a sustainable peace. Where an intervention has not been multilateral, there is great pressure to overcome international political opposition in order to make the peacebuilding process and the construction of the liberal peace multilateral as it is implicitly recognized that a multilateral peace process has more chance of creating a sustainable peace. Furthermore, a vertical and informal form of multilateralism both provides enhanced capacity for a sustainable liberal peace, and also advocates such a peace. Entry into a conflict zone is often predicated on a conservative version of the liberal peace, which is unilateral, with the aspiration of moving towards the orthodox position, which is inherently multilateral. A significant number of examples can be provided for this movement, as Figure 7.2 illustrates, but a significant number also remain mired within the conservative gradation of the liberal peace. No cases can be located within the emancipatory gradation, and indeed, the lack of social justice, and socio-economic well-being and development seems to have marred all international involvements in the post-Cold War era (Paris 2004; Bellamy and Williams 2004; Chandler 2002; Chopra and Hohe, 2004; Cousens and Kumar 2001; Caplan 2002). Clearly, the above diagrams illustrate the tendency for internationals to enter a conflict environment somewhere within the conservative gradation, and then aspire (both the internationals and local recipients included) to move along the axis to the orthodox peace, which is perceived both to be sustainable and to allow the internationals to withdraw.

This requires the development of both horizontal and vertical multilateralism, a combination of which has the effect of guiding recipients' governance frameworks while not denying their sovereignty as more traditional forms of multilateralism might. "Willful" actors are required to drive this, including state and non-state actors, if it is to maintain high levels of legitimacy, particularly with recipient actors. However, experience seems to show that where force is used in a hyper-conservative initial approach, moving along the axis towards the orthodox category tends not to occur quickly. The best illustrations of this appear to be Bosnia and Kosovo, where the political entity (state or not) is weak, and may even be socially and economically unsustainable despite the length of time the internationals have been involved. Where entry is based upon a peace agreement with broad consensus, it often occurs within the conservative gradation but moves rapidly towards the orthodox, as many of the cases in Figure 7.2 indicate. In other words, multilateralism at both international and domestic levels offers a greater chance of a sustainable peace. One of the eternal truths of IR is that for any agreement to be made and then to be implemented, it must be done multilaterally, with both horizontal multilateralism – including that between officials (between state-level actors and international institutions) and non-officials (between private actors, both civilian and militarized) – and a vertical multilateralism between officials, private actors, states and institutions, whether NGO, militarized, or both formal and informal. This is the clearest lesson of the last two decades of attempts to build liberal states and the liberal peace.

Notes

I take responsibility for all errors in this essay as is the custom. Thanks go to Roland Bleiker, Costas Constantinou, Jason Franks, A.J.R. Groom, Ian Hall, Vivienne Jabri, Anthony Lang, Farid Mirabagheri, Nick Rengger, Chandra Sriram, R.J.B. Walker, Alison Watson, and Peter Wallensteen. I would like to thank the many people, local and international, private or official, from East Timor and the DRC to the Balkans, who were willing to talk to me during the course of my fieldwork on which this article is based. I am also grateful to the Leverhulme Trust, the Carnegie Trust, and the Russell Trust for providing funding for various parts of the fieldwork.

1 This phrase indicates a weak consensus between the UN, major states and donors, agencies, and NGOs, that a liberal peace should incorporate a democratic market, democracy, the rule of law, and development, and that all international intervention, both humanitarian or security-orientated should be contingent upon this. This consensus masks a deeper dissensus in terms of the application of resources, the use of force to establish the basis for such a reform, and the efficacy of different actors involved in the many roles this requires.
2 See for example Penn (1693/1993: 5–22).
3 For exceptions see Chopra and Hohe (2004); Paris (2004); Lund (2003).
4 See "Speech of the Special Representative of the Secretary-General for Afghanistan," Opening of 55th Annual DPI/NGO conference, *Rebuilding Societies Emerging from Conflict: A Shared Responsibility*, New York, 9 September 2002.
5 See for example the UN Tribal Liasons Office.
6 See UNSC Resolutions 1401 of 28 March 2002 and 1272 of 25 October 1999.
7 UNSC Resolution 1272 of 25 October 1999.
8 Personal interview with S. Frietas, Program Manager, Democracy and Governance Program, USAID, 11 November 2004.
9 Personal interview with O. Ofstad, Head of Delegation, International Federation of Red Cross and Red Crescent Societies, Dili, 11 November 2004.
10 See Goldstone (2004: 87).
11 In meetings with senior World Bank Staff in Dili, they were at pains to point out their concern about local ownership, and about not offending local politicians and the government, however. Personal interviews, 9 November 2004, Dili.
12 President Xanana Gusmao, "Peacekeeping and Peacebuilding in Timor Leste", *Seminar of the role of the UN in Timor Leste*, Dili, 26 November, 2004.
13 Here Mitrany reflects upon the working peace system without defining what it was to achieve in terms of peace. However, it is clear that he has a somewhat broader notion of the concept than was generally accepted in the policy world at the time.

Part II
Assessing multilateral security institutions

8 Transatlantic relations, multilateralism and the transformation of NATO

Frank Schimmelfennig

Introduction

When the Soviet Union and the Warsaw Pact collapsed at the beginning of the 1990s, NATO lost its most important *raison d'être*: to counter the communist military threat to, and deter a possible attack on, western Europe. This landmark change forced the Western alliance to redefine its relationship to the former enemy, to reappraise its security environment, and to review its organizational set-up, its force structure, and its security strategies and policies.

The transformation of NATO has had two main dimensions. In its external relations, NATO introduced partnership organizations for co-operation with central and eastern European countries (CEECs) and opened the door for new members from this region. In January 1994, NATO agreed on the Partnership for Peace (PfP) program, which deepened security co-operation and consultation between NATO and the CEECs. In 1997, NATO invited the first CEECs (the Czech Republic, Hungary, and Poland) to join the alliance and, in 1999, established the Membership Action Plan (MAP) for the remaining CEECs interested in becoming full members. Seven of them joined NATO in March 2004. In lockstep with the enlargement decisions, NATO upgraded its institutionalized relationship with Russia and Ukraine in 1997 (NATO-Russia Founding Act; Charter on a Distinctive Partnership between Ukraine and NATO) and 2002 (NATO-Russia Council, NATO-Ukraine Action Plan).

Internally, NATO responded to the disappearance of the common Soviet threat and the rise of new, more diverse and unpredictable risks and challenges to the security of its members by developing more flexible and diversified structures. At its 1994 Brussels summit, NATO endorsed the Combined Joint Task Force (CJTF) Concept calling for "easily deployable, multinational, multiservice military formations tailored to specific kinds of military tasks."[1] In 1996, NATO agreed to build a European Security and Defense Identity (ESDI) within NATO, which would permit and support autonomous military operations led by the EU. At the Washington summit of 1999, NATO launched the Defense Capabilities Initiative to equip its forces for new tasks of crisis management and intervention. The Prague summit in October

2002 gave new impetus to the transformation of NATO. In June 2003, NATO defense ministers agreed on a new and streamlined command structure with a single command (Allied Command Operations) with operational responsibility and another command (Allied Command Transformation) responsible for overseeing the transformation of NATO forces and capabilities. In October 2003, NATO inaugurated a highly flexible, globally deployable and interoperable NATO Response Force based on a pool of troops and military equipment.

Finally, and paradoxically at first sight, it was only after the end of the Soviet threat, for which it was established, that NATO became involved in actual warfare, invoked the mutual assistance and consultation articles of the North Atlantic Treaty (NAT) and sent member state troops outside the North Atlantic region – each for the first time in its history. In 1995 and 1999 NATO used its airpower to intervene in Bosnia-Herzegovina and Kosovo and put an end to ethnic violence in these parts of former Yugoslavia. On 12 September 2001, the North Atlantic Council (NAC) agreed to regard the terrorist attacks on New York and Washington as an attack on all alliance members according to Article 5 NAT, and in October 2003 NATO assumed the command and co-ordination of the International Stabilization and Assistance Force (ISAF) in Afghanistan. At the same time, however, NATO member states were deeply split over the war on, and occupation of, Iraq in 2003 and any NATO involvement in it. The strongest opponents of the Iraq war (Belgium, France, and Germany) for some time failed to agree to NATO preparations to protect their ally Turkey against a possible Iraqi counterattack and have rejected any substantial NATO role in Iraq to this day.

It is the aim of this chapter to review the transformation of NATO in the perspective of multilateralism with regard to both institutional structure and actual co-operation. Has NATO become more or less multilateralist in form and practice in the course of its transformation? And how do we explain institutional change and behavioral variation? Following John Gerard Ruggie, multilateralism is defined as a generic institutional form that "coordinates relations among three or more states on the basis of generalized principles of conduct: that is, principles which specify appropriate conduct for a class of actions, without regard to the particularistic interests of the parties or the strategic exigencies that may exist in any specific occurrence." These "generalized organizing principles logically entail an indivisibility among the members of a collectivity with respect to the range of behavior in question" and generate "expectations of 'diffuse reciprocity' " (Ruggie 1993b: 11).

In the first part of this chapter, I describe and explain the flexibilization of NATO, the main feature of its external and internal post-Cold War institutional transformation. In the second part, I assess the multilateral quality of NATO post-Cold War co-operation. Above all, I seek to account for the variations in member state co-operation on the core policies and decisions of the past decade: enlargement and the decisions to intervene in Yugoslavia and the Middle East.

The main argument of the chapter draws on different theoretical approaches. First, I argue that the institutional transformation of NATO has made NATO less multilateralist and this is best explained in functional terms by the nature of the core co-operation problem that the old NATO and the new NATO address. The old NATO faced a common and certain threat and the enforcement problem of extended deterrence: to "keep the Americans in" and to prevent the allies from free-riding under the US nuclear umbrella. The functional response to this situation was a restriction of membership and flexibility.

In contrast, post-Cold War NATO has not been confronted with common or clearly identifiable threats. Within NATO, the core co-operation problem was potential deadlock caused by consensual decision-making under the condition of heterogeneous strategic views, threat perceptions, and security interests. A functional response to this problem was institutional flexibility. With regard to the former Warsaw Pact countries, the main problem was uncertainty resulting from a lack of information on security problems and preferences in this region and a lack of trust. Under these conditions, high flexibility made sense in order to gain knowledge and create trust.

The more flexible and less multilateralist structure of the new NATO does not lead *per se* to a less multilateralist behavior of its members. Rather, behavior varies with the kind of security threats or challenges at issue. Multilateral co-operation has been strongest when core values and norms of the liberal transatlantic community were at stake – either as a result of their massive violation (as in the "ethnic cleansing" in the Balkans) or their strong reaffirmation (as in the candidates for NATO membership). It was weakest in the Iraq case, which was neither located in the core community region nor related initially to the protection of liberal community values. In between are the Afghanistan and Darfur cases. In the absence of a direct common threat, it is their common values that still promote multilateral co-operation between NATO members.

The institutional transformation of post-Cold War NATO: flexibilization

An increase in flexibility has been the hallmark of institutional transformation in post-Cold War NATO. For the purpose of this study, I understand flexibility as the degree to which NATO's rules and arrangements allow member states to choose their level of participation and commitment. Whereas inflexible rules and arrangements bind all member states all of the time, highly flexible or fragmented ones permit varying participation across member states and time. In this regard, the "new NATO" differs markedly from the "old NATO."

Although the NAT is not very specific on this issue, it is clear that collective deterrence and defense was designed to include all member states. Article 5, the most important article of the treaty, reads: "The Parties agree that an armed attack against one or more of them ... shall be considered an attack *against them all* and consequently they agree that ... *each of them* ... will assist the Party or Parties so attacked ..." (my omissions and italics). Moreover, the integrated military command structure and the forward stationing of allied forces (mainly in Germany) in the 1950s were designed to reduce the member states' flexibility in responding to military attacks. As a consequence, member states would have been involved immediately in combat as well as in executing defense plans; their room for political decision-making and maneuvers would have been severely curtailed. To be sure, even during the Cold War, France was able to formally withdraw from military integration (in 1966) while remaining a NATO member and co-operating *à la carte* with its Supreme Command. Many other member states have traditionally had specific arrangements with NATO, for instance, with regard to the stationing of nuclear weapons on their territory. The general thrust of institutional design, however, was to include all member states in the deterrence of the Soviet threat and in the collective defense of NATO territory and to restrict the flexibility of their participation.

In contrast, in the post-Cold War period, the general thrust of institutional design has been reversed. The main transformation decisions of the new NATO have also been decisions in favor of flexibility. According to the CJTF Concept, forces would "vary according to the circumstances"; headquarters would be formed ad hoc; members and partners would contribute "as necessary, using a modular approach, in order to meet the requirements of the specific mission."[2] ESDI permits the use of NATO capacities for operations led by the EU, that is, without US participation. Both follow the principle of "separable but not separate" forces allowing "coalitions of the willing" to take advantage of NATO's organizational assets. In addition, while NATO operations do not require actual participation of all NATO members any more, they are open to participation by non-members, partners or non-partners. For instance, 22 non-NATO countries participated in the Stabilization Force (SFOR) in Bosnia and 19 non-NATO countries did so in the Kosovo Force (KFOR) in Kosovo under NATO command – including, for instance, Argentina and Morocco in both cases.

NATO's partnership arrangements are also based on high flexibility. Since its beginnings in the North Atlantic Co-operation Council, NATO's relations with the CEECs have covered an extremely broad scope of activities, some of which are only weakly related to military security. They range from narrow security issues – such as defense planning, arms control, peacekeeping and, more recently, the fight against terrorism – to issues such as defense economics and conversion, environmental problems emanating from defense-related installations, the military protection of cultural monuments, civil emergency planning, responses to natural and technological disasters, international humanitarian law, and scientific co-operation. Each NATO partner has been able to pick and choose from this long list of potential co-operation activities and to conclude individual work plans and partnership programs. Moreover,

NATO has based its partnership activities explicitly on the principle of differentiation according to which the level and intensity of co-operation varies with the readiness and ability of its partners to meet NATO's political and technical conditions. As a consequence, NATO partnership has resulted in a highly differentiated, diversified, and individualized set of co-operative activities with the non-member countries of central and eastern Europe, some of which – such as Albania, Croatia, and Macedonia – work closely with NATO in preparation for accession to the Alliance, whereas others – such as Belarus – are formal NATO partners with little actual co-operation activity. At any rate, the level of formal and binding commitments in NATO partnership is extremely low.

Thus, if we follow Ruggie's definition, multilateralism has clearly decreased in post-Cold War NATO. Its institutional form is less based on "generalized principles of conduct" but allows more room for "particularistic interests of the parties," the "strategic exigencies that may exist in any specific occurrence," and the divisibility of security co-operation and benefits (Ruggie 1993b: 11). This assessment needs to be qualified in two ways, however. In a pan-European perspective, the formerly exclusive NATO, which offered mutual assistance only for a small group of countries, has expanded its membership considerably and extended its security co-operation to all countries of the region. In addition, the more flexible rules apply equally to all member countries. Although not all of them may be interested in or capable of doing so, each member state is equally entitled to form or join coalitions of the willing and receive institutional support. In other words, NATO does not create *a priori* privileges for certain member states, nor has flexibilization resulted in institutionalized bilateralism – the opposite of multilateralism for Ruggie (1993b: 8–9).

This descriptive analysis is the starting point for the remaining two questions the chapter asks. First, how can we explain the change towards institutional flexibility? Second, how and to what extent is variation in design related to variation in actual co-operation? In other words, does a less multilateral institutional form also produce a less multilateralist behavior of the alliance members?

A functional explanation of flexibilization

According to the functional theory of international institutions, institutional design varies with the type and seriousness of international co-operation problems (Downs et al. 1998; Koremenos et al. 2001a). In the case of security institutions, this general condition can be specified further: design varies with the nature of the threat and the problems of security co-operation that arise from countering it.

In the old NATO, the core threat was clearly identifiable and common to all member states: the Soviet Union. However, while all member states had a common interest in "keeping the Soviets out," their capabilities and vulnerabilities differed. On the one hand, the west European countries were immediately threatened by the massive conventional forces of the Warsaw Pact on their borders, against which they were not capable of defending themselves alone. In addition, most west European countries did not possess nuclear weapons and those that possessed nuclear weapons (Britain and France) had only limited capabilities that might not have been sufficient to deter a conventional or nuclear Soviet attack. For this reason, the west European countries had an interest in a security guarantee by the United States, above all in a place under its nuclear umbrella.

Because of its geographical position, the United States, on the other hand, was not directly threatened by the conventional forces of the Soviet Union and the Warsaw Pact. It usually had a technological edge over the Soviet Union and a superior capability of projecting military power globally. In the early days of NATO, its nuclear capabilities trumped those of the Soviet Union. Later, it has always preserved a credible second-strike capability. Whereas its homeland has generally been safe (with the exception of the Cuban missile crisis), the United States was in a disadvantaged geographical position with regard to the control of the Eurasian landmass. Above all, it sought to deny the Soviet Union access to and control of highly industrialized and wealthy western Europe. For this reason, the United States was interested in a military presence on western European territory and in finding allies for the defense of the region.

The common interests *cum* different capabilities and vulnerabilities created sufficient interdependence between the United States and western Europe to promote the building of a transatlantic alliance, but, as the functional theory of institutions leads us to expect, they also created co-operation problems. I suggest that the enforcement problems of extended deterrence were at the core of the transatlantic alliance. On the one hand, under the US nuclear umbrella, the western European countries had an incentive to minimize their military contributions to the alliance. If, as they assumed, US nuclear capabilities were sufficiently strong to deter the Warsaw Pact from attacking western Europe, why should they invest heavily in expensive conventional military forces (except to pursue their own specific strategic interests)? In a system of mutual nuclear deterrence, investments in conventional defense are militarily irrelevant and rather signal mistrust in the credibility of deterrence. In short, western Europe had the incentive of free-riding under the US nuclear umbrella. On the other hand, the credibility of extended deterrence in a system of mutual nuclear deterrence is always questionable. Whereas the United States had a credible incentive in using nuclear weapons to retaliate against an attack against its own territory, it was doubtful whether it would really use nuclear weapons in the case of a conventional attack on western Europe and thereby invite a Soviet nuclear attack on US territory in retaliation. In short, the United States had the incentive to defect from the nuclear defense of western Europe.[3]

Given these two enforcement problems of extended deterrence, the alliance partners had an interest in making each other's commitments as credible as possible. The United States was keen on committing the Europeans to do as much as possible for their own defense. This would not only reduce the costs of US military engagement in western Europe but, above all, reduce and protract the need to revert to the use of nuclear weapons and thus to test the credibility of extended deterrence. In contrast, western Europe was interested in limiting the US room for discretion and in increasing the pressure on the US administration to use nuclear weapons early in the case of a Warsaw Pact attack.

The nature of the threat and the co-operation problems changed fundamentally with the demise of the Soviet Union and the Warsaw Pact. As the main successor state to the Soviet Union, Russia inherited its nuclear forces but suffered a loss in territory, population, and allies. Above all, however, it was not so much the balance of power but the balance of threats that changed to the advantage of NATO (Walt 1987). Under the Yeltsin presidency of the 1990s, Russia was generally perceived as a country that had terminated the Soviet legacy of enmity to the West and sought a co-operative relationship with Western organizations. Already in its 1991 "Strategic Concept," NATO stated that "the threat of a simultaneous, full-scale attack on all of NATO's European fronts has effectively been removed."[4] Four years later, in its "Study on NATO Enlargement," the organization added, "since then, the risk of a re-emergent large-scale military threat has further declined."[5]

The disappearance of the Soviet threat effectively removed the alliance dilemmas of extended deterrence. The nuclear umbrella ceased to be necessary to guarantee the security of western Europe. The US administration did not have to fear any more that it might be drawn into a nuclear exchange because of the weak conventional forces of its alliance partners, and European governments did not have to be concerned any more about the credibility of the US nuclear security guarantee.

At the same time, however, the clearly identifiable and common threat that had generated the common interest of the alliance members ceased to exist as well. The military interdependence of the United States and western Europe diminished and so did the need for NATO as an organization of collective defense and deterrence. Realist theory therefore expected the end of NATO to follow the end of the Soviet Union and the Warsaw Pact because of the allies' overriding interest in autonomy and the western Europeans' need to balance US hegemony (Waltz 1993). In contrast, the functional theory of international institutions explains the persistence of NATO as a result of high sunk costs stemming from prior investments in the institutionalization of the alliance and of general and specific institutional assets that were seen to be "cost effective in the new security environment" (Wallander 2000). In addition, however, we should observe changes in and adaptations of the institutional design reflecting this new security environment and the new co-operation problems it created.

What were these new co-operation problems? Among NATO members, the absence of a common and clearly identifiable external threat brought the heterogeneity of strategic views and security interests among the allies to the fore. Prominent descriptions of the divergences include global US versus regional European security interests and a militarized foreign policy (attributed to the United States) versus the emphasis on diplomatic, legal and economic tools of foreign policy (attributed to Europe).[6] To be sure, these differences did exist during the Cold War as well and led to debates and conflicts among the allies. Yet the Soviet threat provided a strong focus, which urged the allies to co-operate despite their divergences. The divergence was put into stark contrast again after the 9/11 terrorist attacks on the United States. In the United States, they created an unprecedented sense of insecurity and a strong preference to combat them by the global projection of military force. Both reactions were much weaker in Europe. For NATO as an organization operating on the principle of consensus, the absence of a clear and common threat and the prominence of diverging strategic views and security interests decreased the likelihood of reaching agreement and created the co-operation problem of deadlock or decision-making blockades. Generally speaking, if an individual member state or a group of member states wants to act on a security issue that it considers relevant according to its strategic views and security interests and wants to use NATO resources for that purpose, it is likely to be faced with other member states that do not share its concerns and reject collective action.[7]

In NATO's relations with its former enemies, the CEECs and the successor countries of the Soviet Union, the core problem was uncertainty – about the security preferences of the new and transformed states and about the emergence of new security threats in this region. Would the post-communist regimes consolidate democracy or develop into authoritarian states? Would these states seek friendly relations with the West or follow new anti-Western ideologies rooted in nationalism or traditionalism? What would happen to the enormous armaments of the Soviet Union including its nuclear weapons now located in several independent states? Where would its military technology and knowledge spread? And finally, would the new states develop peaceful relations with each other or would they become mired in new hegemonic struggles and ethnic strife? In other words, the co-operation problems for NATO in this region resulted from both a lack of reliable information about the new security environment and a lack of trust in the newly emerging state actors of the region (see, e.g., Kydd 2001).

Can we attribute the increase in flexibility during NATO's institutional transformation to the change in threats and co-operation problems as the functional theory of institutional design would suggest? More specifically, does the disappearance of a common and clearly identifiable threat – and the concomitant shift from enforcement to deadlock as the core co-operation problem – explain the flexibilization of NATO? And does the emergence of uncertainty in the East account for the flexible design of NATO partnership?

I argue that the functional account is largely plausible. First, international institutions designed to solve an enforcement problem require low flexibility because flexible rules allow countries to decide their level of commitment autonomously and thus further defection and free-riding. Thus, it made sense for old NATO to constrain institutionally the rather flexible treaty commitments to mutual assistance and defense, for instance, through an integrated command and the forward stationing of allied troops. Conversely, the higher flexibility of post-Cold War NATO is a functional response to the deadlock problem it faces. It allows the task-specific creation of "coalitions of the willing", that is, of those member states that share security concerns on specific issues. These coalitions need the basic consent of the Allies to use NATO assets but do not require the participation of those member states with other threat perceptions and security interests. In addition, flexibility allows member states to participate to different degrees reflecting their capabilities and their interests in a security issue. An agreement to make an organization more flexible is likely if all member states expect to need alliance resources and the co-operation of other member states at some point for their specific security concerns but do not expect to generate general consensus and participation.[8]

Co-operation in post-Cold War NATO: varying multilateralism

The final part of the analysis moves from institutional form to international interaction and asks what accounts for the varying degree of multilateralism in post-Cold War NATO policies. The policies I analyze belong to the major post-Cold War decisions of NATO: enlargement and the military interventions and operations in Bosnia-Herzegovina, Kosovo, Afghanistan, Iraq, and Darfur. On the basis of two main indicators – participation and resourcing – I roughly distinguish between areas of strongly and weakly multilateral co-operation. First, if only a part of NATO members agree to a NATO decision or participate in a NATO action, multilateralism in NATO co-operation qualifies as weak. Conversely, an area of strong multilateralism involves the consent and participation of the large majority or all NATO member states. Moreover, strong multilateralism is indicated by a high level of financial and military commitment to a NATO policy.

Table 8.1 gives an overview of multilateral co-operation in the major post-Cold War NATO policies. Whereas multilateral co-operation has been strong overall in NATO's Eastern enlargement and NATO interventions in Bosnia-Herzegovina and Kosovo, it has been weak in the Iraq case and medium weak with regard to military operations in Afghanistan and Darfur.

When the central European governments first expressed their interest in joining NATO in the course of 1991, they were confronted with general reticence among the member states. Although NATO was prepared to establish and expand institutionalized co-operation with the former members of the Warsaw Pact, the expansion of NATO membership was initially rejected. In 1993, a few policy entrepreneurs within alliance governments – most

Table 8.1 Multilateralism in post-Cold War NATO co-operation

Policy	Participation	Resourcing	Multilateralism
Eastern enlargement	Consensual decision	Treaty commitment	Strong
Bosnia-Herzegovina	Consensual decision, NATO operation	Joint military combat and peacekeeping operation	Strong
Kosovo	Consensual decision, NATO operation	Joint military combat and peacekeeping operation	Strong
Afghanistan	NATO sidelined by US-led coalition of the willing, broad participation in war and ISAF	Joint peacekeeping operation with comparatively weak resources	Medium weak
Iraq	Decision blockade, partial participation in war	Training of police forces	Weak
Darfur	Consensual decision, NATO operation in support of African Union	Provision of airlift capacities	Medium weak

notably US National Security Advisor Anthony Lake and German Defense Minister Volker Rühe – began to advocate the expansion of NATO, against an overwhelming majority of member governments and even strong opposition within their own governments. It took until the end of 1994 to make enlargement official NATO policy. Enlargement requires the consensus of all member states, and this consensus was reached in 1997 on the first round of enlargement and in 2002 on the second round (Schimmelfennig 2003: 182–6). Although Eastern enlargement entailed a rather low risk of actual military involvement to defend the new members, the treaty-based commitment to mutual assistance is the strongest commitment that NATO can make. In addition, NATO enlargement caused immediate costs to the member states: the adaptation of NATO's headquarters, staff, and the common infrastructure as well as support for the upgrading and "interoperability" of military forces in the new member states (Geipel 1999). In sum, the consensual decision to expand treaty-based alliance commitments to ten CEECs after initial reluctance and member state divergence qualifies NATO enlargement as a significant policy of strongly multilateral co-operation.

The war in Bosnia-Herzegovina broke out in March 1992. Initially, neither individual member states nor NATO as an organization were prepared and willing to deny Serbia control of the new state and to protect civilians and refugees by military force. NATO repeatedly threatened the Serb forces with air strikes if they attacked UN protected areas and peacekeeping forces, but it was not before 1994 that the NATO threats became more frequent and credible. Yet they could not prevent repeated Serb attacks on the civilian population including kidnappings and killings. In the summer of 1995, however, after Serb forces overran the protected areas of Srebrenica and Zepa and killed 37 people in a shelling of the Sarajevo market place, the major NATO powers (the United States, Britain, and France) overcame their initial policy differences. As a result, NATO decided to exclude the UN from participating in NATO military decisions on Bosnia-Herzegovina and initiated its Operation Deliberate Force. This operation consisted in massive air strikes on Serb forces on the entire territory of Bosnia-Herzegovina, which continued until Serbian commander Ratko Mladic gave in to the NATO ultimatum and agreed to a ceasefire. In December 1995, the Dayton Peace Accord was signed and NATO deployed the 60,000-strong Implementation Force (IFOR) to guarantee the peace and oversee the implementation of the Dayton Accord. In 1996, and until the end of 2004, IFOR was replaced by SFOR. NATO's intervention in Bosnia-Herzegovina constituted the first active combat mission of NATO since its establishment and its first large-scale operational peacekeeping mission. This indicates a high level of resourcing. In addition, the level of participation was high. Not only did the United States, Britain and France agree on a joint military strategy but IFOR and SFOR involved almost all member states and up to 22 partner countries. In sum, multilateral co-operation was strong on both accounts.

The analysis of NATO's involvement in the war in Kosovo comes to a similar conclusion. In 1989, under the leadership Slobodan Milosevic, Serbia abolished the autonomous status that the province of Kosovo with its predominantly ethnic Albanian population had enjoyed since World War II. After almost ten years of peaceful but unsuccessful resistance against Serbian oppression, a Kosovo Liberation Army (UCK) emerged and initiated an armed struggle for the independence of Kosovo in 1998. The Serbian Police and the Yugoslav Army responded with the pillage of Kosovo villages in the summer of 1998; almost 500,000 ethnic Albanians were expelled from their homes. Given the policy convergence already achieved on the similar case of Bosnia-Herzegovina, NATO reacted quickly to the outbreak of violence. Already in June 1998, the alliance began to study possible military options; in October, the NAC authorized activation orders for air strikes. Faced with the threat of NATO bombings, the Serbian leadership accepted a ceasefire and the deployment of an OSCE peacekeeping mission in Kosovo.

In March 1999, however, after Serbia started a new offensive in Kosovo and rejected a peace agreement, NATO initiated air strikes against Yugoslavia (Operation Allied Force) that lasted for 72 days before the Serbian leadership began to withdraw from Kosovo. Operation Allied Force was the result of a consensual decision of the NATO allies, run by the Supreme Allied Command, and politically directed by the NAC. General Wesley Clark, the Supreme Allied Commander Europe at the time, called it "the first Alliance-wide air operation of its type."[9] Although the United States provided most of the military equipment and conducted most of the military operations by far, other allies contributed according to their capabilities. Despite persistent political disagreement on the conduct of the air campaign – and heavy complaints by US officials and militaries on the constraints and inefficiency of "war-by-committee" – alliance cohesion and the intergovernmental steering of the military operation in NATO were preserved until the end (Clark, W. 2002). In addition, NATO provided humanitarian assistance to the ethnic Albanian refugees in Kosovo and the neighboring countries, and led KFOR (established in June 1999) to monitor and enforce the peace. In KFOR, just as in IFOR and SFOR, almost all member states and many partner countries participated. At its full strength, KFOR consisted of approximately 50,000 troops.

In other cases, multilateralism in post-Cold War NATO policy has been much weaker. Compare the interventions in Afghanistan and Darfur with those in Bosnia-Herzegovina and Kosovo. The terrorist attacks on New York and Washington on 11 September 2001 were followed by a strong wave of solidarity and sympathy for the United States in the transatlantic community. For the first time in its history, NATO invoked Article 5 of the Treaty, in effect declaring the attack on the United States an attack on the entire Western alliance. In terms of practical policy convergence, however, the effects have been much weaker. The war in Afghanistan has not been a NATO-led but a US-led military operation – in co-operation with a coalition of willing NATO member countries. Initially, the International Security Assistance Force (ISAF) – established to keep the peace in the country after the defeat of the Taliban regime – was not led by NATO but by individual nations (Britain, Turkey). In February 2003, however, NATO began to support the joint Dutch-German command of ISAF – this was, by the way, the first time that NATO officially provided logistical support to a "coalition of the willing."

In August 2003, NATO took command of ISAF. All NATO member states and many partner countries participate in one way or another in ISAF. Yet compared with the Balkan missions of NATO, the level of resourcing and commitment is much lower. First, ISAF is not a military combat force. US combat forces that are still active in Afghanistan remain outside the command of NATO. Second, in January 2006, ISAF numbered some 9,000 troops – that is around 15 per cent of the size of KFOR in a country about 60 times the size of Kosovo.[10] Moreover, efforts to deploy more forces and to do so in areas outside Kabul needed to be postponed several times because the Allies were unwilling to increase their commitment to the security of Afghanistan. In sum, I rate multilateral co-operation in the Afghanistan case as medium weak.

In the Darfur region of Sudan, a rebellion broke out in 2003, which was brutally suppressed by the government with the help of the *janjaweed*, a mounted Arab militia. The *janjaweed* burnt villages, uprooted crops, raped women, and is estimated to have killed almost 200,000 people. Two million have been displaced. The NATO allies have been united in condemning the acts of the Sudanese government, imposing trade sanctions, giving aid to the displaced people, and putting pressure on the Sudanese government to enter into negotiations with the rebels and to declare a ceasefire in 2004. On request from the African Union (AU) in April 2005, NATO quickly agreed on a package of support measures, most importantly the provision of airlift facilities for AU peacekeepers. In a humanitarian crisis similar to Kosovo in 1998 and 1999, NATO members have thus consensually agreed in the NAC on providing military support. The level of support, however, has remained restricted to small-scale logistical support despite the fact that AU peacekeeping has failed, the ceasefire has broken down and the killings have resumed at the end of 2005. The deployment of NATO troops to Darfur is still ruled out.

In the Iraq case, multilateral co-operation among alliance members has been even weaker. From the beginning, the Bush administration's case and plans for war with Iraq divided the NATO allies. In February 2003, the conflict culminated in probably the most severe crisis in the history of the transatlantic alliance. First, NATO failed to agree to a formal request by the US administration for limited support of NATO. Then, Belgium, France, and Germany blocked advance planning for NATO support of Turkey in the event of a war with Iraq. In response, Turkey called for consultations according to Article 4 of the Treaty. This was the first time in the history of the alliance that Article 4 had been invoked. After a week-long standoff, the crisis could only be formally solved by passing the issue from the NAC to the Defence Planning Committee, on which France does not sit, thereby excluding France from the decision. In the end, whereas NATO would have been ready to support Turkey against a possible Iraqi counterattack (which did not occur), it did not lend support to the "coalition of the willing" that fought the war side by side with the United States. Moreover, the coalition was much smaller than in the Afghanistan case. Also in contrast with the Afghanistan case, NATO has not taken over peacekeeping tasks to assist or replace the coalition combat troops after the regime of Saddam Hussein had been defeated. To this day, the opponents of the war reject any official NATO presence in Iraq. The only minor commitment that NATO was able to make consensually at the Istanbul summit of June 2004 was the training and equipment of Iraqi military forces – with some member states providing training in Europe rather than inside Iraq.

Explaining multilateral co-operation: community values

None of the major post-Cold War NATO decisions was harmonious. Enlargement met with overwhelming resistance from the member governments initially. It took NATO three years to agree on a full-scale air campaign in Bosnia-Herzegovina. NATO was initially sidelined in the case of Afghanistan and could not agree in the case of Iraq. Even in the Kosovo case, in which the general decision to act militarily was quick and rather consensual, the actual conduct of war caused strains among the allies. After the disappearance of the clear and common Soviet threat, against which NATO had originally been established, the allies had to negotiate in each case whether it required a NATO response and was able to generate consensual commitments. The question then is how multilateral co-operation was produced and why it succeeded in some cases but failed in others. Can we attribute the variation to the functional explanation that explained the change in institutional structure best?

Given the high flexibility in NATO's institutional structure, international security co-operation cannot be accounted for by strong institutional effects but must be explained, first, by the need to co-operate to counter a common threat effectively and, second, by the higher efficiency of international co-operation as compared to autonomous action. I argue, however, that co-operation (and its variation) in the post-Cold War period still cannot be explained in this way. In the case of enlargement, the member states did not face a military threat or the growing power of an adversary in Europe that they would need to have balanced by adding new members. Rather, NATO enjoyed a higher degree of security and relative power than at any time before. What is more, given their military and economic weakness, the new central and eastern European members rather diluted than strengthened the military power and effectiveness of NATO (Schimmelfennig 2003: 40–50).

Similarly, neither Bosnia-Herzegovina nor Kosovo were of any major strategic, let alone vital, interest to NATO and its member states. After the end of the Cold War, Yugoslavia had lost its geopolitical relevance. Moreover, there was no need to intervene in order to prevent or stop negative security externalities of the civil wars for the NATO members. By sealing off their borders, NATO countries were able to protect themselves effectively from the consequences: they were able to keep the refugee problem in manageable proportions and were neither threatened by nor drawn into the wars by any of the participants (Hasenclever 2001: 362–80). Thus, in the absence of a relevant threat, security interdependencies, or strategic gains, why should the NATO members have co-operated particularly strongly with regard to enlargement and intervention in the Balkans? At any rate, in the rationalist perspective, the initial divergence of preferences and absence of co-operation is much easier to explain than the eventual policy convergence.

Moreover, it is not clear in this perspective why co-operation should have been weaker in the other cases. At least, Islamist terrorism presented a real and proven security threat to the member states of NATO. In addition, huge geopolitical and energy (oil) interests are at stake in Iraq and Sudan. Even if one argues that the Islamist threat was perceived differently in the United States and Europe, and that the connection between Islamist terrorism and the regime of Saddam Hussein in Iraq was highly doubtful, this might explain the weak co-operation in this case – but not why it was weaker than in the other cases.

As an alternative to functional reasoning, sociological or constructivist institutionalism proposes two main links between institutional design and international co-operation. First, institutional designs may be more or less conducive to processes of institutional learning and socialization (Checkel 2001b, 2005). This line of explanation, however, is not helpful in accounting for the variation in post-Cold War NATO co-operation. All decisions analyzed here were made in the same institutional context (the NAC). In addition, the time dependency of learning and socialization can be dismissed, too, because instances of strongly and weakly multilateralist co-operation occurred almost simultaneously – such as the second round of Eastern enlargement in late 2002 and the Iraq crisis in early 2003.

Second, international organizations institutionalize the fundamental values and norms that constitute the identity of an international community (see, e.g., Abbott and Snidal 1998: 24, and Weber 1994: 4–5, 32). They are established in the treaties and other basic documents of the organization and regularly invoked in its official discourse. In this view, the more these fundamental community values and norms are at stake in a given situation or issue, and the more a proposed collective decision is in line with them and serves to uphold and defend them, the more member state policies will converge. In line with this theoretical argument, co-operation in the alliance will be high if fundamental human rights and liberal-democratic norms are at stake in the transatlantic community. This will either be case, negatively, when they are challenged by grave and systematic human rights violations in the Euro-Atlantic region (such in Bosnia-Herzegovina and Kosovo) or, positively, when they are reaffirmed, strengthened, and expanded (such as in the democratic consolidation of central and eastern Europe that preceded the enlargement of NATO). Either way, the consensual decisions and co-operative actions were not driven by security threats and interests but by the liberal democratic and Euro-Atlantic identity of NATO. NATO members felt compelled to intervene in the civil wars in Yugoslavia insofar as "ethnic cleansing" on the European continent violated the most basic norms of the community and to admit new members from central and eastern Europe insofar as they had embraced liberal democracy and a Western identity.

As the brief case studies have shown, consensus and co-operative action were not the immediate responses of the NATO member states to either the CEECs' bid for membership or the human rights violations on the Balkans. Initially, the member states were reluctant to offer membership to the CEECs or to intervene decisively in Bosnia-Herzegovina precisely because strategic relevance was low and expected costs were high. In both cases, processes of rhetorical action and shaming produced co-operation in the absence of egoistic material and political incentives.

In the enlargement case, the central and eastern European governments and the advocates of enlargement within NATO successfully portrayed the CEECs as traditional members of the Euro-Atlantic community now "returning to Europe" and to liberal democracy. At the same time, they stressed the instability of democratic achievements in their region. In addition, they framed NATO as a democratic community rather than a military alliance, and enlargement as an issue of democracy promotion and protection rather than an issue of military necessity or efficiency. On this basis, they argued the case that NATO's liberal values and norms obliged the member states to stabilize democracy in the CEECs and, for that purpose, to grant them membership in NATO (Schimmelfennig 2003: 230–5). Based on the fundamental identity of the transatlantic community, this framing and justification made it difficult for the opponents to openly oppose enlargement without putting into question their commitment to the community values and norms. It also gave the proponents of enlargement considerable normative leverage in putting this policy on the agenda and work towards its implementation. Thus rhetorically entrapped, the skeptical majority of member states acquiesced in the increasingly concrete planning for NATO enlargement and did not block the enlargement decisions – even though they remained unconvinced of their utility (Schimmelfennig 2003: 242–50).[11]

In the case of Bosnia-Herzegovina, the allies shied away from the risks and costs of an intervention for a long time and could not agree on a common strategy to help. In the summer of 1995, however, it had become clear that low-risk and low-commitment strategies such as humanitarian assistance, peacekeeping, diplomatic mediation efforts, and momentary threats or uses of force were not sufficient to stop the human rights violations and end the plight of the population. In particular, when Serbian forces overran the UN protected areas of Srebrenica and Zepa and killed some 7,000 people who had trusted the UN's and NATO's safety guarantee – while Dutch peacekeeping forces stood by helplessly – Western governments came under strong public criticism and moral pressure to act (Hasenclever 2001: 407–19).[12]

In contrast, the Middle East cases were not only "out of area" but also outside the Euro-Atlantic region to which the identity of NATO applied. Yet the intervention in Afghanistan could be justified as a legitimate act of self-defense against a terrorist organization that not only rejected the fundamental values and norms of the West but also was determined to use violence against NATO member states. This explains the strong show of alliance solidarity after 9/11 and the general readiness of NATO members to join the United States in fighting al-Qaeda and stabilizing Afghanistan. That the war in Afghanistan was not fought under NATO command did not result from a lack of consensus in NATO but from a deliberate choice of the Bush administration to prevent intergovernmental political constraints in the conduct of war. In contrast, the Iraq war failed to generate consensus and policy convergence in NATO because it lacked legitimacy. It was outside the community region, not an act of self-defense and initially not primarily motivated by the defense of community values (although it was later increasingly justified as a war to end tyranny and establish democracy in the Middle East). In the Darfur case, whereas the uncontested perception of the situation as a grave violation of fundamental human rights generated consensual support, the location of the crisis outside the community area prevented this support from going beyond low-level assistance to the regional organization in charge, the AU.

In sum, alliance co-operation varies with the degree to which a security issue was relevant to the identity of the Euro-Atlantic liberal community. Participation is high when NATO action responds to clear and undisputed violations of the Western community's fundamental values, but high participation is only accompanied by high resources when this violation takes place in the transatlantic community region (see Table 8.2). Which alternative explanations could be brought up to challenge the identity-based explanation of multilateral co-operation in NATO? I distinguish between capabilities, hegemony, and partisan alternative explanations and argue that none of them accounts plausibly for the variation in co-operation.

According to the first alternative explanation, the divergence in capabilities is at the core of the co-operation problem in NATO (see, e.g., Kagan 2003). In this view, most European allies lack airlift capacities and globally deployable, usable military forces. Therefore, NATO co-operation becomes increasingly inefficient and useless as the most important security problems move away from the European region. Thus, NATO multilateralism was strong in the European conflicts where the allies' military capabilities were marginally useful in supporting the US armed forces and, above all, in providing peacekeeping forces. By contrast, in the Middle Eastern wars, the capabilities of the allies were too limited for NATO involvement to be useful (with the exception of some allied forces like the British, post-war peacekeeping in Afghanistan, or some EU airlift capacities in Darfur).

Whereas the description of the gap in capabilities is correct, it does not convincingly account for the variation in co-operation. Most importantly, the decisions for or against NATO involvement and individual participation were political, not military decisions. Whereas the decision for NATO-led air strikes in Bosnia-Herzegovina was made consensually, the actual combat involved only a few NATO member states. In the Iraq crisis, it was the US administration that asked for NATO support of the war and preparations for a possible defense of Turkey (in spite of the partners' limited military capabilities). These requests were not rejected because they would have been beyond NATO's capabilities (France would have been able to contribute effectively to the intervention), but because they were contested. Moreover, the Bush administration was highly interested, for reasons of legitimacy, in enlisting as many countries as possible in the coalition, including many that made no or

Table 8.2 Community and multilateralism in post-Cold War NATO co-operation

	Inside community area	*Outside community area*
High legitimacy	High participation and resourcing (Eastern enlargement, Bosnia, Kosovo)	High participation, low resourcing (Afghanistan, Darfur)
Low legitimacy	–	Low participation and resourcing (Iraq)

only minor contributions to the actual warfare. In other words, co-operation in NATO is about coalitions of the *willing*, not coalitions of the *capable*.

According to the second alternative explanation, it was American hegemony and leadership in NATO rather than value commitments that led to co-operation. Indeed, all cases of high policy convergence are cases of strong and essential US leadership. The US administration was the main driving force behind the air campaigns in Bosnia-Herzegovina and Kosovo, and without the US military, the interventions would just not have been possible militarily. The US administration was also the main driving force of NATO enlargement. NATO's main decisions on PfP, the Study on Enlargement, the setting of a date for enlargement, and the selection of new members mirrored US preferences and were predetermined by US domestic decisions (Goldgeier 1999). Nevertheless I argue that it was not the bargaining power of US hegemony but the normative power of US moral entrepreneurship that produced co-operation. First, whereas there is abundant evidence of US use of arguments based on the identity, values, and norms of the Euro-Atlantic community, explicit bargaining was conspicuously absent from the process. There is no evidence – either in newspaper reports or in interviews – of US material threats to the reluctant European allies in the case that they vetoed enlargement. Moreover, US leadership is only successful when it is in line with and legitimated by the fundamental community values. Consequently, it was not sufficient to produce multilateral co-operation when this legitimacy was absent or weak – as in the Iraq crisis. Thus, whereas US leadership may well have been a necessary condition of multilateral co-operation in the cases analyzed here, it was sufficient only in conjunction with value and norm conformance. What is more, when it was successful, US leadership did not need to use bargaining and coercion but consisted mainly in moral entrepreneurship.

Third, it seems at first glance that whereas the cases of strong multilateral co-operation occurred during the Clinton administration, those of weak co-operation fall into the "unilateralist" Bush administration. Yet the second round of NATO enlargement was launched mainly by the Bush administration and consensually approved at the end of 2002 when the Iraq crisis was already looming. In the constructivist perspective, it was approved precisely because the Bush administration argued the case for enlargement on very much the same identity-based grounds as the Clinton administration (Schimmelfennig 2003: 255–60).

Conclusion

In the post-Cold War era, NATO has become more flexible. This change in institutional design can be explained plausibly as a functional response to the disappearance of the common and certain Soviet threat and its replacement with a diversity of less common and clear security issues and with uncertainty about the new security environment in the East. At the same time, however, the more flexible institutional design of post-Cold War NATO, which allows for varying degrees and constellations of co-operation among NATO members, is indeterminate with regard to actual international co-operation. It does not tell us why and how member state policies sometimes converge toward multilateral co-operation and sometimes do not. I have argued in this chapter that, in the absence of a common and clearly identifiable threat to their security, the member states of NATO are mainly held together – and bound to act together – by their common liberal democratic identity and the shared liberal values and norms of the transatlantic community of all member states. Whenever this identity was at stake, member states eventually felt compelled to co-operate, even in the absence of a threat to their own security.

Notes

I thank participants in the Delphi workshop for useful comments on the first draft of this chapter.

1. See NATO Handbook at www.nato.int/docu/handbook/2001/hb1204.htm.
2. See NATO Handbook at *http://www.nato.int/docu/handbook/2001/hb1204.htm* (accessed 26 January 2006).
3. On alliance dilemmas in general, see G.H. Snyder (1984). For conflicting views on the effectiveness of extended deterrence, see Huth (1988); Lebow and Stein (1990).
4. "The Alliances's Strategic Concept agreed by the Heads of State and Government participating in the Meeting of the North Atlantic Council," Rome, 8 November 1991, available at *http://www.nato.int/docu/basictxt/b911108a.htm* (accessed 26 January 2006).
5. "Study on NATO Enlargement" at paragraph 10, available at *http://www.nato.int/docu/basictxt/enl-9501.htm* (accessed 26 January 2006).
6. The most prominent statement of these differences is Kagan (2003).
7. This is different from free-riding insofar as collective action is *not* in the common interest.
8. To be sure, this explanation is plausible but underdetermined: flexibility is not the only rational response to problems of deadlock. For a discussion of other solutions, see, e.g., Héritier (1999: 15–27).
9. See *http://www.nato.int/kosovo/press/p990325a.htm* (accessed 30 January 2006).
10. See "NATO in Afghanistan" online at *http://www.nato.int/issues/afghanistan/index.html* (accessed 30 January 2006).
11. On the mechanism of social influence that is central here, see Johnston (2001).
12. In addition, it must be said that the military situation on the ground had improved due to the Croatian offensive in the west of Bosnia and the pullout of peacekeeping forces. As a result, the risks had decreased with the increase of moral pressure.

9 Persuasion and norm promotion
International institutions in the western Balkans

Geoffrey Edwards and Mladen Tošić

> What we are talking about here are values and standards, values and standards which underpin the European Union, and which Bosnia and Herzegovina must honour if it wishes to move forward in its relations with the EU.
>
> (Ashdown: 2004b)

Introduction

The extent to which international institutions bring about change in the domestic systems of states has long been a matter of inquiry. The academic literature has burgeoned since the end of the Cold War to match and even overtake the examples of multilateral involvement and intervention. It has ranged from the general to the particular, with the role of the EU a frequent focus of study (see for example the issue of *International Organization*, Fall 2005). Yet while there is widespread agreement that institutions such as the EU can and do play a role, the weight and importance to be attached to them varies. On the one hand, much, inevitably, depends on the international context itself as well as the nature of the international institution. On the other hand, central, too, are the circumstances of the target state – whether it is failing, frail, rogue-ish, or post-conflict – and the obduracy or responsiveness of its authorities, the strength and capacities of its domestic institutions, its economy, its geo-strategic position and its conceptions of itself. Moreover, the debate has taken place at a variety of different levels, pitching, for example, positivists against constructivists. Whereas the former might focus on the strategic assessment of costs and benefits and whether incentives outweigh the costs of standing out or defecting, the latter have explored less tangible issues such as identities, norms and cultural practices. There have also been further divisions between enforcement theorists and management theorists, the former focusing more on coercive strategies undertaken by the international institution, the latter on social learning and capacity building (Tallberg 2002). For their part, Finnemore and Sikkink (1998) have pointed to the diverse roles of norm entrepreneurs in bringing about change – not least in holding actors responsible for their violations.

This chapter, taking its lead from the quotation from Paddy Ashdown above, focuses more on norms and on the ability of international institutions to bring about changes in the values and standards of the political actors in Bosnia and Herzegovina (BiH).[1] This is because the preoccupations in the Office of the High Representative (OHR) and generally in the EU–BiH relationship so intimately concern normative structures relating to the rule of law, democracy, human rights and fundamental freedoms. They touch so closely on issues of identity that they both construct and circumscribe the behavior of the various parties and groups in BiH. They also, as Wiener and others have argued, relate closely with the institutional context since strategies and the policies they give rise to are inevitably constructed within such frameworks (Wiener 2004).

In the case of BiH, the institutional framework is particularly complicated because it involves both the basic constitutional structure as well as the interrelated legal and economic elements laid out in Dayton in 1995, together with an overarching framing of the issues through the prospect of EU membership, institutionalized since November 2005 in the negotiations of the Stabilization and Association Agreement (SAA) but in prospect since 1999. To reach the goal of EU accession, BiH is being called on to go through a double transition: firstly, to overcome the legacy of Tito, that is, the legacy of a socialist self-management economy and a single party political system; and, secondly, to vanquish the horrors of war that have dispersed populations through ethnic cleansing and massive population upheaval, deepened the already formalized corruption that existed at all levels of society, and left political power in the hands of nationalist parties seemingly determined to continue the war by political means. This, especially in the case of those in the Republika Srpska (RS), has led to a fierce insistence on maintaining the constitutional position laid down in the Dayton Agreement of 1995. Even if the transition from Titoism to economic liberalism can be comparable, war and its consequences put BiH in a very different position in their development from the countries of central and eastern Europe (CEECs), different as they were from each other (see, for example, Pridham et al. 1997; Henderson 1999; Zielonka and Pravda 2001; Vachudova 2003). The CEECs have not only avoided the experience of war and ethnic cleansing, but they have not had a military presence – whether in the form of the Peace Implementation Force (IFOR), the Stabilization Force (SFOR), both led by NATO, or finally EUFOR, led by the EU – to ensure the implementation and continuation of the peace, or a representative of the international community with such powers as those of the Office of High Representative.

Nonetheless, despite these vital differences, the EU's enlargement to take in the CEECs has been of critical relevance to BiH and the western Balkans for two reasons. Firstly, the success in bringing the CEECs into the EU on the basis of the so-called "Copenhagen criteria" of 1993[2] inspired member states, as Noutcheva put it, "to replicate the model in a region that has been a security concern for the EU for over a decade. The recipe worked once, it was believed it would work a second time" (Noutcheva 2004: 1). This was despite the fact that in the CEECs, as Batt has noted, "the phases of stabilization, transition and integration indeed overlapped, they did basically follow one another. In the western Balkans, EU integration is a *condition* of stabilization, rather than the other way round" (Batt 2004: 19). Insofar as it suggests that all the elements need to be pursued simultaneously, it inevitably creates confusion between Dayton-derived and integration-inspired reform which has been difficult to accept. Secondly, the EU's role has to be put in the whole context of the Union's past relations with the Balkans. The failure of the EU to prevent or to resolve the conflict in the former Yugoslavia, especially in BiH and later in Kosovo, has meant that the EU has now every incentive to prove itself to be a credible foreign policy actor, able to play an active and constructive role in establishing and maintaining peace and stability in Europe – to the extent of using all available foreign and external policy instruments, with membership as the ultimate prospect.

The Copenhagen criteria call not only for the adoption of democratic norms and a liberal economy but also for the administrative capacity actually to implement the *acquis communautaire*. The criteria may have gradually gained substance with the enlargement to the CEECs but they leave, nonetheless, a great deal open for interpretation by the European Commission and the member states at a point when there have been expressions of "enlargement fatigue" if not skepticism about further enlargement as an intermediate necessity. Moreover, the extent to which governments, parties and people in BiH are already clear as to what such a remote goal might mean also remains an open question. Nonetheless, while raising questions of consistency and co-ordination, among others, the "return to Europe" and future membership have been policy goals pursued with determination and ingenuity by both the OHR and the EU, especially in the shape of the European Commission. They have therefore constituted powerful norm entrepreneurs even if not quite in the same way as the non-governmental issue, policy or advocacy networks suggested by, say, Keck and Sikkink (1998). They have, nonetheless, been a vital factor in seeking to mobilize change both through their own actions and by attempting to co-ordinate those of others.

This chapter unfolds in three sections, beginning with an examination of the role of international institutions as norm entrepreneurs and their ability to persuade domestic actors. The second section assesses the contextual framework in which these find themselves in BiH, while the third focuses on the role of the two most prominent international institutions active in BiH, the OHR and the EU, and the impact of the prospect of EU membership. The conclusion points to the dilemma facing international institutions seeking to bring about changes in the values and standards of political actors derived from the experience in BiH.

Entrepreneurs and powers of persuasion

Different paradigms inevitably evoke different approaches to their role. The key issues here are the processes by which the institutions have brought about the transformation that has so far occurred, the "transformative dynamics" as Checkel has termed them (2005). Much of the literature, whether positivist or constructivist, has focused on conditionality – constructivists thereby earning the criticism of Payne for using such material incentives and levers (Payne 2001: 41). But for conditionality to work effectively, the overall objectives and goals have to be clear and acceptable to those targeted and the incentives have to be regarded as credible and valuable, in both the longer and shorter term, not just at governmental level but also more widely among the people. In addition, they have to be seen as being consistently applied both over time within the targeted state and when compared to others. As Schimmelfennig put it, "if international organizations were perceived to subordinate conditionality to other political, strategic or economic considerations, the target state might either hope to receive the benefits without fulfilling the conditions or conclude that it will not receive the rewards in any case" (Schimmelfennig 2005: 5). In the BiH case – as in other instances – not only have there been questions raised about the consistency of EU policies, but there have been doubts as to the credibility of eventual membership and whether all member states are actually committed to western Balkan accession, which inevitably have had an impact on the situation in BiH.

In such conditions of uncertainty, persuasion through the provision or denial of rewards becomes a particularly sensitive issue. Much depends on considerations such as "the depth of cooperation," when the key condition is that the "shadow of the future is long enough that states have to care sufficiently about future payoffs" (Fearon 1998: 270). Or, from a less game-theoretic perspective, the question of the "goodness of fit" has relevance whereby "*the lower the compatibility between European and domestic processes, policies, and institutions, the higher the adaptational pressure*" (Börzel and Risse 2000: 5, emphasis in original). When domestic and European "norms, rules, and the collective understandings attached to them are largely compatible," the pressures are less and compliance and implementation less contested. Both approaches assume states are not ultimately opposed to change. In the BiH case, however, some elements have most certainly been against basic change and participate in the process only with the greatest reluctance and in the absence of alternatives. Others have been against particular policies and norms of behavior.

There has thus been a cycle from which it has proved extremely difficult to break: the greater the pressures for change, the more reluctance has been displayed in embracing it; that has then engendered the greater need for enforcement mechanisms, which in turn has often inhibited policy compliance and acceptance of the desired norms. In the absence of agreement on reforms, the HR has had recourse to more coercive measures. The failure to comply actively with the International Criminal Tribunal for the former Yugoslavia at the Hague (ICTY), for example, as well as continued resistance to policing and defense reforms which had led NATO to reject BiH's application for a Partnership for Peace agreement (PfP), caused the HR to dismiss some 60 party officials and police from their offices in June 2004, including the President of the Serb Democrat Party (SDS) and the Chairman of the RS National Assembly.[3] Nationalist parties resistant to change and hostile to incursions into areas of control have, therefore, been able to exploit such actions with their electorates to reinforce opposition to further change.

Such a spiral of coercive activity, of intervention and sanction in BiH, has been largely tied up in the role of the High Representative and his office (OHR) – with which the EU in its various guises are linked if separate. But implementing Dayton which reflected above all a "logic of consequentialism," while promoting European norms that are a part of "logics of appropriateness" (March and Olsen 2004) in the face of continued resistance, there has been inevitable tension. It has meant behavior by the HR that has often been "explicitly inappropriate" (Finnemore and Sikkink 1998: 897). That raises not only questions about norms and practices but also the likely effectiveness of persuading or inducing local actors to accept different, democratic, liberal norms when the entrepreneurs may have international support but their actions allow for little sense of any local accountability.

What therefore remain important, even for constructivists, are the incentives and a rational assessment of future benefits set against sanctions through imposed conditionality (see, for example, Schimmelfennig and Seidelmeier 2004: 664). The problem for the HR and the EU has been the creation of incentive structures that would encourage such socialization. On the one hand, as Caplan has argued, while outside experts can "encourage 'ownership' of 'best policies' through persuasion", the degree of ownership likely to be achieved will be "much greater if those who must carry out the policies are actively involved in the process of shaping and adapting, if not reinventing these policies in the country itself" (Caplan 2005: 472). It is when, however, local actors reject ownership, and measures have been imposed, that a "dependency syndrome" builds up. As one former HR put it, "every piece of legislation that I impose with my authority as the High Representative, gives politicians in BiH a perfect excuse not to do their job properly" (Petritsch 1999). It may mean that, if the measures are then implemented (which does not necessarily follow), local actors are perforce acting in ways that raise questions about the level or genuineness of any socialization that the institutions might have been hoping for.

The alternative – and key to the EU's approach – has been the emphasis on rewards (especially long-term rewards) if criteria are met. It may be that, as Joseph Stiglitz has declared, "good policies cannot be bought" (quoted in Checkel 2000: 3), but such conditionality remains the favored policy of most international institutions, including the EU. Since all Bosnian actors have signed up to the idea of eventual EU membership, at least in principle, and despite the confusion of Dayton and EU criteria, it is not surprising that there has been frustration on the institutions' part when the Bosnians do not accept EU-generated rules and processes and seem almost to prefer the tougher tactics of persuasion used by the HR.

The confusion of EU and HR criteria raises the possibility that it is less the deliberate refusal of actors to comply than their inability to do so. Tallberg in his 2002 article looks back to theorists such as Oran Young (1992) or Chayes and Chayes (1993) who saw a general propensity to comply (whether through considerations of efficiency, interests or norms) countered or undermined by factors such as the ambiguity of the rules, their lack of transparency which made them difficult to monitor, and the limited capacity to implement them. These, Young described as factors endogenous to the institutional arrangements themselves (as opposed, that is, to exogenous or contextual factors) (Young 1992: 176). In such circumstances, coercive action might be misguided since the emphasis might be better placed on management-orientated measures such as economic and administrative aid and training, with, for Young, considerable importance attached to the institutional design and the arrangements laid out. In the BiH case, it may not only be the political and economic consequences of war that have inhibited political and administrative capacity, but also popular opposition to change.

A rather different dimension to institutional design and capacity building to consider, emphasized by constructivists, is the importance of social learning in bringing about compliance. Social learning, whether by persuasion, argumentation, monitoring and ultimately exposing those who resist the process, emphasizes both the rules by which bargaining should take place and the alternative outcomes possible, including their costs and consequences. It presupposes a degree of acceptance of the parameters of the possible outcomes. But while socialization and even a growing element of Europeanization may be brought about by continuous interaction of the parties involved, it does not necessarily imply more than a strategic calculation of advantage and benefits. The ideas and norms being circulated may resonate with the target audience, but not always in the sense of them becoming more than a part of the political intercourse. That may give them a credibility and an element of legitimacy; it may not guarantee any permanent switch of logic or internalization.

The problem in such approaches is, of course, when non-compliance is actually the preference – even if that may be complicated by a lack of capacity. It is here that Tallberg sees the need for both enforcement and management measures to build capacity, to monitor compliance in order to enhance transparency and expose violations, and to ensure that the legal system can deal with the violators. Transparency also at least invites accountability to a wider audience, both domestic as well as international. At the intra-state level, it allows the various actors to see whether practice and implementation match agreement; at the international level it also encourages greater coordination of effort (Tallberg 2002: 612–13). In the tangled web of the BiH, however, issues of ownership of the reform process are entwined with competing legal systems and principles. Issues of accountability have, too, become blurred given the number of international institutions (the OHR, the EU, the Council of Europe and the OSCE) that are responsible for, or involved in, not just reconstruction but state and democracy building.

Contextual framework

The intimate and complex inter-relationship between the conditions laid down for EU membership and the Dayton Agreement have been of fundamental importance in the BiH's history since the late 1990s. Dayton, after all, set out the constitutional structure for BiH. Opinion as to the compatibility of that structure with continued stability as well as possible membership of the EU has been divided. Cox, for example, has pointed out that there has been "the tendency of peace negotiations to produce highly decentralized constitutional structures, which provide a poor foundation for a state" (Cox 2001: 6). On the other hand, Bose in 2005 argued that "the notion that a (con)federal, consociational structure of government is an inherent obstacle to Bosnia's journey to Europe . . . is sadly misguided" (Bose 2005: 329). The problem was well expressed by the former President of the RS and of BiH's tripartite presidency, Mirko Šarović, who declared in 2003:

> Let's not play games with each other. We had a war here. We wanted to secede and join with Serbia, while people in the Federation wanted an independent Bosnia. We got peace in Dayton that we all accepted. Now, we are not going to give up any bit of our sovereignty that we got at Dayton.
> (International Crisis Group 2003: 21)

And yet, while not seeking to revise Dayton as such, both the HR and the EU have sought to change key powers or competences in the interests of an effective and efficient BiH.

Uncertainty and confusion as to how far such reforms might go in undermining key constitutional and institutional norms and the role of the entities has been at the heart of the opposition. Ahmet Hadžipašić, the Federation Prime Minister, remarked on the inevitability of further centralization of BiH governance, because

> when you make new police regions, you will have to make the same regions for the judiciary. So, once you have made this rationalization in the area of finance, security, and the judiciary, then what is left for us as the entities? We can clean parks and that's about it.[4]

For its part, the RS position was summed up by Mladen Ivanić when he commented that there needed to be a dual-track process, one that kept a decentralised structure "since this is the reflection of reality in BiH." But he recognised, too that "the institutions of BiH must have the authority to fulfil European conditions." The question for him, therefore, was "not a choice between the state or the entities, but to have the state *and* the entities . . . A balance can be found, such as it exists in every federal state."[5]

It not simply a question of constitutional structures, therefore, but also a matter of the practices to which they give rise and which embed them further. Nearly four years of war had concentrated wealth and power structures within the military and political elites in each of the ethnic groupings with the result that there were strong vested interests that were opposed to a strong functioning state, whether decentralized or not. Democratic control and economic liberalization have simply not been in the interests of many of the hard-line nationalist parties and/or those determined to perpetuate a vicious cycle of corruption. Pugh, for example, while seeking to explain how the criminal and shadow economy flourished in Milošević's Yugoslavia and its successor states saw it as a way of enabling people to cope – which was not to excuse "the ruthless, predatory and socially destabilizing role of mafia-networks, or the political grip of rent-seeking, patron-client ties, or nepotism among newly enriched war elites." But, he went on, "such networks and elites retain their power partly because of the services they perform for their followers and dependants" (Pugh 2004: 54).

Control of socially-owned assets provided revenues for nationalist parties and those dependent on them. But the situation was made worse by the, certainly unintended, consequences of the privatization policies urged on BiH by the international community, which reinforced the position of the former war elites, and allowed them to extend their networks beyond their political protectors to those responsible for tackling crime. As Hadžipašić expressed it:

> The people who led the war had status that they wanted to transfer into capital. In order to hold onto this capital they then had to hold onto political power after the war and so we still have local sheriffs who are dominant in politics. Transition is the perfect opportunity for all this. In any system it would be a difficult task. But, during transition it is possible to make and break laws. According to these people the process of transition needs to be as long as possible.[6]

Bureaucracies swollen, even while underpaid, by corrupt networks did not or could not collect taxes; poor services undermined the state and reinforced the need for continuing the services performed by corrupt networks. The vicious circle was made worse by a weak judiciary that could not enforce the law and contracts, thereby making any incoming investment an unattractive proposition. The very institutional incapacity of the state became, as Cox put it "a major obstacle to the peace process in its own right, fostering the conditions of economic and social instability which make a return to open conflict more likely" (Cox 2001: 10).

There was therefore both an unwillingness and a lack of ability to respond to the challenges of post-war reconstruction and transition to an open economy. The international institutions, particularly the OHR and the EU, were thereby able to exercise only limited leverage to bring about voluntary compliance, despite Bosnia's still heavy dependence on external support. But it was no surprise that the EU *qua* Commission in its Report on the preparedness of BiH to negotiate an SAA pointed to the pressing need for more effective governance, a more effective public administration, and an effective judiciary among its 16 points – as well as an independent public broadcasting system (European Commission 2003).

However, foremost among the EU's requirements was compliance with international obligations and especially full co-operation with the ICTY in bringing indicted war criminals before the tribunal. It was a demand that the international community in its various formations had made many times before. Awareness that one of the most wanted war-crime indictees, Ratko Mladić, had remained on the RS pay roll until 2002, suggested more than a lack of commitment on the part of the RS to meeting its obligations. As the chief prosecutor at ICTY, Carla del Ponte, remarked, "I believe there are fundamental systemic weaknesses built into the law enforcement and security structures in Bosnia and Herzegovina, and in particular the Republika Srpska ... The Ministries of Defence and of the Interior of Republika Srpska cannot, by any reasonable standards, be judged to have helped in this regard" (International Crisis Group 2005: 2–3). The EU 2003 Feasibility Study was therefore tied closely not simply to capacity building but also to Bosnian compliance with its international obligations and the conditions already laid down.

Complexity and co-ordination

The transmission of norms to BiH has been made even more difficult by two factors: the complexity of the issues that interconnected the not always easily reconcilable processes derived from Dayton and from European integration, and the multiplicity of norm entrepreneurs. The result has been manifold problems of co-ordination. As one senior EU official admitted,

> The multiplicity of projects and activities, which are complemented by bilateral measures by individual EU member states, cannot hide the fact that the overall record in this field is not altogether encouraging. Not only is there a distinct deficit in co-ordination among the various actors in this field but the resources and the manpower deployed are so far no match for the well-financed and smooth international and interethnic co-operation of criminal networks.
> (Lehne 2004: 118)

Whether a display of rhetoric or not, it was interesting that Ashdown, in reporting that his dismissal of 60 officials was co-ordinated with other measures taken by the United States and EU, declared that "for the first time since Dayton we have initiated a concerted approach to hit those who support war criminals" (Ashdown 2003).

The problem was therefore of long standing and Ashdown accepted that the OHR's relationship with other agencies had not always been easy, especially since each agency had different reporting lines (as, indeed, did he, to the Peace Implementation Council (PIC), to the UN and to the EU). What he had sought to do, by chairing weekly meetings of the principal organizations present in BiH (including SFOR, UNHCR, OSCE, EU, World Bank, and IMF), was to improve co-ordination and as a result raise the quality of work of the international community in BiH (Ashdown 2003). As Solana (to whom Ashdown himself reported, insofar as he was the EU's Special Representative) declared on the tenth anniversary of Dayton:

> a clear lesson from the Balkan dramas is that when the EU, the United States and NATO are united and work together, we can achieve great results . . . The opposite, as the war itself illustrated all too clearly, is also true. Linked to this point that we Europeans have to be willing and able to act ourselves to tackle security situations where we feel more strongly or differently than the United States does.
>
> (Solana 2005)

Even if there was an element of special pleading involved, especially on the last point, the fact remains that the EU and the United States have not always seen wholly eye to eye on BiH and that has had its impact on elites in BiH and the way in which the OHR and the EU have pursued their policies.

The external actors involved in BiH have inevitably had wider, other concerns. The United States, for example, having prevaricated about its involvement when the Europeans had failed to keep the peace in the early 1990s, and again as the crisis broke over Kosovo, had expected that stabilization and reconstruction in BiH would have been achieved in a limited timeframe (Altmann and Whitlock 2004). As the process moved much more slowly than anticipated, it was also overtaken by the events of 9/11, the invasion of Afghanistan and later of Iraq. It then became increasingly difficult for the United States to justify any major presence in Bosnia. At the same time, it wished to retain an influence in the Balkans and has, indeed, taken the lead on several reform processes in BiH, as on defense and on constitutional reform.

But there have been differences of significance between the United States and the EU both towards the Balkans and BiH: Altmann and Whitlock, for example, cite differences over Kosovo with the US more in favor of rapid recognition and the EU concerned about the knock-on effects on BiH (Altmann and Whitlock 2004); Matthiesen cites differences over the United States linking support to countries' non-co-operation with the International Criminal Court in the Hague, even while holding to the policy of co-operation with ICTY (Matthiesen 2004: 17). And it is clear that many in the BiH, especially in the Federation, have looked to the United States for support. This has broadened in the face of the growing prevarication among some EU member states on future accession. As Reljić has remarked, governments increasingly recognized that "by cozying up the United States, they implicitly put pressure on the EU, discouraging Brussels from dropping the Balkan expansion plans." And as he points out, they have the example of successful US pressure on the EU over Turkey's application for membership (Reljić 2005).[7] There are therefore tensions even if US policy has shown signs of movement in that, according to one National Security Council official in March 2002, they were now no longer so much pressing them to implement Dayton as asking them "how they are doing in preparing for a Stabilization and Association Agreement with the EU" (quoted by Vachudova 2003: 158–9).

The EU and the OHR as norm entrepreneurs

A systematic approach to building up the Bosnian state had been adopted by the international community, especially through the PIC, in May 2000. The aim was to work through the OHR to build up core institutions, supported by an effective and merit-based civil service, and to remove obstacles to economic reform – responsibility for the slow pace of domestic implementation being laid "squarely with obstructionist political parties and their allies, both within and outside of BiH" (PIC 2000: 1). That meeting of PIC reaffirmed the go-ahead for the OHR to use to the full the so-called Bonn powers, from the 1997 PIC. Originally, under Dayton, the OHR's purpose had been to facilitate indigenous BiH efforts to implement the agreement. There was growing frustration with the nationalist parties, who were held responsible for the lack of progress, together with endemic corruption, "bureaucratic sclerosis, widespread cynicism among the general public, lost opportunities and wasted international resources on a massive scale" (Ashdown 2003).

The Bonn powers were understood to allow "an unlimited authority to impose laws at any constitutional level, and to dismiss elected representatives, political party officials and public officials" (Cox 2001: 13). By the end of 2000, some 100 laws and binding decisions had been imposed and 57 officials had been dismissed (Cox 2001). Hence the PIC had concluded that any achievements had been the result of international rather than domestic efforts. Paddy Ashdown continued this interventionist policy based on his Mission Implementation Plan (agreed by the PIC in January 2003) with its six core tasks: entrenching the rule of law; ensuring that the peace implementation could not be reversed by extreme nationalists; reforming the economy; strengthening the capacity of institutions, especially at state level; establishing state-level civilian command and control over armed forces, reforming the policing and security sector, and paving the way for Euro-Atlantic integration; and promoting the sustainable return of refugees and displaced persons (International Crisis Group 2003).

Clearly, as the HR and others recognized, such intervention created a dilemma. On the one hand, it enabled him to push even harder against those blocking reforms. As one Council of Europe Assembly Report suggested, "the scope of the OHR is such that, to all intents and purposes, it constitutes the supreme institution vested with power in Bosnia and Herzegovina" (quoted by Caplan 2005: 467). But the Assembly in another report also regretted "that much of the progress achieved in the last two years was a result of the constant pressure by the international community, and in particular the High Representative." It went on to recall that a key objective of BiH's membership in the Council of Europe was to promote domestic ownership and responsibility for reform, adding that "before the responsibilities for running the state are completely transferred to the domestic authorities, the country's leadership will however have to demonstrate a higher degree of political maturity and improve mutual readiness for dialogue and consensus (Council of Europe 2004). Ashdown himself was well aware of the problem, declaring in 2003:

> I have sought to be as sparing as possible in my use of the power to dismiss elected officials. This had come to be seen as an immediate and effective sanction in the absence of efficient courts and against the backdrop of an inadequate system of parliamentary or popular accountability. Yet each dismissal by the High Representative, it could be argued, diminishes the impetus to set in place the kinds of structures of accountability whose absence makes these dismissals necessary. By solving the problems by fiat we remove the incentive for BiH to set in place its own mechanisms for solving the problems.
> (Ashdown 2003)

The problem was how to extricate himself and his office from the ensuing dilemma when "ownership" of the political process of "normalization" and "Europeanization" had clearly not passed to the BiH, whose elites remained largely obdurate in the face of the OHR's activities. That opposition and obduracy, whether determined by vested interests or because political leaders preferred not to compromise their position with their electorates, meant that ideas of partnership for further development within a European framework were continuously being found wanting.

Yet it has been a key assumption of the international institutions that the prospect of EU membership could be the critical driver for reform in BiH and elsewhere in the Balkans. What Paddy Ashdown declared he was pursuing as HR was not "an exit strategy, but rather an entry strategy for BiH into broader European structures, with EU membership as the ultimate goal" (Ashdown 2003). Ashdown's own appointment as the EU's Special Representative was an indication of the EU's commitment. It was of particular importance given the problems of moving from the emphasis on reconstruction in BiH to statebuilding and in the aftermath of Kosovo, that the rationalization of EU policy towards the Balkans included the offer of EU membership once, that is, the Copenhagen criteria had been met (Glenny 2001). The "repackaging" of the various Balkan initiatives into the Stabilization and Association Process was the result. Meeting the conditions laid down by the EU has been seen as critical with all the implications of continuous monitoring to ensure compliance. What the EU sought to avoid, however, was the dilemma created by the OHR and his Bonn powers; if BiH was to show itself capable of undertaking all that European membership entailed, it had to show both capacity and the ability to adapt to European norms.

The offer of prospective membership went along with another indication of the EU's commitment, the move to replace the NATO-led SFOR with an EU-led force. This finally took place in 2004. EUFOR's mission, however, remains very largely that of SFOR yet within different parameters: it is to "provide deterrence and continued compliance" with Dayton, "to achieve core tasks in the OHR's Mission Implementation Plan *and* the Stabilisation and Association Process" (emphasis added), as well as provide support to ICTY and the security environment in BiH in which the police could act against the organized criminal network.[8] Despite therefore the efforts on the part of the Commission's delegation to be seen as separate from the OHR, there remains an inherent inseparability. In that sense, the EU has faced an uphill struggle in terms of its capacity to persuade and to bring about any great rapidity in the process of socialization.

Credibility and consistency

While the 1999 decision was welcomed in BiH, there was a certain sense of unreality about it. It remained too distant a prospect to have any great meaning, not least given the parlous state of the economy. (By 2000, Bosnian GDP was still only 66 per cent of its pre-war levels.) And in any case, there was skepticism that, however remote membership might be, it was not actually being seriously entertained by the EU. Despite the reconfirmation of the possibility of membership at the Thessaloniki European Council of June 2003 and the subsequent EU–West Balkans Summit in the same month, such suspicions were later to be endorsed with, for example, some foreign ministers seeking to exclude wording on EU membership as the final goal for the western Balkans at their meeting in Salzburg in March 2006.[9] Thus although integration has remained the objective – at least in principle – and no one has been prepared to be seen to be an obstacle to it, its remoteness has meant that the EU and even the OHR had relatively little leverage on that basis.

Remoteness of membership compounds the problem of the lack of clarity about what eventual accession might mean, as well as suspicion and confusion about the means to attain it. Too few, even among the elites, really know what membership might entail – as one leader put it:

From my experience, out of 1,000 politicians we have, I think that perhaps only 50 or so know what entry into the EU means, what its consequences might be and its benefits and its costs. Even among that elite there is insufficient education about it and then, because of this, there is a need for arm-twisting on the part of the international community.[10]

Lack of education and sometimes deliberate miseducation about the EU means that the wider public have even less idea of what changes are required of them. Yet their knowledge and acceptance are critical if they are to deny power to the extremist elements, opposed to reform. As one commentator concluded on the 2004 round of enlargement, "it is when politicians from both sides of the political spectrum start identifying their interest with the EU-demanded changes and are willing to invest their own political capital in achieving compliance with these conditions that EU integration becomes the only game in town" (Noutcheva 200: 3). But in BiH, there has not always been either the willingness or the ability to move to compliance with EU norms and values. Without that socialization which ultimately includes the general public, it has become something of a vicious circle, of politicians unwilling to engage with the people, the people unable to understand the issues and therefore reluctant to mandate the politicians.[11] Even those political figures inclined to accept European values have, it is held, had to trim and temper their positions in order to survive.[12] That balancing act has been the primary cause for the frequent imposition of policy by the OHR, which then once again "relieves the domestic institutions of their responsibilities and inhibits the development of accountable government" (European Stability Initiative 2001: 26). And so the cycle threatens once again.

Eliminating the need for such a balancing act has not been helped either by the problems of co-ordination referred to above or by the difficulties experienced by the IC and EU in maintaining clarity and consistency of purpose through different processes at different levels and over an extended time period. The piecemeal approach that characterized the period before 1999 has not wholly been rationalized in the Stabilization and Association Process (SAP) within either BiH or, indeed, the Balkan region. Within BiH, for example, police reform has been particularly problematic in terms both of the norms and standards being transmitted and the solutions proposed. The reform of the various entity police forces emerged as a requirement of the SAP so that it was, in that sense, EU-led although the OHR established the Police Restructuring Commission (PRC) with domestic and international representatives, and the former Belgian prime minister, Wilfried Martens, as Chair. The PRC's Final Report was radical, proposing that local police, hitherto closely allied with the entity structures, should be realigned in areas that would cross entity boundaries. Unlike the defense reform, driven by the OHR and the OSCE with the United States and closer relations with NATO in the background, the EU had explicitly ruled out the possibility of the HR imposing any legislation relating to the SAA conditions, including those on police reform. The result, however, has, in effect, been only agreement to continue to try to reach substantive agreement, and this despite numerous and protracted closed-session meetings between the various domestic and international actors. Since many old and new EU member states have their local policing areas organized along federal and local administrative or community lines, the pressure to delink them in the BiH case was resented and opposed, especially by the RS leaders, even while it was regarded as vital by the EU and HR if crime and corruption were to be effectively tackled. But inconsistencies were made more apparent by the fact that existing and newly created BiH state policing institutions like the State Investigation and Protection Agency (SIPA), the Bosnian FBI, and the State Border Service (SBS), which could have expanded their policing roles in tackling organized and other serious crimes, including war crimes, were experiencing serious shortfalls in funding and staff.[13]

Other European norms have also been misinterpreted or regarded as misdirected. Insofar as the EU has been particularly active in terms of other dimensions of regional policy, it has inevitably sought the greater involvement of local authorities – which sits uneasily with the pressures for centralizing authority in BiH. Issues relating to minority rights are clearly critical and yet there are few models within the existing EU to cite since the principle was introduced only under the Copenhagen criteria to be applied seemingly only to new member states. More generally, Europeanization can sometimes appear at odds with the aim of promoting greater democratization, insofar as it tends to privilege elites over the general public, executives over legislatures and so on (see, for example, Pridham 2002: 954; Grabbe 2001: 1018).

The immediate post-Dayton pressure by the international community to privatize as quickly as possible has been criticized as both simplistic and misguided in conception in that it enriched the war entrepreneurs and their political and judicial networks rather than attract new capital, bring about restructuring or bring in new ideas. In part, Donais argues, this was because international officials and agencies focused on technical issues while those with political responsibilities tended to lack a consistent focus (Donais 2002: 14). The result was that, however unintentionally, nationalist elites, as Pugh has pointed out, were able to control telecommunications (including broadcasting) and energy (electricity, oil and gas) supplies, the revenues from which funded nationalist parties and their parallel structures (Pugh 2004: 56–7). These were consequences that the OHR and EU have had to go to great lengths to counter. Criticism of their efforts was still current in 2002, one group, for example, declaring them to be inadequate for the challenges emerging in the BiH and more generally in the western Balkans in that the instruments required for post-conflict reconstruction and stabilization simply did not tackle the underlying causes of instability: "The danger is no longer ethnic hatred, nationalist extremism or military conflict, but a new crisis of economic and social dislocation" (European Stability Initiative 2002: 4).

A number of other inconsistencies further weaken any commitment to change within the BiH. Vachudova (2003: 154), among others, has pointed to shortcomings on the part of the EU in rejecting some policies which would be particularly helpful in winning and maintaining popular support, such as access to the EU market for agricultural goods and visa-free travel to the EU for Balkan citizens. While there have been improvements in opening up trade, restrictions still apply because of the difficulties such policies would create for EU governments themselves. Yet visa restrictions have meant not simply a sense of isolation – one that has built up since the collapse of the former Yugoslavia and which is likely to increase for Bosniaks and Serbs as Croatian accession talks begin – but they also both deny an important sense of reward and restrict opportunities for a new generation of Bosnian voters of becoming familiar with European values and practices.

Interaction and socialialization?

Such isolation has to be set against the growing involvement of many party leaders in regional and other European political groupings – even if such involvement then also highlights other inconsistencies. BiH membership (and indeed, chairmanship in 2003–4) of the South East European Co-operation Process (SEECP), for example, may not be particularly important in itself (though discussions on improved neighborly co-operation in the Balkans across a range of policy issues of close interest to the EU are of importance), but it nonetheless allows for greater familiarity with developments in other Balkan states. Pevehouse, for one, sees such regional organizations as being particularly useful enabling mechanisms in terms of socialization (Pevehouse 2002: 524) and the BiH Foreign Minister, Mladen Ivanić has endorsed such a view.[14] On the other hand, such meetings and exchanges provide ample opportunity for each country to compare and contrast its treatment at the hands of the international community and EU on such issues as co-operation with ICTY, signing up to the SAA, and PfP membership. However rational it might be for the EU to take account of individual state differences, for those less enamored of change, it creates opportunities to focus on what they might then describe as double standards. Insofar as conditionality is assessed on a country-by-country basis, it also threatens the principles of multilateralism and regional co-operation espoused by the EU (Smith 2003: 83).

Elite familiarity with EU norms is also increasingly apparent through the developing links with EU party foundations and parliamentary groups – which also bring with them further peer pressures. The German party foundations, especially the Konrad Adenauer Stiftung and the Friedrich Ebert Stiftung, have increased their activities in BiH. There has also been increasing co-operation with the party groups in Brussels. The Party for Democratic Progress (PDP), the Party of Democratic Action (SDA), and the Croat Democratic Union (HDZ) have all, for example, become associated as Observers with the European Peoples' Party (EPP). According to one participant this has forced the Bosnian parties "to use a different discourse and behave differently. Every three months we go to Brussels and one is made to explain before one's colleagues what the conflicts we are having within Bosnia are about. This is having a huge impact."[15] It is perhaps then unfortunate that the EPP's President, Wilfried Martens, was responsible for the report on police reform. It has also been among EPP members such as Angela Merkel, the German Chancellor, that the strongest opposition to further enlargement has been expressed and the need for more constructive thinking about alternatives to full membership. Those views may have been directed largely against Turkey, but they have also included a "privileged partnership" for the western Balkans.[16]

The growing intensity of interaction of different levels, formal and informal, makes the actions and intentions of each of the actors significantly more transparent, even if not necessarily more acceptable. To the extent that such interaction is institutionalized, it is often regarded as the harbinger of socialization and Europeanization, and a vital part of the process of inducing actors into the norms and rules of the Union (to paraphrase Checkel 2005: 804). Bosnian elites should, then, have begun on the process – for even if formal relations within the SAP are only very new, the EU has been active in its various policy guises since 1995. According to the Deputy Head of the European Commission's Delegation, the process has begun, if slowly, with differences among the political leaders.[17] Such differences have themselves been welcomed and, indeed, exploited in the interests of opening up schisms that pit one set against another, both then needing to seek allies elsewhere in the system. As Ashdown declared, when discussing how to eliminate the nationalists' stranglehold:

> One of the ways is to vote against their return to power. Frankly . . . this is not very likely to happen . . . There is a different way too. The HDZ in Zagreb is an example of that. This is not the same HDZ as it was under Tudjman. By forcing the nationalist parties to implement reform you get factions within the party. That is the case of Raguz vs. Covic, and you can find the very same elements in other political parties.
> (Ashdown 2004a)

But the process has been a slow one. In terms of the formulation of policies consistent with the process of transition towards potential EU membership, for example, Bosnian attitudes remain ambivalent and/or suspicious. Legislation consistent with the *acquis* has invariably been drawn up by lawyers from the EU and the member states. However, rather than representing the future, the legislation is regarded in the BiH as "sometimes not compatible with our general legal framework or legal culture,"[18] or alien and not easily understood or accepted.[19] Implementing such legislation then becomes politically sensitive and enforcing it sometimes impossible.[20] Such reluctance to implement legislation emphasizes the importance as well as the difficulty of continuous monitoring. It, and the presumption of the political impact of "shaming" non-implementers and violators, are critical elements both in terms of conditionality and social learning. But if the process of non-compliance simply results in action by the OHR in order to keep processes going, then the normative significance of the reforms begins to lose its impact and adaptation becomes regarded with little more than indifference, at best.

Conclusions

Very clearly, the international community – in the form of the OHR and the EU – has brought about changes in the values and standards that prevail in BiH. Both have sought to ensure peace and stability, which has meant tackling the extreme nationalist parties and the corrupt networks that did well out of the war, and bringing BiH into line with the conditions demanded by the EU of those who seek membership. But they have been changes that have frequently been brought about by imposition on the part of the OHR. Critics have therefore argued that, while many of the statebuilding measures are necessary for effective, open and democratic governance in contemporary Europe, their imposition, in the face of opposition from elected leaders, undermines those same values. At a minimum, such an argument would claim, there are limits to the extent that "inappropriate" measures can be taken in the interests of bringing about a logic of appropriateness. On the other hand, the role and powers of the HR have, indeed, created a dilemma. It is, after all, improbable that, in the absence of the Bonn powers, those who have been manipulating the political, economic and judicial systems through corrupt networks would have quietly given up that control in the interests of adapting to the Copenhagen criteria and some future membership of the EU.

But the roles of the HR and the EU raise important questions about compliance with the demands of the international community and the nature of rewards and sanctions. However much the image has been created that "nobody does anything until the IC makes them,"[21] there is a commitment on the part of BiH leaders to European integration. What then becomes confusing is the fact that the HR is also the EU's Special Representative and the EU *qua* Commission has been attempting to separate out the areas covered by the SAP/integration process from that of stabilization, reconstruction and statebuilding, which remain the responsibility of the OHR with its Bonn powers. The primary instrument of both is, of course, persuasion, but for the EU it has become a matter very largely of the use of conditionality to ensure continuous progress towards the possibility of future EU membership. The rewards of compliance are continued movement in opening up the SAP process and continued assistance; sanctions in essence add up to non-movement, but not the withdrawal of aid. For the OHR, there has been the opportunity and frequent recourse to the Bonn powers and the imposition of measures, the removal of officials, party leaders, and so on. For so long as the international community sees the need for reform in the interests of state viability as well as adhesion to the norms of open democracy, sound administration and economic liberalization in opposition to vested political and economic interests, there is likely to be continued need for those powers and the OHR. The inevitable overlap between the norms and standards both the EU and OHR (and OSCE, IMF etc.) wish to see adopted in BiH equally inevitably gives rise to confusion of roles. This, in turn, has provided opportunities for those opposed or reluctant to engage in the transfer to exploit. The clarity and credibility of the message as well as, therefore, the co-ordination of the messengers are vital factors in any successful norm promotion.

Conditionality and monitoring continue to be regarded by the EU as critical in ensuring compliance. It had, after all, worked in the case of the countries of central and eastern Europe who had sought EU membership. The continuous need for the intervention of the OHR indicated that circumstances in BiH were somewhat different and that, despite the rhetoric and lack of alternatives, not all BiH parties were wholly enthusiastic about the changes EU membership seemed to presage. The rush towards privatization and the use of "one size fits all model of economic transformation" (Donais 2002: 14) paid too little attention to the specifics of the BiH case and ignored the possible consequences. In political terms, the legacy of the past – of Tito as well as Milošević and of the war – cast a significantly longer shadow than that of any future within the EU, and skepticism whether the EU actually wanted BiH then made the shadow even darker.

Schimmelfennig and others have been particularly insistent that for conditionality to be effective in bringing about compliance, there needs to be clarity, credibility and consistency. In BiH's case, in the efforts of the HR and the EU, at least as represented by, for example, Ashdown's Mission Statement of 2002 or the European Commission's Feasibility Report of 2003, there were clear principles enunciated. The latter's 16 points, while seemingly numerous, were nonetheless sometimes couched in fairly general terms. The problem has thus been in the application of the policy prescriptions that underlay them, the degree to which they were known and understood among both elites and the wider BiH public, and were acceptable to them. Added to that have been the problems of co-ordination among EU actors, between the institutions responsible for foreign and external policy matters, or the fight against international crime or in establishing the *acquis*. Given the range of policy commitments and the complexity of the situation, such problems of consistency are probably unavoidable. But they have not always helped in winning over a skeptical public or an entrenched politico-economic elite – particularly when access to the media has often been constrained.

Against this, however, to the extent that the process is to be monitored and judged by the EU, issues of "ownership" that have continuously plagued the Bosnian–OHR relationship do not arise in the same way. This is not a peace agreement imposed on warring factions. It is a process leading towards a goal on which all, ostensibly at least, are agreed. However, as we have seen, that commitment is often only partial or faint-hearted. The degree to which European norms and values have become more than superficially accepted is debatable. As the BiH Foreign Minister Ivanić has suggested, any promotion of European values has nearly always had to be balanced by the concern of alienating political support; European values might be entering into Bosnian patterns of thought, but operationalizing them remains unattractive, at least in the short term.[22] So far, it would seem, there is rather more a strategic deployment of acceptable arguments than any internalisation of norms.

However, even here it may be a case for looking to the notion put forward by Elster of "the civilising force of hypocrisy" (Elster 1998: 109–12, quoted by Checkel 2001a) where, however manipulative the motive, the publicity may have a "civilizing" effect and ultimately change preferences. Schimmelfennig, too, has written of rhetorical entrapment in relation to the EU's eastward enlargement (Schimmelfennig 2001) which may work in both the case of BiH elites and the EU, even if that rhetoric may not yet extend to Turkey or even to all Balkan countries. The uncertainties on both sides cannot but perpetuate problems in any BiH socialization process. It is clear that, even if in only quantitative terms, the rate of exposure of BiH elites to European standards and practices has intensified and that has brought a growing familiarity with them. That, combined with what might still only be public lip-service to European norms, creates a momentum or dynamism that establishes its own benchmark against which to hold leaders to account and may yet drive BiH towards a less uncertain future. The problem, however, lies in the extent to which the public knows, accepts and identifies with those norms and the norm entrepreneurs. On that score, there remains rather less optimism that the international institutions have been able to persuade.

Notes

The authors are grateful to those who consented to be interviewed: Renzo Daviddi, Deputy Head of Delegation, European Commission Delegation, BiH, Ahmet Hadžipašić, Prime Minister of the Federation of Bosnia-Herzegovina, Mladen Ivanić, Foreign Minister of Bosnia-Herzegovina, Osman Topčagić, Director of the Directorate for European Integration, BiH, OSCE Staff Member, OSCE Mission to Bosnia-Herzegovina and OHR Staff Members, OHR Sarajevo; and to Tarak Barkawi of the Centre of International Studies, University of Cambridge, for reading an earlier version of this chapter.

1 Lord (Paddy) Ashdown represented both the international community as High Representative from May 2002 until January 2006, when he was replaced by Christian Schwarz-Schilling, and the European Union as a Special Representative in BiH, having been appointed to that post a few months earlier (in March 2002).
2 The Copenhagen criteria – agreed by the Copenhagen European Council of June 1993 – include stable democratic institutions, the rule of law, protection of human and minority rights, an open and functioning economic system and the administrative capacity to implement the *acquis communautaire* and the declared aims of the Union.
3 "List of Removed and Conditionally Removed Officials by the High Representative," 30 June 2004, OHR Press Statement at *http://www.ohr.int/decisions/war-crimes-decs/default.asp?content_id=32747* (accessed 27 April 2006).

4 Interview with Ahmet Hadžipašić, 2006.
5 "The question is not a choice between the state or the entities, but to have the state *and* the entities. There must be some balance here. The key answer is that the state must be authorised to regulate the basic principles and that the entities and the lower levels of government must be bound to behave within the given limits. A balance can be found, such as it exists in every federal state" (Ivanić, interview, February 2006).
6 Hadžipašić, interview, 2006.
7 *EU Observer*, 12 April 2006, which also reported senior US politicians attempting to press the EU to stand firm on membership.
8 For EUFOR's Mission Statement see *http://www.euforbih.org/mission/mission.htm* (accessed 21 April 2006).
9 *EU Observer*, 16 March 2006. While the Salzburg text confirmed the future of the western Balkans in the EU, it also highlighted the EU's ability to absorb further members.
10 Hadžipašić, interview, 2006.
11 As Federation Prime Minister Hadžipašić put it: "The key is when European socialisation comes down to the citizens' level. But we have a barrier here. We cannot fully develop a European strategy if our citizens do not fully understand this and we cannot discuss this with them" (Hadžipašić, interview, 2006).
12 BiH Foreign Minister Mladen Ivanić: "The EU thus creates a solution in Bosnia as it sees fit and . . . there are among Bosnian politicians people who accept these European values as their own. But, I cannot say that they do this fully. They are politicians and must survive. Thus they need to maintain a balance" (Ivanić, interview, 2006).
13 And throughout the process, the EU had its Police Mission (EUPM) offering advice and guidance on best practices at the operational level, while awaiting the political outcome – a role sometimes almost in competition with EUFOR in its role as a stabilization force.
14 "The SEECP leaves positive effects on the domestic scene. The language being used over the past years is far less radical, far more compromising than ever before. I believe that to a significant extent this is the result of the regional element which has become more important over the past years. Thus . . . it is very useful that BiH is a member of such regional organizations" (Ivanić, interview, 2006).
15 Ivanić, interview, 2006.
16 *EU Observer*, 17 March 2006. Mrs Merkel is reported as saying "from my side I would like to say that we should not avoid the term "privileged partnership"."
17 Daviddi, interview, 2006.
18 Ivanić, interview, 2006.
19 Topčagić, interview, 2006.
20 "The biggest problem in implementation is among the politicians. We make the necessary reforms on paper, but then we do all we can not to implement them" (Hadžipašić, interview, 2006).
21 To quote the BiH Director for European Integration, Topčagić (interview, 2006).
22 "The story about European values is a sort of pressure on us, forcing us to do something which does not seem very attractive politically in the short run. But, also, there is the parallel gradual entry of European values into our pattern of thought" (Ivanić, interview, 2006).

10 From "perverse" to "promising" institutionalism?
NATO, EU and the Greek–Turkish conflict

Panayotis Tsakonas

Introduction

The disagreement of the 1980s and 1990s about whether institutions matter or not has given over to a disagreement – or to much less agreement – over the last decade about exactly how institutions affect states' behavior (Martin and Simmons 2001: 43). Thus, the preoccupation of scholars to respond mostly to the realist premise that institutions are epiphenomenal and they can only serve as useful leverages in the hands of the most powerful states to promote their preconceived national interests[1] has been replaced by rational (mainly neo-liberal institutionalist) and social constructivist accounts about how institutions have affected states' behavior.

However, although rational and constructivist efforts have so far generated some promising propositions to better specify the mechanisms of institutional effects and the conditions under which international institutions are expected to lead to the internalization of new roles or interests from their member states,[2] much less has been done on the role institutions play as facilitators of co-operation and conflict management and/or transformation.[3] Bridging "rational-institutionalist" and "constructivist" accounts, this chapter aims at exploring the impact of two of the most successful and prominent international institutions, namely NATO[4] and the European Union, have had on the management and/or transformation of the long-standing Greek–Turkish territorial dispute.

Interestingly, the phenomenon of the Greek–Turkish conflict – which so far has been heavily biased by policy-oriented perspectives – has long constituted an anomaly in the security community of Europe.[5] Especially with regard to NATO, the Greek–Turkish conflict is a case that goes against the conventional wisdom of alliance co-operation, and it is thus dismissed as an exception to the positive identification achieved among the Alliance's other members (Law and McFarlane 1996: 39). The loosening of the structural constraints of the Cold War, the reconstruction of the Alliance's identity, especially after NATO's eastern expansion and the strengthening of the institution's status as "a collective security system" (Wendt 1994: 386; Wendt 1996: 53; Risse-Kappen 1996: 357–99) and a community of "like minded democracies" (Hampton 1998–9: 235), and the strategic upgrading of the eastern Mediterranean region as the new central front of the Alliance seemed to constitute the very factors why the new NATO would be more likely to adopt a bolder approach toward the settlement of the Greek–Turkish dispute. Interestingly though, the Greek–Turkish conflict was exacerbated after the end of the Cold War.

A strong optimism that Greece and Turkey would seek ways of resolving their long-standing territorial dispute also emerged after 1999 due to Turkey's candidacy and potential accession into the EU. It seems, however, that the EU is itself a contentious issue between Greece and Turkey. This is due to the fact that Greece has been a member of the EU since 1981, whereas Turkey, although recognised as a membership candidate at the Helsinki European Council in 1999 and in spite of accession negotiations which began in October 2005, is still generally seen as being a long way from full membership.[6] Interestingly then, the Greek–Turkish dispute may prove to be a "hard case" regarding the impact of the EU on conflict transformation; indeed it may be possible that the EU, due to its particular involvement in this conflict, may have had a detrimental rather than a positive effect.

Overall, it is indeed puzzling how the feelings of mistrust and threat perception between the two states have persisted in institutional contexts that should have led to the emergence of shared norms, understandings and a sense of collective identity, paving the way for the peaceful resolution of their disputes. Although one may argue that these institutional contexts have restrained the two states from full-scale war, they have not succeeded in generating the sense of collectively being part of a security community given that both states have continued to consider military means a rational and justifiable way to relate to each other.

Hence, the examination of the impact NATO and EU have on the management and/or transformation of the Greek–Turkish conflict has both theoretical value and policy relevance. Indeed, the examination of the effects of particular international institutions on the conflict between two states may provide insights into an especially valuable arena, international security, where theorists of all stripes have expected international institutions to be least consequential (Lipson 1984: 1–23; Keohane 1984: 6–7; Grieco 1988: 504; Grieco 1990: 11–14; Mearsheimer 1994–5: 5–49). Moreover, the theoretical inquiry that research should increasingly turn to the question of how institutions matter and emphasize theoretically-informed analysis based on observable implications of alternative theories of institutions (Martin and Simmons 2001: 437) may also be served. An academic inquiry of that kind allows also for a departure from the currently dominant single-issue, single-organization and single-country format to comparative research across time, across states and across international institutions (Simmons and Martin 2002: 205), while the effects of "international socialization" – a process introduced and followed by both NATO and the EU – are to be analyzed in a theory-informed and comparative way (Schimmelfennig 2002: 22; Wichmann 2004: 129).

Last, but not least, the policy relevance of a study examining NATO's and the EU's impact on the Greek–Turkish conflict is directly related to the Greek and Turkish policy makers' ability to better define their countries' future expectations from those two institutions. By analogy, it may also provide NATO and the EU with insights into the limits and/or the unintended effects of their actions, and thus contribute to their ability to refine the strategies they follow in ways that would lead to the positive transformation of the disputants' conflict.

The chapter is divided into three parts. In the first part a review of the relevant literature regarding the role of international institutions in interstate conflict is presented; particular reference is made to research efforts undertaken so far in investigating whether and how NATO and the EU matter in managing and/or transforming the Greek–Turkish conflict. Secondly, two core arguments, which seem to account most for the positive and/or negative impact of EU and NATO on the Greek–Turkish conflict, are presented. A point of methodological nature is also made; it refers to the need to assess NATO and EU institutional effects on the Greek–Turkish dispute by adopting a multi-stage process: one that links an institution's characteristics with certain institutional effects and socialization outcomes. Thirdly, relevant empirical evidence is used to test the chapter's central arguments and to explain why NATO's role is doomed to remain poor and parochial in the years to come, while that of the EU can change the interests and/or the identity scripts of the conflict parties.

Literature review

Institutions and interstate conflict

Unsurprisingly, the ways through which institutions may diminish interstate – and intrastate – conflicts have been the focus of the conflict resolution literature (Rumelili 2006). This literature treats [international and regional] institutions as third parties that have the ability to mediate disputes and provide diplomatic "good offices" (Young 1967; Bercovitch and Langley 1993; Miall 1992), as well as to bridge the parties in conflict or change the nature of the conflict either through various side payments and/or penalties – which are expected to change the conflict parties' cost–benefit calculations about the utility of a negotiated settlement (Stone Sweet and Brunell 1998; Amoo and Zartman 1992) – or through problem-solving [social-psychological] approaches that will change the disputants' perceptions, values and behaviors (Crocker, Hampson, and Aall 1999; Fisher and Keashley 1991: 29–42).

Needless to say that, although a range of capacities exist for the resolution of conflicts among their members, institutions' third-party roles are often constrained by their limited resources and enforcement powers (Amoo and Zartman 1992; Chayes and Chayes 1996). By implication, the main argument of the conflict resolution literature is that institutions seem to be more effective in preventing conflicts in their early stages than by promoting [and monitoring] their member states' and prospective member states' compliance with the institution's fundamental norms, such as democracy and respect of human rights.

Neo-liberal institutionalist accounts of how international institutions may promote peaceful relations argue that institutions can shape state strategies by conveying information, reducing transaction costs – especially those associated with bilateral negotiation, monitoring and verification – and providing opportunities for side payments, linking issue areas, increasing the level of transparency, attenuating the fear of unequal gains, raising the price of defection and discouraging cheating and thus fostering co-operative ventures (Keohane 1984: 146–7; Keohane 1986; Kupchan and Kupchan 1991).

For constructivists, institutions can not only affect states' behavior or strategies; they can also alter their identities by promoting a "common/collective security identity." Providing legitimacy for collective decisions, international institutions – according to constructivist premises – transmit through the "process of socialization" (Schimmelfennig 2000) their norms and rules to their members as well as to prospective member states (Finnemore 1996; Finnemore and Sikkink 1999a). Motivated by ideational concerns to join international institutions, namely the legitimization/justification of their national identity (Hurd 1999), states gradually define their national identities and interests by taking on each other's perspectives, thus building a shared sense of values and identity (Wendt and Duvall 1989; Wendt 1994).

Based on both institutionalist and constructivist premises, much work has been done on the mechanisms that institutions use to transmit their norms both to member states and to prospective members and thus to inducting actors into their norms and rules. Although such work does not explicitly address the linkage between institutional effects and interstate conflicts, its findings on the ways states' behavior is being changed due to the internalization of institutional rules and norms can also tell much about the changes that may follow in states' position over a border conflict. In accordance with this line of reasoning, most recent studies have tried to better specify the mechanisms through which institutions are able to socialize states and state agents, as well as the conditions under which institutions are expected to lead to internalization of new roles and interests (*International Organization* special issue, 2005).

More specifically, these studies have aimed at theoretically highlighting and empirically testing three distinct mechanisms connecting institutions to socializing outcomes – namely "strategic calculation," "role playing" and "normative suasion" – and thus identifying the various causal paths leading to socialization. In accordance with this line of reasoning and building on rationalist and constructivist premises, certain studies suggested that particular socialization mechanisms are usually at work (e.g., "strategic persuasion" and/or "normative suasion") and linked them to particular state behavior and/or policy (Schimmelfennig 2005; Gheciu 2005).

NATO, EU and the Greek–Turkish conflict

Particular efforts have also been undertaken to investigate the effects NATO and the EU have had on the Greek–Turkish conflict. Building on various theoretical strands, research into the effects of NATO and the EU on Greece's and Turkey's strategies toward co-operation and positive identification and, more specifically, into their conflict transformation has shown whether these institutions matter and, more importantly, how they matter even though their impact may have "perverse," undesirable, implications.

As has already been noted, NATO's role in the transformation of the Greek–Turkish conflict has been dismissed as an exception to the positive identification achieved among the other Alliance's members (especially after the end of the Cold War, when it was expected that liberal international institutions such as NATO would facilitate this collective identity and positive identification among its members). By implication, the theoretical expectations of constructivism, that is that institutional linkages not only shape and constrain states' behavioral strategies but also reconstruct their identities and interests, were proved wrong.

Interestingly enough, NATO's positive role in its two members' conflict was also challenged on rational-institutionalist grounds, which would confine the impact of international institutions/organizations to behaviors of states. Indeed, although it was shown that, contrary to realist expectations, institutions (including alliances) do reshape states' definitions of their interests and they do pattern international interactions, they do not, however, always foster co-operation, even among their members. NATO's parochial and/or negative role on the Greek–Turkish conflict was thus explained as a "malfunctioning" of particular rationalist premises and as an indication that certain institutionalist provisions of the Atlantic Alliance have unintentionally exacerbated relations between Greece and Turkey (Krebs 1999).

More specifically, it was argued that the persistence of conflictual relations between Greece and Turkey in the context of their joint membership in NATO was due to three factors: firstly, NATO had created an incentive structure that intensified, rather than mitigated, the two allies' conflict; secondly, arms transfers among NATO's powerful members and the disputants had exacerbated the latter's security dilemma and had triggered a spiral of diplomatic tension; and, thirdly, instead of leading to the amelioration of the two allies' conflict, "issue linkage" and "transparency" – with which NATO had provided the two disputants – have contributed to the deterioration of their conflict (Krebs 1999).

It was also argued that by providing Greece and Turkey with a security blanket against the Soviet threat during the Cold War era NATO had allowed them to shift the focus of their foreign policy from the Soviet threat to their more parochial conflicts and their national issues. Hence, instead of ameliorating Greece's and Turkey's security dilemma, NATO had intensified their dispute. In addition, when the Alliance acted as a facilitator of "issue linkage" it had contributed to the deterioration of the conflict because the multiple issue areas linked together by the Alliance gave Turkey and Greece the opportunity to manipulate these linkages to their political and strategic advantage (since they sought for bargaining leverage), thus broadening the conflict and producing escalating levels of tension (Krebs 1999: 360, 365). Even the Alliance itself – and its fora – became an object of contest.[7]

A series of other institutionalist provisions have also proved unable to produce the fruitful results rational institutionalism expects. For example, "transparency" – which is expected to raise the costs of cheating within an institutional context and thus play a central role in the amelioration of conflict between members of the institution – has not been sufficient to promote co-operation between the two NATO members. By the same token, the "information model" – which stresses the role of institutions in the provision of information and in the learning process – does not seem to apply in the Greek–Turkish dispute and NATO.

Indeed, instead of lessening the one's fears of the expansionist aims of the other, the transparency that NATO's internal mechanisms provided made the power disparities between Greece and Turkey more acute. In the same vein, information about respective military capabilities was seen by Greece and Turkey as a means to get a comparative advantage vis-à-vis the other. By implication, matters then turned on a more "security dilemma" situation, in other words on intentions and motives and on how the one expected the other would use its armed forces (Krebs 1999: 366). In the absence of reassuring information regarding Turkey's goals, Greece viewed Turkish superior capability as a real threat. Therefore, any confidence-building enterprise NATO decided to promote should have gone beyond the conventional knowledge regarding the two states' military capabilities and dealt with the two states' real intentions.

Last, but not least, certain institutional deficiencies of the Alliance had negative effects on the allied rivals' dispute. More specifically, NATO's shortcomings with regard to its potential contribution to a Greek–Turkish confidence-building enterprise were coupled with a particular "institutional impediment" that has so far contributed enormously to the Greek–Turkish arms race, namely NATO's Cascade Program.[8] The latter has in fact violated the spirit of the CFE (Conventional Forces in Europe) Treaty (namely to build-down offensive capabilities), since it simply transposed the problems from the former central front to the flanks. Thus, through NATO's Cascade Program, Greece and Turkey became the principal recipients as the countries with the largest stocks of old Treaty Limited Equipments (TLEs). It is characteristic that, with regard to the volume of weapon systems, by the end of 1995, Greece and Turkey were the greatest importers of military material worldwide.[9]

All in all, rational institutionalist assessment of the role NATO has played in the Greek–Turkish dispute seems to suggest that although NATO has so far succeeded in preventing the Greek–Turkish conflict from turning into a hot war it has unintentionally exacerbated relations between its two members as well as failing to promote co-operation, in the form of confidence- and security-building measures, or to facilitate positive identification among its members, or to provide the confidence it can facilitate the positive transformation of its members' dispute in the future.

From a constructivist perspective, and through a case study of Greek–Turkish relations in the period 1995–9, another study has shown how – by situating Greece and Turkey in different and also liminal/precarious positions with respect to "Europe" – the community-building discourse of the EU reinforced and legitimized the two states' representations of their identities as different from and also as threatening to each other, allowing thus for the perpetuation of their conflicts (Rumelili 2003).

Most recent studies exploring the impact of the EU on the Greek–Turkish conflict, however, suggest a rather promising role for the EU in regard to the positive transformation of the long-standing dispute. Indeed, these studies argue that the EU, especially after 1999 when Turkey was recognized as a membership candidate, can have a positive transformative impact on a series of border conflicts (the Greek–Turkish being one) through four particular "pathways" (Diez, Stetter and Albert 2006: 563–93; Celik and Rumelili 2006: 203–22).

It is worth-noting that these studies view the EU both "as a framework", that can eliminate the bases of interstate conflicts in the long run through democratization and gradual integration, and "as an active player", which can impact border conflicts [also in the short run] through direct and indirect ways. Thus the EU appears as a necessary condition that can have a direct ("compulsory" and/or "connective") as well as an indirect ("enabling" and/or "constructive") impact on the disputants' – especially on Turkey's – strategies towards co-operation and, by implication, on the positive transformation of the two states' conflict.

Argument and methodology

Either from a rational-institutionalist or a constructivist perspective, the relevant literature has so far argued that the Atlantic Alliance has played only a parochial role in the Greek–Turkish conflict. At the same time, a certain amount of optimism has been expressed, especially after 1999, for a promising EU role in the transformation of the Greek–Turkish dispute. Apart from simply sharing the aforementioned pessimism and optimism with regard to NATO and EU impact on the transformation of the Greek–Turkish dispute, this chapter attempts to specify the reasons that NATO's role has always been – and is doomed to remain – poor, while the EU appears as being able to change the interests and/or the identity scripts of the conflict parties.

More precisely, through a comparative assessment of the empirical records of NATO and EU roles in the transformation of the Greek–Turkish conflict, this chapter attempts to specifically show when and under what conditions the two institutions have been able to impact the conflict parties' strategies toward co-operation and conflict transformation. To this end, two interrelated conditions that seem to account most for NATO perverse and EU promising roles in the Greek–Turkish conflict are being developed and empirically tested: Firstly, the type of norms NATO and the EU have exerted on the conflict parties,[10] and the subsequent consequences for the two institutions' legitimacy and credibility appear as a strong determinant for the conflict's positive or negative transformation. In other words, what accounts most for NATO's perverse and EU's promising role in the Greek–Turkish conflict seems to be related to the strength of the norms each institution exerts as well as to the credibility each institution enjoys vis-à-vis the parties in conflict.

Secondly, NATO and EU positive and/or negative effects on the disputants' strategies toward co-operation and positive identification are determined by the "type of socialization" NATO and EU mechanisms produce. To put it differently, whether the institutional mechanisms – by which NATO and EU seek to attain domestic salience and legitimacy – are directed towards the conflict parties' elites only or towards the conflict parties' elites as well as the public and the society does matter because a "thorough" internalization of the institutional rules and norms, and not a solely "elite-driven" one, is a crucial determinant for the positive transformation of the Greek–Turkish dispute.

Interestingly, as a comparison of the empirical records of NATO and EU roles in the transformation of the Greek–Turkish dispute will suggest, the reasons that seem to account for NATO's parochial role in the Greek–Turkish conflict are the ones that should get the credit for a promising role on the part of the EU in the positive transformation of the long-standing dispute.

It should be noted, however, that the fulfillment of the aforementioned conditions also demonstrates the limits of the EU's potential role in the positive transformation of the Greek–Turkish conflict. Indeed, as the EU case demonstrates, to contribute to the positive transformation of a conflict as well as to the disputants' strategies, international security institutions should – apart from fulfilling the aforementioned conditions – also be careful enough to promote the right mix of conditionalities and incentives for distributing rules and norms and for resolving "distributional conflicts."

An additional point of a methodological nature needs particular reference here. It is the basic premise of this chapter that in order to analyze the effects of international institutions on interstate conflicts a multi-stage process should be followed. The aim of this process is twofold: firstly, to integrate institutionalist and constructivist insights into the effects of international institutions on shaping states' interests and identities towards co-operation and positive identification, respectively; secondly, to bring domestic politics more systematically into the study of international institutions (Cortell and Davis 2000) by highlighting the ways different states use the same institutions as well as the ways in which the nature or interests of the state itself are potentially changed by the actions of institutions.

Thus, for assessing the effects of NATO and the EU on the positive and/or negative transformation of the Greek–Turkish conflict, the pathway our analysis follows can be viewed as a multi-stage process that attempts to link an institution's characteristics (norms, views, strategies) with certain institutional effects and/or socializing outcomes. The first stage in this multi-stage process involves an institution's approach towards both the conflict parties and the conflict itself. The issues raised at this stage of analysis refer to particular structural conditions, such as the issue of membership.

In the second stage, particular attention is paid to the mechanisms and to the processes by which international norms stemming from different international institutions can attain domestic legitimacy and salience in different states and so influence foreign policy decisions. The mechanisms that institutions use to exert their norms and influence are thus considered as intervening variables linking input (international institutions' characteristics) and output (conflict transformation and/or conflict parties' strategies towards co-operation and positive identification) (Checkel 2005: 805).

In the third stage, attention turns to the ways institutional actions are perceived, acted upon, manipulated and, most importantly, internalized by the conflict parties' elites and societies. Analysis is at this stage related to the examination of the particular socialization and/or internalization effects of institutional actions and to the domestic degree of salience (Cortell and Davies 2000; Checkel 1997).

Following this multi-stage process in assessing institutional effects on interstate conflicts, the type of impact of a particular institution on the conflict parties can be assessed both from an institutionalist perspective (how institutional action reflects upon the conflict parties' *strategies*) and a constructivist perspective (how institutional action may reconstruct the conflict parties' *identities* and *interests*). Particular inferences can thus be suggested about the reasons that account for NATO and EU positive and/or negative roles in the transformation of the Greek–Turkish conflict.

Empirical illustrations: assessing NATO and EU role and performance

Strength of norms and credibility

Throughout its evolution NATO has been characterized as an exclusive institution whose primary concern was to enhance the security of its members with respect to non-members (Duffield 2006: 638). Moreover, as the prime security institution of the Western community, NATO has always worked as a community-building agency, and international socialization – through "teaching" and "nursing" activities – has been one of its fundamental tasks. The Atlantic Alliance has thus developed and exerted a set of both constitutive and specific norms.[11] The former were interrelated with the collective identity of the Alliance and refer to basic liberal norms, such as democratic political participation and representation, the rule of law and a market-based economy. The latter regulate behavior in individual issue areas and reflect the Alliance's field of specialization, such as norms of international military co-ordination and standardization and norms of civil-military relations.

Especially in the post-Cold War era, NATO has followed an exclusive strategy of community building, which consists in "socialization from the outside," as the Alliance's constitutive norms have been communicated to outsider states by telling them which conditions they should meet before being entitled to join (Schimmelfennig 2003). Specifically in the post-Cold War era and following NATO's transformation, there have been clear references on the part of NATO to democratic – among other – principles as well as to civil dominance over the military. It should be noted at this point that the transmission of such norms has been successful in east and central European states where the prospects of membership induced states to undertake democratic and economic reforms and to settle their outstanding territorial and ethnic conflicts (the examples of Romania and Hungary are striking), but it had played relatively little role in promoting democracy in an already existing NATO member, namely Turkey.

With regard to the conflict between two of its members, Greece and Turkey, the NATO role has been problematic, in terms of two particular issues: the norms and standards being transmitted as well as of the solutions to the conflict proposed.

During the Cold War, NATO's primary concern was to consolidate operational stability and cohesion in the Alliance's southern flank by deterring a Greek–Turkish crisis and/or conflict in the Aegean (Stearns 1992; MacKenzie 1983; Couloumbis 1983). In other words, NATO was interested in regulating behavior in individual issue areas and such a concern reflects the marginal interest that NATO (and the US) had in investing to facilitate the resolution of the two countries' dispute. NATO has also never been interested in making clear to its two allies that there would be costs inherent in any effort by one of the parties to either cheat or defect from the rules agreed within the alliance's institutional context. Such a stance would mean that NATO should be able to play the role of guarantor of any confidence-building enterprise undertaken by the two neighbors but, as the history of NATO relations with its two allies in conflict suggests, NATO did not have such an ability.[12] By implication, the norms NATO has exerted can be valued as specific and/or regulative, that is, in the management of the two allies' conflict,[13] and, most importantly, as particularly weak given that the Alliance had always kept a safe distance from emphasizing the necessity of the resolution of territorial disputes among its members as a precondition for the continuation of their membership (Oguzlu 2004: 461).

By exerting weak and constitutive/regulative norms on the disputants and by maintaining that the ultimate goal was securing operational stability in the Alliance's southern flank (i.e., conflict management), NATO acted as a substitute for more substantive and long-term solutions.[14] By maintaining an attitude of detached concern, hands-off policy and impartiality to the conflict[15] and by offering to the disputants the certainty the Alliance would do whatever it takes to prevent Greece and Turkey from fighting each other in order for stability in the Alliance's flank to be secured, the two allies had no incentive to take responsibility for resolving their own differences. It also gave them little reason to place NATO priorities above their own when it came to force planning and deployment, weapons procurement and other aspects of their national defense policy (Oguzlu 2004: 464). Indeed, with regard to the Greek–Turkish conflict NATO has never been – and never will be – in the position to clearly declare and enforce its commitment to international treaties and international law and/or to recognize in no uncertain terms the status quo of the territorial integrity of its member states.

All the above have resulted in NATO experiencing a low level of credibility and a gradual lessening of its importance as an institutional platform in which the intra-member co-operation process could result in the mitigation of the anarchical effects of the international system.[16] It should be stressed that during the Cold War the credibility of the Alliance was also affected by the preponderant position of the US in NATO and the subsequent US policies vis-à-vis Greece and Turkey. It is not a coincidence that US military sales and aid to Greece and Turkey on a "7-to-10" ratio was interpreted by Greece as a sign of US acquiescence in Turkey's greater geopolitical value and hence, led to Greek thinking that any NATO-framed solution on the Cyprus issue and the Aegean dispute would be likely to favor Turkey at the expense of Greece. By analogy, Turkey interpreted the US "7-to-10" policy as a sign that the US concurred with Greece that Turkey posed a threat to Greece in the Aegean sea.[17]

Moreover, in the post-Cold War era, NATO started losing its attraction for Turkey and Greece as an institution able to define their collective Western/ European identities. The new priorities of the Alliance, namely the promotion of the normative ideational elements of the Western international community in central and eastern European countries through enlargement, reduced the attention paid by the Alliance to Greek–Turkish relations and both countries became marginal to NATO's new identity and missions (Oguzlu 2004: 470–1). Although NATO started as a pan-European co-operative security organization it was gradually transformed into "one of the European security organizations" (Aybet 2000) while, during the 1990s, the EU became the institutional platform upon which Turkey and Greece could prove their European identities and work out their disputes.

It is worth noting that, although the security concerns emerging in the Balkans and the Greater Middle Eastern regions from the second half of the 1990s onwards pushed Greece and Turkey into a position of "front-line states," the consequent promise that NATO might start dealing with the Greek–Turkish conflict in a committed manner was not realized. Faced with increasing "Americanization"[18] of the Alliance and the European acquiescence in US involvement in European security (Art 1996; Duffield 1994–5),

Greece tried to identify its security interests with those of its partners in the EU, whereas Turkey, rebuffed by the EU's gradual discriminatory policies, has had to improve the quality of its strategic security relations with the United States on a more bilateral and less multilateral basis.

NATO has gradually lost its power of attraction in Greek and Turkish eyes and, as a consequence, the credibility of the Alliance as a promising actor has been seriously eroded. Furthermore, the efforts of the European members of the Alliance to develop an autonomous Common Foreign and Security Policy (CFSP) and European Security and Defence Policy (ESDP) has dramatically eroded the multilateral and transatlantic character of NATO and led to a gradual lessening of its importance as an institutional platform in which the intra-member co-operation process could result in the mitigation of the anarchical effects of the international system.

Throughout the Cold War years the European Community (EC) did not have, as the cases of Northern Ireland and Gibraltar indicate, either a clear procedure or an institution to deal with disputes between its members that concerned political issues of high national salience (Alford 1984: 34). Especially with regard to the conflict between Greece, a full member since 1981, and Turkey, an aspirant country since the early 1960s, the EC approach towards the resolution of the conflict has been a hesitant, if not an indifferent, one (Stephanou and Tsardanides 1991). In fact, the EC never decided as a whole to mediate in either managing or resolving the Greek–Turkish dispute. Mainly concerned about keeping both Greece and Turkey anchored to the West, the EC has been purposely kept out of the conflict, thus leaving some space for intervention to either the US or to isolated diplomatic activities of some of its members (Meinardus 1991). Unsurprisingly, the indifference of the EC to the resolution of the conflict has been viewed, interpreted and, most importantly, dealt with differently by the disputants.

Greece's membership of the EC, though largely economically motivated, was also meant to bolster the existing Greek government and, most importantly, to strengthen the country's international position, especially its deterrent capability against Turkey.[19] Enjoying a comparative advantage as a full member of the EC, Greece tried to use the latter as a diplomatic lever against Turkey. As Greek and Turkish analysts argue, the EC collective approach towards the conflict was greatly influenced, if not captured, by Greece's views and desiderata on Cyprus and Greek–Turkish relations (Couloumbis 1994; Guvenc 1998–9). Indeed, successive Greek governments have shown remarkable continuity in using the Cyprus issue for blocking EU-Turkey relations since the 1980s (Kramer 1987; Stephanou and Tsardanidis 1991).[20] At the same time, advancement in relations between the EC and Turkey have remained linked to the exercise of Greece's veto power, unless Turkey first meets particular criteria – related mainly to the state of democracy and the respect for human rights – and/or abandons its revisionist policy in the Aegean.[21]

Unsurprisingly, the EU was perceived by Turkey as just another platform through which Greece, taking full advantage of its position as a member, could exert pressure on Turkey and pursue its national agenda with respect to Turkey. Furthermore, the perception of an EC captured by Greece was negatively interpreted as a reflection of a European reluctance to take Turkey into Europe (Ugur 1999). This reluctance, in turn, fuelled a dominant conviction in Turkish political culture, namely the "Sevres syndrome," or fear of dismemberment as a result of a Western conspiracy (Kirisci and Carkoglu 2003). It is thus evident that by choosing to keep out of the Greek–Turkish dispute, the European Community was exerting rather weak norms over the disputants about the management and/or resolution of their conflict. Indeed, the hesitancy and/or indifference of the EC to intervene in disputes over national issues had negatively affected the EC "third-party" capacity as well as its credibility to act as an honest broker for the resolution of the Greek–Turkish dispute, and overall its ability to have a positive impact on the conflict.

The institutional strengthening of the EC and its genesis into the EU was not followed by a more credible stance towards the Greek–Turkish conflict. Following the Imia crisis in January 1996, some normative pressure was applied on the aspirant Turkey by the European Commission and the European Parliament. The former expressed the EU's solidarity with Greece and warned Turkey that its relationship with the EU was supposed to take place in a context of respect for international law and the absence of the threat or use of force. The European Parliament expressed its concern over Turkey's territorial demands vis-à-vis an EU member and stated that Greece's borders constituted EU borders as well. On a stricter note, the EU Council of Ministers issued a statement in July 1996 urging Turkey to appeal to the International Court of Justice (ICJ) over Imia, to show respect for international law and agreements as well as for EU's external borders, and to declare its commitment to the aforementioned principles. It also considered that disputes should be settled solely on the basis of international law, that dialogue should be pursued along the lines which have emerged in previous contacts between the interested parties and it called for the establishment of a crisis-prevention mechanism.[22] Interestingly, the only result of the normative pressure exerted by these two prominent EU organs and the EU Council on the conflict was the further justification of the dominant perception in the Turkish elite, namely that the EU was being captured by Greece (Rumelili 2004b: 13).

A conflict-resolution proposal was for the first time made on the part of the EU, by an initiative taken by the Dutch Presidency in April 1997. In search of a solution to the continuing exercise of the Greek veto on the EU financial packages offered to Turkey, the Dutch Presidency initiative called for the establishment of a "Committee of Wise Men" (where Greece and Turkey would propose a "wise man" from a third party) who would study the Greek–Turkish problems, identify possible solutions and then refer the problems that could not be resolved to the ICJ. It must be stressed that through the Dutch Presidency proposal the EU had for the first time in its history acted as a typical "third party," without making any explicit link either to Turkey's membership prospects or to Greece's status within the EU (Rumelili

2004b: 15–17). This in turn reflected a move of the EU from its traditional stance of hesitancy or indifference to a new stance towards the conflict, innovative and persuasive, though unfortunately only to a certain sector of the Greek and Turkish elite. It is thus not a coincidence that although the proposal was eventually diluted, due to the strong nationalist opposition it faced within Greece and Turkey, it was followed by the Madrid Declaration in July 1997, which marked a positive step in the two states' search for peaceful relations.

The 1997 European Council in Luxembourg was the first one to introduce the conditionality factor in the EU's intervention in the Greek–Turkish conflict. Thus, the settlement of the Greek–Turkish dispute and the establishment of stable relations with Greece appeared as a condition for strengthening EU links with Turkey. Apparently, the Luxembourg EU decisions were not addressed to both disputants but only to the aspirant Turkey, identifying its dispute with an EU member as an impediment to its candidacy and asking Turkey to comply with this norm and/or condition without offering it, however, the carrot of candidacy. Unsurprisingly, the EU's introduction of a negative conditionality, without being followed by any carrot or reward, was interpreted by Turkey as a policy of "conditional sanctions" imposed by Greece on an ambivalent, if not reluctant, EU with regard to Turkey's membership (Rumelili 2004b: 17–18).

As has been made evident, the EU impact on the transformation of the Greek–Turkish conflict remained parochial prior to the late 1990s. This was not only due to the EU's hesitant, if not indifferent, stance towards the dispute, which had in turn affected negatively its "third-party" capacity as well as its credibility to act as an honest broker. Empirical evidence shows that the EU's impact on the transformation of the Greek–Turkish conflict remained dependent on the weak norms the EU had been exerting since the early 1990s towards the disputants, since the few initiatives taken did not incorporate any membership carrot for the aspirant country and served only to reinforce the latter's perception that the EU's initiatives towards the settlement of the conflict had been "captured" by the disputant who happened to be a member of the EU. It was thus clear that the EU's credibility would remain at a low level and that the EU itself would not have a positive impact on the resolution of the Greek–Turkish dispute.

Things seemed to change dramatically in the late 1990s, however, especially prior to the EU's "big bang" – namely its enlargement to the east. A radically different EU – more supranational, more post-sovereign, more post-modern, more multi-cultural and more demanding – seemed to be emerging. European integration has always been credited with ensuring peace in Europe. Particularly the EU's enlargement process has widely been legitimized by arguing that it will bring peace and stability to a part of Europe that would otherwise be in danger of returning to violent conflict, with possible spill-over to the old member states. Built on core principles, values and norms, the EU sought to export its success story to those who were willing and who could meet the criteria. Pursuing its enlargement task, the new post-Westphalian EU demanded that the candidate countries undergo a radical transformation process following certain principles and adopting the EU Community Law in earnest. Most important, these characteristics were reflected in the norms and rules/conditions encouraged by the EU to states that sought to become members, such as one of the disputants, namely Turkey.

Indeed, prior to the enlargement, the norms and conditions promoted by the EU were both constitutive (e.g., democratization, rule of law, respect of minority and human rights, the role of the military in politics etc.) and specific/regulative (e.g., certain economic and administrative adjustments for harmonizing the state's internal structures to European standards etc.). Moreover, the EU asked states that sought to become members to organize their domestic and foreign policies on the premises that underlie liberal-pluralistic democracy. The EU thus appeared as having a power of attraction stemming from its normative ability to determine the confines of appropriate state behavior in the European theatre.

Especially with regard to the Greek–Turkish conflict, in the 1999 EU Council in Helsinki the EU's role and credibility with regard to its positive transformation and resolution of the dispute was tremendously enhanced.[23] What seemed to make the difference in the EU's transformative ability towards the conflict was a series of issues that may be put under the same heading: exertion of strong norms and positive conditions.

First of all, the EU decisions at Helsinki established the – peaceful – resolution of outstanding border disputes as a community principle (Rumelili 2004a: 9). This in turn meant that the EU was not interested in providing a "patchwork" solution that would either settle for short-term solutions or consolidate the abnormal (to both sides) status quo. Instead, for the first time in the history of the two states' conflict, there was a clear reference[24] to the final forum and/or mechanism the two states should use for resolving/ending their long-standing conflict. By imposing a particular time-framework (2004 was identified as the deadline) and by indicating the final forum to which the disputants might refer for the ending of their conflict (i.e., the ICJ), the EU succeeded in encouraging and, moreover, facilitating substantive and long-term solutions, instead of offering short-run and ad hoc ones.

Secondly, due to the Helsinki decisions, progress on Turkey's candidacy and membership of the EU was linked to the resolution of its border disputes with an EU member. What is of particular importance here is that the strong carrot of candidacy/membership was incorporated along with a positive conditionality. Thus, the EU's stance towards the conflict was viewed, especially by the Turkish elite, as a policy of "conditional rewards," and not – as had been the case in the past – as a policy of "conditional sanctions." The incentives for the disputants to find a better way of resolving their conflict were also increased. For Turkey, the Helsinki European Council Conclusions constituted both an alert and an incentive that "there was light at the end of the tunnel" and therefore Turkey had to successfully address the issues causing instability in a particular part of the Union. They also entailed, implicitly yet clearly, certain commitments for Greece, as the latter would have to enter into a dialogue with the candidate state in order to resolve their dispute, and in case that failed also agree with Turkey what the agenda to be brought before the ICJ for its final verdict to their dispute should be.

Thirdly, the resolution procedure adopted in Helsinki by the EU – namely a "two-step compromise structure" involving first negotiations on all issues followed by adjudication of unresolved issues – reflected a compromise proposal, allowing the disputants not to perceive EU influence as an imposition, but as a deal struck on a balanced distribution of gains.[25] It should be stressed at this point that, besides the EU Council, the European Commission and the European Parliament also contributed, especially after 1999, to the mitigation of the distributional conflicts by "keeping account" of deals struck, compromises made and gains achieved. As examples of effective mechanisms for resolving "distributional conflicts" one may refer to EU Commission Reports and EU Summits and Councils' Conclusions where the progress achieved in Greek–Turkish relations since Helsinki were recorded.[26] Particularly with regard to the conflict between a member state and a candidate state, the EU emphasised the flexibility of the *acquis*[27] in order to accommodate special concerns arising between the disputants. In this manner, disputes perceived by the European Commission as a "series of issue conflicts" were translated into possible solutions through pragmatic approaches.[28]

To sum up, the 1999 EU Summit in Helsinki constituted a breakthrough in the way the EU had intervened in the Greek–Turkish conflict. For the first time the EU adopted a clear and strong position with regard to the dispute between a member and a candidate for membership, in addition to making the long-term goal of the resolution of the conflict a community principle and incorporating the strong carrot of future membership along with a positive conditionality. By applying strong and convincing norms and conditions to a particular inter-state conflict the EU had thus succeeded not only in strengthening its ability to be viewed "as a framework" with potential positive effects in the long run, but also as "an active player" able to impact the conflict through a plethora of ways.

Unfortunately, severe damage to the EU's ability to apply strong norms, and hence to its credibility to positively affect the conflict, occurred at the 2004 EU Summit in Brussels, where as a result of the EU Council's decision that EU-Turkey accession negotiations would start on October 2005 an issue of paramount importance for the resolution of the conflict disappeared.[29] More specifically, the EU decided – obviously with Greece's concession – that the Helsinki timetable urging the two countries to solve their bilateral differences, or else agree by December 2004 to refer them to ICJ, should be withdrawn. Turkey – in addition to the Copenhagen criteria – was now simply asked by the EU to commit to good neighborly relations and resolve any outstanding border disputes in conformity with the principle of peaceful settlement of disputes in accordance with the UN Charter, *including if necessary jurisdiction of the ICJ* (our emphasis). By implication, progress on Turkey's membership would no longer be linked to the resolution of its dispute with Greece, with an obvious decrease in both disputants' incentives (especially Turkey's) to find a way of resolving their conflict. It thus seemed that a resolution of the Greek–Turkish conflict should, for the immediate future, be sought outside the EU context and be achieved sometime in the distant future by a hesitant Greece and a – hopefully – increasingly Europeanized Turkey en route to Brussels.

Depth of internalization

As suggested by the relevant literature, the mechanisms that institutions use to exert their norms are not competing or mutually exclusive and can be differentiated according to the logic of action they follow. Thus, the mechanisms following the "logic of appropriateness" (when actors do what is deemed appropriate) can be either "cognitive" [they teach domestic actors what is deemed appropriate in a given situation] or "normative" [they seek to convince states of their norms]. On the other hand, the mechanisms following the "logic of consequentiality" (based on a cost–benefit analysis, actors choose the action that maximizes their individual utility) may either be "rhetorical" [institutions use social-psychological rewards for compliance and punishment for non-compliance] or "bargaining" [institutions use material threats and promises either directly to coerce a state to follow its norms or indirectly to alter the domestic balance of power in favor of actors that support its norms] (Schimmelfennig 2002: 12–13; Checkel 1999). Needless to say those institutional mechanisms are to be directed towards the conflict parties' elites and/or societies.

Through the aforementioned mechanisms and following particular socialization policies, institutions exert their norms and, most importantly, impact the domestic landscape of the states to be socialized. A useful categorization of the "domestic impact" distinguishes between normative effects and the depth of internalization (Schimmelfennig 2002: 9–10). The former refers to the kind of institutional impact and includes the "formal conception of norms" (mainly seen in the transfer of institutional norms to domestic laws or in the creation of formal institutions that enforce the institutional norm), "the behavioral conception of norms" (measured by the extent the behavior of the states under socialization is consistent with the behavior set by the institutional norm) and the "communicative conception of norms" (related to the ways the communication or discourse among the domestic actors is being affected). The depth of internalization or the "norm salience" (Cortell and Davis 2000: 70–1) refers to the extent the international norm has been transposed into a state's domestic political institutions and culture. By implication one may refer to degrees or levels of internalization and/or salience (high/intermediate/low internalization or high/moderate/low degree of salience). Needless to say, different kinds of normative effects (formal, behavioral, communicative) may also be detected at different levels of internalization or norm salience.

Obviously, it is a rather difficult enterprise to measure the depth of internalization or salience of the institutional norms, rules and conditions. In assessing NATO and EU normative effects and internalization on the Greek–Turkish conflict, empirical evidence is used for the exploration of only measurable effects of NATO and the EU on the conflict, such as changes in the disputants' (especially in Turkey's) institutions and policies, due to internalization of institutional norms (Cortell and Davis 2000: 70). Needless to say, it is a rather difficult enterprise for changes in the domestic political discourse to be objectively assessed, although they seem to be the most important ones. However, an effort will be made to assess changes in the disputants' behaviors and strategies towards co-operation and resolution of their conflict as "deeper" changes in the disputants' interests and identities.

As has already been noted, throughout the Cold War and the post-Cold War era the norms exerted by the Atlantic Alliance with regard to the conflict between two of its allies were weak and regulative, focusing on securing operational stability in the Alliance's southern flank. What is of particular importance, however, is that the particular norms exerted by NATO were directed – and are still being directed – only towards the disputants' elites. Indeed, NATO's regulative norms, basically limited to regulating behavior in individual issue areas between the disputants' governments, such as norms of military co-ordination and standardization, have been transmitted through cognitive and normative mechanisms to the Greek and Turkish elites only. NATO inability to ameliorate the Greek–Turkish security dilemma and provide a sense of collective identity between Greece and Turkey is attributed mainly to the domestic discourse in Greece and Turkey about its role. Specifically, both Greece and Turkey viewed NATO as a strategic instrument to serve their preconceived national interests, rather than as an institutional platform to realize their collective security interests.[30]

It was characteristic in Greek security thinking during the Cold War that NATO was valued more as constraining Turkey than for contributing to collective security against the Warsaw Pact. Indeed, Greek military expenditures have always been more influenced by Turkish military spending than by common alliance defense policy vis-à-vis a common external threat (MacKenzie 1983: 117). The Turkish invasion of Cyprus – an island considered by Greece as an integral part of "Hellenism" as well as of its borders – in July 1974, brought about a major change in Greek strategic thinking. For the majority of the Greek public as well as Greek security analysts and policy makers the fact that "a NATO member, using NATO weapons, had taken 35,000 troops out of the NATO structure in order to occupy another democratic European country" (Moustakis and Sheehan 2000: 96) was ample proof of NATO's inability to play the role of guarantor of Greek–Turkish borders in Cyprus.

By implication, Greece in the mid-1970s found that it had neither institutional nor military safeguards against potential Turkish aggression. Thus, for the majority of the Greek public, NATO was seen to fail since Cyprus and the Aegean disputes were regarded as the results of Turkish expansionism that the West refused to curb (Borowiec 1983: 29–81; Alford 1984: 13). Greece's withdrawal from NATO in the wake of the Turkish invasion of Cyprus in 1974 was a decision taken by the Greek premier Karamanlis for the appeasement of an infuriated public, which blamed the Alliance for "doing nothing" to deter Turkish revisionist policies against Greece and Cyprus.

It is worth noting that a certain amount of anti-Americanism, and by implication of anti-NATOism, seems to be an endemic characteristic of the Greek political and social discourse, reflected in the reaction of the Greek public to the Yugoslav wars, the NATO bombing in Kosovo, the terrorist attacks in New York and on the Pentagon, and more recently during the US invasion of Iraq. This anti-US and anti-NATO stance seems to be something that goes much further than the traditional anti-Americanism of the Left and completely transcends Greece's political spectrum (Michas 2002).

By exerting regulative and short-term norms to Greece's elite and by maintaining an attitude of detached concern, a hands-off policy and impartiality to the conflict, NATO has reinforced these anti-NATO and anti-US feelings and attitudes. Neither has it managed to change the Greek elite's long-standing assumption that the United States and NATO should be more actively engaged in its defense and thus be turned into "security-providing" hegemons.[31] Hence, the participation of Greece in NATO was seen by the Greek elite to be useful as a deterrent factor, a factor of limitation, or one of allied mediation, in an eventual Greek–Turkish confrontation (this was precisely the reason for Greece's reintegration into the Alliance in 1980) but in no case did it take the form of mediation for the resolution of Greek–Turkish differences.

Being a military alliance, NATO regulative rules and norms have been addressed – almost by default – to the military part of the Turkish elite, which has a constitutionally preponderant status and role in Turkish politics. Interestingly enough, the fact that the socialization of the Turkish elite into the Western mentality during the Cold War occurred mainly in the military delayed, if not prevented, the process of democratization in Turkey (Vamvakas 2001). Indeed, almost convinced that the generals would keep Turkey within the orbit of NATO, while managing more successfully the internal instability, the United States – the Alliance's dominant power – co-operated actively during the Cold War with particular Turkish military regimes and signed several defense and economic agreements (Oguzlu 2004: 462).

In the post-Cold War era and following an exclusive "socialization from the outside" strategy of community building, NATO exerted particular constitutive norms by making clear references to democratic principles as well as to civil dominance over the military. Although the transmission of such norms has been relatively successful in east and central European states – where the prospects of membership induced states to undertake democratic and economic reforms – it played relatively little role in promoting democracy in Turkey.

Interestingly, for the Turkish elite the internalization of NATO's post-Cold War identity, which resembled more a pan-European security organization rather than a collective defense alliance, appeared as a way to register its Western, and most importantly, its European identity. As a result Turkey took part in many NATO-led peacekeeping and peacemaking operations in and around Europe and became an ardent participant in NATO's Partnership for Peace. However, this process resulted only in the increase of Turkey's bargaining power and significance in the eyes of the US, rather than in the confirmation of Turkey's European identity (Oguzlu 2004: 468–72). Hence, apart from not internalizing the normative ideational elements of the Western international community, neither did the Turkish elite manage to use NATO as the institutional platform upon which to prove its "Europeanness."

Things have seemed to evolve much more positively with regard to the results produced by the exertion by the EU of strong norms, rules and conditions to the disputants' elites and society. The good news about the potential impact of the EU on the transformation and resolution of the Greek–Turkish conflict is that the EU's strong norms and positive conditions exerted since the 1999 EU summit in Helsinki have started producing some promising results with regard to changes of the disputants' strategies and interests towards co-operation and positive identification. The bad news is that this process seems to have been seriously damaged by the "watering down" of the norms, rules and conditions related to the resolution of the Greek–Turkish conflict decided at the 2004 EU summit in Brussels.

As has been illustrated above, the EU impact on the transformation and resolution of the Greek–Turkish conflict remained parochial until the late 1990s. At the 1999 Helsinki summit the EU put into motion a mix of cognitive, normative, rhetorical, and most importantly, bargaining mechanisms[32] for internalizing a set of strong norms and rules in the disputants' domestic agenda (Tallberg 2002: 609–43). Thus, apart from agreeing on making the resolution of the conflict a community principle and providing the Turkish elite with the strong carrot of candidacy along with a positive conditionality, the EU also actively promoted Turkey's democratization by asking it to proceed with a "small revolution" internally in order for the European *acquis* to be internalized.

The new EU policy of "conditional rewards" was received positively by the Turkish elite, who started reconsidering past views that decisions in the EU were fully captured by Greece. They were now prepared to accept a compromise deal for the resolution of Turkey's long-standing conflict with an EU member.[33] It is worth noting that almost all EU summits and councils' conclusions and decisions from Helsinki onwards have established certain procedures and mechanisms to monitor Turkey's progress in fulfilling the conditions set by the EU.[34] Moreover, the EU compliance system seemed to be operating using a combination of enforcement and management mechanisms in applying norms, which contributed to the EU's ability to combat detected violations, thereby reducing non-compliance to a temporal phenomenon. By implication, the use of carrot and stick by the EU to promote political reforms in Turkey seemed to be having a multi-pathway impact on the Greek–Turkish conflict.

An examination of Turkey's internalization of the European *acquis* after its EU candidacy in 1999 reveals that a "thorough" adoption of the EU's legislation, norms, rules and requirements was put into motion.[35] Most importantly, such a thorough adoption of the *acquis* took place with the participation of, and legitimacy provided by, several political and social actors, beyond those in government. More specifically, these normative and internalization effects of the EU on Turkey took place on a series of levels, namely on "the domestic institutions" level, the "elite" level and the "societal" level.

Various EU Council conclusions ask for certain EU norms and rules (in the form of conditions) to be enmeshed into domestic institutions. Indeed, from 2001 to 2004 various political reform packages were adopted in order to fulfill the Copenhagen political criteria that resulted in deepening Turkey's Europeanization process (Bac 2003: 21). Turkey has so far taken some big steps forward in order to fulfill these conditions and has thus managed – inter alia – to regulate the constitutional role of the National Security Council as an advisory body and in accordance with the practice of EU member states,[36] to fulfil certain economic and legal conditions (e.g., harmonization of the country's legislation and practice with the European *acquis*) and to extend cultural rights of minority groups in practice (allowing mother-tongue broadcasting and education as well as the liberalization of laws restricting freedom of speech and association).

At the elite level, the formal conception of norms (the transfer of EU norms to national laws) had, in turn, certain internalization effects (constitutive effects) on the basic political actors in Turkey. Especially the civil-military elite, which appears as the primary "securitizing actor" able to define the internal and external threats to the state – whose EU membership becomes the primary objective – has slowly, painfully, but steadily entered a process of "de-securitization." It was the EU, especially through the *acquis communautaire*, that increased the chances of successful de-securitization by providing a reference point to legitimize conflict-diminishing policies.

One may at this point stress the change in Turkey's elite interests over the Cyprus issue due to the EU membership incentive and the EU's normative impact on Turkey's political elite (Tsakonas 2001: 1–40). Indeed, despite strong reservations about the role of the EU and veiled threats to EU members that the Turkish Republic of Northern Cyprus (TRNC) would be either integrated into Turkey or that Turkey would withdraw its own candidacy if the Greek-Cypriot administration was accepted as a full member before the Cyprus problem was solved, nothing happened. Quite the contrary, it seemed that there was a general understanding among the Turkish elite that the Cyprus issue had to a great extent been Europeanized and that Turkey would need to reach acceptable compromises with Greece, the Greek Cypriots and the European Union should it aspire to join the EU. Particular credit should be given to the Turkish government, which had firstly neutralized and finally replaced the intransigent Turkish-Cypriot leader Rauf Denktash in order for the Greek-Cypriot community to support the Annan Plan for the reunification of the island. Ironically, the EU had a less positive impact on the Greek-Cypriot elite and the Greek-Cypriot public who rejected the UN Secretary General's plan for the reunification of the island.

Most importantly, at the societal level, Turkey's EU membership candidacy has empowered the domestic actors in both Greece and Turkey who are in favor of promoting Greek–Turkish co-operation, and allowed them to use the EU to legitimize their co-operative policies and activities. Indeed, the explicit link made by the Helsinki Council decisions – between Turkey's progress on EU membership and the peaceful resolution of the Greek–Turkish dispute – has given official and private efforts to promote Greek–Turkish co-operation significance, urgency, and most importantly, legitimacy. Thus, after 1999 a pro-EU coalition (benefited by the EU's mixed strategy of conditions and incentives) emerged, which gradually and steadily gained ground over another vocal "anti-EU" coalition (Onis 2003: 9–34). In addition, Turkey's EU membership candidacy has unleashed funding to civil society efforts directed toward Greek–Turkish co-operation. The effectiveness of the EU in promoting Greek–Turkish co-operation has thus stemmed, not so much from its direct interventions, as from the success of various domestic actors in using the EU as a funder, a symbol and a legitimating handle (Rumelili 2005: 43–54).[37]

In a general sense, the more democratization has taken root, the more diverse societal and political groups have challenged the primacy of the Kemalist understanding of foreign policy. To put it differently, it has gradually become more difficult for the National Security Council, the Foreign Ministry and the Chief of the General Staff, the traditional actors in the Turkish foreign policy-making process, to have the luxury of ignoring what public opinion thinks on foreign policy issues. It seems therefore that the ongoing democratization process in Turkey is continuously having an impact on the process, style and content of Turkey's foreign policy, leading towards a more rationalized and multilateralist stance and a gradual re-definition of Turkey's national interest that is closer to European rules and norms of behavior.[38]

An overall assessment of the normative and internalization effects of the EU on Turkey suggests that the degree of salience or the level of internalization could be characterized as "moderate to high." Indeed, although norms appearing in the domestic discourse have produced some change in Turkey's national agenda as well as in its institutions, they still confront countervailing institutions, procedures and normative claims. However, although for some norms and rules the domestic discourse still admits exceptions, reservations and special conditions, it seems that gradually a legitimization of alternative policies at the elite level has been taking place and the activities of civil society and norms retain more and more salience as a guide to behavior and policy choice.

In the 2004 summit in Brussels, however, there was a setback to the EU's willingness to actively contribute to the resolution of the Greek–Turkish conflict. As noted above, with Greece's concession, the EU decided to withdraw the Helsinki timetable, which had set December 2004 as a deadline for the resolution of the conflict either through an agreement between the disputants or via the compulsory reference of the Greek–Turkish dispute to the ICJ. The 2004 Brussels decision thus had certain consequences not only for the credibility of the EU to be "an active player" in the resolution of the Greek–Turkish conflict but also for its ability to be viewed "as a framework" with potential positive effects in the long run.

Indeed, from 1999 to 2004 the EU made the long-term goal of the resolution of the conflict a community principle and exerted clear and strong rules and norms to the disputants.[39] Most importantly, the strength of the norms the EU exerted after 1999, being supported and transcended by a mix of cognitive, normative, rhetorical and bargaining mechanisms, managed to achieve a moderate degree of internalization by Turkey, the disputant whose behavior deviated more from institutional norms. It would seem, by de-linking progress on Turkey's membership with the resolution of its dispute with Greece, the 2004 EU summit decreased both disputants', especially Turkey's, incentives to search for a – solely bilateral – compromise solution.

Even worse, a series of other developments may further exacerbate the EU's ability to constructively intervene and contribute to the resolution of the Greek–Turkish conflict. Indeed, in the years to come the resolution of the Greek–Turkish conflict is expected to become even more secondary to the EU's priorities in its enlargement policy (Celik and Rumelili 2006: 208). Moreover, representations of Turkey as "non-European," especially after the rejection of the European Constitution by France and The Netherlands, have resurfaced in many EU countries, Greece included, as the European identity discourse began to emphasize the "non-European" characteristics of Turkey. Such developments may move Turkey back to an ambiguous, if not threatening, institutional position in relation to the EU and thus have detrimental consequences for the resolution of its conflict with Greece.

Conclusions

The examination of the impact NATO and the EU have had on the management, transformation and/or resolution of the Greek–Turkish conflict has both theoretical value and policy relevance. Building on various theoretical strands, research – on the effects of NATO and the EU on Greece's and Turkey's strategies toward co-operation and positive identification and, more specifically, on their conflict transformation – has shown whether and mainly how these institutions matter.

The relevant literature has so far argued for a parochial role of the Atlantic Alliance in the Greek–Turkish conflict while a certain amount of optimism has been expressed, especially after 1999, for a promising EU role in the transformation of the Greek–Turkish dispute. Through a comparative assessment of the empirical records of NATO and EU roles in the transformation of the Greek–Turkish conflict, this chapter argues that two interrelated conditions seem to account most for NATO's perverse role and the EU's promising role in the Greek–Turkish conflict.

The first is related to the strength of the norms the two institutions have exerted on the conflict parties, while the second concerns the "type of socialization" and/or the depth of internalization the two institutions' mechanisms have produced. Specifically, and in accordance with recent findings, which argue that compliance crises tend to occur when the implementation of intergovernmental agreements is not backed by a public discourse at the societal level (Zurn and Joerges 2005), empirical findings show that in order for a "thorough" internalization to take place institutional norms should be directed at both the elite and the public. This chapter also draws attention to the need for international security institutions that fulfill the aforementioned conditions to be careful to promote the right mix of conditionalities and incentives to the disputants in order to positively contribute to the transformation and/or resolution of an inter-state dispute.

Notes

1 Structural realism believes that international institutions matter only at the margins of international relations, and whatever power they have is derived from the power of their members (Mearsheimer 1994–5).
2 See the special issue of *International Organization* on "International Institutions and Socialization in Europe" (2005).
3 The literature distinguishes between conflict management (regulation of conflictual relations) and conflict transformation (the transformation of subject positions from incompatibility/antagonism to compatibility/tolerance).
4 We here adopt Keohane's remark that "alliances are institutions" (Keohane 1988: 74). However, Russett's and Oneal's point that "the ways alliances affect interstate relations will not be the same as the ways that institutions with economic functions operate" (Russett and Oneal 2001: 166) is also taken into account.
5 Greece and Turkey have been allies in NATO since 1952. They have also been associate members of the European Community since 1961 and 1963, respectively. Greece became a full member in 1981, and Turkey became a candidate of the EU in 1999. However, despite their joint participation in and/or close association with these institutions, Turkey and Greece have continued to maintain antagonistic relations. In addition to armed conflict over Cyprus in 1974, Turkey and Greece have been in numerous near-war situations in 1964, 1967, 1976 and in 1996, over Cyprus and the continental shelf, airspace and small islets in the Aegean.
6 Greece has in the past vetoed financial protocols in relation to the Association Agreement with Turkey, and caused a delay in the conclusion of a Customs Union between Turkey and the EU. Although these issues are now largely settled, many Turkish politicians see Greece as an enemy inside the EU, causing unfavorable and unjustified treatment.
7 As Monteagle Stearns has noted: "instead of enabling them to reconcile their differences by direct negotiation, their [Greece and Turkey] common alliance with the United States and Western Europe often appears to act as an impediment. Bilateral disputes acquired multilateral dimension." See Stearns (1992: 5).

NATO, EU and the Greek–Turkish conflict 247

8 After the end of the Cold War, NATO's policy made provisions for the transference of the comparatively more sophisticated weapon systems of certain countries (e.g., United States, Germany), which had to be reduced under the CFE Treaty, to those NATO member states that had obsolete weapon systems, in order to streamline the latter.
9 See Koucik and Kokoski (1994: 36). In accordance with NATO's Cascade Program, Greece received 986 tanks, 350 ACVs and 403 artillery pieces, while Turkey received 922 tanks, 800 ACVs and 203 artillery pieces.
10 Responding to Paul Kowert and Jeffrey Legro's remark that "the literature has generally been biased toward studying those norms that *have* affected state policies" (Kowert and Legro 1996), this chapter deals with an institution whose weak norms have failed in affecting the policies of two of its members that are in conflict in a way that would promote the adoption of co-operative strategies.
11 For the distinction between "constitutive" and "regulative" norms, see Dessler (1989: 454).
12 One of the most recent examples of NATO's failure to play the role of guarantor of a particular confidence-building enterprise taking place within the Alliance's institutional context was during an Alliance exercise named Destined Glory in September 2000. During that exercise – whose main goal was to build confidence between Greece and Turkey – in the Aegean, NATO failed to make clear, especially to the Turkish side, that any defection of what had been discussed and agreed within the context of the Alliance would entail certain costs for the party that decided to defect. However, although none of the participants expressed a reservation or an objection to the exercise plans during the initial phase of the planning in NATO Headquarters, Turkey decided some days after the beginning of the exercise to prohibit the flights of the participating Greek aircraft over the Greek islands of Lemnos and Ikaria, which according to Turkey should be demilitarized. Although NATO's Office of the Legal Adviser rejected Turkish claims, Turkey insisted on preventing Greek aircraft from executing their NATO missions by intercepting them while flying above the Greek island of Lemnos. The closing of Turkish national airspace to Greece's aircraft participating in the exercise, which Turkey had previously harassed and intercepted, rendered Greece's further participation impossible and compelled it firstly to ask for the suspension of the exercise and then to withdraw from it. It would have been particularly useful had NATO managed to ensure the participation of all forces in the entire area of the exercise as well as to conduct the exercise as previously agreed during its planning phase. Unfortunately, NATO's mismanagement of the particular exercise sent wrong messages to the party that decided to deviate from the scenario agreed within the alliance's institutional context, given that Turkey's determination to exploit the conduct of a NATO exercise in order to score politically against Greece did not entail any costs. Most importantly, it made NATO's ability to play the role of guarantor of any confidence-building enterprise between Greece and Turkey rather questionable.
13 For some analysts this is related to internal power configuration, namely to NATO's continuing dependence on US preponderance and sufferance.
14 Gallarotti's work on "adverse substitution" is very telling about the destabilizing effects of International Organizations (IOs). According to Gallarotti, an IO is prone to failure when it – inter alia – serves as a substitute (i.e., a less costly and less viable multilateral scheme offering short-run and ad hoc solutions) for more substantive and long-term solutions (i.e., managing the conflict, not resolving it). In his words: "the institution provides a 'patch work' solution that consolidates the abnormal to both sides' status quo and thus reduces the incentives for disputants to find a better way of resolving it." See Gallarotti (2001: 381–2).
15 Contrary to Tuschoff's observation regarding the perceived impartiality of NATO

high-level military commanders, which has enabled them to resolve conflicts and gain national concessions on disputed issues (Tuschoff 1999: 140–61), the Greek–Turkish case aptly demonstrates that NATO has never been in the position to serve as a neutral actor in politically charged situations.

16 This did not mean, however, that the Alliance had ceased to be perceived by successive Greek governments as a potential provider of security against the "Turkish threat." See Tsakonas and Tournikiotis (2003). For reference to particular examples regarding successive Greek governments' efforts to get a formal security guarantee, see Dimitras (1985).

17 For these remarks, see Oguzlu (2004: 466).

18 With an increase in the United States' relative power vis-à-vis the European members of the Alliance, in the post-Cold War era NATO has mainly remained a political instrument of the US Government. Decisions about enlargement, the definition of the new missions of the Alliance and of the geopolitical boundaries of the Alliance have mainly reflected the concerns and priorities of the successive US governments in the 1990s. As such, NATO has gradually turned out to be a state-centric platform for the US to enlist possible allies in their global-scale security initiatives and undertakings. See Layne (2000) and Croft (2000).

19 In the words of one senior Greek official: "Turkey would thus think twice to attack an EU member state." See *The Economist*, 26 July 1975, and *The Guardian*, 19 May 1976 (as quoted in Valinakis 1997: 279). See also the speeches of the premier, Constantine Karamanlis, in *Kathimerini* [Greek daily], 11 April 1978 and 1 January 1981, as quoted in Valinakis (1997: 283).

20 It was not until March 1995 that Greece decided to lift its veto towards the EU-Turkey Customs Union agreement. In exchange for the removal of the Greek veto on the Customs Union, accession negotiations between the EU and Cyprus would begin in March 1998. Cyprus would thus be included in the next round of enlargement accession negotiations. With regard to Turkey's European orientation, decisions made in Luxembourg and Cardiff, in January and June 1998 respectively, further burdened the already tense and fragile Greek–Turkish security agenda, as the postponement of Turkey's accession negotiations remained linked to Greece's deliberate policy of keeping the doors of the EU closed.

21 In 1986, Greece vetoed the resumption of the Association relationship between Turkey and EC and the release of frozen aid to Turkey. A year later, when Turkey applied for EC membership, Greece was the only member that openly opposed referring the application to the EC Commission for an Opinion. See Guvenc (1998–9). It is characteristic that even up to the EU-Turkey Association Council in April 1997, Greece maintained its veto and continued blocking EU aid to Turkey worth 375 million ECUs. As explained by the then Greek Minister of Foreign Affairs, Theodoros Pangalos, the veto was to be maintained until Turkey stopped disputing Greek sovereignty in the Aegean. See Athens News Agency, Daily Bulletin, 30 April 1997, statement by Foreign Minister Pangalos.

22 Declaration adopted by the Fifteen Ministers of Foreign Affairs of the EU at the General Affairs Council on 15 July 1996, Brussels, SN 3543/96.

23 Turkey's eligibility for EU membership after Helsinki depended on resolving two issues: its border conflict with an EU member-state, Greece, and the Cyprus issue. With regard to Greek–Turkish relations, Helsinki made it clear to Turkey that it had four years – until 2004 – to resolve the conflict with neighboring Greece before the rather critical review that would assess Turkey's path towards the European Union took place. Paragraph 4 of the Helsinki European Council Conclusions states: "[. . .] the European Council stresses the principle of peaceful settlement of disputes in accordance with the United Nations Charter and urges candidate States to make every effort to resolve any outstanding border disputes and other related issues. Failing this they should within a reasonable time bring the dispute

to the International Court of Justice. The European Council will review the situation relating to any outstanding disputes, in particular concerning the repercussions on the accession process and in order to promote their settlement through the International Court of Justice, at the latest by the end of 2004." Regarding the Cyprus issue, the Helsinki European Council reiterated in Paragraphs 9a and 9b that although a political settlement of the Cyprus problem would facilitate Cyprus's accession to the EU, this very settlement would not be a precondition for accession. At the same time, the European Council ambiguously stressed that "all relevant factors" would be taken into account for the final decision on accession. The fifteen Heads of State and Government of the European Union have sent a clear message to Turkey that the division of Cyprus must end by the date of the next EU meeting at the latest. After that date, even a divided Cyprus would become member of the Union. In that sense, Turkey, which illegally occupies the northern part of the island, could no longer block the accession of Cyprus to the European Union. See Helsinki European Council Conclusions, online at *http://www.europa.eu.int/council/off/conclu/dec99_en.htm*.

24 Both the Helsinki Conclusions and the provision on Greek–Turkish relations, in the "medium-term priorities" of the Accession Partnership, do refer to the resolution of the two states' outstanding border disputes.

25 For this remark, see Rumelili (2004b: 14). The approach adopted in the Helsinki Summit is indeed different from past approaches. For example, the EU Council of Ministers stated in July 1996 (after the Imia crisis) that "the cases of disputes created by territorial claims, such as the Imia islet issue, should be submitted to the International Court of Justice." Similarly, the Luxembourg Council Decisions of December 1997 urged "the settlement of disputes, in particular, by legal process, including the ICJ."

26 Commission discourses also include references to the continuous improvement in relations between Greece and Turkey. The improvement is sometimes linked with words like "significantly" (EU Commission Regular Report 2001: 89) or "dramatically" (EU Commission Regular Report 2004: 52). In this context, the Regular Reports refer to the signing of bilateral agreements that aim to deepen the co-operation between the two countries (EU Commission Regular Report 2003: 41 and EU Commission Regular Report 2002: 18 and 44), agreement on a number of confidence-building measures (2004: 2003: 41; 2002: 44; 2001: 31), the exploratory talks in the Aegean that started in March 2002 (EU Commission Regular Reports in 2004 and 2002: 18 and 44) as well as symbolic movements such as the "official visit" of the Turkish PM to Greece and his "private visit to Western Thrace where he called on the Turkish-speaking Muslim minority to contribute to Greece's prosperity" (EU Commission Regular Report 2004) and the public commitments at the highest level to continued rapprochement (EU Commission Regular Report 2003: 41). In some documents, there have also been references to the Greek–Turkish rapprochement at the level of civil society (EU Commission Regular Report 2001: 89). The evolution of Turkish foreign policy and its perception of security interests towards EU standards has also been recorded, though the Greek–Turkish dispute remains unresolved (EU Commission Report, October 2004). See Pace (2005).

27 The EU *acquis*, also known as *acquis communautaire*, concerns the "legal order" of the Union.

28 According to the EU Commission discourse, Greek–Turkish conflict appears as a series of "issue conflicts": "There are a number of contentious issues in the Aegean area between Turkey and an EU Member State, Greece, including disputes about the demarcation of the continental shelf. Turkey also challenges sovereignty over various islets and rocks. The boundaries of the two territorial waters and airspace are also problematic" (Regular Report 1998: 51). The European

Commission sees the role of the EU as a forum where the Greek–Turkish dispute can be discussed in the context of political dialogue (Regular Report 2001: 33) while the use of carrot and stick to promote political reforms in Turkey could be seen to have a multi-pathway impact on the Greek–Turkish conflict. See Pace (2005).

29 The government that emerged from the parliamentary elections in March 2004, burdened with the rejection of the Annan Plan by the Greek/Cypriots and hesitant to pay the cost that a compromise settlement with Turkey before the Helsinki deadline (i.e. the end of 2004) would entail, opted for a transference of the dispute's resolution to the future. For an analysis of Greece' "socialization" strategy vis-à-vis Turkey, see Tsakonas (2007).

30 There is a plethora of examples, both during the Cold War and in the post-Cold War era, that verify this thesis. Back in mid-1950s Greece argued for the establishment of a NATO patrol-boat base on the island of Leros, which was vetoed by Turkey because the latter considered that this Dodecanese island – in accordance with the 1923 Lausanne and 1947 Paris treaties – should remain demilitarized. See Iatrides (2000: 32–46). By analogy, Turkey was constantly vetoing the inclusion of the island of Lemnos in the planned military exercises of the Alliance in the region in order to prevent the promotion of Greece's goals through NATO; see Karaosmanoglu (1988: 85–118).

31 Several cases during the Cold War and after can be reviewed to illustrate Greece's attempts to get from either NATO or the US a formal security guarantee. They include Premier Andreas Papandreou's request in 1981 to the Alliance to provide Greece with a security guarantee against another ally, namely Turkey. The rejection of such a request by the Alliance led to Papandreou's refusal to sign the particular NATO summit final communiqué; the same request was posed again in 1990 to the US government in return for its access to military bases and other facilities in Greece. See Dimitras (1985); Tsakonas and Tournikiotis (2003).

32 Making use of its bargaining power means that EU conducts policies through which it addresses primarily the political leadership of the conflict parties. This is probably the most obvious way through which the EU attempts to exert influence. In its relations with Turkey the EU has, on the one hand, repeatedly used the "carrot" of a future membership in order to "convince" the Turkish government not only to pursue conflict transformation vis-à-vis the Cyprus conflict or the contested border issues with Greece, but also to engage in far-reaching constitutional and economic reforms. On the other hand, the "stick" of threatening suspension of financial assistance has in the past been used by the EU to exert political pressure on Turkey and normative power.

33 On elite receptivity as a factor essential to the socialization process, see Ikenberry and Kupchan (1990: 284).

34 After Helsinki and in order to prepare for membership, the Accession Partnership called upon Turkey to prepare a National Program for the Adoption of the Acquis (NPAA), which should be compatible with the priorities established in the Accession Partnership. The purpose of the Accession Partnership was to set out the specific short-term and medium-term priorities and intermediate objectives for political, economic and legal/administrative reforms in a single framework, and touch upon Turkey's internal, as well as external, front. In July 2003, the Turkish government revised its National Programme on the Adoption of the Acquis in line with changes and political reforms adopted since 2001.

35 For a good account of the political and legal reforms which have been stimulated since Turkey's EU candidacy, see Bac (2003: 17–31).

36 A development that has had certain repercussions for the Turkish military ability to solely define the issues that concern the country's national interest.

37 Especially after 1999, again slowly but steadily, one could notice, both within

Turkey and the TRNC, the surfacing of a plethora of political parties, business associations and civil society organizations which have challenged the "orthodox" well-established Turkish policy on Cyprus and started demanding that Turkey and TRNC cease adopting a skeptical view of the EU and the accession of the island to the EU.

38 Our focus on the institutional effects on Turkey's foreign policy behavior is mainly related to the fact that, as theory suggests, convergence effects appear when institutions exert their greatest influence on precisely those states whose behavior deviates substantially from institutional norms. See Martin and Simmons (2001). In the Greek–Turkish dyad, Turkey is undoubtedly the one of the disputants whose behavior deviates more from institutional norms. Hence, the assessment of the EU's ability to exert its normative and internalization effects on Turkey's foreign policy.

39 Based on the observation that the level of internalization of the EU's norms and rules on Turkey has been a moderate one, we consider the EU norms and rules as particularly strong. This assessment follows Cortell and Davis' remark that "the strength of a norm is a function of its level of "institutionalization", namely of the norm's tenets in the states' constitutional, regulative and/or judicial systems." See Cortell and Davis (2000: 70).

11 Evaluating multilateral interventions in civil wars

A comparison of UN and non-UN peace operations

*Nicholas Sambanis and
Jonah Schulhofer-Wohl*

Introduction

As the prevalence of civil war around the world peaked in the mid-1990s, the international community responded by increasing the number of peacekeeping operations to end those wars and prevent their recurrence. Both the number and scope of peacekeeping operations expanded drastically after the end of the Cold War. The UN took the lead in those efforts, but other regional organizations and individual countries also engaged in peacekeeping activities. The UN had some spectacular failures in Somalia and Rwanda, but also some impressive successes, in Cambodia, El Salvador, Mozambique, and elsewhere. The record of non-UN peacekeeping is less well-known. Have peacekeeping operations by organizations other than the UN had the same overall success rate as UN peace operations? This is the question that we address in this chapter. The evidence that we present suggests that the UN has been much more successful in peacekeeping than other organizations. We analyze that evidence and suggest some possible explanations for this empirical fact.

UN officials and advocates see the UN's legitimacy as one of its key virtues. The UN "premium" of international legitimacy as an impartial mediator is often seen as a critical component of UN peacemaking and peacekeeping.[1] Legitimacy is distinct from the organization's resources and technical capabilities, and derives from its commitment to maintain peace and order in accordance with the rules of the UN Charter. Thus the UN's legitimacy is not necessarily a characteristic of other actors engaged in peacekeeping (individual countries or regional organizations), even if those actors have the capabilities to engage in peacekeeping. These assertions, evident in journalistic accounts, case studies of UN peacekeeping, and speeches by diplomats and UN officials, skirt key policy questions. Why might UN operations be more likely to achieve good peacebuilding results than non-UN operations? Are the mechanisms behind UN success fundamentally unavailable to non-UN operations? We address this question in this chapter, by suggesting some possible explanations. These explanations do not resolve the debate. Rather, they highlight the fact that we do not yet know why there is a difference in the relative effectiveness of UN and non-UN peacekeeping and point the way to more research that could resolve this puzzle.

The literature on peace operations has provided several, often conflicting perspectives on the effectiveness of UN and non-UN peacekeeping. Several studies describe potential advantages and disadvantages of UN and non-UN approaches to peacekeeping (see, e.g., Diehl 1993), and case studies offer detailed accounts of the histories of particular operations (see, e.g., Durch 1996). But a theoretical account of the differences between the two types of UN missions is in short supply. There are also only a few empirical analyses of the differences between UN and non-UN missions. Here, the results that authors have presented are not consistent. Heldt and Wallensteen (2005) have observed that UN peace operations appear to be more successful than non-UN operations because the former, while succeeding at the same rate as the latter, tend to be deployed in more difficult conflict environments. Yet, Heldt (2004) is cited in the same study, arguing that, controlling for the degree of mission difficulty, UN and non-UN operations appear not to differ in their rate of success. Fortna's (2004a) analysis finds that peace missions (UN and non-UN missions combined) have had a positive effect on continued peace, but this result is driven by the effects of UN missions.

We compare the effects of UN and non-UN peace operations by building on Doyle and Sambanis' (2000, 2006) ecological model of peacebuilding. According to the model, there are three main dimensions to the peacebuilding "space" after civil war. Levels of war-related hostility, pre- and post-war levels of local capacities, and available international capacities interact to deliver specific post-conflict outcomes. The higher the levels of hostility, and the lower the local and international capacities, the lower will be the probability of a successful transition to peace. The main measure of international capacities in the Doyle and Sambanis model is UN peacekeeping. UN operations are successful if they respond to the type of co-ordination or co-operation problem facing parties to the conflict. In other words, not all types of peace operations work all the time. Their empirical analysis has shown that UN peace operations have a robust, large and statistically significant positive effect on the probability of peacebuilding success and that this effect is larger in the short run. All types of UN mandates can have a positive effect, though consent-based operations make the larger difference. A central conclusion of this work that we bring to our analysis is that an operation affects peacebuilding success through its interaction with the characteristics of the conflict.

All types of peace operations should, in principle, have a positive effect if they offer sufficient international capacities to counteract the negative effects of hostility and to compensate for deficiencies in local capacities. Thus, on the basis of Doyle and Sambanis (2000, 2006), our prior belief is that non-UN operations are no less likely to have a positive effect on peacebuilding than UN-operations themselves. This is grounded in the more theoretical literature on external or "third party" intervention, which analyzes intervention in conflict abstractly, in contrast to the vast majority of the literature on peace operations as such. We provide support for this prior belief by offering an overview of the conventional wisdom on the differences between UN and non-UN peace operations. Here, we indicate that perceived differences between the two types in fact vary across both UN and non-UN operations, such that the two may not necessarily be understood as natural categories. Note that in contrast to the literature on peace operations as such, more theoretically orientated studies of external or "third party" interventions in conflict, whether formal or empirical, apparently proceed based on this assumption. Historical evidence on pre-UN peace operations also supports this claim (see Heldt and Wallensteen 2005).

We test our hypothesis about the effectiveness of non-UN operations empirically, using data from Doyle and Sambanis (2006). We find that the data do not support our hypothesis and that non-UN operations have no significant effect on peacebuilding success, in contrast to UN operations, which have a large significant positive effect. This result is robust across multiple models employing different operationalizations of the dependent variable, different controls, and different econometric assumptions. We find support for the idea that the presence of a non-UN peace operation in the same conflict may complement the effectiveness of a multidimensional UN operation.[2] We postulate several possible explanations for the result that non-UN operations have no significant effect on peacebuilding success and we explore the differences between the outcomes of UN and non-UN peace operations as a way to analyze the determinants of the composition of a peace operation.

Literature review

The perceived differences between UN and non-UN peace operations are many. Non-UN operations, which could range from efforts by regional organizations to multinational undertakings, or potentially even intervention by a single state, are thought to be subject to problems of impartiality, bias, logistics, vulnerability to domestic politics, and lack of financial, technical and coercive resources.[3] Interestingly enough, the reverse of all of these problems have also been noted as potential advantages of non-UN operations, as are some additional characteristics: the potential for operational stability in contrast to regularly reviewed and renewed UN mandates, and greater local and external support based on the ability to incorporate stakeholders (Diehl 1993). These often directly contradictory advantages and disadvantages lead us to conclude that both UN and non-UN operations vary in their avoidance of the problems listed above and their provision of the services hypothesized as needed to build peace. The logic is that falsification of purported regularities in the differences between UN and non-UN peace operations implies that variation in the characteristics of peace operations exists, regardless of their source.

Yet while a large body of literature treats abstractly external intervention in conflict, a category to which peace operations undoubtedly belong, and analyzes its characteristics and effects as varying in ways that are not inherent to a particular actor,[4] we feel obliged to falsify one additional set of claims about differences between UN and non-UN operations. Non-UN operations are held to lack the special kind of "moral authority" the UN confers on its undertakings (Dorn 1998) or require accountability to the UN itself (Weiss, Forsythe, and Coate 2004). Some may also see them as lacking the unique legitimacy of UN operations (Bellamy and Williams 2005). Such analyses allude to the existence of something like a UN "brand" that enhances peace operations by its essence, not its characteristics. (We could call this the primordialist theory of peacekeeping!) Thus, Diehl (2000: 357) concludes that:

> A best-case scenario would be a peacekeeping operation organized by the United Nations, with full support of the major powers and put in place following a comprehensive peace agreement between two states. Both protagonists would be strongly supportive of the operation as would any regional actors. The peacekeeping operation might be assigned monitoring functions and be located along a narrow international border in a sparsely populated area that would make detection of military and other movements easy, while not offering opportunities for the peacekeepers themselves to come under fire.

Such claims for the existence and operational benefits of UN legitimacy are made regularly and forcefully, not just by UN officials but in debates on foreign affairs, and are not exclusive to discussions of peace operations but appear more generally, even in the literature on international institutions.[5] In addition to our skepticism, purely on logical grounds, of treating differences between UN and non-UN operations as innate, increased scrutiny of intra-state operations undertaken by the UN particularly from the early 1990s onward, but also during the Cold War (e.g., ONUC in the Congo), provides evidence that legitimacy, however defined, varies from one UN operation to the next. On a general level, depending on the context, individuals may believe the UN's actions to be part of a US-sponsored, or at least Western-sponsored, project, implying lack of legitimacy.[6] On a more micro-level, allegations of misconduct also taint the UN.[7] The UN still retains substantial credibility as an impartial mediator, but even impartial UN missions can have effects that some of the parties to an intra-state conflict can consider to be biased.[8] Hence the legitimacy of UN intervention may not always be a constant and it may not always explain why UN missions seem to be more effective than non-UN missions.

Relevant to the debate about the merits of UN and non-UN peace operations is the pre-UN history of peace interventions. Heldt and Wallensteen (2005) describe two instances of peace operations under the auspices of the League of Nations. In the first, following the Versailles Treaty, the League administered the Saar region of Germany and deployed police there, while the French controlled security. For a 1935 referendum on the status of the region, which occurred peacefully, the League deployed a 3,300-strong force of British, Italian, Dutch and Swedish troops for the period December 1934 to February 1935 because Germany would not accept that the referendum be held with the French having the security role. In the second case, the League assisted in verifying the withdrawal of 110,000 to 130,000 foreign troops from the Spanish Civil War, by organizing an observer mission of 12 members, known as the International Military Commission. Finally, Heldt and Wallensteen (2005) note the peacekeeping use of Swedish and Norwegian troops in Schleswig in 1849 and 1850 following a war between Denmark and Germany. They explain that the peacekeepers were "tasked to maintain law and order . . . until a peace agreement could be established," which indeed occurred in July 1850, and was followed by their withdrawal. These examples, in disparate settings and geopolitical contexts, further illustrate that it need not be the case that the UN endows peace operations with something that other actors are fundamentally unable to provide.[9]

Our argument

Based on an ecological model of peacebuilding, we argue that the effect of peace operations should not differ across organizations, controlling for the relevant elements of these operations. The specifics of an operation and how well it is matched to the characteristics of the conflict should affect peacebuilding success. To develop this line of argument further, we specify the characteristics of conflict to which peace operations should respond in order to facilitate peacebuilding.

The resolution of conflict is characterized by co-ordination and co-operation problems, with some conflicts reflecting entirely one or the other, and others reflecting a mix of the two, either simultaneously or in sequences. Co-ordination problems have a payoff structure that gives the parties no incentives to unilaterally move out of equilibrium, once they reach equilibrium.[10] It is well established that the best strategy to resolve co-ordination problems is information provision and improvement of the level of communication between the parties.[11] Communication gives the parties the ability to form common conjectures about the likely outcomes of their actions. Without the ability to communicate, they will not choose the most efficient outcome.

In a game of pure co-ordination, both parties want to pursue compatible strategies. But if neither knows the rules or what the other party prefers, they will be tempted to experiment, to try one and then another of the strategies, and this of course can be costly. Co-ordination can be readily achieved by credible information on rules, payoffs, and the parties' compliance with the rules or stated preferences. Once the rule is known or the other parties' preferences are clear, co-ordination can be achieved. UN monitors or observers

Interventions in civil wars: a comparison 257

can assist such communication and help the parties co-ordinate to an efficient outcome.

One formulation of a co-ordination problem is the "assurance" game. The classic story (as told by the eighteenth-century French philosopher Jean Jacques Rousseau) is a stag hunt in which catching the stag depends on all the hunters co-operating. But if a rabbit suddenly appears, some of the hunters may be tempted to defect in order to catch the rabbit which, though less desirable than the hunter's share of the deer, can be caught (in this story) by one hunter on his own. If all chase the rabbit, they divide the rabbit. Here, if players A and B can choose between strategies of co-operation and defection, we get a payoff structure such as the following: mutual co-operation yields an equal payoff (4, 4) for players A and B, as each gets a half-share of the deer. When A co-operates and B defects, A gets 0 and B gets 3 (the rabbit); correspondingly when A defects and B co-operates, A gets 3 and B, 0. When both defect, each gets 1.5 (a half-share of the rabbit). In this case, peacekeeping needs to be more involved than in the previous co-ordination game. In both cases communication should be sufficient, but the temptation to defect out of fear that another hunter will do so first (even though this is rational for neither) requires more active facilitation and continual reassurance. Information alone may not be enough; the peacekeepers may need to provide regular reports on each party's compliance, and so reduce the costs of communication between the parties and allow them to co-ordinate their strategies.[12] The more the peacekeepers need to increase the costs of non-co-operation, the more we move from a co-ordination game to a game of co-operation.

In the more complicated framework of actual peace processes, many parties that have a "will" to co-ordinate lack the "way." Co-ordination is promoted when parties receive assistance in capacity building, demobilizing armies and transforming themselves from military factions to coherent political parties. Such assistance permits them to act rationally according to their preferences, rather than incoherently.

By contrast, co-operation problems create incentives to renege on agreements, particularly if the parties discount the benefits of long-term co-operation in favor of short-run gain. In one-shot games of co-operation the parties will try to trick their adversaries into co-operating while they renege on their promises. A well-known example is the Prisoner's Dilemma. Two accomplices in police custody are offered a chance to "rat" on their partner. The first to rat gets off and the "sucker" receives a very heavy sentence. If neither rats, both receive light sentences (based on circumstantial evidence); and, if both rat, both receive sentences (but less than the sucker's penalty). Even though they would be better off trusting each other by keeping silent, the temptation to get off and the fear of being the sucker make co-operation extremely difficult.

Co-operation problems are much more difficult to solve. How can co-operation failure (defection) be avoided? In the classic Prisoner's Dilemma one-shot game, we always end up at double defection (both rat) unless there is some external enforcement mechanism. Conditions of repeated play (iteration) may produce co-operation in infinite-horizon games even without external enforcement, but not if there is a visible end to the game.[13] Short-term defection from agreements may even be possible from iterated games if one of the parties discounts the future severely. Strong third party involvement would be necessary to support effective co-operation, unless the parties' agreements are self-enforcing. However, self-enforcement of peace agreements in internal conflicts may be impossible for at least three reasons.

First, many conflicts are characterized by power asymmetry, which implies that the costs of co-operating while other parties are defecting may be extremely large for the weaker party. In internal conflicts, a settlement implies that the rebels would need to disarm, making themselves vulnerable to an attack by the state, even if the state can later renege on the agreement. Walter (1997) argues that this is the "critical barrier" to negotiated settlement in civil wars. The potential for time-inconsistent behavior by the state makes the settlement non-credible.

Second, internal conflicts – especially of the ethnic variety – can escalate to the point where one or more of the groups are eliminated, forcibly displaced, or weakened to the point of not having any bargaining leverage. This seems to have been the strategy of the *genocidaires* in Rwanda, and of the Serbs in the Bosnian war. This also implies that the potential gains from short-term defection for the stronger party could be infinite if such defection could eliminate the weaker party from future bargaining. Thus, the usual long-term benefits to co-operation in iterated play need not be greater than short-term gains from defection.

Third, in computer-simulated results of iterated prisoner's dilemma games (where the solutions from iterated play come from), players have access to strategies that cannot be replicated in real life. For example, tit-for-tat punishment strategies of permanent exclusion of one of the parties may be feasible in a simulated environment, but are not realistic in actual civil wars. Parties that defect from peace agreements cannot be permanently excluded from further negotiation, so reciprocal punishment strategies against defection are implausible.[14] This should increase the discounting of expected future costs of short-term violations by parties who can expect to be included in future negotiations regardless of their previous behavior.

Given these enforcement problems, strong peacekeeping is necessary in internal conflicts resembling co-operation problems to increase the parties' costs from non-co-operation, or reduce the costs of exploitation, or increase the benefits from co-operation – and ideally all three at once. Can peacekeeping have such an impact? And if so, how? The literature suggests that peacekeepers can change the costs and benefits of co-operation by virtue of the legitimacy of their UN mandate, which induces the parties to co-operate; by their ability to focus international attention on non-co-operative parties and condemn transgressions; by their monitoring of and reporting on the parties' compliance with agreements; and by their function as a trip-wire that would force aggressors to go through the UN troops to change the military status quo.

Ultimate success, however, may depend less on changing the incentives for existing parties within their preferences and more on transforming preferences – and even the parties themselves – and thus turning a co-operation problem into a co-ordination problem. The institution-building aspects of peacebuilding can be thought of as a revolutionary transformation in which voters and politicians replace soldiers and generals; armies become political parties; and war economies, peace economies. Reconciliation, when achieved, is a label for these changed preferences and capacities. To be sure, the difficulty of a transformative strategy cannot be overestimated. Most post-war societies look a great deal like they did prior to the war. However, if, for example, those who have committed the worst war crimes can be prosecuted, locked up and thus removed from power, the prospects for peace rise. The various factions can begin to individualize rather than collectivize their distrust and hostility. At minimum, the worst individuals are no longer in control.[15]

Therefore, even where enforcement is used at the outset, the peace must eventually become self-sustaining and consent must be won if the peace enforcers are ever to exit and have their work remain complete. As consensual peace agreements can rapidly erode, forcing peace enforcers to adjust to the strategies of "spoilers," their success or lack of success in doing so tends to be decisive in whether a sustainable peace follows.

These structural differences between co-operation and co-ordination problems imply that different peacekeeping strategies should be used in each case. Strong intervention strategies, such as multidimensional peacekeeping or enforcement with considerable international authority, are needed to resolve co-operation problems, whereas weaker peacekeeping strategies, such as monitoring and traditional peacekeeping, are sufficient to resolve co-ordination problems. Weak peacekeeping has no enforcement or deterrence function. Stronger peacekeeping through multidimensional operations can increase the costs of non-co-operation for the parties and provide positive inducements by helping rebuild the country and restructure institutions so that they can support the peace. Enforcement may be necessary to resolve the toughest co-operation problems.[16] Not all civil war transitions are plagued by co-operation problems. Some wars resemble co-ordination problems, whereas frequently both types of problems occur, in which case intervention strategies must be carefully combined or sequenced (Doyle and Sambanis 2006). Table 11.1 illustrates how peacebuilding strategies can be matched successfully with different types of conflict.

In our empirical analysis, we will consider if UN and non-UN peace operations match the right mandate to the right peacebuilding ecology. Peacebuilding success would depend on the assignment of the right mandate to each case. Thus, if we find systematic differences between the UN and other organizations in the design of appropriate mandates, this could be a

Table 11.1 Matching problem type and strategy type

		Peacebuilding strategy	
		Weak	Strong
Conflict type	Co-operation	Ineffective/counter-productive	Best
	Co-ordination	Best	Inefficient

source of difference in the success rates of peace missions from these different organizations.

Data

The dataset used is from Doyle and Sambanis (2006). It covers all peace processes after civil war from 1945 until the end of 1999,[17] coding 145 civil wars in that period. Wars that were ongoing as of 31 December 1999 and/or wars in which there had been no significant peace process prior to that point were dropped.[18] If a peace process started and failed immediately, a failure of the peace was coded in the first month of the peace process.[19] Rules for coding the start and end of a civil war, including criteria used to separate civil wars from other forms of political violence and to distinguish bouts of civil war in the same country are reproduced from Doyle and Sambanis (2006) in the Appendix, where we also provide a list of civil wars and peace operations.[20]

Dependent variable

We analyze peacebuilding using several measures. The main dependent variables are sovereign and participatory peace two years after the end of the war. These are coded as combinations of four intermediate variables.

Sovereign peace is attained when there is no war recurrence, no residual violence, and no divided sovereignty. The resumption of civil war in a country is captured in the *Warend* variable, with a suffix to indicate the time elapsed after which this outcome is evaluated. *Warend2* indicates whether there is still peace two years after the end of civil war: it is coded 1 if civil war has not re-started after two years and 0 otherwise.[21] The variable *No Residual Violence* (*Noviol*) codes lower-level, or residual, violence after the war, referring to what other datasets call intermediate armed conflict – about 200 deaths per year[22] – and the presence of mass violations of human rights, such as politicide, genocide, widespread extra-judicial killings, torture, and mass imprisonments of the political opposition. If there is no evidence of these events two years after the end of the war, then *Noviol*=1; otherwise it equals 0. The suffix again indicates the time period of evaluating outcomes (*Noviol2* refers to residual violence two years after the war's end). Finally, the government's ability to exercise its sovereignty throughout the country's territory is a component of peacebuilding. If state sovereignty is undivided, then *Sovereign* = 1. If there is *de facto* or *de jure* partition or regional autonomy that obstructs government control of an area of the country, then this criterion is not satisfied and *Sovereign* = 0. Thus, sovereign peace two years after the war (*pbs2lr3*) is coded 1 if *Warend2* = 1, *Noviol2* = 1, and *Sovereign* = 1; and 0 otherwise.

Participatory peace adds a measure of political openness to sovereign peace, based on the country's polity score two years after the end of the war (*pol2*). This is the difference of the regime's democratic and autocratic characteristics.[23] The variable ranges from 0 (extreme autocracy) to 20 (maximum democracy).[24] The cutoff point used is a low score of 3 on that scale. Regimes that fall below this cutoff point are coded as participatory peace failures – we are effectively coding the "peace of the grave" in completely authoritarian regimes as peacebuilding failures. All other regimes above this very low threshold are considered successes, if they also satisfy the sovereign peace criteria.

These coding rules imply that several cases – those where the UN has not departed for at least two years before the end of the dataset, December 1999 – must be excluded from the analysis.[25] PB (peacebuilding) outcomes are coded for 119 cases with non-missing data for any of the explanatory variables. There are 84 participatory peace failures (69.42 per cent) and 37 successes (30.58 per cent).[26] Achieving sovereign peace is easier, with 68 failures and 53 successes.[27]

Explanatory variables

The ecological model of peacebuilding posits that the variables that determine success fall into three categories: level of hostility, local capabilities, and international capacities. Peace operations are the key measure of international capacities. We use all the controls from Doyle and Sambanis' core model (2006): For level of hostility, we control for the log of the number of deaths and displacements (*Logcost*),[28] the type of war (ethno-religious or not) as *Wartype*,[29] the number of factions (*Factnum*), and whether a peace treaty was ever signed by the majority of the parties (*Treaty*).[30] For local capacities, we control for socio-economic development proxied by electricity consumption per capita (*idev1*)[31] and dependence on natural resources, proxied by primary commodity exports as a percentage of GDP (*isxp2*) or oil-dependence (*oil*). Finally, for international capacities, in addition to UN (and non-UN missions), we control for foreign economic assistance, proxied by the amount of net current transfers per capita to the balance of payments of the country (*transpop*).[32]

We describe in more detail only the variables relating to UN and non-UN peace operations. The variables of interest are the presence and mandate of peace operations, which are a large portion of the international capacities in the model. Mandate proxies for the mission's strength, its technical and military capabilities, and the level of international commitment.[33] Coding reflects the types of missions:[34] fact-finding and mediation (*mediate*);[35] observer missions (*observe*); traditional peacekeeping (*tradpko*); multidimensional peacekeeping (*multipko*); and enforcement with or without transitional administration (*enforce*). A categorical variable (*unmandate*) captures the different mandate types. The binary indicator *unintrvn* identifies all cases of UN intervention, while the categorical variable *unops* lumps together monitoring missions (observer and traditional peacekeeping operations) and the more intrusive missions (multidimensional, enforcement, and transitional administration). Combined multidimensional and enforcement are also grouped together into a variable labeled *strongUN*, because strong missions should be more effective in difficult peacebuilding ecologies. The variable *PKO* combines all Chapter VI UN peacekeeping missions, excluding observer and enforcement missions. Finally, the variable *Ch6* identifies all missions authorized under Chapter VI of the UN Charter (i.e., it excludes enforcement missions).[36] These different versions of the UN's involvement will allow us to develop a more nuanced argument about the conditions under which UN is likely to help build self-sustaining peace. UN mandates were coded based on a close reading of each operation's operational guidelines, status of forces agreements (where available), and a review of UN documents that indicated how much of the mandate was actually implemented.[37]

Non-UN peace operations were coded using Heldt (2002) and supplemented in most cases with additional research. There are two versions of a non-UN peace operation variable. The first, *nonunops*, is coded exactly as the *unops* variable but for non-UN operations, thus distinguishing between strong and weak operations by grouping observer and traditional non-UN operations together and grouping multidimensional, enforcement, and transitional non-UN operations together. The second, *nonUN*, captures the presence of any non-UN operation. In order to deal with overlapping UN and non-UN operations, if bilateral or regional involvement took place in the context of a UN mandate, then we code a UN peace operation. But in some cases, both a UN mission and a separate third-party peace operation took place simultaneously and we code both in those cases.[38]

Our data include 34 UN peace operations (13 observer missions, 8 traditional peacekeeping missions, 7 multidimensional peacekeeping missions, and 6 cases of enforcement or transitional administration) and 44 cases of non-UN peace operations (broken down into 15 observer missions, 12 traditional peacekeeping missions, and 17 peace enforcement or transitional administration missions).

The effects of UN and non-UN peace operations compared

We estimate the effects of peace operations using logistic regression. First, we examine participatory peace two years after the war (*pbs2s3r3*) as the measure of peacebuilding success. Table 11.2 presents our results.

Table 11.2 The effect of UN and non-UN peace operations on participatory peace

Explanatory variables	Models			
	1.1	1.2	1.3	1.4
Peace operations				
Strong UN	**3.2456**	**3.4546**	–	–
(*StrongUN*)	(1.1108)	(1.1755)	–	–
Any UN	–	–	**2.1809**	**2.0856**
(*Unintrvn*)	–	–	(0.6532)	(0.6570)
Strong non-UN mandate	0.1568	–	−0.3569	–
(*Nonunops*)	(0.4191)	–	(0.4066)	–
Any non-UN	–	0.6749	–	−0.4219
(*NonUN*)	–	(0.6904)	–	(0.6575)
Level of hostilities				
Ethnic war	**−1.5963**	**−1.5566**	**−1.6221**	**−1.6451**
(*Wartype*)	(0.5132)	(0.5114)	(0.4934)	(0.4930)
Deaths and displaced	**−0.3201**	**−0.3150**	**−0.3405**	**−0.3468**
Natural log (*Logcost*)	(0.1338)	(0.1332)	(0.1453)	(0.1438)
Number of factions	**−0.6259**	**−0.6610**	−0.5989	−0.5861
(*Factnum*)	(0.2389)	(0.2539)	(0.2554)	(0.2553)
Signed peace treaty	**1.5182**	**1.4326**	**1.6933**	**1.6835**
(*Treaty*)	(0.7088)	(0.7030)	(0.7300)	(0.6900)
Local capacities				
Electricity consumption with	**0.0006**	**0.0006**	0.0004	0.0004
missing values imputed	(0.0003)	(0.0003)	(0.0003)	(0.0003)
(*Idev1*)				
Primary commodity exports/	**−7.8379**	**−7.9091**	**−7.6404**	**−7.8397**
GDP (*Isxp2*)	(2.2256)	(2.2556)	(2.1070)	(2.1742)
Other international capacities				
Net transfers per capita	**3.75e–06**	**3.57e–06**	**3.15e–06**	**3.03e–06**
(*Transpop*)	(1.25e–06)	(1.26e–06)	(1.06e–06)	(1.07e–06)
Constant	**5.3781**	**5.3388**	**5.5585**	**5.6150**
	(1.5016)	(1.5153)	(1.6300)	(1.6145)
Observations	119	119	119	119
Pseudo-R^2	33.68%	34.21%	32.98%	32.50%
Log-likelihood	−48.92	−48.53	−49.43	−49.79

Logistic regression; reported are coefficients and robust standard errors in parentheses; **bold** indicates significance at the 0.05 level; *italics* indicate significance at the 0.05 level with one-tailed test.

Models 1.1 and 1.2 control for the effects of combined multidimensional and enforcement operations (*strongUN*). Here, none of the operationalizations of non-UN operations – whether presence (*nonUN*) or strength (observer and traditional operations versus multidimensional, enforcement, and transitional authority operations) – has a statistically significant effect on participatory peace two years after the war. Models 1.3 and 1.4 control for the presence of any UN operation (*unintrvn*). Again, no operationalization of non-UN operations has a statistically significant effect.

Next, we look at the different components of the participatory peace definition. We begin by dropping the undivided sovereignty criterion (*pbs2s3_nosov*) and present these results in Table 11.3.

The substantive result of no statistically significant effect of non-UN operations from Table 11.2 does not change if we use a different concept and measure of peacebuilding success or if we change the model specification. But there appears to be an interaction effect between UN and non-UN peace operations. First, the coefficient on *strongUN* in Model 2.1 is larger than the coefficient on *strongUN* in Model 2.3 (at 2.74 compared to 2.35), the only difference between the two specifications being that model 2.3 does not control at all for non-UN operations, whereas Model 2.1 controls for *nonunops*. Both *strongUN* coefficients are statistically significant at the 0.05 level. Similarly, a comparison between Model 2.1 and Model 2.7 indicates that, when *strongUN* is controlled for, the coefficient on *nonunops* is slightly more than 168 per cent of the equivalent result when no controls for UN operations are in place, at 0.4542 compared to 0.2698, while its standard error decreases, from 0.3119 to 0.3059, an almost two per cent reduction. Second, this effect appears to be particular to the relationship between non-UN operations and the category of multidimensional and enforcement UN operations. A comparison between Model 2.1 and Model 2.8 shows that the coefficient on *nonUN*, denoting the presence or absence of any kind of non-UN peace operation, in fact decreases once the *strongUN* control is added. Additionally, the point estimates of the non-UN operation coefficients change systematically from Models 1.3 and 1.4 to Models 2.5 and 2.6. Each of these models controls for the presence of UN operations only. However, Models 2.5 and 2.6 drop the undivided sovereignty requirement from the coding of the dependent variable while Models 1.3 and 1.4 include this. These results may suggest that non-UN operations act to freeze the situation on the ground rather than re-establishing undivided sovereignty in the country receiving the intervention.

Models 2.1 and 2.2 look at how changing the control for natural resources affects the results. Whether we control for the ratio of primary commodity exports to GDP (*isxp2*) or oil export dependence (*oil*), our results are unaffected. Model 2.3 drops the control for non-UN operations to establish a baseline with which to compare other results. Models 2.5 and 2.6 use any UN intervention as a control and consider both operationalizations of non-UN operations. Finally, Models 2.7 and 2.8 drop the controls for UN operations and just look at strong non-UN operations or the presence of any non-UN operation, but non-UN missions do not "soak up" the significance of UN missions in those regressions. Thus, any interaction between UN and non-UN missions runs in the direction of non-UN missions enhancing the effects of UN missions.

Next, we examine different components of participatory peace at the two-

Table 11.3 The effect of UN and non-UN peace operations on participatory peace, without the undivided sovereignty criterion

Explanatory variables	Models							
	2.1	2.2	2.3	2.4	2.5	2.6	2.7	2.8
Peace operations								
Multidim PKO and enforce (*StrongUN*)	**2.7395** (0.9457)	**2.6299** (0.9398)	**2.3487** (0.8667)	—	—	—	—	—
UN enforcement (*Enforce*)	—	—	—	−0.9456 (0.8502)	—	—	—	—
Any UN intervention (*Unintrvn*)	—	—	—	—	**1.9956** (0.6309)	**1.9843** (0.6266)	—	—
Strong non-UN (*Nonunops*)	0.4542 (0.3059)	0.2702 (0.3444)	—	0.0622 (0.3550)	0.1353 (0.2978)	—	0.2698 (0.3119)	—
Any non-UN mission (*NonUN*)	—	—	—	—	—	0.4360 (0.7205)	—	0.6641 (0.7026)
Level of hostility								
Ethnic war (*Wartype*)	−1.0374 (0.4752)	**−0.9299** (0.4700)	**−0.9678** (0.4650)	**−0.8822** (0.4586)	**−1.0627** (0.4644)	**−1.0473** (0.4656)	**−0.9873** (0.4604)	**−0.9548** (0.4595)
Deaths and displaced Log (*Logcost*)	**−0.2525** (0.1066)	**−0.2964** (0.1127)	**−0.2234** (0.1087)	**−0.2623** (0.1043)	**−0.2684** (0.1140)	**−0.2652** (0.1127)	**0.2182** (0.0986)	**−0.2111** (0.0987)
Number of factions (*Factnum*)	**−0.3622** (0.1880)	**−0.3535** (0.1764)	−0.3212 (0.1934)	−0.1829 (0.1594)	−0.3666 (0.2214)	−0.3706 (0.2169)	−0.1845 (0.1663)	−0.1964 (0.1695)
Signed peace treaty (*Treaty*)	0.9159 (0.6355)	0.8572 (0.6568)	1.0263 (0.6454)	**1.2471** (0.6189)	0.9754 (0.6468)	0.9443 (0.6621)	**1.2922** (0.5977)	**1.2445** (0.6211)
Local capacities								
Electricity consumption with missing values imputed (*Idev1*)	**0.0011** (0.0003)	**0.0014** (0.0004)	**0.0012** (0.0003)	**0.0013** (0.0003)	**0.0010** (0.0003)	**0.0009** (0.0003)	**0.0010** (0.0003)	**0.0010** (0.0003)

(Continued overleaf)

Table 11.3 Continued.

	Models							
Explanatory variables	2.1	2.2	2.3	2.4	2.5	2.6	2.7	2.8
Primary commodity Exports/GDP (*lsxp2*)	−4.6842 (1.9025)	—	−4.0516 (1.8604)	—	−4.5714 (1.9612)	−4.5817 (1.9226)	−4.7730 (1.8035)	−4.7171 (1.7189)
Oil export dependence (*Oil*)	—	−2.0626 (0.5180)	—	−2.1940 (0.5414)	—	—	—	—
Other international capacities								
Net transfers per Capita (*Transpop*)	**3.30e−06** (1.54e−06)	**3.78e−06** (1.72e−06)	**3.61e−06** (1.46e−06)	*3.47e−06* (1.82e−06)	**2.70e−06** (1.37e−06)	*2.51e−06* (1.47e−06)	*2.94e−06* (1.59e−06)	*2.71e−06* (1.65e−06)
Constant	**3.2961** (1.2370)	**3.4191** (1.2685)	**2.8671** (1.2667)	**2.7216** (1.1553)	**3.5229** (1.4178)	**3.4774** (1.3984)	**2.5802** (1.1185)	**2.5073** (1.1043)
Observations	119	119	119	119	119	119	119	119
Pseudo-R^2	27.45%	30.34%	25.75%	25.96%	28.15%	28.35%	22.49%	22.73%
Log-likelihood	−56.05	−53.82	−57.37	−57.20	−55.51	−55.36	−59.88	−59.70

Logistic regression; reported are coefficients and robust standard errors in parentheses; **bold** indicates significance at the 0.05 level; *italics* indicate significance at the 0.05 level with one-tailed test.

year evaluation point. We consider war recurrence (*warend2*) alone, and then war recurrence and residual violence (*warnoviol2*). Table 11.4 presents our results.

Neither UN nor non-UN peace operations have a statistically significant effect if we look only at war recurrence (Models 3.1 and 3.2). Strong UN operations, however, have a positive statistically significant effect on no war recurrence and no residual violence (Models 3.3 and 3.4). Here, the effect of strong UN operations is significant at the 0.05 level with a single-tailed test in Model 3.3 and significant at the 0.05 level in Model 3.5. We return to this result when we look at war recurrence in the longer term, using survival analysis methods that allow us to account for the right-censoring effect that is inherent in the coding of our dependent variable in the logit regressions.

Finally, we consider sovereign peace (*pbs2lr*) rather than any version of participatory peace. These results are presented as Table 11.5. Here, as in Tables 11.2 and 11.3 we see that strong UN operations have a positive, statistically significant effect on peacebuilding (here, sovereign peace). Non-UN operations, however operationalized, still do not have a statistically significant effect on the measure of peacebuilding.

Immediately of note considering all the results is that non-UN peace operations do not have the effect hypothesized in any of the short-run models. The coefficients of the three non-UN variables, across all specifications of the model, are not statistically significant. We have confirmed that non-UN missions are not significant using alternative estimation methods for the short run (propensity score matching and selection models) and they also apply to long-term models (survival models of the duration of the peace).

One complication is that it is often difficult to clearly distinguish biased military interventions by non-UN actors from peacekeeping interventions. In the case of UN intervention, the article of the Charter which authorizes those interventions allows us to make this classification, and the rules of engagement as well as the mandate of the mission are often quite different if the UN mission is authorized under Chapter VII of the UN Charter as compared to Chapter VI (no consent is required in the former). In non-UN missions, it is harder to make this distinction and this is consequential, since partial intervention may well have different effects than impartial intervention. Some (Regan 2002) have shown that partial military intervention prolongs the duration of civil war, for example. Sorting out those non-UN peace missions that had a clear enforcement mandate and could therefore more easily be confused with war-making rather than peacekeeping, we found that the results on non-UN peace missions did not change and even consent-based non-UN peacekeeping did not have a significant impact on any of the ways that we used to code peacebuilding success.

Average numbers of deaths and displacements, levels of development, numbers of factions, and net current transfers are roughly equal in cases of UN and non-UN peace missions as compared to the null category in each

Table 11.4 The effect of UN and non-UN peace operations on components of participatory peace

	Dependent variable			
	No war recurrence		No war recurrence or residual violence	
Explanatory variables	Models 3.1	3.2	3.3	3.4
Peace operations				
Multidimensional PKO and enforce (*StrongUN*)	1.1891	1.3339	*1.8791*	**2.0805**
	(1.1132)	(1.1448)	(0.9934)	(1.0534)
Strong non-UN (*Nonunops*)	−0.0500	–	0.1619	–
	(0.2324)	–	(0.2366)	–
Any non-UN mission (*NonUN*)	–	0.2184	–	0.7066
	–	(0.5288)	–	(0.5626)
Level of hostility				
Ethnic war (*Wartype*)	−0.0941	−0.0889	−0.3143	−0.2850
	(0.4623)	(0.4641)	(0.3691)	(0.3696)
Deaths and displaced log (*Logcost*)	*−0.2303*	*−0.2368*	−0.1289	0.1311
	(0.1343)	(0.1348)	(0.1044)	(0.1027)
Number of factions (*Factnum*)	**−0.2400**	**−0.2572**	**−0.3542**	**−0.3819**
	(0.1308)	(0.1253)	(0.1395)	(0.1297)
Signed peace treaty (*Treaty*)	−0.7356	−0.7879	0.1241	0.0318
	(0.5133)	(0.5074)	(0.4930)	(0.5071)
Local capacities				
Electricity consumption with missing values imputed (*Idev1*)	0.0007	0.0006	**0.0007**	**0.0006**
	(0.0004)	(0.0004)	(0.0003)	(0.0003)
Primary commodity exports/GDP (*Isxp2*)	**−2.6247**	**−2.6752**	−2.6838	−2.7680
	(1.2698)	(1.2884)	(1.7769)	(1.8438)
Oil export dependence (*Oil*)	–	–	–	–
	–	–	–	–
Other international capacities				
Net transfers per capita (*Transpop*)	4.33e–06	4.13e–06	5.82e–06	5.43e–06
	(2.81e–06)	(2.69e–06)	(4.91e–05)	(4.45e–06)
Constant	**4.7218**	**4.8116**	**2.5196**	**2.5815**
	(1.6954)	(1.7033)	(1.0952)	(1.0806)
Observations	119	119	119	119
Pseudo-R^2	18.79%	18.86%	17.05%	17.78%
Log-likelihood	−58.54	−58.49	−68.41	−67.82

Logistic regression; reported are coefficients and robust standard errors in parentheses; **bold** indicates significance at the 0.05 level; *italics* indicate significance at the 0.05 level with one-tailed test.

Table 11.5 The effect of UN and non-UN peace operations on sovereign peace

	Models	
Explanatory variables	4.1	4.2
Peace operations		
Multidim. PKO and enforce (*StrongUN*)	**2.1437**	**2.3773**
	(1.0448)	(1.0907)
Any UN (*Unintrvn*)	–	–
	–	–
Strong non-UN (*Nonunops*)	−0.2149	–
	(0.2908)	–
Any non-UN (*NonUN*)	–	0.1518
	–	(0.5184)
Level of hostilities		
Ethnic war (*Wartype*)	*−0.8230*	*−0.8245*
	(0.4408)	(0.4439)
Deaths and displaced natural log (*Logcost*)	*−0.1751*	*−0.1817*
	(0.1071)	(0.1039)
Number of factions (*Factnum*)	**−0.5652**	**−0.5884**
	(0.1823)	(0.1807)
Signed peace treaty (*Treaty*)	0.7204	0.6181
	(0.5326)	(0.5329)
Local capacities		
Electricity consumption with missing values imputed (*Idev1*)	0.0002	0.0002
	(0.0003)	(0.0003)
Primary commodity exports/GDP (*Isxp2*)	−4.5695	−4.7591
	(2.9392)	(3.0470)
Other international capacities		
Net transfers per capita (*Transpop*)	**4.57e–06**	**4.29e–06**
	(2.14e–06)	(2.17e–06)
Constant	**4.1604**	**4.2488**
	(1.1313)	(1.1034)
Observations	119	119
Pseudo-R^2	22.87%	22.55%
Log-likelihood	−63.07	−63.33

Logistic regression; reported are coefficients and robust standard errors in parentheses; **bold** indicates significance at the 0.05 level; *italics* indicate significance at the 0.05 level with one-tailed test.

case; and non-UN missions are no more likely than UN missions to intervene in harder-to-resolve ethno-religious wars or in wars with more factions. So, it does not seem to be the case that the relative ineffectiveness of non-UN peacekeeping is because non-UN missions become involved in harder conflicts, with a lower *ex ante* probability of success.[39] Also, comparing mean values of the other covariates for strong peace missions only again does not reveal any systematic difference between UN and non-UN missions. For example, average levels of development and primary commodity export dependence are about the same in cases of UN and non-UN enforcement.[40] Some indicators of the levels of hostility point to a harder peacebuilding ecology in cases of non-UN enforcement. For example, deaths and displacements are somewhat higher for non-UN enforcement cases. But other hostility indicators point in the opposite direction: the number of factions, for example, is not significantly different in UN and non-UN cases; and UN enforcement has been used exclusively in ethno-religious wars, which are harder to resolve, while the same is not true for non-UN peace missions.

Thus, in terms of our earlier theoretical discussion, summarized in Table 11.1, it is not clear that the reason for the differential effectiveness of UN and non-UN missions is any major difference in assigning the right mandate to the right case. This comparison, however, is complicated by the fact that non-UN missions do not field multidimensional missions, so we are left with comparing enforcement missions here (and we could do the same for observer missions). But the fact that non-UN missions are missing this valuable combination of limited enforcement and civilian administration that we find in UN multidimensional missions can by itself help explain at least part of the difference in the relative effectiveness of UN and non-UN missions. Since that multidimensional mandate is judged to be necessary in some conditions – where local capacities are low and hostility is high, while a peace treaty forges some degree of local consent for international assistance – the fact that non-UN peace missions have not responded with such a multidimensional mandate can be considered a strategic failure that could explain at least partially the results that we have presented here.

We should return, however, to our earlier discussion of a possible interaction effect between non-UN and UN operations (see discussion of Table 11.3). We looked more closely at that by separating non-UN missions in which advanced industrialized countries and/or countries with advanced militaries participated, and all others. "Advanced" country missions include missions with troops from the United States, Europe, Canada, Australia, New Zealand, and CIS countries; 25 out of 44 non-UN missions are from the group of "advanced" countries. If we replace our control for non-UN missions with one that counts only those 25, we find no substantive change in the results with respect to participatory peace, which is not surprising because those missions typically focused on monitoring and/or enforcement and not on building capacities for self-sustaining peace (see Table 11.6, Model 5.1). With respect to war recurrence alone, those missions are also non-significant (p-value is 0.105), but they are much more significant than UN missions and have double the coefficient (Model 5.2).

When we turn to a longer-term analysis of war recurrence using survival models, we find that UN missions are in fact effective in preventing war recurrence (see Table 11.7, Model 6.1) whereas non-UN missions are not (p-value = 0.11; Model 6.2). But, when we add both together, they become much more significant both jointly and individually (Model 6.3). The reason that

Table 11.6 Non-UN operations involving the participation of advanced militaries and peacebuilding

	Models	
Explanatory variables	Participatory peace 5.1	War recurrence 5.2
Peace operations		
Any UN (*Unintrvn*)	**1.8324**	0.7857
	(0.7657)	(0.6967)
Militarily advanced non-UN (*nonUNdev*)	0.3878	1.4785
	(0.8725)	(0.9122)
Level of hostilities		
Ethnic war (*Wartype*)	**−1.6237**	−0.1498
	(0.5454)	(0.4904)
Deaths and displaced natural log (*Logcost*)	**−0.3423**	**−0.2754**
	(0.1288)	(0.1207)
Number of factions (*Factnum*)	**−0.5598**	*−0.2531*
	(0.2559)	(0.1530)
Signed peace treaty (*Treaty*)	**1.6460**	−0.6548
	(0.6391)	(0.5450)
Local capacities		
Electricity consumption with missing values imputed (*Idev1*)	0.0004	0.0004
	(0.0004)	(0.0005)
Primary commodity exports/GDP (*Isxp2*)	**−7.8817**	**−3.1213**
	(3.0456)	(1.5620)
Other international capacities		
Net transfers per capita (*Transpop*)	2.72e–06	3.64e–06
	(1.82e–06)	(2.75e–06)
Constant	**5.4456**	**5.2836**
	(1.6263)	(1.5271)
Observations	119	119
Pseudo-R^2	32.36%	20.57%
Log-likelihood	−49.89	−57.26

Logistic regression; reported are coefficients and robust standard errors in parentheses; **bold** indicates significance at the 0.05 level; *italics* indicate significance at the 0.05 level with one-tailed test.

non-UN missions seem to have no effect may well be because regional peacekeeping that is led by less developed countries has had a very poor performance record, with about half of those missions ending in peacebuilding failure. By contrast, in three out of four non-UN missions from "advanced" states, the peace had not failed at the end of our analysis time. It is also the case that there was a slightly higher chance that a UN mission with a substantial mandate (enforcement missions or peacekeeping) would be present in cases where the non-UN mission was fielded by advanced states, so the combined presence of UN and non-UN missions would have both expanded

Table 11.7 Non-UN operations involving the participation of advanced militaries and war recurrence (survival model of peace duration)

	Models		
	6.1	6.2	6.3
Peace operations			
Any UN (*Unintrvn*)	**0.4746**	–	**0.4122**
	(0.1527)	–	(0.1273)
Militarily advanced non-UN (*nonUNdev*)	–	0.4127	*0.3548*
	–	(0.2277)	(0.1975)
Level of hostilities			
Ethnic war (*Wartype*)	1.4318	1.3090	1.2702
	(0.3841)	(0.3262)	(0.3045)
Deaths and displaced natural log (*Logcost*)	*1.1111*	*1.1248*	*1.1362*
	(0.0698)	(0.0735)	(0.0752)
Number of factions (*Factnum*)	1.0808	1.0673	1.1135
	(0.0915)	(0.0943)	(0.0783)
Signed peace treaty (*Treaty*)	1.1596	0.9553	1.2377
	(0.3438)	(0.2170)	(0.2853)
Local capacities			
Annual rate of growth of GDP (*gdpgrofl*)	**0.9602**	**0.9594**	**0.9566**
	(0.0111)	(0.0101)	(0.0112)
Electricity consumption with missing values imputed (*Idev1*)	**0.9995**	0.9996	0.9997)
	(0.0002)	(0.0003)	(0.0002)
Primary commodity exports/GDP (*Isxp2*)	**4.9813**	3.1924	**5.2200**
	(2.3920)	(1.2118)	(2.4227)
Other international capacities			
Net transfers per capita (*Transpop*)	0.1000	0.1000	0.1000
	(1.00e–06)	(1.19e–06)	(1.21e–06)
Wald χ^2	**68.91**	69.29	70.68
Observations:	129	129	129
Log-likelihood:	–270.72	–270.52	–268.06

Cox regression; reported are hazard ratios and robust standard errors clustered by country in parentheses; **bold** indicates significance at the 0.05 level; *italics* indicate significance at the 0.05 level with one-tailed test.

the technical capacity and enforcement potential of the mission and would have given a clear signal of international interest, which could help explain why success was more likely in those cases.

So we see more evidence in favor of a mutually reinforcing relationship between UN and non-UN missions, if those missions come from countries with the resources and technical capacities to keep the peace. The fact that the effects of non-UN missions are restricted to preventing a resumption of violence and do not extend to higher-order, participatory peace leads us to conclude that there should be a division of labor in peacebuilding missions, with the UN performing the capacity-building functions while enforcement and policing are delegated to missions from advanced countries.

Conclusion: an empirical result and a new research question

The sharp difference in the results for UN and non-UN missions is instructive and worth further study. Critics of non-UN operations might contend that they appear to be much more ineffective in lending support to peacebuilding if non-UN actors are the primary agents for two widely cited reasons: non-UN operations lack impartiality and do not have adequate resources or technical capabilities (including training and organizational knowledge). We have not yet been able to determine why non-UN missions are less effective than UN missions, though our results that non-UN missions from advanced countries tend to do better than other non-UN regional peacekeeping would suggest that differences in the peacekeepers' technical capacities, resources, and military training are part of the answer. (As was the case with our analysis in Tables 11.2 to 11.5, excluding the cases of non-UN enforcement and keeping only cases of consent-based non-UN peacekeeping did not change the results substantively.)

There are other candidate explanations that our data do not allow us to fully evaluate. One common conjecture is that non-UN missions do not benefit from the UN's legitimacy premium and suffer because they are not perceived as impartial and thus fail to reassure the parties at critical junctures of the peace process. The key question remains, however, what the effect of controlling for perceived impartiality would be in our models. There have been non-UN missions that have been perceived as being at least as impartial as some UN missions, so if we were able to measure and control for this in our analysis, it is possible that the significance and magnitude of the effects of non-UN operations could increase. Controlling for perceived impartiality could also affect the significance and magnitude of the coefficients for UN operations. However, measuring perceived impartiality of a UN mission may be too difficult if not impossible.[41]

Studies of the relative merits of UN and non-UN peace operations have been asking the wrong question. It is not whether UN and non-UN peace operations have different impacts empirically – our results show that they undoubtedly do – but why the composition of non-UN peace operations and their suitability to the task of peacebuilding differs in the aggregate from these characteristics of UN operations. Framing the debate between the two "types" of operations in this way is important from a theoretical and policy perspective. As we have argued in this chapter, the logic employed by proponents of innate differences between UN and non-UN peace operations is not clear. While there may well exist a legitimacy premium for UN missions, it is far from evident that this alone can account for the sharp differences that we have found. Rather than assume that the UN's legitimacy explains these differences, a better approach would be to isolate at a high level of detail those aspects of peace operations that are important for success and to ensure that whatever the originating organization or state, a peace operation possessed these characteristics.

Doyle and Sambanis' (2006) ecological model of peacebuilding provided the basis for our analysis in this chapter. We have argued that expanding that model to incorporate factors that explain the gap between UN and non-UN operations would enhance its explanatory power. By explaining why there are differences between UN and non-UN peace operations, we could learn more about what explains the UN's success at peacebuilding. This will have important implications for the peacebuilding literature more generally. Understanding that certain peace operations are more successful than others is a critical first step, and that is the step that we have made in this chapter. Pursuing this line of research further promises to generate policy recommendations on how to design any type of peace operation for the maximum positive impact on peacebuilding. Still, indicating only how peace operations can be improved begs the question of why such change has not already occurred. A new challenge for analysts of peacekeeping and policymakers is to grasp the political process by which peace operations are created and fielded. If not all peace operations have the characteristics that allow them to achieve peacebuilding success, we need to understand the origins of this deficiency.

Notes

1 Bellamy and Williams (2005); see also United Nations (2005).
2 See the results of our Models 2.1, 2.9 and 2.10.
3 See Diehl (1993) for an excellent summary of these concerns in the case of regional and multi-national operations and also Weiss, Forsythe, and Coate (2004).
4 For examples, see Mason and Fett (1996); Regan (1996, 2000, 2002); Balch-Lindsay and Enterline (2000); Elbadawi and Sambanis (2000); Siquiera (2003); and A. Smith and Stam (2003).
5 See Barnett (1997) and Claude (1966).
6 See Paris (2002) for a discussion of understanding the UN in this light.
7 See, for example, complaints about sexual abuse by UN peacekeepers in Burundi, Congo, Haiti, Ivory Coast, Kosovo, Liberia, and Sierra Leone (C. Lynch, "Officials Acknowledge 'Swamp' of Problems and Pledge Fixes Amid New Allegations in Africa, Haiti." *Washington Post*, 13 March 2005, p. A22) and complaints about organizational malfeasance at headquarters during the Rwandan genocide (Gourevitch 1998).
8 A good example is given by several UN missions where a consent-based mandate was eventually transformed into an enforcement mandate due to the parties' lack of co-operation, which often stemmed from the parties' realization that the UN would be an obstacle to their aims (since, if the UN maintains the status quo in a situation where one of the parties believes that it can change the status quo through the use of force, then it follows that the UN's impact is not "impartial" in the ordinary sense of the term since it benefits the parties that are more committed to the peace). There are also other examples where the UN's motives for intervening are doubted by one or more of the parties. For accounts of Patrice Lumumba's

accusations that ONUC was acting on behalf of the CIA, see Doyle and Sambanis (2006).
9 A test of the proposition that UN operations are more effective because they carry greater legitimacy is difficult because we cannot measure the legitimacy of the intervening party directly. A conceivable test of this proposition would be to consider legitimacy as the residual category. We would then need to be able to capture all other differences between UN and non-UN operations. If a difference in the efficacy of UN and non-UN operations persists, we might then be able to attribute it to legitimacy.
10 See Morrow (1994) and Kreps (1990) for a precise definition of co-ordination and collaboration games.
11 For a summary see Keohane and Axelrod (1986).
12 Regional powers can play this role, if organized by an impartial party with broad legitimacy. See Doyle, Johnstone and Orr (1997) for a discussion of the role played by the "Friends of the Secretary-General" in the El Salvador negotiations.
13 By contrast, even in finite, yet multiple-iteration games, if the timing of the game's end is not known, players can be expected to play as if they were engaged in an infinite horizon game. But if the endgame is visible, then finite game strategies will be used.
14 As an impartial third party, the UN cannot formally exclude parties from negotiations. The inclusion of the Khmer Rouge in the negotiations leading to the Paris Accords over the Cambodian civil war is a case in point. Moreover, exclusion of parties from the terms of the settlement can generate grievances that lead to renewed fighting.
15 See Bass (2000); and, for the difficulties, Snyder and Vinjamuri (2003–4).
16 Strong peacekeeping is different from peace enforcement. Strong peacekeeping can only deter or punish occasional violations. If the violations are systematic and large-scale, a no-consent enforcement operation might be necessary.
17 One civil war in the dataset started in 1944, but all peace processes started after 1945.
18 In a few cases, a war was ongoing in 1999, but a serious peace effort had taken place earlier (and obviously failed). Those cases are included, but the analysis remains robust if they are dropped.
19 These are cases where a military victory fails to end the war (e.g., Afghanistan in 1992) or where the UN intervenes to end the fighting, but fails (e.g., Angola; Sierra Leone; Somalia). We do not include any peace processes that started after 31 December 1999 and this causes us to lose a few UN missions (e.g., UNAMA in Afghanistan; MONUC in the Democratic Republic of the Congo (DRC); UNAMSIL in Sierra Leone).
20 Sambanis (2004) contains an extensive discussion of the definition of civil war used in these data.
21 Details on the coding of war resumption are given for each country in the online supplement to Doyle and Sambanis (2006) and in comments inserted in their dataset.
22 See, e.g., Gleditsch et al. (2001).
23 This uses the Polity dataset (version 2000). For the years in which Polity scores are missing (i.e., they indicate regime transition or war in the country), scores are interpolated. The "Polity2" series of the 2002 version of the database is already interpolated by the Polity database coders (Marshall and Jaggers 2004).
24 This is computed as democracy (ranging from 0 to 10) plus 10 minus autocracy (also ranging from 0 to 10).
25 These are all cases where the UN has not yet failed by any of the criteria. So, dropping them from the analysis should make it harder to find significant effects for UN missions.

26 Two of these cases are dropped due to missing data in our models, but can be included in other specifications if imputed values are used for some of the covariates.
27 Using a five-year cutoff point, there would be 74 participatory peace failures and 35 successes; and 58 sovereign failures and 51 successes. Doyle and Sambanis (2006) also code an alternative version of PBS, where all ambiguous cases are either dropped (if the criteria for coding a civil war may not be met) or re-coded as the opposite outcome (if the initial coding of PB outcome was questionable). For participatory peace two years after the war, the alternative version has 78 failures and 25 successes (for a total of 103 observations).
28 Since there is a large variance in this variable, the natural log is used. Deaths and displacements are combined. Doyle and Sambanis (2006) provide comments and sources for the coding of each case in their online supplement in the document labeled "Civil War coding" and as comments in the spreadsheet and single-record version of their dataset.
29 See Sambanis (2002). There is not much documentation in the literature for the classification of wars into "ethnic" or "non-ethnic" varieties. Doyle and Sambanis (2006) use their own coding, based on a set of detailed notes on each conflict, to test the robustness of the original *Wartype* variable used in Doyle and Sambanis (2000).
30 Doyle and Sambanis (2006) post supplementary information online, including a comparison of the coding of *Treaty* across several datasets for cases shared in common. The definition of *treaty* is different from that in Doyle and Sambanis (2000). Where coding differs from the coding of other authors, they provide a summary explanation, including a description of the case and excerpts from the actual treaty text.
31 This measure is highly correlated with income: 77.67 per cent with Fearon and Laitin's (2003) income series (*gdpen*) and 79.78 per cent with the income series (*aclplvs*) in Przeworski et al. (2000).
32 This variable is sometimes measured several years away from the war's start or end. Doyle and Sambanis (2006) used data from the IMF's International Financial Statistics to code this variable. See IMF (various years).
33 Mandates should be correlated with numbers of troops and budgets for UN missions. Sometimes they are not, which indicates planning failure at the level of the Security Council.
34 *Unmandate* includes peacekeeping and enforcement mandates as well as serious efforts at peacemaking and mediation that are not followed up by a peacekeeping operation. The variable *untype* excludes cases of mediation.
35 These were cases of UN mediation or peacemaking without, however, a follow-up peacekeeping mission.
36 There is little ambiguity about the coding of UN mandate types. Doyle and Sambanis (2006) discuss this issue in detail in their supplement. The results are robust to recoding several cases according to suggestions made by other scholars or in cases where Doyle and Sambanis (2006) thought the mandate was ambiguous, and are sometimes better.
37 See the online supplement for Doyle and Sambanis (2006) for a list of supporting documents, including summaries of the mandate, list of functions actually performed by each mission, information on changes in mission mandate over time, and copies of relevant UN documents.
38 The cases of non-UN third-party peace operations and information on these missions (names, deployment dates, departure dates, and mandates) are given in the online supplement to Doyle and Sambanis (2006).
39 This is evident by comparing the results of equality of means tests for all the variables in the model, sorted by UN intervention and then by non-UN intervention.

40 There are only a few cases to compare: the average (with 6 cases) for UN missions is .17 while for non-UN (17 cases) it is .18. Electricity consumption per capita levels are also about the same (608 versus 633 kWh).
41 For an interesting effort, see Heldt (2001), who coded whether the force commander of a UN operation was from the same ethnic group as the majority of the population in the war-affected country. The difficulty here would be to ascertain if the selection effect is overcome by coding the identity of the force commander. In some cases, such high-level assignments may be random, yet in others they may well reflect an assessment at headquarters of the likely effect of the force commander's identity on the prospects for successful discharge of the peacekeepers' mandate.

Appendix to Chapter 11

A: Coding criteria for civil wars (from Doyle and Sambanis 2006)

An armed conflict is classified as a civil war if:

a. The war takes place within the territory of a state that is a member of the international system[i] with a population of 500,000 or greater.[ii]
b. The parties are politically and militarily organized and they have publicly-stated political objectives.[iii]
c. The government (through its military or militias) must be a principal combatant. If there is no functioning government, then the party representing the government internationally and/or claiming the state domestically must be involved as a combatant.[iv]

---

i   This includes states that are occupying foreign territories that are claiming independence (e.g., West Bank and Gaza in Israel, and Western Sahara in Morocco). A strict application of this coding rule could drop those cases where the international community (through the UN) rejects the state's claims of sovereignty on the occupied territories.
ii Countries could be included after their population reaches the 500,000 mark, or from the start of the period if population exceeds the 500,000 mark at some point in the country series. If a civil war occurs in a country with population below the threshold, we could include it and flag it as a marginal case. Cases of civil war close to the 500,000 mark are Cyprus in 1963 (578,000 population) and Djibouti in 1991 (450,000 population). Use of a per capita death threshold to code civil war would allow the population threshold to be relaxed.
iii This should apply to the majority of the parties in the conflict. This criterion distinguishes insurgent groups and political parties from criminal gangs and riotous mobs. But the distinction between criminal and political violence may fade in some countries (e.g., Colombia after 1993). "Terrorist" organizations would qualify as insurgent groups according to this coding rule, if they caused violence at the required levels for war (see other criteria). Non-combatant populations that are often victimized in civil wars are not considered a "party" to the war if they are not organized in a militia or other such form, able to apply violence in pursuit of their political objectives.
iv Extensive indirect support (monetary, organizational, or military) by the government to militias might also satisfy this criterion (an example is Kenya during the ethnic clashes in the Rift Valley). However, in such cases it becomes harder to distinguish civil war from communal violence. In other cases, where the state has collapsed, it may not be possible to identify parties representing the state as all parties may be claiming the state and these conflicts will also be hard to distinguish from inter-communal violence (e.g., Somalia after 1991).

d. The main insurgent organization(s) must be locally represented and must recruit locally. Additional external involvement and recruitment need not imply that the war is not intra-state.[v] Insurgent groups may operate from neighboring countries, but they must also have some territorial control (bases) in the civil war country and/or the rebels must reside in the civil war country.[vi]
e. The start year of the war is the first year that the conflict causes at least 500–1,000 deaths.[vii] If the conflict has not caused 500 deaths or more in the first year, the war is coded as having started in that year only if cumulative deaths in the next three years reach 1,000.[viii]
f. Throughout its duration, the conflict must be characterized by sustained violence at least at the minor or intermediate level. There should be no three-year period during which the conflict causes fewer than 500 deaths.[ix]
g. Throughout the war, the weaker party must be able to mount effective resistance. Effective resistance is measured by at least 100 deaths inflicted on the stronger party. A substantial number of these deaths must occur in the first year of the war.[x] But if the violence becomes effectively one-

---

v   Intra-state war can be taking place at the same time as inter-state war.
vi This rule weeds out entirely inter-state conflicts with no local participation. The Bay of Pigs, for example, would be excluded as a civil war because the rebels did not have a base in Cuba prior to the invasion. Some cases stretch the limits of this definitional criterion: e.g., Rwanda in the late 1990s, where ex-FAR recruits with bases in the DRC engaged in incursions and border clashes against government army and civilians. If this is a civil war, then so is the conflict between Lebanon-based Hezbollah and Israel (assuming the other criteria are met).
vii This rule can be relaxed to a range of 100–1,000 since fighting might start late in the year (cf. Senegal or Peru). Given the lack of high-quality data to accurately code civil war onset, if no good estimate of deaths is available for the first year, onset can be coded at the first year of reported large-scale armed conflict provided that violence continues or escalates in the following years. Note that in the dataset, start/end month is also coded where possible. In some cases, coding rules can be used to identify the start month (e.g., in cases where the war causes 1,000 deaths in the first month of armed conflict). But in most cases, the month only indicates the start of major armed conflict or the signing of a peace agreement, which can gives a point of reference for the start/end of the war, respectively.
viii This rule also suggests when to code war termination if the three-year average does not add up to 500. In such a case, the end of the war can be coded at the last year with more than 100 deaths unless one of the other rules applies (e.g., if there is a peace treaty that is followed by more than six months of peace).
ix This criterion makes coding very difficult, as data on deaths throughout the duration of a conflict are hard to find. However, such a coding rule is necessary to prevent one from coding too many war starts in the same conflict or coding an ongoing civil war for years after the violence has ended. Three years is an arbitrary cut-off point, but is consistent with other thresholds found in the literature. Data notes (see online supplement to Doyle and Sambanis 2006) give several examples of cases where the coding of war termination has been determined by this criterion. A more lenient version would be a five-year threshold with fewer than 500 deaths.
x   This criterion must be proportional to the war's intensity in the first years of the war. If the war's onset is coded the first year with only 100 deaths (as often happens in low-intensity conflicts), then it would not be possible to observe effective resistance in the first year of the war if effective resistance was defined as 100 deaths suffered by the state.

sided, even if the aggregate effective resistance threshold of 100 deaths has already been met, the civil war must be coded as having ended and a politicide or other form of one-sided violence must be coded as having started.[xi]

h. A peace treaty that produces at least six months of peace marks an end to the war.[xii]

i. A decisive military victory by the rebels that produces a new regime should mark the end of the war.[xiii] Since civil war is understood as an armed conflict against the government, continuing armed conflict against a new government implies a new civil war.[xiv] If the government wins the war, a period of peace longer than six months must persist before we code a new war (see also criterion k).

j. A ceasefire, truce, or simply an end to fighting mark the end of a civil war if they result in at least two years of peace.[xv] The period of peace must be longer than what is required in the case of a peace agreement, as we do not have clear signals of the parties' intent to negotiate an agreement in the case of a truce/ceasefire.[xvi]

---

xi This criterion distinguishes cases in which insurgent violence was limited to the outbreak of the war and, for the remainder of the conflict, the government engaged in one-sided violence. A hypothetical example is a case where insurgents inflicted 100 deaths on the government during the first week of fighting and then the government defeated the insurgents and engaged in pogroms and politicide for several years with no or few deaths on the government's side. If it is not possible to apply this rule consistently to all cases (due to data limitations), then periods of politicide at the start or end of the war should be combined with war periods. This implies that civil wars will often be observationally equivalent to coups that are followed by politicide, or other such sequences of different forms of political violence.

xii Treaties that do not stop the fighting are not considered (e.g., the Islamabad Accords of 1993 in Afghanistan's war; the December 1997 agreement among Somali clan leaders). If several insurgent groups are engaged in the war, the majority of groups must sign. This criterion is useful for the study of peace transitions, but may not be as important if researchers are interested in studying, for example, civil war duration.

xiii Thus, in secessionist wars that are won by the rebels who establish a new state, if a war erupts immediately in the new state, a new war onset would be coded in the new state (an example is Croatia in 1992–5), even if the violence is closely related to the preceding war. A continuation of the old conflict between the old parties could now count as an inter-state war, as in the case of Ethiopia and Eritrea who fought a war in 1998–2000, after Eritrea's successful secession from Ethiopia in 1993.

xiv This criterion allows researchers to study the stability of military victories. Analysis of the stability of civil war outcomes would be biased if an end to civil war through military victory was coded only when the victory was followed by a prolonged period of peace. This would bias the results in favor of finding a positive correlation between military outcomes and peace duration. This criterion is important to analyze war recurrence, but not necessarily war prevalence.

xv Peace implies no battle-related deaths, or, in a lenient version of this criterion, fewer deaths than the lowest threshold of deaths used to code war onset – i.e., fewer than 100 deaths per year.

xvi These situations are different from those where there is no violence as a result of armies standing down without a ceasefire agreement, which would fall under criterion f.

k. If new parties enter the war over new issues, a new war onset should be coded, subject to the same operational criteria.[xvii] If the same parties return to war over the same issues we generally code the continuation of the old war, unless any of the above criteria for coding a war end apply for the period before the resurgence of fighting.

Using these coding rules, Doyle and Sambanis (2006) code 145 civil war starts from 1944 to 1999 (2.08 per cent of 6,966 non-missing observations in an annual frequency time-series cross-sectional dataset, covering 161 countries). Without coding new war onsets in countries with already ongoing civil wars, the number of civil wars is 119 (1.93 per cent of 6,153 non-missing observations). Out of these cases, 20 may be called "ambiguous" – that is, they may not meet one or more of the coding rules. Doyle and Sambanis (2006) consider these as sufficiently close to the concept of civil war as to include them in the analysis.

---

xvii These incompatibilities must be significantly different or the wars must be fought by different groups in different regions of the country. For example, three partially overlapping wars would be coded in Ethiopia (Tigrean, Eritrean, Oromo) from the 1970s to the 1990s. New issues alone should not be sufficient to code a new war, as there is no "issue-based" classification in the definition of civil war. Such a rule could be applied if civil wars were classified into categories – e.g., secessionist wars versus revolutions over control of the state. In addition to having new issues, most parties must also be new before a new war onset can be coded.

Appendix to Chapter 11

B: Civil wars starting in 1945–1999 and short-run peacebuilding outcomes*

Country	War start	War end	Sovereign peace	Participatory peace	Type of UN operation	Type of non-UN operation
Afghanistan	1978	1992	Failure	Failure	None	None
Afghanistan	1992	1996	Failure	Failure	None	None
Afghanistan	1996	2001	.	.	None	Enforcement
Algeria	1962	1963	Success	Failure	None	None
Algeria	1992	.	.	.	None	None
Angola	1975	1991	Failure	Failure	Observer mission	None
Angola	1992	1994	Failure	Failure	Traditional PKO	None
Angola	1997	2002	Failure	Failure	Traditional PKO	None
Angola	1994	1999	.	.	None	None
Argentina	1955	1955	Success	Success	None	None
Argentina	1975	1977	Failure	Failure	None	None
Azerbaijan	1991	1994	Failure	Failure	None	Observer mission
Bangladesh	1974	1997	Success	Success	None	None
Bolivia	1952	1952	Success	Success	None	None
Bosnia	1992	1995	.	.	Enforcement	Enforcement
Burundi	1965	1969	Failure	Failure	None	None
Burundi	1972	1972	Success	Failure	None	None
Burundi	1988	1988	Failure	Failure	None	None
Burundi	1991	.	.	.	None	Observer
Cambodia	1970	1975	Failure	Failure	None	None

(Continued overleaf)

B: Civil wars starting in 1945–1999 and short-run peacebuilding outcomes* (Continued)

Country	War start	War end	Sovereign peace	Participatory peace	Type of UN operation	Type of non-UN operation
Cambodia	1975	1991	Success	Success	Multidimensional PKO	None
Central African Republic	1996	1997	.	.	Multidimensional PKO	Traditional PKO
Chad	1965	1979	Failure	Failure	None	Traditional PKO
Chad	1980	1994	Failure	Failure	None	Traditional PKO
Chad	1994	1997	Success	Success	None	None
China	1946	1949	Failure	Failure	None	None
China	1947	1947	Success	Failure	None	None
China	1950	1951	Success	Failure	None	None
China	1956	1959	Success	Failure	None	None
China	1967	1968	Success	Failure	None	None
Colombia	1948	1966	Failure	Failure	None	None
Colombia	1978	.	Failure	Failure	None	None
Congo (Brazzaville)	1993	1997	Failure	Failure	None	None
Congo (Brazzaville)	1998	1999	.	.	None	None
Congo-Zaire	1960	1965	Failure	Failure	Enforcement	None
Congo-Zaire	1967	1967	Success	Failure	None	None
Congo-Zaire	1977	1978	Failure	Failure	None	None
Congo-Zaire	1996	1997	Failure	Failure	None	None
Congo-Zaire	1998	2001	.	.	Observer mission	Observer mission
Costa Rica	1948	1948	Success	Success	None	Observer mission
Croatia	1992	1995	Success	Success	Enforcement	Observer mission
Cuba	1958	1959	Failure	Failure	None	None

Cyprus	1963	Failure	Failure	Traditional PKO	Traditional PKO
Cyprus	1974	Failure	Failure	Traditional PKO	None
Djibouti	1991	Success	Success	None	None
Dominican Republic	1965	Success	Success	Observer mission	Traditional PKO
El Salvador	1979	Success	Success	Multidimensional PKO	Traditional PKO
Egypt	1994	Success	Success	None	None
Ethiopia	1974	Success	Success	None	None
Ethiopia	1978	Success	Success	None	None
Ethiopia	1976	Failure	Failure	None	None
Georgia	1991	Failure	Failure	None	Traditional PKO
Georgia	1992	Failure	Failure	Observer mission	Enforcement
Greece	1944	Success	Success	Observer mission	Traditional PKO
Guatemala	1966	Failure	Failure	None	None
Guatemala	1978	Success	Success	Multidimensional PKO	None
Guinea-Bissau	1998	.	.	None	Traditional PKO
Haiti	1991	Failure	Failure	Multidimensional PKO	Enforcement
India	1989	Failure	Failure	None	None
India	1984	Success	Success	None	None
India	1989	.	.	None	None
India	1990	.	.	None	None
India	1946	Success	Success	None	None
Indonesia	1950	Failure	Failure	None	None
Indonesia	1953	Failure	Failure	None	None
Indonesia	1956	Failure	Failure	None	None
Indonesia	1976	Failure	Failure	None	None

(Continued overleaf)

B: Civil wars starting in 1945–1999 and short-run peacebuilding outcomes* (Continued)

Country	War start	War end	Sovereign peace	Participatory peace	Type of UN operation	Type of non-UN operation
Indonesia	1975	1999	.	.	Enforcement	Enforcement
Indonesia	1990	1991	Failure	Failure	None	None
Indonesia	1999	2002	.	.	None	None
Iran	1978	1979	Failure	Failure	None	None
Iran	1979	1984	Failure	Failure	None	None
Iraq	1959	1959	Failure	Failure	None	None
Iraq	1961	1970	Success	Failure	None	None
Iraq	1974	1975	Failure	Failure	None	None
Iraq	1985	1996	Failure	Failure	None	Enforcement
Iraq	1991	1993	Failure	Failure	None	Enforcement
Israel	1987	1997	Success	Success	None	None
Israel	2000	.	.	.	None	None
Jordan	1970	1971	Success	Failure	None	Observer mission
Kenya	1963	1967	Success	Failure	None	None
Kenya	1991	1993	Failure	Failure	None	None
Korea	1948	1949	Success	Success	None	None
Laos	1960	1973	Failure	Failure	None	Observer mission
Lebanon	1958	1958	Success	Success	Observer mission	Traditional PKO
Lebanon	1975	1991	Failure	Failure	Traditional PKO	Enforcement
Liberia	1989	1990	Failure	Failure	None	Enforcement
Liberia	1992	1997	Failure	Failure	Observer mission	Enforcement

Country	Year	Year	Result	Result	Enforcement	Enforcement
Liberia	1999	.	Success	.	None	None
Mali	1990	1995	Success	Success	None	None
Moldova	1991	1992	Failure	Failure	None	Traditional PKO
Morocco/Western Sahara	1975	1991	Failure	Failure	Observer mission	None
Mozambique	1976	1992	Success	Success	Multidimensional PKO	None
Myanmar/Burma	1948	1951	Failure	Failure	None	None
Myanmar/Burma	1948	1988	Failure	Failure	None	None
Myanmar/Burma	1960	1995	Failure	Failure	None	None
Namibia	1973	1989	Success	Success	Multidimensional PKO	None
Nepal	1996	.	.	.	None	None
Nicaragua	1978	1979	Failure	Failure	None	None
Nicaragua	1981	1990	Success	Success	Observer mission	Observer mission
Nigeria	1967	1970	Success	Failure	None	None
Nigeria	1980	1985	Failure	Failure	None	None
Oman	1971	1975	Success	Failure	None	None
Pakistan	1971	1971	Success	Success	None	None
Pakistan	1973	1977	Failure	Failure	None	None
Pakistan	1994	1999	.	.	None	None
Papua New Guinea	1988	1998	.	.	None	Traditional PKO
Paraguay	1947	1947	Success	Success	None	None
Peru	1980	1996	Failure	Failure	None	None
Philippines	1950	1952	Success	Success	None	None
Philippines	1972	1992	Failure	Failure	None	None
Philippines	1971	.	Failure	Failure	None	None
Russia	1994	1996	Failure	Failure	None	None

(Continued overleaf)

B: Civil wars starting in 1945–1999 and short-run peacebuilding outcomes* (Continued)

Country	War start	War end	Sovereign peace	Participatory peace	Type of UN operation	Type of non-UN operation
Russia	1999	.	.	.	None	None
Rwanda	1963	1964	Failure	Failure	None	None
Rwanda	1990	1993	Failure	Failure	Traditional PKO	Observer mission
Rwanda	1994	1994	Success	Success	Observer mission	Enforcement
Senegal	1989	1999	.	.	None	None
Sierra Leone	1991	1996	Failure	Failure	None	Enforcement
Sierra Leone	1997	2001	Failure	Failure	Traditional PKO	Enforcement
Somalia	1988	1991	Failure	Failure	None	None
Somalia	1991	.	Failure	Failure	Enforcement	None
South Africa	1976	1994	Success	Success	Observer mission	Observer mission
Sri Lanka	1971	1971	Success	Success	None	None
Sri Lanka	1983	2002	Failure	Failure	None	Enforcement
Sri Lanka	1987	1989	Success	Success	None	None
Sudan	1963	1972	Success	Failure	None	None
Sudan	1983	2002	Failure	Failure	None	Observer mission
Syria	1979	1982	Success	Failure	None	None
Tajikistan	1992	1997	.	.	Observer mission	Enforcement
Thailand	1966	1982	Success	Success	None	None
Turkey	1984	1999	.	.	None	None
Uganda	1966	1966	Success	Success	None	None
Uganda	1978	1979	Failure	Failure	None	None

Uganda	1981	1987	Failure	None	None
Uganda	1990	1992	Failure	None	None
Uganda	1995	.	.	None	None
United Kingdom	1971	1998	.	None	None
USSR	1944	1948	.	None	None
USSR	1944	1947	.	None	None
USSR	1944	1950	.	None	None
USSR	1944	1948	.	None	None
Vietnam	1960	1975	Success	Failure	None	Observer mission
Yemen Arab Republic	1948	1948	Success	Success	None	None
Yemen	1994	1994	Success	Success	None	Observer mission
Yemen Arab Republic	1962	1970	Success	Success	Observer mission	Observer mission
Yemen Peoples Rep.	1986	1986	Success	Failure	None	None
Yugoslavia	1991	1991	Failure	Failure	Traditional PKO	None
Yugoslavia	1998	1999	.	.	Enforcement	Enforcement
Zimbabwe	1972	1979	Failure	Failure	None	None
Zimbabwe	1983	1987	Success	Success	None	.

* Note: This list includes some cases that are not included in the analysis. Ongoing wars, for example, are excluded. The USSR wars are excluded due to missing data in several of our variables, and because they started before the start of our analysis period. There are some differences between our civil war list and some others in the literature.

12 Why no UN Security Council reform?

Lessons for and from institutionalist theory

Erik Voeten

This chapter is based on the premise that institutional reform and the absence thereof are revealing about the effects of institutional design on outcomes, or at least how governments perceive these effects to be. In the past fifteen years, we have witnessed major institutional reforms and innovations in the international arena. The EU broadened, deepened, and moved increasingly towards a supranational decision-making structure. NATO accepted ten new member states and modernized its military command structure. The international trade system was transformed fundamentally by the replacement of GATT with the World Trade Organization (WTO) and its highly legalized dispute-resolution mechanism. The World Bank responded to pressure by non-governmental organizations (NGOs) and others to formally incorporate environmental issues into their decision-making procedures (Nielson and Tierney 2003). And, the creation of the International Criminal Court (ICC) and the Kyoto Protocol, while not embraced universally, signal that there is considerable appetite in many parts of the globe for new and extended institutional solutions to global issues.

At the same time, some institutional configurations have remained remarkably stable. The UN Security Council (UNSC) is an important example. What makes the UNSC's institutional persistence so interesting is that its activities have changed rather dramatically with the Cold War's ending. The Council has not only initiated many more sanctions and peacekeeping missions, but it has also broadened the scope of what it can do – at times not shying away from authorizing the use of force to topple regimes. Moreover, states, including great powers, are paying more attention to the UNSC than ever before. Whereas the absence or presence of UN authorization had little bearing on the use of force in the Cold War period, the absence of such authorization is now widely lamented and appears to affect the depth and breadth of multilateral co-operation in a non-trivial manner (Voeten 2005).

This upsurge in activity has not been paired with a "constitutive moment" similar to what occurred at the ends of World Wars I and II. At those junctures, multilateral security institutions were purposively designed by the victors of the latest grand war, perhaps with the objective to "lock in" favorable institutional structures that would outlast the immediate power advantages that resulted from the last war (Ikenberry 2001). The UNSC is the quintessential example of this: it granted permanent membership and veto power to the five "victors" of World War II, while excluding the defeated powers[1] and raising an entry barrier for potential rising powers.

The antiquated nature of the UNSC's institutional structure has invited incessant calls for institutional reform,[2] varying from carefully crafted diplomatic proposals to Thomas Friedman's cavalier suggestion that veto powers ought to be elected by the fans of the UN such that France could be "voted off the island".[3] Discussing the latest reform effort, the December 2004 report by the High-Level Panel on Threats, Challenges, and Change (hereafter: the High-Level Panel), UN Secretary-General Kofi Annan argued that this is "most decisive moment for the international system since the UN was founded in 1945."[4] Yet, while governments have expressed consensus support to make the UNSC "more representative, efficient and transparent" in numerous anniversary UNGA (General Assembly) resolutions,[5] the issue has barely advanced beyond discussions by blue-ribbon committees and low-level diplomats.[6] Bruce Russett captures the general sentiment well: "been there and not done that" (Russett 2005: 155).

Why has the activity of the UNSC increased so much, but its institutional structure changed so little? The typical answers are that the end of the Cold War allowed the UNSC to become more active, while the persistence of the UNSC's institutional structure can be attributed to institutional "stickiness." These accounts are not entirely inaccurate. Yet, they are limited. Most importantly, if institutional design matters, then it is problematic to rely on a theory that privileges continuity to explain institutional design while singling out a massive exogenous shock as the explanation for increased activity. Institutionalists argue that fundamental institutional change generally occurs in response to an exogenous shock that undermines the mechanisms that generate continuity (e.g., Pierson 2000). The end of the Cold War represents precisely the kind of external shock that could be expected to lead to a "critical juncture" for institutional change (Ikenberry 2001). Moreover, the very same factors that created an increased demand for multilateralism are likely to also create a demand for institutional adjustments. If the relevance of the end of the Cold War resides in a normative shift towards a set of global liberal norms that generate new demand for multilateralism, then we would surely expect this normative shift to be reflected in institutional changes. If the end of the Cold War is relevant primarily for the shift in the balance of power (or threats), then we would expect the institutional structure of the UNSC to be adjusted to that new power structure.

In this chapter, I evaluate various plausible explanations for the UNSC's institutional persistence in the context of its increased activity. I argue that in order to understand these issues, we need a fuller appreciation of how the UNSC fits in its strategic environment. Strategic explanations should fare well in the context of the UNSC: there are relatively few actors, with well-defined interests, bargaining over high stakes. Yet, analyses of the UN tend to assume away strategic behavior[7] and/or look at the UN in isolation from the outside world. As Stanley Hoffmann put it:

> It has always been a problem that specialists of international politics dealing primarily with the diplomatic and strategic scene dismissed the UN from their analyses, whereas lawyers and political scientists specialized in the study of the UN's political functions tended to lock themselves up, so to speak, within the UN and to look at the world outside only dimly, as it was filtered into and through the UN.
> (Hoffmann 1998: 179)

I argue that the UNSC forms an institutional solution to two sets of problems that arise from the incompleteness of any contract that seeks to regulate uses of force, while not outright forbidding them. The UNSC is asked to make decisions on whether particular uses of force by states are appropriate and if (and how much) collective action should be produced in response to threats to international peace and security. From the perspective of institutional design, this solution is sub-optimal. The task of determining the appropriateness of interventions is best delegated to an independent (neutral) institution, such as a court, and the determination of public good production to a majoritarian (political) institution. Yet, the optimality of such a dual institutional solution collapses once we take into account the problem of enforcement: the UNSC cannot actually prevent individual states from going it alone in the absence of its blessing. Moreover, the willingness of individual states to go it alone can sometimes be critical for the production of collective goods.

I show how this availability of outside options profoundly affects issues of institutional design, and thus, reform. Perhaps most importantly, it curtails the extent to which formal institutional power translates into "real world" power. Analyses of formal bargaining power in the UNSC typically conclude that the veto players distribute the gains equally among themselves and that non-permanent members are virtually powerless (e.g., O'Neill 1997; Winter 1996). If this were true, there would be little reason for non-permanent members to abide by UNSC decisions and help finance peacekeeping operations. Moreover, veto powers that possess more outside options have greater bargaining power than veto powers that have fewer resources, despite equal institutional status. Hence, in practice, informal decision-making practices reflect asymmetric capabilities, even if these are not reflected in the UNSC's formal institutional structure. This chapter then, points to the limits of the expected effects of formal institutions, and thus institutional reform, in the context of enforcement problems.

The chapter proceeds with a brief sketch of the increase in UNSC activity following the end of the Cold War or, perhaps more accurately, the start of the first Gulf War. It then discusses various common explanations for institutional persistence. The following sections introduce the issues that arise in delegating decisions regarding uses of force to an international institution and provide some simple illustrations of how outside power affects bargaining in an institution such as the UNSC. The chapter concludes with some implications for institutionalist theory, as well as for the debates surrounding UNSC reform.

The post-gulf war explosion in UNSC activity

Figure 12.1 plots temporal variation in an important indicator of institutional activity: the occurrence of Chapter VII resolutions between 1946 and 2004. Chapter VII resolutions have the unique property among UN decisions that they are binding upon all member states of the United Nations, regardless of whether they have a seat at the UNSC. The UNSC can invoke Chapter VII in response to the "existence of any threat to the peace, breach of the peace, or act of aggression" (UN Charter, Article 39). Chapter VII resolutions are used to authorize sanctions as well as uses of force by UN troops, regional organizations, or individual member states. Hence, they can reasonably be understood as the most important decisions that the UNSC takes.

Between 1946 and 1990, the UNSC adopted only 22 resolutions under Chapter VII. The two most important cases were the Congo peacekeeping force (ONUC) and the Korean War (1950). In the latter case, authorization was possible only due to the temporary absence of the USSR in protest at the exclusion of the People's Republic of China from the Council. In anticipation of deadlock when the USSR would retake its seat, the UNGA adopted the

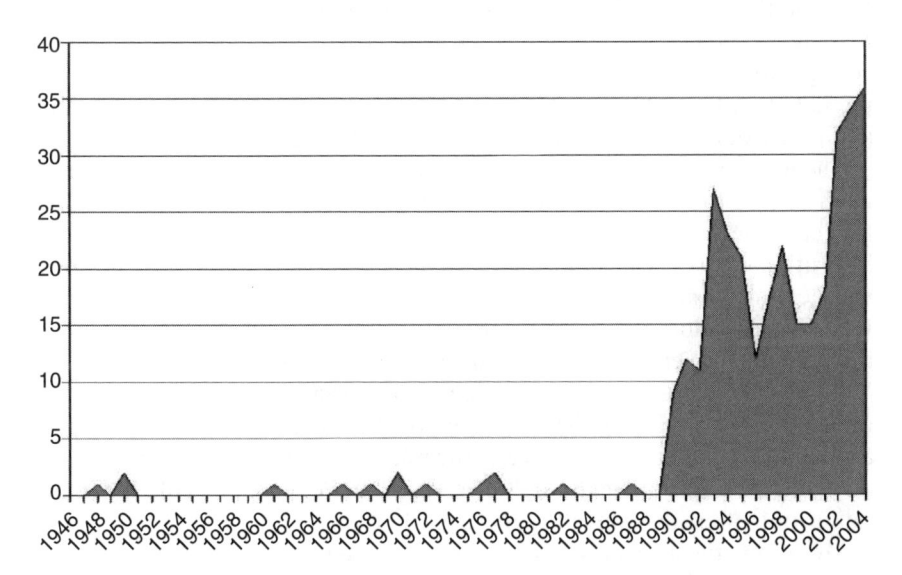

Figure 12.1 Annual number of Chapter VII resolutions, 1946–2004.

1950 "Uniting for Peace Resolution," which allowed the UNGA to take responsibility in security affairs if the SC were unable to act. It has been invoked ten times, most notably in 1956 to order the French and British to stop their military intervention in the Suez Canal and to create the UN Emergency Force to provide a buffer between Egyptian and Israeli forces.

UN involvement in important international crises became increasingly rare after the late 1960s, a development that Ernst Haas labeled "regime decay" (Haas 1983). The UN had little or no say in the major Cold War interventions, such as the Soviet invasion of Afghanistan and the US military action in Vietnam, nor in smaller interventions, such as the US military actions in Grenada and Panama. Between 1977 and the start of the Gulf War, the UNSC adopted only two resolutions under Chapter VII. By contrast, between 1990 and 2004, the Council approved 304 Chapter VII resolutions. Moreover, these resolutions carried actual consequences. The main objectives of most of the Cold War "first-generation" peacekeeping missions were to maintain a neutral position and monitor a situation. Many of the peacekeeping missions of the 1990s had much more ambitious mandates and operated in much more difficult environments. During the Cold War, there was only one UN-commanded mission that used force beyond traditional peacekeeping principles (Congo) and one in which the UNSC authorized interested parties to exercise force (Korea). Between 1990 and 2001, the UNSC authorized such extensive uses of force in 17 different countries across all continents (Jakobsen 2002).

Explanations for institutional persistence

Why did the UNSC suddenly became so active without adjusting its decision-making structure? Most accounts, explaining why suboptimal institutional configurations persist, rely in some way on the notion of path dependence: the idea that the path of previous outcomes matters in determining current and future outcomes (e.g., Hall and Taylor 1996; Page 2006; Pierson 2000).

The most frequently-used argument along these lines is that the UN's creators sought to lock-in institutional arrangements by raising a high barrier for change in the Charter (e.g., Russett 2005). Yet, on closer inspection, these institutional barriers are mild relative to most other international institutions. Charter amendments require approval from two-thirds of the members of the UNGA and ratification by two-thirds of the members of the UN, including the permanent members of the Security Council (UN Charter, Article 108). Virtually all international governmental organizations require unanimous ratification for amending their founding treaties. This includes the IOs, such as the WTO, that have been successfully reformed or created since the end of the Cold War. Yet, there are only five states that can individually block the ratification of an amendment to the UN Charter.

Moreover, the lessons from the 1963 Charter reform, which expanded ECOSOC and the Council, illustrate that the dynamics of the ratification process can pressurize the permanent members. France and the Soviet Union voted against Council expansion in the UNGA, whereas the US and UK abstained. China abstained on the second part of the proposed amendment that expanded ECOSOC. Thus, all five permanent members expressed reservations during the Assembly votes. Nevertheless, all five veto powers had ratified the amendments within two years of these votes, presumably in response to pressures from the non-aligned states whose allegiance in the Cold War conflict was at stake (Bourantonis 2005; Luck 2003).

One may counter that institutional obstacles make certain reforms unlikely, if not impossible, in particular reform of the veto. Yet, veto power only transfers to real world influence to the extent that countries that do not possess it attach value to the UNSC's decisions. UNSC reform poses a problem of co-ordination: if the rest of the world agreed on a single proposal, it would be very difficult to refuse for the five veto powers, as long as the proposal remained within some boundaries that maintain the utility of the UNSC to the permanent members (see also Axelrod 1998). Although the permanent five are powerful, other states have considerable potential leverage. Japan and Germany could cease paying the UN's bill; India, Brazil, and South Africa could co-opt developing nations to ignore UNSC decisions. In response to such actions or the threat thereof, the UNSC's authority would decline rapidly, and with it the value of veto power.

Yet, we do not observe meaningful threats to discontinue co-operation with the UNSC in the absence of reform nor meaningful attempts at co-ordinating reform proposals. Instead, the leading aspirant members have largely relegated the issue to blue-ribbon committees and low-level diplomats (Urquhart 2005). Some leaders publicly claim aspirations to permanent member status, while privately admitting that the issue is not pushed or even that they perceive more downsides than upsides to permanent membership.[8] The second and third largest contributors to the UN (Japan and Germany) continue to contribute to the UN and maintain laws that insist on UN authorization as a condition for active military participation in interventions, despite their exclusion from permanent membership.[9] Thus, even though the institutional barriers to reform are real, we still need to explain why outsiders continue to value the UNSC's decisions and make only tepid attempts to reform the institution.

A second theoretical argument is that institutions tend to generate increasing returns, which in turn raise the cost of institutional adjustments (e.g., Pierson 2000). For example, Wallander argues that in the process of "keeping the Russians out, the Americans in, and the Germans down" NATO also developed a set of general assets that could be mobilized to deal with new security missions (Wallander 2000). These assets were not optimal, in the sense that the United States and the Europeans would probably have devised a different institutional structure had they designed one from scratch after the Cold War, but their availability helped ensure the preservation of NATO. While the UN developed some assets during the Cold War that were useful afterwards, especially in the area of peacekeeping, it is difficult to see how these would foreclose changes in the decision-making rules that control the use of these assets.

A third, and more persuasive, line of reasoning follows from the path dependence literature's focus on issues of timing and sequencing (Pierson 2000). The concept of path dependence implies that individual incidents may turn out to be formative moments that shape a path of institutional development, while foreclosing others. It is plausible that the first Gulf War had a considerable influence on expectations about the role of the UNSC in the post-Cold War world. It is important to appreciate how sudden the shift was. When the United States invaded Panama in December 1989, it did not even consider asking for UNSC approval. A UNGA resolution deploring the intervention had no discernible impact on domestic public or elite support for the intervention, and neither did a UNSC resolution that the US vetoed (Luck 2002: 64). After the Gulf War, the UNSC became, as former US Secretary of State James Baker put it, the "natural first stop for coalition building" (Baker 1995: 278). *Ex ante*, the first Gulf War was highly controversial. *Ex post*, the war was widely cited as the most successful multilateral effort ever.[10]

It is thus conceivable that the Gulf War experience made the UNSC the focal point for future collaborative actions (Voeten 2005). Moreover, the event may have impressed upon elites and citizens that satisfactory multilateral solutions are possible even with unsatisfactory decision-making procedures. Nevertheless, we still need to explain why this institution could perform this role. The next section explores this issue, starting with the question why states would delegate authority to the UNSC in the first place?

Enforcement and optimal institutional design

Rationalist explanations of institutional design usually build on some version of contract theory. This is the branch of economic theory concerned with explaining why, when, and how authority relations emerge in a specific type of anarchical environment: markets (for an overview, see Bolton and Dewatripont 2005).[11] Contract theorists start with the observation that uncertainty, hidden information or more broadly "transaction costs" prevent otherwise beneficial co-operation (trade) from occurring. These inefficiencies occur in part because authority, generally defined as "the right to pick a decision in an allowed set of decisions" (Simon 1951), is not appropriately allocated. In response, actors may create contracts that define authority relationships and compensation schemes that provide incentives for improved levels of exchange. Questions of institutional design arise because parties to a long-term contract generally cannot anticipate all future states of the world to which the contract may apply and/or cannot agree on a common description of the complete state space. This implies that at the contract stage, parties have to decide how control rights, decision-making rules, discretion, and so on should be distributed among the contracting parties.

When states contemplate how to regulate future uses of force, they cannot anticipate all future instances in which the exercise of force may serve the purposes of the contracting parties. Thus, although the UN Charter explicitly forbids the use or threat of force "against the territorial integrity or political independence of any state, or in any manner inconsistent with the Purposes of the United Nations" (UN Charter Article 2, para. 4), the Charter also explicitly recognizes two general circumstances under which the use of force does serve the purposes of the UN: when it is exercised as individual or collective self-defense against armed attacks (Article 51) or when it otherwise constitutes a collective action against the "existence of any threat to the peace, breach of the peace, or act of aggression" (Article 39). To continue the economic analogy, the exceptions allow the use of force to protect property rights (sovereignty) and to produce public goods (peace).

The UNSC can be understood as an institutional solution that addresses the inherent conflicts of interests that arise in interpreting these exceptions. The remainder of this section explores the demands on such an institutional solution.

Collective actions to preserve the peace

How do states determine that a threat to the peace warrants a collective response? Chapter VII of the Charter explicitly grants the Council authority over this. Article 39 states that "The Security Council shall determine the existence of any threat to the peace, breach of the peace, or act of aggression and shall make recommendations, or decide what measures shall be taken [. . .] to maintain or restore international peace and security." UNSC decisions can authorize uses of force by regional organizations or "coalitions of the willing,"[12] and they can authorize peacekeeping missions executed and financed by the members of the UN. Such missions deliver public goods, in that they produce something (peace/stability) that is non-excludable and enjoyed by most or all status-quo powers, although some benefit more than others in individual cases (Bennett et al. 1994).

Models of public good provision predict that poor nations will be able to free-ride off the contributions of wealthier nations and that the public good will be underprovided because contributors do not take into account the spillover benefits that their support confers to others.[13] The UNSC may help alleviate underprovision and free-riding in three ways. First, the fixed burden-sharing mechanism for peacekeeping operations provides an institutional solution that helps reduce risks of bargaining failures and lessens transaction costs.[14] Second, the delegation of decision-making authority to a small number of states may facilitate compromise on the amount of public good that ought to be produced (Martin 1992: 773). Third, the UNSC helps states pool resources (Abbott and Snidal 1998). The existence of selective incentives induces some states to incur more than their required share of the peacekeeping burden. For example, Kuwait paid two-thirds of the bill for the UN Iraq–Kuwait Observation Mission through voluntary contributions. Australia proved willing to shoulder a disproportionate share of the peacekeeping burden in East Timor. States are more likely to make such contributions when these add to the efforts of others in a predictable manner.

From the perspective of contract theory, the main question of institutional design is: what decision-making rule yields the optimal level of public goods? A general result is that some form of (qualified) majority rule is *ex ante* Pareto efficient (e.g., Bolton and DeWatripont 2005). Before knowing precisely what issues will arise, participants have an incentive not to insist on veto rights. Under very general conditions, each actor is better off occasionally contributing to public goods that the actor would not have approved than to absorb the underprovision of public goods that would result from granting each actor veto power. The delegation of authority to an institution governed by (qualified) majority voting rules helps solve the time inconsistency problems that prevent actors from realizing this trade-off.

The *ex ante* efficiency of majority rule collapses, however, when institutional decisions are not enforceable (see Maggi and Morelli 2003). The intuition is that, in the absence of enforcement, the time inconsistency issue is not resolved: states may act upon their incentives to undermine individual unfavorable decisions. Expectations regarding such behavior undermine the willingness of other states to contribute more than they would under a voluntary scheme in the hope that the long-term benefits of co-operation exceed the short-term benefits of shirking. In the shadow of enforcement issues, the Pareto efficient solution is therefore to grant veto rights to those with the ability to undermine the institutions' decisions.

Two points are especially relevant. First, this argument implies not just that permanent members are unlikely to give up their veto power, but also that a more majoritarian or inclusive institution may not be better at producing public goods. The history of the "Uniting for Peace" procedure is illustrative. As mentioned before, the Western powers used the temporary absence of the USSR in 1950 to grant the UNGA authority to take measures to preserve international peace and security if the UNSC were deadlocked. This procedure was invoked on ten different occasions. It could no longer be used effectively after the early 1960s, when the US and the West lost their near-automatic majority in the UNGA. After that, the UNGA still passed many resolutions related to security, but they were routinely ignored and produced few public goods. For example, US President Ronald Reagan famously claimed that the 1983 UNGA resolution condemning the United States for its intervention in Grenada "didn't upset his breakfast at all" (quoted in Luck 2002: 63).

Second, it is important to appreciate that enforcement problems are the key to the limited effectiveness of majoritarian institutions in the international system. As enforcement problems were solved, veto rights could be and have been lifted. For example, the EU has switched from unanimity to qualified majority rule on many issues where strong enforcement procedures of EU decisions have been realized, for instance through the ECJ, whereas unanimity rule is preserved on those issues where the institution has few enforcement capabilities, most notably issues of immigration and security.[15]

These arguments should not be taken to imply that the precise design of the UNSC is optimal from the perspective of public good production. The UNSC's voting rules contains clear inefficiencies from the perspective of an institution that produces public goods. The UNSC grants veto power to actors that should not have it. For example, China has temporarily blocked peacekeeping missions in Guatemala and Macedonia for the simple reason that government officials in those countries had interactions with, or made statements about, Taiwan. From an efficiency standpoint, China should not have the ability to single-handedly block those efforts given that it contributes very little to peacekeeping efforts. Similarly, Japan and Germany should be given more incentives to help produce public goods by granting them greater responsibilities.

If the UNSC was truly just about producing public goods, reforms along the lines suggested above should not be terribly controversial and could marginally improve institutional performance. However, the determination of whether force can and should be used also deals with considerable distributional conflict over the extent to which the missions are indeed in the public interest or reflect the needs and wants of a set of countries and/or governments. Those issues, discussed in the following sections, complicate matters considerably.

Self-defense

The self-defense exception is open to *ex post* opportunism: states may and frequently do resort to expanded conceptions of self-defense in attempts to justify unilateral uses of force (Schachter 1989). This issue could potentially be resolved by assigning an independent institution, such as a court, the task to evaluate the validity of the claims for self-defense. This has not occurred. There is little impetus in the High-Level Panel Report[16] or elsewhere to grant the ICJ a greater role in this regard nor does the Panel favor rewriting Article 51 to identify more precisely when uses of self-defense are permitted. The Panel's treatment of the issue (paragraphs 188–192) pertains mostly to the question of whether preventive uses of force could be justified under Article 51, which the Panel rejects. The discussion is a thinly disguised judgment that the US invasion of Iraq was illegal. The Panel is clearly worried about the erosion of a norm ("allowing one to so act is to allow all") but offers no suggestion for institutional reform other than to point to the necessity of UNSC authorization for such actions.

The UNSC has little formal authority on this matter. States must report self-defense uses of force to the UN – something that they have not always done (Schachter 1989). The Council is not, however, assigned the task of assessing the legitimacy of self-defense claims. In practice, however, states do behave "as if" Council authorization makes questionable uses of the self-defense concept more acceptable, as illustrated by Resolution 1373, which reaffirms the right of the United States to act forcefully in its self-defense against terrorist activities and de facto legitimized the US military action in Afghanistan.[17]

Presumably, governments care about UNSC resolutions authorizing force in the name of self-defense because they are concerned about their general reputation for upholding norms and rules that regulate uses of force. They may do so out of an inherent appreciation for these norms, to please domestic publics, or because they believe that others are more likely to co-operate with states that show a general inclination to comply with rules and norms. One should be aware, however, that the judgment whether a particular use of self-defense is permitted is ultimately a political one and not subject to judicial review. Thus, one should not expect judgments that are independent or consistent from a legal perspective and it is not entirely clear what the value is of lamenting the lack of such consistency – though it is a prominent theme in the legal literature.[18]

It is also unclear what the value would be of reforms that seek to institutionalize new rules for the use of force, given the necessary incompleteness of such rules and the absence of independent arbitration. Such rules will be upheld only if they become generally accepted norms outside the institutional setting of the UNSC (i.e., they must be self-enforcing). Any new institutional adoption of rules for the use of force will likely reflect, rather than instigate, such norm acceptance.

The fact that the acceptance or rejection of self-defense claims is ultimately determined through a political process also implies that some states will be more likely than others to obtain the blessing of a multilateral institution. To understand more precisely how this affects the functioning of the institution, we need to turn to an analysis of how the outside power of states interacts with formal institutional rules, an exercise that will be undertaken in the next section. Such an analysis is also important to better understand the manner in which the authorization of collective actions and the evaluation of appropriate unilateral uses of force are related. Collective action authorized by the UNSC has been most extensive and effective when there has been a strong lead state, such as Australia in East Timor or the United States in the first Gulf War (e.g., Fearon and Laitin 2004). The willingness of a state to "go it alone" helps solve the free-rider problem in the production of public goods. Yet, generally states are only willing to do this if they are granted leeway in executing the intervention. As such, the UNSC cannot simultaneously restrict military interventions by outside actors to unambiguous uses of self-defense *and* be effective at maintaining international peace and security.

Outside power and formal institutions

Institutionalists generally claim that power is "important," but they rarely explicitly model its consequences for institutional behavior or design (see also Brooks and Wohlforth 2005 and Voeten 2001). This omission results at least partly from the perception that the toolkit of institutional analysis is unsuitable for the analysis of power asymmetries. For example, in a special issue on the rational design of institutions published in *International Organization*, the motivation for de-emphasizing the role of power was the absence of "compelling results" in the formal literature (Koremenos et al. 2001b: 1067).

Here I will use insights from a very simple bargaining model to shed light on this issue (see also Voeten 2001). The illustration is based on a fairly straightforward situation of heterogeneous preferences over outcomes, as depicted in Figure 12.2. One of the permanent members, typically the United States, prefers to act militarily in response to some situation. At least one other veto power prefers a milder response, such as sanctions, or even no response. This describes the basic strategic dilemma that states faced for example in Iraq's invasion of Kuwait, the removal of Aristide from power in Haiti, ethnic cleansing in Kosovo, or Iraq's failure to comply with weapons inspections. When there is distributional conflict among the veto powers, no multilateral agreement exists that defeats the status quo (no action). Hence, any proposal between the ideal points of powers 1 and 3 will be vetoed, and stalemate is the result.[19]

Now suppose that veto power 1 has the ability to act unilaterally or with a few allies. In that case, she could just act alone and not bother with a multilateral institution at all. However, veto power 1 may have some incentive to sway others to co-operate. UNSC authorization may encourage burden-sharing, it may decrease the perception among citizens at home and abroad that the military action is threatening or it may in some other way enable the continuance of beneficial co-operation (see Voeten 2005).

Suppose for the moment that the benefit of UNSC authorization is exogenous and in utility terms equivalent to a policy compromise at point M. This assumption implies that everything else being equal, veto power 1 prefers to have UNSC authorization rather than not have it.[20] If this is true, then there exists a point along the continuum in Figure 12.2 where Power 1 is indifferent between the disutility of a compromise and the absence

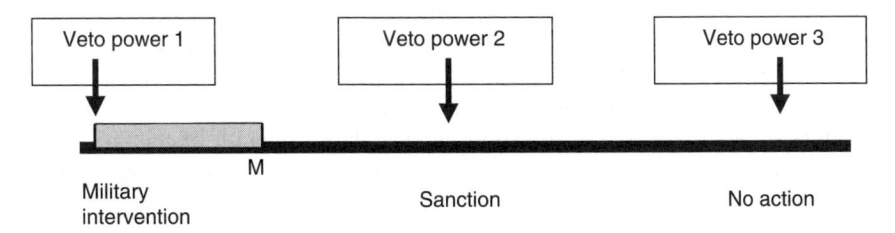

Figure 12.2 Bargaining with heterogeneous preferences: the effects of outside options.

of multilateral agreement. That is: Power 1 prefers any multilateral action between her ideal point and point M to going at it alone. Similarly, veto powers 2 and 3 prefer these multilateral agreements to unilateral action by Power 1, which would create a (from their perspectives) undesirable military intervention over which they would have no influence. Thus, the presence of a credible outside option and some incentive for co-operation combine to create a bargaining range where none exists in the absence of the outside option.

This very simple analysis has a few relevant implications. First, it points to a straightforward way in which the end of the Cold War increased UNSC activity. Two characteristics of the Cold War were that there were two veto powers that both had extensive outside options *and* who were reliably on opposite sides of the spectrum (like powers 1 and 3 in Figure 12.2). It is easy to see that in such a scenario UNSC action can do little but help maintain a status quo (first-generation peacekeeping), even if there were some inherent advantages to multilateralism. Asymmetric outside options, however, create the possibility that the UNSC can act in the absence of harmony among the five veto powers.

This is exactly the opposite conclusion from those who argue that unipolarity has killed the UNSC (e.g., Glennon 2003). The bargaining perspective suggests that unipolarity made multilateral actions possible in cases where bipolarity did not. The evidence for the latter view is that the most extensive UN authorizations of force were almost all in cases where the US either implicitly or explicitly threatened to act outside the Council. This is certainly true for the first Gulf War, Somalia, Haiti, Bosnia,[21] Kosovo,[22] and Afghanistan.

Second, the current UNSC is not just a forum based around great power consent for collective actions, but it has also become an institution that offers states the possibility of imposing some measure of constraint on a superpower. This is a rather different purpose than originally intended by the Charter. The value of veto power to individual states in exercising the latter task is at best mixed. In the world sketched by Figure 12.2, the policy preferences of a new veto power affect outcomes only under rare circumstances.[23] The new permanent member could potentially use its leverage to obtain some side-payments. But there might also be downsides to having the formal power to veto a multilateral initiative. For example, in the lead-up to the Iraq war, Gerhard Schröder was able to acquire the domestic benefits of opposing the war, while much of the US ire was directed at France, the country with the power to block UNSC authorization of the mission. Most states will want some measure of constraint on the US but few states will want to be in the position to apply that constraint. To current UNSC members, veto power confers some measure of status and influence that is difficult to give up,[24] but that status may not be sufficiently valuable to outsiders in comparison to the resources that would be necessary to acquire it.

Third, in the absence of bargaining failures, institutional reforms would be irrelevant. In the simple world of Figure 12.2, states would always be able to achieve a multilateral compromise at point M and avoid unilateral actions. In reality, bargaining failures prevent this from occurring. The argument is essentially identical to rationalist explanations for war (Fearon 1995). Given that war is costly, there always exists some Pareto improving agreement that does not result in war. Similarly, if unilateralism is costly, then there should be some multilateral solution that benefits all.

Bargaining failures can have many causes. I discuss two. First, states may have asymmetric information.[25] For example, veto power 1 may know how much it is willing to compromise in exchange for UNSC authorization, but others may not. Player 1 will have difficulties credibly communicating her willingness to compromise, given that she has incentives to under-report her willingness to do so. Second, domestic politics may interfere. For example, the rise of nationalism made it virtually impossible for Russia to publicly agree to the Kosovo intervention. At the same time, Russia worked hard to avoid an intervention over which it had no say. Russia's foreign minister Igor Ivanov traveled to Belgrade on 12 March to try to persuade Milosevic to accept a peacekeeping force – the same force the Russians had been objecting to so far in the UNSC.[26] Some newspaper reports even suggested that Russia effectively participated in the NATO force by allowing its vessels to transport military supplies.[27]

A similar story applies to French opposition over the Iraq war. A French general met with General Command staff on 16 December 2002 to discuss the details of a French contribution of 10,000 to 15,000 troops and French President Jacques Chirac told his troops to prepare for action in a speech at the Ecole Militaire on 7 January 2003 (Cantaloube and Vernet 2004; Cogan 2003). Clearly there was room for a compromise, but things changed, apparently at least in part for domestic political reasons.

Given that bargaining failures are likely, adding more states with veto power would surely make the UNSC less able to act. Similarly, reforms that enhance the transparency of UNSC debates may increase stalemate. Public speeches in formal settings tend to raise the cost of withdrawing from a position, while generally having only minimal persuasive impact. There is some value to negotiating behind closed doors (Goldstein and Martin 2000).

Conclusions

What does all this tell us about the extent to which institutional reform could make the UNSC perform better? One major hindrance to improving the UNSC is that the institution is called upon to solve two rather distinct political problems: the initiation of collective actions to produce public goods (e.g., Sudan) and the imposition of some measure of constraint on the exercise of force by a superpower (e.g., Iraq). From an efficiency perspective, the two tasks pose different demands on institutional design. Moreover, the extent to which an individual use of force fits either case is a matter of fierce contestation. Hence, there is no straightforward way to redesign the institutional structure that would address the concerns separately.

First, consider the case of the Sudan (Darfur). The UNSC's failure here is its inability to produce an extensive response that potentially could have prevented genocide. To a large extent, this failure results from a lack of willingness among the great powers to contribute resources. We could, however, redesign the UNSC to marginally improve the incentives for participation. For example, a country with a low general willingness to contribute to global public goods should not be able to block resolutions out of private concerns (China). Also, giving wealthy countries such as Japan and Germany positions of responsibility could plausibly enhance their perceived interest in attempting to stop genocide far away.

In the case of the latest Iraq war, it is much less clear if and how the UNSC has failed. To some, the UNSC has failed in that it did not prevent the US intervention. More realistically, the UNSC can achieve two things in a case like Iraq. First, if a multilateral solution fails, this failure should be perceived as costly by the offending state. If this is so, then it raises the cost of future unilateral actions. From this perspective, the UNSC may not have failed at all. Second, a multilateral compromise could have been achieved that would have given other states more control over the intervention. Depending on the outcome, this might have been perceived as a failure or as a success. Regardless of this, the demands on institutional design are clearly different from the Sudan case. For example, whereas China has, despite some recent changes, not been a major contributor to collective actions, it is obviously a necessary participant in evaluating the political expedience of an intervention.

What institutional reform is necessary, then, depends strongly on what function we expect the UNSC to perform. One could argue, for instance, that a body that decides by weighted majority rule and that would consist of only democratic states, would be respected more in the US and hence could impose greater constraints on it (greater value of M in Figure 12.2). Yet, it is unclear why we would expect such a body to respond more effectively to global crises. Moreover, a majoritarian body runs the risk of making itself irrelevant by making decisions that are not enforceable.

The main implication for the institutionalist literature is the need to go beyond the "power also matters" approach towards institutional design. If power matters, then it should be modeled explicitly, rather than separated from the effects of institutions. This chapter has illustrated some extremely simple ways to do this. I would contend that the toolkit of formal models is very suitable to explicitly model the impact of power asymmetries. In game theoretic terms, power resides in the ability to commit oneself. This is not mere "cleverness" (Krasner 1991), but may stem from having the military capacity to pursue interventions unilaterally. At the same time, power does have other sources, such as the ability to raise audience costs, ability to delay, and specific institutional features such as agenda-setting or veto power. How formal institutional power transfers into actual bargaining power should be higher on the agenda of institutionalist research.

More generally, the analysis points to the limits of the impact that institutional reform and design have when decisions need to be self-enforcing and non-institutionalized power asymmetries matter. When we take into account the interaction with its external environment, the stakes for institutional reform appear to be much lower than when we lock ourselves up inside the UNSC. This may explain, for instance, why the push for institutional reform comes primarily from high-level bureaucrats within the foreign ministries of countries such as Germany and Japan, rather than from the executives of those countries. The bureaucracies may care a great deal about the prestige attached to formal membership, while the executives care more about actual influence and may be wary of the additional responsibilities attached to permanent membership.

While the impact of institutional design is constrained, the particularities of formal institutions are certainly not completely irrelevant. Outcomes realized through multilateral institutions look different from outcomes that are not, though not in ways that we can understand without a proper analysis of power asymmetries and enforcement problems. Moreover, the current decision-making procedures do contain certain inefficiencies that increase the chance for bargaining failures and lead to an underproduction of public goods (peace). Nevertheless, the benefits of clever constitutional engineering will likely be relatively small both for the production of public goods as well as for the private interests of individual states.

Notes

An earlier version of this paper was presented at the workshop Assessing Multilateralism in the Security Domain, Delphi, 3–5 June 2005. I thank the participants at that workshop, especially Dimitris Bourantonis and Arturo Sotomayor, for useful comments and suggestions.

1 This exclusion was formalized in the Charter through the so-called Enemy Clauses, which have never been repealed.
2 For extensive analyses of the history of UN reform, see Bourantonis (2005) and Luck (2003).
3 Friedman, T. (2003) "Vote France off the Island," *New York Times*, 9 February 2003.
4 These precise words are from a speech given at the Banqueting House, Whitehall, London, 10 February 2005 (http://www.una-uk.org/10feb05/sgspeech.html) and refer explicitly to a similar statement in his 4 December 2003 UNGA speech in which he installed the Panel.
5 See the 2005 *World Summit Outcome*, the 2000 *Millennium Declaration*, and the *Declaration on the Occasion of the Fiftieth Anniversary of the United Nations* from 1995. The 2005 text reads (point 153): "We support early reform of the Security Council – an essential element of our overall effort to reform the United Nations – in order to make it more broadly representative, efficient and transparent and thus to further enhance its effectiveness and the legitimacy and implementation of its

decisions. We commit ourselves to continuing our efforts to achieve a decision to this end and request the General Assembly to review progress on the reform set out above by the end of 2005."

6 As Brian Urquhart writes, on the High-Level Panel report: "In the past many excellent and forward-looking ideas have died a dismal death being torn to pieces by junior diplomats in the committees of the General Assembly" (Urquhart 2005: 185). From the UNGA session following the 2005 World Summit, there is little evidence the High-Level Panel report will experience a different fate.

7 For example, by assuming that states engage in "role-oriented" behavior and hence are not opportunistic (Frederking 2003).

8 This statement is based on conversations with various long-time participants in negotiations over UN reform. The latter part of the statement holds especially for countries such as Mexico and Argentina, who would prefer not to have Brazil become their permanent representative but at the same time see little benefit in obtaining an institutional position that would likely bring them into unwanted conflict with the US, given that domestic public opinion would likely force these countries to frequently offer resistance to US initiatives.

9 For Japan, see Law Concerning Co-operation for United Nations Peacekeeping Operations and Other Operations (the International Peace Co-operation Law) originally passed in June 1992. For Germany, see especially the ruling by the *Bundesverfassungsgericht* [Federal Constitutional Court] 90, 286, 12 July 1994.

10 For instance, having voted against the war became a serious liability for 2004 Democratic presidential candidate John Kerry.

11 Even though the nature of the anarchical environment in international politics differs from that of a market, international relations theorists have long recognized that the existence of transaction costs and asymmetric information provide a compelling *raison d'être* for international institutions (for an overview, see Martin and Simmons 1998). As such, scholars have used the tools of contract theory, in particular principal–agent theory, to explore if, when, why, and how states delegate authority to IOs (e.g., Pollack 1997; Nielson and Tierney 2003).

12 There is some debate as to the legal standing of this (Blokker 2000).

13 This paragraph is adopted from Voeten (2005).

14 A fixed burden-sharing system was put in place in 1973 by UNGA Resolution 310.

15 I have taken some liberties in interpreting Maggi and Morelli, who argue that the EU uses qualified majority rule on issues that are less "important." I believe that the enforcement interpretation more accurately reflects their formal results and the data.

16 The ICJ receives one mention, on page 12, acknowledging that "disputes were remedied under the International Court of Justice."

17 UNSC Resolution 1373, 28 September 2001.

18 For example, on the application of the self-defense concept in Resolution 1373, see Farer (2002).

19 For a discussion of how vote buying may alter this, see Voeten (n.d.).

20 We may show how this benefit arises endogenously either from domestic interactions or from reputation effects through repeated interactions, but such an analysis would contribute little to the issues at stake here and unnecessarily complicate matters.

21 The most forceful UN resolutions were adopted only after the US threatened to unilaterally lift the arms embargo against Bosnian Muslims (see Christopher 1998).

22 The authorization of KFOR after the intervention had taken place. This is a somewhat different case from the others.

23 They only matter if the new veto power's ideal point is smaller than M. For more, see Voeten (2001).

24 For example on Russia, see Bourantonis and Panagiotou (2004).
25 For a formal analysis of this argument, see Voeten (2001).
26 "Igor Ivanov rectifies mistakes of Americans," *Izvestia*, 12 March 1999.
27 "Russia is already participating in NATO operations in Balkans," *Izvestia*, 10 March 1999.

13 The reform and efficiency of the UN Security Council

A veto players analysis

*Aris Alexopoulos and
Dimitris Bourantonis*

Introduction

Since the beginning of the 1990s, we observe a growing number of proposals to increase the representativeness of the UNSC. The reasoning behind these proposals is that in this way the UNSC will improve its efficiency in the implementation of its decisions. However, there are counter-arguments, which tend to dominate the debate, that a potential enlargement or a more demanding decision rule almost by definition will reduce the decision capacity of the body. Most scholarly accounts of UNSC reform, while in favor of UNSC enlargement, take it as a self-evident truth that its bigger size would weaken its decision-making capacity and in other words its ability to act swiftly and effectively. Russett (2005: 161) for instance, argues that "anything ... that increases the number of players that have leverage in its [i.e., the UNSC] negotiations throws one more bucket of sand into the wheels of rapid and decisive action by the Council." Reviewing the history of UNSC reform Sutterlin (1987: 4) has underlined that "to be an effective body in dealing with threats to the peace, the Council had to be small and capable of quick decisions." In the same line of reasoning, Wallensteen (1997: 106), Weiss (2003: 149), Caron (1993: 567), the members of the UN Secretary-General's High-Level Panel on Threats, Challenges and Change and others[1] have called for a trade-off between better representation through Council enlargement and efficiency. Their convictions that "concern for efficiency argues for a relatively small Council," or that "a Security Council of 21 or 25 members would hardly improve effectiveness" or "the number of members must be kept small for the sake of efficient argument" as such sound like axioms or arbitrary judgments. With this work we examine various scenarios of reform of the UNSC, based on enlargement and change in the decision rule, and obtain that a reduced decision capacity is not always the case. We will show that there are types of reform that may lead in the opposite direction, to increase the decision capacity of the body.

The central element in the decision structure of the UNSC is the veto power, which either institutionally or positionally the involved players hold. It is this reason, which drives us to apply, by analogy, to such an international decision structure, the work of Tsebelis (2002) on the role of veto players in decision-making games, a theory produced to explain the functioning of domestic political institutions. To do so, the chapter is organized in three sections. Firstly, we introduce the tools of Tsebelis's veto players theory needed in the analysis of the various reform scenarios. Secondly, based on the main findings we analyze the current functioning of the UNSC. Thirdly, we discuss the decision capacity of the system under alternative reform scenarios on the membership and institutional arrangements of the future UNSC.

The veto players theory and its implications on international decision-making

According to Tsebelis' theory, veto players are individual or collective decision makers whose agreement is necessary for the change of the status quo (SQ). In his book, following spatial analysis, Tsebelis arrives at the key proposition that the SQ is preserved as the number of veto players increases, and at the same time the diversity of their policy preferences over the policy at stake increases as well.

This argument is drawn upon the complementary analytic concepts of *winset* and *core* of a decision-making system. Tsebelis defines as the core of a political system the set of points that cannot be defeated by any other point of the space within which decision makers choose over policies (Tsebelis 2002: 21–6). If the status quo of a policy belongs to this set, then it is undefeatable and the decision makers cannot agree to replace it with a new policy output. Equally, if the core of a political system is an empty set, then decisions over changing the SQ are possible. All the points that can defeat the SQ belong to its winset. The larger the winset, the easier it is for the veto players of the system to agree upon a change of the status quo. Additionally, since the variety of policy alternatives is wider, the possibility for the decision makers to agree upon a policy outcome in far distance from the SQ is also greater. Therefore, the decision capacity of a political system can be measured either with the winset or with the core. The larger the winset, the larger is the decision capacity; or, equivalently, the smaller the core, the larger is the decision capacity of the system. For our analysis, in order to measure the decision capacity of the UNSC for each of the reform scenarios, we will use the concept of *core*. The size of the core depends on the decision rule, the number and the location on space of the ideal points of the veto players of the system.

Tsebelis shows in his theory that the core expands as the majority rule becomes more demanding, starting from simple to qualified majority and unanimity (Tsebelis 2002: 39–41). The core also expands, the more distant the veto players' ideal policy points are. The increased number of veto players does not necessarily lead to the increase of the core. If these veto players are located closer among them than their fewer predecessors, then the core is smaller. Tsebelis (2002: 30–2) shows that a core of three decision-makers can by greater than a core of five, if the five players are located inside the core of the three.

We can observe this possibility in Figure 13.1, where we locate two decision bodies, one with three members (A1, A2, A3), which compose the triangle A1A2A3 on the two-dimension policy plane, and the other body with five members (B1, B2, B3, B4, B5), which compose the pentagon B1B2B3B4B5. The pentagon is contained within the triangle. The core of the first body is the triangle, so if the SQ is located within this triangle the members A1, A2 and A3 cannot reach an agreement to change it. All points inside the triangle cannot be defeated by unanimity among the three veto players of the decision body A. Under the same reasoning, the five members of the decision body B cannot reach by unanimity an agreement to change the SQ if this is located within the pentagon B1B2B3B4B5. Since the pentagon is contained within the triangle, it is also smaller than A1A2A3. As we earlier discussed, the core is a measurement of the decision capacity of the correspondent decision body. The smaller the core, the greater the capacity of the decision body, since there are more points of the space outside the core over which the veto players may agree by unanimity to replace the status quo. In our case, the decision capacity under unanimity of A1, A2, A3 is smaller than the decision capacity of the larger set of B1, B2, B3, B4, B5 though closer located veto players.

The reader can also verify that the same number of decision makers, when located with a greater distance between them than the first time, produce a

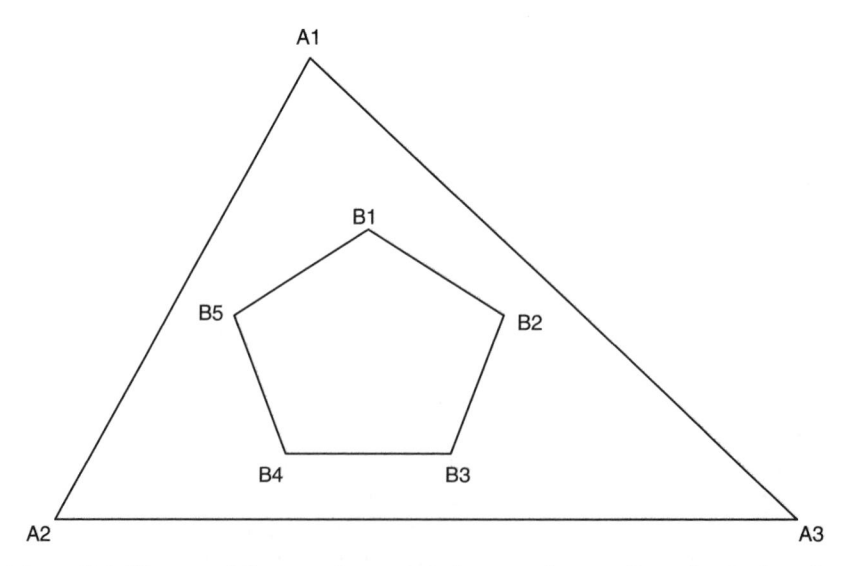

Figure 13.1 Three- and five-member unanimity cores in two dimensions, where five members can reach a decision more easily than a three-member decision body that is more distant.

greater core. The important element is the location of the ideal preference points of the players in the decision game, and not the number of the players.

Applying the above-mentioned theoretical propositions on the functioning of the UNSC, we compose the following argument for the proposed reform scenarios: The increase of the membership of the UNSC does not necessarily correspond to a reduced capacity to make decisions. The key element is the location of the policy preferences of the new members in the policy space regarding the SQ. Hence, it is not the increase of the members of the UNSC alone, but its combination with the divergence of the decision makers' security policy preferences in the UNSC that produces less collective action for the promotion of the international security.

In the following parts we will examine in more detail the current functioning and various reform scenarios of the UNSC, in terms of their decision capacity, based on the argument raised above, about the number and the location of veto players, incorporating in our analysis specific alternative member states. We will show that the important element to produce a more efficient UNSC is not the number of veto players in the decision process but the distance of their preferences over two distinct forms of enforcement actions that are available to the UNSC under Chapter VII of the UN Charter (i.e., sanctions or use of armed force) and their economic development agenda.

Analyzing the current structure of the UNSC

Statistical evaluation by different scholars (Kim and Russett 1996; Voeten 2000) of the roll-call votes in the UNGA has produced conflicting evidence over the dimensionality of the voting behavior of the states.[2] Further examination with more data from the post-Cold War era remains to be done in order to produce more consistent results. Due to the lack of this empirical evidence and taking into account the long-lasting debate in the scholarship over the sources of conflict in international politics, we decide to work on a two-dimensional space, although unidimensionality could provide simplicity in our analysis.[3] But this simplicity comes at the cost of generalizability of the results. For example, while in a single dimension there is always a median voter, in more than one dimension a median voter rarely exists; actually the probability of existence of such a voter is 0 (zero).

These generalizability restrictions do not apply to our two-dimensional representation. In addition, this representation of the decision-making of the UNSC allows us to incorporate trade-offs in the players' security policy preferences without losing clarity in the presentation of the arguments. We choose to represent the decision-making of the UNSC by a system of two axes, where across the horizontal axis we measure the economic agenda of a member of the UNSC. To be more specific, we examine whether it pursues the restructuring of its external debt with the advice of the IMF[4] and the World Bank, whether it tries to expand into new foreign markets, or whether it is embarked upon environmental protection negotiation at a world level. We assume that the economic agenda of the states is related to their level of development. We pick as an indicator for the development level the extensively used GDP per capita despite its shortcomings in representing the real level of development.[5] The reason is that we adopt the position that the economic agenda of governments abroad is very closely related to the living standards of their citizens. What the states pursue in international fora mirrors the need of their voters for employment, consumption, free time, and quality of life in general. Along the vertical axis we measure whether the member state of the UNSC prefers sanctions or the use of armed force to safeguard peace. With these two variables we try to bridge the liberal and realist traditions in international relations literature. The foreign economic policy agenda is formed according to liberal intergovernmentalism arguments (Moravcsik 1997) for representing domestic political and economic interests abroad. We assume that a two-stage game (Putnam 1988) occurs, in which the economic agenda of the state players is formed domestically at first and then negotiated abroad. Despite the increased possibility that, in general, domestic actors, governments and international organizations may be engaged in a super game, which takes place simultaneously in two nested arenas, the domestic and the international (Tsebelis 1990), we believe that this is not very probable in the case of decision making within the Security Council structure. Here, the countries come to negotiate having already fixed their economic policy preferences. The security agenda of the states is formed according to realist assumptions for geopolitical interest formation. In the third part of the paper we will try to locate, on the produced two-dimensional policy space, the members of the UNSC according to these variables.

Let us now turn to the decision rule of the UNSC. In the current structure of the UNSC, what is needed for a decision to be validated is not only to reach a qualified majority, around 60 per cent (9/15), but also that none of the permanent members uses its veto privilege in order to block the decision. In other words a decision at the UNSC can be reached when two conditions occur simultaneously: (1) qualified majority with a threshold at 60 per cent, and (2) no use of veto by any of the current five permanent members, namely US, UK, France, China and Russia.

Translating the above decision conditions in the language of veto players theory, the core of the decision system of the UNSC is the convexification of two cores – "the unanimity core" consisting of the five permanent members and "the 60 per cent qualified majority core" of the whole UNSC. Since we have already discussed the way the unanimity core is identified, it is now time to do the same for the qualified majority core and also discuss the convexification of the two cores in a UNSC-like decision body.

In Figure 13.2 we select any 15 points, which correspond to the members of the current composition of the UNSC. Any selection (say 8 ... 12) of five points could play the role of the five permanent members of the UNSC, which hold the privilege of veto power. The 8 ... 12 pentagon composed of

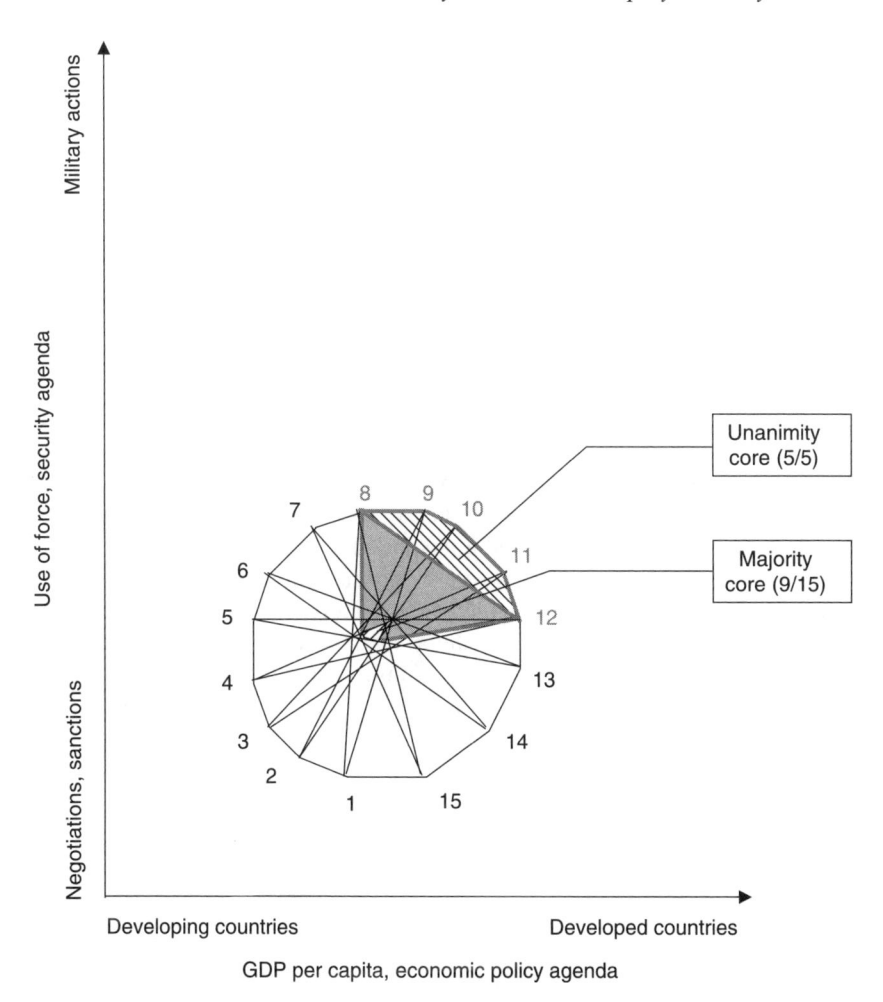

Figure 13.2 A fifteen-member decision body in a two-dimensional policy space.

these points constitutes "the unanimity 5/5 core" of this set of decision-makers. We can also divide the fifteen members several times, picking 9 out of 15 points and creating 9/15 majorities. The lines, such as the one drawn through the points 1 and 8, which can leave 9 points on the one side of them, including 1 and 8, are called "9/15 qualified majority dividers" (q-dividers in Tsebelis 2002: 52). We draw all the possible q-dividers, creating each time an enneagon (say the 1, 8, 9 ... 15). Anywhere within each enneagon the correspondent veto players cannot unanimously (9/9) agree to change the SQ if the last is located within the enneagon. This enneagon constitutes the unanimity core of the nine selected players. If we now select all possible enneagons, their intersection constitutes the area within which no point can be defeated by any 9/15 majority. This intersection is the hatched small polygon in Figure 13.2 and represents the "9/15 qualified majority core" of the fifteen-player decision-making body.

In the case of the UNSC, if the status quo on a peace crisis is laid within the five permanent members' unanimity core, no matter whether it is not contained within the "60 per cent qualified majority" core, no draft resolution can be adopted by the UNSC, since it will be vetoed as less preferred by at least one of the permanent members. If the SQ lies outside the five permanent members' unanimity core and within the "60 per cent qualified majority" core of the fifteen members of the UNSC, it again cannot be defeated by any other draft resolution since it will not be supported by at least 9/15 votes. If the SQ lies outside both cores, but within the area contained by the straight lines that connect the extreme points of the unanimity and the 9/15 core, it again cannot be defeated. Actually, if the draft resolution is closer to one of the two cores, then it will be vetoed by the members of the other core since the draft proposal moves things away from their ideal policy preferences. Therefore, the core of the UNSC is the area that covers and connects the two cores and represents their convexification – the hatched and shaded areas in Figure 13.3.

The greater the differences between the permanent and the non-permanent members of the UNSC and the greater the preference dispersion (less homogeneous) inside these two groups, the greater is the size of the core of the UNSC, and, hence, the greater the possibility for unilateral or (let us say) non-collective actions under UNSC auspices. In the case of non-decision for the UNSC, there are two possible policy outcomes: either mostly unilateral

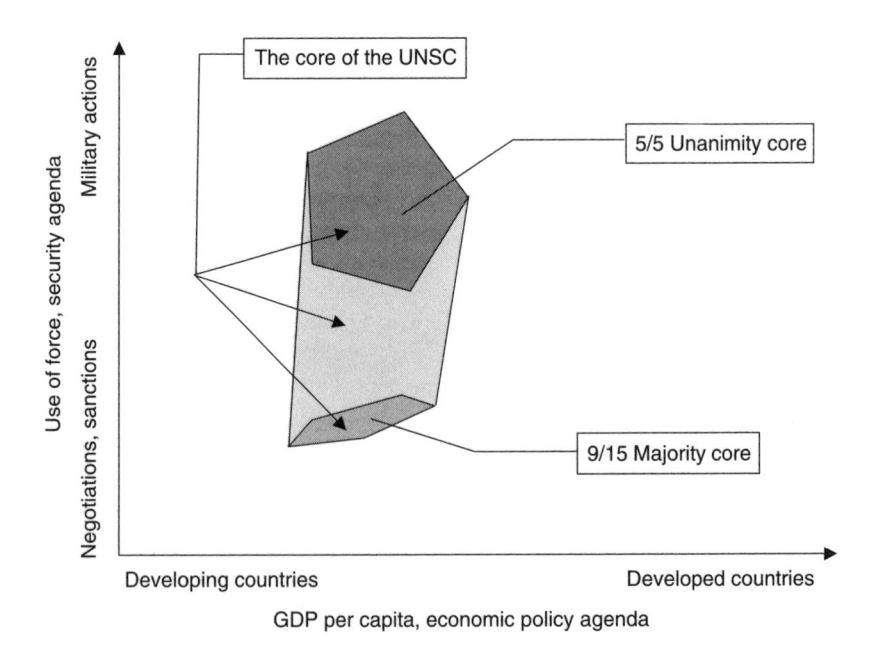

Figure 13.3 The core of the UNSC.

actions occur outside the UNSC or peace violation remains bleeding. The core of the UNSC could serve as a measure of multilateralism in the collective security agenda. The larger the core, the fewer multilateral actions take place under UNSC auspices.

We should mention here, based on Greenberg's theorem,[6] that "the 9/15 qualified majority core" does not always exist in a two-dimensional policy space, since 9/15<2/(2+1). If the preferences of the fifteen members of the decision body are homogeneous enough, the "9/15 qualified majority core" may shrink and disappear. In this case, only within the "five permanent members' unanimity core" is the SQ security case unbeatable. Outside this area we can form draft resolutions, which can be voted for both by the five permanent members and by a combination of nine of the total fifteen members of the UNSC.

Analyzing the main UNSC reform scenarios

In order to obtain a complete picture of the various implications of the above-presented theoretical arguments for the location of the ideal preference points of the member states and the potential changes of the current decision rule to the decision capacity of the UNSC, we are going to examine the following reform scenarios. Firstly, we examine two cases in both of which the potential new members hold veto power. In one case, the new members belong to the developed economies and in the other to the developing ones. In turn, we compose the scenario where none of the new permanent members has individual veto power. In this case, we examine the impact of the new members on the rest of the tripartite decision core, the qualified majority core and the area between the two cores. Thirdly, we examine the scenario where, although no change occurs in the current composition of the permanent members of the UNSC, we allow the relocation of its permanent members on our preference map. Finally, we examine the decision capacity of the UNSC under a potential change of its decision rule, with the presentation of a scenario where the required qualified majority becomes more demanding.

We start our discussion on the various reform scenarios trying to locate both the permanent and the candidate members of the UNSC on the two-dimensional space according to their ideal policy preferences. As mentioned above, the two dimensions are, on the vertical axis, the type of enforcement measures (i.e., the imposition of sanctions or the use of armed force) preferred by states supporting the UNSC actions under Chapter VII of the UN Charter and, on the horizontal axis, states' GDP per capita as an index of their international economic policy preference. Without losing in generalizability, we indicatively choose to quantify coercion on a scale from 0 to 120, where zero stands for the preference of economic sanctions and 120 for the use of military force to deal with threats to the peace, breaches of the peace and acts of aggression. A mix of economic sanctions and threat of using military force lies in between the two extremes.

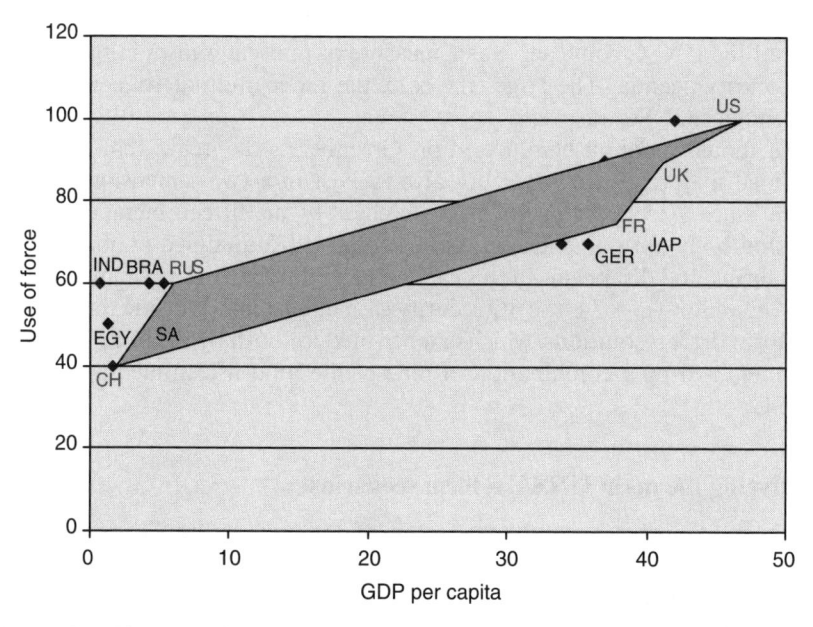

314 *Aris Alexopoulos and Dimitris Bourantonis*

Figure 13.4 The UNSC's preference mapping.

We start our mapping exercise by locating on our policy space the permanent members of the UNSC. What matters in this picture is not the absolute mark but the relative distance between the states. The US, being the most active and taking initiatives for peacemaking, holds the highest score on the scale favoring military force. The UK is the closest to US ideal position; however, in our measurement exercise it obtains a slightly lower score due to segments of domestic pacifists' constraints incorporated into the governing Labor party. Because of both pacifist constraints in the French political system and the anti-US legacy in foreign policy, we locate France close to US but even lower than the UK. Russia, in most of the cases discussed in the UNSC, usually votes in favor of respect for national sovereignty and blocs proposals for the use of military force; for this reason, it takes a much lower grade in our scale. China is in line with Russia, but much more in favor of respect for national sovereignty and against the use of military force, so it takes the lowest grade.

New permanent members with veto power

We now turn our examination on how a reform scenario works by adding, as new permanent members of the UNSC, Germany and Japan – which hold a high probability of becoming the new members of the body. Germany's ideal point on our space is very close to France and the UK. Its GDP per capita and its security policy preference after its post-Cold War transformation resemble those of its major European allies. Actually, Germany for years came close to resembling a civilian power acting with self-imposed constraints in its foreign and security policy. Since the emergence of a new security environment, in the aftermath of the Cold War, the foreign and security policy of Germany has been under a process of change, normalization and emancipation, indicating the country's willingness to display less of a profile of a civilian power and more of a profile of a normal state. Its growing self-image as a great power and its resistance to the US vision of a unipolar world has led Germany to assume more responsibility on the international stage, while continuing to give prominence to multilateralism, especially through the context of the UN and NATO. To this end, Germany has progressively accepted the necessity of taking part in international military operations around the globe. However, in line with the pacifist sentiments of the German public, as four out of five Germans believe that the UN endorsement should be secured before the use of coercive means to deal with international threats or breaches of the peace (Pew Global Attitudes Project 2004), Berlin recognizes force as a last resort. Germany would support the use of force under a UNSC mandate only if its major European partners agreed to participate in such a multilateral action. Based on the above analysis we locate Germany inside or marginally outside the unanimity core of the five permanent members of the current UNSC.

The other front-runner for taking a permanent post at the UNSC is Japan. Japan's traditional pacifism led the state to pursue for many years the role of a global civilian power. However, in the wake of the 11 September terrorist attacks and the rising threat perceptions of North Korea (and China), pacifist and isolationist sentiments have been significantly weakened and a new political and military posture has emerged. This posture drives Japan to become "a global ordinary power" by two means: firstly, by enhancing its military capability for its self-defense in response to feared external threats, as Japan is already one of the world's largest spenders on national defense, and secondly, by assuming a more active role in international security activities. With Japanese policy-making deriving less from ideology than from more pragmatic considerations, the main partisan disagreements among the various political parties competing for power have eased and there is an emerging consensus on foreign and security policy issues, based on two main pillars: alliances with Western countries, principally with the US, and pro-UN orientation. However, differences between the major political parties over these two pillars "are likely to be a question of emphasis with regard to each pillar, rather than disputes over fundamental issues" (Inoguchi and Bacon 2006: 17). As far as Japan's policy vis-à-vis the UN is concerned, there is a shift away from a stance that would tolerate no change in its role as passive observer or an actor engaged only in "checkbook diplomacy" by simply contributing money to the UN, towards assuming "international responsibilities" which permanent membership in the UNSC entails. After Japan's involvement in the war against Afghanistan and its military support for the US-led war against Iraq in 2003, the clamor in Japan is pervasive for pushing its policy preferences toward playing a more active role in UN affairs, including the endorsement of the use of force. To this end, the major Japanese political forces are prone to make revisions to the pacifist contribution and more specifically to the so-called no-war clause of Article 9, which, according to 1992 Diet legislation, allows the participation of Japan in peacekeeping operations, but still prohibits the country from taking part in military operations under Chapter VII of the UN Charter. For this reason, we believe that in the near future the ideal point of Japan will also be inside or on the borders of the current unanimity UNSC core.

Hence, our analysis drives us to the conclusion that a potential enlargement of the UNSC with Germany and Japan as its new permanent members that would also hold the privilege of institutional veto, will not change the decision capacity of the Council, since the ideal points of the new members are within the current unanimity core of the five old members.

Other candidates, however, with a much lower GDP per capita are India, Brazil, Egypt and South Africa. New members from the pool of developing economies spread to a significant degree the ideal points of the members of the UNSC across the foreign economic policy variable in our preference mapping exercise. This is enough to drive us to the conclusion that, contrary to the case of Japan and Germany, a potential enlargement of the UNSC with developing countries holding veto power increases the size of the unanimity core and reduces its decision capacity.

New permanent members without veto power

We move our discussion to the examination of the most popular reform scenarios. These reform proposals (see the scenarios of the High-Level Panel) do not propose the expansion of veto to new members, so the unanimity core in the new decision structure remains unchanged. In this case, the proposed new members, no matter whether they hold a permanent or a non-permanent post, will affect the rest of the tripartite decision core, the qualified majority core and the area between the two cores. In order to examine the impact of the above-mentioned developing states as permanent members and speculate on the implications of such an enlargement for the UNSC's decision capacity, we need to locate their ideal points not only according to their GDP per capita but also across the security policy dimension. We do this exercise by examining India, South Africa, Brazil and Egypt, which so far have shown greater probability of becoming the new permanent members, without, however, any veto power in a potential UNSC reform.

In the interest of *realpolitik* and national interest, India attempted from the early 1990s onward to redefine its foreign policy, in order to suit the requirements of a greatly altered international order. Its commitment to the Non-Aligned Movement (NAM) – a guiding factor in its foreign policy – eased as its foreign policy began to shift towards more pragmatism and its increasing self-awareness that it has the potential to emerge, due to its strategic importance and its military capability, as a great power in its own right. As a result, India has underplayed the role of the leader of the NAM, it has come closer to the West, especially to US, and has discarded the anti-great power impulses that shaped its foreign policy during the Cold War. India, as an ardent supporter of multilateralism through the UN, is expected to develop as a permanent member of the UNSC a stronger sense of international responsibility, as part of its great-power ambitions, and give its vote for the imposition of sanctions in cases that fall within Chapter VII of the UN Charter. However, as far as the tension between the old and the new directions remains an enduring one in India's foreign policy, doubts are thrown upon India's ability to push its preferences still further to endorse the use of force. Such ability will depend on the nature of the issue and the circumstances prevailing in India's domestic politics at the particular time when an issue is being considered by the UNSC. The above analysis leads us to locate India closer to the pacifist side with a moderate inclination to the use of force to invade countries and we mark its ideal security preference somewhere close to that of Russia.

Regarding the case of South Africa, mainly due to its recent transformation to a democratic system of governance, this state has shown a lack of ability to articulate a coherent foreign policy agenda that would enable it to establish a distinctive niche for itself in world affairs. As a middle power, it is characterized by a tendency to pursue multilateral approaches to world issues, a tendency to embrace compromise positions in international disputes and a willingness to maintain a degree of autonomy in relation to major powers (Cilliers 1999). As an African state, it has been too assertive of "African renaissance," which has become a central element of the country's international objectives. Being very active in grappling with the continent's problems and having a leadership role within the African Union and the NAM (Hamill and Lee 2001: 37), where it acts as a champion of the underdog on the basis of anti-North bias, South Africa is committed to non-interference and to solution of conflicts by political rather than coercive means. Evidence of this can be found in the leading role it played towards the adoption by the African Union of the "Ezulwini Consensus," a document that contains the African position on UN issues.[7] The document is highly critical even of the imposition of sanctions, which according to the African states could be decided by the UNSC only if a strict set of conditions was met. Taking all this into account, one can assume that South Africa as a permanent member of the UNSC would hardly go further to endorse the use of force, so its mark on our scale is the lowest.

Egypt now views its international role as a mediator, particularly in solving disputes between various Arab states in an effort to shape the norms of intra-Arab relations and trying to advance the peace process between Israel and the Arabs. Its mediating role in intra-Arab disputes has been welcomed by most Arab states, which have given credence to Egypt playing that role, viewing it as entirely consistent with the notion of "Arabness" (Alterman 2005: 359). As a bridge to the Arab world and as a broker in the Israeli-Palestinian conflict, Egypt has enhanced its value to the US, the relationship with which remains a keystone of Egypt's foreign policy. As has been pointed out, sometimes Egypt exploits its role as a broker and "frequently helps frame an agenda that is much more to U.S. liking than would otherwise be the case" (Alterman 2003: 4). In all probability, Egypt, as a permanent member of the UNSC, in which most of the issues concern Middle East and Africa, would do its outmost to sustain the profile of mediator. It seems unlikely to support the use of force under a UN mandate except in acts of aggression that constitute blatant violations of the principle of non-intervention similar to that the Arab region experienced in 1990 when Iraq invaded Kuwait.[8] Should Egypt have supported the use of force under Chapter VII of the UN Charter, it might have undermined its ability to maintain, internally and externally, its profile of mediator. Egypt, which along with the other NAM countries has accused the UNSC of "increasingly resorting to Chapter VII of the UN Charter as an umbrella for addressing issues that do not necessarily pose a threat to international peace and security,"[9] is against the imposition of any "preventive" sanctions.[10] This drives us to argue that Egypt is in favor of "targeted" sanctions as a last resort under strict conditions and only after all means of peaceful settlement have been exhausted. Therefore, we give to Egypt the same mark as South Africa.

At last, we try to locate Brazil on our map. In recent years, Brazil's foreign policy has departed from its traditional tendencies of aloofness, that was mainly due to the serious domestic (political and economic) problems it had to address, toward developing a more assertive and pragmatic role in its region and even broadly in the wider international context. Despite the fact that Brazil maintains a strong notion of sovereignty and is guided in the conduct of its international relations by the principles of non-intervention, non-interference and the peaceful solution of disputes, enshrined in the 1988 Constitution, it has in practice employed double standards in its policy vis-à-vis enforcement actions under Chapter VII of the UN Charter. It seeks to play the dominant role in regional crisis management without resorting to the use of sanctions or armed force. For instance, Brazil, as non-permanent member of the UNSC, did not vote for UNSC Resolution 940 of 1994, which authorized the member states to "use all necessary means to facilitate the departure from Haiti of the military leadership."[11] At the broader international level, Brazil has maintained that the UNSC can make use of its powers under Chapter VII "in clear exceptional circumstances" as in Somalia in 1994 and Iraq in 1991.[12] Brazil voted in favour of UNSC Resolution 897 of 1994, which reaffirmed the obligation of states to fully implement the embargo imposed by Resolution 733 of 1992. It also supported Resolution 678 of 1990 during the Gulf War by using the

UN Security Council: a veto players analysis 319

argument that it was about an invasion that took place outside the Latin American region.[13] Based on the above evidence we give Brazil the same mark as Russia and India.

Based on the above comparative evaluation, we observe that, despite the dominant impression within the security policy community and also within wider public opinion, the security policy preference of these less developed countries converges with the ideal points of the current permanent members from the pool of the developed economies (see Figure 13.4 on page 314). More specifically, we observe this trend of convergence in contrast to divergence across the economic variable of our mapping exercise. This may lead us to assert that the size of the qualified majority core and its distance from the unchanged unanimity core will change only marginally. So it is reasonable to argue that, even with the addition of this type of countries to the bundle of permanent members, the decision capacity of the UNSC might stay unchanged and in any case would not be reduced dramatically.

The potential relocation of the current permanent members of the UNSC

Another aspect we want to examine, in order to obtain a complete picture of the various implications of the location of member states' ideal preference points for the decision capacity of the UNSC, is the potential relocation of the current permanent members on our preference map. Suppose we take a hypothetical, but realistic scenario for the decision capacity of the UNSC 20 to 25 years from now without any reform in its current function. The new element that will change drastically the size of the unanimity core of the UNSC is the transfer of Russia and China to the bundle of developed countries. Both are fast-growing economies, especially China, which has taken off and perhaps in less than 30 years' time will land close to the average GPD per capita of western European economies such as Germany, France, and the UK. This development would make the unanimity core of much smaller size and, therefore, the decision capacity of the UNSC would increase accordingly. In this case, the blocking role of non-permanent members from the less developed states would be increased. The location of the ideal preference points of these countries might influence the qualified majority core and the area between the two cores (see Figure 13.3 on page 312) in such a way that the total core of the UNSC might be larger than the current core, which includes a larger unanimity core. The loss in unbeatable points in the unanimity core, due to the convergence of China and Russia with the rest of the current permanent members, could be compensated by new points in the two other parts of the total UNSC core. However, we must not forget that these states may be located on our space in such a way that the q-core (the small polygon in Figure 13.3) is empty. In this case these countries have no impact on the decision capacity of the UNSC. If the five permanent members reach an agreement on a draft proposal outside their

320 *Aris Alexopoulos and Dimitris Bourantonis*

unanimity core they will also obtain a majority of 9/15 to make it a UNSC resolution.

A scenario with a more demanding decision rule

Let us now examine another element in a potential reform proposal. What happens to the qualified majority core if we change the decision rule and make it more demanding by moving it, let us say, from 9/15 to 10/15?

It is easy to verify[14] that the shaded polygon representing the 9/15-majority core in Figure 13.2 will also expand. This drives us to the conclusion that the decision capacity of the fifteen-member body, with its composition remaining unchanged, will be reduced. We can also see, as in the case of any unanimity core (see Figure 13.1), that if the ideal points of the members change by moving apart from their current position, then the "9/15 core" will expand too. However, we can observe a smaller 10/15 than a 9/15 "qualified majority core" by adding new members in the decision body which hold ideal points on our two-dimensional space in such a way that makes the initial 9/15 core to shrink. Hence, we cannot predict whether the decision capacity of the UNSC will decrease if we just enlarge it and make its decision rule more demanding.

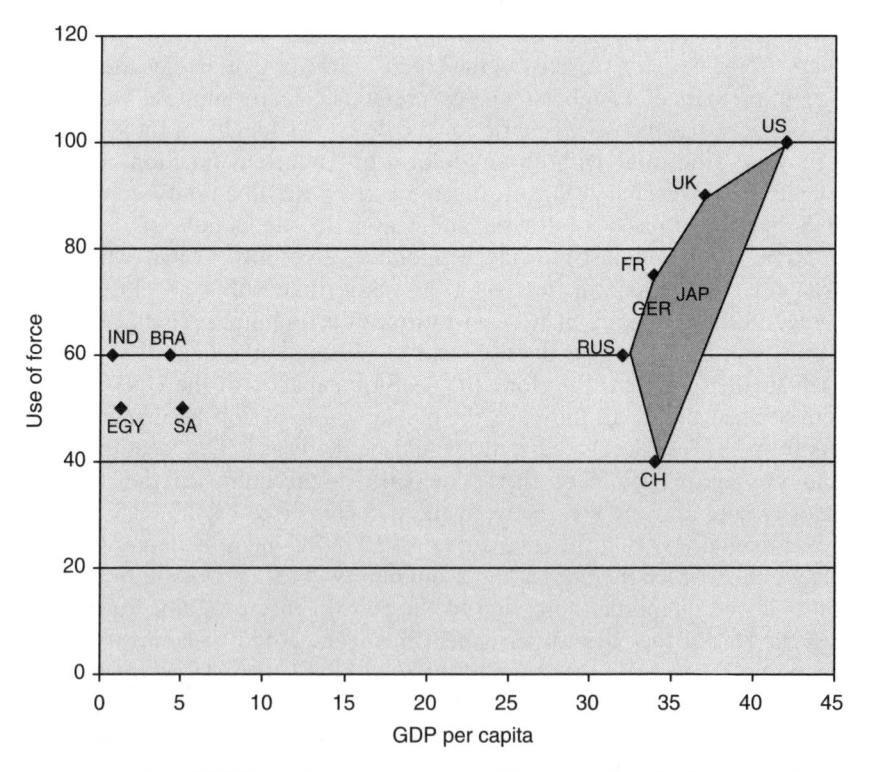

Figure 13.5 The UNSC's preference mapping in 25 years: a hypothetical scenario.

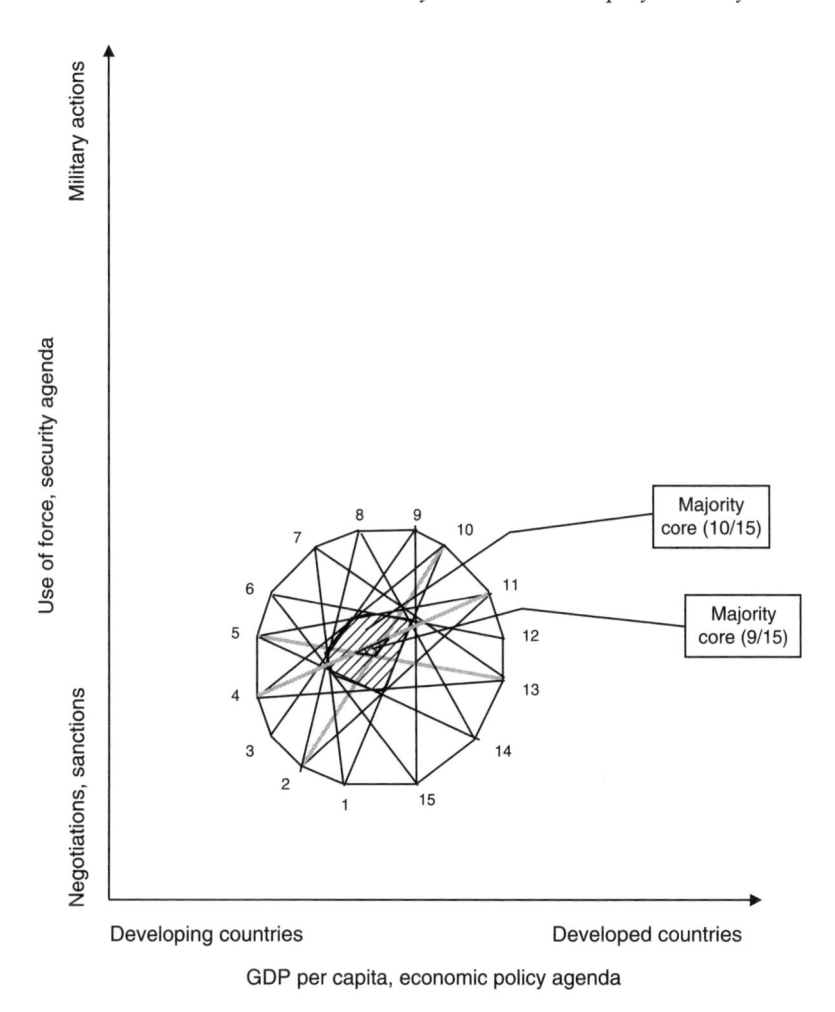

UN Security Council: a veto players analysis 321

Figure 13.6 A fifteen-member decision body in a two-dimensional policy space, with majority core 10/15 (compared with a majority core 9/15).

The knowledge of the new size of the body is not enough to drive us to a safe inference. In order to determine the outcome of such an exercise we also need to know the exact position of the ideal preference points of all the members of our modified decision body.

Concluding remarks

Our discussion may be summarized as follows. According to Tsebelis' veto players theory, the important element for the decision capacity of the UNSC is not its size but the location of the ideal preference points of its members and the decision rule according to which these members vote for the proposed draft resolutions. We have shown that it is misleading to connect, as many used to do, enlargement with less decision capacity in the UNSC. We have shown that we could have a UNSC larger than the current one, with more permanent members equipped with institutional veto power, which could however arrive at a decision with less difficulty than the current, smaller UNSC. We examined the various reform scenarios based on the main analytical tool provided by the veto players theory, according to which, the larger the core is, the smaller is the decision capacity of a decision body. We have found that the three parts of the core of the UNSC may be reshaped in various and many times opposite directions, which make prediction of its decision capacity an extremely demanding exercise. However, we managed to show that the key element in the solution of this puzzle is the positioning of the member states on the decision space, and not the size of the decision body.

Finally, we want to exclusively state that our motivation to do this work was not to embark upon a normative discussion of the future of the UNSC. On the contrary, we tried to limit ourselves to positive discussion, locating our arguments on the same side as those who believe that the fruitful way to do social science is not to mix the two cognitive worlds. We also share the opinion that positive evidence may help a better normative discussion based on feasible goals and more efficient means. If the goal is a more efficient UNSC, we have shown that this has nothing to do with its size. If the goal is to increase the legitimacy of the decisions of the UNSC, and we want to do this based on input legitimacy, we could increase its size in order to make it more representative without losing in efficiency. On the contrary, the efficiency might be improved if we chose, as new members, states with ideal preference points over security and foreign economic policy located in such a way as to drive the current decision core to shrink.

Notes

1 See Laurenti (1997: 11); Russett et al. (1997: 155); Blum (2005: 632); Zacher (2003: 11), Reisman (1993: 96).
2 Kim and Russett (1996) arrived at the conclusion that there are two significant, underlined factors in the voting behavior of states: the issue of self-determination of states and the promotion of political rights in domestic politics. Some years later, with the same data set, Voeten (2000) showed these results of factor analysis were false, with an alternative method called nominate model and concluded that the post-Cold War voting behavior of states in the UNGA is one-dimensional, according to hegemonic or antihegemonic preference of the states in the world security system.
3 For arguments in favor of unidimentionality, see also Frieden (2004).
4 Dreher, Sturm and Vreeland (2006) argue and provide evidence that there is a positive correlation between a country's participation in IMF programmes and the coincidence of this country being a member of the UNSC. The IMF loans provided to these countries increased during their service on the UNSC and decreased before and after the service.

5 Kim and Russett (1996: 648) in their statistical evaluation of the roll-call votes of the UNGA find strong correlation between the first dimension produced by factor analyzing the data, the self-determination dimension, and GNP per capita, with a coefficient of very high negative value (−7.5). For indicative arguments in favor of or against the use of GDP for measuring the power and influence of countries on foreign affairs, see also the discussion in Fearon (2005).
6 According to Greenberg (1979), a core always exists if $q<n/(n+1)$, where q is the decision rule and n the dimensionality of the policy space.
7 See "The Common Position of the Proposed Reform of the United Nations: The Ezulwini Consensus," African Union, Executive Council, 7th Extraordinary Session, 7–8 March 2005.
8 During the Gulf War of 1991, Egypt supported the use of force under the terms of Resolution 678 of the UNSC.
9 See "Comments of the Non-Aligned Movement on the Observations and Recommendations Contained in the Report of the High-Level Panel on Threats, Challenges and Change," UN Doc. A/59/565 and A/59/565 CORR.1, 28 February 2005, p. 6.
10 Ibid., p. 17.
11 See Resolution 940 adopted by the UNSC on 31 July 1994.
12 See the remarks of Mr Castro, Permanent Represntative of Brazil to the UN, in UN Doc. S/PV.3334, 4 February 1994, pp. 27–8.
13 See the remarks of Mr Sardenberg, Permanent Representative of Brazil to the UN, in UN Doc. S/PV.3413, 31 July 1994, p. 9.
14 Tsebelis and Yataganas show the same for a seven-member decision body and a 5/7 decision rule. See G. Tsebelis and X. Yataganas (2005) "The Treaty of Nice, the Convention Proposal, and the Treaty Establishing a Constitution for Europe: A Veto Players Analysis", *European Constitutional Law Review* 1(3): 429–51.

References

Abbott, K. and Snidal, D. (1998) "Why States Act through Formal International Organizations", *Journal of Conflict Resolution* 42(1): 3–32.

Abbott, K., Keohane, R., Moravcsik, A., Slaughter, A-M. and Snidal, D. (2000) "The Concept of Legalization", *International Organization* 54(3): 401–19.

Acharya, A. (1991) "Association of Southeast Asian Nations: 'Security Community' or 'Defence Community'?", *Pacific Affairs* 64(2): 159–78.

Acharya, A. (1999) "A Concert of Asia", *Survival* 41(3): 84–101.

Acharya, A. (2001) *Constructing a Security Community in Southeast Asia: ASEAN and the Problem of Regional Order*, London: Routledge.

Acharya, A. (2004) "How Ideas Spread: Whose Norms Matter? Norm Localization and Institutional Change in Asian Regionalism", *International Organization* 58(2): 239–76.

Acharya, A. and Tan, S.S. (2004) "Introduction", in S.S. Tan and A. Acharya (eds), *Asia-Pacific Security Cooperation: National Interests and Regional Order*, Armonk, NY: ME Sharpe.

Acharya, A. and Tan, S.S. (2006) "Betwixt Balance and Community: America, ASEAN, and the Security of Southeast Asia", *International Relations of the Asia-Pacific* 6(1): 37–59.

Ackerman, B., and Golove, D. (1995) "Is NAFTA Constitutional?", *Harvard Law Review* 108(4): 799–929.

Adler, E. and Barnett, M. (1998a) "A Framework for the Study of Security Communities", in Adler and Barnett (eds) *Security Communities*, Cambridge: Cambridge UP, pp. 29–65.

Adler, E. and Barnett, M. (eds) (1998b) *Security Communities*, Cambridge: Cambridge UP.

Alford, H. (2000) *Organization Evolving*, Thousand Oaks, CA: Sage.

Alford, J. (1984), *Greece and Turkey: Adversity in Alliance*, New York: St. Martin's Press.

Allison, R. (2004) "Regionalism, Regional Structures and Security Management in Central Asia", *International Affairs* 80(3): 463–83.

Alter, K.J. (2000) "The European Union's Legal System and Domestic Policy: Spillover or Backlash?", *International Organization*, 54(3): 489–518.

Alterman, J. (2003) "The United States and Egypt: Building the Partnership", *Middle East Note*, Washington, DC: Center for Strategic and International Studies.

Alterman, J. (2005) "Dynamics Without Drama: New Options and Old Compromises

in Egypt's Foreign Policy", *Cambridge Review of International Affairs* 18(3): 357–69.
Altmann, F.L. and Whitlock, E. (eds) (2004) *European and US Policies in the Balkans*, Berlin: Stiftung Wissenschaft und Politik.
Alvesson, M. (1993) *Cultural Perspectives on Organizations*, New York: Cambridge UP.
American Society of International Law (1999) Forum on Kosovo, 93(4), October.
Amoo, G.S. and Zartman, I.W. (1992) "Mediation by Regional Organizations: The Organization for African Unity (OAU) in Chad", in J. Bercovitch and J.Z. Rubin (eds) *Mediation in International Relations. Multiple Approaches to Conflict Management*, New York, St. Martin's Press, pp. 131–48.
Anderson, B. (1983) *Imagined Communities: Reflections on the Origin and Spread of Nationalism*, New York: Verso.
Anderson, B. (1991) *Imagined Communities: Reflections on the Origins and Spread of Nationalism*, London: Verso.
Anderson, J., Ikenberry, G.J. and Risse, T. (eds) (2008) *The End of the West? Crisis and Change in the Transatlantic Order*, Ithaca, NY: Cornell UP.
Anderson, J., Ikenberry, G.J. and Risse, T. (eds) (forthcoming) *The End of the West? The Crisis of the Transatlantic Relationship*, Ithaca, NY: Cornell UP.
Anderson, K. (2004) "Humanitarian Inviolability in Crisis: The Meaning of Impartiality and Neutrality for U.N. and NGO Agencies Following the 2003–2004 Afghanistan and Iraq Conflicts", *Harvard Human Rights Journal*, 17 (Spring): 41–74.
Annan, K. (2000) *We The Peoples: The Role of the United Nations in the 21st Century*, New York: United Nations.
Annan, K. (2002) "Democracy as an International Issue", *Global Governance*, 8(2): 134–42.
Apthorpe, R. (2001) "International Emergency Relief Aid in Kosovo 1999–2000: Was it Humanitarian or Not?", paper presented at Kosovo and the Changing Face of Humanitarian Action Conference, Uppsala, Sweden, May.
Arquilla, J. and Ronfeldt, D. (2001) *Networks and Netwars: The Future of Terror, Crime, and Militancy*, Santa Monica, CA: RAND Corporation.
Art, R. (1996) "Why Western Europe Needs the United States and NATO", *Political Science Quarterly* 111(1): 1–39.
ASEAN (2003a) "Declaration of ASEAN Concord II (Bali Concord II)", Online at <http://www.aseansec.org/15160.htm> (accessed on 23 February 2006).
ASEAN (2003b) *ASEAN Statistical Yearbook*, Jakarta: The ASEAN Secretariat.
ASEAN (2004) "ASEAN Security Community Plan of Action", Online at <http://www.aseansec.org/16827.htm> (accessed on 26 April 2005).
Ashdown, P. (2003) "The Rule of Law in a Post-War Society: The Latest Developments from Bosnia and Herzegovina", 80 Club Lecture, 19 June.
Ashdown, P. (2004a) "Yes, I did go to Karadzic", OHR Press Office, 24 January.
Ashdown, P. (2004b) Press Interview, 30 June, CEPS *Europa-South East Monitor*, Issue 56.
Asmus, R., Everts, P. and Isernia, P. (2003) *Power, War, and Public Opinion. Thoughts on the Nature and Structure of the Trans-Atlantic Divide*, Washington, DC: Transatlantic Trends.
Augustine of Hippo (427/1991), *City of God*, XIX, 13: 1, London: Penguin Classics.
Axelrod, R. (1998) "How to Negotiate for Reform of the UN Security Council", Online at <http://www-personal.umich.edu/~axe/>.

References

Axelrod, R. and Keohane, R. (1986) "Introduction" and "Conclusion," in K. Oye (ed.) *Cooperation Under Anarchy*, Princeton: Princeton UP.

Aybet, G. (2000) *A European Security Architecture after the Cold War: Questions of Legitimacy*, Houndmills: Macmillan Press.

Ba, A.D. (2005) "On Norms, Rule-breaking, and Security Communities: A Constructivist Response", *International Relations of the Asia-Pacific* 5(2): 255–66.

Bac, M.M. (2003) "Turkey's Political Reforms and the Impact of the European Union", *South European Society and Politics* 10(1): 17–31.

Bahr, E. (2003) *Der deutsche Weg. Selbstverständlich und Normal*, München: Karl Blessing Verlag.

Bailes, A.J.K. (2003) "Armament and Disarmament in the Caucasus and Central Asia: An Introduction" in A.J.K. Bailes et al. (eds) *Armament and Disarmament in the Caucasus and Central Asia*, Stockholm: SIPRI, policy paper, no. 3, pp. 1–7.

Baker, J.A. (1995) *The Politics of Diplomacy: Revolution, War and Peace, 1989–1992*, New York: Putnam's Sons.

Balch-Lindsay, D. and Enterline, A.J. (2000) "Killing Time: The World Politics of Civil War Duration, 1820–1992", *International Studies Quarterly* 44(4): 615–42.

Barnett, M. (1997) "Bringing in the New World Order: Liberalism, Legitimacy, and the United Nations", *World Politics* 49(4): 526–51.

Barnett, M. (2005) "Humanitarianism Transformed", *Perspectives on Politics*, 3(4): 723–40.

Barnett, M. and Finnemore, M. (1999) "The Politics, Power, and Pathologies of IOs", *International Organization* 53(4): 699–732.

Barnett, M. and Finnemore, M. (2004) *Rules for the World: International Organizations and World Politics*, Ithaca, NY: Cornell UP.

Bass, G.J. (2000) *Staying the Hand of Vengeance: The Politics of War Crimes Tribunals*. Princeton, NJ: Princeton UP.

Batt, J. (2004) "Introduction: The Stabilization/Integration Dilemma", in J. Batt (ed.) *The Western Balkans: Moving On*, Chaillot Paper No. 70, Paris: Institute for Security Studies.

BBC World Service (2005) "In 18 of 21 Countries Polled, Most See Bush's Re-election as Negative for World Security", London: BBC World Service 22-Nation Poll on Bush's Re-election, 19 January.

Beetham, D. (1985) *Max Weber and the Theory of Modern Politics*, New York: Polity.

Beitz, C. (1979) *Political Theory and International Relations*. Princeton, NJ: Princeton UP.

Beitz, C. (1994) "Cosmopolitan Liberalism and the States System", in C. Brown (ed.) *Political Restructuring in Europe: Ethical Perspectives*, London: Routledge, pp. 123–36.

Bellamy, A, and Williams, P. (2004) Special Issue on Peace Operations and Global Order, *International Peacekeeping* 10(4): 1–212.

Bellamy, A.J. and Williams, P.D. (2005) "Who's Keeping the Peace? Regionalization and Contemporary Peace Operations", *International Security* 29(4): 157–95.

Bendor, J., Glazer, A. and Hammond, T. (2001) "Theories of Delegation", *Annual Review of Political Science* 4: 235–69.

Bennett, A., Lepgold, J. and Unger, D. (1994) "Burden-Sharing in the Persian Gulf War", *International Organization* 48(1): 39–75.

Bercovitch, J. and Langley, J. (1993) "The Nature of Dispute and the Effectiveness of International Mediation", *Journal of Conflict Resolution* 37(4): 670–91.

Berman, S. (2003) "Islamism, Revolution, and Civil Society", *Perspectives on Politics*, 1(2): 257–72.
Best, G. (1994) *War and Law since 1945*, Oxford: Clarendon Press.
Blair, T. (1999) "Doctrine of the International Community", speech delivered to the Economic Club of Chicago, 22 April. Online at <http://www.globalpolicy.org/globaliz/politics/blair.htm>.
Bleiker, R. (2000) *Popular Dissent, Human Agency, and Global Politics*, Cambridge: Cambridge UP.
Blokker, N. (2000) "Is the Authorization Authorized? Powers and Practice of the UN Security Council to Authorize the Use of Force by Coalitions of the Able and Willing", *European Journal of International Law* 11(3): 541–68.
Blum, Y. (2005), "Proposals for UN Security Council Reform", *American Journal of International Law* 99(3): 632–49.
Bobbitt, P. (2002) *The Shield of Achilles: War, Peace, and the Course of History*, New York: Anchor Books.
Bocheva, L. and Martin, L. (2001) "Institutional Effects on Satte Behavior: Convergence and Divergence", *International Studies Quarterly* 45(1): 1–26.
Boli, J. and Thomas, G. (eds) (1999) *Constructing World Culture: International Nongovernmental Organizations Since 1875*, Stanford, CA: Stanford UP.
Bolton, P. and Dewatripont, M. (2005) *Contract Theory*, Cambridge: MIT Press.
Borowiec, A. (1983), *The Mediterranean Feud*, New York: Praeger.
Börzel, T.A. and Risse, T. (2000) *When Europe Hits Home: Europeanization and Domestic Change*, European Integration online Papers (EIoP) Vol. 4, No. 15, Online at <http://www.eiop.or.at/eiop/texte/2000-015a.htm>.
Börzel, T.A. and Risse, T. (2004) *One Size Fits All! EU Policies for the Promotion of Human Rights, Democracy and the Rule of Law*, paper prepared for the Workshop on Democracy Promotion, 4–5 October, Center for Development, Democracy and the Rule of Law, Stanford University–Heidelberg–Berlin: Institution.
Bose, S. (2005) "The Bosnian State a Decade after Dayton", *International Peacekeeping* 12(3): 322–35.
Bouchet-Saulnier, F. (2000) "Between Humanitarian Law and Principles: The Principles and Practices of "Rebellious Humanitarianism" ", Online at <http://www.msf.org/msfinternational/invoke.cfm?component=article&objectid=6589C8A5-DC2C-11D4-B2010060084A6370&method=full_html>.
Bourantonis, D. (2005) *The History and Politics of UN Security Council Reform*, London: Routledge.
Bourantonis, D. and Panagiotou, R. (2004) "Russia's Attitude towards the Reform of the United Nations Security Council, 1990–2000", *Journal of Communist Studies and Transition Politics* 20(4): 79–102.
Bradol, J.H. (2004) "The Sacrificial International Order", in F. Weissman (ed.) *In the Shadow of "Just Wars": Violence, Politics, and Humanitarian Action*, Ithaca, NY: Cornell UP, pp. 1–22.
Braml, J. (2004) "Die religiöse Rechte in den USA", SWP-Studie, S 35. Berlin: Stiftung Wissenschaft und Politik, September.
Brooks, S. and Wohlforth, W. (2002) "American Primacy in Perspective", *Foreign Affairs* 81(4): 20–33.
Brooks, S. and Wohlforth, W. (2005) "International Relations Theory and the Case against Unilateralism", *Perspectives on Politics* 3(3): 509–24.
Bukovansky, M. (2002) *Legitimacy and Power Politics*. Princeton, NJ: Princeton UP.

Bulmer, S., Jeffery, C. and Paterson, W.E. (2000) *Germany's European Diplomacy: Shaping the Regional Milieu*, Manchester: Manchester UP.
Burchell, G., Gordon, C. and Miller, G. (eds) *The Foucault Effect: Studies in Governmentality*, Hemel Hempstead, Herts: Harvester Wheatsheaf.
Burns, J.F. (2002) "Political Realities Impeding Full Inquiry into Afghan Atrocity", *New York Times*, 29 August.
Byers, M. (1999) *Custom, Power, and the Power of Rules: International Relations and Customary International Law*, Cambridge: Cambridge UP.
Caldeira, G.A. and Gibson, J.L. (1995) "The Legitimacy of the Court of Justice in the European Union: Models of Institutional Support", *American Political Science Review* 89(2): 356–77.
Calhoun, C. (2004) "A World of Emergencies: Fear, Intervention, and the Limits of Cosmopolitan Order", Online at <http://www.google.com/search?q=cache:JrRXlGFxbucJ:www.ssrc.org/programs/calhoun/publications/a_world_of_emergencies.pdf+%22World+of+Emergencies%22&hl=en>.
Camacho, C., Higgins, T. and Luger, L. (2003) "Moral Value Transfer from Regulatory Fit: "What Feels Right *Is* Right" and "What Feels Wrong *Is* Wrong" ", *Journal of Personality and Social Psychology* 84(3): 498–510.
Cambell, D. (1992) *Writing Security*, Minneapolis: University of Minnesota Press.
Cantaloube, T. and Vernet, H. (2004). *Chirac contre Bush: l'Autre Guerre*, Paris: Jean-Claude Lattes.
Caplan, R. (2002) *A New Trusteeship? The International Administration of War-torn Territories*, The Adelphi Papers, Oxford: Oxford UP.
Caplan, R. (2005) "Who Guards the Guardians? International Accountability in Bosnia", *International Peacekeeping* 12(3): 463–76.
Caporaso, A. (1993) "International Relations Theory and Multilateralism: The Search for Foundations" in J.G. Ruggie (ed.) *Multilateralism Matters: The Theory and Praxis of an Institutional Form*, New York: Columbia UP, pp. 51–90.
Caporaso, J. (1992) "IR Theory and Multilateralism", *International Organization* 46(3): 599–632.
Carlson, C. (2003) "Central Asia: Shanghai Cooperation Organization Makes Military Debut", Online at <http://globalsecurity.org/military/library/news/2003/08/mil-03085-rfel54708.htm> (accessed on 5 May 2005).
Caron, D. (1993) "The Legitimacy of the Collective Authority of the Security Council", *American Journal of International Law* 87(4): 552–88.
Carothers, T. (1999) *Aiding Democracy Abroad*, Washington, DC: Carnegie Endowment for International Peace.
Carr, E.H. (1938) *The Twenty Years' Crisis, 1919–39: An Introduction to the Study of International Relations*, London: Macmillan.
Carter, A.B. (1999–2000) "Adapting US Defense to Future Needs", *Survival* 41(4): 101–23.
Carter, A.B. and Perry, W.J. (1999) *Preventive Defense: A New Security Strategy for America*, Washington, DC: Brookings Institution.
Carter, W.H. (1936) in the Foreword to C. Van Vollenhoven, *The Law of Peace*, London: Macmillan.
Cassese, A. (1999) "*Ex Iniuria Ius Oritur*: Are We Moving Towards International Legitimation of Forcible Humanitarian Countermeasures?", *European Journal of International Law* 10(1): 23–30.
Ceadal, M. (1987) *Thinking about Peace and War*, Oxford: Oxford UP.

Celik B.A., and Rumelili, B. (2006) "Necessary but not Sufficient: The Role of the EU in Resolving Turkey's Kurdish Question and the Greek-Turkish Conflicts", *European Foreign Affairs Review* 11(2): 203–22.

Chan, S. (1997) "In Search of Democratic Peace: Problems and Promise", *Mershon International Studies Review* 41(1): 59–91.

Chandler, D. (2002) *From Kosovo to Kabul: Human Rights and International Intervention*, London: Pluto.

Chandler, D. (2004) "The Responsibility to Protect: Imposing the "Liberal Peace" ", *International Peacekeeping* 11(1): 59–81.

Chayes, A. and Chayes, A. (1993) "On Compliance", *International Organization* 47(2): 175–205.

Chayes, A. and Chayes, A. (eds) (1996) *Preventing Conflict in the Post-Communist World: Mobilizing International and Regional Organizations*, Washington, DC: Brookings Institution.

Checkel, J.T. (1997) "International Norms and Domestic Politics: Bridging the Rationalist-Constructivist Divide", *European Journal of International Relations* 3(4): 473–95.

Checkel, J.T. (1998) "The Constructivist Turn in International Relations Theory", *World Politics* 50(2): 324–48.

Checkel, J.T. (1999) "Why Comply? Constructivism, Social Norms and the Study of International Institutions", Oslo, ARENA Working Paper, no. 24.

Checkel, J.T. (2000) "Compliance and Conditionality", ARENA Working Paper, WP 00/18.

Checkel, J.T. (2001a) "Taking Deliberation Seriously", ARENA Working Paper, WP 01/14.

Checkel, J.T. (2001b) "Why Comply? Social Learning and European Identity Change", *International Organization* 55(3): 553–88.

Checkel, J.T. (2005) "International Institutions and Socialization in Europe: Introduction and Framework", *International Organization* 59(4): 801–26.

Choo, J. (2003) "The Geopolitics of Central Asian Energy" in J. Sperling, S. Kay and S.V. Papacosma (eds) *Limiting Institutions? The Challenge of Eurasian Security Governance*, Manchester: Manchester UP, pp. 112–77.

Chopra, J. (2000) "The UN's Kingdom of East Timor", *Survival* 42(3): 27–39.

Chopra, J. and Hohe, T. (2004) "Participatory Intervention", *Global Governance* 10(3): 289–305.

Christopher, W. (1998) *In the Stream of History: Shaping Foreign Policy for a New Era*, Palo Alto, CA: Stanford UP.

Cilliers, J. (1999) *An Emerging South African Foreign Policy?*, Institute for Security Studies, Occasional paper, no. 39, April.

Clark, A.M. (2001) *Diplomacy of Conscience: Amnesty International and Changing Human Rights Norms*, Princeton, NJ: Princeton UP.

Clark, I. (2001) *The Post-Cold War Order*, Oxford: Oxford UP.

Clark, W. (2002) *Waging Modern War*, New York: Public Affairs Press.

Claude, I. (1966) "Collective Legitimization as a Political Function of the United Nations", *International Organization* 20(3): 367–79.

Cogan, C. (2003) *French Negotiating Behavior: Dealing with La Grande Nation*, Washington, DC: Institute of Peace.

Coicaud, J.-M. (2001) "International Organizations, the Evolution of International Politics, and Legitimacy", in J.-M. Coicaud and V. Heiskanen (eds) *The Legitimacy of International Organizations*, Tokyo and New York: United Nations UP, pp. 189–220.

Congressional Research Service [CRS] (1993) *Treaties and Other International Agreements: The Role of the United States Senate*, Washington, DC: Government Printing Office.

Constas, D. (ed.) *The Greek–Turkish Conflict in the 1990s: Domestic and External Influences*, New York: St. Martin's Press, pp. 157–163.

Cooley, A. and Ron, J. (2002) "The NGO Scramble", *International Security* 27(1): 5–39.

Cooper, R. (2003) *The Breaking of Nations*, London: Atlantic Books.

Cortell, A.P. and Davis, J.W. (1996) "How Do International Institutions Matter? The Domestic Impact of International Rules and Norms", *International Studies Quarterly* 40(4): 451–78.

Cortell, A.P. and Davis, J.W. (2000) "Understanding the Domestic Impact of International Norms: A Research Agenda", *International Studies Review* 2(1): 65–87.

Couloumbis, T. (1983) *The United States, Greece and Turkey: The Troubled Triangle*, New York: Praeger.

Couloumbis, T. (1994) "Introduction: The Impact of EC Membership on Greece's Foreign Policy Profile", in P. Kazakos and P.C. Ioakimidis (eds) *Greece and EC Membership Evaluated*, London: Pinter Publishers, pp. 189–98.

Council of Europe Assembly (2004) "Honouring of Obligations and Commitments by Bosnia and Herzegovina", Doc. 10200, 4 June.

Council of Europe Assembly (2005) "The Way towards the Future of Bosnia and Herzegovina Goes through The Hague", 21 June.

Council on Foreign Relations (2005) *In Support of Arab Democracy: Why and How*, Task Force Report 54, New York: Council on Foreign Relations.

Cousens, E. and Kumar, C. (2001) *Peacebuilding as Politics*, Boulder, CO: Lynne Rienner.

Cox, M. (2001) "State Building and Post-Conflict Reconstruction: Lessons from Bosnia", CASIN Project, Online at <http://www.209.85.129.104/search?q=cache:I5JZMwbF_rEJ:www.casin.ch/web/pdf/cox.pdf+Marcus+Cox,+state+building+and+postconflict+reconstruction&hl=en&ct=clnk&cd=1>.

Cox, R.W. (1981) "Social Forces, States and World Orders: Beyond International Relations Theory", *Millennium: Journal of International Studies* 10(2): 126–55.

Crocker, A.C., Hampson, O.F. and Aall, P. (1999) "Multiparty Mediation and the Conflict Cycle" in Crocker, Hampson and Aall (eds) *Herding Cats: Multiparty Mediation in a Complex World*, Washington, DC: United States Institute of Peace, pp. 19–45.

Croft, S. (2000) "The EU, NATO and Europeanization: The Return of Architectural Debate", *European Security* 9(2): 1–20.

Crone, D. (1993) "Does Hegemony Matter? The Reorganization of the Pacific Political Economy", *World Politics* 45(4): 501–25.

Crozier, M. (1964) *The Bureaucratic Phenomenon*, Chicago: University of Chicago Press.

Curtis, D. (2001) "Politics and Humanitarian Aid: Debates, Dilemmas, and Dissension", in *Humanitarian Policy Group Report* 10, POLIS at the University of Leeds and CAFOD Conference, London: Overseas Development Institute, 1 February.

Cusimano, M. (2000) "Beyond Sovereignty: The Rise of Transsovereign Problems", in M. Cusimano (ed.) *Beyond Sovereignty: Issues for a Global Agenda*, Boston and New York: Bedford/St. Martin's, pp. 1–40.

Cutts, M. (1998) "Politics and Humanitarianism", *Refugee Survey Quarterly* 17(1): 1–15.
Daalder I. and Lindsey, J. (2003) *American Unbound: The Bush Revolution in Foreign Policy*, Washington, DC: Brookings Institution.
Daalder, I. and O'Hanlan, M. (2001) *Winning Ugly: NATO's War to Save Kosovo*. Washington, DC: Brookings Press.
Dawisha, K. and Parrott, B. (eds) (1997) *Conflict, Cleavage, and Change in Central Asia and the Caucasus*, Cambridge: Cambridge UP.
Deering, C.J. and Maltzman, F.M. (1999) "The Politics of Executive Orders: Legislative Constraints on Presidential Power", *Political Research Quarterly* 52(4): 767–83.
Dehio, L. (1948) *Gleichgewicht oder Hegemonie. Betrachtung über ein Grundproblem der neueren Staatengeschichte*, Krefeld: Scherpr.
Deibert, R.J. and Gross Stein, J.G. (2002) "Hacking Networks of Terror", *International Organization Dialogue* 1(1): 1–14.
Der Derian, J. (2001) *Virtuous War*, Boulder, CO: Westview Press.
Dessler, D. (1989) "What's at Stake in the Agent-Structure Debate?", *International Organization* 43(3): 441–73.
Deutsch, K., Burrell, S. and Kann, R. (1957) *Political Community and the North Atlantic Area: International Organization in the Light of Historical Experience*, Princeton, NJ: Princeton UP.
Diamond, L. (1996) "Is the Third Wave Over?", *Journal of Democracy* 7(3): 20–37.
Dibb, P. (1995) *Towards a New Balance of Power in Asia*, Adelphi Paper 295, Oxford: Oxford UP.
Diehl, P.F. (1993) "Institutional Alternatives to Traditional U.N. Peacekeeping: An Assessment of Regional and Multinational Options", *Armed Forces and Society* 19(2): 209–30.
Diehl, P.F. (2000) "Forks in the Road: Theoretical and Policy Concerns for 21st Century Peacekeeping", *Global Society* 14(3): 337–60.
Diez, T., Stetter, S., and Albert, M. (2006) "The European Union and Border Conflicts: The Transformative Power of Integration", *International Organization* 60(3): 563–93.
DiMaggio, P. and Powell, W. (1991) *The New Institutionalism in Organizational Analysis*, Chicago: University of Chicago Press.
Dimitras, P. (1985) "Greece: A New Danger", *Foreign Policy* 78(19): 134–50.
Dimitrova, A. and Pridham, G. (2004) "International Actors and Democracy Promotion in Central and Eastern Europe: The Integration Model and its Limits", *Democratization* 11(5): 91–112.
Dobbin, F. (1994) "Cultural Models of Organization: The Social Construction of Rational Organizing Principles", in J. Martin (ed.) *The Sociology of Culture*, Boston: Basil Blackwell, pp. 117–41.
Donais, T. (2002) "The Politics of Privatization in Post-Dayton Bosnia", *Southeast European Politics* 3(1): 3–19.
Dongfeng, R. (2004) "The Central Asia Policies of China, Russia and the USA, and the Shanghai Cooperation Organization Process: A View from China", Online at <http://www.editors.sipri.se/pubs/CentralAsiaSCO.pdf> (accessed on 15 January 2006).
Donini, A. (2004) *The Future of Humanitarian Action: Implications of Iraq and Other Recent Crises*, Medford, MA: Tufts University, Feinstein International Famine Center.

Donno, D. and Russett, B. (2004) "Islam, Authoritarianism, and Female Empowerment: What Are the Linkages?", *World Politics* 56(4): 582–607.

Dorn, W. (1998) "Regional Peacekeeping is not the Way", *Peacekeeping and International Relations* 27(3/4): 1–3.

Dosch, J. (2003) "Changing Security Cultures in Europe and Southeast Asia: Implications for Inter-Regionalism", *Asia Europe Journal* 1(4): 483–501.

Downs, G.W., Rocke, D.M. and Barsoom, P.N. (1996) "Is the Good News about Compliance Good News about Cooperation?", *International Organization* 50(3): 379–406.

Downs, G.W., Rocke, D.M. and Barsoom, P.N. (1998) "Managing the Evolution of Multilateralism", *International Organization* 52(2): 397–419.

Doyle, M. (1983) "Kant, Liberal Legacies, and Foreign Affairs", *Philosophy and Public Affairs* 12(3): 205–35.

Doyle, M. and Sambanis, N. (2000) "International Peacebuilding: A Theoretical and Quantitative Analysis", *American Political Science Review* 94(4): 779–801.

Doyle, M. and Sambanis, N. (2006) *Making War and Building Peace: United Nations Peace Operations*. Princeton, NJ: Princeton UP.

Doyle, M., Johnstone, I. and Orr, R. (eds) (1997) *Keeping the Peace: Multidimensional UN Operations in Cambodia and El Salvador*, Cambridge: Cambridge UP.

Dreher, A., Sturm, J-E. and Vreeland, J. (2006), "Does Membership on the UN Security Council Influence IMF", Swiss Federal Institute of Technology, Working Paper, No. 131.

Duffield, J. (1994) "Explaining the Long Peace in Europe: The Contributions of Regional Security Regimes", *Review of International Studies* 20(4): 269–88.

Duffield, J. (1994–5) "NATO's Functions after the Cold War", *Political Science Quarterly* 109(5): 763–87.

Duffield, J. (2006) "International Security Institutions: Rules, Tools, Schools or Fools?", in R.A. Rhodes, S.A. Binder and B. Rockman (eds) *The Oxford Handbook of Political Institutions*, Oxford: Oxford UP, pp. 633–53.

Duffield, M. (2001) *Global Governance and the New Wars: The Merging of Development and Security*, New York: Zed Press.

Dunn, D. (2003) "Myths, Motivations and 'Misunderestimations': The Bush Administration and Iraq", *International Affairs* 79(2): 279–98.

Durch, W.J. (ed.) (1996) *UN Peacekeeping, American Politics and the Uncivil Wars of the 1990s*, New York: St. Martin's Press.

Eberwein, W-D. (1995) "The Future of International Warfare: Toward a Global Security Community?", *International Political Studies Review* 16(4): 341–60.

Eisenstadt, S.N. and Giesen, B. (1995) "The Construction of Collective Identity", *European Journal of Sociology* 36: 72–102.

Elbadawi, I. and Sambanis, N. (2000) "External Interventions and the Duration of Civil Wars", paper presented at the workshop on the Economics of Civil Violence, Princeton University, NJ, 18–19 March.

Elgström, O. and Jönsson, C. (2000) "Negotiation in the European Union: Bargaining or Problem-solving, *Journal of European Public Policy* 7(5): 684–704.

Ellwood, D. (ed.) (1989) *The Marshall Plan Forty Years After: Lessons for the International System Today*, The Bologna Center of the Johns Hopkins University School of Advanced International Studies.

Elman, M.F. (1999) "The Never-Ending Story: Democracy and Peace", *International Studies Review* 1(3): 87–103.

Elster, J. (ed.) (1998) *Deliberative Democracy*, New York: Cambridge UP.
Elster, J. (1999) *Alchemies of the Mind: Rationality and the Emotions*, Cambridge: Cambridge UP.
Emmerson, D.K. (2005) "Security, Community, and Democracy in Southeast Asia: Analyzing ASEAN", *Japanese Journal of Political Science* 6(2): 165–85.
Eriksson, M. and Wallensteen, P. (2004) "Appendix 3A. Patterns of Major Armed Conflicts, 1990–2003", in *SIPRI Yearbook 2004: Armaments, Disarmament and International Security*, Oxford: Oxford UP.
Europäische Union (2005) *Vertrag über eine Verfassung für Europa*. Luxemburg: Amt für Amtliche Veröffentlichungen der Europäischen Gemeinschaften.
European Commission (2003) COM (2003) 692, *Report from the Commission to the Council on the Preparedness of Bosnia and Herzegovina to Negotiate a Stabilisation and Association Agreement with the European Union*, Brussels, 19 November.
European Council (2003) *A Secure Europe in a Better World – European Security Strategy*, Brussels: European Institute for Security Studies, 12 December.
European Stability Initiative (ESI) (2004) *Governance and Democracy in Bosnia and Herzegovina: Post Industrial Society and the Authoritarian Temptation*, Online at <http://unpan.un.org/intradoc/groups/public/documents/UNTC/UNPAN018624.pdf> (last accessed 17 April 2006).
European Union Council (2004) "EU Solidarity Programme on the Consequences of Terrorist Threats and Attacks (revised/widened CBRN Programme) – Adoption", DG 1, 15480/04, 1 December.
Falk, R. (2002) "Revisiting Westphalia, Discovering Post-Westphalia", *Journal of Ethics* 6(4): 311–52.
Farer, T. (2002) "Beyond the Charter Frame: Unilateralism or Condominium Frame?", *American Journal of International Law* 96(2): 359–64.
Fearon, J.D. (1995) "Rationalist Explanations for War", *International Organization* 49(3): 379–414.
Fearon, J.D. (1997) "Signaling Foreign Policy Interests: Tying Hands versus Sinking Costs", *Journal of Conflict Resolution* 41(1): 68–90.
Fearon, J.D. (1998) "Bargaining, Enforcement, and International Cooperation", *International Organization* 62(2): 269–305.
Fearon, J.D. (2005) "Reforming International Institutions to Promote International Peace and Security", Paper prepared for the International Task Force on Global Public Goods, 6 January.
Fearon, J.D. and Laitin, D.D. (2003) "Ethnicity, Insurgency, and Civil War", *American Political Science Review* 91(1): 75–90.
Fearon, J.D. and Laitin, D.D. (2004) "Neotrusteeship and the Problem of Weak States", *International Security* 28(4): 5–74.
Festić, A. and Rausche, A. (2004) "War by Other Means: How Bosnia's Clandestine Political Economies Obstruct Peace and State Building", *Problems of Post-Communism* 51(3): 27–34.
Finnemore, M. (1993) "International Organizations as Teachers of Norms: The United Nations Educational, Scientific, and Cultural Organization and Science Policy", *International Organization* 47(4): 556–97.
Finnemore, M. (1996) *National Interests in International Society*, Ithaca, NY: Cornell UP.
Finnemore, M. and Sikkink, K. (1998) "International Norm Dynamics and Political Change", *International Organization* 52(4): 887–917.

Finnemore, M. and Sikkink, K. (1999a) "International Norms and Political Change", in P. Katzenstein, R. Keohane and S. Krasner (eds) *Exploration and Contestation in the Study of World Politics*, Cambridge, MA: MIT Press, pp. 247–78.

Finnemore, M. and Sikkink, K. (1999b) "Taking Stock: The Constructivist Research Program in International Relations and Comparative Politics", *Annual Reviews of Political Science* 4: 391–416.

Fisher, J.R., and Keashley, L. (1991) "The Potential Complementarity of Mediation within a Contingency Model of Third Party Intervention", *Journal of Peace Research* 28(1): 29–42.

Fleishman, J.L. and Aufses, A.H. (1976) "Law and Orders: The Problem of Presidential Legislation", *Law and Contemporary Problems* 40(3): 1–45.

Forsythe, D. (2005) *The Humanitarians: The International Committee of the Red Cross*, New York: Cambridge UP.

Fortna, V.P. (2004a) "Does Peacekeeping Keep Peace? International Intervention and the Duration of Peace After Civil War", *International Studies Quarterly* 48(2): 269–92.

Fortna, V.P. (2004b) "Interstate Peacekeeping: Causal Mechanisms and Empirical Effects", *World Politics* 56(4): 481–519.

Foucault, M. (1991) "Governmentality", in G. Burchell, C. Gordon and P. Miller (eds) *The Foucault Effect: Studies in Governmentality*, Hemel Hempstead, Herts: Harvester Wheatsheaf, pp. 87–104.

Franck, T. (1999) "Lessons of Kosovo", *American Journal of International Law* 93(4): 857–60.

Fravel, M.T. (2005) "Regime Insecurity and International Cooperation: Explaining China's Compromises in Territorial Disputes", *International Security* 30(1): 46–83.

Frederking, B. (2003) "Constructing Post-Cold War Collective Security", *American Political Science Review* 97(3): 363–78.

Frieden, J. (2004) "One Europe, One Vote? The Political Economy of European Union Representation in International Organizations", *European Union Politics* 5(2): 261–76.

Friis, L. and Murphy, A. (2000) "Turbo-charged Negotiations: the EU and the Stability Pact for South Eastern Europe", *Journal of European Public Policy* 7(5): 767–86.

Fukuyama, F. (2004) *State Building: Governance and Order in the Twenty-First Century*, London: Profile.

Gallant, N. and Stubbs, R. (1997) "APEC's Dilemmas: Institution-building Around the Pacific Basin", *Pacific Affairs* 70(2): 203–18.

Gallarotti, G. (2001) "The Limits of International Organization: Systemic Failure in the Management of International Relations" in L. Martin and B. Simmons (eds) *International Institutions*, Cambridge, MA: MIT Press, pp. 365–403.

Gardner, L.C. (1984) *A Covenant with Power: American and World Order from Wilson to Reagan*, New York: Oxford UP.

Garton, A.T. (2001) "Is There a Good Terrorist?" *New York Review of Books*, 29 November: 30–3.

Geipel, G.L. (1999) "The Cost of Enlarging NATO", in J. Sperling (ed.) *Two Tiers or Two Speeds? The European Security Order and the Enlargement of the European Union and NATO*, Manchester: Manchester UP, pp. 160–80.

Gerhards, Jürgen, and Michael Hölscher (2005) *Kulturelle Unterschied in der*

Europäischen Union. Ein Vergleich zwischen Mitgliedsländern, Beitrittskandidaten und der Türkei. Wiesbaden: VS Verlag für Sozialwissenschaften.

Gheciu, A. (2005) "Security Institutions as Agents of Socialization? NATO and the 'New Europe' ", *International Organization* 59(4): 973–1012.

Giddens, A. (1991) *Modernity and Self Identity in the Late Modern Age*, Cambridge: Polity Press.

Gill, B. (2004) "China's New Security Multilateralism and its Implications for the Asia-Pacific Region", in *SIPRI Yearbook 2004: Armaments, Disarmament and International Security*, Oxford: Oxford UP, pp. 381–8.

Gilpin, R. (1981) *War and Change in World Politics*, Princeton, NJ: Princeton UP.

Gleason, G. and Shaihutdinov, M.E. (2005) "Collective Security and Non-State Actors in Eurasia", *International Studies Perspectives* 6(2): 274–84.

Gleditsch, N.P., Strand, H., Eriksson, M., Sollenberg, M. and Wallensteen, P. (2001) "Armed Conflict, 1945–99: A New Dataset", *Journal of Peace Research* 39(5): 615–37.

Glennon, M.J. (2003) "Why the Security Council Failed", *Foreign Affairs* 82(3): 16–35.

Glenny, Misha (2001) Memorandum submitted to the Select Committee on Foreign Affairs 27 March 2001, Online at <http://www.publications.parliament.uk/pa/cm2001/cmselect/cmfaff/246/1021303.htm> (last accessed 22 December 2004).

Goldgeier, J.M. (1999) *Not Whether but When: The US Decision to Enlarge NATO*, Washington, DC: Brookings Institution.

Goldsmith, J.L. and Posner, E.A. (2005) *The Limits of International Law*, New York: Oxford UP.

Goldstein, J. and Martin, L. (2000) "Legalization, Trade Liberalization, and Domestic Politics: A Cautionary Note", *International Organization* 54(3): 503–632.

Goldstone, A. (2004), "UNTAET with Hindsight", *Global Governance* 10(1): 83–98.

Gordon, P.H. (1998) "Europe's Uncommon Foreign Policy", *International Security* 22(1): 74–100.

Gourevitch, P. (1998) *We Wish To Inform You That Tomorrow We Will be Killed With Our Families*, New York: Farrar, Straus & Giroux.

Grabbe, H. (2001) "How Does Europeanization Affect CEE Governance? Conditionality, Diffusion and Diversity", *Journal of European Public Policy* 8(6): 1013–31.

Greenberg, J. (1979), "Consistent Majority Rule over Compact Sets of Alternatives", *Econometrica* 47(3): 627–36.

Greenberg Research (1999) *The People on War Report: ICRC Worldwide Consultation on the Rules of War*, Geneva: International Committee of the Red Cross, October, Online at <http://www.icrc.org/icrceng.nsf>.

Grieco, J.M. (1988) "Anarchy and the Limits of Cooperation: A Realist Critique of the Newest Liberal Institutionalism", *International Organization* 42(3): 485–507.

Grieco, J.M. (1990) *Cooperation among Nations: Europe, America, and Non-tariff Barriers to Trade*, Ithaca, NY: Cornell UP.

Guang, P. (2005) "The Astana Summit. A New Stage in the Development of the Shanghai Cooperation Organization", *Asia-Europe Journal* 3(4): 501–6.

Gusmao, X. (2004) "Peacekeeping and Peacebuilding in Timor Leste", *Seminar on the Role of the UN in Timor Leste*, Dili, 26 November.

Guvenc, S. (1998–9) "Turkey's Changing Perception of Greece's Membership in the European Union", *Turkish Review of Balkan Studies* 4: 103–30.

Haacke, J. (2003) "ASEAN's Diplomatic and Security Culture: A Constructivist Assessment", *International Relations of the Asia-Pacific* 3(1): 57–87.

Haas, E. (1983) "Regime Decay: Conflict Management and International Organizations, 1945–1981", *International Organization* 37(2): 189–256.
Habermas, J. (2002) "Letter to America", *The Nation*, 16 December.
Haftendorn, H., Keohane, R. and Wallander, C. (1999) *Imperfect Unions. Security Institutions over Time and Space*, Oxford: Oxford UP.
Hall, P. and Taylor, R. (1996) "Political Science and the Three New Institutionalisms", *Political Studies* 44(5): 936–57.
Halliday, F. (2001) "The Romance of Non-State Actors", in D. Josselin and W. Wallace (eds) *Non-State Actors in World Politics*, London: Palgrave, pp. 21–37.
Hamill, J. and Lee, D. (2001) "A Middle Power Paradox? South African Diplomacy in the Post-Apartheid Era", *International Relations* 15(4): 33–59.
Hampton, M.N. (1998–9) "NATO, Germany and the United States: Creating Positive Identity in Trans-Atlantia", *Security Studies* 8(2/3): 235–69.
Hampton, M.N. and Sperling, J. (2002) "Positive/Negative Identity in the Euro-Atlantic Communities: Germany's Past, Europe's Future?", *Journal of European Integration* 24(4): 281–302.
Hanrieder, W. (1978) "Dissolving International Politics: Reflections on the Nation-State", *American Political Science Review* 72(3): 1276–87.
Hansen, A. (2004) "Security and Defence: The EU Police Mission in Bosnia-Herzegovina" in W. Carlnaes, H. Sjursen and B. White (eds) *Contemporary European Foreign Policy*, London: Sage, pp. 173–85.
Hardt, M. and Negri, A. (2000) *Empire*, Cambridge, MA: Harvard UP.
Harnisch, S. and Maull, H.W. (2001) "Introduction", in Harnisch and Maull (eds) *Germany as a Civilian Power? The Foreign Policy of the Berlin Republic*, Manchester: Manchester UP, pp. 1–9.
Harper, J.L. (1996) *American Visions of Europe*, New York: Cambridge UP.
Hasenclever, A. (2001) *Die Macht der Moral in der Internationalen Politik. Militärische Interventionen Westlicher Staaten in Somalia, Ruanda und Bosnien-Herzegowina*, Frankfurt: Campus.
Hasenclever, A., Mayer, P. and Rittberger, V. (1997) *Theories of International Regimes*, Cambridge: Cambridge UP.
Hassner, P. (2002) *The United States: The Empire of Force or the Force of Empire?*, Chaillot Papers No. 54, Paris: Institute for Security Studies, European Union.
Havel, V. (1999) "Kosovo and the End of the Nation-State", *New York Review of Books*, 10 June, pp. 4–6.
Hawkins, D., Lake, D., Nielson, D. and Tierney, M. (eds) (2005) *Delegation Under Anarchy: States, International Organizations, and Principal Agent Theory*, book manuscript.
Hayner, P.B. (2001) *Unspeakable Truths: Confronting State Terror and Atrocity*, New York: Routledge.
Held, D. (1995) *Democracy and the Global Order*, Cambridge: Polity.
Heldt, B. (2001) "Conditions for Successful Intrastate Peacekeeping Missions", Working Paper, National Defence College of Sweden, June.
Heldt, B. (2002) "Peacekeeping Operations by Regional Actors, 1948–2000", Unpublished paper, National Defence College of Sweden, 18 November.
Heldt, B. (2004) "UN-led or Non-UN-led Peacekeeping Operations?", *IRI Review* 9(2): 113–38.
Heldt, B. and Wallensteen, P. (2005) *Peacekeeping Operations: Global Patterns of*

Intervention and Success, 1948–2004, Sandöverken: Folke Bernadotte Academy Publications.
Hemmer, C. and Katzenstein, P.J. (2002) "Why is There No NATO in Asia? Collective Identity, Regionalism, and the Origins of Multilateralism", *International Organization* 56(3): 575–607.
Henderson, K. (ed.) (1999) *Back to Europe*, London: UCL Press.
Héritier, A. (1999) *Policy-Making and Diversity in Europe: Escaping Deadlock*, Cambridge: Cambridge UP.
Herrmann, R.K. 2004. "George W. Bush's Foreign Policy", in C. Campbell and B. Rockman (eds) *The George W. Bush Presidency*, Washington, DC: CQ Press, pp. 191–225.
Herz, J.H. (1957) "The Rise and Demise of the Territorial State", *World Politics* 9(4): 473–93.
Higgins, E.T. (2000) "Making a Good Decision: Value from Fit", *American Psychologist* 55(11): 1217–30.
Hoare, Q. and Nowell-Smith, G. (eds) (1972) *Selections from the Prison Notebooks of Antonio Gramsci*, London: Lawrence & Wishart.
Hoffmann, S. (1998) *World Disorders: Troubled Peace in the Post-Cold War Era*, Lanham, MD: Rowman & Littlefield.
Holsti, K.J. (1995) "War, Peace and the State of the State", *International Political Science Review* 16(4): 310–39.
Holsti, O.R. (1996) *Public Opinion and American Foreign Policy*, Ann Arbor, MI: Michigan UP.
Holsti, O.R. (2001) "Public Opinion and Foreign Policy", in R. Lieber (ed.) *Eagle Rules: Foreign Policy and American Primacy in the 21st Century*, Englewood Cliffs, NJ: Prentice Hall, pp. 16–46.
Holzgrefe, J.L. and Keohane, R. (eds) (2004) *Humanitarian Intervention*, New York: Cambridge UP.
Homer-Dixon, T.F. (1995) "On the Threshold: Environmental Changes as Causes of Acute Conflict", in S. Lynn-Jones and S. Miller (eds) *Global Dangers: Changing Dimensions of International Security*, Cambridge, MA: MIT Press, pp. 43–83.
Horowitz, D. (1985) *Ethnic Groups in Conflict*, Berkeley and Los Angeles: University of California Press.
Houghton, R. and Robertson, K. (eds) (2001) "Humanitarian Action: Learning from Evaluation", ALNAP Annual Review Series, London: Overseas Development Institute.
Howard, M. (1993) "The Historical Development of the UN's Role in International Security", in A. Roberts and B. Kingsbury (eds) *United Nations, Divided World: The UN's Roles in International Relations*, New York: Oxford UP.
Howard, M. (2000) *The Invention of Peace and War*, London: Profile Books.
Howell, W.G. (2003) *Power Without Persuasion: The Politics of Direct Presidential Action*, Princeton, NJ: Princeton UP.
Huelshoff, M.G., Sperling, J. and Hess, M. (2005) "Is Germany a "Good European"? German Compliance with EU Law", *German Politics* 14(3): 354–70.
Hunjoon, K. and Sikkink, K. (2007) Do Human Rights Trials Make a Difference?, paper presented at the annual meeting of the American Political Science Association, Chicago, Illinois, August 30–September 2.
Huntington, S.P. (1968) *Political Order in Changing Societies*, New Haven, CT: Yale UP.
Huntington, S.P. (1999) "The Lonely Superpower", *Foreign Affairs* 78(2): 35–49.

Hurd, I. (1997) "Security Council Reform: Informal Membership and Practice" in B. Russett (ed.) *The Once and Future Security Council*, New York: St. Martin's Press, pp. 135–52.
Hurd, I. (1999) "Legitimacy and Authority in International Politics", *International Organization* 53(2): 379–408.
Hurd, I. (2005) "The Strategic Use of Liberal Internationalism: Libya and the UN Sanctions, 1999–2003", *International Organization* 59(3): 495–526.
Huth, P. (1988) *Extended Deterrence and the Prevention of War*, New Haven, CT: Yale UP.
Hyde-Price, A. (2000) *Germany and the European Order: Enlarging NATO and the EU*, Manchester: Manchester UP.
Iatrides, J.O. (2000) "NATO and Aegean Disputes: The Cold War and After", in A. Chircop, A. Gerolymatos and J.O. Iatrides (eds) *The Aegean Sea After the Cold War. Security and Law of the Sea Issues*, London: Macmillan, pp. 32–46.
Ignatieff, M. (ed.) (2001) *Human Rights as Politics and Idolatry*, Princeton, NJ: Princeton UP.
Ignatieff, M. (2003) *Empire Lite: Nation-building in Bosnia, Kosovo and Afghanistan*, London: Vintage.
IISS (2004) *The Military Balance, 2004–2005*, Oxford: Oxford UP.
Ikenberry, G.J. (1989) "Rethinking the Origins of American Hegemony", *Political Science Quarterly* 104(3): 375–400.
Ikenberry, G.J. (2000) *Whither Pax Americana? Balance of Power, Hegemony, and the Future of American Preponderance*, manuscript. Washington, DC.
Ikenberry, G.J. (2001) *After Victory: Institutions, Strategic Restraint, and the Rebuilding of Order After Major War*, Princeton, NJ: Princeton UP.
Ikenberry, G.J. (2002) "America's Imperial Ambition", *Foreign Affairs* 81(5): 44–60.
Ikenberry, G.J. (2003) "State Power and the Institutional Bargain: America's Ambivalent Economic and Security Multilateralism", in R. Foot, S.N. MacFarlane and M. Mastanduno (eds) *U.S. Hegemony and International Organizations: The United States and Multilateral Institutions*, New York: Oxford UP, pp. 49–70.
Ikenberry, G.J. (2005) "Ruling Unipolarity: American Power and the Logic of International Order", unpublished paper.
Ikenberry, G.J. and Kupchan, C.A. (1990) "Socialization and Hegemonic Power", *International Organization* 44(4): 283–315.
Ikenberry, G.J. and Tsuchiyama, J. (2002) "Between Balance of Power and Community: The Future of Multilateral Security Co-operation in the Asia-Pacific", *International Relations of the Asia-Pacific* 2(1): 69–94.
IMF (1949–98) *Financial Statistics*, Washington, DC: IMF.
IMF (2004) *Direction of Trade Statistics Yearbook 2004*, Washington, DC: IMF.
IMF (2006) World Economic Outlook Database, September.
Inoguchi, T. and Bacon, P. (2006) "Japan's Emerging Role as a "Global Ordinary Power" ", *International Relations of the Asian-Pacific* 6(1): 1–21.
International Commission on Intervention and State Sovereignty (2001) "The Responsibility to Protect", Ottawa: International Development Research Centre.
International Crisis Group (2003) "Bosnia's Nationalist Governments: Paddy Ashdown and the Paradoxes of State Building", Balkans Report no. 146, 22 July.
International Crisis Group (2005) "Bosnia's Stalled Police Reform: No Progress, No EU", Europe Report No. 164, September.

International Organization (2005) Special Issue on "International Institutions and Socialization in Europe", 59(4): 860–1079.
Jabri, V. (1996) *Discourses on Violence*, Manchester: Manchester UP.
Jackson, R. (1990) *Quasi-States*, New York: Cambridge UP.
Jakobsen, P.V. (2002) "The Transformation of United Nations Peace Operations in the 1990s", *Cooperation and Conflict* 73(3): 267–82.
Jepperson, R.L., Wendt, A. and Katzenstein, P.J. (1996) "Norms, Identity, Culture and National Security", in P.J. Katzenstein (ed.) *The Culture of National Security: Norms and Identity in World Politics*, New York: Columbia UP, pp. 33–74.
Jervis, R. (2002) "Theories of War in an Era of Leading Power Peace", *American Political Science Review* 96(1): 1–14.
Jervis, R. (2003) "The Compulsive Empire", *Foreign Policy* 137 (July/August): 82–7.
Jonson, L. (1998) *Russia and Central Asia: A New Web of Relations*, London: Royal Institute of International Affairs.
Johnston, A.I. (2001) "Treating International Institutions as Social Environments", *International Studies Quarterly* 45(4): 487–515.
Judah, T. (2002) *Kosovo: War and Revenge*, New Haven, CJ: Yale UP.
Kagan, R. (2002) "Power and Weakness", *Policy Review* 113 (June–July), Online at <http://www.policyreview.org/JUN02/kagan.html>.
Kagan, R. (2003) *Of Paradise and Power. America and Europe in the New World Order*, New York: Knopf.
Kang, D. (2003) "Getting Asia Wrong: The Need for New Analytical Frameworks", *International Security* 27(1): 57–85.
Kant, I. (1795/1983) "To Perpetual Peace. A Philosophical Sketch", in T. Humphrey (ed.) *Immanual Kant. Perpetual Peace and Other Essays on Politics, History, and Morals*, Indianapolis: Hackett, pp. 107–43.
Karaosmanoglu, L.A. (1988) "Turkey and the Southern Flank: Domestic and External Contexts" in J. Chipman (ed.) *NATO's Southern Allies: Internal and External Challenges*, London: Routledge, pp. 85–118.
Katzenstein, P. (1996) *The Culture of National Security*, New York: Columbia UP.
Katzenstein, P. (1997) "The Cultural Foundations of Murakami's Polymorphic Liberalism", in K. Yamamura (ed.) *A Vision of a New Liberalism? Critical Essays*, Stanford, CA: Stanford UP, pp. 23–40.
Katzenstein, P.J. (2002) "September 11 in Comparative Perspective: The Antiterrorism Campaigns of Germany and Japan", *Dialogue-IO* 1(1): 45–56.
Kaufman, S.J. (2001) *Modern Hatreds: The Symbolic Politics of Ethnic War*, Ithaca, NY: Cornell UP.
Kay, S. (2003) "Geopolitical Constraints and Institutional Innovation: The Dynamics of Multilateralism in Eurasia," in J. Sperling, S. Kay and S.V. Papacosma (eds) *Limiting Institutions? The Challenge of Eurasian Security Governance*, Manchester: Manchester UP, pp. 125–43.
Keck, M. and Sikkink, K. (1998) *Activists beyond Borders: Transnational Advocacy Networks in International Politics*, Ithaca, NY: Cornell UP.
Kelly, C. (1998) "On the Relief-to-Development Continuum", *Disasters* 30(2): 174–5.
Kelsen, H. (1948) "Collective Security and Collective Self-Defense under the Charter of the United Nations", *The American Journal of International Law* 42(4): 783–96.
Keohane, R.O. (1984) *After Hegemony: Cooperation and Discord in the World Political Economy*, Princeton, NJ: Princeton UP.

Keohane, R.O. (1986) "Reciprocity in International Relations", *International Organization* 40(1): 1–27.
Keohane, R.O. (1988) "Alliances, Threats, and the Uses of Neorealism", *International Security* 13(1): 169–76.
Keohane, R.O. (1989) *International Institutions and State Power: Essays in International Relations Theory*, Boulder, CO.: Westview Press.
Keohane, R.O. (2001) "Governance in a Partially Globalized World", *American Political Science Review* 95(1): 1–13.
Keohane, R. and Axelrod, R. (1986) "Achieving Cooperation Under Anarchy", in K. Oye (ed.) *Cooperation Under Anarchy*, Princeton, NJ: Princeton UP, pp. 226–45.
Keohane, R.O. and Martin, L.L. (1995) "The Promise of Institutionalist Theory", *International Security* 20(1): 39–51.
Khoo, N. (2004) "Deconstructing the ASEAN Security Community: A Review Essay", *International Relations of the Asia-Pacific* 4(1): 35–46.
Kim, S.Y. and Russett, B. (1996) "The New Politics of Voting Alignments in the United Nations General Assembly", *International Organization* 50(4): 629–52.
King, G. and Ragsdale, L. (1988) *The Elusive Executive: Discovering Statistical Patterns in the Presidency*, Washington, DC: Congressional Quarterly Press.
Kirchner, E.J. and Sperling, J. (2007) *Governing European Security*, Manchester: Manchester UP.
Kirisci, K. and Carkoglu, A. (2003) "Perceptions of Greeks and Greek-Turkish Rapprochement by the Turkish Public", in B. Rubin and A. Carkoglu (eds), *Greek-Turkish Relations in an Era of Détente*, London: Frank Cass.
Knaus, G. and Fox, M. (2004) "Bosnia Herzegovina: Europeanisation by Decree?", in J. Batt (ed.) *The Western Balkans: Moving on*, EU-ISS Chaillot Paper 70, pp. 55–68.
Knock, T.J. (1992) *To End All Wars: Woodrow Wilson and the Quest for a New World Order*, New York: Oxford UP.
Koremenos, B., Lipson, C. and Snidal, D. (2001a) "The Rational Design of International Institutions", *International Organization* 55(4): 761–99.
Koremenos, B., Lipson, C. and Snidal, D. (2001b) "Rational Design: Looking back to Move Forward", *International Organization* 55(4): 1051–82.
Koucik, S. and Kokoski, R. (eds) (1994) *Conventional Arms Control: Perspectives on Verification*, Oxford: Oxford UP.
Kowert, P. and Legro, J. (1996) "Norms, Identity and their Limits: A Theoretical Reprise" in P. Katzenstein (ed.) *The Culture of National Security: Norms and Identity in World Politics*, New York: Columbia UP, pp. 451–97.
Krahenbuhl, P. (2000) "Conflict in the Balkans: Human Tragedies and the Challenge to Independent Humanitarian Action", *International Review of the Red Cross* 837: 11–29.
Kramer, H. (1987) "Turkish Application for Accession to the European Community and the Greek Factor", *Europa Archiv* 42(10): 605–14.
Krasner, S.D. (1991) "Global Communications and National Power: Life on the Pareto Frontier", *World Politics* 43(3): 336–66.
Krasner, S.D. (1995–6) "Compromising Westphalia", *International Security* 20(3): 115–51.
Krasner, S.D. (1999) *Sovereignty: Organized Hypocrisy*, Princeton, NJ: Princeton UP.
Krasner, S.D. (2001) "Abiding Sovereignty", *International Political Science Review* 22(3): 229–51.

Krebs, R. (1999) "Perverse Institutionalism: NATO and the Greco-Turkish Conflict", *International Organization* 53(2): 343–77.

Krell, G. (2003) *Arroganz der Macht, Arroganz der Ohnmacht. Der Irak, die Weltordnungspolitik der USA und die Transatlantischen Beziehungen*, HSFK-Report 1/2003, Frankfurt/Main: Hessische Stiftung Friedens- und Konfliktforschung.

Kreps, David M. (1990) *Game Theory and Economic Modeling*, Oxford: Clarendon Press.

Kritz, N.J. (1996) "Coming to Terms with Atrocities: A Review of Accountability Mechanisms for Mass Violations of Human Rights", *Law and Contemporary Problems* 59(4): 127–52.

Kritz, N.J. (1999) "War Crime Trials: Who Should Conduct Them – and How", in B. Cooper (ed.) *War Crimes: The Legacy of Nuremberg*, New York: TV Books, pp. 168–82.

Kubbig, B.W. (1988) *Amerikanische Rüstungskontrollpolitik: Die innergesellschaftlichen Kräfteverhältnisse in der ersten Amtszeit Reagans (1981–1985)*, Frankfurt/Main: Campus.

Kull, S. (2005) *Opportunities for Bipartisan Consensus: What Both Republicans and Democrats Want in US Foreign Policy*, Baltimore, MD and Menlo Park, CA: PIPA/ Knowledge Networks Poll, 18 January.

Kupchan, C. (2003) *The End of the American Era: U.S. Foreign Policy and the Geopolitics of the Twenty-First Century*, New York: Alfred A. Knopf.

Kupchan, C. and Kupchan, C. (1991) "Concerts, Collective Security and the Future of Europe", *International Security* 16(1): 114–61.

Kupchan, C. and Kupchan, C. (1995) "The Promise of Collective Security", *International Security* 20(1): 52–61.

Kutnjak, I.S. and O'Connor, S.T. (2005) "The Bosnian Police and Police Integrity", *European Journal of Sociology* 2(4): 428–64.

Kydd, A. (2001) "Trust Building, Trust Breaking: The Dilemma of NATO Enlargement", *International Organization* 55(4): 801–28.

Lang, T. (ed.) (2003) *Just Intervention*, Georgetown,: Georgetown UP.

Laurenti, J. (1997) *Reforming the Security Council: What American Interests?*, UNA-USA Occasional Paper Series, New York, United Nations Association of the United States.

Law, M.D. and McFarlane, S.N. (1996) "NATO Expansion and European Regional Security" in D.G. Haglund (ed.) *Will NATO Go East? The Debate Over Enlarging the Atlantic Alliance*, Kingston, Ontario: Queen's University Center for International Relations.

Layne, C. (2000) "U.S. Hegemony and the Perpetuation of NATO", *Journal of Strategic Studies* 23(3): 59–92.

Leader, N. (2000) *The Politics of Principle: The Principles of Humanitarian Action in Practice*, London: Overseas Development Institute.

Lebow, R.N. and Stein, J.G. (1990) "Deterrence: The Elusive Dependent Variable", *World Politics* 42(3): 336–69.

Lehne, S. (2004) "Has the 'Hour of Europe' Come at Last? The EU's Strategy for the Balkans", in J. Batt (ed.) *The Western Balkans: Moving on*, EU-ISS Chaillot Paper 70, pp. 111–24.

Leifer, M. (1996) *The ASEAN Regional Forum: Extending ASEAN's Model of Regional Security*, Adelphi Paper 302, Oxford: Oxford UP.

Liberman, P. (2006) "An Eye for an Eye: Public Support for War against Evildoers", *International Organization* 60(3): 687–722.

Liberman, P. (2007) "Crime, Punishment, and War", *International Security*, forthcoming.
Linklater, A. (1998) *The Transformation of Political Community*, Columbia: University of South Carolina Press.
Linz, J. and Stepan, A. (1996) *Problems of Democratic Transition and Consolidation*, Baltimore, MD: Johns Hopkins UP.
Lipson, C. (1984) "International Cooperation in Economic and Security Affairs", *World Politics*, 37(1): 1–23.
Lipson, C. (1991) "Why Are Some International Agreements Informal?", *International Organization* 45(4): 495–538.
Lipson, C. (2003) *Reliable Partners: How Democracies Have Made a Separate Peace*, Princeton, NJ: Princeton UP.
Loescher, G. (2001) *The UNHCR and World Politics: A Perilous Path*, New York: Oxford UP.
Long, W.J. and Brecke, P. (2003) *War and Reconciliation: Reason and Emotion in Conflict Resolution*, Cambridge, MA: MIT Press.
Luck, E.C. (2002) "The United States, International Organizations, and the Quest for Legitimacy", in S. Patrick and S. Forman (eds) *Multilateralism and U.S. Foreign Policy*, London: Lynne Rienner, pp. 47–74.
Luck, E.C. (2003) *Reforming the United Nations: Lessons from a History in Progress*, New Haven, CT: Academic Council on the United Nations System, Working paper.
Lund, M.S. (2003) "What Kind of Peace is Being Built: Taking Stock of Post-Conflict Peacebuilding and Charting Future Directions", paper presented on the 10th Anniversary of Agenda for Peace, International Development Research Centre, Ottawa, Canada, January.
Lund, M., Barnett, R. and Hara, F. (1998) "Learning from Burundi's Failed Democratic Transition, 1993–1996", in R. Barnett (ed.) *Cases and Strategies for Preventive Action*, New York: Century Foundation, pp. 47–92.
Lutz, E. and Sikkink, K. (2000) "International Human Rights Law and Practice", *International Organization* 54(3): 633–59.
Lynn-Jones, S. and Miller, S. (1995) "Introduction", in Lynn-Jones and Miller (eds) *Global Dangers: Changing Dimensions of International Security*, Cambridge, MA: MIT Press, pp. 3–14.
MacFarlane, N. (2000) "Politics and Humanitarian Action", *Occasional Papers*, Institute for International Studies, Providence, RI: Brown University.
MacKenzie, K. (1983) "Greece and Turkey: Disarray on NATO's Southern Flank", *Conflict Studies* no. 154, London: Institute for the Study of Conflict.
Macrae, J. (1998) "Death of Humanitarianism? An Anatomy of the Attack", *Disasters* 22(4): 309–17.
Macrae, J. (1999). "Aiding Peace . . . and War: UNHCR Returnee Reintegration and the Relief–Development Continuum", *New Issues in Refugee Research* 14, Geneva: UNHCR.
Macrae, J. and Leader, N. (eds) (2000) *Terms of Engagement: Conditions and Conditionality in Humanitarian Action*, London: Overseas Development Institute.
Macrae, J., Collinson, S., Buchanan-Smith, M., Reindorp, N., Schmidt, A., Mowjee, T. and Harmer, A. (2002) *Uncertain Power: The Changing Role of Official Donors in Humanitarian Action, Humanitarian Policy Group Report 12*. London: Overseas Development Institute.
Maggi, G. and Morelli, M. (2003) "Self Enforcing Voting in International

Organizations", NBER Working Paper No. W10102, September, Online at <http://ssrn.com/abstract=468789>.
Malcom, N. (1999) *Kosovo: A Short History*, New York: NYU Press.
Mandelbaum, M. (2002) *The Ideas that Conquered the World*, New York: Public Affairs.
Mansfield, E.D. and Snyder, J. (1995) "Democratization and the Danger of War", *International Security* 20(1): 5–38.
Mansfield, E.D. and Snyder, J. (2002) "Incomplete Democratization and the Outbreak of Military Disputes", *International Studies Quarterly* 46(4): 529–50.
March, J.G. and Olsen, J.P. (1989) *Rediscovering Institutions: The Organizational Basis of Politics*, New York: Free Press.
March, J.G. and Olsen, J.P. (1998) "The Institutional Dynamics of International Political Orders", *International Organization* 52(4): 943–69.
March, J.G. and Olsen, J.P. (2004) "The Logic of Appropriateness", *ARENA Working Papers* 04/09.
Margolis, L. (1986) *Executive Agreements and Presidential Power in Foreign Policy*, New York: Praeger.
Marshall, Monty, and Jaggers, Keith (2004) Polity IV Project. Codebook and Data Files, Online at <http://bsos.umd.edu/cidcm/inscr/polity> [Accessed on 25 March 2005].
Martin, J. (1992) *Cultures in Organizations: Three Perspectives*, New York: Oxford UP.
Martin, L.L. (1992) "Interests, Power, and Multilateralism", *International Organization* 46(4): 765–92.
Martin, L.L. (1993) "The Rational State Choice of Multilateralism", in J.G. Ruggie (ed.) *Multilateralism Matters: The Theory and Praxis of an Institutional Form*, New York: Columbia UP, pp. 91–121.
Martin, L.L. (2000) *Democratic Commitments: Legislatures and International Cooperation*, Princeton, NJ: Princeton UP.
Martin, L.L. (2005) "The President and International Commitments: Treaties as Signaling Devices", *Presidential Studies Quarterly* 35(3): 440–65.
Martin, L.L. and Simmons, B. (1998) "Theories and Empirical Studies of International Institutions", *International Organization* 52(4): 729–57.
Martin, L.L. and Simmons, B. (2001) "Theories and Empirical Studies of International Institutions", in L.L. Martin and B. Simmons (eds), *International Institutions*, Cambridge, MA: MIT Press, pp. 437–65.
Mason, T.D., and Fett, P.J. (1996) "How Civil Wars End: A Rational Choice Approach", *Journal of Conflict Resolution* 40(4): 546–68.
Matthiesen, P. (2004) "The Western Balkans – the EU, NATO and the US – Expectations versus Reality", in F-L. Altmann and E. Whitlock (eds) *European and US Policies in the Balkans*, Berlin: Stiftung Wissneschaft und Politik, pp. 15–9.
Mattli, W. and Slaughter, A-M. (1995) "Law and Politics in the European Union: a Reply to Garrett", *International Organization* 49(1): 183–90.
Maull, H.W. (1990) "Germany and Japan: The New Civilian Powers", *Foreign Affairs* 69(5): 91–106.
Mayer, K.R. (1999) "Executive Orders and Presidential Power", *Journal of Politics* 61(2): 445–66.
Mayer, K.R. and Price, K. (2002) "Unilateral Presidential Powers: Significant Executive Orders, 1949–99", *Presidential Studies Quarterly* 32(2): 367–86.
McCubbins, M. and Sullivan, T. (eds) (1987) *Congress: Structure and Policy*, New York: Cambridge UP.

Mead, M. (1990) "Warfare is Only an Invention–Not a Biological Necessity" in D. Hunt (ed.) *The Dolphin Reader*, 2nd ed, Boston: Houghton Mifflin, pp. 415–21.

Mead, W.R. (2001) *Special Providence: American Foreign Policy and How It Changed the World*, New York: Knopf.

Mearsheimer, J.J. (1990) "Back to the Future: Instability in Europe after the Cold War", *International Security* 15(1): 5–56.

Mearsheimer, J.J. (1994–5) "The False Promise of International Institutions", *International Security* 19(3): 5–49.

Mearsheimer, J.J. (1998) "The False Promise of International Institutions", in M.E. Brown, O.R. Coates, S.M. Lynn-Jones and S.E. Millar, *Theories of War and Peace*, Cambridge, MA: MIT Press, pp. 329–83.

Mearsheimer, J.J. (2001) *The Tragedy of Great Power Politics*, New York and London: W.W. Norton.

Meinardus, R. (1991) "Third-Party Involvement in Greek-Turkish Disputes" in D. Constas (ed.) *The Greek – Turkish Conflict in the 1990s*, New York: St. Martin's Press.

Meinecke, F. (1929) *Idee der Staatsräison in der Neueren Geschichte*, München: R. Oldenburg.

Merkl, P.H. (2005) *The Rift Between America and Old Europe: The Distracted Eagle*, London: Routledge.

Merlinguen, M. and Ostrauskaite, R. (2005) "Power/Knowledge in International Peacebuilding: The Case of the EU Police Mission in Bosnia", *Alternatives* 30(3): 297–323.

Mertus, J. (1999) *Kosovo: How Myths and Truths Started a War*, Berkeley, CA: University of California Press.

Meyer, J. (1991) "Institutionalized Organizations: Formal Structure as Myth and Ceremony", in W. Powell and P. DiMaggio (eds) *The New Institutionalism in Organizational Analysis*, Chicago: University of Chicago Press, pp. 41–62.

Meyer, J. and Rowan, B. (1977) "Institutional Organizations: Formal Structure as Myth and Ceremony", *American Journal of Sociology* 83(2): 340–63.

Miall, H. (1992) *The Peacemakers: Peaceful Settlement of Disputes since 1945*, New York: St. Martin's Press.

Michas, T. (2002), "America the despised – Letter from Athens", *The National Interest*, Online at <http:// www.findarticles.com> [accessed on 15 November 2006].

Millett, S.M. (1990) *The Constitutionality of Executive Agreements: An Analysis of United States v. Belmont*, New York: Grand Publishing.

Milward, A.S. (1992) *The European Rescue of the Nation-State*, Berkeley, CA: University of California Press.

Minear, L. (1999) "The Theory and Practice of Neutrality: Some Thoughts on the Tensions", *International Review of the Red Cross* 833: 63–71.

Minear, L. (2002) *The Humanitarian Enterprise: Dilemmas and Discoveries*, Bloomfield, CT: Kumarian Press.

Minear, L. and Smilie, I. (2004) *The Charity of Nations*, Bloomfield, CT: Kumarian Press.

Minear, L., van Baarda, T., and Sommers, M. (2000) "NATO and Humanitarian Action in the Kosovo Crisis", *Occasional Papers*, Institute for International Studies, Providence, RI: Brown University.

Minow, M. (1998) *Between Vengeance and Forgiveness: Facing History after Genocide and Mass Violence*, Boston: Beacon Press.

Mitrany, D. (1975) *The Functional Theory of Politics*, London: Martin Robertson.

Moe, T.M. (1990) "Political Institutions: The Neglected Side of the Story", *Journal of Law, Economics, and Organization* 6 (Special Issue): 213–53.
Moe, T.M. and Howell, W.G. (1999a) "The Presidential Power of Unilateral Action", *Journal of Law, Economics, and Organization* 15(1): 132–79.
Moe, T.M. and Howell, W.G. (1999b) "Unilateral Action and Presidential Power: A Theory", *Presidential Studies Quarterly* 29(4): 850–73.
Moravcsik, A. (1997) "Taking Preference Seriously: A Liberal Theory of International Politics", *International Organization* 51(4): 513–53.
Moravcsik, A. (2003) "Striking a New Transatlantic Bargain", *Foreign Affairs*, 82(4): 74–89.
Moravcsik, A. and Vachudova, M.A. (2002) "National Interests, State Power and EU Enlargement", Center for European Studies, Harvard University, Working Paper No. 97.
Morgan, P. (1993) "Multilateralism and Security: Prospects in Europe", in J.G. Ruggie (ed.) *Multilateralism Matters: The Theory and Praxis of an Institutional Form*, New York: Columbia UP, pp. 327–64.
Morris, N. (1999) "UNHCR and Kosovo: A Personal View from within UNHCR", *Forced Migration Review* 5(August): 14–17.
Morris, P. (1999) "Humanitarian Interventions in Macedonia: an NGO Perspective", *Forced Migration Review* 5(August): 18–19.
Morrow, J. (1994) *Game Theory for Political Scientists*. Princeton, NJ: Princeton UP.
Moustakis, F. and Sheehan, M. (2000) "Greek Security Policy after the Cold War", *Contemporary Security Policy* 21(3): 95–115.
Muller, H. (1993) "The Internalization of Principles, Norms, and Rules by Governments: The Case of Security Regimes", in V. Rittberger (ed.) *Regime Theory and International Relations*, Oxford: Oxford UP, pp. 361–90.
Muller, H. (2003) *Terrorism, Proliferation: a European Threat Assessment*, Chaillot Paper No. 58, Paris: Institute for Security Studies.
Nabers, D. (2003) "The Social Construction of International Institutions: The Case of ASEAN +3", *International Relations of the Asia-Pacific* 3(1): 113–36.
Nagel, T. (1988) "War and Massacre", in S. Scheffer (ed.) *Consequentialism and Its Critics*, Oxford: Oxford UP, pp. 51–73.
Narine, S. (1998) "ASEAN and the Management of Regional Security", *Pacific Affairs* 71(2): 195–214.
Nathan, J.A. and Oliver, J.K. (1994) *Foreign Policy Making and the American Political System*, 3rd edn, Baltimore, MD: Johns Hopkins Press.
Nau, H.R. (2002) *At Home Abroad. Identity and Power in American Foreign Policy*, Ithaca, NY: Cornell UP.
Nielson, D. and Tierney, M. (2003) "Delegation to International Organizations: Agency Theory and World Bank Environmental Reform", *International Organization* 57(2): 241–76.
Noutcheva, G. (2003) "Europeanisation and Conflict Resolution", *Europa South-East Monitor*, CEPS, no. 49, October.
Noutcheva, G. (2004) "The EU and the Western Balkans", *Europa South-East Monitor* CEPS, no. 58, September.
Nye, J.S. (1990) *Bound to Lead: The Changing Nature of American Power*, New York: Basic Books.
Nye, J.S. (2002) *The Paradox of American Power: Why the World's Only Superpower Can't Go It Alone*, Oxford: Oxford UP.

Nye, J.S. (2003) "US Power and Strategy After Iraq", *Foreign Affairs* 82(4): 60–73.
Nyers, P. (1999) "Emergency or Emerging Identities? Refugees and Transformations in World Order", *Millennium* 28(1): 1–26.
O'Brien, P. (2004) "Politicized Humanitarianism: A Response to Nicolas de Torrente", *Harvard Human Rights Journal* 17: 31–9.
O'Neill, B. (1997) "Power and Satisfaction in the Security Council", in B. Russett (ed.), *The Once and Future Security Council*, New York: St. Martin's Press, pp. 59–82.
Office of the President *see* US President's Office
Ogata, S. (2005) *The Turbulent Decade*, New York: Norton Press.
Oguzlu, H.T. (2004) "The Promise of NATO in the Construction of Cooperative Turkish-Greek Relations", *Review of International Affairs* 3(3): 458–78.
Oneal, J.R. and Russett, B.M. (1997) "The Classic Liberals were Right: Democracy, Interdependence, and Conflict, 1950–1985", *International Studies Quarterly* 41(2): 267–93.
Onis, Z. (2003) "Domestic Politics, International Norms and Challenges to the State: Turkey-EU Relations in the Post-Helsinki Era", *Turkish Studies* 4(1): 9–34.
Orbinski, J. (1999) "Kosovo: Aid Under Siege Once Again: The Principles, Roles, and Responsibilities of Humanitarian Action were Challenged at a Fundamental Level During the Kosovo Crisis", Online at <http:// nato.int>.
Orru, M., Biggart, N.W. and Hamilton, G. (1991) "Organizational Isomorphism in East Asia", in W. Powell and P. DiMaggio (eds) *The New Institutionalism in Organizational Analysis*, Princeton, NJ: Princeton UP, pp. 361–89.
Osgood, R.E. (1953) *Ideals and Self-Interest in America's Foreign Relations. The Great Transformation of the Twentieth Century*, Chicago: Chicago UP.
Overseas Development Institute, Disasters Emergency Committee, et al. (2000) *Independent Evaluation of Expenditure of DEC Kosovo Appeal Funds*. Phases I and II, April 1999–January 2000. London: Disasters Emergency Committee.
Owen, J.M. (1994) "How Liberalism Produces the Democratic Peace", *International Security* 19(1): 87–125.
Owen, J.M. (1997) *Liberal Peace, Liberal War. American Politics and International Security*, Ithaca, NY: Cornell UP.
Pace, M. (2005) "EU Policy-Making Towards Border Conflicts", *Working Paper Series in EU Border Conflicts Series*, No. 15, University of Birmingham.
Page, S. (2006) "Path Dependence", *Quarterly Journal of Political Science* 1(1): 87–115.
Paris, R. (2002) "International Peacebuilding and the "Mission Civilisatrice" ", *Review of International Studies* 28(4): 637–56.
Paris, R. (2004) *At War's End*, Cambridge: Cambridge UP.
Patrick, S. (2002) "Multilateralism and Its Discontents: The Causes and Consequences of US Ambivalence" in S. Patrick and S. Forman (eds) *Multilateralism and U.S. Foreign Policy: Ambivalent Engagement*, Boulder, CO: Lynne Rienner, pp. 1–44.
Payne, R.A. (2001) "Persuasion, Frames and Norm Construction", *European Journal of International Relations* 7(1): 37–61.
Penn, W. (1693/1993) *An Essay towards the Present and Future Peace of Europe*, London: Everyman.
Perlo-Freeman, S. and Stålenheim, P. (2003) "Military Expenditure in South Caucasus and Central Asia" in A.J.K. Bailes et al., *Armament and Disarmament in the Caucasus and Central Asia*, Stockholm: SIPRI, pp. 7–20.

Petritsch, Wolfgang (1999) "Report to the PIC Steering Board Meeting in Brussels", October, Brussels: Peace Implementation Council.
Pevehouse, J.C. (2002) "Democracy from the Outside-In? International Organizations and Democratization", *International Organization* 56(3): 515–49.
Pew Research Center (2002) *Americans and Europeans Differ Widely on Foreign Policy Issues*, Washington, DC: Pew Research Center for the People and the Press, April.
Pew Research Center (2002) *What the World Thinks in 2002*, Pew Global Attitudes Project, Washington, DC: Pew Research Center for the People and the Press.
Pew Research Center (2003) *Views of a Changing World. Report*, Pew Global Attitudes Project, Washington, DC: Pew Research Center for the People and the Press, June.
Pew Research Center (2004) *A Year after Iraq War. Mistrust of America in Europe Ever Higher, Muslim Anger Persists*, Pew Global Attitudes Project, Washington, DC: Pew Research Center.
Pew Research Center (2005) *Trends 2005*, Washington, DC: Pew Research Center for the People and the Press.
Pfeffer, J. and Salancik, G. (2003) *The External Control of Organizations: A Resource Dependence Perspective*, Stanford, CA: Stanford UP.
PIC (2000) "Declaration of the Peace Implementation Council", 24 May, Brussels: Peace Implementation Council.
Pictet, J. (1979) *The Fundamental Principles of the Red Cross*, Geneva: Henry Dunant Institute.
Pierson, P. (2000) "Increasing Returns, Path Dependence, and the Study of Politics", *American Political Science Review* 94(2): 251–67.
Plato (c. 360 BC 1941) "The Allegory of the Cave", trans. F. MacDonald Cornford, *The Republic of Plato*, Oxford: Oxford UP.
Pogge, T. (2002) *World Poverty and Human Rights*, Cambridge: Polity.
Pollack, M. (1997) "Delegation, Agency, and Agenda Setting in the European Community", *International Organization* 51(1): 99–134.
Pond, E. (2004) *Friendly Fire. The Near-Death of the Transatlantic Alliance*, Pittsburgh, PA and Washington, DC: European Union Studies Association/Brookings Institution Press.
Porter, T. (1999) "Coordination in the Midst of Chaos: The Refugee Crisis in Albania", *Forced Migration Review* 5: 20–3.
Porter, T. (2000) "The Partiality of Humanitarian Assistance – Kosovo in Comparative Perspective", *Journal of Humanitarian Assistance*, Online at <http://www.jha.ac/articles/a057.htm>.
Posen, B. (2003) "Command of the Commons: The Military Foundation of US Hegemony", *International Security* 28(1): 5–46.
Powell, R. (1991) "Absolute and Relative Gains in International Relations Theory", *American Political Science Review* 85(4): 1303–20.
Power, S. (2002) *A Problem from Hell: America and the Age of Genocide*, New York: Basic.
Pridham, G. (2002) "EU Enlargement and Consolidating Democracy in Post-Communist States – Formality and Reality", *Journal of Common Market Studies* 40(1): 953–73.
Pridham, G., Herring, E. and Sanford, G. (eds) (1997) *Building Democracy: the International Dimension of Democratisation in Eastern Europe*, Leicester: Leicester UP.

Przeworski, A., Alvarez, M., Cheibub, J. and Limongi, F. (2000) *Democracy and Development: Political Institutions and Well-being in the World, 1950–1990*, New York: Cambridge UP.

Pugh, M. (2002) "Peacekeeping and Critical Theory", paper presented at the BISA Conference, LSE, London, 16–18 December.

Pugh, M. (2004) "Rubbing Salt into War Wounds. Shadow Economies and Peace-building in Bosnia and Kosovo", *Problems of Post Communism* 51(3): 53–60.

Pupavac, V. (2001) "Therapeutic Governance: Psycho-Social Intervention and Trauma Risk Management", *Disasters* 25(4): 358–72.

Putnam, R.D. (1988) "Diplomacy and Domestic Politics", *International Organization* 42(3): 427–61.

Putnam, T. (2002) "Human Rights and Sustainable Peace", in S.J. Stedman, D. Rothchild and E. Cousens (eds) *Ending Civil Wars: The Implementation of Peace Agreements*, New York: Lynne Rienner, pp. 237–71.

Randel, J. and German, T. (2002) "Trends in the Financing of Humanitarian Assistance", in J. McRae (ed.) *The New Humanitarianism: A Review of Trends in Global Humanitarian Action, Humanitarian Policy Group Report*, London: Overseas Development Institute, pp. 12–28.

Regan, P. (1996) "Conditions for Successful Third Party Interventions", *Journal of Conflict Resolution* 40(1): 336–59.

Regan, P. (2000) *Civil Wars and Foreign Powers: Outside Interventions and Intrastate Conflicts*, Ann Arbor, MI: University of Michigan Press.

Regan, P. (2002) "Third-Party Interventions and the Duration of Intrastate Conflict", *Journal of Conflict Resolution* 46(1): 55–73.

Reisman, M. (1993) "The Constitutional Crisis in the United Nations", *American Journal of International Law* 87(1): 83–100.

Reljić, D. (2005) "The Western Balkans without a Plan for the Future", *SWP Comments*, 31 July.

Report of the Secretary-General's High Level Panel on Threats, Challenges, and Change (2004) New York: United Nations.

Richmond, O. (2002) *Maintaining Order, Making Peace*, London: Palgrave.

Richmond, O. (2004a) "The Globalisation of Approaches to Conflict", *Cooperation and Conflict* 39(2): 129–50.

Richmond, O. (2004b) "UN Peace Operations and the Dilemmas of the Peacebuilding Consensus", *International Peacekeeping* 10(4): 83–101.

Richmond, O. (2005) *The Transformation of Peace*, London: Palgrave.

Rieff, D. (2002) *A Bed for the Night: Humanitarianism in Crisis*, New York: Simon and Schuster.

Riesman, W.M. (1999) "Kosovo's Antimonies", *American Journal of International Law* 93(4): 860–2.

Risse, T. (2000) "Let's Argue!: Communicative Action in World Politics", *International Organization* 54(1): 1–39.

Risse, T. (2002) "U.S. Power in a Liberal Security Community", in J. Ikenberry (ed.) *America Unrivaled. U.S. Unipolarity and the Future of the Balance of Power*, Ithaca, NY: Cornell UP, pp. 260–83.

Risse, T. (2003) "Beyond Iraq: The Crisis of the Transatlantic Security Community", *Die Friedens-Warte* 78(2–3): 173–93.

Risse, T. (2006) "The Crisis of the Transatlantic Security Community", in I. Peters (ed.) *Transatlantic Tug-of-War: Prospects for US–European Cooperation*, Berlin: LIT Verlag, pp. 11–141.

Risse, T., and Sikkink, K. (1999) "The Socialization of International Human Rights Norms into Domestic Practice", in T. Risse, S. Ropp and K. Sikkink (eds) *The Power of Human Rights: International Norms and Domestic Change*, Cambridge: Cambridge UP, pp. 1–38.

Risse, T., Ropp, S. and Sikkink, K. (1999) *The Power of Human Rights*, New York: Cambridge UP.

Risse-Kappen, T. (1988) *The Zero Option. INF, West Germany, and Arms Control*, Boulder, CO: Westview.

Risse-Kappen, T. (1995) *Cooperation among Democracies. The European Influence on U.S. Foreign Policy*, Princeton, NJ: Princeton UP.

Risse-Kappen, T. (1996) "Collective Identity in a Democratic Community: The Case of NATO", in P. Katzenstein (ed.) *The Culture of National Security: Norms and Identity in World Politics*, New York: Columbia UP, pp. 357–99.

Roberts, A. (1999) "NATO's "Humanitarian War" Over Kosovo", *Survival* 41(3): 102–23.

Roggo, B. (2000) "After the Kosovo Conflict, a Genuine Humanitarian Space: A Utopian Concept or an Essential Requirement?", *International Review of the Red Cross*, 837: 31–47.

Rotberg, R.I. and Thompson, D. (eds) (2000) *Truth vs. Justice: The Morality of Truth Commissions*, Princeton, NJ: Princeton UP.

Roth, K. (2001) "The Case for Universal Jurisdiction", *Foreign Affairs* 80(5): 150–4.

Ruggie, J.G. (1992) "Multilateralism: The Anatomy of an Institution", *International Organization* 46(3): 561–98.

Ruggie, J.G. (ed.) (1993a) *Multilateralism Matters. The Theory and Praxis of an Institutional Form*, New York: Columbia UP.

Ruggie, J.G. (1993b) "Multilateralism: The Anatomy of an Institution", in J.G. Ruggie (ed.) *Multilateralism Matters*, New York: Columbia UP, pp. 3–47.

Ruggie, J.G. (1994) "America and Multilateralism after the Cold War", *Political Science Quarterly* 109(4): 553–70.

Ruggie, J.G. (1998) *Constructing the World Polity*, London: Routledge.

Rumelili, B. (2003) "Liminality and Perpetuation of Conflicts: Turkish-Greek Relations in the Context of Community-Building by the EU", *European Journal of International Relations* 9(2): 213–48.

Rumelili, B. (2004a) "The European Union's Impact on the Greek–Turkish Conflict: A Review of the Literature", *Working Paper Series in EU Border Conflicts Series*, no. 6.

Rumelili, B. (2004b) "The Microprocesses of Hegemonic Influence: The Case of EU and Greece/Turkey", *EUBORDERCONF Project*, Bogazici University/University of Birmingham.

Rumelili, B. (2005) "Civil Society and the Europeanization of Greek–Turkish Cooperation", *South European Society and Politics* 10(1): 43–54.

Rupnik, J. (2005) European Parliament, Committee on Foreign Affairs, 25 January, *Centre d'Etudes et de Recherches Internationales*, Online at <http://europa-eu-un.org/articles/sl/article_4265_sl.htm>.

Russett, B. (1993) *Grasping the Democratic Peace*, Princeton, NJ: Princeton UP.

Russett, B. (2005) "Security Council Expansion: Can't and Shouldn't", in *Reforming the United Nations for Peace and Security*, New Haven, CT: Yale Center for the Study of Globalization, pp. 153–66.

Russett, B. and Oneal, J. (2001) *Triangulating Peace. Democracy, Interdependence, and International Organizations*, New York and London: W.W. Norton.

Russett, B., O'Neil, B. and Sutterlin, J. (1997) "Breaking the Restructuring Logjam", in B. Russett (ed.) *The Once and Future Security Council*, London, Macmillan: pp. 153–69.

Sambanis, N. (2002) "Do Ethnic and Non-Ethnic Civil Wars Have the Same Causes? Organization and Interests in Ethnic Insurgency", Working Paper, Yale University, 17 October.

Sambanis, N. (2004) "What Is A Civil War? Conceptual and Empirical Complexities of an Operational Definition", *Journal of Conflict Resolution* 48(6): 814–58.

Schachter, O. (1989) "Self-Defense and the Rule of Law", *American Journal of International Law* 83(2): 259–77.

Scheffer, D.J. (2000) "The U.S. Perspective on the ICC," in S.B. Sewall and C. Kaysen (eds) *The United States and the International Criminal Court*, New York: Rowman & Littlefield, pp. 119–36.

Schelling, T. (1960) *The Strategy of Conflict*, Cambridge, MA: Harvard UP.

Schimmelfennig, F. (2000) "International Socialization in the New Europe: Rational Action in an Institutional Environment", *European Journal of International Relations* 6(1): 109–39.

Schimmelfennig, F. (2001) "The Community Trap: Liberal Norms, Rhetorical Action and the Eastern Enlargement of the European Union", *International Organization* 55(1): 47–80.

Schimmelfennig, F. (2002) "Introduction: The Impact of International Organizations on the Central and Eastern European States – Conceptual and Theoretical Issues", in R. Linden (ed.) *Norms and Nannies. The Impact of International Organizations on the Central and East European States*, Lanham, MD: Rowman & Littlefield, pp. 1–29.

Schimmelfennig, F. (2003) *The EU, NATO and the Integration of Europe. Rules and Rhetoric*, Cambridge: Cambridge UP.

Schimmelfennig, F. (2005) "The International Promotion of Political Norms in Eastern Europe: a Qualitative Comparative Analysis", Harvard University, Center for European Studies /Central and Eastern Europe, Working Paper 61.

Schimmelfennig, F. (2006) "Strategic Calculation and International Socialization: Membership Incentives, Party Constellations, and Sustained Compliance in Central and Eastern Europe", *International Organization* 59(4): 827–60.

Schimmelfennig, F. and Sedelmeier, U. (2004) "Governance by Conditionality: EU Rule Transfer to the Candidate Countries of Central and Eastern Europe", *Journal of European Public Policy* 11(4): 661–79.

Schmitt, C. (1996) *The Concept of the Political*, Chicago: University of Chicago Press.

Schneckener, U. (2002) *Netzwerke des Terrors. Charakter und Strukturen des transnationalen Terrorismus*, Berlin: Stiftung Wissenschaft und Politik, December.

Schöllgen, G. (2003) *Der Auftritt. Deutschlands Rückkehr auf die Weltbühne*, Berlin: Propyläen Verlag.

Schulz, W.F. (2001) *In Our Own Best Interest: How Defending Human Rights Benefits Us All*, Boston: Beacon.

SCO (Shanghai Co-operation Organization) (2001a) *Declaration on the Creation of*

the Shanghai Cooperation Organization, Online at <http://russia.shaps.hawaii.edu/fp/russia/sco_1_20010620.html> [accessed on 5 May 2005].
SCO (Shanghai Co-operation Organization) (2001b) *Charter of Shanghai Cooperation Organization*, Online at <http://www.sectsco.org/news_detail.asp?id=96&LanguageID=2> [accessed on 5 May 2005].
SCO (Shanghai Co-operation Organization) (2001c) Shanghai Communiqué, Online at <http://www.missions.itu.int/~kazaks/eng/sco/sco04.htm> [accessed on 5 May 2005].
SCO (Shanghai Co-operation Organization) (2004) Tashkent Declaration of the Heads of the States Participating in the Shanghai Co-operation Organization, Online at <http://www.sectsco.org/news_detail.asp?id=119&LanguageID=2> [accessed on 5 May 2005].
Scott, W.R. (1987) "The Adolescence of Institutional Theory", *Administrative Studies Quarterly* 32(4): 493–511.
Scott, W.R. (1995) *Institutions and Organizations*, Thousand Oaks, CA: Sage.
Scott, W.R. and Meyer, J. (1993) *Organizational Environments: Ritual and Rationality*, Beverly Hills, CA: Sage.
Scott-Flynn, N. (1999) "Coordination in Kosovo: The Challenge for the NGO Sector", Humanitarian Practice Network.
Searle, J.R. (1999) "I married a computer", *New York Review of Books*, 8 April, pp. 37–8.
Segal, G. (1996) "East Asia and the "Constrainment" of China", *International Security* 20(4): 107–35.
Setear, J.K. (2002) "The President's Rational Choice of a Treaty's Preratification Pathway: Article II, Congressional-Executive Agreement, or Executive Agreement?", *Journal of Legal Studies* 31(1): 5–39.
Sewall, S.B. and Kaysen, C. (eds) (2000) *The United States and the International Criminal Court*, New York: Rowman & Littlefield.
Shambaugh, D. (2004–5) "China Engages Asia: Reshaping the Regional Order", *International Security* 29(1): 64–99.
Shanghai Co-operation Organization *see* SCO
Shklar, J. (1964) *Legalism*. Cambridge, MA: Harvard UP.
Simma, B. (1999) "NATO, The UN and the Use of Force: Legal Aspects", *European Journal of International Law* 10(1): 1–22.
Simmons, B.A. (2000) "International Law and State Behavior: Commitment and Compliance in International Monetary Affairs", *American Political Science Review* 94(4): 819–35.
Simmons, B.A. and Martin, L.L. (2002) "International Organizations and Institutions", in W. Carlsnaes, T. Risse, and B.A. Simmons (eds) *Handbook of International Relations*, London: Sage.
Simon, H. (1951) "A Formal Theory of the Employment Relationship", *Econometrica* 19(3): 299–305.
Simon, S. (1996) "Alternative Visions of Security in the Asia Pacific", *Pacific Affairs* 69(3): 381–96.
Simon, S. (1998) "The Limits of Defense and Security Cooperation in Southeast Asia," in J. Sperling Y. Malik and D. Louscher (eds) *Zones of Amity, Zones of Enmity: The Prospects for Economic and Military Security in Asia*, Leiden: Brill, pp. 62–75.
Siquiera, K. (2003) "Conflict and Third-Party Intervention", *Defence and Peace Economics* 14(6): 389–400.

Slim, H. (1997) "Doing the Right Thing: Relief Agencies, Moral Dilemmas, and Moral Responsibility in Political Emergencies and War", *Disasters* 21(3): 244–57.

Slim, H. (2002a) "By What Authority? The Legitimacy and Accountability of Non-governmental Organisations", *Journal of Humanitarian Assistance*, Online at <http://www.jha.ac/articles/a082.htm>.

Slim, H. (2002b) "Claiming a Humanitarian Imperative: NGOs and the Cultivation of Humanitarian Duty", paper presented at the Seventh Annual Conference of Webster University on Humanitarian Values for the 21st Century, Geneva, 21–22 February.

Slim, H. (2002c) "Military Intervention to Protect Human Rights: The Humanitarian Agency Perspective", *Journal of Humanitarian Assistance*, Online at <http://www.jha.ac/articlesa084.htm>.

Slim, H. (2004a) "Politicizing Humanitarian Action According to Need", presentation to the 2nd International Meeting on Good Humanitarian Donorship, Ottawa, 21–22 October.

Slim, H. (2004b) "Protecting Civilians: Putting the Individual at the Humanitarian Centre", in Office of the Co-ordinator of Humanitarian Assistance (ed.) *The Humanitarian Decade: Challenges for Humanitarian Assistance in the Last Decade and into the Future*, vol. II, New York: United Nations Press, pp. 154–70.

Slomp, G. (1996) "Hobbes, Feminism, and Liberalism", Political Studies Association Conference, University of Glasgow.

Smith, A. and Stam, A. (2003) "Mediation and Peacekeeping in a Random Walk Model of Civil and Interstate War", *International Studies Review* 5(4): 115–35.

Smith, K.E. (2003) *European Union Foreign Policy in a Changing World*, London: Polity Press.

Smith, M. (1996) "The EU as an International Actor," in J.J. Richardson (ed.) *European Union: Power and Policy-Making*, London: Routledge, pp. 247–62.

Smith, M.G. (2003) *Peacekeeping in East Timor*, Boulder, CO: Lynne Rienner.

Smith, T. (1994) *America's Mission: The United States and the Worldwide Struggle for Democracy in the Twentieth Century*, Princeton, NJ: Princeton UP.

Snyder, G.H. (1984) "The Security Dilemma in Alliance Politics", *World Politics* 36(4): 461–95.

Snyder, J. (2000) *From Voting to Violence*, London: W.W. Norton.

Snyder, J. (2002) "Anarchy and Culture: Insights from the Anthropology of War", *International Organization* 56(1): 7–46.

Snyder, J. and Vinjamuri, L. (2003–4) "Trials and Errors: Principle and Pragmatism in Strategies of International Justice", *International Security* 28(3): 5–44.

Solana, J. (2005) "Dayton @ 10: Drawing Lessons from the Past", Policy Dialogue organised by EPC and King Baudouin Foundation, Brussels, 25 November, S382/05.

Solingen, E. (1998) *Regional Orders at Century's Dawn: Global and Domestic Influences of Grand Strategy*, Princeton, NJ: Princeton UP.

Soutou, G.H. (2000) "Was there a European Order in the Twentieth Century? From the Concert of Europe to the End of the Cold War", *Contemporary European History* 9(3): 329–33.

Spiro, P.J. (2001) "Treaties, Executive Agreements, and Constitutional Method", *Texas Law Review* 79(5): 961–1033.

Stålenheim, P., Omitoogun, W., and Perdomo, C. (2005) "Military Expenditures," in SIPRI, *SIPRI Yearbook 2005*, Oxford: Oxford UP, pp. 307–44.

Stanley, H.W. and Niemi, R.G. (2001) *Vital Statistics on American Politics, 2001–2002*, Washington, DC: CQ Press.

Stearns, M. (1992) *Entangled Allies: US Policy towards Greece, Turkey and Cyprus*, New York: Council on Foreign Relations.

Stedman, S.J. (1997) "Spoiler Problems in Peace Processes", *International Security* 22(2): 5–53.

Steinbruner, J.D. (2000) *Principles of Global Security*, Washington, DC: Brookings Institution Press.

Stephanou, C. and Tsardanides, C. (1991) "The EC Factor in the Greece–Turkey–Cyprus Triangle" in D. Constas (ed.) *The Greek–Turkish Conflict in the 1990s: Domestic and External Influences*, New York: St. Martin's Press, pp. 207–30.

Stockton, N. (1998) "In Defence of Humanitarianism", *Disasters* 22(4): 352–60.

Stockton, N. (2002) "Strategic Coordination in Afghanistan", ECHO/ Afghanistan Research and Evaluation Unit, August.

Stockton, N. (2004) "The Changing Nature of Humanitarian Crises", in Office of the Co-ordinator of Humanitarian Assistance (ed.) *The Humanitarian Decade: Challenges for Humanitarian Assistance in the Last Decade and into the Future*, vol. II, New York: United Nations Press, pp. 15–38.

Stoddard, A. (2002) "Trends in US Humanitarian Policy", in J. Macrae, *The New Humanitarianisms: A Review of Trends in Global Humanitarian Action*, Humanitarian Policy Group Report, 11, London.

Stone Sweet, A. and Brunell, T.L. (1998) "Constructing a Supranational Constitution: Dispute Resolution and Governance in the European Community", *American Political Science Review* 92(1): 63–81.

Strand, J., Rapkin, D. and Scales, P. (2005) Weighted Voting, Relative Voting Power, and UN Security Council Reform, paper presented in the annual meeting of the International Studies Association, Honolulu, 1–5 March.

Suchman, M. (1995) "Managing Legitimacy: Strategic and Institutional Approaches", *Academy of Management Review* 20(3): 571–610.

Suhrke, A. (2001) "Peacekeepers as Nation-builders: Dilemmas of the UN in East Timor", *International Peacekeeping* 8(4): 1–20.

Suhrke, A., Barutciski, M., Sandison, P. and Garlock, R. (2000) *The Kosovo Refugee Crisis: An Evaluation of UNHCR's Emergency Preparedness and Response*, Geneva: UNHCR, February.

Sumner, G.W. (1911) *War and Other Essays*, New Haven, CI: Yale UP.

Sutterlin, J. (1997) "The Past as Prologue", in B. Russett (ed.) *The Once and Future Security Council*, London and New York: Macmillan, pp. 1–13.

Talbott, S. (1984) *Deadly Gambits*, New York: A. Knopf.

Talbott, S. (1988) *The Master of the Game: Paul Nitze and the Nuclear Arms Race*, New York: A. Knopf.

Tallberg, J. (2002) "Paths to Compliance: Enforcement, Management, and the European Union", *International Organization* 56 (3): 609–43.

Terry, F. (2002) *Condemned To Repeat?*, Ithaca, NY: Cornell UP.

Thatcher, M. and Stone Sweet, A. (2002) "Theory and Practice of Delegation to Non-Majoritarian Institutions", *West European Politics* 25(1): 1–22.

Towell, P. (1998) "Aspiring NATO Newcomers Face Long Road to Integration", *Congressional Quarterly* 56(6): 275.

Tribe, L.H. (1995) "Taking Text and Structure Seriously: Reflections on Free-Form Method in Constitutional Interpretation", *Harvard Law Review* 108(6): 1221–303.

Trofimov, D. (2003) "Arms Control in Central Asia", in A.J.K. Bailes et al. *Armament and Disarmament in the Caucasus and Central Asia*, Stockholm: SIPRI, pp. 46–56.

Tsakonas, P. (2001) "Turkey's Post-Helsinki Turbulence. Implications for Greece and the Cyprus Issue", *Turkish Studies* 2(2): 1–40.

Tsakonas, P. (2007) *A Breakthrough in Greek-Turkish Relations? Understanding Greece's Socialization Strategy*, Basingstoke and New York: Palgrave, forthcoming.

Tsakonas, P. and Tournikiotis, A. (2003) "Greece's Elusive Quest for Security Providers: The 'Expectations–Reality Gap' ", *Security Dialogue* 34(3): 301–14.

Tsebelis, G. (1990) *Nested Games,*: University of California Press.

Tsebelis, G. (2002) *Veto Players: How Political Institutions Work*, Princeton, NJ: Princeton UP.

Tuschoff, C. (1999) "Alliance Cohesion and Peaceful Change in NATO", in H. Haftendorn, R.O. Keohane, and C.A. Wallander (eds) *Imperfect Unions: Security Institutions over Space and Time*, Oxford: Oxford UP, pp. 140–61.

Ugur, M. (1999) *The European Union and Turkey: An Anchor/Credibility Dilemma*, Aldershot, Hants: Ashgate.

United Nations Development Programme (2004) *Human Development Report 2004*, New York: Oxford UP.

United Nations High-Level Panel on Threats, Challenges, and Change (2004) *A More Secure World: Our Shared Responsibility*. New York: United Nations, A/59/565, 2 December.

United Nations (2005) *Year in Review 2004: United Nations Peace Operations*, New York: United Nations Dept of Public Information.

Urquhart, B. (2005) "Brief Notes on the Report of the High-level Panel on Threats, Challenges and Change" in *Reforming the United Nations for Peace and Security* New Haven, CT: Yale Center for the Study of Globalization, pp. 183–5.

US President's Office (2002) *The National Security Strategy of the United States of America*, Washington, DC: The White House, September. (Also online at http://whitehouse.gov/nsc/nss.html)

US President's Office (2006) *The National Security Strategy of the United States of America, 2006*, Washington, DC: White House.

Vachudova, M.A. (2003) "Strategies for Democratization and European Integration in the Balkans", in M. Cremona (ed.) *The Enlargement of the European Union*, Oxford: Oxford UP, pp. 141–60.

Valinakis, Y. (1997) *With Vision and Program: Foreign Policy for a Greece with Self-Confidence*, Thessaloniki: Paratiritis [in Greek].

Vamvakas, P.I. (2001) "States in Transition and Defensive Alliances: Greece and Turkey in NATO" (Unpublished PhD thesis, Boston University, Graduate School of Arts and Sciences).

Vaughan, D. (1996) *The Challenger Launch Decision*, Chicago: University of Chicago Press.

Vaux, T. (2001) *The Selfish Altruist*, Sterling, VA: Earthscan Publishing.

Vedby Rasmussen, M. (2003) *The West, Civil Society, and the Construction of Peace*, London: Palgrave.

Vejvoda, I. (2004) *US Policy towards Southeast Europe: Unfinished Business in the Balkans*, Testimony to the US Senate Committee on Foreign Relations, 14 July.

Voeten, E. (2000) "Clashes in the Assembly", *International Organization* 54(2): 185–217.

Voeten, E. (2001) "Outside Options and the Logic of Security Council Action", *American Political Science Review* 95(4): 845–58.

Voeten, E. (2005) "The Political Origins of the United Nations Security Council's Ability to Legitimize the Use of Force", *International Organization* 59(3): 527–57.
Voeten, E. (n.d.) "A Strategic Approach to Understanding Security Council Authority", in in B. Cronin and I. Hurd (eds) *International Authority and the UN Security Council*, Cambridge: Cambridge UP, forthcoming.
de Waal, A. (1997) *Famine Crimes*, Bloomington: Indiana UP.
Wæver, O. (1998) "Insecurity, security, and asecurity in the West European non-war Community", in E. Adler and M. Barnett (eds) *Security Communities*, Cambridge: Cambridge UP, pp. 69–118.
Walker, R.B.J (1992) *Inside/Outside: International Relations as Political Theory*, Cambridge: Cambridge UP.
Wallander, C.A. (2000) "Institutional Assets and Adaptability: NATO After the Cold War", *International Organization* 54(1): 705–35.
Wallensteen, P. (1997) "Representing the World: A Security Council for the 21st Century", in R. Dahl (ed.) *The Politics of Global Governance*, Boulder, CO: Lynne Rienner, pp. 103–15.
Walt, S.M. (1987) *The Origins of Alliances*, Ithaca, NY: Cornell UP.
Walter, B.F. (1997) "The Critical Barrier to Civil War Settlement", *International Organization* 51(3): 335–64.
Waltz, K. (1978) *Theory of International Politics*, New York: Random House.
Waltz, K. (1979) *Theory of International Politics*, Reading, MA: Addison-Wesley.
Waltz, K. (1993) "The Emerging Structure of International Politics", *International Security* 18(2): 44–79.
Wanandi, J. (2005) "Towards an Asian Security Community", *Asia-Europe Journal* 3(3): 323–32.
Ward, M.D. and Gleditsch, K.S. (1998) "Democratizing for Peace", *American Political Science Review* 92(1): 51–61.
Warner, D. (1999) "The Politics of the Political/Humanitarian Divide", *International Review of the Red Cross* 833: 109–18.
Weber, S. (1993) "Shaping the Postwar Balance of Power: Multilateralism in NATO", in J.G. Ruggie (ed.), *Multilateralism Matters: The Theory and Praxis of an Institutional Form*, New York: Columbia UP, pp. 233–92.
Weber, S. (1994) "Origins of the European Bank for Reconstruction and Development", *International Organization* 48(1): 1–38.
Weiss, T. (1999) "The Humanitarian Identity Crisis", *Ethics and International Affairs* 13: 1–42.
Weiss, T. (2003) "The Illusion of UN Security Council Reform", *Washington Quarterly* 26(4): 147–61.
Weiss, T., Forsythe, D. and Coate, R. (2004) *The United Nations and Changing World Politics*, 4th edn, Boulder, CO: Westview Press.
Wendt, A. (1994) "Collective Identity Formation and the International State", *American Political Science Review* 88(2): 391–425.
Wendt, A. (1996) "Identity and Structural Change in International Politics", in Y. Lapid and F. Kratochwil (eds) *The Return of Culture and Identity in IR Theory*, Boulder, CO: Lynne Rienner, pp. 47–66
Wendt, A. (1999) *Social Theory of International Politics*, Cambridge: Cambridge UP.
Wendt, A. and Duvall, R. (1989) "Institutions and International Order" in E. Czempiel

and J. Rosenau (eds) *Global Changes and Theoretical Challenges: Approaches to World Politics for the 1990s*, Lexington, MA: Lexington Books, 51–74.

Weschler, L. (2000) "Exceptional Cases in Rome: The United States and the Struggle for an ICC," in S.B. Sewall and C. Kaysen (eds) *The United States and the International Criminal Court*, New York: Rowman & Littlefield, pp. 85–111.

Wessels, W. (1997) "An Ever Closer Fusion? A Dynamic Macropolitical View on Integration Processes", *Journal of Common Market Studies* 35(2): 267–99.

Wheeler, N. (2000) *Saving Strangers*, New York: Oxford UP.

White House *see* US President's Office

White, N.D. (1993) *Keeping the Peace*, Manchester: Manchester UP.

Wichmann, N. (2004) "The Hand that Rocks the Cradle: Do Norms Matter?" *International Studies Review*, 6(1): 129–30 [book review].

Wiener, A. (2004) "Contested Compliance: Interventions on the Normative Structure of World Politics", *European Journal of International Relations* 10(2): 189–234.

Wiles, P. (2001) "The Kosovo Emergency: The Disasters Emergency Committee Evaluation", paper presented at Kosovo and the Changing Face of Humanitarian Action Conference, Uppsala, Sweden, May.

Wilmer, F. (1998) "The Social Reconstruction of Conflict and Reconciliation in the Former Yugoslavia", *Social Justice* 25(4): 90–113.

Wilson, W. (1983) Address to the Senate, 22 January 1917, in Arthur S. Link et al. (eds), *The Papers of Woodrow Wilson*, vol. 40, Princeton, NJ: Princeton UP, pp. 533–9.

Winter, E. (1996) "Voting and Vetoing", *American Political Science Review* 90(4): 813–24.

Wohlforth, W.C. (1999) "The Stability of a Unipolar World", *International Security* 24(1): 5–41.

Wolfers, A. (1962) "Collective Security versus Collective Defense" in A. Wolfers (ed.) *Discord and Collaboration: Essays on International Politics*, Baltimore, MD: Johns Hopkins UP, pp. 181–216.

Woodward, B. (2002) *Bush at War*, New York: Simon & Schuster.

Woodward, B. (2004) *Plan of Attack*. New York: Simon & Schuster.

WorldAudit.org (n.d.) "World Audit Democracy Statistics", Online at http://www.worldaudit.org/statpage.htm [accessed on 2 February 2006].

Worldviews 2002 (2002) Chicago: The Chicago Council on Foreign Relations and the German Marshall Fund of the United States.

Wright, Q. (1964) *The Study of War*, Chicago: University of Chicago Press.

Yom, S.L. (2002) "The Future of the Shanghai Cooperation Organization", Online at <http://www.fas.harvard.edu/-asiactr/haq/200204/0204a003.htm> [accessed on 23 October 2004].

Yoo, J.C. (2001) "Laws as Treaties? The Constitutionality of Congressional-Executive Agreements", *Michigan Law Review* 99(4): 757–852.

Young, O. (1967) *The Intermediaries: Third Parties in International Crises*, Princeton, NJ: Princeton UP.

Young, O. (1992) "The Effectiveness of International Institutions: Hard Cases and Critical Variables" in J. Rosenau and E.O. Czempiel (eds) *Governance Without Government: Order and Change in World Politics*, Cambridge: Cambridge UP, pp. 160–94.

Zacher, M. (2003) "The Conundrums of Power Sharing: The Politics of Security

Council Reform", Paper prepared for the Conference on the United Nations and Global Security, University of British Columbia, 18–19 September.

Zielonka, J. and Pravda, A. (eds) (2001) *Democratic Consolidation in Eastern Europe: International and Transnational Factors*, vol. 2, Oxford: Oxford UP.

Zurn, M. and Joerges C. (eds) (2005) *Law and Governance in Postnational Europe: Compliance Beyond the Nation-State*, New York: Cambridge UP.

Index

Note: *italic* page numbers denote references to Figures/Tables.

Abu Grahib 79
accountability 57–8, 207–8
Acharya, A. 134n9
Acheson, Dean 34, 36
adverse substitution 247n14
Afghanistan 3, 4, 6; bilateral aid 147; Islamabad Accords 279nxii; Japanese involvement 315; NATO 14, 185, 191, *192*, 194, 195, 198; Northern Alliance 53–4; peacebuilding 171–2, 175, 176, 177, *177*, 281; Soviet invasion of 292; transatlantic security co-operation 80–1; unilateralism 168; US military action in 43, 298, 300; US threats to NGOs in 148
African Union (AU) 195, 317
al-Qaeda 3, 198
Albania 54, 187
Albanian Force (AFOR) 154
Albright, Madeleine 45
Alexopoulos, Aris 16–17, 306–23
Algeria 281
alliances 110, *111*
Altmann, F.L. 211
amity 109, *111–12*, 113, 114, *126*, 131, 132–3
amnesties 50, 54, 55, 56
Amnesty International 49
anarchy 102, 128, 163
Anderson, Benedict 117
Angola 147, 157, *177*, 281
Annan, Kofi 46, 152, 289
anti-Americanism 87, 91, 241
Anti-Ballistic Missile (ABM) treaty 38, 63–4, 84
Arab states 317–18
Argentina 281, 304n8
arms control 64, 67, 68
ASEAN +3 129

ASEAN Regional Forum (ARF) 129
ASEAN Security Community (ASC) 123
Ashdown, P. 202, 210–11, 212, 213, 218, 220
Asia-Pacific region 36, 129–30
Asia-US relations 28, 30–1
Asian Pacific Economic Co-operation (APEC) 21, 31, 35, 36, 37
Asmus, R. 88–9
Association of Southeast Asian Nations (ASEAN) 114, 117–18, 122–3, 125, 128–30, 133
"assurance" game 257
"Atlanticists" 97, 98
atrocities 49–51, 53, 56, 57
Aufses, A.H. 62
Australia 37, 168, 296, 298
autonomy 24, 40–1, 103, 108
Azerbaijan 281

Baker, J.A. 36, 294
Balkans 6, 85, 169, 202–22; ethnic cleansing 14; international socialization 14, 15; peacebuilding 172, 173, 175, 177; security concerns 233; transatlantic security co-operation 80–1; *see also* Bosnia and Herzegovina; Kosovo; Yugoslavia, former
Bangladesh 281
bargaining failures 300–1, 303
Barnett, Michael 11, 136–62, 164
Batt, J. 204
Belarus 187
bilateral agreements 9–10, 30–1, 60; executive agreements versus treaties 68–72, 76; multilateral versus bilateral agreements 72–5, 76
bilateral aid 146, 155
Bin Laden, Osama 85

Blair, Tony 97, 161n33
Bobbitt, Phillip 102
Bolivia 281
Bose, S. 208
Bosnia and Herzegovina (BiH) 15, 202–22, 281, 300; complexity and co-ordination 210–12; contextual framework 208–10; credibility and consistency 214–17; genocide strategy 258; humanitarian intervention 140, 143, 150; interaction and socialization 217–19; Kosovo comparison 152, 154; NATO intervention 184, 191, 192–3, 195–6, 197, 198, 199–200; peacebuilding 171, 175, 176–7, *177*, 178; refugees 156; weak consensus 168; *see also* Balkans; Yugoslavia, former
Bourantonis, Dimitris 1–17, 306–23
Boutros-Ghali, Boutros 141
Brahimi, Lakhdar 51
Brazil 293, 304n8, 316, 318–19
Brecke, Peter 56
Brown, Gordon 97
Brunei 114
Brunell, Thomas 124
Brussels European Council Summit (2004) 238–9, 242, 244–5
Brussels Pact 34
Burma *see* Myanmar
Burt, Richard 93
Burundi 43, 48, 281
Bush, George Sr. 36, 74
Bush, George W. 6, 21, 38, 43, 44, 65; aversion to multilateralism 72; national interest 119; National Security Strategy 45, 80, 97; NATO co-operation 200; neo-conservatives 92–3; opposition to 78, 79, 87, 89; Reagan comparison 91–2; religious vote 86–7

Cambodia: ASEAN 114; Paris Accords 275n14; peace operations 169, 173, 177, 252, 281–2
capacity building 207, 257, 273
capitalism 92, 94
Caplan, R. 206
Care International 150
Caron, D. 306
Carothers, Thomas 48
Carter, James 74
Cascade Program 228
ceasefires 279
censorship 47
Central African Republic 282
central and eastern European countries (CEECs): Balkans comparison 203; EU enlargement 203–4, 220; NATO 36–7, 183, 186–7, 190, 191–2, 196, 197–8, 232; transmission of democratic norms 241
central Asia 114, *115*, 116–17, 120–2, *121*, 125–8, *126*
Chad 282
Chayes, A. 207
Checkel, J.T. 205
Cheney, Dick 92
China 58, 282; ASEAN relations with 128–9; defense expenditure 134n7; Shanghai Co-operation Organization 114, 116, 117, 120–2, 127; UN Security Council 291, 293, 297, 302, 314, 319
Chirac, Jacques 301
Chopra, Jarat 174
Churchill, Winston 33
civil peace 166–7, 174, *176*
civil wars 252–87
civilianized security community *112*, 113–14, 133
Clark, Wesley 193
Clinton, Bill 36, 37, 152; multilateral agreements 74–5; national interest 119; NATO co-operation 200; transatlantic disagreement 81
"coalitions of the willing" 81, 90, 91, 97, 99, 191
coercion 23, 202, 207; *see also* military force
Cold War 1, 39, 85, 136; arms race 92; end of 7–8, 78, 81, 130, 139, 288, 289; European conflict resolution 234; India 317; multilateral agreements 72; NATO 131, 186, 233, 240; peacekeeping missions 292; threats to peace 140; UN assets 293–4; UN Security Council 293, 300
collective action 290, 295–7, 298, 301
collective defense 110, *111*, 113, 130–2, 133, 185–6; *see also* collective security
collective identity: European Union 132; institutions 226; NATO 130, 227, 231–2; southeast Asia 117, 129; state interests 105; transatlantic relationship 79, 84–9, 91, 98; *see also* identity
collective security 110, *111*, 113; European Union 133; institutions 226; League of Nations 31; NATO 223, 240; UN Security Council 313; *see also* collective defense
Colombia 282
Combined Joint Task Force (CJTF) 183, 186
Common Foreign and Security Policy (CFSP) 124, 234

"complex humanitarian emergencies" 142
concerts 110–13, *111*, 129–30, 132
conditionality 205, 246; Bosnia and Herzegovina accession to the EU 217, 219, 220; Turkey accession to the EU 236, 237, 242
Conference on Security Co-operation in Europe (CSCE) 36
conflict resolution: co-operation problems 256, 257–9, *260*; co-ordination problems 256–7, 259, *260*; European Union 132; Greek–Turkish conflict 232, 234, 235, 238, 239, 242, 245; humanitarianism 144; institutional role 225–6; regulation 108
Congo (Brazzaville) 282
Congo (Zaire): humanitarian funding 147, 157; peacebuilding *177*; relief agencies 154; UN missions 282, 291, 292
Congress 61, 62, 63, 70, 73, 99
conservatives 92–4, 95, 97, 98, 99
constitutional peace 166, *176*
constructivism 12, 15, 41n1, 205; civil peace 167; Greek-Turkish conflict 229; humanitarianism 158; institutions 223, 226, 227, 230; interstate conflict 231; liberal peace 164; NATO 196–7, 200; normative change 45, 46, 51–2, 54; social learning 202, 207
contract theory 294–5, 296, 304n11
Conventional Forces in Europe (CFE) Treaty 228, 247n8
co-operation: central Asia 116; contract theory 294; Greek-Turkish conflict 227, 229, 230, 244, 245; institutional bargain 25, 26; liberal peace 167, 170; multilateralism definition 7; NATO 14, 186–7, 189–90, 191–200, 201; neo-institutionalism 12; peace operations 256, 257–9, *260*; peacebuilding consensus 168; post-Westphalian state 133; state identity 105; UN Security Council 299, 300; US institution building 31
co-operative security 110, *111*, 128
Copenhagen criteria 203, 204, 214, 216, 219, 243
core concept 307–9, 310–13, 319–20
corruption 165, 209, 216, 219
Cortell, P.A. 251n39
cosmopolitanism 137, 143, 164
Costa Rica 282
Cox, M. 208, 209, 212
credibility 60, 214, 220; European Union 230, 235, 236; NATO 230, 233; United Nations 255

crime: Bosnia and Herzegovina 209, 210, 214, 216; transnational 1, 124–5
crisis management 4
critical theory 164
Croatia 52, 187, 279nxiii, 282
Crozier, Michael 25
Cuba 282
Cyprus: civil war classification 277nii; Greek-Turkish conflict 233, 234, 240–1, 243–4, 246n5, 249n23, 251n37; peace operations 283

Darfur: NATO 14, 185, 191, *192*, 194–5, 198, 199; UN Security Council failure 302; *see also* Sudan
Davis, W.J. 251n39
Dayton Agreement (1995) 193, 203, 206, 208, 210, 212
"de-securitization" 243
decision-making: institutional reforms 288; UN Security Council 15–16, 290, 292–3, 295–7, 302, 306, 309–13, 316, 319–22; veto-player analysis 306–9, 310–13, 321–2
Deering, C.J. 62
democracy 31, 32, 44, 46, 57, 134n1; Bosnia and Herzegovina 203, 219; compliance with institutional norms 226; Copenhagen criteria 221n2; enlargement doctrine 36; European policy elites 96; humanitarianism 137, 160; liberal peace 168; National Security Strategy 45; NATO norms 37, 231–2; promotion of 47–9, 99, 120, 197; Turkey 234; US/European values 85; US neo-conservatives 92, 94
democratic peace hypothesis 102
democratization 4, 48–9, 165; Bosnia and Herzegovina 216; EU accession conditions 237; EU resolution of interstate conflicts 229; liberal peace 164, 169, 170; Turkey 241, 242, 244
Democrats 70, 72, 73, 75, 76, 94, 96
Derrida, Jacques 160n2
deterrence 110, 186, 188, 189
Deutsch, Karl W. 84
developing countries 2
development 143–4, 149, 160, 170
Diehl, P.F. 255
dispute resolution 110, 238, 248n23; *see also* conflict resolution
Djibouti 277nii, 283
doctrine of full interchangeability 61
domestic politics: bargaining failures 301; Europe 95–8; international institutions and interstate conflict 230; United

States 60, 61, 64, 69–70, 91–5; *see also* political factors
Dominican Republic 283
Donais, T. 216
Doyle, M. 253, 254, 260, 261, 274, 277–80
Dreher, A. 322n4
drug trafficking 1, 2, 4
Duffield, J. 8, 13
Duffield, M. 142
Dunant, Henry 158

earmarking of funds 146–7, 148
East Timor 43, 48, 53, 118; Australia role 168, 296, 298; peacebuilding 169, 173–4, 175, 176–7, *177*
eastern Europe *see* central and eastern European countries
Economic and Social Council (ECOSOC) 292–3
economic development 309, 310
economic power 82
economic relations 80, 89–90
Edwards, Geoffrey 14–15, 202–22
Egypt 49, 283, 292, 316, 317–18
Eisenstadt, S.N. 85
El Salvador 50, 55, *177*, 252, 283
Elster, J. 221
emotion 56–7
enforcement 202, 207, 302, 303; NATO 188–9; peace operations 258, 259, 262, 263, 270, 273; UN Security Council 290, 296–7, 309, 313; *see also* military force
enmity 109, 110, *111*, 113; central Asia *126*, 127; southeast Asia *126*, 129
environmental issues 1, 2, 81
Eritrea 279nxiii
Ethiopia 279nxiii, 280nxvii, 283
ethnic cleansing 14, 53, 185, 197, 203; Kosovo 153, 155, 299; relief agencies 150
ethnic conflict 48, 57, 269, 270
Europe: immigration 3; NATO 130–1, 188–90, 199; post-Westphalian hypothesis 102, 103; security policy orientation 26; state attributes 114, *115*; system properties *121*, 123–5; transatlantic relationship 10, 28–9, 30, 32–5, 78–100, 188–9; *see also* central and eastern European countries; European Union
European Central Bank (ECB) 119, 124
European Commission 204, 210, 220, 235, 238, 249n26, 249n28
European Community (EC) 234–5
European Court of Justice (ECJ) 124, 132, 297

European Defence Community (EDC) 34
European Parliament 235, 238
European Peoples' Party (EPP) 217–18
European Security and Defence Identity (ESDI) 183, 186
European Security and Defence Policy (ESDP) 234
European Union (EU) 119, 202, 288; Bosnia and Herzegovina 203, 205, 206–7, 208–11, 212–21; defense expenditures 135n11; enforcement procedures 297; enlargement 43, 203–4, 221, 236–7; Greek-Turkish conflict 15, 223, 224–5, 229–31, 233–9, 240, 242–6; as "neutral mutant" 103; post-Westphalian states 114; security multilateralism 125, *126*, 132–3; socialization 14; transatlantic relationship 10, 80; *see also* Europe
European Union Force (EUFOR) 203, 214
evasion hypothesis 62–3, 69–70, 71
Everts, P. 88–9
executive agreements 60–77; multilateral versus bilateral agreements 72–5, 76; theoretical framework 61–7; treaties versus 67–72, 76

Finnemore, Martha 51–2, 54, 57, 164, 202
Fleishman, J.L. 62
flexibility 185–91, 196
force *see* military force
Fortna, V.P. 253
France: defense expenditure 135n11; "Gaullists" 96–7; Iraq war 195, 300, 301; military force 120; NATO 33, 186, 193; public attitudes towards the United States 87; UN Security Council 293, 314; US institution building 29
free markets 164, 168; *see also* market economy
free speech 47, 48
free trade 32, 94
Friedman, Thomas 289
Fuchs, Peter 162n46
fused security community *112*, 114

Gallarotti, G. 247n14
Gardner, Lloyd 35
"Gaullists" 96–7, 98
General Agreement on Tariffs and Trade (GATT) 288
genocide 49, 52, 53, 150, 258, 302
Georgia 283
Germ Weapons Convention 38
Germany 29, 78, 81, 119, 133;

"Atlanticists" 97; defense expenditure 135n11; division of 30; League of Nations peace operation 256; NATO 33, 34; public attitudes towards the United States 87; UN funding 293; UN Security Council 297, 302, 303, 314–15, 316
Giesen, B. 85
governance: East Timor 173–4; peace 169–70
governmentality 170
Great Britain: "Atlanticists" 97; defense expenditure 135n11; NATO 33, 193; power 58; public attitudes towards the United States 87, 91; US institution building 29; *see also* United Kingdom
Greece: anti-Americanism 241; human rights trials 55; peace operations 283; Turkey conflict 15, 223–51
Greenberg, J. 313, 323n6
Grenada 292, 296
Guantanamo Bay 79
Guatemala *177*, 283, 297
Guinea-Bissau 283
Gulf War (1991) 6, 85, 140; Brazil support for 318–19; UN Security Council 292, 294, 298, 300
Gusmao, Xanana 174

Haas, Ernst 292
Habermas, Jürgen 78
Hadžipašić, Ahmet 208, 209, 222n11
Haiti *177*, 283, 299, 300, 318
Hassner, P. 92
Havel, Vaclav 161n33
hegemony 30–1, 82–3, 164, 171, 200
Heldt, B. 253, 255–6, 262
Helsinki European Council Summit (1999) 224, 237–8, 242, 244, 248n23, 249n25
Herz, John 102
Hezbollah 278nvi
Higgins, Tory 50
High Level Panel on Threats, Challenges and Change 289, 297, 304n6, 306
High Representative (HR) 205–6, 207, 213, 215, 216, 219
Hitler, Adolf 85
Hoffmann, Stanley 290
Holbrooke, Richard 39
Holsti, Kal 134n1
Howell, W.G. 62
Hull, Cordell 32
human rights 46, 48, 136; Afghanistan 172; Bosnia and Herzegovina 203; compliance with institutional norms 226; Copenhagen criteria 221n2; EU accession conditions 237; European policy elites 96; humanitarianism 137, 138, 140, 142, 143–4, 150, 160; justice for perpetrators of atrocities 49–51, 52, 53–4, 55, 57; liberal peace 164, 168, 169, 170; Turkey 234; US/European values 85, 197
Human Rights Watch 49, 156
human security 139, 164
humanitarianism 11, 85, 136–62, 171; classical versus solidarist 144, *144*; definition of 136; humanized multilateralism 137–8, 139–41, 145; Kosovo intervention 151–7; organizational culture 150–1; politicization of 137–8, 139, 142–5, 151, 155, 156–7, 159; principal-agent analysis 145–8; sociological institutionalism 148–9; *see also* peace operations
humanity 137, 139, 143, 150

identity 104–5, *105*, *115*, 164; Bosnia and Herzegovina 203; central Asia *115*, 116, 127; European *115*, 118–19, 132, 245; fused security community 114; NATO *115*, 118–19, 130, 131, 199, 201, 223; security referent 108; southeast Asia *115*, 117, 128, 129; Turkey 242; *see also* collective identity
Ifantis, Kostas 1–17
Ignatieff, M. 172
Ikenberry, G. John 9, 21–42, 82
immigration 1, 2, 3
impartiality: humanitarian intervention 137, 138, 143, 144, 148, 156–7, 162n40; peace operations 273
imperialism 82–3, 117
impermanent alliances 110, *111*
Implementation Force (IFOR) 193, 194, 203
independence 137, 138, 148
India 58, 120, 283, 293, 316–17
Indonesia 55, 114, 117, 122, 128, 283–4
"information model" 228
institutional peace 166, *176*
institutionalism 11, 12; Greek-Turkish conflict 227, 228–9; institutional change 289; interstate conflicts 230, 231; liberal 166, 167; neo-liberal 23, 158, 226; power 299, 302, 303; sociological 138, 145, 148–9, 151, 158, 196–7; United States 29, 31–2; *see also* international institutions
insurgent groups 277niii, 278

364 *Index*

interaction context 109
interdependence 84, 89–90; Europe 119; southeast Asia 118, 129
interests 105, *105*, 106–7, 109, *109*, *115*; central Asia *115*, 117; Europe *115*, 119–20, 132; southeast Asia *115*, 118, 129; United States *115*, 119, 131
international civil society 109–10, *112*
International Committee of the Red Cross (ICRC) 53, 143, 158
International Court of Justice (ICJ) 235, 238, 239, 249n23, 297
International Criminal Court (ICC) 43, 52, 56, 288; European support for 80; transatlantic disagreement 81; US rejection of 21, 38, 49
International Criminal Tribunal for Yugoslavia (ICTY) 49, 52–3, 54, 206, 210, 211–12, 214, 217
international financial institutions (IFIs) 164, 172, 173
International Force for East Timor (INTERFET) 168
international institutions 7–8, 11–13; Bosnia and Herzegovina 208; enforcement issues 296–7; interstate conflicts 15, 224, 225–6, 230–1, 246; security community concept 84; transatlantic relationship 90–1; *see also* international organizations
international law 5, 31, 149; civilianized security community 113; interstate disputes 235; nation-state sovereignty 78
International Monetary Fund (IMF) 211, 309, 322n4
international organizations (IOs) 83, 88, 163; adverse substitution 247n14; amendment to founding treaties 292; conditionality 205; liberal peace 168; principal-agent analysis 145–6; vertical multilateralism 165, 172; *see also* international institutions; non-governmental organizations
international relations 44, 45, 46, 81, 101, 163
International Stabilization and Assistance Force (ISAF) 184, 194
Iran 43, 49, 79, 284
Iraq 3, 6, 7; bilateral aid 146; censorship 47; geopolitical and oil interests 196; Greek anti-Americanism 241; illegality of US invasion 297; invasion of Kuwait 318; Japanese involvement 315–16; NATO 14, 185, 191, *192*, 195, 197, 198; opposition to war against 78, 84, 87, 89, 184, 300, 301; peacebuilding 171, 172, 175, 176, 177, *177*, 284; political polarization 49; preventive attack 45; regime change 92; strategic dilemma 299; transatlantic relationship 91, 98, 99; UN Security Council 302; unilateralism 168; US promotion of international change 43; US threats to NGOs in 148; *see also* Gulf War
Ireland 85–6
Isernia, P. 88–9
Islamic public opinion 48–9
Israel 146, 278nvi, 284, 292, 317–18
Italy 135n11
Ivanic, Mladen 208–9, 217, 220–1, 222n12

Japan: APEC 37; ASEAN relations with 128–9; UN funding 293; UN Security Council 297, 302, 303, 314, 315–16; US institution building 29, 30
Jervis, Robert 44–5
Jordan 284
justice 46, 164, 165; liberal peace 169; perpetrators of atrocities 49–51, 52–4, 55–6, 57
Justice and Home Affairs (JHA) 124

Kagan, R. 78, 82, 88
Kantianism 96
Karzai, Hamid 51
Katzenstein, Peter 30–1
Kazakhstan 114, 116, 134n7
Keck, M. 204
Kennan, George 34
Kenya 284
Keohane, Robert 17n1, 246n4
Kerry, John 86, 304n10
Kim, S.Y. 322n2, 323n5
Korea 284
Korean War 291–2
Kosovo 4, 43, 45, 85, 300; criminal trials 52; ethnic cleansing 53; EU/US differences 211; Greek anti-Americanism 241; humanitarianism 11, 138, 146, 151–7, 159; NATO intervention 184, 191, *192*, 193–4, 195, 196, 200; peacebuilding 171, 175, 176–7, *177*, 178; Russian domestic pressures 301; strategic dilemma 299; UN mission 173; weak consensus 168
Kosovo Force (KFOR) 186, 194
Kowert, Paul 247n10
Krasner, Stephen 103
Kupchan, C. 99, 100
Kurds 140
Kuwait 296, 299, 318

Kyoto Protocol 21, 38, 288
Kyrgyzstan 114, 116, 117, 120, 134n7

Lake, Anthony 36, 191–2
Laos 114, 129, 284
League of Nations 21, 28, 31, 255–6
Lebanon 284
legalism 52, 54, 71, 72
legitimacy: Greek–Turkish conflict 244; humanitarian intervention 139, 140, 151; international norms 231; multilateralism as source of 7; NATO *199*, 200; sociological institutionalism 138; UN Security Council 322; United Nations 252, 255, 273–4, 275n9; United States 82, 99
Legro, Jeffrey 247n10
Lehne, S. 210
liberal democracies 83, 85
liberal institutionalism 166, 167
liberal internationalists 43, 44, 46, 96, 166
liberal peace 163–79; *see also* peace
liberalism 40, 96, 163, 167
Liberia 284–5
"light footprint approach" 171, 172
logic of appropriateness 50, 51–4, 57, 108, 149, 219, 239
logic of consequences 50, 51, 54–6, 57, 239
logic of emotions 50, 56–7
Long, William 56

Macedonia 54, 153, 187, 297
Madrid Declaration (1997) 236
Malaysia 114, 117, 118, 129
Mali 285
Maltzman, F.M. 62
management theorists 202, 207
Mansfield, Edward 134n1
March, James 54
market economy 85, 96, 119, 232; *see also* free markets
Marshall Plan 34, 35
Martens, Wilfried 215, 218
Martin, Lisa 9–10, 12, 60–77
Matthiesen, P. 211
Mayer, K.R. 62
Mearsheimer, J.J. 81
Medécins Sans Frontières (MSF) 154
Merkel, Angela 97, 218
Mexico 2, 37, 304n8
Meyer, J. 149
Middle East 48–9, 198, 199, 233, 317–18
military force: central Asia *115*, 116; collective security 113; Egypt 318; Europe 96, *115*, 120; Germany 315; humanitarian emergencies 150–1; Japan 315; National Security Strategy 94; self-defense 297–8; southeast Asia *115*, 118; state attributes 105, *105*, 106, *115*; UN Charter 295; UN Security Council 291, 301, 310, 313–14, *320*, *321*; United States 88–9, *115*, 299
Milosevic, Slobodan 151, 193, 209, 220, 301; ethnic cleansing 153, 155; Hitler comparison 85; trial of 43, 52–3
Mitrany, D. 167, 174
Mladić, Ratko 210
modernization theory 57, 58
Moe, Terry 23, 25, 62
Moldova 285
Morocco 285
Mozambique 50, *177*, 252, 285
multilateralism: critique of 9, 43–4; definitions of 139, 184, 187; European policy elites 96, 97; European Security Strategy 80; executive agreements versus treaties 68–72, 76; forms of security multilateralism 108–14, 125–33; Germany 315; horizontal 11, 164–5, 168, 171, 172–3, *176*, 178; humanization of 11, 137–8, 139–41, 145, 157, 158, 159; India 317; institutional bargain 22, 23–7, 32–5, 39–40; institutional change 289; "instrumental" 79; multilateral versus bilateral agreements 72–5, 76; NATO co-operation 14, 185, 191–200, 201; non-state actors 164; peace 165–7, 169–70, 171–7, 178–9; peacebuilding 168–9; security institutions 7–8; state attributes 10–11, 101, 104–6, 114–20; state system properties 101, 106–7, 120–5; traditional notions of 163, 164; UN Security Council 299–300, 302, 313; United States 5–6, 9–10, 21–3, 27–41; vertical 11, 164–5, 167, 168, 169, 171–5, *176*, 178–9
Myanmar 114, 117, 118, 122, 129, 285

Nabers, D. 134n9
Namibia 50, *177*, 285
Nathan, J.A. 62
National Security Strategy 45, 79, 80, 93–4, 97
nationalism 203, 206, 216, 218, 219
neo-conservatives 38, 43, 45, 92–4, 95, 96, 99
neo-institutionalism 12
neo-liberal institutionalism 23, 158, 226
neo-liberalism 147, 160, 164, 165
neo-realism 12, 81, 90
Nepal 285

neutrality 137, 138, 144, 148
"new public management" 147
Nicaragua *177*, 285
Nigeria 285
Non-Aligned Movement (NAM) 316–17, 318
non-governmental organizations (NGOs) 142, 146, 159, 163, 288; Kosovo 154, 155; liberal peace 167, 168, 174; US threats to 148; vertical multilateralism 172; *see also* international organizations
non-interference 122, 317, 318
non-state actors 11, 13, 105, 163–4, 166; liberal peace project 170, 178; post-Westphalian state 102
normative frameworks 107, *107*, 108; central Asia 121–2, *121*; Europe *121*, 124–5; southeast Asia *121*, 123; United States *121*
norms 7, 11, 108–9, *109*, 289; Bosnia and Herzegovina 203, 205–6, 214, 216, 217, 220–1; central Asia *126*, 127; civilianized security community *112*, 113; collective defense *111*; collective security *111*; concerts 110, *111*; Copenhagen criteria 204; EU security multilateralism *126*; European 132, 205–6, 214, 216, 217, 220–1, 236–7, 242; fused security community 114; Greek-Turkish conflict 230, 235, 236–7, 238, 239–45, 246, 251n38; human rights 143; humanitarianism 158–9; internalization of 230, 239–45, 246; international socialization 14; NATO 14, 131, 197, 198, 200, 201, 231–2, 240, 241; norm entrepreneurs 47, 50–2, 170, 202, 204, 206, 210, 212–14, 221; normative change 46–7, 51–4, 58; political order 50; salience 231, 239–40, 244; security co-operation 110; social constructivism 12, 51; southeast Asia *126*, 129; sovereignty principle 106; strength of 251n39; transatlantic relationship 79, 90, 91, 98; transmission of institutional 226; US instrumental view of 125; US security multilateralism *126*; use of force 298; vertical multilateralism 164, 165; *see also* values
North America Free Trade Agreement (NAFTA) 21, 35, 36, 37
North Atlantic Council (NAC) 184, 193, 195
North Atlantic Treaty Organization (NATO) 1, 14, 81, 183–201, 288; assets 293; Bosnia and Herzegovina 206; expansion of 21, 22, 35, 36–7, 187, 191–2, 195–8, 200; flexibilization 185–91, 200–1; Greek-Turkish conflict 15, 223–5, 227–30, 231–4, 240–2, 245–6; humanized multilateralism 141; institutional bargain 33–4, 35; Kosovo intervention 11, 151–7, 168; new members 68, 71; post-Cold War agreements 68; post-Westphalian states 114; security multilateralism 125, 130–2, 133; transatlantic relationship 90–1, 100, 118–19; US institution building 29, 30
North Korea 315
Noutcheva, G. 203–4, 215
nuclear deterrence 188, 189
Nuclear Non-Proliferation Treaty 79
nuclear smuggling 1, 4
Nuclear Test Ban Treaty 21

Office of the High Representative (OHR) 203, 204, 206, 210, 211, 212–16, 219–20
Ogata, Sadako 153, 162n37
Oliver, J.K. 62
Olsen, Johan 54
Oman 285
Oneal, J. 246n4
Organization for European Economic Co-operation (OEEC) 34–5
Organization for Security and Co-operation in Europe (OSCE) 211
organizational culture 149, 150–1
Orru, M. 148–9
Oxfam 156

pacifism 314, 315, 316, 317
Pakistan 3, 65, 120, 285
Palestinian territories 43, 49, 146
Panama 292, 294
Papandreou, Andreas 250n31
Papua New Guinea 285
Paraguay 285
participatory peace 261, 262–7, *268*, 270, *271*, 281–7
Partnership for Peace (PfP) program 183, 200, 206, 217, 242
path dependence 294
Payne, R.A. 205
peace 163–79; ceasefires 279; as governance 169–70; gradations of 171–7; participatory 261, 262–7, *268*, 270, *271*, 281–7; sovereign 260–1, 267, *269*, 281–7; *see also* peacebuilding
Peace Implementation Council (PIC) 211, 212
peace operations 15–16, 139, 141, 252–87; advanced military participation 270–2,

271, 272, 273; co-operation problems 256, 257–9, *260*; co-ordination problems 256–7, 259, *260*; data 260–2; literature review 254–6; mandate 261–2, 267, 270, 271, 274n8; objectives of 292; Turkey's participation 242; UN Security Council 288, 295–6; war recurrence 260, 267, *268,* 270–1, *271; see also* humanitarianism
peacebuilding 11, 15–16, 163, 165, 168–9, 178; division of labour 273; ecological model 253, 256, 261, 274; gradations of liberal peace 171–7; humanitarianism 137, 160; peace as multilateral governance 169–70; strategies *260*; UN versus non-UN operations 259–60, 261, 262, 267, 270, 273, 274
persuasion 205, 206, 226
Peru 285
Pevehouse, J.C. 217
Philippines 114, 117, 128, 285
Pinochet, Augusto 43
police reforms 215–16
political factors: Bosnia and Herzegovina 209, 212, 213, 214–16, 217–19, 220; humanitarianism removal from 136–7; multifaceted concept of security 5; participatory peace 261; politicization of humanitarianism 137–8, 139, 142–5, 151, 155, 156–7, 159; *see also* domestic politics
Porter, T. 153, 156–7
positivism 202, 205
post-Westphalian state 10–11, 102–4, 107, 114, 132, 133–4
postmodernism 164
Powell, Colin 93, 136
power 106, *107,* 302–3; central Asia 120–1, *121*; Europe *121,* 123–4, 132; institutional bargain 22–7, 40; post-war distribution of 28, 35; southeast Asia *121,* 122, 128; UN Security Council 16, 290, 299–301; United States 9, 22, 39, 82–3, *121,* 124
power politics 44–5
Power, Samantha 45–6
pre-emptive action 4, 6, 38, 94
president of the United States 10, 60, 61–3, 64–5, 67, 69–70, 72–5
preventive use of force 45, 81, 94, 297
principal-agent analysis 138, 145–8, 151, 158, 304n11
principled activists 45
Prisoner's Dilemma 257–8
privatization 209, 220

Programme of Action on Illicit Trade in Small and Light Arms 38
Przeworski, Adam 47
public goods provision 290, 295–6, 297, 301, 303
Pugh, M. 209, 216
Putin, Vladimir 65

rationalist approaches 12–13, 15, 41n1; contract theory 294; explanation for war 301; Greek-Turkish conflict 223, 227, 228–9
Reagan, Ronald 63, 74, 75, 99, 296; Bush comparison 91–2; opposition to 78; unilateralism 93, 98
realism 12, 40, 44–5, 46, 83, 163; European policy elites 96; geopolitical interests 310; institutions 223, 227; NATO 189; structural 246n1; US neo-conservatives 92, 93, 95; use of force 106; victor's peace 166
reconciliation 56–7
refugees 1, 2, 3; Bosnia and Herzegovina 212; Kosovar Albanians 153, 194; Kurdish 140; Serbia 156
regime change 81, 92
regional organizations (ROs) 163, 168, 172
regionalism 36, 37
regulator 108, *109, 126,* 128, 130
reliability 60, 63–7, 69–70, 72, 76
relief agencies 137, 142, 144, 150–1, 153–7, 159–60, 162n43
religion: fundamentalism 2, 5; US voting patterns 86–7
Reljić, D. 212
Republicans 70, 72, 73, 74, 76
Republika Srpska (RS) 203, 208, 210, 216
resource dependence 149, 151, 161n22
Rice, Condoleeza 45, 93
Richmond, Oliver 11, 163–79
Riesman, Michael 152
Risse, Thomas 10, 78–100
Robinson, Mary 51
Rousseau, Jean-Jacques 257
Ruggie, John Gerard 7, 46, 134n2, 166, 184, 187
Rugova, Ibrahim 151
Rühe, Volker 191–2
rule of law 48, 49, 54, 55, 57, 165; Afghanistan 172; Bosnia and Herzegovina 203, 212; civilianized security community 114; Copenhagen criteria 221n2; EU accession conditions 237; humanitarianism 142; institutionalization of 56; liberal peace 164, 169; NATO norms 232

368   Index

Rumsfeld, Donald 92
Russett, B. 246n4, 289, 306, 322n2, 323n5
Russia: defense expenditure 134n7; domestic politics 301; NATO relations with 131, 183, 189; peace operations 285–6; Shanghai Co-operation Organization 114, 116, 117, 120–2, 127; UN Security Council 314, 319; US agreements with 63, 65; *see also* Soviet Union, former
Rwanda: civil war classification 278nvi; environmental degradation 2; genocide strategy 258; humanitarian agencies 143, 150, 152; peace operations 43, *177*, 252, 286; war crimes tribunal 53

Saddam Hussein 3, 85, 140, 196
Sambanis, Nicholas 15–16, 252–87
sanctions 219; national policy preferences 313, 317, 318; Sudan 194; UN Security Council 288, 291, 299, 310, 313, *321*
Šarović, Mirko 208
Schimmelfennig, Frank 14, 183–201, 205, 220, 221
Schröder, Gerhard 96, 98, 300
Schulhofer-Wohl, Jonah 15–16, 252–87
Schuman Plan 34
Scott, W.R. 149
security: expansion of concept 141, 145; forms of security multilateralism 108–14, 125–33; human 139, 164; multifaceted concept of 5; new discourse of 3–4; new security agenda 1–3; state attributes 104–6; state system properties 106–7; statist conception of 136
security community concept 84, 130, 133, 224
security dilemmas: central Asia 127; forms of security multilateralism 110; Greek-Turkish conflict 227, 228
security referent 108, *109*, 110, 113, 114; central Asia 125–7, *126*; European Union *126*, 132; NATO 130; southeast Asia *126*, 128; United States *126*
self-defense 295, 297–8
self-determination 49, 322n2, 323n5
self/other distinction 85
Senate 61, 62, 64, 65, 67
Senegal 286
September 11th 2001 terrorist attacks 3, 4–5, 78, 83, 93, 131, 184, 190, 194
Serbia 52–3, 152, 156, 192–3, 198, 208, 258
Seselj, Vojeslav 52–3
Shanghai Co-operation Organization (SCO) 114, 116–17, 121–2, 125–8, 133

Shklar, Judith 52
Sierra Leone: humanitarian funding 157; mixed tribunal 56; peacebuilding 168, 171, 175, 176–7, *177*, 286
signaling 60, 63, 64–5, 67, 69–72, 76
Sikkink, Kathryn 51–2, 54, 57, 202, 204
Simmons, B. 12
Singapore 58, 114, 117, 128, 129
Slim, Hugo 159
Snyder, Jack 9, 43–59, 134n1
social constructivism *see* constructivism
social learning 202, 207
socialization 14, 52, 231, 239; ASEAN 123; Bosnia and Herzegovina 15, 214, 215, 217, 218, 221; Greek-Turkish conflict 224, 225, 230, 241, 246; international institutions 226; NATO 231, 232
sociological institutionalism 138, 145, 148–9, 151, 158, 196–7
"soft power" 82
Solana, Javier 152, 211
solidarist humanitarianism 144, *144*
Solingen, Etel 49
Somalia 140, 279nxii, 300; aid agencies 150; peacebuilding 172, 177, *177*, 252, 286; UN Security Council powers 318
South Africa 50, 55, 286, 293, 316, 317
South East European Co-operation Process (SEECP) 217
southeast Asia 114, *115*, 117–18, 120, *121*, *126*, 128–30
sovereign control 105–6, *105*, *115*; central Asia *115*, 116; Europe *115*, 119; southeast Asia *115*, 118; United States *115*
sovereign peace 260–1, 267, *269*, 281–7
sovereign recognition 106, *107*, 108; central Asia 121, *121*; Europe *121*, 124; southeast Asia *121*, 122–3; United States *121*
sovereignty 78, 103, *107*, 108, 166; central Asia 127; collective defense 113; European Union 132–3; fused security community 114; NATO 130, 131; peace operations 260–1, 264; positive 142; post-Westphalian state 102; southeast Asia 129
Soviet Union, former (USSR): Cold War 1, 39; dissolution of 116, 183, 189; peace operations 287; as threat to NATO 187–8; UN Security Council 291, 293; US agreements with 68, 71; US institution building 33; *see also* Russia
Sperling, James 10–11, 101–35
Srebrenica massacre 43, 53, 193, 198

Index   369

Sri Lanka 286
Stabilization and Association Agreement (SAA) 203, 210, 212, 215, 217
Stabilization and Association Process (SAP) 214, 215, 218, 219
Stabilization Force (SFOR) 186, 193, 194, 203, 211, 214
state of nature 109–10, *111*
states 10–11, 101–35, 163–4; attributes 104–6, 114–20; bargaining failures 300–1; enforcement issues 296; forms of security multilateralism 108–14, 125–33; humanitarianism 145, 146–8, 151, 159; institutional bargain 22, 23–7, 40; interstate conflict 224, 225–6, 229, 230–1, 246; post-Westphalian 10–11, 102–4, 107, 114, 132, 133–4; self-defense 297–8; system properties 101, 106–7, 120–5; UN voting behavior 322n2
Stearns, Monteagle 246n7
Stiglitz, Joseph 206
Stockton, N. 156
Strategic Concept (NATO) 141, 153, 189
Sturm, J-E. 322n4
Sudan: geopolitical and oil interests 196; humanitarian funding 147; NATO actions 194–5; peace operations 286; relief agencies 154; UN Security Council failure 302; *see also* Darfur
Sutterlin, J. 306
Sweet, Alec Stone 124
Syria 286
systematic country reviews 35

Taiwan 297
Tajikistan 114, 116, 117, 120, 134n7, 286
Talbott, Strobe 141
Tallberg, J. 207
Tan, S.S. 134n9
territoriality 102, 103
terrorism 1, 3, 4–5; insurgent groups 277niii; rise of transnational 78, 83; threat to NATO 196; transatlantic relationship 79, 80, 88; *see also* September 11th 2001 terrorist attacks
Thailand 114, 118, 122, 128, 129, 286
threats 3, 140, 141; NATO 131, 187–8, 189, 190, 196, 201; UN Security Council role 290, 295–7; US/European views 88
torture 49, 53
Tošić, Mladen 14–15, 202–22
transatlantic relationship 10, 78–100, 118–19, 188–9; collective identity 84–9; end of the Cold War 81; European domestic issues 95–8; multilateral institutions 90–1; rise of transnational terrorism 83; transnational interdependence 89–90; US domestic issues 91–5; US power 82–3
transnational crime 1, 124–5
transparency 207, 226, 227, 228, 301
treaties 61, 63–6, 67–72, 76
Truman, Harry S. 34, 36
truth commissions 50, 55, 56
Tsakonas, Panayotis 1–17, 223–51
Tsebelis, George 16, 307–8, 321
Turkey: EU accession 212, 218, 221, 224, 236–9, 242–5, 248n23; Greece conflict 15, 223–51; Iraq war 184, 195, 199; Kurdish refugees 140; peace operations 286; US aid agreements with 65
Tuschoff, C. 247n15

Uganda 147, 286–7
Ukraine 131, 183
uncertainty 190, 200
unilateralism 6–7, 9, 38–9, 79, 95, 168, 301; critique of 43–4; European policy elites 96; National Security Strategy 94; neo-conservatives 92–3; opposition to US 84, 97; peacebuilding 171, 175, *177*; presidential actions 62, 63; transatlantic relationship 10, 90, 91, 97, 98; UN Security Council 299, 300, 312–13
unipolarity 35, 39–40, 82, 83, 94–5, 300
United Kingdom (UK): Iraq war 81; military force 120; peace operations 287; UN Security Council 293, 314; *see also* Great Britain
United Nations (UN): analyses of 290; Bosnian conflict 192, 193; humanitarianism 146; Japan 315–16; liberal peace 168, 169; peace operations 15–16, 141, 172, 173, 252–6, 258–9, 261, 262–74; security concept 141; transatlantic disagreement 81
United Nations Assistance Mission in Afghanistan (UNAMA) 171–2
United Nations Charter: dispute resolution 238, 248n23; enforcement actions 309, 313, 318; institutional persistence 292; peace operations 252, 262, 267; use of force 295, 318
United Nations Development Program (UNDP) 171
United Nations General Assembly (UNGA) 289, 292, 294, 296, 309, 322n2, 323n5
United Nations High Commissioner for Refugees (UNHCR) 140, 149, 153, 155, 161n34, 211

United Nations Security Council (UNSC) 16–17, 56, 141, 288–305; bargaining 299–301; collective action 290, 295–7, 298; explosion in activity 291–2; institutional persistence 288, 289–90, 292–4; Kosovo intervention 151–2; reform scenarios 313–19; self-defense 297–8; threats to peace 140; veto-player analysis 306–23

United Nations Transitional Administration in East Timor (UNTAET) 173, 174

United States (US): ambivalence about multilateralism 5–6, 9, 21–3; anti-Americanism 87, 91, 241; ASEAN relations with 128–9; Balkans 211–12; Cold War 1; defense expenditure 120, 135n11; democracy promotion 47; Greek-Turkish conflict 233, 234, 250n31; humanitarian funding 157; institution building 27–40; instrumental view of norms 125; international tribunals 49; Islamic public opinion against 48–9; military agreements 9–10, 60–77; military force 120, 299; national interest 119; NATO 130–1, 188–90, 193–4, 199–200, 248n18; peacebuilding 171; policy lock-in of other states 22, 26, 27, 29, 32–3, 35, 37, 40–1; power 58, 124; security multilateralism *126*; self-defense 298; state-building 172; transatlantic relationship 10, 28–9, 30, 32–5, 78–100, 188–9; UN Security Council 293, 296, 300, 302, 314; unilateralism 6–7, 10, 38–9, 43, 44–5, 79, 90, 91–2, 97; war hawks 46; *see also* North Atlantic Treaty Organization

Universal Declaration of Human Rights 5
universalism 164
Urquhart, Brian 304n6
Uzbekistan 114, 116, 120, 122

Vachudova, M.A. 216–17
values: Bosnia and Herzegovina 219; European 220–1, 222n22; NATO 185, 197, 198, 200, 201; transatlantic relationship 79, 85, 89, 91, 97; US neo-conservatives 92; *see also* norms
Vaughan, D. 150
veto powers 289, 290, 293, 296–7, 299–301, 306–23
victor's peace 166, 167, 170, *176*
Vietnam 114, 129, 287, 292
Voeten, Erik 16, 288–305, 322n2
Vreeland, J. 322n4

Wæver, Ole 125
Wallander, C.A. 293
Wallensteen, P. 253, 255–6, 306
Walter, B.F. 258
Waltz, K. 81
war 28, 107, *107*; central Asia *121*, 122, 127; civil 252–87; collective security *111*, 113; concerts 110, *111*; EU states 132; Euro-Atlantic *121*, 125; humanization of 158; rationalist explanations for 301; rules of 53, *111*; security regulator 108; southeast Asia *121*, 123; *see also* peace operations
war crimes 49, 52, 54, 210, 259
Warsaw Pact 183, 185, 188, 189, 191, 240
Weapons of Mass Destruction (WMD) 1, 2, 5
Weiss, T. 306
Whitlock, E. 211
Wilson, Woodrow 28, 29, 31–2
winsets 307
Wolfowitz, Paul 45, 92
World Bank 172, 174, 211, 288, 309
World Trade Organization (WTO) 21, 35, 80, 288, 292

Yemen Arab Republic 287
Yemen Peoples Republic 287
Young, Oran 207
Yugoslavia, former 49, 53, 85, 184, 196; bilateral aid 146; Greek anti-Americanism 241; NATO intervention 197; peace operations 287; refugees 2; *see also* Balkans; Bosnia and Herzegovina; Kosovo; Serbia

Zimbabwe 287